THE LONG ARC OF LEGALITY

The Long Arc of Legality breaks the current deadlock in philosophy of law between legal positivism and natural law by showing that any understanding of law as a matter of authority must account for the interaction of enacted law with fundamental principles of legality. This interaction conditions law's content so that officials have the moral resources to answer the legal subject's question 'But, how can that be law for me?' David Dyzenhaus brings Thomas Hobbes and Hans Kelsen into a dialogue with HLA Hart, showing that philosophy of law must work with the idea of legitimate authority and its basis in the social contract. He argues that the legality of international law and constitutional law are integral to the main tasks of philosophy of law, and that legal theory must attend both to the politics of legal space and to the way in which law provides us with a 'public conscience'.

DAVID DYZENHAUS is University Professor of Law and Philosophy, University of Toronto, Canada. He works on legality under stress, an interest that he developed as a law student in apartheid South Africa. As one of the leading theorists of the rule of law, his work both reshapes philosophy of law and connects its most abstract concerns to the practical dilemmas human rights lawyers face.

THE LONG ARC OF LEGALITY

Hobbes, Kelsen, Hart

DAVID DYZENHAUS
University of Toronto

CAMBRIDGE
UNIVERSITY PRESS

CAMBRIDGE
UNIVERSITY PRESS

Shaftesbury Road, Cambridge CB2 8EA, United Kingdom

One Liberty Plaza, 20th Floor, New York, NY 10006, USA

477 Williamstown Road, Port Melbourne, VIC 3207, Australia

314–321, 3rd Floor, Plot 3, Splendor Forum, Jasola District Centre, New Delhi – 110025, India

103 Penang Road, #05–06/07, Visioncrest Commercial, Singapore 238467

Cambridge University Press is part of Cambridge University Press & Assessment, a department of the University of Cambridge.

We share the University's mission to contribute to society through the pursuit of education, learning and research at the highest international levels of excellence.

www.cambridge.org
Information on this title: www.cambridge.org/9781009048866

DOI: 10.1017/9781009049054

First published 2022
First paperback edition 2023

A catalogue record for this publication is available from the British Library

Library of Congress Cataloging-in-Publication data
Names: Dyzenhaus, David, author.
Title: The long arc of legality : Hobbes, Kelsen, Hart / David Dyzenhaus, University of Toronto.
Description: Cambridge, United Kingdom ; New York, NY, USA Cambridge University Press, 2021. | Includes bibliographical references and index.
Identifiers: LCCN 2021034737 (print) | LCCN 2021034738 (ebook) | ISBN 9781316518052 (hardback) | ISBN 9781009048866 (paperback) | ISBN 9781009049054 (epub)
Subjects: LCSH: Rule of law–Philosophy. | Law–Philosophy.
Classification: LCC K3171 . D992 2021 (print) | LCC K3171 (ebook) | DDC 340/.11–dc23
LC record available at https://lccn.loc.gov/2021034737
LC ebook record available at https://lccn.loc.gov/2021034738

ISBN 978-1-316-51805-2 Hardback
ISBN 978-1-009-04886-6 Paperback

For Louise and Carole

CONTENTS

PREFACE

'The arc of the moral universe is long, but it bends toward justice', said Martin Luther King, Jr. I make a similar claim about the long arc of legality, the arc of the idea of government under law. Legality's arc bends towards justice of a special kind, the justice intrinsic to the legal order of the modern state. I trace the trajectory of that arc from Thomas Hobbes to Hans Kelsen and HLA Hart, the foremost legal positivist philosophers of the twentieth century.

Hobbes is one of the founders of legal positivism if by that label we mean that there is no more to law than what people have 'posited' or put in place in order to organize the common life of their society. In the modern era, the power to make law is centralized in the institutions of the state. Law is made by those who have authority to do so within the legal order of the modern legal state. Why, then, have philosophers spent so much time on constructing a theory to explain the role of law in our common life? The reason is the tricky transition from 'power' to 'authority'. How is sheer political power transformed into legal right, the right to tell legal subjects – those subject to the state's power – what to do?

Hobbes, Kelsen and Hart all thought that a theory of law must account for law's authority, but without making such authority depend on a source outside legal order, whether divine will or some secular ideal of justice. Thus, legal positivists traditionally reject rival 'natural law' theories because such theories do, in their view, trace the authority of law to some moral source outside legal order. That leaves positivists with the arduous task of solving the puzzle of legal authority – how law transforms might into right – without reliance on anything external to law.

I argue that their legal theories do contain a solution to that puzzle. Law's authority is due to the fact that legal order affords to its officials resources which enable adequate answers to legal subjects who ask 'But, how can that be law for me?' That's a long answer and it takes a long book to set out. It requires following me through a close reading of texts by my principal figures, often against the orthodox understanding of their work, and with Kelsen and Hart at times against their self-understanding.

It is against Kelsen's and Hart's self-understanding, as I argue that they could not help but become natural lawyers in their bid to understand law in the register of authority. They needed to incorporate (and in fact largely did) many of the insights associated with Gustav Radbruch, Lon Fuller and Ronald Dworkin, the twentieth-century natural lawyers who argued both that there are moral resources which ground law's authority and that these resources are wholly internal to legal order.

My reading is not, however, or so I claim, against Hobbes's self-understanding, at least because he was untroubled by our labels like 'legal positivism' and 'natural law'. His philosophy of law is a theory of the positive law of the modern legal state in which ultimate legal authority is understood as power exercised in compliance with an extensive list of the 'laws of nature'. He, of course, also claimed the state has authority because its subjects must accept that they consented to be ruled by its law. They consent through contracting with each other in the state of nature to put in place the state and its representative in the sovereign who rules in their name. That may seem to make the source of authority both external and deeply troubling, as it relies on the fiction of an original social contract to arrive at the conclusion that the sovereign has unlimited authority. Subjects are under a duty to obey the law, whatever its content. For this reason, legal positivists since Bentham have rejected social contract theory in general and Hobbes's version of it in particular, as have contemporary natural lawyers.

Proper attention to Hobbes's legal theory shows, however, that the legal order of the modern legal state internalizes the social contract in the way in which law mediates the relationship between ruler and subject. Moreover, the same attention to Kelsen and Hart, in particular to parts of their work which may seem anomalous at first, shows that they could not help but rely on the social contract idea in their attempts to solve the puzzle of legal authority. In so doing, they also committed themselves to Hobbes's view that the law of a society amounts to a 'public conscience'. Law has a moral quality to it just in being law and so must be given appropriate weight by both legal officials and subjects in their deliberations.

In support of these controversial claims, I show how they help us to understand contemporary debates about the constitution of the modern legal state and the way in which its legal order relates to 'law beyond the state', in particular international law. But, as I also show, engagement with these debates is necessary because the internal legal order of the state cannot be understood without engaging in these debates. Questions about constitutionalism and the legality of international law are integral to the main tasks of philosophy of law.

Three caveats are in order. First, I claim in the Introduction that this book is in part an 'homage' to Hart. One reviewer suggested that this claim may seem a little disingenuous since I am highly critical of Hart in these pages and Kelsen emerges from them as the 'real hero'. But I do stand by that claim. I have been reading and rereading Hart's *The Concept of Law* for over forty years. Each time, and right up until the present, I have discovered some new and profound insight in his deceptively pellucid prose and my arguments here are largely prompted by an engagement over these years with his legal theory.

Second, the reader must contend not only with length, but also with the many quotations which populate the text. One participant in a manuscript workshop commented that I should make my own voice emerge more from the thickets of names and quotations. But I came to appreciate more as I revised the manuscript why my argument needs those names and quotations. That argument consists in my best possible assembly of ideas developed by philosophers of law who have made their task explaining the authority of the modern legal state, and the quotations are necessary to support those interpretations of their work which on occasion go against the grain of orthodoxy.

Third, the ideas assembled are those of dead white Western men. Even my living interlocutors are almost all white Western men. And dead or alive, their task is unsurprisingly one of elucidating a theory of a form of state developed in the West. Their and my legal theories are thus in some deep sense parochial, or, as I would prefer to say, situated in a particular kind of experience. In Chapter 6, I suggest that legal theory should in general be so situated. For the moment, I claim only that understanding this form of state is worthwhile because, whatever its origins, it has been exported to pretty much the rest of the world. In addition, while that export was undertaken in the service of empire, colonialism and neocolonialism, it is important to get the legal theory of that state right if we want to understand how law can be both an instrument of oppressive state power and a source of resistance.

The attempt to understand how law enables resistance as well as oppression began when I was a law student in the 1970s in apartheid South Africa. In the version set out in these pages, it began when Alberto Puppo and Raymundo Gama invited me to spend a week in 2015 giving lectures in the Eduardo García Máynez Seminar at ITAM (Instituto Tecnológico Autónomo de México). The topic of the seminar was philosophy of international law and I put together as a basis for my lectures a very rough manuscript composed of my work-in-progress – the first draft of this book – with a focus (new for me) on international law. I thank Alberto, Raymundo and the students who participated in the seminar for their generosity in engaging with this draft.

Since then I have worked on and off on trying to wrestle that manuscript into better shape. I intended to finish it during the academic year 2016/17 when I had a fellowship at the Wissenschaftskolleg zu Berlin. While the Wissenschaftskolleg proved a most productive place to do sustained research, I discovered that I could not proceed before developing my view of the debate between Kelsen and Hart about the legality of international law, a task which consumed the year. That debate became pivotal to my argument and I thank the Wissenschaftskolleg for this wonderful opportunity.

The academic year 2020/1 gave me the time I needed for a final set of revisions and I thank the Guggenheim Foundation which awarded me a fellowship for this period.

In the meantime, the manuscript has been through many drafts and I owe thanks to a number of people who have helped me in this process. The most important intervention was a manuscript workshop which Geneviève Cartier organized at the Montreal campus of her university in June of 2018. I thank Geneviève and Sherbrooke University for making this event possible and also all those who participated in a day and a half of intense discussion of the manuscript: Evan Fox-Decent, Colin Grey, Hoi Kong, Hugo Lafrenière, Finn Makela, Mark Walters and Jacob Weinrib. Hugo, I should mention, provided me with a summary of the entire discussion as well as with detailed comments on a draft of the Introduction.

I have over the years enlisted several talented students at my university as research assistants, both writing memoranda on discrete topics and giving me no-holds-barred criticism of my drafts. My thanks go to Haim Abraham, Manula Adhihetty, Ryan Deshpande, Matthew Oliver, Kerry Sun and Andy Yu. Manula deserves a special mention for a set of careful and challenging comments on the bulk of my penultimate draft. I also thank the students in my MA Philosophy of Law seminar in 2018 on whom I inflicted a draft of the whole manuscript, especially Eric Wilkinson whose term paper 'Hart and the Moral Foundation of Law' helped me to formulate some key thoughts.

Several colleagues from outside my university have contributed greatly to this project over the years, and I thank them for their friendship and their scholarly support. Geneviève Cartier, Evan Fox-Decent and Mark Walters need another mention in this context and my enduring thanks go as well to Trevor Allan, Rueban Balasubramaniam, Nehal Bhuta, Hassan Jabareen, Santiago García Jaramillo, Murray Hunt, Aileen Kavanagh, Matthew Lewans, Karin Loevy, Janet McLean, Tom Poole, Arie Rosen, Kristen Rundle, Benjamin Straumann, Rayner Thwaites and Lars Vinx. I also thank three anonymous reviewers for Cambridge University Press for their detailed and helpful comments on the project.

The University of Toronto and my two homes in it in Law and Philosophy continue to provide an excellent environment for scholarship and Ed Iacobucci, Dean of Law, during most of this period, and Martin Pickavé, Chair of Philosophy, were unstinting in their support. Three colleagues and friends have been especially influential as I worked through my arguments. Jutta Brunnée and Karen Knop have patiently tried to educate me in international law over the years, informally in our 'international law drinks' sessions, more formally through being willing each to teach a seminar with me, with Karen on 'Foreign Relations Law' and with Jutta on 'The Rule of Law in International Law Theory'. I have been resisting Arthur Ripstein's attempts to turn me into a Kantian for many years, but there is hardly an issue canvassed in this book unmarked by our conversations.

Four other institutions have been tremendously important to me in the writing of the book. First, I have taught several times as a Global Visiting Professor in the Law School of New York University. My colleagues in legal theory there have been most important to the development of my ideas, especially Richard Brooks, Benedict Kingsbury, Lewis Kornhauser, Mattias Kumm, Liam Murphy, Richard Stewart and Jeremy Waldron. The same is true of the students, most of all in my Jurisprudence course in 2018 on whom I tried out many of my arguments as we went through *The Concept of Law* together. In particular, Alma Diamond, Teng Li and Meir Yarom have provided me with novel insights into old problems.

Second, there is the University of the Witwatersrand in Johannesburg where I studied political theory and law and had my first academic position. The seeds of the ideas in this book were all planted there by my teachers. I have recorded before my special debt to John Dugard. John taught me Jurisprudence, though he did not regard himself as a theorist, and only taught the course because he thought it important that students be concerned with the legal nature of the apartheid state. That course set me on the inquiry in which I am still engaged forty years on. John's real passion, however, was for international law, a field in which he achieved great eminence. His International Law course was in fact my favourite in my LLB degree and here I have attempted to return to the rest of the issues to which John introduced me.

Third, there is the University of Oxford where, in my DPhil thesis, I made my first sustained attempt to set out a view of the legal nature of the apartheid state under the direction of my main supervisor, Ronald Dworkin. For our first session, I presented Dworkin with a Marxist and positivist analysis of some judgments in which judges differed about how to interpret apartheid law. 'But', he asked, 'who do you think was right?' That question changed the course of my thesis and I hope to have made more progress towards answering it since 1988, the year I defended the thesis. It gives me much pleasure to put the final touches to that answer back in Oxford, and I thank All Souls College for the visiting fellowship during which I completed this book.

Fourth, I thank Cambridge University Press and its dedicated staff, not only for agreeing to publish this book, but also for publishing the three collections Tom Poole and I edited which came out of workshops we organized, and which facilitated a collaboration most important to the development of my arguments. Finola O'Sullivan has been my editor at the Press throughout a relationship which began in 2004 when I gave the JC Smuts Memorial Lectures to the Faculty of Law at Cambridge. Sadly, she will be gone from that role before this book is published. I will be far from alone in sorely missing her singular warmth and dedication to her authors.

Last, there are some more personal thanks. I have discussed the issues I grapple with here with Cheryl Misak since we met as graduate students in Oxford. Her influence on my work has been immense. Much more important is everything else she contributes, together with our children Alexander and Sophie, to my happiness. My dedication is to my sisters, Louise Spitz and Carole Lewis, for more than sixty years of love and care.

Introduction

I.1 The Puzzle of Authority

Philosophy of law has long been in a state of deadlock, unable to make progress in solving the puzzle of law's authority – that law is both a matter of right and might. This book seeks to break the deadlock.[1] It does so by going back to the work of HLA Hart, who in 1958 set solving that puzzle as the main task for legal theory in 'Positivism and the Separation of Law and Morals' with his lapidary claim: 'Law surely is more than the gunman situation writ large'.[2] I argue that the task can be accomplished through exploiting the rich resources in Hart's own legal theory. But I do so in a way closed to him by the idea he claimed was central to his tradition in his 1958 manifesto for legal positivism: his Separation Thesis that there is no necessary connection between law and morality.

The thought that we should abandon the Separation Thesis will not seem like news to Hart's successors, who have taken to claiming that legal positivism is not committed to this thesis, even that Hart himself never upheld it.[3] But, as I will explain, the claim that Hart never advanced the thesis is wrong and the connection my arguments display is far stronger than any of his successors acknowledge. The resources I muster from Hart's legal theory show that one cannot elaborate a theory of law's authority without elaborating a theory of its legitimate authority, where legitimacy is actual legitimacy. Law's authority is a matter both of what legal subjects in fact accept and what they have reason to accept.

[1] In *What Makes Law: An Introduction to Legal Philosophy* (Cambridge: Cambridge University Press, 2014), Liam Murphy suggests that the deadlock cannot be broken and that we should move on in practical ways.

[2] HLA Hart, 'Positivism and the Separation of Law and Morals', in Hart, *Essays in Jurisprudence and Philosophy* (Oxford: Clarendon Press, 1983) 49, at 59.

[3] For example, Leslie Green, 'Positivism and the Inseparability of Law and Morals' (2008) 23 *New York University Law Review* 1035.

Law's authority does not, then, as Hart's most influential successor Joseph Raz has argued, amount to a claim to rule legitimately which must be made even when the law on behalf of which its officials make the claim is utterly immoral and even when the officials are completely insincere.[4] Rather, as Hart always suggested, the central task of philosophy of law is to understand the authority law *has*, not the authority it merely *claims*. Moreover, law's authority cannot be explained as de facto authority – what it has a matter of fact – but which may not amount to legitimate or de jure authority, despite the reliance by both Hart and his successors on that distinction.

As I argue, the idea that there could be an illegitimate legal authority is a contradiction in terms: an unauthoritative authority. What makes law authoritative is that the officials who speak in its name can answer satisfactorily the legal subject's question 'But, how can that be law for me?' The legal order of what I will refer to as the 'modern legal state', in Hart's words the 'distinctive structure of a municipal legal system',[5] affords to its officials resources which enable them to answer that question and so to maintain their order as a legal order. A legal order is therefore one in which the law has de jure authority.

My main thesis is that the legal subject's question should be at the centre of philosophical inquiry into law. But on my argument the legal subject and the modern legal state are two sides of the same coin. I do not attempt to buttress the claim that as a matter of history the conceptions emerge together, although I believe this to be the case. However, I try to show that if philosophy of law is to progress beyond deadlock, it must both make its conceptions of state and subject explicit and appreciate the tight, indeed unbreakable, relationship between the two.

In my account, a theory of law's authority has three elements. First, it explains authority as compliance with fundamental principles of legality – the right-giving basis of legal order. Second, it gives to officials a role in interpreting enacted law in the light of such principles. It thus offers a theory of the role of official interpretation of the law in maintaining legal order. Given the first and second elements, the principles make up a grammar of legality in that enacted laws which are not interpretable in the light of the principles have a dubious claim to authority. If enough dubious laws are enacted, the order begins to shift from one of legal right

[4] Joseph Raz, 'Authority, Law, and Morality', in Raz, *Ethics in the Public Domain: Essays in the Morality of Law and Politics* (Oxford: Oxford University Press, 1994) 194.

[5] HLA Hart, *The Concept of Law* (Oxford: Clarendon Press, 1994, 2nd ed.), 17.

to one of unmediated coercive power. Thus, to be legal, to count as valid law, law must be interpretable in a way which respects the fundamental principles. Third, the way in which these two elements combine in a single legal theory requires invoking what I call a 'constitutionalist idea'. This is the idea of an ongoing practice which constitutes legitimate authority of the sort early modern political theorists set out in versions of the social contract. These theorists substituted for the divine right of the monarch a secular basis for the authority of the modern legal state, one produced by the voluntary interaction of the very individuals who are subject to that authority.

Interpretability is key. Laws which are not interpretable in light of fundamental principles of legality lose their claim to authority because they do not bear the marks of having been enacted with legal right. They are 'illegal laws', laws which lack the quality of legality. Conversely, when laws are interpretable in this way, legal officials will be able to justify to the legal subject their exercise of authority. They will be able to answer adequately the question 'But, how can that be law for me?' For legality mediates the conversion of public policy into the enacted law applied by officials to legal subjects. This process of mediation, whereby political judgments are converted into legal content, brings the fundamental principles to bear on the determination of the law which the officials apply. In this way, the officials maintain the constitutionalist idea through a dynamic process of juridical production.

All three elements are to be found in Hart, though in a distorted form which can be corrected only by setting them in the long arc of legality – an arc which stretches from Thomas Hobbes in the seventeenth century to the other major legal positivist thinker of the twentieth century, Hans Kelsen.[6] Hobbes's and Kelsen's contributions to my argument are not, however, through an account of their place in a chronological history of ideas. Rather, it is through the way their theories help to provide a more satisfactory theory of legal authority than if we suppose that the main protagonists are confined, on the one hand, to Hart followed by Raz in the legal positivist camp, and on the other, to Lon Fuller and Ronald

[6] Why Hobbes, that is, why not Rousseau, Kant or any other classic philosopher of law and politics? The answer is that Hobbes is *the* theorist of the modern legal state, as I hope to demonstrate in this book. I will set out my reasons for not opting for a Kantian legal theory in Appendix II.

Dworkin in the natural law camp with their distinct attempts to show a necessary connection between law and morality.[7]

In making this argument, I seek to vindicate the insight in a passing remark in Michael Oakeshott's essay on the rule of law that there is a 'vision of a state in terms of the rule of law' which 'hovers over the reflections of many so-called "positivist" modern jurists'.[8] In this essay, Oakeshott set out an account which owes most to Hobbes, though he acknowledged that its roots can be found in other early modern as well as modern theorists. Kelsen is the positivist jurist he had in mind.[9]

Oakeshott's insight is profound. While Hobbes and Kelsen are not often linked[10] and Kelsen hardly mentioned Hobbes let alone acknowledged any debt to him, they both chose to explain the law of the modern legal state as a matter of both rightful authority and coercive power. Since they understood that to explain law as a matter of authority is to explain it as de jure authority, they focused on the way in which legality plays a crucial role in transforming political might into legal right.

Here and throughout it is important to bear in mind that the right in issue here is not right at large but (in accordance with the first element sketched above) *jus* or legal right, the idea of right intrinsic to legal authority. The whole of this book is an exercise in unpacking this idea, which is also the idea which animates terms like the 'rule of law' and 'legality'. Such terms are the closest English comes to conveying the connotations of *jus* and its equivalents – *Recht*, *droit*, *diritto* – as well as the other words which European languages (except for Polish) have for expressing the distinction between law in the sense of made or enacted law and law in the sense of legal right. It is the right or authority implicit in the kind of political rule which establishes in enacted or positive law its judgments about how the subjects of rule should act. In so doing, lawmakers accept that the content of their judgments will be determined

[7] An omission from my cast list, and thus for the most part from this book, is the natural lawyer John Finnis and his major work *Natural Law and Natural Rights* (Oxford: Clarendon Press, 1980). I explain why in Appendix III.

[8] Michael Oakeshott, 'The Rule of Law', in Oakeshott, *On History and Other Essays* (Indianapolis: Liberty Fund, 1999) 129, at 175.

[9] See my 'Dreaming the Rule of Law', in Dyzenhaus and Thomas Poole, eds, *Law, Liberty and State: Oakeshott, Hayek and Schmitt on the Rule of Law* (Cambridge: Cambridge University Press, 2015) 234.

[10] Though see Norberto Bobbio, *Thomas Hobbes and the Natural Law Tradition* (Chicago: Chicago University Press, 1993, Daniela Gobetti, trans.) and Bobbio and Danilo Zolo, 'Hans Kelsen, the Theory of Law and the International Legal System: A Talk' (1998) 9 *European Journal of International Law* 355, at 358–9.

in accordance with the discipline which the requirements of legality – of government under law – imposes.

The right-giving basis of legal order resides in its fundamental principles of legality. In Hobbes, these are his laws of nature the 'Science' of which he said is 'the true and onely Moral Philosophy',[11] and of which Oakeshott observed that they amount to 'no more than an analytic break-down of the intrinsic character of law, ... the *jus* inherent in genuine law'.[12] In his much neglected chapter 26 'Of Civill Lawes' in *Leviathan* (1651), Hobbes made clear that legal officials, in maintaining these laws, a task which includes the activity of judges in interpreting enacted law, do the job of preserving the social contract by which subjects have agreed with each other to regard the law – the commands of their sovereign – as binding on them.

The social contract is usually understood as a once and for all act in the state of nature with civil society its product. But the continued existence of such a society depends on the maintenance of the civil laws which provide the framework for the subjects' interaction with both one another and the state in an ongoing dynamic process. Put differently, a civil society must be fully governed by law – both enacted law and fundamental principles of legality – for the 'mutuall Relation between Protection and Obedience'[13] to obtain. To the extent it is not so governed, the social contract becomes ever more friable. To the extent that it is so governed, the social contract is renewed.

The social contract and the protection–obedience relationship are thus the two major components of the constitutionalist idea. Indeed, in early modern political thought, they were conceived as two closely connected though distinguishable ideas, both of which were required to make up a complete contract: the *Gesellschaftsvertrag* or contract of the whole of the society to be ruled by one sovereign and the *Herrschaftsvertrag* which, as Ernest Barker put it, 'in the sense of government, is based on a contract between ruler and subjects'.[14] Barker noted correctly that with Hobbes, once the political community is formed, there is no further contract

[11] Thomas Hobbes, *Leviathan* (Cambridge: Cambridge University Press, 1996, Richard Tuck, ed.), 110.

[12] Oakeshott, 'The Rule of Law', 173.

[13] Hobbes, *Leviathan*, 491.

[14] Ernest Barker, 'The Theory of the Social Contract in Locke, Rousseau and Hume', in Barker, *Essays on Government* (Oxford: Clarendon Press, 1960, 2nd ed.) 86, at 90. Emphasis removed.

between the 'sovereign Leviathan' and the community so that the state is subject to 'none of the limits of a contract of government'.[15]

But, as I show, the role of officials in maintaining the order of civil law makes possible the mutual relationship of protection and obedience and that relationship does the work of a contract of government. Hence, Barker was wrong to suppose that Hobbes's sovereign is unlimited,[16] though, as I argue at various points, the issue is more that the sovereign is legally constituted, and as such may not as sovereign violate fundamental principles of legality. For the present, I want to note that in general presence matters more than name. So long as there is present in a legal theory, first, an idea of what legitimates the legal order – what gives it the quality of legality which distinguishes it from the gunman writ large – and, second, a sense of how that idea achieves traction in the relationship between ruler and subject, one is trafficking in a constitutionalist idea, the functional equivalent of a complete social contract.[17]

Of the thinkers on whom I focus, Hobbes and Kelsen understood this best and so offered, as I show, the most satisfactory accounts of how the three elements of a theory of law's authority combine. But these elements became inevitable as soon as Hart made the puzzle of legal authority the main task for legal theory. For since 1958 there is general agreement that law cannot be reduced to the coercion attached to the commands of a legally unlimited sovereign, as Hart's predecessors Jeremy Bentham and John Austin had argued. Rather, law has to be understood both as a matter of authority and of the fundamental rules or norms which both constitute such authority and condition its exercise through official interpretation.

There is also general agreement that, as Hart argued in his 1961 classic *The Concept of Law*, an understanding of law as authoritative requires adopting the 'internal point of view' of those subject to the law who accept it as such. They follow its injunctions not because they fear punishment – the claim Hart rejected in Bentham's and Austin's 'command theory' of law – but because they regard it as the right thing to do. '[T]he coercive power of law presupposes its accepted authority';[18] and

[15] Ibid, 92.

[16] Though see ibid, note 1 at 92 for Barker's perceptive qualifications to this claim which I set out in Chapter 2.

[17] For an analysis of the persistence of the social contract idea, even in thinkers who purported to reject it such as Hume and Bentham, see JW Gough, *The Social Contract: A Critical Study of Its Development* (Oxford: Clarendon Press, 1957, 2nd ed.).

[18] Hart, *The Concept of Law*, 203.

I follow Hart in supposing that the kind of acceptance at stake is not reducible to hypothetical acceptance, an idea of what would be accepted if only individuals were rational or reasonable. It is, or at least is also and mainly, actual or factual acceptance.[19]

Hart always resisted the idea that such acceptance is tantamount to moral endorsement. As Raz put it in an homage to his teacher, Hart remained 'the heir and torchbearer' of Bentham's and Austin's positivism, a 'great tradition in the philosophy of law which is realist and unromantic in outlook'. That tradition, Raz continued, 'regards the existence and content of the law as a matter of social fact whose connection with moral or any other values is contingent and precarious'. '[C]entral', then, to Hart's 'whole outlook' is 'the rejection of the moralizing myths which accumulated around the law', so that he shares the 'Benthamite sense of the excessive veneration in which the law is held in common law countries, and its deleterious moral consequences'. Raz also mentioned that Hart's 'fear' was 'evident ... that in recent years legal theory has lurched back in that direction'.[20]

It is only at this point that real disagreement between contemporary legal positivists and natural lawyers begins, though it is not about whether law is a matter of social fact. Like Hart's claim that law is a matter of authority as well as coercion, there is general agreement that law is a matter also of facts, including facts about coercion. Disagreement arises because of the claim made in the 'lurch' that if law is to be understood as a matter of authority, that requires finding a moral basis for the authority of law. It is this disagreement which leaves legal theory caught, as it were, between might and right.

The lurcher was, of course, Dworkin, Hart's successor in the Chair of Jurisprudence in Oxford. Raz's description captures well a sense among Oxford philosophers of law that Dworkin's own version of 'moralizing myth' amounted to an awkward though short-lived distraction. However, Hart had worked hard behind the scenes and somewhat illicitly to ensure Dworkin's succession to his chair, a fact of more than biographical interest.[21] While Hart had been so impressed by Dworkin's performance

[19] In Chapter 3, I argue that acceptance is a mix of both, in which actual acceptance dominates.

[20] Raz, 'Authority, Law, and Morality', 194.

[21] Nicola Lacey, *A Life of HLA Hart: The Nightmare and the Noble Dream* (Oxford: Oxford University Press, 2004), 291–3. Lacey reports at 186 that Hart was already troubled by Dworkin's criticisms at the time Dworkin was an undergraduate law student in Oxford.

as an undergraduate law student in Oxford that it is alleged he stole Dworkin's Jurisprudence paper from the examination office as a souvenir, much more important must have been Hart's perception of the importance to philosophy of law of the sweeping challenge to legal positivism in two of Dworkin's first published papers, 'Model of Rules I' and 'Model of Rules II'.[22] There Dworkin argued that judges who follow his 'interpretive theory' of law will in any 'hard case' – a case in which there is reasonable disagreement about what the law requires – do their duty by disinterring the principles which justify the law in fact relevant to the legal question and selecting the answer which shows the law in its best moral light. In his view, this argument undermined three main positivist theses.

First, he had shown that law is more than a matter of facts. It is also a matter of the principles implicit in the law which rise to the surface in hard cases. It followed, second, that one could reject the positivist claim that when judges must resort to principles, the judges are by definition not deciding according to law because they are exercising discretion – an act of legislation. In other words, since law is both a matter of fact and principles, in hard cases judges will find that the law does not run out and so they do not have to legislate an answer. The principles will supply the legal reasons which permit judges to reason that their decisions are fully justified by the law. Finally, to show the law in its best light is to show it in its best moral light. Since Dworkin took the most basic of such principles to be the liberal principle that individuals should be treated with equal concern and respect, he argued that law's connection with moral values is neither contingent nor precarious. He thus rejected the Separation Thesis which Hart took as the hallmark of the positivist tradition. In sum, Dworkin's challenge to legal positivism was that the authority of law is de jure since it is based on the liberal moral principles implicit in the law of any legal order.[23]

In mounting this challenge, Dworkin accepted Hart's argument that law is to be understood as a matter of authority and from the internal point of view. Indeed, since judges generally present their judgments as

[22] In Ronald Dworkin, *Taking Rights Seriously* (London: Duckworth, 1981, 3rd impression) 14 and 46.

[23] In *Law's Empire* (London: Fontana, 1986), Dworkin developed this argument in setting out an account of what he called 'associative obligation', the obligations of a community constituted by law. See 195–202. I develop a similar idea here through what I term a 'jural community'.

fully determined by law, he maintained that the adoption of the internal point of view as the lens for legal theory supported his position. But because Dworkin never denied that 'the existence and content of the law' is in part 'a matter of social fact' he made, so legal positivists suggested, his claim about law's connection with morality hostage to facts about the law established by the lawmakers of a particular society. To the extent that lawmakers were determined to use the law as an instrument of an oppressive, discriminatory and deeply illiberal ideology, the part of the law reflective of that ideology would expand and eventually make impossible any judicial attempt to show the law in a moral light. Any judicial interpretation, to use Dworkin's terminology, would have to 'fit' so large an amount of relevant law which as a matter of fact exhibited explicitly immoral content that the best 'justification' of the law would be one which promoted that content.[24] As Raz put this point in the essay which opened with his homage to Hart, Dworkin's claim that judges should decide hard cases in 'accordance with the prevailing spirit behind the bulk of the law' would have required a 'South African judge to use his power to extend apartheid'.[25]

Dworkin always tried to avoid confronting this criticism, and in his last word on it said that, while 'the puzzle of evil law' has had a 'prominent place in seminars on legal theory', it is of 'almost no practical importance' because philosophers of law agree that judges should refuse to apply such law, even if they disagree about the reasons they may rely on in doing so.[26] He never, though, found a satisfactory way to respond to the criticism, one in which Hart joined with what Dworkin once called 'uncharacteristic vehemence'.[27]

We will see that such vehement moments in Hart's responses to his foils in his otherwise temperate approach are revealing. As was the case with Hart's tone in dismissing others of his time who argued for a necessary connection between law and morality – Radbruch and Fuller[28] – vehemence on his part showed that their positions touched a crucial nerve in his theory. Indeed, he confessed in his last collection of

[24] See Ronald Dworkin, 'Hard Cases', in Dworkin, *Taking Rights Seriously* 81.

[25] Raz, 'Authority, Law, and Morality', 209.

[26] Ronald Dworkin, *Justice for Hedgehogs* (Cambridge, MA: Belknap Press, 2011), 410.

[27] Ronald Dworkin, 'A Reply by Ronald Dworkin', in Marshall Cohen, ed., *Ronald Dworkin and Contemporary Jurisprudence* (London: Duckworth, 1984) 247, at 257.

[28] Hart, 'Positivism and the Separation of Law and Morals', 72–5. In fairness, Hart's remarks about Fuller were more temperate but still disparaging – for example, Hart, 'Lon L Fuller: *The Morality of Law*', in Hart, *Essays in Jurisprudence and Philosophy* 343,

essays that a legal theory is implausible which tries to explain law as a matter of authority when it does not resort to some basis in morality for the claim of right implicit in a claim to authority. This confession comes in the course of not only Hart's last and also intemperate attack on Dworkin but also in an expression of concern about Raz's own injection through his idea of the legitimacy claimed by law of a 'moral component' into a positivist theory of law's authority.[29]

Hart was not much troubled by Raz's idea that officials must at least pretend to believe, however insincerely, that the laws they enforce are legitimate because he thought that the idea lacks any moral content and so fails to threaten the Separation Thesis. But his rejection of both Dworkin's claim that there is a basis in moral principles for law's authority and Raz's moral component left him with a position which he acknowledged in his *Essays on Bentham* might seem 'paradoxical or even a sign of confusion' to 'many' because it entails that 'judicial statements of the subject's legal duties need have nothing to do with the subject's reasons for action'.[30] Nevertheless, he asserted that legal theory could make do with the idea of the 'rule of recognition', the most fundamental rule of a modern legal state. The rule specifies the ultimate criteria of validity for all the other rules of a legal order and, through the practice of the officials who in fact accept it, constitutes legal authority.[31]

These *Essays on Bentham* are Hart's most important sequel to 'Positivism and the Separation of Law and Morals' and *The Concept of Law*. They make clear Hart's enduring debt to Bentham for having 'brought into political and legal theory a new and uncompromisingly positivist train of thought'. Hart acknowledged that the roots of Bentham's and his own theories of authority lie in Hobbes's account of law as the command of a sovereign. As he noted, Bentham shared with Hobbes the thought that both the 'legislative power' and 'political society … itself' are 'human artefacts', in Hobbes's view, the product of a social contract between those who find themselves subject to that power, the members of that political society. But as Hart also noted, Hume's 'criticism of the theory of the social contract' had had the effect,

at 363, perhaps because, as I indicate later, Hart considered Fuller's main insights to be easily absorbed into his legal theory.

29 HLA Hart, *Essays on Bentham: Jurisprudence and Political Theory* (Oxford: Clarendon Press, 1982), 147–61.

30 Ibid, 262–8, at 267.

31 Hart, *The Concept of Law*, 94–9.

on Bentham's own account, that the 'scales fell from [his] eyes', so that Bentham rejected as a misleading fiction Hobbes's idea that the command constituted law because it was given to 'subjects already under a prior obligation arising from their contract with each other to obey him'.[32]

Hart applauded Bentham's attempt to move away from Hobbes's constitutionalist idea of the social contract by founding obligation in a fact about legal order – in the 'disposition of the people', or what Austin called the 'habit of obedience'.[33] He also applauded Bentham's struggles to come to terms with another fact – that sovereignty or ultimate legal authority is legally limited. In contrast, Austin had followed Hobbes (or so Hart thought) in simply stipulating that the sovereign was by definition not subject to legal limit. But as Hart's 1958 critique of the command theory of law showed, he regarded it as a mistake to try to do without any such idea, a mistake which issued in the conclusion that the commander is 'uncommanded' – 'the gunman situation writ large'.[34] Here Hart found Bentham a more subtle thinker than Austin. He suggested that Bentham in his struggles on this score had done the groundwork for locating the basis of legal authority in an actual social practice, understood from the internal point of view of the participants in the practice, and not, as in Austin, located in facts about what people merely have a habit of doing.[35]

However, as Hart had begun to argue in 1958, the salient practice for legal theory is not that of all those subject to law. Rather, it is the practice of the officials who maintain the fundamental rules of a legal order and, in maintaining them, manifest their acceptance of such rules as providing them with 'authoritative legal reasons'. As he put it in his response to Raz: 'When a judge of an established legal system takes up his office he finds that though much is left to his discretion there is also a firmly settled practice of adjudication, according to which any judge of the system is required to apply in the decision of cases the laws identified by specific criteria or sources.'[36]

32 Hart, *Essays on Bentham*, 221. Jeremy Bentham, *A Fragment on Government* (Cambridge: Cambridge University Press, 1988), 51.

33 John Austin, *Lectures on Jurisprudence or the Philosophy of Positive Law*, vol. 1 (London: John Murray, 1885, 5th ed.), 220–1.

34 Hart, 'Positivism and the Separation of Law and Morals', 59.

35 Hart, *Essays on Bentham*, 222–5.

36 Ibid, 158.

Hart thus sought to reinstate a constitutionalist idea at the centre of a theory of legal order. But he wanted to do so without invoking anything that smacked of the social contract and the thought that such an idea legitimates the order. He suggested he could achieve this by explaining both that acceptance could be confined to officials and that their acceptance in no way implied moral endorsement, which is why he wanted to ward off Raz's moral component. He omitted to note, however, that Raz had taken from Kelsen the idea that there is a peculiarly legal point of view which the jurist or official must adopt – the view of the legal subject who regards the law as a legitimate legal authority. Raz named this figure Kelsen's 'legal man', the legal subject who adopts 'the law as his personal morality, and as exhausting all the norms he accepts as just'.[37]

Hart's omission of the detail that in dismissing Raz on this one point he was also dismissing Kelsen can be explained by the fact that Hart thought he had successfully demolished Kelsen's Pure Theory of law in earlier works. Thus, Kelsen hardly figures in *Essays on Bentham*, as is the case in philosophy of law today where, if he is discussed, it is usually through the partial and obscuring lens Hart provided in the two essays he devoted to Kelsen, as well as in his marginal remarks in *The Concept of Law*. Indeed, Hart's vehemence when it came to criticism of his foils who argued for a necessary connection between law and morality is more than matched by his tone when it came to his fellow positivist Kelsen, whom he accused variously of making 'perverse', 'confused', 'profoundly mistaken', 'highly idiosyncratic' and 'content-obsessed' arguments, and of putting forth a 'comic' theory based on a 'useless' central idea.[38]

Three things worried Hart in particular about Kelsen's Pure Theory. First, he took it to be a version of the command theory since Kelsen argued that all legal norms are instructions to officials to apply sanctions to disobedient subjects.[39] Second, while Kelsen put forward his own

[37] Joseph Raz, 'Kelsen's Theory of the Basic Norm', in Raz, *The Authority of Law: Essays on Law and Morality* (Oxford: Clarendon Press, 1983) 122, at 142–3.

[38] Hart, *The Concept of Law*, 236, and HLA Hart, 'Kelsen Visited' and 'Kelsen's Doctrine of the Unity of Law', in Hart, *Essays in Jurisprudence*, 286 and 309, at 302, 313, 321. In an interview in 1988, Hart said that Kelsen's 'central error was his . . . "content-obsession"; this led him to attempt to determine the question whether laws belong to the same or different systems solely by an examination of their content'. HLA Hart, 'Answers to Eight Questions', in Luís Duarte D'Almeida, James Edwards and Andrea Dolcetti, eds, *Reading HLA Hart's The Concept of Law* (Oxford: Hart Publishing, 2013) 279, at 290. The irony here will be become evident as I develop my argument, since on my account blame for that error should be laid at Hart's door.

[39] Hart, *The Concept of Law*, 35–8.

version of the Separation Thesis in the slogan that 'law can have any content', he also argued that it is not possible for two valid norms to be in a genuine conflict. For example, if a norm of a moral order prohibits killing while the norm of a legal order requires it through imposing an obligation to perform military service, someone eligible for such service will have to choose which normative order to regard as valid.[40] Hart thought that not only do valid norms come into genuine conflict but also that to deny such conflict, as in this example, precludes moral criticism of the law one recognizes as valid.[41] The denial, in other words, obscures the moral clarity which the Separation Thesis brings in permitting the legal subject to 'speak plainly' and say that valid 'laws may be law but too evil to be obeyed'.[42]

Hart thus thought that Kelsen had, despite his positivism, fallen into one of the two traps he suggested in 1958 inhere in the claim of the natural law tradition that an extremely unjust law cannot be law – *lex injusta non est lex*. For that claim leads either to the 'anarchist' mistake in supposing that a law one finds to be immoral is not really law or to the opposite reactionary mistake of 'obsequious quietism' in supposing that X should be obeyed just because X is the law.[43] Kelsen, Hart clearly supposed, had fallen into the second trap and, on Raz's reading of Kelsen's legal man, Hart would be entirely correct.

Most important though for Hart was his third concern, Kelsen's 'useless' candidate for the constitutionalist idea – the *Grundnorm* or basic norm which states that the constitution of a legal order, and thus all its valid laws, is to be obeyed. Unlike Hart's rule of recognition, the basic norm is not read off the practice of legal officials. It is stipulated by those who wish to make sense of legal order as a meaningful order of norms, as a unity rather than a conflicting plurality of competing authoritative demands. The basic norm for Kelsen is the key to legal theory because it explains how law transforms might into legal right.[44]

40 Hans Kelsen, *General Theory of Law and State* (Cambridge, MA: Harvard University Press, 1945, Anders Wedberg, trans.), 375.

41 Hart, 'Kelsen Visited', 302–3.

42 Hart, 'Positivism and the Separation of Law and Morals', 77.

43 Ibid, 53–4, quoting Bentham.

44 See, for example, Hans Kelsen, *Die philosophischen Grundlagen der Naturrechtlehre und des Rechtspositivismus*, where he says that the attempt by the positivist jurist to comprehend law as an objective order through the medium of the *Grundnorm* entails that 'in a certain sense might is transformed into right', in Hans Klecatsky, René Marcic and Herbert Schambeck, eds, *Die Wiener rechtstheoretische Schule: Hans Kelsen, Adolf*

Hart, however, dismissed it as redundant to an explanation of the authority of law. It sufficed to observe, he argued, that, as a matter of actual official practice, there exists a rule which stipulates criteria for the recognition of valid laws and that officials manifest their acceptance of this rule by applying the criteria and criticizing those who do not.[45]

Hart's claim that one should look no further than to the fact of accepted rule to explain law's authority is considered by his critics and by some of his followers to be wrong; Raz's Kelsen-inspired introduction of his moral component is the most prominent example of the latter. But there seems to be little interest in Anglo-American legal theory in investigating whether Kelsen's basic norm might do better, in large part because Hart's dominance means that it is taken on trust that he had successfully disposed of the figures in what he recognized as his own tradition – Bentham and Austin – as well as Kelsen. As a result, philosophy of law can work in Hart's paradigm, as shaped by Raz, with occasional pauses to rebuff the lurchers, Fuller and then Dworkin, who attempt to revive one or other version of the natural law idea that there is a necessary connection between law and morality. At the same time, positivism can incorporate some useful insights they provided, along with some further insights gleaned from Kelsen, though with these insights scrubbed of any features which trouble the Separation Thesis.

Like Raz's essay from which I quoted, my book is in part an homage to Hart, though one which dwells on moments in his work which his successors regard as either mistakes or mere afterthoughts to his main arguments, a status Hart himself signalled by postponing these moments to the end of his analysis in both 'Positivism and the Separation of Law and Morals' and *The Concept of Law*. In addition, he treated the topics discussed in these moments – the relationship between law and justice, between law and morality and, in *The Concept of Law*, between municipal law and public international law – as if they were discrete, each waiting for the application of the legal theory he had developed earlier.

As I show, this strategy permitted Hart to divide and conquer his foils at the same time as he incorporated into his legal theory their insights in

Merkl, Alfred Verdross, vol. 1 (Vienna: Europa Verlag, 1968) 281, at 339. I refer to the translation which appears as an appendix to Kelsen, *General Theory of Law and State*, 389 under the title 'Natural Law Doctrine and Legal Positivism' (Wolfgang Herbert Kraus, trans.). For the relevant passage, see 437, where '*die Transformation der Macht zu Recht*' (Kelsen's emphasis) is translated blandly as 'the transformation of power into law'.

[45] Hart, *The Concept of Law*, 293.

order to strip them of content to the point where they did not endanger the Separation Thesis. I also argue that a successful account of law's authority – of what Hart once called 'legal legitimacy'[46] – requires, first, that the topics he regarded as mere afterthoughts, waiting for the application of a fully elaborated theory, are made central to the account, and second, that the insights of Hart's foils which he incorporated into his legal theory be appreciated more on their own terms.

Consider in the first regard that Hart at the outset of *The Concept of Law* asserted that international law is 'only a relatively small and unimportant part of the most famous and controversial theories of law',[47] and relegated its treatment to the last chapter in which it turned out not to be law properly so-called, at least not law in the sense of law validated by a rule of recognition. Kelsen, in contrast, argued that the authority of the modern legal state cannot be understood other than through the place of all such states in the international legal order, which required that one fully integrate a theory of international law as law properly so-called into one's general theory of law.

In the second regard, consider that when Hart introduced Radbruch to philosophy of law in English in 1958 he observed that Radbruch's claim that extreme injustice is no law was due to his 'considered reflections' on the Nazi experience which had 'led him to the doctrine that the fundamental principles of humanitarian morality were part of the very concept of *Recht* or Legality and that no positive enactment or statute, however clearly it was expressed and however clearly it conformed with the formal criteria of validity of a given legal system, could be valid if it contravened basic principles of morality'.[48] Hart added that this 'doctrine can be appreciated fully only if the nuances imported by the German word *Recht* are grasped'.[49]

But Hart did not pause to grasp the nuances. Instead, he moved immediately to invective, saying that Radbruch and others were guilty of 'extraordinary naïvety' in supposing that the positivist view that an utterly immoral law could still be a law had played a role in the Germans

46 See Hart, 'Answers to Eight Questions', 298. Though see also Hart, *The Concept of Law*, 55–6 where, in discussing deviation from rules in contrast to mere habits, Hart said that with the former 'deviation from the standard is generally accepted as a *good reason* for making it'. His emphasis. It follows, ibid, that in such cases 'criticism for deviation is regarded as *legitimate* or justified in this sense'. My emphasis.

47 Ibid, 4.

48 Hart, 'Positivism and the Separation of Law and Morals', 74.

49 Ibid, 74–5.

becoming insensitive to the 'demands of morality' and hence 'subservient to state power'. It sufficed, in his view, to repeat Austin's claim that natural law positions like Radbruch's are 'stark nonsense', as demonstrated by the example of a man condemned to death for a trivial offence, who claims that the law is not law because it is immoral, but who is refuted because 'the court of justice will demonstrate the inconclusiveness of . . . [his] reasoning by hanging . . . [him] up, in pursuance of the law of which . . . [he had] impugned the validity'.[50]

Hart's refusal to explore the nuances of *Recht* at this point is due to his understanding of the debate in legal theory as between legal positivism and what he took to be the two strands of the natural law tradition, corresponding to the two traps he had diagnosed in 1958 of anarchism and quietism. As he set these out in 1961, one strand states that there are principles 'of true morality or justice, discoverable by human reason without the aid of divine revelation even though they may have a divine origin'. Law to be law must comply with these principles – *lex injusta non est lex*. The other strand argues that there is a 'widely diffused though not necessarily universal, recognition of a moral obligation to obey the law, even though this may be overridden in particular cases by a stronger moral obligation not to obey particular morally iniquitous laws'.[51] But, as in his reliance on Austin's example to answer Radbruch, Hart took the former strand to be what I call 'positivism with a minus sign': the law of a legal order is all of its positive laws as identified by its criteria of validity with those laws subtracted which are extremely unjust by some moral standard external to legal order. He supposed that this strand is refuted by the existence of immoral laws and wicked legal systems, just as he later claimed of Dworkin's interpretive theory. In regard to the latter strand, he perceived only a grain of truth to it. While there must be at least some group of individuals who accept the law as duty-imposing, not only may they be a distinct minority – the officials – but their reasons for taking such an internal point of view need not be moral reasons, or even pretend moral reasons, as we saw from Hart's response to Raz.[52]

Hart did not list a third natural law position, one which I show Hobbes pioneered in *Leviathan*. It holds that the principles are discoverable by human reason. But they are not to be found in some natural order of things which tends towards some kind of telos or end, as thinkers from

[50] Ibid, 73.
[51] Hart, *The Concept of Law*, 156–7.
[52] Ibid, 117.

Aristotle through Aquinas to John Finnis have supposed. Rather, these principles are entirely internal to a legal order in that no legal order worthy of the name could fail to instantiate them. Moreover, conformity to these principles will sustain a relationship of reciprocity between ruler and ruled, something like Hobbes's relation between protection and obedience.

Hart thought therefore that he did not have to consider this position as one within the natural law tradition since he understood the tradition as appealing to moral standards external to law. He did though confront it on several occasions in the form Fuller gave it of the principles of legality necessary for legal order to exist. Hart argued either that he could accept Fuller's basic insights into his own theory while deflating their moral pretensions, just as he did with the second strand of natural law, or that the principles are not necessary to legal order.[53] But in both cases, Hart effected a kind of rapprochement with a position which, in my view, is the best candidate for a viable natural law position. Moreover, his failure to discuss the nuances in Radbruch's account of law as *Recht* meant both that he could attempt to ignore the fact that Radbruch's account elaborated a theory based on this kind of position and that he could attempt to respond more easily to the position, once he had repackaged it in the next part of his essay.

In this book I treat this third position as *the* natural law one and use the vocabulary of natural law in elaborating it, for example, in talking about the 'nature' of law,[54] not only because this is the accurate way to describe it but also because it is the position which provides the account of the authority of law with the three elements sketched above. I have already tried in previous work to show that such a position is the best candidate for solving the puzzle of authority. In *Hard Cases in Wicked Legal Systems: South African Law in the Perspective of Legal Philosophy*,[55] I argued against Dworkin that the puzzle of authority, as raised by the existence of valid or authoritative evil law, is of practical importance. At the same time, I argued against legal positivism that a study of the actual

[53] See Jeremy Waldron, 'Positivism and Legality: Hart's Equivocal Response to Fuller' (2008) 83 *New York University Law Review* 1135.

[54] See Lorraine Daston, *Against Nature* (Cambridge, MA: MIT Press, 2019) for an account of why appeals to the natural order of things in normative theories are both hard to escape and should not be feared, so long as one sees there is a plurality of such orders available.

[55] *Hard Cases in Wicked Legal Systems: South African Law in the Perspective of Legal Philosophy* (Oxford: Clarendon Press, 1991).

adjudication of such cases reveals that they support the claim that there is a necessary connection between law and morality.

The title was adapted from Dworkin's claim that a study of such cases is 'not very important . . . from the practical point of view, because the judgments we make about foreign wicked legal systems are rarely hinged to decisions we have to take'.[56] However, in the line preceding the claim about the 'practical point of view', he had said that wicked legal systems 'should be treated . . . like hard cases that turn on which conception of law is best rather than easy cases whose proper resolution we already know and can therefore use to test for any particular conception for adequacy'.[57] That claim seemed to make wicked legal systems quite important. After all, for Dworkin hard cases provide the resource for working out both the content of rival conceptions of law and for adjudicating between their substantive merits. The 'hard case' of authority in a wicked legal system should, that is, provide us with insight into the 'easy case' of the authority of a morally decent system. In this regard, I argued that when a deeply immoral ideology becomes 'the prevailing spirit behind the bulk of the law',[58] so the very fabric of legal order is rent to the point where those who wield political power can no longer claim to be governing according to law.

This argument relied mainly on Fuller's attempt to show that there are eight formal 'desiderata' or principles of legality with which the law of any legal order must largely comply, for example, generality, publicity and non-contradiction, and that these principles amount to an 'inner morality' of law.[59] That judges were able to show the law in its best moral light depended on their legal order being in good shape as a *legal* order, in good shape from the perspective of legality.

Dworkin, we should note, had been just as dismissive of Fuller's legal theory as Hart and later Raz.[60] In their view, even if Fuller were right, at

56 Dworkin, 'A Reply by Ronald Dworkin', 260.

57 Ibid. See also Dworkin, *Law's Empire*, 108: 'The question of wicked legal systems . . . is not one but many questions, and they all arise, for legal theory, at the level where conceptions compete.'

58 Raz, 'Authority, Law, and Morality', 209.

59 Lon L Fuller, *The Morality of Law* (New Haven: Yale University Press, 1969, revised ed.), 38–44.

60 Ronald Dworkin, 'Philosophy, Morality, and Law: Observations Prompted by Professor Fuller's Novel Claim' (1965) 113 *University of Pennsylvania Law Review* 672; Hart, *The Concept of Law*, 206–7. See further, Joseph Raz, 'The Rule of Law and Its Virtue', in Raz, *The Authority of Law* 210, at 223–6.

most compliance with such principles would make law a more effective instrument of policy, which would make its connection with morality entirely contingent. But I showed that in the circumstances of apartheid South Africa the possibility of judges adjudicating along Dworkinian lines depended on lawmakers abiding by the principles. In other words, the presence of the more substantive moral principles which for Dworkin make law a matter of principle is dependent on the legal order's compliance with the formal principles which figure in Fuller's theory of legality. Further, the more that possibility waned, the more this was because governmental power became arbitrary in that it was unmediated by law, whether law is understood as a matter of fact or of fact and principles. It followed that as long as legal order prevailed, so there was a moral quality to the law.

But this was only a first step. One case study, even if successful, can have only limited application to a debate in philosophy of law as it is vulnerable to the charge of parochialism, a charge that positivists levelled in more or less polite forms against Dworkin. For his positivist critics allege that his legal theory is at best a mere 'theory of adjudication', not a general theory of law, and at worst a theory of how judges in a particular place during a particular period were able to decide hard cases on the basis of liberal principle. It is, that is, an account best suited to the period during which Dworkin both received his legal education and put in place the foundations of his legal theory: the 'Warren Court', roughly 1953–69, when, under the leadership of Earl Warren, the US Supreme Court developed a far-reaching liberal jurisprudence, enabled by its constitutional authority to invalidate legislation which conflicted with its sense of constitutionally protected rights.

To counter this kind of charge, I sought in the second edition of *Hard Cases in Wicked Legal Systems* to situate better my argument in its intellectual context.[61] For I had begun to trace its roots in Hobbes's theory of the authority of the modern legal state, whereas in the first edition Hobbes had the role of the villain in the piece, the thinker whose authoritarian political theory explains why legal officials might suppose that their duty was to apply the law as it in fact requires, whatever its content. As I argued in the second edition and elsewhere, and as Oakeshott indicated, the Austinian view that the sovereign – the ultimate legal authority – is not subject to law is true of Hobbes only to the extent

[61] See my *Hard Cases in Wicked Legal Systems: Pathologies of Legality* (Oxford: Oxford University Press, 2010, 2nd ed.).

that in his legal theory the sovereign may change positive law at will. Austin failed therefore with Hart and most other readers of Hobbes to appreciate the way in which the sovereign is for Hobbes subject to law in another sense, the sense of *Recht* or *jus*. In addition, I had become more aware of how Hart's own theory contains unexploited resources for attending to the puzzle of legal authority. These resources included Hart's concessions, intended and unintended, to the various strands of the natural law tradition.

Here I show that, once these concessions are assembled together from the places where Hart's divide and conquer strategy scattered them, the third natural law position emerges from his own 'positivist' theory, though with both the moral standards and the official activity he deemed external to legal order, and thus outside the scope of philosophy of law, fully internalized. Moreover, with these elements internalized, it becomes not only plausible but even necessary to accept the second natural law strand Hart identified – that there is a 'widely diffused though not necessarily universal, recognition of a moral obligation to obey the law, even though this may be overridden in particular cases by a stronger moral obligation not to obey particular morally iniquitous laws'.[62] That, in turn, requires accepting the first strand in that one accepts that law to be law must meet the standards set by the *jus* of *lex*, by law's own internal standards of justice.

In order to show all this, I need to take a further step in setting out the long arc of legality. Kelsen's Pure Theory is the main new player. As I show, in the two essays Hart devoted to criticism of Kelsen he missed entirely the most important dimension of Kelsen's legal theory – that it is above all a dynamic legal theory. Such a theory tries to capture a crucial feature of the modern legal state: it is the state which engages in the fully law-governed production of legal norms.[63] It thus differs from a static theory in that it includes the dynamic process of legal change within the scope of philosophy of law while a static theory consigns change to some extra-legal space.

Kelsen himself thought that the biggest mistake in Hart's tradition, what he called the 'analytical jurisprudence' of John Austin, is that it 'regards law as a system of rules complete and ready for application,

[62] Hart, *The Concept of Law*, 156–7.

[63] Hans Kelsen, 'The Pure Theory of Law and Analytical Jurisprudence' (1941) 55 *Harvard Law Review* 44.

without regard to the process of their creation'.[64] Now in 1958, Hart had emphatically rejected the view that his positivist tradition supports a theory of adjudication according to which 'the law was a closed logical system in which judges deduced their decisions from premises'. 'The root of this evil', Hart said, is a 'preoccupation with the separation of powers and Blackstone's "childish fiction" (as Austin termed it) that judges only "find," never "make," law'.[65] For the same reason, Hart would have repudiated Kelsen's attribution of a static theory of law to his own amendments to Austin's command theory.

As we will see, Kelsen's diagnosis of the problem in Hart's tradition is spot on. Hart's inability to move away from a static understanding of legal order stemmed from his explicit assumption that one can construct a theory of law by focusing on the distinctive structure of a municipal legal system and from two implicit assumptions. First, that the paradigm of such a system is one in which there is parliamentary supremacy and in which moral norms act only as an external and extra-legal check on the already determined content of the law. Such norms, that is, provide a source for criticizing the content of the law as it is and thus for reforming it. But they are not conceived as intrinsic to law so that it is part of the officials' obligation of 'fidelity to law',[66] to use Fuller's term, to work out the content of the law in light of such principles. Second, municipal systems are as a matter of fact independent from each other in that they are sealed against penetration by the legal norms of other systems, including the norms of international law. As a corollary, norms from one system enter another only by permission of the other.[67]

As a result, Hart built into his general theory of legal order contingent features of his own, in particular the dualistic stance that international legal norms become law properly so-called from the internal point of view of the officials of that order only when the norms have been explicitly incorporated by positive law. And, as Kelsen argued, this kind of dualism will recur throughout such a theory, most notably, as dualism about the relationship between law and morality, that is, the Separation Thesis.

[64] Ibid, 49.

[65] Hart, 'Positivism and the Separation of Law and Morals', 66.

[66] Lon L Fuller, 'Positivism and Fidelity to Law: A Reply to Professor Hart' (1958) 71 *Harvard Law Review* 630.

[67] See, notably, Hart, *The Concept of Law*, 296–7, the endnote to 121.

These assumptions confine Hart and the others in his tradition to explaining the static dimension of law, and their attempts to adapt their theories to account for the dynamic dimension are in deep tension with any commitment to the Separation Thesis. In this tradition, Austin alone frankly recognized that the assumptions make it very difficult, perhaps impossible, for its adherents to recognize either constitutional law or public international law as law properly so-called.[68] Even in the legal order which they take as their model – the UK order of parliamentary supremacy – the common law turns out to be not quite law properly so-called.[69] Rather ironically, then, Hart's legal positivism, which still shapes philosophy of law today, turns out to be utterly parochial, not only a (flawed) legal theory of one municipal structure, UK-style parliamentary supremacy but also of that structure at a time when Hart and others were struggling to make sense of the death throes of empire, though without explicit engagement with the implications of those throes for their theories.[70] It also turns out that Hart's theory proves incapable on its own terms of making a move away from the command theory of law. While it will take this whole book to make this argument, I wish to note its important themes at the outset, the first of which has to do with the distinction between static and dynamic theories of law.

I.2 Static versus Dynamic Theories of Law

On my argument to come, it turns out that the fundamental divide in philosophy of law is neither between legal positivism and natural law theory, nor between theories of law and theories of adjudication. Rather, the divide is between static theories of law, as espoused by Bentham, Austin, Hart and Raz, and dynamic theories, as espoused by Hobbes,

[68] Austin, *Lectures on Jurisprudence*, vol. 1, 177, 204.

[69] As AWB Simpson showed in a brilliant essay, 'The Common Law and Legal Theory', in Simpson, ed., *Oxford Essays in Jurisprudence* (Oxford: Oxford University Press, 1973, 2nd series) 77. The attempt to remedy this defect led to the development of 'inclusive legal positivism' which holds that dynamic theories such as Dworkin's are plausible but only when a legal order has as a matter of contingent fact incorporated moral principles into its positive law. In contrast, 'exclusive legal positivists' maintain that only facts can be a ground for legal validity. See Appendix I. I treat Hart's legal positivism in its exclusive version, which it must take if it is to retain its hold on the Separation Thesis.

[70] See Coel Kirkby, 'Law Evolves: The Uses of Primitive Law in Anglo-American Concepts of Modern Law, 1861–1961' (2018) 58 *American Journal of Legal History* 535.

Kelsen, Radbruch, Fuller and Dworkin, with Kelsen the philosopher of law who set out the fullest account of such a theory.

First, and as suggested, static theories are aware of the dynamic dimension of legal order and do attempt to grapple with it. But their allegiance to their static model makes these attempts vain and mainly serves to highlight tensions in their theories. In contrast, dynamic theories are not only fully aware of law's static dimension but also give that dimension a role in their theories. In other words, dynamic theories integrate the 'is' and the 'ought' of law – law's factual side and its normative side. In doing so, they also respond to the tensions which beset their static counterparts by explaining how a mark of legal order is that it is already designed, though could always be better designed, to respond institutionally to such tensions. In other words, the tensions are not theoretical. Rather, they are tensions diagnosed by the theory which can as such receive an institutional solution, which brings me to a second theme – conflicts between norms.

I.3 Conflicts between Norms

I generally use the term 'very unjust' rather than 'evil' or 'wicked' to describe the kind of law which creates the puzzle of unjust law, namely the puzzle which arises when the content of a law is deeply immoral, yet it appears that because the law is valid it has some normative force. As I have explained, I want to explore the legal philosophical project of understanding the transformation of power into authority brought about by the establishment of the modern legal state. In this vein, when it comes to the moral standards which law must meet in order to be law, no natural law position should argue for the anarchist position that law is not law merely because it seems unjust to me, that is, from my moral perspective external to the law. Rather, law ceases to be law when it fails by its own internal moral standards, standards which maintain the equal status as persons of the individuals whom law addresses.

The natural law position of the kind I develop here holds that there is a moral order immanent in the law as we find it, in social facts about the law as it is, and this moral order responds to the problem of extremely unjust laws. The position thus takes its place with other natural law positions in the 'theodistic tradition' which supposes that God's works in the world as we find it are for the best according to some intrinsic moral order. As Susan Neiman explains in her illuminating work on evil in modern thought, secular positions which claim that the world as we find it contains the moral resources we need to resolve our problems fit within this tradition.[71]

Legal positivism is part of an opposing tradition in that it does not suppose that the legal world as we find it has the resources to respond to such injustice, so it consigns the problem elsewhere; we might say, it expels the problem from the legal to the moral system. The difference between using 'very unjust' (and therefore potentially manageable by law) and 'evil' (and therefore inherently unmanageable by law) as the description of such laws should therefore indicate which tradition one belongs to, though actual debate is not precise in this way.

Consider that in the debate I describe in Chapter 1 Hart rejected natural law positions because they share a 'romantic optimism that all the values that we cherish ultimately will fit into a single system, that not one of them has to be sacrificed or compromised to accommodate another'.[72] And he quoted the following lines as an expression of the optimism he rejected: 'All Discord Harmony not understood | All partial evil Universal Good.'[73] These lines are from Alexander Pope's philosophical poem, *Essay on Man*, which as Neiman shows is a central text in the theodistic tradition.[74]

Dworkin's title of his last work, *Justice for Hedgehogs*, may be seen as a direct riposte to Hart. The Greek poet Archilochus said that 'the Fox knows many things, but the hedgehog, knows only one big thing', a contrast made popular by Isaiah Berlin in his essay, 'The Hedgehog and the Fox'.[75] And Dworkin, on the first page of his book, declared himself a hedgehog and placed himself in the camp of those who see the normative world through the lens of one value – Kant's principle of dignity – in contrast to foxes, who think that a plurality of values is needed.[76]

But the more important reason for using 'very unjust' rather than 'wicked' or 'evil' to describe the issue confronting philosophy of law is that 'wicked' and 'evil' have distorting distancing effects on the way philosophers of law think about the problem. Standardly, the problem

[71] Susan Neiman, *Evil in Modern Thought: An Alternative History of Philosophy* (Princeton: Princeton University Press, 2002), 7–8.

[72] Hart, 'Positivism and the Separation of Law and Morals', 77.

[73] Ibid.

[74] Neiman, *Evil in Modern Thought*, 31–6.

[75] Isaiah Berlin, 'The Hedgehog and the Fox', in Berlin, *Russian Thinkers* (London: The Hogarth Press, 1978) 22, at 22.

[76] Dworkin, *Justice for Hedgehogs*, 1.

is thought to be one which dwells in other often distant times or places: the Nazi state, the antebellum USA with its laws permitting both slavery itself and the Fugitive Slave laws which required that fugitives be returned to their masters, and the racist laws of the South African state during apartheid.

Recall that Dworkin suggested that we should not take the puzzle of very unjust law too seriously because it is 'not very important ... from the practical point of view, because the judgments we make about foreign wicked legal systems are rarely hinged to decisions we have to take'.[77] As I pointed out in Section I.1, that seems wrong. On Dworkin's own terms, the hard case of legitimacy in an unjust legal system should provide us with an insight into the easy case of the legitimacy of a morally decent system, just as in Dworkin's legal theory it is through the adjudication of hard cases that we can learn about what makes a case easy.

But the point I want to make goes further. The problem, properly characterized as one about very unjust law, should matter to those who think that their legal orders are more or less just, or at any rate not too unjust, because it helps to alert them to problems of injustice which might be otherwise hard for them to detect. Law itself helps in this regard in that the commitment to governing legally, that is, in accordance with fundamental principles of legality, helps to bring certain kinds of injustice to the surface as problems which the legal order needs to solve in order to maintain itself in good shape. It follows that the puzzle of very unjust law is a permanent problem for legal theory. One might even say with only slight exaggeration that it is *the* problem for legal theory, if philosophy of law is principally about explaining law's authority. It is a permanent problem for us, whoever we are, in that injustice is often hard to see, especially by those who are its beneficiaries or at least not its immediate victims, and even sometimes by the victims themselves.

This last set of claims might appear to be so obvious as to be trite. But what makes them neither obvious nor trite is that they are claims about law's role in both justice and injustice. The idea that law can be both sword and shield – both the instrument of injustice and a bulwark against it – is hardly novel and the rule of law is usually and rightly invoked to explain the way in which law can be a bulwark against injustice, though its role as bulwark is not that easy to explain in the face of very unjust laws. However, explanations of the virtue of the rule of law tend to see its

[77] Dworkin, 'A Reply by Ronald Dworkin', 260.

virtue as merely formal, as with legal positivists like Hart and Raz, or as too substantive, as with natural lawyers like Dworkin. If, as Hart put it in 1958, all that the rule of law can do when it comes to 'hideously oppressive' laws is ensure that they are applied with the 'most pedantic impartiality',[78] abiding by the rule of law will make matters morally worse. The bad moral content of particular laws will be reproduced time and again. Or, as Raz put the same point in what may be the most widely cited essay on the rule of law in the last fifty years, one should not confuse the rule of law with the 'rule of good law'. He went on:

> A non-democratic legal system, based on the denial of human rights, on extensive poverty, on racial segregation, sexual inequalities, and religious persecution may, in principle, conform to the requirements of the rule of law better than any of the legal systems of the more enlightened Western democracies.[79]

The innocent-seeming 'in principle' is what undermines Raz's argument. For *in practice* the rule of law affords the legal subject the opportunity to ask independent legal officials to answer the question posed by the figure I claimed should be at the centre of legal philosophical inquiry: the legal subject who asks 'But, how can that be law for me?' Those officials will in the first instance try to draw on the resources of legal principle which enable an answer to that question. But even if they find that they cannot provide an adequate answer, that does not show that Hart and Raz are proved correct. For the inadequacy may stem from their lowly place in the hierarchy of the normative structure of the legal order and officials higher up the hierarchy may be better placed to offer an adequate answer.

Moreover, in Kelsen's 'monistic' account of the relationship between states and the international legal order, the issue may only get a solution when it moves to the international level. In this regard, I argue that Kelsen's monism responds to the problem Hart detected of the pluralism of values without indulging in 'romantic optimism' precisely because he saw legal order as responding dynamically to conflicts between norms, that is, without supposing that such conflicts can be worked out harmoniously within one static worldview. However, as I now explain, I will not, and indeed could not, provide a comprehensive account of writings which stretched over more than half a century and in which Kelsen

[78] Hart, 'Positivism and the Separation of Law and Morals', 81.
[79] Raz, 'The Rule of Law and Its Virtue', 211.

changed his mind on many important issues. Instead, I attempt to show that Kelsen's Pure Theory is not an exercise in the heaven of concepts, but a deeply pragmatic account of legal theory's answerability to experience, itself based on law's answerability to the experience of the legal subject.

I.4 Kelsen's Pragmatism

My account is mainly of Kelsen in the 1920s and early 1930s, a period when he was developing both a general theory of law which integrated international law, and, in what Kelsen regarded as an entirely separate inquiry, a theory of democracy. I will later question Kelsen's view that his inquiry into democracy was so distinct from his general legal theory. For now, I want to emphasize that, unlike Hart who first developed his theory of the modern legal state and then applied that theory to international law, Kelsen integrated international law into his general legal theory. In doing so, he set out a theory of law which was cosmopolitan and took as one of its main tasks the development of an understanding of how different legal systems relate juridically to each other. This task included not only the relationship between each municipal system and the international legal order but also the relationship between the private law norms of different municipal systems, that is, the field of private international law which pertains to cases in which a court must consider a norm from a different jurisdiction because of some connection of the parties to that jurisdiction. Still Kelsen's theory remains one of the modern legal state, as that state is constituted within an international legal order of such states. As such it is parochial at least in that it is a theory of a politically contingent phenomenon of the West, albeit one exported to much of the world.

That feature naturally makes Kelsen vulnerable to the charge that his theory will neglect other kinds of law which are not state-produced, notably, customary law and Indigenous law, as well as law 'beyond the state', by which is meant much more than international law because it includes 'transnational law', 'global law' and so on. It also exposes him to the charge that his theory, like others, is an apology for imperialism, colonialism and all that travels with a nineteenth-century discourse of civilization, of what Article 38(1) of the Statute of the International Court of Justice describes as the 'general principles of law recognized by civilized nations'.

Both charges can be answered to the extent possible only by the argument of the whole book. Here are the nutshell versions. I have already pointed out that Hart's focus on the state – on the 'distinctive structure of municipal law' – led to an account of international law in the last chapter of *The Concept of Law* as not law properly so-called. But it is the way Hart focused on the state more than the focus per se that is the problem. For his focus was shaped by the assumptions which in combination make his legal theory highly parochial: a theory of the state in which the ultimate legal authority is a supreme parliament. In fact, things are worse in that the concept of the state is largely missing in his tradition, so that the role his conception of the modern legal state plays in his philosophy of law is largely subterranean.[80]

In contrast, the concept of the state is front and centre in Kelsen's legal theory, as it was in the European tradition of *Staatsrechtslehre* in which he worked. That title is hard to translate as it combines in one neologism 'state', 'legal right' and 'teaching'. I take it to indicate that one should approach the puzzle of legal authority through the lens of the legitimate authority of the modern legal state.[81] Moreover, it requires understanding all law as public law, which not only involves a rejection of those influential Kantian legal theories which give priority to private law over public law but also dropping any hard and fast distinction between the two.[82]

In contrast to Hart's dualisms between law and morality and public international law and municipal or domestic law, as well as the Kantian dualism about private and public law, Kelsenian legal theory presents an uncompromisingly monistic view of legal order in which there is one basic norm for all valid legal orders. But, once adapted in a way I sketch in this book, such monism makes possible the study of legal order in all its plurality of forms. Indeed, as I try to show, putting the state front and centre has in Kelsen's hands the somewhat paradoxical effect of decentring the state, since in order to understand the authority of any particular legal state, one must understand it in relation not only to international law but also to the private law of other states. More important is the state

[80] As pointed out by the evocative title of Janet McLean, *Searching for the State in British Legal Thought: Competing Conceptions of the Public Sphere* (Cambridge: Cambridge University Press, 2012).

[81] See my 'The Idea of a Constitution: A Plea for *Staatsrechtslehre*', in Dyzenhaus and Malcolm Thorburn, eds, *Philosophical Foundations of Constitutional Law* (Oxford: Oxford University Press, 2016) 9.

[82] See Appendix II.

itself is decentred in that with the birth of the modern legal state is born the legal subject, the juridical conception of the human individual as free and equal before the law.

Moreover, Kelsen's legal theory is, to use Raz's description of Hart, both 'realist and unromantic in outlook', indeed, much more realistic than Hart's tradition, though I will suggest that 'pragmatic' rather than 'realist' captures better what is at stake in these debates because of Kelsen's attention to the life of the law as lived experience, to adapt Oliver Wendell Holmes.[83] For the moment, I note that Kelsen much more than Hart took the legal world as we find it seriously as the object of philosophical inquiry, since in his theory facts about the actual experience of law must be accounted for by theory, not discounted because of prior moral commitments, notably those entailed by the Separation Thesis. In regard to the other charge of apology, I rely largely on Hart's analysis of the pathologies of legal order.

I.5 Law's Pathologies

I have already indicated my claim that Hart's *The Concept of Law* is haunted by the death throes of the British Empire. But at the same time his book is more sensitive than perhaps any other classic of philosophy of law to law's potential to be an instrument of oppression as much as liberation.[84] Consequently, it is deeply sensitive to the point that 'however great the aura of majesty or authority the official system may have, its demands must in the end be submitted to a moral scrutiny'.[85]

While I argue that Hart went wrong in claiming that acceptance of authority could be confined to the officials of the system, he was absolutely right to make a theme of philosophy of law the 'pathologies' which arise when there is a 'breakdown in the complex congruent practice' of both officials and subjects which sustains a legal order.[86] He was also absolutely right to emphasize that the breakdown will occur when the 'solid gains' brought by the invention of the form of rule of the modern legal state are outweighed because its 'centrally organized power' is used

[83] Oliver Wendell Holmes, 'The Common Law', in Richard A Posner, ed., *The Essential Holmes* (Chicago: University of Chicago Press, 1992) 229, at 237: 'The life of the law has not been logic: it has been experience.' See Chapter 6.

[84] Hart, *The Concept of Law*, 118.

[85] Ibid, 210.

[86] Ibid, 118.

for 'the oppression of numbers with whose support it can dispense'.[87] I show that when one brings together Hart's remarks on the pathologies which follow a denial of the gains to a significant part of the population, scattered though these remarks are throughout *The Concept of Law*, they help to elaborate the juridical context in which officials are unable to answer adequately the legal subject's question 'But, how can that be law for me?'

In one of these passages, Hart remarked that if a system 'is fair and caters genuinely for the vital interests of all those from whom it demands obedience, it may gain and retain the allegiance of most for most of the time, and will accordingly be stable'. That is, most will 'look upon its rules from the internal point of view as accepted standards of behaviour' and thus not from the external point of view of 'malefactors or mere helpless victims' upon whom 'these legal standards have to be imposed by force or threat of force'. However, the system 'may be narrow and exclusive', 'run in the interests of the dominant group, and it may be made more repressive and unstable with the latent threat of upheaval'.[88]

This picture presents a stark distinction between who is within what I call the 'jural community' – the community of legal subjects who have full status before the law – and who is without. But Hart usefully blurred this distinction when he continued: 'Between these two extremes various combinations of these attitudes are to be found, often in the same individual.'[89] The idea of a combination of attitudes provides a fertile terrain for exploring legal theory through the lens of the question 'But, how can that be law for me?' The combination is not, however, as Hart seemed to indicate, of attitudes alone, because one must take into account the reasons for attitudes. I argue that the pathologies arise when there is a 'breakdown in the complex congruent practice' of both the officials and the subjects which sustains a legal order and that the breakdown happens when a significant part of the jural community is relegated to the status of second-class citizenship.

The idea of second-class citizenship does not here pertain to one's political standing in the sense of X is a citizen of Canada. Rather, it pertains to one's juridical standing, one's standing before the law. This second-class citizen has one foot in the space of first-class citizenship or full status before the law, with the other in a space of law-created inferior

[87] Ibid, 202.
[88] Ibid, 201–2.
[89] Ibid, 202.

status. Such second-class status is much more *legally* problematic than the status of slavery, so long as the enslaved persons are relentlessly consigned to the status of objects or things. For if one is legally recognized as having status as a legal subject for some purposes but not for others, the parts of the law which seem to relegate one to inferior status are put into question by those parts which do not when a legal challenge is mounted to the inferior status.

Inquiry into the complexities of this status is for Hartian positivists not a matter of legal theory because its problems arise outside the 'core' of 'settled' law, in the 'penumbra' of unsettled law.[90] Hence, officials decide on their answers in an act of discretion, ultimately unconstrained by law. In other words, such problems are excluded from the scope of legal theory by the static nature of Hart's legal theory. His way of conceiving the tensions which arise for the second-class citizen supposes that the content of the problematic law has already been determined, so that the only issue for the legal subject is whether to criticize or disobey the law.

In contrast, for a dynamic legal theory, the question of the content of the law is located one step back when legal subjects ask an official to determine the law in a way which can adequately respond to them. Such tensions arise because the problem raised by the individual who cannot get an adequate answer to the question 'But, how can that be law for me?' becomes most acute when the individual is a member of group which has second-class status. In this way, the singular question 'for me?' provides both a lens on the structural problems created by positive law which affect whole groups and an opportunity for individuals in those groups to take a stand on their legal rights.

The standing of legal subjects – their right to get an answer to the question of how the law responds to their place within the jural community – was central to Dworkin's interpretive theory, as evident in the distinction he adhered to throughout his career between 'legislative rights' and 'legal rights'. The former are 'rights that the community's lawmaking powers be exercised in a certain way'. The latter are 'political rights, but a special branch because they are properly enforceable on demand through adjudicative and coercive institutions without need for further legislation or lawmaking activity'. It is these rights that give rise to the 'political obligation' 'to obey *whatever* laws lawmaking institutions adopt'.[91]

[90] Hart, 'Positivism and the Separation of Law and Morals', 64.
[91] Dworkin, *Justice for Hedgehogs*, 407. My emphasis.

In making this distinction, Dworkin presupposed the idea of the legal subject's standing before the law which animates the argument of my book. As he observed, the distinction is between two kinds of *political* rights. The politics of that demand are best revealed, I argue, not by trying with Dworkin to generate a complete legal theory from a theory of adjudication, but, more along Kelsenian lines, by situating a theory of adjudication within a dynamic general legal theory. In doing so, we can appreciate better what I call the 'politics of legal space', the difference made by the fact that politics is conducted in a space constructed by law. We can see why legal theory is best conceived as 'political legal theory', a theory of law which explains not only the features of legal orders as they are but also the role of those features in what we can think of as the 'rule-of-law project'. This is a project in which the interaction of politics and law is designed so that legal subjects are subject to the rule of law, not to the arbitrary power of a gunman writ large.

The idea of second-class citizenship already relies on the metaphor of space, as that subject's problematic status arises because one foot is in the space of full equality before the law while the other is in the space of inferiority. I show that this interaction of legal spaces within a state can itself be illuminated by the interaction of a legal space with a space unregulated by law, for example, a space where unmediated political discretion rules, as well as with legally regulated spaces outside of a particular state, both the spaces of other states and the space regulated by public international law.

The way in which law regulates the spaces within a state as well as the way in which those spaces interact with others will determine where a state is placed on what I call the 'continuum of legality'. This term is inspired by Fuller's contention that legal orders can be more or less compliant with the rule of law, but must be to a large extent compliant if they are to be law-governed, to be a *legal* order, as opposed, for example, to an order of legally unmediated political power.[92] The closer a state is to the end of the continuum where there is largely compliance with legality, the more adequate will be the answers to the legal subject's question. Correspondingly, the closer it is to the other end, to ceasing to be a legal state since unmediated political discretion not law rules, the less adequate such answers will be. There is, however, authority or legal

[92] Fuller, *The Morality of Law*, 39–40.

legitimacy (to use Hart's term) to the answer at either end, ranging from a lot to very little.

But even when an answer has as much legal legitimacy as it is possible to have, it is not legitimacy all things considered but only as much legitimacy as legality by itself can impart. There are other kinds of legitimacy, notably what we can think of as political legitimacy (the legitimacy imparted when laws are the results of democratic procedures) and moral legitimacy (the legitimacy imparted when the content of laws accords with one's moral principles). The idea of moral legitimacy brings me to my last theme: the individual legal conscience.

I.6 The Individual Legal Conscience

While I explore the way in which these different kinds of legitimacy are related, my main inquiry is into legal legitimacy, what Hart called in his 1958 account of the moral virtues of the Separation Thesis the 'specific character of the authority of a legal order'.[93] Hart claimed that Bentham had contributed to an understanding of such authority in his 'simple' 'recipe' for 'life under a government of laws': '"*to obey punctually; to censure freely*"'.[94] Bentham himself called the recipe the 'motto of a good citizen',[95] and it is hardly, despite Hart's claim, 'simple'. It requires that legal subjects obey the law while maintaining their freedom to criticize it, which assumes that law, or at least laws enacted under a government of laws – the government of a modern legal state, has an authority to which the good citizen must accord weight.

It is this stance which I call the 'individual legal conscience' – the mindset of the subject who accords appropriate moral weight to the law. Now Bentham clearly thought that the laws of such a government deserve this kind of respect from a citizen when and only when the government has managed with some success to have its laws live up to the 'fundamental axiom' of his utilitarian political philosophy that 'it is the greatest happiness of the greatest number that is the measure of right and wrong'.[96] Put differently, the authority law has is measured by its

93 Hart, 'Positivism and the Separation of Law and Morals', 53.
94 Ibid, 53. Bentham's emphasis.
95 Bentham, *A Fragment on Government*, 10.
96 Ibid, 3.

accordance with an external moral measure, in Bentham's case utility.[97] On that view, there is no puzzle of legal authority. Law can be understood, as the command theory suggests, as a matter of coercion or might since its rightness is not internally generated. Put differently, the gunman writ large becomes legitimate when and only when his commands in fact benefit the individuals subject to his coercive power. The puzzle of legal authority arises, then, only when philosophers of law try to explain the authority law has just in being law. Notice, however, that a puzzle of authority remains – the puzzle of moral authority – even if one supposes that law is, in the words of one of Hart's successors, 'normatively inert' so that all the normative action is at the external moral level.[98] As Robert Paul Wolff argued in *In Defense of Anarchism*,[99] if one follows Kant in supposing that the 'autonomous man' is one who 'gives laws to himself, or who is self-legislating', it seems to follow that a 'morally legitimate state is a logical impossibility'.[100]

I seek only to resolve the puzzle of legal authority, not the puzzle of moral authority. However, it is worth noting at this stage that Raz's theory of legal authority was developed initially as an attempt to respond to Wolff;[101] and I try to show that solving the puzzle of legal authority can help in responding to, if not resolving, the puzzle of moral authority. Indeed, the solution to the puzzle of law's authority might even indicate why the puzzle of moral authority should be left unresolved because there is a moral worth to supposing, with Hart, that 'however great the aura of majesty or authority the official system may have, its demands must in the end be submitted to a moral scrutiny'.[102]

The same theme of the need to subject oneself to collective judgment while maintaining a grip on one's own sense of right and wrong is also to be found at the end of Berlin's influential essay 'Two Concepts of Liberty' in his observation that the mark of a 'civilized man' is to be able to 'realize the relative validity of one's convictions ... and yet stand for

[97] Indeed, the label 'Separation Thesis' is retrospectively bestowed on the distinction between law and morality which Hart referred to in 1958 as the 'utilitarian distinction' – 'Positivism and the Separation of Law and Morals', 78.

[98] John Gardner, *Law as a Leap of Faith* (Oxford: Oxford University Press, 2012), 23.

[99] Robert Paul Wolff, *In Defense of Anarchism* (Berkeley: University of California Press, 1998).

[100] Ibid, 14, vii.

[101] Raz, 'Legitimate Authority', in Raz, *The Authority of Law* 3, at 25–7.

[102] Hart, *The Concept of Law*, 210.

them unflinchingly'.[103] In many respects, such sentiments resonate with those to be found in the works of Weimar-era social democrats or left liberals, who were committed to the success of Germany's first experiment in democratic constitutionalism. Most notably, the sentiments resonate with themes in Kelsen's major contribution to political theory, in particular in his account of the way in which legality plays a role in sustaining a commitment to democracy in an age in which citizens have to negotiate the 'torment of heteronomy', that is, the torment produced by the partial forfeiture of autonomy.[104]

The stance recommended by such thinkers requires that good citizens recognize both the primacy they should give to their own judgments and that in a secular era those judgments have to be viewed as relative to the individual, with the consequence that the collective understanding of the common good must generally trump the individual's. Such an ethical stance will lead to a stance of qualified deference to positive law, in particular to rule by the statutes enacted by a democratic parliament which are general in form and which apply for the most part prospectively, so that legal subjects may guide their conduct by the law.

The stance, we should note, does not indulge in what we saw Raz call earlier an 'excessive veneration' of the law. For there is a gap between excessive veneration and other positive attitudes. If a government which observed the rule of law had by that fact to observe conditions which improved the lives of those subject to the law, it would follow that law would deserve our respect because of its moral qualities, even if we recognize that bad laws might have in the end no conclusive moral claim on us because their immoral content so clearly outweighs the moral quality they necessarily have.

Of course, if there is reason to accord law moral weight just because it is law, that reason complicates our moral deliberations more than if law has no such weight. But even if there is such reason, the conclusion that the law is too unjust to be obeyed is still perfectly open to us, so long as the reason does not lead to excessive veneration. Indeed, we might even think there is such reason in the face of the fact that governments have

[103] Isaiah Berlin, 'Two Concepts of Liberty', in Berlin, *Four Essays on Liberty* (Oxford: Oxford University Press, 1969) 118, at 172. Berlin was quoting here from Joseph Schumpeter.

[104] See Hans Kelsen, *The Essence and Value of Democracy* (Lanham: Rowman and Littlefield, 2013, Nadia Urbinati and Carlo Invernizzi Accetti eds, Brian Graf, trans.), 7, where the translator gives 'agony of heteronomy' as the translation.

used, and will no doubt in the future use, law as an instrument of quite systematic immoral policy. This fact would make us not want to venerate, let alone excessively venerate, law. But still we might think that when we condemn such immorality we do so because the overwhelming badness involved in a systematic use of law as an instrument of immorality easily outweighs the moral good there is to government under law. We might even say that what has gone wrong is not only the institutionalization of injustice but also the fact that law has been made the instrument of injustice. Notice in this regard that we usually think it appropriate to speak of government *ab*using the form of law to promote immoral policies, and not of a simple 'use', which implies that the form is generally better suited to promoting something worthy of our respect. So my thought is that we should be alert to the possibility of a more moderate position on the relationship between law and morality than one that would cause us to 'lurch' to a stance of excessive veneration of the law.

Only Kelsen's legal theory is, on my argument to come, capacious enough to accommodate the following pivotal ideas of philosophy of law of the last sixty years or so, all of which are needed to fill out this moderate position: Hobbes's idea that the law is a 'publique Conscience';[105] Hart's idea of the authority law has in terms of practice-based acceptance and his concern about preserving the space for moral criticism; Kelsen's own idea of legal order as a hierarchy of norms unified by the basic norm; Radbruch's claim that extreme injustice is no law; Fuller's idea that any legal order will to some large extent comply with formal principles of legality which condition the content of law; and Dworkin's elaboration of the role of substantive moral principles implicit within the positive law in judicial interpretation.

In addition, this Kelsenian legal theory allows us to understand not only why the legal subject is the central figure of philosophy of law but also why legal orders are capable of providing answers to the subject's question 'But, how can that be law for me?' It thus completes the long arc of legality which starts in Hobbes's argument that it is a social contract which underpins the authority of law under conditions of modernity, as only that constitutionalist idea can explain both authority as compliance with fundamental principles of legality and the official duty to interpret enacted law in the light of such principles.

I now offer a quick roadmap of the book.

[105] Hobbes, *Leviathan*, 223.

I.7 A Quick Roadmap

Chapter 1, 'The Puzzle of Very Unjust Law I: Hart and Dworkin', sets out the way in which the deadlock in legal theory about authority arose by focusing on the debate between Hart and Dworkin about the natural law claim that extremely unjust law is not law. I argue that, while Hart and others were right to see that the existence of unjust laws and legal systems poses a serious challenge to Dworkin's legal theory, Hart's own theory is vulnerable to that same challenge. Moreover, it is so because the puzzle of extremely unjust law leads to the puzzle of legal authority.

I continue to explore these issues in Chapter 2, 'The Puzzle of Very Unjust Law II: Hobbes', where I argue that both puzzles start to look quite different when they are placed within a tradition of inquiry about legal authority anchored in one of the great texts of Western philosophical jurisprudence, Hobbes's *Leviathan*. I show, against the orthodox reading of Hobbes, that he presents a sophisticated and profound theory of the modern legal state as it was beginning to emerge, one which articulates the complex relationship between a commitment to government under law and the fundamental principles of legality which such government must observe if it is to maintain its authority.

Chapter 3, 'The Constitution of Legal Authority / The Authority of Legal Constitutions', argues that the solution to the puzzle of authority starts in seeing how legal authority is constituted by a constitutionalist idea, and I show that Kelsen's basic norm and Hart's rule of recognition are functional equivalents of the social contract in Hobbes. With the much maligned idea of a social contract restored to its proper place in legal theory, one can also see how the central authority relationship is not between lawmakers and legal officials; rather, it is between those who make law and legal subjects, with legal officials mediating that relationship by the fundamental principles of legality so that they are able to answer the legal subject's question.

Chapter 4, 'The Janus-Faced Constitution', extends the argument about constitutionalism to the relationship between the legal space of national legal orders with public international law, and that between the private law norms of one national legal order with another, namely, private international law. I adopt the lens of the monism/dualism debate in public international law to argue for a version of Kelsen's preferred 'international law monism' which seeks to make sense of his opposition to all kinds of dualism in legal theory: dualism about the relationship between national and public international law; dualism about the relationship between different national jurisdictions; and dualism about the relationship between law and morality. The argument shows not only that this kind of monism permits there to coexist a plurality of different normative orders – the various national legal orders, the international legal order – but also that this kind of monism is required to comprehend why there could be pluralism in the first place. It establishes the converse of the traditional motto of the USA, *E pluribus unum* – 'Out of plurality, unity' – by showing that 'Out of unity, plurality'.

Chapter 5, 'The Politics of Legal Space', explores more fully the metaphor of space deployed in Chapter 4 in my attempt to understand better why within the space of a modern legal state the subject can get an answer to the question 'But, how can that be law for me?', so long as the state remains legal. In particular, I want to explore the difference made within a state between, on the one hand, the interaction of a legal space with a space of no-law and, on the other, an interaction of two legal spaces. This exploration relies on Ernst Fraenkel's analysis of the Nazi state as a Dual State in order to show why formal principles of legality, as developed first by Hobbes and then Fuller, condition the content of positive law in a way which makes a Dworkinian interpretive approach available to legal officials, including judges.[106] I contrast the Dual State with other ideal types of state – the Rule-of-Law State, the Apartheid State and the Parallel State, with the last based on the legal order of Israel and the Occupied Territories. I argue that when a state moves further along the continuum of legality from the Rule-of-Law State end towards the Dual State end, so its legal order becomes ever more pathological, until the point where it ceases to be a legal state. Finally, based on an account of the USA before the Civil War, I suggest that all modern legal states are in fact 'Hybrid States' which contain elements of all four ideal types, with the result that the types serve mainly to help place a state on the continuum of legality.

In Chapter 6, 'Legality's Promise', I return to the themes of this Introduction, in particular to the claims Hart made on behalf of the Separation Thesis. I argue that the Separation Thesis caused Hart to distort not only his own attempt to understand law as a matter of authority but also hampered the progress of philosophy of law in general. Most importantly, philosophy of law must shed the thesis if it is to

[106] Ernst Fraenkel, *The Dual State: A Contribution to the Theory of Dictatorship* (Oxford: Oxford University Press, 2017).

recognize the full implications of understanding law in the register of authority. Only then can we explore the thought that a legal order constitutes a particular kind of political community, a jural community made up of legal subjects who are entitled to get an answer when they pose the question 'But, how can that be law for me?'

This is a community which has established a public record or fund of compulsory values which are distinct from other values which the community regards as important in that those who do not accept the values will be subject to sanctions and in which the content of the compulsory values is determined in a formal process of argumentation. The statutes and other positive law artefacts which are the basis of this fund are, in Kelsenian terms, only 'fragments'[107] of complete laws because their content cannot be fully known until the law is applied to those in the community.

This process is formal, though not in the sense that the laws have a content which is revealed either by logical deduction or by the exclusively factual tests on which Hart's legal positivism insists. Rather, it is formal in the Kelsenian sense that, while the positive law is taken as a given, the officials who interpret and implement it are committed to treating it as the law of an order, as a unity, so that they can give an answer to the subject who asks 'But, how can that be law for me?' Legal order, as it is conceived by political legal theory, provides a kind of laboratory for a society to work out what its compulsory fundamental values are and should be. The political legal theory which explains law in this way is doubly pragmatic. It requires that legal theory be answerable to the lived experience of the law and explains how the law itself is answerable to the way it is experienced.

Finally, I have included three Appendices which deal more briefly with matters which are highly relevant to my arguments but which would amount to distractions if included in the text and are yet are too long for footnotes. Appendix I discusses the debate between 'inclusive' and 'exclusive' legal positivism and its relation to my themes, in particular my account of the place of private international law in philosophy of law. Appendix II contains a Kelsenian response to the claim made by Kantian private law theorists that, not only is the distinction between private and public law basic to legal theory, but also that private law has a kind of

[107] This is Hart's term in *The Concept of Law*, 35, referring to Kelsen, *General Theory of Law and State*, 63.

primacy over public law in the construction of legal order. Appendix III discusses the natural law theory of John Finnis and explains why, on my argument, it is not so much a theory based on *jus* or *Recht* but rather a variant of legal positivism, a 'variant of concern' (as we say these days) in that the authority of law is contingent on its being the vehicle for a troublingly conservative social philosophy.

1

The Puzzle of Very Unjust Law I

Hart and Dworkin

In the short chapter 'Law' in *Justice for Hedgehogs*, Ronald Dworkin said that 'the puzzle of evil law' has had a 'prominent place in seminars on legal theory' although it is of 'almost no practical importance'.[1] The puzzle, in his view, is primarily about cases where judges find themselves faced with the problem of enforcing an evil law. Should we say that the judges must not enforce it because it is very unjust, or that they must not enforce it because it is not law? Since philosophers of law agree on the practical outcome – judges must not enforce evil law – Dworkin claimed that the 'ancient jurisprudential problem is sadly close to a verbal dispute'.[2]

Dworkin's claim was wrong. He was always reluctant to confront the puzzle of such law and only ever did so when taxed by his critics. I argue that the fact that both he and HLA Hart came to propose different solutions with the same practical effect – Dworkin that such law is not law and Hart that it is law but too immoral to enforce – shows not that the dispute is verbal but that the problem confronts their positions with equal force. The puzzle of evil law, or 'very unjust law' as I call it for reasons explained in the Introduction, is as much a problem for legal positivism as it is for natural law theories. In addition, we will see that this old jurisprudential problem sets the stage for the most important implication of the overall argument of this book.

Dworkin did not dispute the features of law on which legal positivists focus – that law is made by human beings and that its content is to a large extent determined by the contingent facts of the public record. But if, as he argued, the moral domain and the legal domain are one, we need also

[1] Ronald Dworkin, *Justice for Hedgehogs* (Cambridge, MA: Belknap Press, 2011), 410. Sections 1.1–1.3 of this chapter are based on my 'Dworkin and Unjust Law', in Wil Waluchow and Stefan Sciaraffa, eds, *The Legacy of Ronald Dworkin* (Oxford: Oxford University Press, 2016) 131. I thank Oxford University Press for permission to reuse this material.

[2] Dworkin, *Justice for Hedgehogs*, 412.

to accept both that morality is made by human beings and that its content is to a significant extent determined by the contingent facts of the public legal record. It would follow that there is what Hart once denied – 'a moral legislature with competence to make and change morals, as legal enactments make and change law'.[3] In other words, Dworkin must accept Hobbes's claim, elaborated in Chapter 2, that the legal subject must regard the law as 'the publique Conscience, by which he hath already undertaken to be guided'.[4]

Section 1.1 sketches the puzzle which very unjust law poses for legal theory. Section 1.2 shows that it confronts Hart's legal positivism as starkly as it does any natural law theory, while Section 1.3 sets out Dworkin's unsuccessful attempts to solve the puzzle, culminating in his claim that it presents a merely verbal dispute. In Section 1.4, I suggest that the puzzle helps to explain both why philosophy of law seems to be deadlocked and why current attempts to break the deadlock are unproductive. As I signalled in the Introduction, the puzzle of very unjust law leads to the puzzle of legal authority – how law can be a matter of both right and might – and these attempts eliminate one or other of these elements.

1.1 Is There a Puzzle Regarding Very Unjust Law?

In *Justice for Hedgehogs*, Dworkin seemed to strengthen his natural law commitments. He declared it a mistake for legal theory, one he himself had made, to engage in an exercise of bridge-building between 'two different intellectual domains' or 'systems': (1) law, which 'belongs to a particular community', and (2) morality, which does not, because 'it consists of a set of standards that have imperative force for everyone'. Law, on this mistaken view, is 'made by human beings' and it is a contingent fact what its content is, whereas morality is 'not made by anyone . . . and it is not contingent on any human decision or practice'.[5] Hence, he suggested that we should replace the 'two-systems' picture of legal theory with a 'one-system picture'.[6] Legal rights are political rights, but a special branch because they are properly enforceable on demand

[3] HLA Hart, *The Concept of Law* (Oxford: Clarendon Press, 1994, 2nd ed.), 177.

[4] Thomas Hobbes, *Leviathan* (Cambridge: Cambridge University Press, 1996, Richard Tuck, ed.), 223.

[5] Dworkin, *Justice for Hedgehogs*, 412.

[6] Ibid, 402.

through adjudicative and coercive institutions without need for further legislation or lawmaking activity'.[7] Moreover, in the manuscript version of *Justice for Hedgehogs*, though not in the book, Dworkin said that it would be 'counterintuitive' to suppose that 'most of the subjects of most of the political communities over history had no moral duty to obey the laws of their community'.[8]

The puzzle of very unjust law thus faces Dworkin's theory because, with other natural lawyers, he accepted that in any legal order the following kinds of social fact count in determining the content of the law: facts about the criteria for determining whether a law is a valid law of that order, for example, whether the legislature followed the formal steps required for enacting a bill into law; whether there is in fact an entrenched bill of rights or other constitutional document which explicitly or by implication gives judges the authority to declare an otherwise valid statute invalid because it violates the constitution; facts about who has the authority to make, interpret and enforce the law; facts about the interpretive practices of the legal order, for example, whether there is a doctrine of precedent; and so on. It is this factual dimension of determining the law which explains why we can distinguish between, say, the law of the USA and that of Canada, and why we do not suppose that we can find out the law of either by asking what law those countries would ideally have made.

Natural lawyers can then be understood as supposing that, in addition to social facts, morality necessarily plays a part in determining the content of the law. Consider that Dworkin's 'interpretivism' holds that in a 'hard case', one in which lawyers reasonably disagree about the answer to the legal question, the judge should decide by developing a principled justification of the relevant positive law which shows it in its best light. Whatever theory best explains why one lawmaker would have enacted most of the relevant law also gives the answer to the legal question posed by the case. It is the 'one right answer'; the answer the judge is under a legal and moral duty to give.[9]

[7] Ibid, 407.

[8] Quoted in Susanne Sreedhar and Candice Delmas, 'State Legitimacy and Political Obligation in *Justice for Hedgehogs*: The Radical Potential of Dworkinian Dignity' (2010) 90 *Boston University Law Review* 737, at 746.

[9] This full version of this theory was set out first in 'Hard Cases', in Ronald Dworkin, *Taking Rights Seriously* (London: Duckworth, 1981, 3rd impression) 81 and refined in Ronald Dworkin, *Law's Empire* (London: Fontana, 1986).

Dworkin's position can thus be plausibly understood as claiming that the authority of law (as he would put it, law's ability to justify coercion) is grounded by that theory, which plays its role at a second stage in the interpretive process. At the first stage, the judge determines what answers to the question fit the facts about the relevant law. At the second, the judge selects the answer given by the best theory of that law.

If this were the correct understanding of Dworkinian interpretivism, it would replicate the dualism of two-systems legal theories. It would suppose that at the first stage the issue for the judge is the domain of facts about the law which provides the raw materials – the 'preinterpretive' data[10] – which have to be ascertained before one considers at the second stage what theory best justifies those facts. But if the best theory of why those are the facts is to be considered the 'moral' theory of that legal order, his interpretive model seems to make the morality of law hostage to the contingent facts of the legal historical record. As his positivist critics pointed out, in a 'wicked legal system', one explicitly and relentlessly dedicated to extreme injustice, the only available theory of the law will surely be the repugnant ideology of which the law is the instrument. The perverse result is that a judge in such a system is under a legal and a moral duty to apply the repugnant ideology in hard cases since that ideology grounds the authority of the law in that order. For this reason, Dworkin's critics used the apartheid legal order as an example which showed why interpretivism should be rejected.[11]

Dworkin's move to an explicitly one-system theory was prefigured by his rejection in response to this kind of objection of the impression that there is a process with two discrete stages, one focusing on the dimension of 'fit', the other on the dimension of moral 'soundness'. Rather, he

[10] Ibid, 65–6.

[11] As Joseph Raz wrote in 1985, Dworkin's position would seem to 'require a South African judge to use his power to extend Apartheid'; Joseph Raz, 'Authority, Law, and Morality', in Raz, *Ethics in the Public Domain: Essays in the Morality of Law and Politics* (Oxford: Oxford University Press, 1994) 194, at 208. For extended discussion of this claim, see David Dyzenhaus, *Hard Cases in Wicked Legal Systems: Pathologies of Legality* (Oxford: Oxford University Press, 2010, 2nd ed.). It was not only critics of Dworkin who came to this conclusion. In 1984 a South African law professor, and adherent of Dworkin's interpretivism, argued that at that stage in apartheid a judge had no choice but to see that the best and perhaps only explanation of the law was a white supremacist ideology. Because it followed that the judges' legal duty was to decide their cases in accordance with that ideology, their moral duty was to refuse to participate in the legal order, and so he called on the liberal judges on the South African bench to resign: Raymond Wacks, 'Judges and Injustice' (1984) 101 *South African Law Journal* 266.

emphasized, there is only one stage because the inquiry into fit will be framed by the judge's moral theory of the legal order as a whole. But the bigger the role Dworkin's theory gave to a judge's moral theory in determining the content of the law, the less it seemed that he was offering a theory of law. Rather, he seemed to be developing an account of the kind of liberal morality to which he thought legal orders should aspire, which had contingently been manifested in some.[12]

We will also see in Section 1.3 that this move landed Dworkin in a dilemma between the natural law position that very unjust laws are invalid and the legal positivist position that they are valid, but we should say that they should be disobeyed because they are so unjust. I have indicated that he sought in *Justice for Hedgehogs* to draw the sting from this dilemma by saying that it did not matter which limb one embraces because all will agree on the practical outcome – the judge should not enforce such laws. But the obvious positivist response is that the limb which requires the judge to deny that a valid law is law replicates the mysteries of the natural law tradition, one which ultimately precludes 'the possibility of morally illegitimate legal systems'.[13] In contrast, legal positivism, with its focus on law as a matter of social facts, can support the limb which permits the judge to avoid mystery and say, 'This law is valid but too unjust to apply.' Moreover, since positivism denies in its Separation Thesis that there is any necessary connection between law and morality, it does not appear to face any puzzle.

If this conclusion were so easily reached, there would be no puzzle about very unjust law for philosophy of law and philosophers of law would all be positivists. Seminars in legal theory would not have to discuss the merits of natural law positions, unless they were focused on the history of legal thought. In that case, natural law could be brought out briefly from the dustbin of debunked theories, in much the same way as the command theory of Hart's utilitarian predecessors Bentham and Austin gets a cursory glance in such seminars, usually through the lens of Hart's summaries of their position. And just as Dworkin suggested that the problem of very unjust law is an unproductive distraction, at times legal positivists suggest that legal theory is needlessly distracted by natural law positions, since these are not general theories of law but

[12] See, for example, the essays collected in Ronald Dworkin, *Freedom's Law: The Moral Reading of the American Constitution* (Cambridge, MA: Harvard University Press, 1996).

[13] Scott Shapiro, *Legality* (Cambridge, MA: Belknap Press, 2011), 49.

projects for legal reform or (the charge against Dworkin) parochial theories of adjudication suited to perhaps only one jurisdiction.

But even if there is no puzzle of very unjust law for legal positivism, positivists have been much preoccupied with its existence. In *The Concept of Law*, Hart devoted considerable space to explaining just why legal positivism's 'wider concept of law', one which includes the study of valid legal rules with an unjust content, is to be preferred to the 'narrow concept' of the natural law tradition, which he thought must deem such rules not to be law and thus not fit for jurisprudential analysis.[14] And positivism's facility with dealing with such law, exemplified in the Nazi legal system, is the motif of much of Hart's 1958 article, 'Positivism and the Separation of Law and Morals', which set the stage both for *The Concept of Law* and for debates in philosophy of law in the latter half of the last century.[15]

Hart is best understood as arguing that positivism should be accepted because it has the correct theory of the nature of law and that an additional distinct advantage of the theory is its facility with clarifying the moral issues raised by very unjust law.[16] But his preoccupation with such law could lead one to suppose that one should adopt legal positivism because of that facility.[17] Indeed, Scott Shapiro, who has provided the most recent major restatement of a legal positivist position, complains that

> [w]hether trying to debunk the law's pretensions to authority, or constructing a general theory of law, legal positivists have spent an excessive amount of time focusing on morally inadequate systems and tailoring their theories to fit those regimes. Their obsession with the Nazis and the Problem of Evil, however, has blinded them to a basic jurisprudential truth; a wicked regime is a botched legal system, much as 'the Earth is flat' is a failed scientific theory.[18]

Shapiro is not admitting here that legal positivism has a problem responding to such law. Rather his point is that we should take as our

[14] Hart, *The Concept of Law*, 209–12.

[15] HLA Hart, 'Positivism and the Separation of Law and Morals', in Hart, *Essays in Jurisprudence and Philosophy* (Oxford: Clarendon Press, 1983) 49.

[16] See Leslie Green, 'The Morality in Law', in Luís Duarte D'Almeida, James Edwards and Andrea Dolcetti, eds, *Reading HLA Hart's The Concept of Law* (Oxford: Hart Publishing, 2013) 177, at 203–7.

[17] Liam Murphy, 'Better to See Law This Way' (2008) 23 *New York University Law Review* 1088.

[18] Shapiro, *Legality*, 391.

paradigm not the ways in which law can be used as an instrument of injustice but law when it is doing what we think law in its nature does; in Shapiro's view, this involves establishing plans which make it possible in complex societies to solve pressing moral problems which only the institution of law can solve. Like Dworkin, Shapiro regards very unjust law as a distraction from what should be the main project of philosophy of law, though unlike Dworkin, he regards the existence of very unjust law as a refutation of any natural law position, because the content of a society's legal plan could just as well be apartheid ideology as, say, liberal democracy.[19]

However, as I argue in Section 1.2, and as Shapiro acknowledges, a different problem does arise for legal positivism.[20] Recall that the problem of very unjust law seems to arise directly for natural law positions because of their claim about some necessary connection between law and morality. On the other side of the ledger, their claim about morality makes it easier for them to explain that law is not only a matter of social facts but also something which has authority over its subjects.[21] And we can plausibly suppose, as I suggested in my sketch of Dworkin's interpretive theory, that if law had the moral basis to it which a natural law position claims, that basis would ground law's claim to authority, as Hart acknowledged.

In *The Concept of Law*, Hart identified as one of the three 'recurrent issues' of legal philosophy the fact that both moral and legal rules share a vocabulary of obligation: 'they withdraw certain areas of conduct from the free option of the individual to do as he likes'. Moreover, he said that the idea 'of justice ... seems to unite both fields' and justice 'is both a virtue specially appropriate to law and the most legal of virtues. We think and talk of "justice *according to* law" and yet also of the justice or injustice *of* the laws.'[22] These facts alone, Hart said, 'suggest the view that law is best understood as a "branch" of morality or justice' which leads to the assertion that 'an unjust law is not a law'. But that assertion, he continued, has the 'same ring of exaggeration and paradox if not falsity, as "statutes are not laws" or "constitutional law is not law"'. It has

[19] See my 'Legality without the Rule of Law? Scott Shapiro on Wicked Legal Systems' (2012) 25 *Canadian Journal of Law and Jurisprudence* 183.

[20] Shapiro, *Legality*, 49.

[21] There is an important difference between saying that law has authority and that it claims authority, as I explain in Section 1.2.

[22] Hart, *The Concept of Law*, 6–7. His emphasis.

that ring because of the important differences between legal and moral rules.[23] Not least among these differences, as I have already mentioned, is his view that moral rules and principles are immune 'from deliberate change'; hence, 'the idea of a moral legislature with competence to make and change morals, as legal enactments make and change law, is repugnant to the whole notion of morality'.[24]

In other words, Hart argued for a dualist or two-systems picture, according to which law is contingent and subject to deliberate change by the body empowered to make that change, whereas morality is not. Yet Hart also warned against overreacting to natural law claims in a way which reduces law to facts without any explanation of the vocabulary of obligation which law and morality share.[25] He rejected the command model of law – according to which law is the commands of a legally unlimited sovereign backed by threats – in part because, as he put it, '[l]aw surely is not the gunman situation writ large, and legal order is surely not to be thus simply identified with compulsion'.[26]

Such acknowledgement presents legal positivism with its own puzzle – how to generate the 'ought' of legal authority from the 'is' of social facts. Positivism sets itself the task of showing that the social facts of law are somehow also normative facts, but without making the mistake of supposing that the obligations which arise from these facts are moral in nature. I discuss that puzzle throughout this book. In this chapter, I want simply to show that Hart's incorporation of a specifically legal idea of authority into philosophy of law raises very starkly for legal positivism the kinds of problem which in Section 1.3 we will see also plague Dworkin's position. Indeed, the problem of very unjust law, whether it manifests itself in the relation between legal subject and law or judge and law, serves mainly to point to a deeper problem about how to reconcile our intuitions that law is both a matter of fact, including facts about coercion, and a matter of authority. That deeper problem manifests itself when a judge must apply such a law to an individual.

[23] Ibid, 8.

[24] Ibid, 175, 177.

[25] Ibid, 8. Hart mentions here Oliver Wendell Holmes's dictum that 'The prophecies of what the courts will do in fact, and nothing more pretentious, are what I mean by the law.' But he clearly had in mind as well Bentham's and Austin's command theory of law. I discuss Holmes's position in Chapter 6.

[26] Hart, 'Positivism and the Separation of Law and Morals', 59.

1.2 The Puzzle for Legal Positivism

In part IV of 'Positivism and the Separation of Law and Morals', Hart addressed the topic of very unjust law in an engagement with Gustav Radbruch, the German philosopher of law. After the Second World War, Radbruch, in reaction to the horrors of National Socialism and what he regarded as German lawyers' complicity in the Nazi rise to power, advanced what became known as the 'Radbruch Formula': extreme injustice is no law.[27] We saw in the Introduction that Hart observed that when Radbruch made the claim that extreme injustice is no law, the 'law' he had in mind was *Recht* and that his 'considered reflections' on law in the Nazi period had

> led him to the doctrine that the fundamental principles of humanitarian morality were part of the very concept of *Recht* or Legality and that no positive enactment or statute, however clearly it was expressed and however clearly it conformed with the formal criteria of validity of a given legal system, could be valid if it contravened basic principles of morality.[28]

Hart added that this 'doctrine can be appreciated fully only if the nuances imported by the German word *Recht* are grasped'[29]

Hart, as I observed, did not pause to examine these nuances. Instead, he vehemently rejected Radbruch's claim that law's role as an instrument of Nazi immorality should undermine the positivist commitment to the Separation Thesis. In particular, he was affronted by Radbruch's suggestion that the German legal profession's commitment to a positivist view of law had contributed to the horrors because the 'positivist slogan "law is law"' lay behind their failure to 'protest against the enormities they were required to perpetrate in the name of law'.[30] He accused Radbruch of 'naïveté' because he had only 'half digested the spiritual message of liberalism', the message in fact delivered by legal positivism: 'law is law' tells us that law 'is not morality'; hence, it should not be thought to 'supplant morality'.[31]

Hart supposed that the point is sufficiently made by quoting a paragraph in which Austin imagines a law which makes punishable by death

27 Gustav Radbruch, 'Statutory Lawlessness and Supra-statutory Law' (2006) 26 *Oxford Journal of Legal Studies* 1 (Bonnie Litschewski Paulson and Stanley L Paulson, trans.).
28 Hart, 'Positivism and the Separation of Law and Morals', 74.
29 Ibid.
30 Ibid, 73.
31 Ibid, 74–5.

an 'act innocuous, or positively beneficial'. I am tried and condemned for committing this act and object that it is 'contrary to the law of God', that is, to natural law. Austin said that 'the court of justice will demonstrate the inconclusiveness of my reasoning by hanging me up, in pursuance of the law of which I have impugned the validity'.[32] Hart endorsed Austin's claim that this example shows that those who say that human laws cease to be law if they conflict with 'the fundamental principles of morality' are talking 'stark nonsense'.[33] Rather, they should 'speak plainly' and say 'that laws may be law but too evil to be obeyed'.[34]

Hart suggested that he could add support for this position by going beyond a 'mere academic discussion' to a problem of legal practice, the issue raised by the 'Grudge Informer Case'. In this case, as he understood things, a postwar German court found that a woman was guilty of the crime of illegal deprivation of liberty for turning in her husband during the war for making derogatory remarks about Hitler. Such remarks were considered a crime under two Nazi statutes, and so the woman claimed that what she did was not illegal. Thus, the court had to rely, Hart thought, on the Radbruch Formula in order to claim that the Nazi statutes were not really law.[35]

In Hart's view, the Radbruch Formula obscures the moral dilemma raised by the case: should one leave the woman unpunished or should one 'sacrifice a very precious principle of morality endorsed by most legal systems', the principle against retroactive punishment?[36] The formula does so because it requires the judges to pretend that valid law was not really law. The only way for the dilemma to be candidly faced if one thinks that the woman should be punished is, Hart asserted, for the

[32] Ibid, 73.

[33] Ibid.

[34] Ibid, 77.

[35] Both Hart and Fuller relied on a flawed report of the case, as HO Pappe pointed out in 'On the Validity of Judicial Decisions in the Nazi Era' (1960) 23 *Modern Law Review* 260. The court did not invalidate the laws but came to the conclusion that the woman was guilty because she was the 'indirect perpetrator' of the crime of illegal deprivation of liberty. For my own discussion as well as my translation of the case, see 'The Grudge Informer Case Revisited' (2008) 23 *New York University Law Review* 1000. In chapter 9 of *The Concept of Law*, 304, Hart said that Pappe's analysis should be 'studied', but did not himself take the time to respond to it, in my view, because of his inability to let go of the assumption that the law can have any content despite the fact that in this same chapter he disputed that assumption.

[36] Hart, 'Positivism and the Separation of Law and Morals', 76–7.

legislature, fully conscious of the moral sacrifice involved, to 'enact a frankly retrospective law'.[37]

Hence, Hart supposed that a correct moral appreciation of this difficult problem is facilitated by the Separation Thesis and that the thesis is an important corrective to the sense in Germany that the decisions of postwar courts which deployed the formula signalled the triumph of natural law over legal positivism, a reaction Hart described as 'hysteria'.[38] Legal positivism, in contrast to natural law, permits us to 'speak plainly' by using 'a moral condemnation which everybody can understand' and which 'makes an immediate and obvious claim to moral attention'. In contrast, an assertion that 'these evil things are not law' is one 'many people do not believe' and it raises 'a whole host of philosophical issues before it can be accepted'.[39]

Most participants in the debate which followed Hart's essay and Lon Fuller's response to it failed to notice that Hart implicitly relied on a difference between two perspectives in play in part IV. There is the perspective of legal subjects confronted by a very unjust law and thus with the moral evaluation of law's claim that they are under a duty to *obey* the law. And there is the judicial perspective in which judges are confronted by the same law, but with a question which has at least to be framed differently, even if we suppose that the answer is no different. For the judge's question is whether they are under a duty to *apply* the law to whomever it affects, thus facing the affected subject with the question whether to obey the law, as interpreted by the judge.

It might seem that Hart should have supposed that his own implicit formula – 'Disobey unjust law, but don't deny its validity' – needs only a slight adaptation for the situation of judges: 'Don't apply unjust law, but don't deny its validity.' However, Hart followed Austin in rejecting this option. Notice Austin's deliberate use of the phrase 'court of *justice*'. His point was that the justice the law demands may be something we should morally condemn; as Hart put it in the next part of his essay, the 'justice in the administration of the law' is 'not justice of the law'.[40] It seems that the judge qua judge is not entitled to refuse to apply the law and that Hart committed himself to the same view in reserving to the legislature the authority to retrospectively criminalize grudge informing. For while

[37] Ibid, 76.
[38] Ibid.
[39] Ibid, 77–8.
[40] Ibid, 81.

Hart's main point was that something goes wrong when one pretends that a valid law is not law, in 1958 he suggested it was impermissible for a judge to refuse to apply an unjust law, let alone invalidate it.

Now we might suppose that the question of whether judges have the authority to invalidate a statute is to be resolved by looking at facts about the jurisdiction and that Hart assumed that postwar German judges did not at that time have such authority. But why did he deny to judges the option of refusing to *apply* unjust law if 'law is law' in the way in which the Separation Thesis insists we understand that slogan? One possible answer is that the judicial role is such that judges are under both a moral and a legal duty to apply the law as they find it. They are thus precluded from considering the moral considerations external to law on which the legal subject should rely when it comes to the question of obedience, or from confronting the kind of moral dilemma which Hart thought was at stake in the Grudge Informer Case. In other words, very unjust law does not confront judges with a moral dilemma, since (to use Fuller's terminology) judges subscribe to an 'ideal of fidelity to law'[41] which requires them to uphold the law, no matter how immoral its content.

Early in *The Concept of Law*, Hart seemed to reinforce the idea that judges have a standing duty to apply the law, whatever its content. He argued that 'obedience' misleadingly describes what judges do when they apply the law since a legal subject can obey the law without supposing that this is the 'right thing' to do; for example, because the subject fears punishment. Judges, in contrast, must adopt the 'internal point of view' according to which the 'rule of recognition' – the ultimate rule of the legal order which certifies the validity of particular rules – provides 'a public, common standard of correct judicial decision'.[42] Indeed, if judges do not adopt that internal point of view, one of the 'two minimum conditions necessary and sufficient for the existence of a legal system' no longer obtains.[43] It should follow that judges are under a standing obligation to apply the law of their jurisdiction, whatever its content, which distinguishes their normative situation from that of legal subjects. In addition, Hart emphasized that one has to appreciate that the problem

[41] Lon L Fuller, 'Positivism and Fidelity to Law: A Reply to Professor Hart' (1958) 71 *Harvard Law Review* 630.

[42] Hart, *The Concept of Law*, 116–17.

[43] Ibid. See Thomas Mertens, 'Radbruch and Hart on the Grudge Informer: A Reconsideration' (2002) 15 *Ratio Juris* 186, at 202–4, for careful discussion of these issues.

of morality and justice for a subject who had to decide whether to obey an unjust law is 'very different' from the problem the postwar courts faced.[44]

However, at one point in *The Concept of Law* Hart changed tack. When he returned to the issues of Radbruch and the Grudge Informer Case, he revised his 1958 view and said that a judge faced with a very unjust law should say: 'This is law; but it is too iniquitous to be applied or obeyed.'[45] On that revision, the judge would be saying: 'As a judge it is my duty to apply the law; the law requires that you not be punished; but I am going to punish you, because that is what my duty requires.' The obvious tension here can be resolved if one's position is that there is a standing moral duty on judges to apply the law, even when its content is unjust, though with the following rider: if the content of the law is very unjust, the judge must weigh the moral duty to apply the law against the moral duty not to apply it. This position does seek to respond to the moral complexity of the situation. But the complexity is not illuminated by the Separation Thesis which denies that law as such has any moral quality to it. The complexity is illuminated, that is, only by a legal theory which can explain why the law requires official fidelity, albeit that the requirement may be outweighed by a countervailing duty. In sum, the Separation Thesis does not help to illuminate what Hart wishes to illuminate – the *moral* complexity of the situation.[46]

In this light, one of the reasons Hart advanced for adopting the 'wider' or positivist concept of law which regards very unjust law as morally but not legally problematic is weakened because the wider concept fails to assist 'our moral deliberations'.[47] Does that leave intact the other reason Hart advanced – that positivism is superior to natural law theories

[44] Hart, *The Concept of Law*, 211.

[45] Ibid, 208.

[46] See Fuller, 'Positivism and Fidelity to Law', 656. It does not help to put the matter into a kind of indirect speech. Raz, as I point out later in this section, offers the suggestion that we might consider the judge's duty here in the same light we consider such statements as, 'As a Catholic, my duty is . . . ' But he also argues that judges must consider their legal duty to apply the law as a duty from the moral perspective. See Raz, 'Incorporation by Law' (2004) 10 *Legal Theory* 1. Nor does it help to suggest that the duty to apply the law might be a non-moral duty, that is, a duty which is morally but not normatively inert. As we saw in the Introduction, and will see again in this chapter, while Hart claimed that the judicial duty to apply the rule of recognition could rest on non-moral reasons, he recognized that an idea of authority based on non-moral reasons made his account of authority highly problematic.

[47] Hart, *The Concept of Law*, 209.

because of the way it assists 'our theoretical inquiries'?[48] Hart thought it does. Natural law's 'narrower' concept of law excludes from legal philosophy rules which are legally valid but beyond the moral pale; and it is the task of legal philosophy to 'group and consider together as "law" all rules which are valid by the formal tests of a [legal] system . . . , even though some of them offend against a society's own morality or against what we may hold to be an enlightened or true morality'.[49]

However, a natural lawyer can respond to Hart's claims about moral deliberation by pointing out that his concept of law fails to bring to light the moral complexity caused by the existence of very unjust law because the concept cannot explain why a judge is faced in this situation by a conflict of duties. That conflict in turn indicates why Hart's concept of law does not aid theoretical inquiry. Instead, we need a legal theory which can explain the conflict as one between duties of the same kind – that the judge is pulled in one direction by the moral duty to apply the law and in another by the moral duty not to.

Hart generally dealt with this kind of problem by seeking to avoid it. Recall that he said of the principle against retroactive punishment that it is 'a very precious principle of morality endorsed by most legal systems'.[50] But the principle is not a free-standing moral principle which most legal systems just happen to endorse. Rather, it is a moral principle which is also legal in that it has a place only within the institutional structure of a legal order. If it did not have that place, if the order permitted punishment for acts which were not crimes at the time they were committed, one would have reason to doubt both that what was happening was 'punishment' and the order's claim to be 'legal'. Moreover, if Hart had acknowledged that the principle is a moral principle of legality, he would have been better equipped to explain why the postwar judges had a duty to apply the law as found, which was not dependent on a contingent fact about their legal order. Rather, the judges had a duty to uphold principles of legality, including the principle against retroactive punishment, because the internal point of view of judges anywhere requires a commitment to such principles. They are among the 'conditions necessary and sufficient for the existence of a legal system'.[51]

[48] Ibid.

[49] Ibid.

[50] Hart, 'Positivism and the Separation of Law and Morals', 76–7.

[51] Hart, *The Concept of Law*, 116–17.

Notice that this point suffices to make the issue more than a failure to account for moral complexity. Hart's focus can be seen as narrower than that of natural law because it does not include whatever feature of law gives it the moral quality which produces such complexity; for example, a legal/moral principle such as the principle against retroactivity, or whatever else might ground a standing obligation on judges to apply the law. Of course, Hart could respond as he did in part V of the 1958 essay, and was to do so more elaborately in his later critiques of Fuller, that even if such principles are necessary features of law, compliance with them is 'unfortunately compatible with very great iniquity'.[52] But this response is rife with problems as it exemplifies what I alluded to in the Introduction as Hart's divide and conquer strategy when it came to his foils.

Consider that Hart distinguished between part IV of his 1958 essay, on Radbruch, and part V, on legality and justice, by saying that the former dealt with the situation raised by a single law with clearly unjust content while the latter dealt with the challenge to the Separation Thesis which arises when one analyses a 'legal system considered as a whole'.[53] Part V thus provides Hart's take on the 'nuances imported by the German word *Recht*' which Radbruch elaborated in setting out his formula. By skipping discussion of the nuances in part IV and postponing the discussion to part V, Hart cleared the way for dealing in part IV with Radbruch on his own terms instead of confronting Radbruch's actual argument.

Hart did not refer to Fuller in part V. But as I show in Chapter 6, he responded there to Fuller's embryonic argument that legal order must by and large comply with principles of legality and that such compliance imparts a moral quality to law.[54] Hart's response was (perhaps deliberately) ambiguous. On the one hand, he appeared to argue that no important connection between law and morality emerges out of the fact that law must conform to principles of legality to be law, because even though the principles of legality are moral, the moral quality they give to law is so weak that it is easily outweighed by other moral considerations. On the other hand, he indicated, as Joseph Raz was to argue in a later essay on the rule of law,[55] that, in the positivist view, such principles are

52 Ibid, 207.

53 Hart, 'Positivism and the Separation of Law and Morals', 78.

54 See Fuller's discussion of 'The Problem of the Inconsiderate Sovereign', in Lon L Fuller, *The Law in Quest of Itself* (Boston: Beacon Press, 1940), 34–41.

55 Raz, 'The Rule of Law and Its Virtue'.

not moral. They serve only to make law into a more effective instrument of the goals enacted into law. This ambiguity allowed Hart and Raz at times to acknowledge that the principles are moral while denying that law must by and large comply with them and at other times to acknowledge that law must by and large comply with the principles while denying that compliance imparts any moral quality to law. In other words, by dividing Fuller's singular argument into two, Hart and Raz made it easier for themselves to appear to conquer each.[56]

Hart's objection that natural law theory narrows the scope of philosophy of law by consigning the study of unjust laws to some other discipline than philosophy of law can also be matched by an objection that positivism consigns all moral questions which arise about very unjust law to other disciplines, thus impoverishing philosophy of law. To say with Austin that '[t]he existence of law is one thing, its merit or demerit another',[57] is to assert that the other thing – the question of obedience to law – is a matter for moral, not legal philosophy.

Similarly, Hart argued in part III of his 1958 essay that in cases where it is controversial what the law requires, judges must legislate by deciding the matter in accordance with their view of what law ought to be, thus consigning theories of adjudication such as the one Dworkin was to develop to political theory. Hart offered two reasons why one should not infer from the necessity of such judicial reliance on 'oughts' that there is a necessary connection between law and morality. First, this kind of decision usually takes place in the 'penumbra' of uncertainty about what the law requires, in contrast to the determinate 'core' of settled law.[58] Hence, all philosophy of law can say about such decision-making is that it amounts to an act of discretion or judicial legislation based, at least ultimately, on extra-legal considerations.

Second, even if it is the case that the judge can find some prescription in the law as to how the case must be decided, the content of that prescription will be contingent on facts about the law of that legal order, so we should see that the legal 'oughts' operative in that legal order might be highly immoral. Hart offered as an example of the latter an ought which he thought might have informed the interpretation of the Nazi judges who convicted and sentenced to death the husband of the Grudge

[56] For discussion of Hart's changing position, see Jeremy Waldron, 'Positivism and Legality: Hart's Equivocal Response to Fuller' (2008) 83 *New York University Law Review* 1135.

[57] Hart, 'Positivism and the Separation of Law and Morals', 52.

[58] Ibid, 62–72.

Informer: 'What sentence would both terrorize the public at large and keep the friends and family of the prisoner in suspense so that both hope and fear would cooperate as factors making for subservience?'[59] He noted that the 'prisoner of such a system would be regarded simply as an object to be used in pursuit of these aims', but, he said, this would 'still be an intelligent and purposive' decision and 'from one point of view the decision would be as it ought to be'.[60]

The first reason was for Hart the more important one. He offered the second as a kind of *ad hominem* refutation of those who might 'invite' us to accept a different description, one offered by a Dworkinian account of adjudication whose main features Hart succinctly and presciently outlined in 1958.[61] In other words, the first reason is that 'legislation' accurately describes what judges generally do in such cases. The second reason points out that those who suggest that there are values inherent in the law which determine right answers are committed to supposing absurdly that the immoral point of view Hart sketched in his example can tell judges what they morally speaking ought to do.

Hart appeared to think that the kind of ought in his example, while deeply immoral, is legally unproblematic. Consider, however, the point of view of the prisoner who has to regard himself as, in Hart's own words, 'an object to be used in pursuit of these aims'. Why may the prisoner not draw on the resources of Hart's legal positivism and say that he is the victim of a gunman situation writ large, not a legal order which purports to exercise authority over him? Put differently, it is one thing for Austin to say that the execution of the condemned man in the example Hart quoted in 'refutation' of Radbruch proves the man's mistake in saying that the law was no law, since Austin's theory of law *is* that law is the commands of an uncommanded commander backed by threats. But it is altogether another thing for Hart, who rejected the command theory, to say of the person objectified in this way that he should regard as authoritative the law which consigns him to prison and execution: that he should regard the law as having changed his normative situation, however undeniably it changed his physical situation.

Moreover, a law which told judges to impose the harshest sentence possible in a bid to intimidate the population, no matter what the criminal law of their land directed them to do, would be a very odd

59 Ibid, 70.

60 Ibid.

61 Ibid, 68–9.

law, legally speaking. It would tell judges to act arbitrarily in violation of the criminal law directly relevant to their decision. As HO Pappe pointed out, the law did not in fact tell judges to act so, since large parts of pre-Nazi German law survived into the Nazi period, including the law on punishment which required that punishment be proportionate to the offence.[62] That point is, of course, subject to the challenge that the presence of a legal resource such as a requirement of proportionality was entirely contingent. But as I have suggested, and argue in Chapter 5, if a legal order is present, judges will have such resources available to them. For the moment, we can note that Pappe also claimed that one should be a little slower than Hart in getting to the conclusion that such an ought – one from 'a point of view' which made the wishes of party officials the standard – could be made into a legal standard, another issue for later.[63]

Hence, the question of the role of legal oughts in the interpretive process, which Hart thought he could put aside when he dealt with Radbruch and the Grudge Informer Case, complicates his assumption in part IV that the problem is how to respond to law which is clearly law and clearly unjust. For there is a prior question in the situation of very unjust law about both whether there is law at all and, if there is, what its content is. For that prior question to emerge, a concept of law is needed which does not suppose either that law can have any content whatsoever or that when a particular law appears to have a very unjust content, the situation is morally but not legally problematic. What underpins these suppositions is the assumption that the content of law is to be found in the 'core': what can be certified as valid law with a factually determined content. That entails adopting what I called in the Introduction a 'static' model of law, one in which law properly so-called is law the content of which can be derived by factual tests. It thus contrasts with a 'dynamic' model in which law properly so-called is also the law produced by creative though law-governed official interpretation.

It is not that a static model is unaware of such dynamic activity, only that it considers that it is located outside of law and so its study can be consigned to other disciplines, for example, political theory. It is the model which underpins both parts III and IV, which is important because Hart could ignore the nuances in Radbruch's theory in part IV only by assuming that the problem Radbruch's formula addresses is that

62 Pappe, 'On the Validity of Judicial Decisions in the Nazi Era', 271.
63 Ibid, 271–2. See Chapter 5.

of particular laws which have both been certified as valid and as having a determinate, immoral content. He could thus reduce the formula to positivism with a minus sign: the law of a legal order is all of its positive laws as identified by its criteria of validity with those laws subtracted which are extremely unjust by some moral standard external to legal order. That in turn permitted him to deal with the nuances of *Recht*, the justice peculiar to legal order, in part V as if these had no bearing on the situation he analysed in part IV or the problem of adjudication with which he dealt in part III.

I come back to Radbruch's theory and its nuances in Chapter 6. For the moment, consider that in part V of the 1958 essay Hart mentioned 'the normally fulfilled assumption that a legal system aims at some form of justice colours the whole way in which we interpret specific rules in particular cases, and if this normally fulfilled assumption were not fulfilled no one would have any reason to obey except fear (and probably not that) and still less, of course, any moral obligation to obey'.[64] He went on to say that if there were not some group which received the benefit of protection from the law, the system would 'sink to the status of a set of meaningless taboos' and 'no one denied those benefits would have any reason to obey except fear and would have every moral reason to revolt'.[65]

Now Hart in part V was responding, as I mentioned, to Fuller's embryonic position that law must comply with principles of legality to be law and that such compliance imparts a moral quality to the law.[66] Hart conceded that legal orders do all overlap with morality in that they afford morally valuable protections to individuals, for example, in criminal law and property law. He also conceded that there is, 'in the very notion of law consisting of general rules, something which prevents us from treating it as if morally it is utterly neutral'. 'Generality', Hart said, requires '[n]atural procedural justice' which consists of 'principles of objectivity and impartiality in the administration of the law' and 'which are designed to ensure that rules are applied to only to what are genuine cases of the rule or at least to minimize the risks of inequalities in this

[64] Hart, 'Positivism and the Separation of Law and Morals', 79.

[65] Ibid, 82.

[66] In Chapter 6, I argue that attention to Radbruch's actual theory, rather than to Hart's caricature of it in part IV, shows that Hart in part V in substance reinvented that theory, though in a fashion distorted by the Separation Thesis.

sense'.[67] But such concessions do not, Hart claimed, undermine the Separation Thesis. The protections do not have to be afforded to everyone, and laws 'that are hideously oppressive' can be applied with the 'most pedantic impartiality'.[68]

However, this claim leaves in place and indeed sharpens the question raised by part II of the 1958 essay in which Hart argued that law must be understood in the register of authority. Why should we think that law, on the assumption that it is more than the gunman writ large, governs the lives of those who get no protection and who are deprived of it by hideously oppressive commands backed by force? In fact, Hart's concessions also complicate parts III and IV because if there are legal reasons for thinking that in the normal case 'some form of justice colours the whole way in which we interpret specific rules in particular cases', it should follow that judges confronted by an unjust law face a legal problem, not merely a clash between legal and moral duty. Such a problem requires them to ask the following: 'Does the law really have that unjust content despite the fact that the legislature seems in fact to have stipulated exactly it?' And if their answer to that question is 'Yes', they are driven by legal duty to confront the Radbruch Formula, since if they apply that content to the oppressed group, they are carrying out a gunman's commands, not implementing law.

The deep issue here is the role of authority in Hart's conception of law. If law's authority is a central feature of legal order which any philosophy of law must explain, legal positivism is faced with the puzzle of very unjust law. If the commands of the powerful are incapable of sustaining a claim to be exercised with right on those subject to their power, the commands lack authority, and therefore seem to lose a claim to legal status.

Hart would, of course, have thought that this argument merely reproduces Radbruch's 'naïveté'. In *The Concept of Law* he described 'an extreme case' in which 'the internal point of view with its characteristic use of normative legal language (This is a valid rule) might be confined to the official world'. He went on to say that such a society 'might be deplorably sheeplike; the sheep might end in the slaughter-house'. But, he added, 'there is little reason for thinking that it could not exist or for denying it the title of legal system'.[69] Hart's point was that if there is a

[67] Hart, 'Positivism and the Separation of Law and Morals', 81.
[68] Ibid.
[69] Hart, *The Concept of Law*, 117.

'rule of recognition' – the ultimate rule of a legal order for the certification of its other rules – and that rule certifies a rule as valid, the rule has authority, whatever its content.[70] But if the only reason legal subjects follow the rules is that they are sheeplike, that is, they think that the fact that a rule has been validly made is reason enough to obey it, they are making the rather large mistake, on Hart's own argument, of only 'half digesting' the message of legal positivism. They regard the 'primary' rules identified by the officials of the system as valid in terms of the system's 'secondary' rule of recognition as requiring their obedience whatever the content of those rules. Full digestion, in contrast, would lead them to decide whether or not to obey on the basis of their extra-legal moral evaluation of the content.[71]

From a natural law perspective, the mistake is to suppose that compliance with criteria of validity suffices to bestow authority on a rule. Recall that Hart in 1958 suggested that a natural law perspective inclines legal subjects to fall into one of two opposite traps, the anarchist trap of supposing that because a law is immoral it is invalid and the reactionary trap of 'obsequious quietism', of supposing that because a law is valid it must be moral.[72] Here we see what we can think of as the 'validity trap' which Hart's positivism encounters in supposing that a sufficient condition for the authority of particular laws is that they meet the formal criteria of validity specified by a legal order's rule of recognition.

In contrast, a natural law position which argues that law's authority is grounded on some moral basis beyond such certification will not make it so easy for individuals to become sheep. Nor, despite positivists' claims to the contrary, does it follow from the fact that individuals accept that law has a moral quality that their stance will be one of obsequious quietism. Rather, the individuals must weigh their duty to obey the law against the dictates of conscience. This is a morally complex situation, the complexity of which may better be appreciated by a natural law position about the moral quality of law which makes plausible law's claim to authority.

In sum, when Hart's position is viewed through the lens of his responses to the issue of very unjust law, we can see why such law

[70] Ibid, 94–5.

[71] In contrast, as Hart points out, ibid, 117, in a 'primitive society' – one in which there are only primary rules and where acceptance must be both by the whole society and content-dependent – 'the rules must be widely accepted as setting critical standards for the behaviour of the group'. See my Chapter 3.

[72] Bentham's phrase, see Hart, 'Positivism and the Separation of Law and Morals', 54.

presents a puzzle for his version of legal positivism. But we can also see why important developments within his tradition of legal philosophy make the puzzle more acute. I have in mind here primarily Raz's argument that it is in the nature of law that law must claim legitimate authority and that judges are committed to endorsing that claim.[73] I should note, and will note again, that Raz's argument is hardly unequivocal.

The direction of Raz's argument is from the nature of authority to the nature and limits of law. On his account, an entity which is capable of claiming authority, which satisfies the 'non-moral conditions' for being an authority, is one that can communicate a judgment to others on what the balance of reasons applicable to them requires.[74] That judgment provides those subject to the authority with an 'exclusionary reason', a reason which excludes the subject from acting on the basis of conflicting reasons.[75] Moreover, in order to do its exclusionary work, the content of the judgment must be ascertainable without revisiting the issue of what the balance of reasons requires – it must be determinable as a matter of fact, not by moral argument. This Raz calls the 'strong social thesis'.[76]

Raz says that in claiming to have determined the balance of reasons, the entity claims not only authority but also legitimate authority. Whether it has such authority will depend both on whether its judgment is right and whether those subject to it would in fact better serve their own interests by following the authority's judgment than by following their own. The entity thus must satisfy the conditions set by what Raz calls the 'normal justification thesis'.[77]

On this account, judges, in telling parties what the law is that applies to them, are committed to endorsing law's claim to legitimate authority. As Raz explains, because legal officials are in the business of telling subjects what their obligations are, they must give the appearance of allying themselves with the claim. In other words, the officials – those who 'use'[78] the law – must at least pretend to believe that the laws they

[73] See Raz, 'Authority, Law, and Morality'.

[74] Ibid, 199–202.

[75] Joseph Raz, 'Legitimate Authority', in Raz, *The Authority of Law: Essays on Law and Morality* (Oxford: Clarendon Press, 1983) 3, at 22.

[76] Joseph Raz, 'Legal Positivism and the Sources of Law', in Raz, *The Authority of Law* 37, at 47–8.

[77] Raz, 'Authority, Law, and Morality', 198.

[78] Joseph Raz, 'Kelsen's Theory of the Basic Norm', in Raz, *The Authority of Law* 122, at 141.

enforce are just, even if they do not in fact so believe.[79] They act as if they adopt the point of view of the figure Raz names the 'legal man' whom he claims to find in Kelsen: the legal man adopts 'the law as his personal morality, and as exhausting all the norms he accepts as just'.[80]

In Raz's view, then, an understanding of legal orders as authoritative involves understanding their claim to have legitimate authority, which requires the figure of the man who accepts the legitimacy of the legal order because he equates justice with the content the laws happen to have. In turn, the jurist must explain legal order from the legal man's point of view. Raz claims that presupposing this figure is perfectly consistent with the claim that legal orders are rarely just, so that in general their claim to legitimate authority fails. If that is correct, he would make no concession to the natural law claim that there is an intrinsic connection between law and morality. Yet he also says that his argument shows that the 'gap' between legal positivists and natural lawyers is not 'as unbridgeable as is sometimes imagined' because legal positivism must adopt in somewhat modified form two 'semantic theses' usually associated with natural law.

First, there is the thesis that 'normative terms like "a right", "a duty", "ought" are used in the same sense in legal, moral and other normative contexts'. The second thesis is that 'legal statements are moral statements'; to say that someone has a legal duty to repay a debt is to assert a moral duty to repay the debt 'arising out of the law'.[81] Positivists, Raz suggests, are tempted to reject the second thesis, since they argue that law is a matter of social fact and its value is always a further question. While if the law is in force there will be some who make what Raz calls 'fully committed statements' – statements that endorse the law's claim to legitimacy – it is possible for others to make the same statements from

[79] Or at least this is what I take Raz to be saying, in 'Legal Validity', in *The Authority of Law* 146, at 154–5, including 155, note 13. See HLA Hart, *Essays on Bentham: Jurisprudence and Political Theory* (Oxford: Clarendon Press, 1982) 127, 155–7, at 155: 'Raz's final view, after hesitation, seems to be that one necessary condition [if a legal system … is to constitute the law of a particular society] is that there be on the part of judges either belief or at least the pretence of belief in the moral justifiability of the law'.

[80] Raz, 'Kelsen's Theory of the Basic Norm', 142–3; see also Raz, 'The Purity of the Pure Theory', in Stanley L Paulson and Bonnie Litschewski Paulson, eds, *Normativity and Norms: Critical Perspectives on Kelsenian Themes* (Oxford: Oxford University Press, 2007) 237. Raz's claim to find this figure in Kelsen is not uncontroversial. See Stanley L Paulson, 'The Weak Reading of Authority in Hans Kelsen's Pure Theory of Law' (2000) 19 *Law and Philosophy* 131 and my Chapter 3.

[81] Raz, 'Legal Validity', 159.

their point of view but without endorsing it, just as a knowledgeable Catholic can inform an ignorant Jew about what his religious duties are without endorsing the Jewish faith.[82] The jurist and the lawyer can make statements from the point of view of the legal man while leaving as a further question whether those statements should be endorsed. That shows, Raz thinks, why positivist legal theory must accept the first semantic thesis. But it also shows that the second thesis must be accepted because the 'not committed detached' statements of the lawyer or jurist are 'parasitic on the full-blooded normative statements' of the legal man.[83]

Recall though that for Raz officials, including judges, have at least to give the appearance of making the same 'full-blooded normative statements', which can only mean that they must give the appearance of morally endorsing the legal order and its particular laws. They adopt, that is, the stance of the legal man. The implications of this account are not that easy to settle. Here are two candidates:

1. If law does not live up to the normal justification thesis, it is illegitimate, lacks authority, and therefore is not law. That is, if the moral conditions for having authority are set by the normal justification thesis, and if satisfying those conditions is necessary for law to have authority, then satisfying the non-moral conditions does not suffice for an artefact to be law, even if properly produced by those who have authority to make law.
2. The de facto authority of the law is one thing, established by satisfying the non-moral conditions, but the legitimate or de jure authority is another, since it requires satisfying the moral conditions. In that case, Raz's account would be no different from Hart's, with Raz's claim about a moral component to judicial duty no more than, as we will see Hart said of Dworkin's theory, an 'idle but confusing decoration'.[84]

[82] Ibid, 156–7.
[83] Ibid, 159.
[84] Yet another possibility is that Raz thinks that among the non-moral conditions which have to be satisfied is that the law must claim to have legitimate authority and officials must endorse that claim. In this respect, his account would be similar to Robert Alexy's Radbruch-inspired legal theory; see, for example, Alexy, 'On Necessary Relations between Law and Morality' (1989) 2 *Ratio Juris* 167, at 176–7. Thus, the Nazis had law as long as Nazi officials made such claims, and despite the fact that Nazi law was wholly illegitimate. But that seems to make a legal order's existence turn not on the rule of recognition, various institutions, etc. Instead, it turns on a very formal claim which will always be satisfied – that at least the officials will claim and likely think that the order they serve is

Now Hart, unlike Raz, argued that the law *has* authority, not merely that it *claims* authority. He disagreed with the command theorists in that they did without a theory of law's authority. The command theory is compatible with a claim that *the* law of a particular system has authority, for example, when the gunman is a democratic legislature which decides social policy according to the axiom of utilitarianism in promoting the greatest happiness of the greatest number. But in that case the authority is not 'of *law*'; rather, it is the authority of '*the* law', and law has authority not because it is law but because it is made by a body which has legitimacy. In other words, law as such has no claim to either authority or legitimacy and we do not need the idea of authority to explain the nature of law.

Notice that if one adopts this option, there is no problem in saying that if the law has authority, the authority it has is legitimate, because these two judgments are one and the same and purely external. But that is tantamount to adopting option (2). In that case, in limiting his argument to saying that the law claims legitimate authority and then stipulating that the law has the authority it claims only when it satisfies the normal justification thesis, Raz would resurrect Bentham's and Austin's position. The only difference would be that the legitimating source external to law is not the kind of utilitarianism which is operationalized by a sovereign, democratic legislature. Rather, it is a liberal philosophy of autonomy operationalized by individuals who, as John Stuart Mill argued, pursue 'our own good in our own way', a premise which requires that we take each individual to be sovereign 'over himself, over his own body and mind'.[85]

I mentioned in the Introduction that Raz's theory of authority attempts a solution to the puzzle of moral authority set by Robert Paul Wolff's *In Defense of Anarchism*,[86] in which Wolff argued that if one follows Kant in supposing that the 'autonomous man' is one who 'gives laws to himself, or who is self-legislating', it follows that a 'morally

legitimate. See further Raz, 'Legitimate Authority', 8–9. Raz has refined and amended his theory of authority many times, for example, *Between Authority and Interpretation* (Oxford: Oxford University Press, 2009). These refinements and amendments are largely, in my view, the product of his struggle to respond to the problem set out in the text.

[85] John Stuart Mill, *On Liberty*, in *John Stuart Mill, Three Essays: On Liberty, Representative Government, The Subjection of Women* (Oxford: Oxford University Press, 1984) 5, at 18, 15.

[86] Robert Paul Wolff, *In Defense of Anarchism* (Berkeley: University of California Press, 1998).

legitimate state is a logical impossibility'.[87] The normal justification thesis is Raz's answer. It tells subjects that a morally legitimate state is one which tells them to do what they should in any case do, and is better at determining what they should do than they are. But that answer comes at the cost of ridding philosophy of law of the puzzle of legal authority. Law has no intrinsic authority so there is no point inquiring into what Hart called the 'specific character of the authority of a legal order'.[88] Law, that is, has authority when and only when it contains reasons which satisfy the normal justification thesis.

It is significant that Hart explicitly acknowledged that legal positivism is unable to resolve the puzzle of legal authority when he expressed his concern that Raz's analysis of what Hart called 'authoritative legal reasons'[89] threatened to undermine the Separation Thesis.[90] Hart argued that Raz's analysis should be rejected, first, because it is unrealistic. He suggested that judges need form no views about the moral merits of the law in accepting that they are under a standing duty to apply it, whatever the merits of its content; something he took Raz to recognize in his thought that the judges could be insincere in associating themselves with the legal man. Here Hart relied on the claim he advanced in *The Concept of Law*, that the obligations of the legal realm can be accepted on the basis of 'many different considerations':

> calculations of long term interest; disinterested interest in others; an unreflecting inherited or traditional attitude; or the mere wish to do as others do. There is no reason why those who accept the authority of the system should not examine their conscience and decide that, morally, they ought not to accept it, yet for a variety of reasons to continue to do so.[91]

Second, Hart rejected Raz's account in so far as it presupposes a 'cognitive account of moral judgement in terms of objective reasons for action'.[92] 'Far better adapted to the legal case', he asserted, is a non-cognitive theory, according to which 'to say that an individual has a legal obligation to act in a certain way is to say that such action may be

87 Ibid, 14, vii.
88 Hart, 'Positivism and the Separation of Law and Morals', 53.
89 Hart, *Essays on Bentham*, 243.
90 Ibid, 153.
91 Hart, *The Concept of Law*, 203.
92 Hart, *Essays on Bentham*, 158–9.

properly demanded from him according to legal rules or principles regulating such demands for action'.[93]

Hart did note a difficulty for his argument. The virtue of Raz's account, he suggested, is that it responds to the idea that when a subject is stated to have a duty to act contrary to his own sense of his interests, it is assumed that there exist reasons that are objective in that they 'exist independently of his subjective motivation'.[94] On this assumption, 'it would be difficult to deny that legal duty is a form of moral duty' because that denial would seem to entail that there were 'two independent "worlds" or sets of objective reasons, one legal and the other moral'. And Hart conceded that his non-cognitive account of legal reasons seems committed to the 'paradoxical' and even confused conclusion that 'judicial statements of a subject's legal duties need have nothing directly to do with the subject's reasons for action'.[95] He also conceded that his account of judicial acceptance had become 'whittled down' to the point where it seemed quite different from the idea as he had 'first introduced it in the model of a simple society whose members accepted a commander's words as . . . [authoritative legal] reasons for doing what he commands them to do'.[96] This latter kind of acceptance Hart described as 'full blooded' to contrast it with 'institutionalized "whittled down"' forms of acceptance. But in neither case 'need there be, though there may often be, belief in the moral legitimacy of the legislature or the pretence of such belief'.[97]

Hart therefore detected a problem for positivist legal theory. If one of the features of law which requires explanation is law's authority, the command theory must be rejected. Something is required which attends to the way in which law provides reasons of a special kind to subjects – authoritative legal reasons. Hart's term 'full blooded' does not help to address this problem. It seems to mean something like 'vigorous' or 'robust' and is very close to 'fully committed' or 'fully normative', the terms Raz used in the passages to which Hart objected, and in which he made the argument that judges must give the impression that the rule they accept they have a duty to apply is one which legal subjects have a duty to follow.[98]

93 Ibid, 159–60.
94 Ibid, 266–8.
95 Ibid.
96 Ibid.
97 Ibid, 268.
98 Raz, 'Legal Validity', 153, including note 13.

The exchange between Hart and Raz does, however, help to illuminate the path forward. Raz's point can be put as follows. When Hart talked of 'official acceptance', he tended to think of the relationship of acceptance as one between the officials, on the one hand, and the fundamental rules of the legal order, on the other. Acceptance refers to the voluntary cooperation of each official with every other in upholding secondary rules, that is, besides the rule of recognition, rules that govern the production, enforcement and interpretation of primary rules. But these officials do not have to have any regard for the individuals who are subject to their decisions. Once they have determined what the law is, they simply declare it, apply it or enforce it.

But, as Hart acknowledged in his response to Raz, his own account then seems committed to the 'paradoxical' and even confused conclusion that 'judicial statements of a subject's legal duties need have nothing directly to do with the subject's reasons for action'.[99] Moreover, in a philosophical obituary of Hart, Raz concluded that because Hart's rule of recognition is to be explained as a matter of the facts about its existence, which include the fact that criticisms are made of those who deviate from its duties, he put forward a non-cognitivist, 'sanction theory of rights and duties'.[100] In other words, Hart put forward a position of the sort he thought he had rejected in rejecting the command theory of law.[101]

The path forward, then, is to find a way of bringing the legal subject into the picture so that we can understand why legal officials must make decisions which do respond to the subjects' reasons for action. To adapt Hart above, philosophy of law would not then deny that legal duty is a form of moral duty and so would not have to suppose that there are 'two independent "worlds" or sets of objective reasons, one legal and the other moral'.

The rest of this book is devoted to describing the path. But we can note right now that Hart took a tentative step onto it in chapter 9 of *The Concept of Law*, 'Laws and Morals'. There he said that 'a minimum of justice is realized whenever human behaviour is controlled by general rules publicly announced and judicially applied'. If law is to function as a system of social control, its rules 'must be intelligible and within the capacity of most to obey, and in general they must not be

[99] Hart, *Essays on Bentham*, 266–8.

[100] Joseph Raz, 'HLA Hart (1907–1992)' (1993) 5 *Utilitas* 145, at 149.

[101] Hart, *The Concept of Law*, chapter 3, 'The Variety of Laws'.

retrospective'.[102] His explicitly Hobbesian argument was that both law and morals must have a minimum content if they are to 'forward the minimum purpose of survival which men have in associating with each other' and that 'in the absence of this content' men would have 'no reason for obeying voluntarily any rules'.[103] The point about reasons for obedience is important.[104] These reasons for obedience must be addressed at least to the natural facts of human vulnerability, approximate equality, limited resources and limited understanding and will.[105] This 'natural necessity', he stated, has to qualify the 'positivist thesis that "law may have any content"'.[106]

Later in that chapter, Hart said that judges 'may often display' what he called 'characteristic judicial virtues': 'impartiality and neutrality in surveying the alternatives; consideration for the interest of all who will be affected; and a concern to deploy some acceptable principle as a reasoned basis for decision'.[107] Hart was, I think, deliberately coy about the status of these virtues within his general argument about the necessary minimum content of natural law.[108] But I assume that he saw them as the characteristics of the role of a judge who wishes to be true to the judicial role, the role whereby judges understand themselves as operating in a system of authority rather than a gunman situation writ large, and understand their legal order as catering to the minimum content of natural law he sketched.

Now imagine such a judge confronted by a law which requires that a whole group of people be treated inequitably, for example, one of the segregationist statutes of the apartheid regime.[109] That judge must – a matter of *legal duty* – struggle to find an interpretation which displays both consideration for the interest of all those who will be affected and a concern to deploy some acceptable general principle, derived from the relevant legal materials, as a reasoned basis for a decision. It is a struggle because a law which explicitly institutionalizes inequality on its face does

[102] Hart, *The Concept of Law*, 206–7.
[103] Ibid, 193.
[104] Ibid, 194.
[105] Ibid, 194–200.
[106] Ibid, 199.
[107] Ibid, 205.
[108] In my view, his coyness is symptomatic of the kinds of issues about the rule of law and legality which arise in his challenges to Fuller, as depicted by Waldron, 'Positivism and Legality: Hart's Equivocal Response to Fuller'.
[109] See my *Hard Cases in Wicked Legal Systems*.

not display such consideration and is hard to interpret in a way which displays some acceptable general principle. That creates a tension internal to the judicial perspective, since the judicial virtues are prominent among the norms judges accept as defining the judicial role. Most concretely, the judge will have a hard time answering the legal subject who asks 'But, how can that be law for me?'

Put differently, if the commands of the powerful are incapable of sustaining a claim to be exercised with right on those within their power, the commands lack authority, and therefore start to lose their grip on a claim to legal status. For such commands undermine the mutual relationship between protection and obedience Hobbes outlined in *Leviathan*[110] and which Hart depicted as follows, in giving a snapshot in chapter 8 of *The Concept of Law* of his argument to come in chapter 9:

> It seems clear that the sacrifice of personal interest which such rules *demand* is the price that must be paid in a world such as ours for living with others, and the protection they *afford* is the minimum which, for beings such as ourselves, makes living with others worth while. These simple facts constitute . . . a core of indisputable truth in the doctrines of Natural Law.[111]

Hart's own treatment of this kind of issue relied on a clear distinction between an in-group which gets protection from the law and an out-group which does not. As I have indicated, he thought that the in-group could be small, confined to the officials of the system, and the system would still be a legal system, albeit in a deplorable state.[112] Only if there were no one in the in-group at all would the system become one in which there was the appearance of law but what passed for law had sunk to 'the status of a set of meaningless taboos'.[113] Hart thus did not generally attend to the important issues that arise for philosophy of law when one is in the in-group for some purposes but not for others. However, as I noted in the Introduction, he clearly saw that within any jural community between the one extreme of being altogether in the out-group, and thus regarding the law as a matter of might, and the other extreme of being fully in the in-group, and thus regarding the law as a matter of right, 'various combinations of these attitudes are to be found, often in

[110] Hobbes, *Leviathan*, 491.
[111] Hart, *The Concept of Law*, 181. His emphasis.
[112] Ibid, 117. Compare 90–1.
[113] Hart, 'Positivism and the Separation of Law and Morals', 81.

the same individual'.[114] As I suggested, the idea of a combination of attitudes provides a fertile terrain for exploring legal theory through the lens of the question 'But, how can that be law for me?' The combination is not, however, of attitudes alone, because it must include the reasons for attitudes. The pathology arises when a 'breakdown in the complex congruent practice' of both officials and subjects which sustains a legal order occurs; and such an occurrence takes place when a large part of the jural community is relegated to the status of second-class citizens.[115]

It seems fair to say, then, that Hart must have held the view that the 'normal' or 'healthy' case of a legal order is one in which power is exercised authoritatively. To be a first-class citizen or full legal subject in such an order is to be able to accept that the legal order as a whole and its particular laws offer one the kind of reasons which are understandable as addressing one's interests. Even when such subjects strongly disagree with the content of the law, they must be in a position to recognize that the legal order as a whole serves the interests which are in the character of a legal order to serve and that its particular laws are interpretable in light of those interests. When they ask the question 'But, how can that be law for me?' a judge mindful of the judicial virtues can give a satisfactory answer.

Hart would, of course, have objected that in any case in which the judge may display these virtues in order to respond to a legal question raised by the parties, the judge has to exercise an extra-legal discretion as such a question will arise precisely because the positive law determines no answer. And Dworkin's response to this objection preoccupied legal theory thereafter. He sought to show that ultimately at stake in such cases is the question of the political ideal which law serves and that legal positivism, despite the denials of its proponents, gives an answer which informs the way judges who endorse a positivistic ideal decide these cases.[116] Because legal positivists responded to Dworkin by asserting that there is a categorical distinction between a theory of law and a theory of adjudication, with the latter outside the scope of philosophy of law because it is a political theory about how judges should decide in the

[114] Hart, *The Concept of Law*, 202.

[115] Indeed, he seemed at times to think there was no problem. See his treatment of a segregationist law, ibid, 161 and my Chapter 6.

[116] Dworkin, *Law's Empire*.

penumbra of unsettled law, legal theory has long appeared to be deadlocked.[117]

But my argument so far helps to soften that distinction in that it shows that Hart's legal theory is committed to an outline of a theory of the role of adjudication in maintaining legal order, albeit not to a substantive theory about how judges should decide hard cases. On Hart's theory, judges should come up with an answer to the legal question which meets two criteria. First, it shows how the law responds to legal subjects in a way which respects their subjectivity – their ability to respond to reasons. Second, the answer rests on a justice-like general principle supported by the relevant legal materials, a principle which shows that the legal subjects are such because they are not outside the class whose interests the law protects, even if the protection is rather minimal.

In sum, when Hart and Raz following him made the issue of law's authority central to their inquiry into the nature of law, they found themselves caught in a dilemma between an account of authority which seemed vacuous because legal obligations are seen as morally inert, as in Hart, and one which came perilously close to a natural law account which builds moral aspirations into the concept of law, as in Raz. It is for such reasons, in my view, that Hart, after stating his resistance to Raz's suggestion that judges must associate themselves with the legal order's claim to legitimate authority, delivered the withering criticism of Dworkin sketched in Section 1.3. But my argument in this section has been that the moment Hart made the idea of authority central to his account of the nature of law, he confronted positivist legal theory with the puzzle of very unjust law and blurred the divide between his position and natural law.

1.3 The Puzzle for Dworkin

When Dworkin put the omniscient judge Hercules at centre stage of his interpretivism, he both reconfigured the debate about very unjust law and made himself vulnerable. On the one hand, he reconfigured the debate because the issue of very unjust law had traditionally been understood as one about the appropriate stance of the individual faced with such law, whereas in Dworkin's account the focus is on judges. On the other hand, because the moral quality of law seemed to come from the

117 See Liam Murphy, *What Makes Law: An Introduction to Philosophy of Law* (Cambridge: Cambridge University Press, 2014).

fact that correct answers to hard cases were constructed in the light of the best theory of the positive law, it also seemed that Dworkin made interpretivism hostage to facts about the positive law.

On Dworkin's view, interpretation has two dimensions, 'fit' – 'What range of answers is plausibly consistent with as much as possible of the relevant positive law?' – and 'justification' – 'What answer is given by the theory that best justifies that law?'[118] The vulnerability arises if, on the dimension of fit, the facts about the law of a jurisdiction overwhelmingly point to an underpinning immoral ideology of which the positive law was the instrument. It seems to follow that, on the other dimension of soundness, the theory which best 'justifies' the law is the one which shows it in a very bad moral light.

In his first response to this kind of challenge, Dworkin contemplated that a situation might arise where the 'institutional right is clearly settled by established legal materials . . . and clearly conflicts with background moral rights'.[119] The institutional right, he said, 'provides a genuine reason, the importance of which will vary with the general justice or wickedness of the system as a whole, for a decision one way, but certain considerations of morality present an important reason against it'. In this situation, he concluded, the only options open to the judge are to lie, by saying that 'the legal rights are different from what he believes they are', or to resign, which will 'ordinarily be of little help', or to stay in office and hope 'against odds, that his appeal based on moral grounds will have the same practical effect as a lie would'. Dworkin also said that he agreed with Hart's argument for candour in the 1958 essay that it would be 'unwise to make this lie a matter of jurisprudential theory'. Hence, the 'accurate description' is 'that legal and moral rights here conflict'. That description, Dworkin went on, applies to both easy and hard cases, so that 'in spite of the influence that morality must have on the answer in a hard case', 'jurisprudence must report the conflict accurately, leaving to the judge both the difficult moral decision he must make and the lie he may be forced to tell'.[120]

Hart seized on this set of remarks, as well as a passage in which he reported Dworkin's concession that in a wicked legal system the

118 See, for example, Dworkin, 'Hard Cases', 121–3.

119 Ronald Dworkin, 'Appendix: A Reply to Critics', in Dworkin, *Taking Rights Seriously* 291, at 326–7, responding to Kent Greenawalt, 'Policy, Rights and Judicial Decisions' (1977) 11 *Georgia Law Review* 991.

120 Ibid.

'"soundest theory of the law"' could include morally repugnant principles sanctioning an absolutist dictatorship or morally odious policies like 'blacks are less worthy of concern than whites'.[121] In Hart's view, these concessions 'surrender the idea that legal rights and duties are a species of moral right and duties', leaving Dworkin's theory with the 'truism' that there will be a moral justification for good law but not for very unjust law, that is, with a position 'indistinguishable from legal positivism'.[122] The only answer Dworkin could have to this criticism, Hart suggested, is the 'last-ditch' and 'hopeless' defence that individuals in a wicked legal system have a moral right that judges treat like cases alike, whether this is a matter of deciding a case by reference to settled law or by reference to the least bad principles underpinning unsettled law when the law is indeterminate. Since there can be no moral reason for repeating 'past evil', he concluded that this defence failed when it came to settled law. Dworkin's moral terminology here amounted to 'an idle but confusing decoration to the positivist simple conclusion'. Hart added that when the law is unsettled, there can be no moral reason for extending principles merely because they are the least morally odious available.[123]

Dworkin's response started by noting the 'uncharacteristic vehemence' of Hart's criticism.[124] It consisted of two parts, a structure which remained constant through to *Justice for Hedgehogs*. The first part was a criticism which I will not spend much time on here, both because Dworkin did not elaborate it, and because my detailed account of Hart in Section 1.2 was intended in part to explain why the criticism is on the mark. It is that if positivists wish to claim that their legal theory clarifies the moral complexity of the situation of a judge faced with applying a very unjust law, they must suppose that the fact that there is law supplies a moral reason of some kind to the judge to apply that law. The fact that there is law either affects the moral situation, something Dworkin's theory seeks to explain, or if it is morally inert, as Hart seemed to insist,

[121] Hart, *Essays on Bentham*, 150, quoting from Dworkin, 'Appendix: A Reply to Critics', 343.

[122] Hart, *Essays on Bentham*, 150–1. Hart added that there cannot in any case be any individual expectations when the law is indeterminate, that is, because (at least on the positivist account) the law supplies no answer in such cases.

[123] Ibid, 152–3. However, as we have seen in this chapter, Hart's criticism of Radbruch was even harsher, and I suggested in the Introduction that Hart's tone on such occasions usually indicated a sense of vulnerability.

[124] Dworkin, 'A Reply by Ronald Dworkin', 257.

the judge is not in a moral dilemma.[125] The contribution of Section 1.2 is thus in part to show that Dworkin was right to claim that legal positivism finds itself in a dilemma on this issue. But, as I now explain, it also prepares the way for seeing why he could not escape a similar dilemma.

The second part of Dworkin's response offered a new set of options to the situation of a judge starkly faced with a clearly unjust law, though he did, we should note, express doubts that such situations will easily arise.[126] The response supports a different set of options for the judge, replacing the previous three – lie, resign, apply the law and make a moral protest – with two. The judge declares the law invalid because it is unjust, not merely because of the injustice of the particular law but because the law partakes of the pervasive injustice of a wholly illegitimate system. Alternatively, the particular law is unjust, but the system is on the whole legitimate, or at least not altogether illegitimate, in which case the judge should recognize the law as valid but refuse to apply it.

Dworkin used the analogy of an ill-advised and vague promise. For example, I promise a friend who is also my employee to fire another employee.[127] Suppose that the best interpretation of the promise is that it was made from a flawed conception of friendship which required the employee be fired despite having done nothing wrong. If one thinks there is any kind of moral reason to keep such a promise, the reason cannot depend on the principles which figured in working out its content; rather, it must have its source in the 'morality of promise-keeping'.[128]

On this analogy, one should see that it is a mistake to suppose with Hart that Dworkin's account of 'how legal rights are identified in hard cases' supplies the reasons for supposing that those rights, 'once identified, have some claim to be enforced in court'.[129] In terms Dworkin coined later, Hart had confused the question which is the legal philosopher's focus, the question of the 'grounds of law' – 'the circumstances in which particular propositions of law should be taken to be sound or true' – with the political philosopher's question about the 'force of

[125] Ibid, 259. Fuller, 'Positivism and Fidelity to Law', 656, had made exactly this criticism in 1958.

[126] Dworkin, 'A Reply by Ronald Dworkin', 299, note 4. In Chapter 5, I argue that Dworkin should have relied more on such doubts.

[127] Ibid, 257–8.

[128] Ibid, 258. For the most elaborate account of this point, see Dworkin, *Justice for Hedgehogs*, 407–9.

[129] Dworkin, 'A Reply by Ronald Dworkin', 257.

law' – 'the relative power of any true proposition of law to justify coercion in different sorts of exceptional circumstance'.[130]

This new response raised two different issues. First, it requires an explanation of how a very unjust legal system could supply moral reasons. Second, is that explanation tied to the 'exceptional circumstances' of a very unjust legal system or does it also tell us why morally decent legal systems create moral reasons? Dworkin confronted only the first issue. In my view, the second is the more important and in fact gives the answer to the first by explaining, along lines suggested by Fuller and Radbruch, why the sheer existence of legal order puts in place the resources required for officials to supply such reasons. That answer is set out in Chapters 5 and 6. For the moment, I want to suggest that the need to confront the second issue is supported by the problem Dworkin encountered in seeking to respond only to the first.

Dworkin argued that if an unjust legal system is a source of moral reasons for judges to apply its laws, that arises from the fact that there is a 'general political situation' such that 'the central power of the community has been administered through an articulate constitutional structure the citizens have been encouraged to obey and treat as a source of rights and duties, and that the citizens have in fact done so'.[131] His point was only that if there were such reasons, the situation would be the source of the reasons, not that the existence of such a situation suffices to supply the reasons. Indeed, in *Justice for Hedgehogs*, he said that since the Nazi order was wholly illegitimate it faced judges with a 'prudential' rather than a moral dilemma because there was no force to Nazi edicts. In contrast, in the antebellum situation of American judges from northern states faced with a duty by constitutionally authorized Fugitive Slave Acts to return fugitives to their situation of slavery, there was a moral reason. The US legal order, Dworkin suggested we may assume, 'was sufficiently legitimate so that its enactments generally created political obligations':[132]

> The structuring fairness principles that make law a distinct part of political morality – principles about political authority, precedent, and

[130] Dworkin, *Law's Empire*, 110.

[131] Dworkin, 'A Reply by Ronald Dworkin', 258.

[132] Dworkin, *Justice for Hedgehogs*, 411. I discuss the juridical situation of such enslaved persons in Chapter 5. Dworkin had set out this view many years before. See his 'The Law of the Slave-Catchers', *Times Literary Supplement*, 5 December 1975, 1437, a review of Robert M Cover, *Justice Accused: Antislavery and the Judicial Process* (New Haven: Yale University Press, 1975).

> reliance – gave the slaveholders' claims more moral force than they otherwise would have had. But their moral claims were nevertheless and undoubtedly undermined by a stronger moral argument of human rights. So the law should not have been enforced.[133]

Hence, it is better to say in this situation 'what most lawyers would say that the Act was valid law but too unjust to enforce'. For that 'expresses nuances' which the claim that there was no law there 'smothers'. 'It explains why the judges confronted with the Act faced, as they said, a moral dilemma and not simply a prudential one.'[134]

But there is something else which helps to explain why judges in both the Nazi era and in the antebellum USA faced a dilemma, however described, so long as they had moral convictions condemning the injustice of the content of the *artefact* which confronted them. I use this term for the moment in an attempt not to prejudge whether the Fugitive Slave statutes were law and whether there were legal rights, because for one side in the debate to call something 'law' implies that it supplies a special kind of moral reason for judges to enforce it, while for the other side nothing of the sort is implied, since law is morally inert.

The artefact confronts the judges because it was produced in accordance with whatever formal procedures their political order recognizes to mark the distinction between, on the one hand, the rights people think they should have, and, on the other, whatever it is they have in virtue of the artefacts that have in fact been produced. As Dworkin said, such a distinction can only be made 'in a community that has developed some version of what Hart called secondary rules: rules establishing legislative, executive, and adjudicative authority and jurisdiction'.[135] And it is rights of the latter sort – institutional or legal rights – which 'people are entitled to enforce on demand, without further legislative intervention, in adjudicative institutions that direct the executive power of sheriff or police'.[136]

Now, despite my attempt to keep the description clean of talk of rights, it has crept in, as it did for Dworkin in the passage quoted above when he talked about the slaveholders' 'weak moral claims'. The problem is that he at times insisted that there is law in these situations only in the 'preinterpretive sense', that is, artefacts which are candidates for valid

[133] Dworkin, *Justice for Hedgehogs*, 411.
[134] Ibid.
[135] Ibid, 405.
[136] Ibid.

law.[137] There is, then, law in this sense along a political range of legal orders. They range from liberal democratic to liberal but not democratic, to democratic but not liberal, to thoroughly illegitimate. These orders are in the range because they all have secondary rules which make the distinction possible between law in this sense and the rights people should have. Of course, not all political orders have such rules, in which case they may have no claim to be legal orders. But since Dworkin conceded that the presence of secondary rules gives rise to the distinction, he appeared to concede everything to positivism, as Hart argued. Dworkin seemed then stuck with the truism that it is only in just legal systems, those which contingently incorporate principles of liberal morality, that legal duties are also moral duties.

It follows from Dworkin's concession that he was faced with the kind of 'theoretical dilemma' he diagnosed for Hart: the dilemma between saying that there is law for the oppressed group despite the fact that law supplies them with no moral reasons and saying that there is no law for that group because it fails to give them such reasons.[138] That theoretical dilemma becomes a practical dilemma for judges who have to consider applying an artefact which they must see as legal to individuals who the judges know should not consider the artefact as legal.

Given that, unlike both Hart and Raz, Dworkin supposed that law generally does supply moral reasons, as well as his embrace in *Justice for Hedgehogs* of a one-system picture of law and morality, the problem of very unjust law might seem even sharper for his position than it is for theirs. Moreover, his responses to that problem at times seemed to place him on the wrong side of the positivist/natural law divide in that he consigned the problem of the injustice of very unjust law to morality, thus presupposing the two-systems picture of the relationship between law and morality he wished to reject. The impression that Dworkin has a harder time than do legal positivists is, however, misleading. As I have argued, the problem of very unjust law confronted Hart's legal positivism as soon as he made an explanation of the authority of law central to his inquiry into the nature of law. And, as I show in Section 1.4, it highlights problems with Raz's influential account of the authority of law as well as with recent work in philosophy of law which seeks to take legal philosophical inquiry in a new direction.

[137] Dworkin, *Law's Empire*, 65–6.

[138] See TRS Allan, 'Law, Justice and Integrity: The Paradox of Wicked Laws' (2009) 29 *Oxford Journal of Legal Studies* 705.

1.4 Taking Law Seriously

The title of this section is a play on that of one of the main events in philosophy of law in the twentieth century, the publication of Ronald Dworkin's *Taking Rights Seriously*. These now somewhat neglected essays are, in my view, Dworkin's most exciting contribution to philosophy of law, for they required legal philosophers to start responding to the challenge Dworkin posed – that law is best understood as a matter of moral and political principle.

In the 'Introduction',[139] which got little attention even at the time of publication, Dworkin presented the arguments of the book as swimming against the tide of what he called the 'ruling theory of law'.[140] This was Jeremy Bentham's combination in one 'general theory' of law of a normative part, utilitarianism, with a conceptual part, positivist legal theory. According to Dworkin, in the second half of the twentieth century this general theory had split into two separate endeavours: on the one hand, 'law and economics', the investigation of law as a mechanism for maximizing utility, and, on the other, Hartian legal positivism.[141]

My sense is that in the last few years the tide has turned dramatically. Not only is philosophy of law taking rights seriously, as Dworkin advocated, but it is taking them so seriously that law is vanishing from the scope of legal philosophical inquiry. Hence the title of this section. The challenge now is that the turn is so extreme that philosophers of law need to think about taking their subject seriously.

For now we have Scott Shapiro arguing that a moral ideal is part of the concept of law so that law has to be understood in terms of a master plan to serve that ideal.[142] In addition, we have Mark Greenberg arguing that legal obligations are a subset of moral obligations,[143] and Scott Hershovitz that our legal practices do not generate obligations that are distinctively legal but at best moral rights and obligations some of which we label legal.[144] Even Raz, Dworkin's arch antagonist in the debates over these forty years, has said that when we make the assumption that our legal system is legitimate and binding, 'we cannot separate law from morality as two independent points of view, for the legal one derives

[139] Ronald Dworkin, 'Introduction', in Dworkin, *Taking Rights Seriously*, vii.
[140] Ibid, ix.
[141] Ibid.
[142] Shapiro, *Legality*.
[143] Mark Greenberg, 'The Moral Impact Theory of Law' (2014) 123 *Yale Law Journal* 1289.
[144] Scott Hershovitz, 'The End of Jurisprudence' (2015) 124 *Yale Law Journal* 1160.

what validity it has from morality'.[145] It follows for him that judges are subject to law only when they are subject to morality.[146] That is a big assumption. But Raz, while saying that of course not all legal systems do 'enjoy moral legitimacy', nevertheless proceeds on the 'assumption that the legal systems we are considering enjoy such legitimacy'.[147] He does not specify what these systems are, nor explain why we should make this assumption, one hardly distant from a line we saw appear in the manuscript version of *Justice for Hedgehogs* where Dworkin said that it would be counterintuitive to think that 'most of the subjects of most of the political communities over history had no moral duty to obey the laws of their community'.[148] Finally, for some time now, legal positivists have been asserting, implausibly, that Hart never defended the thesis that there is no necessary connection between law and morality.[149]

So it seems that Dworkin's challenge was too successful, in which case the pendulum has swung too far, at least with some of these interventions, in particular those of Greenberg and Hershovitz, since they seem to want to go beyond Dworkin to the point where, to put things a little provocatively, all that matters is a one-system picture of morality. We need no longer worry about law. At least, we need not worry about it in the sense in which Hart and Dworkin worried about it: that there is, as Hershovitz puts it, a distinct domain of 'legal quasi-normativity' which requires explanation – that there are 'distinctively legal rights, obligations, privileges, and powers, which can and do differ from their moral counterparts'.[150]

That we need to ask whether philosophers of law should take law seriously seems a rather strange proposition. But suppose that it were the

[145] Raz, 'Incorporation by Law', 6–7.

[146] Ibid, 8.

[147] Ibid, 6–7.

[148] Quoted in Sreedhar and Delmas, 'State Legitimacy and Political Obligation in *Justice for Hedgehogs*', 746.

[149] Leslie Green, 'Positivism and the Inseparability of Law and Morals'.

[150] Hershovitz, 'The End of Jurisprudence', 1174. For a critique of these one-system theories, see Hasan Dindjer, 'The New Legal Anti-Positivism' (2020) 26 *Legal Theory* 181. Dindjer, after arguing convincingly that these theories have trouble accounting for even morally unproblematic law, suggests at 212–13 that his argument does not dispose of the challenge to legal positivism since 'one might hold that one can get from social facts to legal facts only via some intervening moral explanation, yet deny that the legal facts thereby explained are themselves just more moral facts'. That description well captures the argument of my book.

case that a crude emotivism – a theory that moral claims do no more than express our emotions – is correct as a matter of meta-ethics. Then philosophers interested in ethics should study the emotions if they want to understand the role that moral judgments play in our lives. Moreover, Bentham's utilitarianism is a kind of emotivism (a point I come back to in Chapter 6) – morality is served in producing the greatest happiness of the greatest number. Emotivism also underpins the command theory of law's understanding of how to produce the habit of obedience of legal subjects. Lawmakers should attach a sanction to each command sufficient to make is more pleasurable to obey than to suffer the pain which will attend disobedience. Emotivism, that is, completes the picture of how to unify hedonistic utilitarianism with the command theory of law because for law to do its job of transmitting correct judgments of utility to legal subjects, moral calculation amounts to nothing more than the calculus of pleasure over pain.[151]

Now suppose it is the case that not emotivism but moral realism – the theory that moral judgments reflect certain objective facts in the world – which is correct as a matter of meta-ethics. The turn in philosophy of law to studying law in terms of its moral impact, judged by independently derived objective standards of morality, seems to be driven by this kind of meta-ethical theory. It has exactly the same kind of result on its object of study – law – as emotivism. Philosophy of law need no longer have 'law' as part of its inquiry.

If reductionism of either sort took our inquiry forward, there would be no problem with foregoing the idea that there is a distinct domain of legal normativity. But in the case of law, reduction to morality can no more escape the problems generated by the puzzle of very unjust law than can Hart's legal positivism or Dworkin's interpretivism. On their one-system picture, as Hershovitz and Greenberg appear to understand it, no unjust law could provide a reason for a judge to enforce it. And, as we have seen, Dworkin seemed to vacillate between the one-system and the two-systems pictures in responding to the problem of the very unjust legal system.

A useful distinction has been drawn in this regard by Nicos Stavropolous in the entry 'Legal Interpretivism' in the *Stanford Encyclopedia of Philosophy* between 'hybrid interpretivism' and 'pure

[151] See, for example, Ross Harrison, *Bentham* (London: Routledge and Kegan Paul, 1983), 192–4.

non hybrid interpretivism'.[152] Hybrid interpretivism is really Hartian legal positivism plus a Dworkinian theory of adjudication.[153] We identify the relevant legal materials using the rule of recognition, and then try to come up with an answer that shows the materials in their best light by setting out a scheme of principles which justifies both the materials and the answer.

Stavropolous points out that this methodology is not faithful to the basic interpretivist idea that institutional history becomes relevant only when political ideals make it so.[154] Pure interpretivism, in contrast, is faithful to that idea.[155] But it remains the case that the relevant institutional history is the one which we do in fact have, not the one we would ideally like to have. The question then arises: why start with that history? Stavropolous says that the reason has to do with the legality of a claim – only claims grounded in past institutional practices are permissibly recognized and enforced. And he notes, without elaboration, that there is some similarity to Kelsen's view that legality is at bottom a boundary separating permissible coercion exercised in the name of the community and impermissible coercion not so exercised.[156] In this perspective, law does not drop out of the picture altogether. But to the extent that it stays in, it is difficult to see how pure interpretivists can escape the dilemma which has been the focus of this chapter.

Consider that Hershovitz's claim is that legal philosophy should be concerned with practical questions, not metaphysical ones. How do our legal practices affect our moral rights, obligations, privileges and powers? In that case, there does not seem to be something called law which is playing an independent role in our inquiry. Nevertheless, when it comes to the Fugitive Slave Act, Hershovitz says that '[w]hatever its moral faults, it was a duly enacted statute and our working theory is that federal marshals are legally obligated to enforce it'.[157] But he also says that there could be no moral obligation to enforce the statute, and therefore no legal obligation either. Moreover, he suggests that we should say of the federal marshals who were charged with enforcing the Act that they had an

[152] Nicos Stavropolous, 'Legal Interpretivism', http://plato.stanford.edu/entries/law-interpretivist/, *Stanford Encyclopedia of Philosophy*, first published 14 October 2003; substantive revision 8 February 2021.

[153] Ibid, 10–17.

[154] Ibid, 16.

[155] Ibid, 17–23.

[156] Ibid, 24–30, at 26.

[157] Hershovitz, 'The End of Jurisprudence', 1160.

obligation to enforce the acts of Congress unless the acts were morally repugnant. But we don't, he adds, want such officials thinking of themselves as moral arbiters of the acts of Congress. It is morally permitted, even required, to build some 'moral obtuseness' into the system despite the fact that, he concedes, it might be good if the marshals experience conflict and even recognize that there are occasions for stepping outside their role and declining to enforce a statute. Hence, one can distinguish, or so he claims, between legal and moral obligations.[158]

This rather bewildering set of claims demonstrates that there is no escape from what Hershovitz calls at one point the 'fly-bottle' of quasi-normativity despite his argument that we should jettison the idea that there is a distinct kind of legal normativity.[159] At best, he seems to be reinventing Radbruch, or at least Hart's understanding of Radbruch's position: extreme injustice is no law with the reservation that only supreme or superior courts are well placed to make that judgment.

Imagine, for example, that an enslaved person in antebellum America escapes to a northern state only to be captured by a federal marshal, and finds no friendly abolitionist lawyer to take the matter beyond the summary procedure which certifies that rendition back to slavery is required by law. The enslaved person has been told of pure interpretivism and protests to the marshal on being led off in shackles that what the marshal is doing is illegal. I have in mind here, of course, Austin's claim which we saw Hart quote with approval above.

> Suppose an act innocuous, or positively beneficial, be prohibited by the sovereign under penalty of death; if I commit this act, I shall be tried and condemned, and if I object to the sentence, that it is contrary to the law of God . . . the Court of Justice will demonstrate the inconclusiveness of my reasoning by hanging me up, in pursuance of the law of which I have impugned the validity.[160]

Austin's claims are at the centre of a new book by one of the last 'old school' legal positivists, Frederick Schauer, *The Force of Law*.[161] That book, which seeks to resurrect the command theory of law for legal philosophy, relies entirely on the idea of force as coercive force, that is, not the force of authority. But it seems to me to be the flip side of what we can think of as moral realist, pure interpretivism. One obeys the law,

[158] Ibid.
[159] Ibid, 1162, 1187.
[160] Quoted in Hart, 'Positivism and the Separation of Law and Morals', 73.
[161] Frederick Schauer, *The Force of Law* (Cambridge, MA: Harvard University Press, 2014).

Schauer claims, only if one's exclusive reason for obeying the law is the law's say-so. If I have reasons for doing what the law tells me to do which are independent of the fact that law so commanded me, for example, I think that doing that thing is in any case the right thing to do, I have not obeyed the law: 'there is a crucial difference between doing something because of the law and doing something for law-independent reasons that happens to be consistent with the law'.[162]

Schauer thus rejects Hart's claim in *The Concept of Law* that we should replace Oliver Wendell Holmes's 'bad man', who wants to know what the law is simply to avoid the pain which attends non-compliance, with a figure Hart dubbed the 'puzzled man', who wants to know what the law requires, not so he can know what he can get away with, but in order to obey simply because it is required by the law.[163] Schauer concludes that Hart, in framing the issue of obedience as an opposition between the bad man (who cares only for self-interest) and the puzzled man (who wants to know what the law is so he can follow it) ignored the 'moral person', the person who acts for reasons other than self-interest and who does not need law's prescriptions to do the right thing.[164]

The difference between Schauer's moral person, on the one hand, and Hershovitz's and Greenberg's position, on the other, is only that Schauer has no doubt about the legal status of the unjust law and is interested in establishing why it counts as a formally valid law. Schauer, to put things differently, remains concerned with the law. However, Schauer makes what seems to me a significant error. He paraphrases the passage from Austin as saying that Austin was 'insisting that the defendant's view of the morality or justice of a law was largely beside the point. The hangman has the last word. More specifically, Austin was arguing against Blackstone's version of natural law theory, according to which an unjust law is no law at all.'[165] Schauer goes on:

> although Austin, as with Bentham before him, fully recognized the possibility of criticizing the law–evaluating its merit or demerit–he recognized as well that a subject's ability to criticize the substance of the law was largely irrelevant to the operation of the law as it actually existed. For Austin the legal system was not a debating society. It was not the place where a law's merit or demerit could be discussed, and that was precisely

[162] Ibid, 49.
[163] Quoting from Hart, *The Concept of Law*, 40.
[164] Schauer, *The Force of Law*, 59. His emphasis.
[165] Ibid.

> and only because the law possessed the means of enforcing *its* view of a law's merit and validity.[166]

But the legal systems familiar to us are in significant part a 'debating society' as their courts and tribunals are sites where lawyers and others debate among other things the question of what the law is on a matter and, on a Dworkinian approach, the issue in such debates is at one and the same time what the law is in light of a conception of what it ought to be. Moreover, while Bentham and Austin rejected this kind of interpretive understanding of the judicial role, they did agree that their legal system was in significant part a debating society. The difference between them is that Bentham, who held in contempt the legal elites of his day, wanted to eradicate this kind of debate within the legal order to the greatest extent possible. In his view, utilitarian expertise is best located in the legislature, and the content of its decisions should be transmitted through legislation to legal subjects without unelected legal officials being given the opportunity to impose their views on the law. However, total legal certainty is not achievable and correspondingly judges will have on occasion to make determinations of what the law requires based on their sense of right and wrong. Bentham therefore advocated that judicial decisions should be stripped of precedential force to ensure that to the extent such debate took place it had minimal legal effect. In contrast, Austin distrusted democracy because he thought that the masses were ill-educated and that utilitarian expertise is rather to be found in elites such as the judicial elite. So he was content with the fact, as he saw it, that such debate is quite central to legal order.[167]

What Bentham and Austin principally shared is a conception of law as a transmitter from lawmaker to legal subject of the content of the judgments of those best suited to calculate overall utility. Where they differed, as just indicated, is in their location of utilitarian expertise. But once the judgment is made, it must be transmitted to those subject to it in a way which permits its content to be preserved untarnished by the moral judgments of others involved in implementing the judgments. Correspondingly, the legal subjects, whose compliance with the judgments is necessary for utility to be served, must be motivated to comply for reasons other than their moral endorsement of the content of

[166] Ibid, 16. His emphasis.

[167] John Austin, *Lectures on Jurisprudence or the Philosophy of Positive Law*, vol. 1 (London: John Murray, 1885, 5th ed.), Lecture III and 218–19.

particular laws or their views about the legitimacy of the system as a whole. Sanctions are the most efficient way of motivating such compliance.

In other words, the command theory of law and its particular conception of law as a command backed by sanctions whose content can be determined as a matter of factual reasoning is shaped by the substantive normative concerns of Bentham's and Austin's utilitarian political theories. Moreover, with that shaping certain theoretical questions are excluded, most significantly questions about the authority of law which have to do with claims of right or legitimacy internal to the legal order. Elites rule legitimately when they make judgments which accord with utility, a matter which can only be adjudicated by an exercise of calculation external to law.

We are back at this point with what we saw Dworkin term a general theory of law, one which unites a normative with a conceptual part. Notice that on this understanding of the command theory of law, it is a one-system theory, and indeed a kind of pure interpretivism.[168] The theory of law to which it provides answers is driven by a fundamental political ideal which tells us why legal materials must be taken seriously, and further, offers a conception of how to understand such materials, as positive law, and of how to interpret them – in a way which relies on factual tests to derive their content.

Dworkin contested this one-system theory at every level. In his introduction to *Taking Rights Seriously*, he said that chapters 1 to 3, which included the critique of legal positivism for not being able to account for the role of principles in legal argument, contained his conceptual critique of legal positivism, and that chapter 4, 'Hard Cases', provided a bridge between the conceptual part and the normative theory of rights outlined in the rest of the collection. Dworkin said of chapter 4 that the most important distinction in it is between two forms of political rights: background rights against the community as a whole and more specific institutional rights – legal rights – against a decision made by an institution. 'Legal rights may then', he said, 'be identified as a distinct species of a political right, that is, an institutional right to the decision of a court in its adjudicative function.'[169] As I have remarked, this distinction

[168] In *Justice for Hedgehogs*, Dworkin made the same point at 486, note 6, when he called Bentham a 'closet interpretivist'.

[169] Dworkin, *Taking Rights Seriously*, xii.

remained pivotal to his thinking about law throughout his work, as can be seen in his short chapter 'Law' in *Justice for Hedgehogs.*

It is this distinction which pure interpretivists wish to eliminate. As a result, law matters to philosophy of law only when an artefact produced in accordance with criteria of validity is judged by an independently established set of moral standards to be worthy of having an impact on those subject to the power of those who produced the artefact. That leaves the endeavour of working out the details of what is involved in producing those artefacts to those who might follow Schauer in his bid to revive the command theory of law and to understand law as a matter of coercive force, not authority. Legal theory would then not be so much deadlocked, as divided into camps which had nothing to say to one another because neither would think that the other was inquiring into law.

In my view, a large part of this problem comes out of the commitment to the kind of moral realism which at the moment travels with pure interpretivism, one which seems to assume not only that there are moral facts but also that these facts are both universal and timeless. Recall Dworkin's statement of the problematic two-systems picture: there are 'two different intellectual domains' or 'systems': (1) law, which 'belongs to a particular community'; and (2) morality, which does not, because 'it consists of a set of standards that have imperative force for everyone'. Law, on this mistaken view, is 'made by human beings' and it is a contingent fact what its content is, whereas morality is 'not made by anyone ... and it is not contingent on any human decision or practice'.[170]

Dworkin did not dispute that law is made by human beings, nor that its content is to a large extent determined by the contingent facts of the public record. However, if the moral domain and the legal domain should be seen as one, we may have to accept not only that morality is made by human beings but also that its content is in part determined by the contingent facts of the public record. We would then have to reject the kind of moral realism sketched in this section. It would follow that there is what Hart denied: 'a moral legislature with competence to make and change morals, as legal enactments make and change law'.[171] In other words, the law does, in Hobbes's phrase, provide us with a public conscience – the topic of Chapter 2.

[170] Dworkin, *Justice for Hedgehogs*, 400.
[171] Hart, *The Concept of Law*, 177.

2

The Puzzle of Very Unjust Law II

Hobbes

Most readers acquainted with Hobbes will think that a chapter on Hobbes and the puzzle of very unjust law must be rather short. After all, Hobbes is infamous for arguing that the law the sovereign makes not only can have any content but also that the content it happens to have is by definition just. He thus seems to have offered a radical version of a one-system theory about the relationship between law and morality in which morality is collapsed into the content of the positive law of a particular jurisdiction. Moreover, in a well-known passage, he explicitly denied the existence of such a thing as fundamental law, thus excluding a role for fundamental principles of legality in his legal theory.[1] In short, he seemed to rule out the kind of puzzle of very unjust law which we saw in Chapter 1 flummoxed both Hart and Dworkin.

Chapter 2 is long in part because it takes some time to explain why this orthodox view of Hobbes is wrong. While Hobbes in one sense excluded the possibility of very unjust law, he was troubled by a category of 'iniquitous law', that is, positive law which seems on its face to violate one of the many laws of nature the modern legal state must observe if it is to be maintained. This category points to an insight crucial to my argument. Very unjust law is suspect as law because of the way it undermines the equality of the legal subjects it targets, their equality before the law. That is not all. It is also the case that this targeting imposes a cost on legal order. As the cost rises, legal order begins to change into another kind of order altogether, one of unmediated coercive power. An important clue in this respect was offered by Hobbes immediately after his denial of the category of fundamental law. He said that one may still 'very reasonably distinguish Lawes in that manner' because such a law in 'every Common-wealth is that, which being taken away, the

[1] Thomas Hobbes, *Leviathan* (Cambridge: Cambridge University Press, 1996, Richard Tuck, ed.), 199. Hereafter, *Leviathan*.

Common-wealth faileth, and is utterly destroyed; as a building whose Foundation is destroyed'.[2]

Even more important when it comes to the length of this exposition of Hobbes is that, with the orthodox view corrected, we have in place the outline of a theory of the modern legal state capable of breaking the deadlock sketched in Chapter 1, thus providing the basis for a solution to the puzzle of law's authority. That basis resides in the way Hobbes properly configured the three elements of a successful theory of such authority: the fundamental principles of legality (despite his apparent denial that there are such things); the role of officials in interpreting the principles; and the constitutionalist idea which combines the first two elements in the contract of authorization whereby individuals in the state of nature agree with each other to create the state and obey the sovereign individual or body who represents them. The remaining chapters serve to elaborate and update that theory in order to complete the long arc of legality.

Section 2.1 explains Hobbes's neglect in philosophy of law as due to his reputation as an early command theorist. Section 2.2 shows that the factor which most set Hobbes apart from that tradition, his claim that legal authority is always de jure, reveals when elaborated that Hobbes set out not a command theory but a sophisticated mix of what we think of today as natural law and legal positivist elements. Section 2.3 applies the resources of this theory to three examples of very unjust law which Hobbes himself confronted.

Together these three examples permit me in Section 2.4 to sketch an interpretive spectrum at one end of which judges are under a duty to invalidate an apparently valid sovereign act while at the other end the legality of the act is in doubt but not severely enough to warrant its invalidation. I also discuss some of the implications of the spectrum for what we can think of as a 'political legal theory', a theory of political order as legal order.

2.1 Hobbes and Legal Positivism

Hobbes's legal theory presents some of the key elements of a command theory of law. Law is the commands of the sovereign, the sovereign is not subject to the law of any other body and is the one who is in fact obeyed.

[2] Ibid, 199–200.

He is thus usually regarded as an early legal positivist, yet hardly figures in contemporary debates in philosophy of law except as a kind of whipping boy because of one stark difference between his command theory and that of Bentham and Austin. As we have seen, a feature of the latter is that sanction is one of the constitutive elements of their theory since it is fear of sanctions which motivates subjects' general habit of obedience. But Hobbes did not have as part of his definition of law that each command comes with a sanction to motivate compliance. Rather, he said that 'Law in generall, is not Counsell, but Command; nor a Command of any man to any man; but only of him, whose Command is *addressed to one formerly obliged to obey him.*'[3]

The basis of legal order is not therefore coercion. Rather, it is an obligation which derives from the social contract between the individuals in the state of nature whose agreement constitutes the state and authorizes the sovereign to act in their name. It might seem to follow from that difference that Hobbes is a moral as well as a legal positivist. Not only is it the case that there is nothing more to law than what one with de facto power happens to command. It is also the case that those who find themselves subject to that power must regard the commands as issued with right, as de jure, and therefore as legitimate or just, drawing as Hobbes does on the etymology of *jus*tice in *jus*. The figure Joseph Raz names 'Kelsen's legal man' – the legal subject who adopts 'the law as his personal morality, and as exhausting all the norms he accepts as just'[4] – would be Hobbes's legal subject too, with the difference that for Hobbes the content of the law must be sincerely taken by both officials and subjects as just.

The basis for this view of Hobbes is that, in his political theory, the state is created by a covenant between individuals in the state of nature who thereby unify themselves into one person. The state cannot by itself act, so it has to be represented by the sovereign person (if one) or persons (if a group) and in the act of covenanting the individuals authorize the sovereign to secure the common peace and their safety. Since the sovereign acts in their name, they must understand that they own all its laws since they are ultimately the authors of the law. Put differently, since the sovereign always acts with right, de jure, they cannot accuse it of injustice because that would be to claim that it acted without the right it has

[3] Ibid, 183. My emphasis.

[4] Joseph Raz, 'Kelsen's Theory of the Basic Norm', in Raz, *The Authority of Law: Essays on Law and Morality* (Oxford: Clarendon Press, 1983) 122, at 142–3.

through their authorization. Hobbes also emphasized that so long as one is in a condition of subjection to a sovereign's laws, it does not matter how that condition came about. The subject will be deemed to have consented to the sovereign's rule. De facto power over a subject is de jure authority.

In chapter 29 of *Leviathan*, 'Of those things that Weaken, or tend to the Dissolution of a Common-wealth', Hobbes drove the claim further. There he set out the doctrines 'repugnant to' civil society which if not rejected by the individuals in that society will prove the internal causes of its disintegration. One such doctrine is that '*whatsoever a man does, against his Conscience is Sinne*'. It follows from that doctrine that no one would 'dare to obey the Soveraign Power, farther than it shall seem good in his own eyes'.[5] The transition from the state of nature to civil society, he suggested, is from a state where the individual has 'no other rule to follow but his own reason' to a civil society in which he accepts the public judgments of the sovereign about 'Good and Evill'[6] because he has contracted with all other individuals so to do. The public or enacted laws of a civil society are the repository of the society's values which the individuals in that society must take as moral. Hence, an individual who is subject to the law of a sovereign should see that 'the law is the publique Conscience, by which he hath already undertaken to be guided'.[7]

This is the case, Hobbes argued, whatever form the government takes, whether monarchic, aristocratic or democratic, though he expressed a clear preference for the first.[8] Moreover, as I mentioned in the Introduction, he deliberately did not pair the contract in the state of nature – the societal contract or *Gesellschaftsvertrag* – with a contract of government or *Herrschaftsvertrag*. There can, in Hobbes's view, be no contract between ruler and ruled because such a contract would undermine the societal contract which must authorize the sovereign 'without stint', that is, give it unlimited authority.[9]

Because the image of law as our public conscience requires us to take our compulsory moral values to be those legislated by an all-powerful sovereign, liberals reject it out of hand. At most, liberals concede that one can make a case for such a requirement when the law is the product of a

5 *Leviathan*, 223. His emphasis.
6 Ibid.
7 Ibid.
8 Ibid, chapter 19.
9 Ibid, 114.

democratic process. But in that case, liberals insist, the legitimacy of the law derives from the fact that the process is democratic and not from its moral quality as law. In addition, even if there are reasons to obey law because it is democratically made, these are reasons independent of the content of the laws – reasons to do with the merits of the democratic process.

For liberal theory, then, it remains for the individual conscience to judge the merits of the content of the law and, if it is morally offensive, conscientious objection becomes an issue. Put differently, if private conscience is to have the priority it should enjoy, it must rely on standards of justice independent of the will of the state or of the collective, no matter that the will is both expressed in law and that the law is democratically made. As we have seen Hart put it, 'the idea of a moral legislature with competence to make and change morals, as legal enactments make and change law, is repugnant to the whole notion of morality'.[10]

It is above all Hobbes's moral positivism which is supposed to distinguish Hobbes from later English legal positivists, that is, Bentham, Austin and Hart. For since 1958, when Hart published the manifesto for legal positivism which still shapes debates in philosophy of law today, it has been taken for granted in the English-speaking world that legal positivism rejects utterly any thought that individuals should substitute the dictates of the law for the dictates of private conscience. Indeed, as we saw in the Introduction, Hart argued that legal positivism's insistence that law is no more than the rules recognized as valid in a particular society enables the good citizen to establish the priority of private conscience over 'positive morality',[11] the values which happen to be accepted in a society, whether embedded in law or in social conventions. For legal positivism makes clear to the citizen that the content of the law is the product of historical and political contingency and, as such, there is no necessary moral quality to law.[12]

Philosophers of law thus generally assume that the sole link between Hobbes and the legal positivist tradition is that Bentham and Austin took from Hobbes the idea that valid law is to be found in the commands of a

[10] HLA Hart, *The Concept of Law* (Oxford: Clarendon Press, 1994, 2nd ed.), 177.

[11] For the distinction between 'critical' and 'positive' morality, see HLA Hart, *Law, Liberty, and Morality* (Oxford: Oxford University Press, 1962), 20.

[12] HLA Hart, 'Positivism and the Separation of Law and Morals', in Hart, *Essays in Jurisprudence and Philosophy* (Oxford: Clarendon Press, 1983) 49.

legally unregulated sovereign. There is much to this assumption. We have just encountered Hobbes's definition of civil law: law is the command not 'of any man to any man: but only of him, whose Command is addressed to one formerly obliged to obey him'.[13] In addition, again in chapter 29, Hobbes set out his 'regress' argument to counter the repugnant doctrine that '*he that hath the Soveraign Power, is subject to the Civill Lawes*'.[14] He argued that the sovereign cannot be subject to any such legal limit because it would follow that the one who enforced the limit would be the true sovereign, who cannot be subject to any legal limit, and so on. So here we have both the definition of law as the command of the sovereign and the claim that the sovereign itself is not subject to law.

That is supposed to be the only link between Hobbes and the command theorists since in his *Lectures on Jurisprudence*, Austin, following Bentham, roundly rejected the idea that there is a moral quality to law: 'The existence of law is one thing; its merit or demerit another.'[15] He also explicitly rejected social contract theories because he found the idea of the original covenant incoherent. Such theories, he argued, take the basis of political obedience in calculations of utility and turn it into a doctrine 'darkly conceived and expressed' which seeks the 'extension of the empire of right and justice' – a justice which is 'absolute, eternal, and immutable', not a 'creature of law' but 'anterior to every law; exists independently of every law; and is the measure of or test of all law or morality'.[16] Hence in these respects Hobbes puts forward a very different position from Bentham and Austin.

Hart, in turn, rejected both the idea that the sovereign is legally unlimited and the claim that all law consists of commands backed by sanctions. As we know, in his version of legal positivism, every sovereign is legally limited by the fundamental rules with which it must comply if it wishes its directives to be recognized as law. The foundational rule of the legal order is the secondary rule of recognition, which certifies the validity of all other rules, and which exists as a matter of social fact in the practice of legal officials. The officials maintain this rule because they accept that they are under a duty so to do, though their reasons for taking

[13] *Leviathan*, 183.

[14] Ibid, 224. His emphasis.

[15] John Austin, *Lectures on Jurisprudence or the Philosophy of Positive Law*, vol. 1 (London: John Murray, 1885, 5th ed.), 233.

[16] For further discussion, see my 'Austin, Hobbes, and Dicey' (2011) 26 *Canadian Journal of Law and Jurisprudence* 411.

that as their duty can be various, and should not therefore be thought of as amounting to their moral endorsement of the practice, even if it is likely that many of them do endorse it.[17]

Since, with Bentham and Austin, Hart rejected Hobbes's moral positivism, and since he also rejected the command theory of law, his legal positivism can be viewed as making a complete break with Hobbes. It is perhaps for this reason that Hobbes does not figure at all in 'Positivism and the Separation of Law and Morals' and hardly at all in *The Concept of Law*. In the latter, Hobbes gets only two insubstantial mentions in the text and one in the notes, the last of which was Hart's suggestion that his idea of a minimum content of natural law has some affinity with the Hobbesian thought that law must serve the human interest in survival.[18]

There are, however, more substantial references to Hobbes in Hart's *Essays on Bentham*.[19] There Hart acknowledged Hobbes's role in sketching the elements of the command theory of law, though he was anxious to stress the difference between Hobbes and Bentham.[20] Bentham and not Hobbes should be taken as the founder of legal positivism, because the 'very centre, and . . . the sane and healthy centre' of legal positivism is Bentham's 'insistence' on a 'morally neutral' or 'normatively neutral' 'vocabulary for the use in the discussion of law and politics'. In contrast, Hobbes 'had treated the commands of the Sovereign that make law as issued to those who are under an obligation to obey him'. Bentham's most important innovation in legal theory was to reject Hobbes's view that the legal subject has an 'antecedent obligation' to obey the sovereign and to substitute 'flatly descriptive and normatively neutral' terms to describe law. Hart added that the 'central tenet of positivism' – that 'the 'morality of law is [not] relevant to the validity of law' – was under a 'new and sophisticated attack . . . by my distinguished American successor in the Oxford Chair of Jurisprudence', referring of course to Dworkin, and his theory of the role of substantive moral principles implicit in the law.[21]

But in *Essays on Bentham*, Hart did more than acknowledge Hobbes's role in setting out a command theory. He found in Hobbes's distinction between command and advice the source of his own idea of a

[17] Hart, *The Concept of Law*, 26–49, 100–23.
[18] Ibid, 63, 191, 299–300.
[19] HLA Hart, *Essays on Bentham: Jurisprudence and Political Philosophy* (Oxford: Clarendon Press, 1982).
[20] Ibid, 27, 28, 221, 225, 244, 252.
[21] Ibid, 28. See 221 and 225 for the same point.

'peremptory reason' which Hart took to be the first feature of 'authoritative legal reasons',[22] the kind of reasons law gives to both its subjects and its officials. Hart referred here to chapter 25 of *Leviathan*, 'Of Counsell', where Hobbes says: 'Command is when a man saith, *Doe this*, or *Doe not do this*, yet without expecting any other reason than the Will of him that sayes it.'[23] Hobbes, said Hart, 'meant that the commander characteristically intends his hearer to take the commander's will instead of his own as a guide to action and so to take it in place of any deliberation or reasoning of his own'.[24]

Hart identified a second feature of the kinds of reasons the law gives which he did not attribute to Hobbes. Authoritative legal reasons are 'content-independent', 'intended to function as a reason independently of the nature or character of the actions to be done'.[25] Put another way, and in accordance with the Kelsenian slogan, law can have any content and yet its directives are to be taken by legal subjects as peremptory reasons for action. As I argue in Section 2.2.3, a lot turns on how one interprets this feature, on whether – to use terms I have relied on so far – one understands content-independence through the lens of a static or a dynamic model of law. Hobbes, I suggest, adopted a dynamic lens while Hart following Bentham and Austin, and with Raz following him, adopted a static one.

Now Hart rejected Bentham's and Austin's sanction-based accounts of the force of such reasons, that is, why the subject accepts them as peremptory, as well as both Hobbes's idea of prior antecedent obligation and Dworkin's attempt to update that idea. But he also rejected, as we have seen, a central part of Raz's account of the authority of law, despite the fact that Raz not only took over both features Hart had identified but also elaborated them in a way that made his account perhaps the most influential theory of authority of the last fifty years or so. As I explained in Chapter 1, Raz captures the feature of peremptoriness in his idea of an 'exclusionary reason', a reason which excludes subjects from acting on the basis of their own assessment of the balance of reasons.[26] To do its exclusionary work, the content of the judgment must be ascertainable without revisiting the issue of what the balance of reasons requires – it

22 Ibid, 244, 252–3.
23 *Leviathan*, 176. His emphasis.
24 Hart, *Essays on Bentham*, 252–3.
25 Ibid, 254.
26 Joseph Raz, 'Legitimate Authority', in Raz, *The Authority of Law* 3, at 22.

must be determinable as a matter of fact, not by moral argument. This Raz calls the 'strong social thesis' and it explains how authoritative legal reasons can be both peremptory and content-independent.[27] The subject treats the fact that the authority said 'Do X!' as the reason to do X. Hence, the merit of doing X is not the reason to do it, and the subject is able to determine the content of what to do without engaging in evaluative argument. In addition, Raz put forward the idea that the law must not only possess the features which make it an authority in fact but also must claim legitimate authority.

Hart rejected the upshot of this last idea which he took to be that judges must either believe or pretend to believe in the 'moral legitimacy' of the law of their legal order.[28] But he noted that rejection left him in a difficult position, in effect a two-systems or dualist view that there are 'two independent "worlds" or sets of objective reasons, one legal and the other moral'. He thus conceded that his non-cognitive account seems committed to the 'paradoxical' and even confused conclusion that 'judicial statements of a subject's legal duties need have nothing directly to do with the subject's reasons for action'.[29]

Hart therefore detected a puzzle for philosophy of law. If one of the features of law which requires explanation is law's authority, sanction-based accounts of law will not do. Something is needed which attends to the way in which law provides reasons of a special kind to subjects – authoritative legal reasons. Of course, if authoritative legal reasons were always moral reasons of some kind, their force would be more easily explained. But since, in line with his tradition from Bentham on, that is, excluding Hobbes but including Raz, Hart was not willing to countenance that such reasons always have a moral quality to them, he confessed that he was at something of loss.

It was, however, a comfort to Hart that we can understand what I refer to as the *structure* of authoritative legal reasons in the way suggested by Hobbes – that they are content-independent, peremptory reasons for action – without resolving the 'larger issue between the legal positivist and his critics' of how to understand what I will refer to as the *force* of such reasons, where 'force' means 'normative force', not the force of

[27] Ibid, 47–8.

[28] Hart, *Essays on Bentham*, 156–7. In fact, Raz was rather ambiguous about this issue, as we saw in Chapter 1, and as Hart acknowledged.

[29] Hart, *Essays on Bentham*, 266–7.

coercion.[30] Hart thus left unresolved a debate with the result that, as we saw in Section 1.4, philosophy of law seems torn between, on the one hand, a moral realist account of law in which law is no longer taken seriously and, on the other, a return to the command theory of law and the claim that law is nothing more than the gunman situation writ large.

Hobbes, I now argue, disagreed with Hart. He agreed that peremptoriness is a feature of authoritative legal reasons but rejected the idea of content-independence, or at least content-independence as Hart and Raz understand it. Hart and Raz, that is, suppose that content-independence requires that the content be determinable as a matter of fact, without any reliance on moral considerations or argument. And that understanding presupposes a static model of law.

For Hobbes, in contrast, the larger issue – the force of such reasons – is closely connected to his understanding of their structure in two important respects. First, his account of their structure is nested within his political theory. Structure is not a matter of morally neutral description but of normative argument. Second, the structure of authoritative legal reasons conditions their content in a way which explains their force. Legal reasons cannot have any content whatsoever since their content must be interpretable as consistent with the laws of nature, a requirement which presupposes a dynamic model of law.

This disagreement is important because only if one sides with Hobbes is one able to explain, as Hart wanted, law as a matter of authority. Indeed, despite his insistence that authority is always de jure authority, Hobbes began *Leviathan* by stating that his aim was to avoid the traps we saw Hart detect in natural law thought of adopting either the anarchist's perspective or that of 'obsequious quietism'.[31] For in the Dedication he said that he wished to pass 'unwounded' between those 'who contend, on one side for too great Liberty, and on the other side for too much Authority'.[32] Hobbes called the figure who accords the state too little authority the 'Foole', who asserts that even in an established civil society he is entitled to disobey the law when he calculates that disobedience will better serve his interests.[33]

The Foole trades on Hobbes's argument that self-interest is the basis for entering civil society. If that argument is correct, why, the Foole asks,

[30] Ibid, 268.
[31] Hart, 'Positivism and the Separation of Law and Morals', 54. Emphasis removed.
[32] *Leviathan*, 3.
[33] Ibid, 101.

should he not follow self-interest within civil society? Hobbes offered several different answers: the Foole is wrong to reason from the condition of the state of nature to the condition of civil society because in the latter there is security; the Foole is counting on luck in not being caught for his infractions of the law and that is an unreasonable basis for calculation of benefit; the Foole is putting himself in the position in which he can count only on himself. He thus relinquishes the protection of the sovereign with the result that he will be considered an unreliable member of any society and will find himself a general outcast.[34]

It is unclear that this slew of prudential considerations can shake the Foole. He can retort that he might factor all these possibilities into his calculation and still reach the conclusion that he will benefit from breaking the law because he will not be caught. But it is important that Hobbes did not think his primary audience is composed of individuals who reason only on the basis of the Foole's understanding of self-interest. He defined the Foole as the one who says 'there is no such thing as Justice'.[35] The Foole is thus no ordinary criminal but someone who denies the very basis of civil society in denying that there is such a thing as justice. He is what we might think of as a self-conscious and self-declared outlaw. And Hobbes's primary audience is individuals who do accept there is such a thing as justice once they are members of a civil society, a society in which there is peace and stability secured by – to use Max Weber's formulation – a state which has a monopoly on the legitimate use of force.

Hobbes contrasted the Foole with another figure – the 'Just man', one who 'taketh all the care he can, that his Actions may be all Just'.[36] The Just Man is someone who abides by the laws of nature in the state of nature even though that puts him at severe risk. Thus, Hobbes said that what 'gives to humane Actions the relish of Justice, is a certain Noblenesse or Gallantnesse of courage, (rarely found,) by which a man scorns to be beholding for the contentment of his life, to fraud, or breach of promise'.[37] While he thought that in the state of nature it is irrational so to behave, he also argued that things are very different once civil society is established because in the civil condition all have the security and stability to be just men without putting themselves at risk.

[34] Ibid, 102–3.
[35] Ibid, 101.
[36] Ibid, 103–4.
[37] Ibid.

It is, as I now argue, the Just Man who accepts that the law is a public conscience. But he is not doomed by Hobbes to taking an uncritical stance towards the law, for the question he asks does not suppose that the law has a content which is both determinate and fixed. The Just Man's question is 'But, how can that be law for me?' It presupposes legal subjects who regard themselves as under a duty to obey the law because government under law serves their interest in equality and so they expect that the law to which they are subject will prove interpretable as serving that interest.

2.2 The Legal Constitution of Sovereignty

In this section, I present shorter (and revised) versions of arguments I have made in more detail elsewhere as my aim is to persuade by the coherence of the package of points rather than by the discrete arguments for each point.[38] The package displays the connection between three basic points, each of which is set out in one of the subsections in Section 2.3: the sovereign is a legally constituted artificial person; Hobbes's laws of nature are part of the legal constitution of sovereignty; in constituting sovereign authority, the laws of nature condition the content of the civil law in a way which makes plausible Hobbes's claim that there is an antecedent obligation of obedience to the sovereign such that the subject should regard the law as a public conscience.

The three points together show that the understanding of the Hobbesian sovereign as legally unlimited is wrong, despite his apparent assertions to the contrary. But the mistake is not demonstrated by finding limits on sovereign authority of the sort we associate with an entrenched bill of rights which gives judges the authority to invalidate statutes which violate the rights. Rather, the Hobbesian sovereign is a legally constituted sovereign. As such, its political authority manifests itself when it rules by

[38] This chapter, and in particular this section, are based on the following: 'How Hobbes met the "Hobbes Challenge"' (2009) 72 *Modern Law Review* 488; 'Hobbes on the Authority of Law', in Dyzenhaus and Thomas Poole, eds, *Hobbes and the Law* (Cambridge: Cambridge University Press, 2012) 186; 'Dreaming the Rule of Law', in Dyzenhaus and Thomas Poole, eds, *Law, Liberty and State: Schmitt, Hayek and Oakeshott on the Rule of Law* (Cambridge: Cambridge University Press, 2015) 234; 'The Public Conscience of the Law' (2014) 43 *Netherlands Journal of Legal Philosophy* 115; 'The Public Conscience of the Law From Hobbes to Hart' (2015) 45 *Ragion Pratica* 565; 'Thomas Hobbes and the Rule by Law Tradition', in Martin Loughlin and Jens Meirhenrich, eds, *The Cambridge Companion to the Rule of Law* (Cambridge: Cambridge University Press, 2021) 261.

law. Justice resides in rule by law, in ruling in a way which lives up to *jus*. Moreover, rule by law entails, as we would say today, ruling in accordance with the rule of law, which in turn entails ruling in accordance with fundamental legal principles which condition the content of the law.

These connections have not been noticed by most Hobbes scholars because they generally skip over Hobbes's chapter 26, 'Of Civill Lawes', pausing only to notice his definition of law as the command of the sovereign,[39] the paragraph in which he sets out his view that the sovereign is legally unlimited,[40] and his puzzling claim that the 'Law of Nature, and the Civill Law, contain each other, and are of equall extent'.[41] Such partial attention to chapter 26 produces a highly misleading context for understanding Hobbes's legal theory. The conjunction of claims that law is the command of the sovereign and that the sovereign is legally unlimited is thought to explain Hobbes's place as the founder of the command theory of law. Once Hobbes's theory is so conceived, the puzzle about his claim about the equal containment of civil and natural law is too easily solved. The nineteen laws of nature, discussed at length in chapters 14 and 15 of *Leviathan*, are held to be of equal extent with the civil law only in that the content of the civil law should be taken by legal subjects as an accurate guide to the content of natural law. Thus, as one philosopher has argued, if the sovereign orders all mediators to be killed on sight, this must be taken as the correct interpretation of Law 15 – '*That all men that mediate Peace, be allowed safe Conduct.*'[42] This position entails that the 'true function' of Hobbes's extensive account of the laws of nature, 'and the only one that cannot be eliminated, is to provide the most absolute ground to the norm according to which there is no other valid law than positive law'.[43] The function of the laws of

[39] *Leviathan*, 184.

[40] Ibid, 186.

[41] Ibid, 185.

[42] Ibid, 108. His emphasis. See Mark C Murphy, 'Was Hobbes a Legal Positivist?' (1995) 105 *Ethics* 846.

[43] Norberto Bobbio, *Thomas Hobbes and the Natural Law Tradition* (Chicago: Chicago University Press, 1993, Daniela Gobetti, trans.), 148. The same point is made by SA Lloyd in the title of her paper, 'Hobbes's Self-effacing Natural Law Theory' (2001) 82 *Pacific Philosophical Quarterly* 187. That is, the laws of nature ground the political obligation of subjects but disappear once civil society is up and running. In *Morality in the Philosophy of Thomas Hobbes: Cases in the Laws of Nature* (Cambridge: Cambridge University Press, 2009), 273, Lloyd argues that Hobbes's summary of the laws of nature in the maxim '*Do not that to another, which thou wouldest not have done to thyself*' (*Leviathan*, 109, his emphasis) amounts to the 'reciprocity theorem' that if we want others to submit to

nature is, that is, to give rise to the authoritarian conclusion that legal subjects must take the law of their sovereign to be binding, whatever its content.

But, as I now argue, this conclusion does not follow because the function of the laws of nature is to condition the content of the sovereign's laws in a way which makes it possible for legal subjects to understand its rule as a matter of right rather than unmediated coercive power. As we saw Michael Oakeshott suggest,[44] the laws of nature provide a standard of right or justice which is internal to law – the *jus* of *lex*. The puzzle of very unjust law does arise for Hobbes when it is difficult for a judge who is tasked with interpreting the law to come to a conclusion which does not offend one or more of the laws of nature, though he characterized it as a problem of iniquity, not injustice. Moreover, if the conclusion is offensive in this way, the consequences go beyond the particular case because the offence undermines the relationship between protection and obedience which undergirds the civil condition.

2.2.1 *The Validity Proviso*

I recalled in Section 2.1 the distinction between the *Gesellschaftsvertrag* and the *Herrschaftsvertrag* and in the Introduction I mentioned that Ernest Barker, in his discussion of this distinction, had rightly said that with Hobbes, once the political community is formed, there is no further contract between the 'sovereign Leviathan' and the community so that the state is subject to 'none of the limits of a contract of government'.[45] Here I wish to introduce the footnote qualification of this most perceptive historian of political thought:

political authority we must do so as well. So much is true. But it only captures a small part of the operation of the laws of nature and if they are self-effacing, there is no role for law in maintaining another reciprocal relationship – the functional equivalent of the governmental contract in the relationship of protection and obedience between ruler and ruled. I think that much the same can be said of Gerald Gaus's several illuminating attempts to solve the puzzle of authority in both Hobbes's political philosophy and in the public reason literature inspired by John Rawls. See, for example, Gaus, 'Hobbes's Challenge to Public Reason Liberalism: Public Reason and Religious Convictions in Leviathan', in SA Lloyd, ed., *Hobbes Today: Insights for the 21st Century* (New York: Cambridge University Press, 2013) 155.

[44] Michael Oakeshott, 'The Rule of Law', in Oakeshott, *On History and Other Essays* (Indianapolis: Liberty Fund, 1999) 129, at 173.

[45] Ernest Barker, 'The Theory of the Social Contract in Locke, Rousseau and Hume', in Barker, *Essays on Government* (Oxford: Clarendon Press, 1960; 2nd ed.) 82, at 92.

> On the other hand, we have to notice (1) that in the theory of Hobbes every subject covenants with every other, in one and the same act, to form a society *and to obey a government*, and a subject will therefore break a sort of contract with the government (not with the ruler, but with other subjects) if he refuses to obey; (2) that in the theory of Hobbes, as it eventually develops, the ruler is bound to give protection to the lives of his subjects, and if he fails to do so they may rebel – so after all there *is* an implicit contract between ruler and subjects, which the ruler may himself break.[46]

I argue here that these two points amount to much more than a qualification, which requires taking into account a complicating factor. When Hobbes set out the social contract in *Leviathan*, he presented it as breaking down into either two separate contracts, or, better, as two stages of one.[47] For he told us that when the 'Common-wealth' – that is, the state – is 'instituted' by consensus, at the same time, by majority vote, the contracting individuals decide on the form of government, which may, as he explained later, be monarchic, aristocratic or democratic.[48]

In insisting that the form of government must be decided on in the same moment, while remaining agnostic about its form, Hobbes expressed his indifference to the kind of constitution.[49] But that indifference is not about whether there will be a constitution. There must be one, though at the abstract level of political theory, Hobbes found more important than the kind of constitution the way in which any constitution must manifest itself in a public order of law. In this fashion, he turned the social contract into a constitutionalist idea.

On the one hand, there is the *Herrschaftsvertrag* or governmental contract in the form of an ongoing practice which constitutes the

46 Ibid, 98, note 1. His emphasis.

47 See JW Gough's illuminating, and Barker-inspired, account in *The Social Contract: A Critical Study of its Development* (Oxford: Clarendon Press), 109–10.

48 *Leviathan*, 121. This is the opening paragraph of Hobbes's chapter 18 on 'sovereignty by institution', which sets out the inalienable rights of the sovereign. In the next chapter, on 'sovereignty by acquisition', Hobbes claims that the rights are the same and consent is to be presumed when the sovereign takes authority by conquest and the conquered individuals remain under the sovereign's protection. This chapter is often interpreted as part of his general argument that might begets right. I do not contest that interpretation. However, I add that might begets right only when it issues in the relationship of protection and obedience, which in effect creates the same normative bond between ruler and ruled as sovereignty by institution. It follows that sovereignty by institution is the paradigm for sovereignty in general.

49 See Lars Vinx, 'Constitutional Indifferentism and Republican Freedom' (2010) 38 *Political Theory* 809.

authority of the modern legal state. On the other hand, that practice presupposes the *Gesellschaftsvertrag* or societal contract made by individuals in the state of nature. Put differently, Hobbes made the crucial move in developing a social contract theory for the modern legal state by turning the *Herrschaftsvertrag* into a juridical relationship between ruler and ruled, one mediated by a dynamic process of application of the law in which the officials answer the legal subject's question 'But, how can that be law for me?'

As I now show, the first step in understanding Hobbes's social contract theory lies in seeing how the sovereign is legally constituted at least in that its lawmaking is subject to the equivalent of a Hartian rule of recognition, despite the orthodox view of Hobbes as having argued that there can be no formal legal limits on sovereign authority. This 'regress argument' occurs in chapter 29 as Hobbes's response to one of the doctrines which undermines the state:

> A fourth opinion, repugnant to the nature of a Common-wealth, is this, *That he that hath the Soveraign Power, is subject to the Civill Lawes.* It is true, that Soveraigns are all subject to the Lawes of Nature; because such lawes be Divine, and cannot by any man, or Common-wealth be abrogated. But to those Lawes which the Soveraign himselfe, that is, which the Common-wealth maketh, he is not subject. For to be subject to Lawes, is to be subject to the Common-wealth, that is to the Soveraign Representative, that is to himselfe; which is not subjection, but freedome from the Lawes. Which errour, because it setteth the Lawes above the Soveraign, setteth also a Judge above him, and a Power to punish him; which is to make a new Soveraign; and again for the same reason a third, to punish the second; and so continually without end, to the Confusion, and Dissolution of the Common-wealth.[50]

The passage is commonly understood to say that the sovereign is legally unlimited. However, Hobbes was clear that it is only enacted law which does not bind the sovereign. He took care to affirm in this passage, as in many other places in *Leviathan*, that the sovereign is subject to the laws of nature, though this affirmation is in general thought to be defused by his parallel claim that the sovereign's answerability for infractions of the laws of nature is to God, not to its subjects,[51] a claim I address in Section 2.3.

[50] *Leviathan*, 224. His emphasis.

[51] Ibid, 148.

Hobbes made a further argument to the conclusion that the sovereign is legally unlimited in chapter 26, 'Of Civill Lawes', in which he sets out his account of the interaction of enacted law with the laws of nature:

> The Soveraign of a Common-wealth, be it an Assembly or one Man, is not Subject to the Civill Lawes. For having power to make, and repeale Lawes, he may when he pleaseth, free himselfe from that subjection, by repealing those Lawes that trouble him, and making of new; and consequently he was free before. For he is free, that can be free when he will: Nor is it possible for any person to be bound to himselfe; because he that can bind, can release; and therefore he that is bound to himselfe only, is not bound.[52]

However, this passage does not say that the sovereign in being free from subjection to civil law is legally unlimited. Rather, it tells us something about the legal constitution of sovereignty because it clarifies what Hobbes meant in chapter 29 when he said that the sovereign is subject only to itself.[53] The sovereign, as we learn from chapter 16, 'Of Persons, Authors, and things Personated', is an artificial person. It must therefore express itself by artificial means, through law. So its will must take legal form before a subject need take notice of it. As Hobbes was to put the matter later in *Behemoth*:

> For by disobeying Kings, we mean the disobeying of his laws, those his laws that were made before they were applied to any particular person; for the King, though as a father of children, and a master of domestic servants command many things which bind those children and servants yet he commands the people in general never but by a precedent law, and as a politic, not a natural person.[54]

Hence, the freedom from being bound by enacted law Hobbes emphasized is the liberty to change the law at will, which, given the point about the artificial nature of the sovereign, is the freedom to enact a law to abrogate or to amend an existing law. Until the point where that liberty is exercised, the person or people who occupy the sovereign office, as well as the officials to whom they have delegated authority, must act in accordance with the law.

Hobbes, then, did not have in mind that the sovereign could make law without complying with public criteria for lawmaking. Rather, he had in

[52] Ibid, 184.
[53] Ibid, 224.
[54] Thomas Hobbes, *Behemoth or the Long Parliament* (London: Frank Cass, 1969, Ferdinand Tönnies, ed.), 51.

mind the equivalent of Hart's rule of recognition. The sovereign may at will change any law, including the public criteria for valid legal change, so long as it complies with those criteria when it enacts the new law. In other words, the sovereign is free to make whatever law it likes provided it complies with the public criteria which permit both officials and subjects to recognize what counts as valid law in their legal order. I call this condition the 'validity proviso'.

Hobbes did say some things which are in tension with this argument. He asserted that the subject is entitled to bring suit against his sovereign – 'the Liberty to sue for his right, as if it were against a Subject'.[55] But, in the same breath, he qualified the assertion by saying that if the sovereign demands something not on the ground of law but 'in Vertue of his Power',[56] there is no legal action possible because subjects must take themselves to have authorized all that the sovereign does in virtue of its power. In addition, in *De Cive* Hobbes said that when the subject brings suit against the sovereign, the sovereign will be final judge in the matter and could not give 'an unfair judgement'. He appeared to mean that when the sovereign has issued a final interpretation of what the law requires, its judgments must be regarded as constituting right reason, even if they appear to be in tension with – or even contradictory to – one of the laws of nature.[57] The same would appear to be true of the situation in which the sovereign is not acting as final interpreter of the law but as supreme legislator.

Notice, however, that these qualifications create rather different kinds of tension. The first is a tension between two arguments – one for the legal constitution of sovereignty and one which claims that sovereignty amounts to legally unlimited power. The second is a tension within the argument for the legal constitution of sovereignty. It does not pit legality against power but points to a problem internal to legal government when the sovereign acts in a way which seems inconsistent with one of the laws of nature. I now turn to exploring the second tension, as it helps to explain why the sovereign's authority is legally constituted both by the public criteria for what counts as law and, in a sense I will clarify, by the

[55] *Leviathan*, 153.

[56] Ibid.

[57] Thomas Hobbes, *On the Citizen* (Cambridge: Cambridge University Press, 1998, Richard Tuck and Michael Silverthorne, eds), 85. However, Hobbes did not offer this as the reason, but somewhat puzzlingly said 'as though (the equity of the cause being well understood) he could not give wrong judgment'.

laws of nature. That explanation in turn both helps to address the first tension and to see why Hobbes could claim that the law should be understood as a public conscience.

2.2.2 *The Legality Proviso*

Recall that, in setting out the regress argument, Hobbes repeated his constant claim that the sovereign, while not subject to any legal limit, is subject to the laws of nature.[58] Since Hobbes also said that the sovereign is answerable only to God for its infractions of the laws of nature, and since the sovereign is in any case the person with ultimate authority in regard to what the laws require, this subjection may seem of no practical import. However, it brings into play a second proviso, which I call the 'legality proviso': the laws the sovereign makes must be interpreted, and so must be interpretable, in light of the laws of nature.

The key here is Hobbes's conception of the judicial role. Early in *Leviathan*, in chapter 5, 'Of Reason, and Science', Hobbes set out the problem that no individual's reason, nor group of individuals' reasons, can be guaranteed to deliver certainty about the solution to any controversy. He offered as a rational solution that the parties to a controversy should choose an arbitrator whose decision they must understand as constituting right reason:[59]

> And therefore, as when there is a controversy in an account, the parties must by their own accord, set up for right Reason, the Reason of some Arbitrator, or Judge, to whose sentence they will both stand, or their controversie must either come to blowes, or be undecided, for want of a right Reason constituted by Nature; so it is also in all debates of what kind soever; And when men that think themselves wiser than all others, clamor and demand right Reason for judge; yet seek no more, but that things should be determined, by no other mens reason but their own, it is as intolerable in the society of men, as it is in play after trump is turned, to use for trump on every occasion, that suite whereof they have most in their hand.[60]

The passage prepares the way for the introduction of the sovereign as the arbitrator of the political and other disputes whose decisions legal subjects must take for right reason if they are to avoid the slide into the

[58] *Leviathan*, 224.
[59] Ibid, 32–3.
[60] Ibid.

'dissolute condition of masterlesse men' – the condition of the state of nature.[61] The orthodox interpretation of Hobbes is that the example tells us that it matters more in a conflict that the conflict is resolved or settled by a definitive decision than how it is resolved. A principle of 'settlement' might seem, then, what makes it rational to submit to arbitration, and thus by parity of reasoning to the decisions of an all-powerful political sovereign, whatever the content of the decision of the arbitrator or of the sovereign.[62]

If this interpretation captured the whole of Hobbes's argument, his solution to the problem of the state of nature would be wholly procedural. But as he made clear, there is much more to arbitration than a principle of settlement, one which can be satisfied by the parties' agreement to abide by, say, the outcome of a coin toss. Once the conflicting parties' consent constitutes an arbitrator, that person is not merely a natural individual. Rather, it is an artificial person in that it takes on a role in which at least four of the other laws of nature are implicated. Law 11 is the law of equity, that '*if a man be trusted to judge between man and man*, it is a precept of the Law of Nature, *that he deal Equally between them*'.[63] And because, says Hobbes, 'every man is presumed to do all things in order to serve his own benefit, no man is a fit arbitrator in his own cause', which gives us Law 17.[64] For the same reason, Law 18 holds that no individual is to be judge who '*has in him a natural cause of partiality*'.[65] Law 19 is that in controversies of fact the judge must give credit to the witnesses.[66]

These last four laws are both procedural and substantive in that they affect, without determining, the content of any decision by an arbitrator who is faithful to the moral discipline of his role. Moreover, when the parties submit a dispute to an arbitrator, they do so not only in the expectation that it will give a decision which provides a definitive resolution to the dispute, and so permit them to avoid fighting it out by whatever means they choose. They also submit in the expectation that the decision will accord with the laws of nature which set out what we might

61 Ibid, 128.
62 For discussion of the role of this principle in positivistic legal theory, see Jeremy Waldron, 'The Concept and the Rule of Law' (2008) 43 *Georgia Law Review* 1, at 6.
63 *Leviathan*, 108. His emphasis.
64 Ibid, 109.
65 Ibid. His emphasis.
66 Ibid.

think of as the moral discipline of the arbitrator's role, the equivalent of what we saw Hart call 'judicial virtues'.[67]

The authority of the arbitrator comes, then, not only from the consent of the parties to abide by its decision but also from the kind of decision which makes it rational to submit to arbitration. A complaint by one of the parties that the decision is flawed because the arbitrator failed to act in accordance with these constraints of role is different in kind from the complaint which Hobbes rules out that the party simply does not like the way the arbitrator settled the dispute. Moreover, when the arbitrator is a judge in civil society, it is subject to more than the natural law discipline of role. It is also under a duty to decide in accordance with the positive law enacted by the ultimate judge, the sovereign. But that the arbitrator is still subject to the laws of nature has the result that for Hobbes the specific authority of law comes not only from the fact that law provides an institutionally conclusive way of settling a dispute because it provides determinate conclusions about the obligations of legal subjects. Law's authority also comes from the fact that the arbitrator is under a duty to base its conclusions about what the law requires on sound reasons, reasons which include the laws of nature.[68] In play here is not only a principle of settlement but also a principle of justification.

Hobbes did see differences between the situation of the arbitrator in the state of nature and the judge in a civil society. The legal order of civil society has to be staffed by subordinate judges because all laws require interpretation,[69] and good judges, in his view, are judges who, in interpreting the written law, rely on their understanding of the 'unwritten' law, the laws of nature.[70] Moreover, one should not think that there is anything illegitimate in judges interpreting the positive law through the lens of the laws of nature, because it would be a great insult if subordinate judges were to attribute to the ultimate judge, the sovereign, an intention to flout the laws.[71]

It is telling that Hobbes regarded subordinate judges as under a duty to the sovereign to interpret its positive law as if it complied with the laws of nature. This duty flows not to a natural individual, even if the sovereign

[67] Hart, *The Concept of Law*, 205.

[68] I adapt here the illuminating argument in Kenneth Winston, 'Introduction', in Winston, ed., *The Principles of Social Order: Selected Essays of Lon L Fuller* (Oxford: Hart Publishing, 2001) 11, at 36–7.

[69] *Leviathan*, 190–1.

[70] Ibid, 95–6.

[71] Ibid, 194.

happens to be one natural individual, as the quotation above from *Behemoth* makes clear. From the judicial perspective, and indeed from the perspective of all the officials of the order, the sovereign is the artificial person who makes the written laws which they must interpret in light of the laws of nature. That is, the sovereign is a legal sovereign in two senses: it is the person or body which has the authority to make laws provided that it complies with both the validity proviso (the public criteria recognized for certifying that a law is valid) and the legality proviso (the laws of nature).

Moreover, the validity proviso is normatively subordinate to the legality proviso. The latter is not set out in the main discussion of the laws of nature in chapter 15, 'Of other Lawes of Nature'. Rather, it is to be found in chapter 26 where Hobbes says legal order requires 'not only a Declaration of the Law, but also sufficient signes of the Author, and Authority' in order to comply with an 'Evident Law of Nature, that no man ought to weaken' sovereign power.[72] Such signs, however, do not by themselves authorize the sovereign. Rather, they serve only as 'Verification' of the laws, as 'but the Testimony and the Record'. The signs do not, then, by themselves amount to 'the authority of the Law; which consisteth in the Command of the Soveraign only'.[73]

This relationship between the provisos gives rise to the question of what happens when a law which clearly complies with the validity proviso clearly violates the legality proviso. The answer to this question is complex. It is important, first, to notice that Hobbes did contemplate such conflicts. Those who have sovereign power cannot by definition commit injustice, since justice is a property of law. But they can commit 'Iniquity'.[74] It follows that while subjects cannot accuse their sovereign of injustice, they can challenge it on the basis of iniquity – of failing to comply with one of the laws of nature. More accurately, as I will elaborate in Section 2.2.4, while Hobbes is generally allergic to public debate about contentious issues (one of his main reasons for preferring monarchy to democracy as a mode of government), he not only permitted but also even required that a constrained kind of moral deliberation take place about the *jus* of *lex*. For he clearly allowed a legal subject to challenge a law which if literally interpreted would lead to tensions with one or more of the laws of nature. The challenge is put on the basis that a judge should

72 Ibid, 189.
73 Ibid.
74 Ibid, 124.

try to find a more reasonable interpretation of the law, one consistent with relevant laws of nature. That *jus* is not external to *lex*: 'The Law of Nature, and the Civill Law, contain each other, and are of equall extent.'[75]

The second complicating factor is that if the sovereign seeks to give away any of the rights of sovereignty which are essential to the office of sovereign, the 'Grant is void'.[76] It follows that a subordinate judge could declare void, for example, an abdication of the sovereign right of 'judicature':

> of hearing and deciding all controversies, which may arise concerning Law, either Civill, or Naturall, or concerning Fact. For without the decision of Controversies, there is no protection of one Subject, against the injuries of another; the Lawes concerning *Meum* and *Tuum* are in vaine; and to every man remaineth, from the naturall and necessary appetite of his own conservation, the right of protecting himselfe by his private strength, which is the condition of Warre; and contrary to the end for which every Common-wealth is instituted.[77]

The example is important because if such a grant in a law which meets the validity proviso is void, a question is raised about the legality of a law which abolishes any of the essential features of the judicial role; for example, a law which required judges to ignore the facts, or to decide partially, say, in a dispute between a member of some favoured group and a member of some disfavoured group. Correspondingly, a question must arise in regard to the legality of laws which are obviously iniquitous, that is, laws which directly relegate a group to second-class status instead of requiring judges to give judgments which have that effect.

There is, in my view, a two-part answer implicit in Hobbes's legal theory and it does not require that we infer an authority for judges to invalidate laws which violate the laws of nature though do not go the distance of purporting to abrogate or grant away an entire right of sovereignty. The first part is negative and has to do with the strain which such laws put on the sovereign–subject relationship when the sovereign does things which make it difficult for subjects to understand themselves in 'the mutuall Relation between Protection and Obedience' which Hobbes says on the last page of *Leviathan* is the 'designe' of the book to expose.[78] The second part is positive and has to do with the quality of

75 Ibid, 185.
76 Ibid, 127.
77 Ibid, 125. His emphasis.
78 Ibid, 491.

the civil condition legal subjects enjoy when the sovereign does not so act – the quality of civil liberty under a regime of public laws. Sections 2.2.3–2.2.5 offer a sketch of these parts, beginning with the positive one.

2.2.3 *Hobbes's Theory of the Role of Adjudication*

Hobbes is well known for his opposition to the common lawyers of his day and their theory of the role of judges in legal order, which is pretty much the same theory refined centuries later in Dworkin's interpretivism. Hobbes's foil here was Sir Edward Coke, the eminent common law jurist and judge.

Coke's best-known claim is in a dictum in his judgment in *Dr. Bonham's Case*: 'it appears in our books, that in many cases, the common law doth control Acts of Parliament, and sometimes adjudge them to be void; for when an act of Parliament is against Common right and reason, or repugnant, or impossible to be performed, the Common Law will control it, and adjudge such an Act to be void'.[79] Such a claim was naturally anathema to Hobbes. But in *Leviathan*, he quoted and focused on three different propositions. First, '[t]hat the Common Law, hath no Controuler but the Parlament'.[80] Second, that '[the law is] an Artificiall perfection of Reason, gotten by long study, observation, and experience'.[81] The third is an example from Coke's writings of a law which requires punishment of the innocent:

> If a man . . . that is Innocent, be accused of Felony, and for feare flyeth for the same; albeit he judicially acquitteth himselfe of the Felony; yet if it be found that he fled for the Felony, he shall notwithstanding his Innocency, Forfeit all his goods, chattells, debts, and duties. For as to the Forfeiture of them, the Law will admit no proofe against the Presumption in Law, grounded upon his flight.[82]

Hobbes perceived the threat in the first proposition to be that it seeks to make 'the Legislative Power depend on private men, or subordinate judges',[83] that is, it contains much the same message as Coke's dictum in *Dr. Bonham's Case*. The second proposition is to much the same effect.

[79] Edward Coke, *The Selected Writings and Speeches of Sir Edmund Coke*, vol. 1 (Indianapolis: Liberty Fund, 2003; Steve Sheppard, ed.), 275.
[80] *Leviathan*, 186.
[81] Ibid, 187.
[82] Ibid, 193.
[83] Ibid, 186.

It answers the question of 'whose Reason . . . shall be received for Law' by asserting that it is the reason of the lawyers because of their study of and experience in the practice of the law.[84] The third proposition Hobbes treated with scorn, as an example of the absurdities which arise when the 'Presumption' of judges is taken to be a presumption of law.[85]

While the first two propositions should be as obnoxious to Hobbes as the dictum from *Dr. Bonham's Case* lest they attempt to dilute sovereign power, he treated them with some respect. Notice that the proposition that the common law has no controller but parliament on its face concedes that the common law is subordinate to parliament, though Hobbes seemed to suspect that it opens the way to giving common law principles a higher status than statute. However, he chose to take the proposition at face value and said that it is true but not of legal order in general. Its truth is contingent on there being in place a particular kind of legal order, one in which a parliament is the supreme legislative power in contrast, for example, to a legal order in which a monarch is sovereign.[86]

When it comes to the proposition about lawyers and the artificial reason of the law, Hobbes understood it as seeking to make sense of the lawyers' claim, with which he agreed, that 'Law can never be against reason'.[87] But he offered two objections to the claim that the reason is artificial. The first is already indicated – that the reason of lawyers and 'subordinate judges' reduces to their subjective views of right and wrong and that leads to 'contradiction' and 'discordance' in the law.[88] The only way to avoid this problem is to see that the reason of the law is the

> Reason of this our Artificiall Man the Common-wealth, and his Command, that maketh Law: And the Commonwealth being in their Representative but one Person, there cannot easily arise any contradiction in the Lawes; and when there doth, the same Reason is able, by interpretation, or alteration, to take it away.[89]

The second objection is that if the reason of the law is taken to be the artificial reason of lawyers, one must consider that the 'long study' of the law may possibly 'encrease, and confirm erroneous Sentences' and that 'where men build on false grounds, the more they build, the greater is the

[84] Ibid, 187.
[85] Ibid, 193.
[86] Ibid, 186.
[87] Ibid, 186–7.
[88] Ibid, 187.
[89] Ibid.

ruine'.[90] It is in some tension with the first objection because its focus is not discordance but concordance – judges as a group treating past (possibly bad) decisions as binding precedent, with, as we saw Hart put it in Chapter 2, the 'most pedantic impartiality'.[91] Hobbes repeated this objection later in the chapter in his discussion of the judicial interpretation of statute law, set within the context of his general legal theory. It is in that context that he poured scorn on Coke's dictum about the legal presumption in the case of the innocent man who fled when charged with felony.

Hobbes began that account by saying that before validly enacted laws can become binding there is another 'very material' condition to be met: the laws have to be given an 'authentique Interpretation', a condition necessary because 'All Laws, written, and unwritten, have need of Interpretation.'[92] Here the judge's duty is to give a 'reasonable interpretation', which is the interpretation which accords with the laws of nature lest he insult the sovereign by supposing that his intention could be other than 'Equity'. If the judge cannot reach a reasonable judgment, he should 'respit Judgement till he have received more ample authority'; the judge should, that is, defer judgment and consult the sovereign.[93] Thus, legislative intention was for Hobbes a matter of construction by judges in light of their understanding of the laws of nature, which makes his account of judicial interpretation of statute law quite similar to that put forward by the common lawyers, save for Hobbes's hostility to precedent.[94]

But even that hostility is qualified because Hobbes did not oppose a doctrine of precedent when it comes to 'mutable' laws or statutes.[95] Even a mistaken interpretation by a judge of statute law binds into the future. It is true that its force into the future depends on the sovereign

90 Ibid.

91 Hart, 'Positivism and the Separation of Law and Morals', 81.

92 *Leviathan*, 190.

93 Ibid, 192.

94 In *A Dialogue between a Philosopher and a Student, of the Common Laws of England*, Hobbes insists again that it is natural or human reason, not Coke's idea of artificial reason, that is the 'Life of the Law'. See Thomas Hobbes, *A Dialogue Between a Philosopher and a Student, of the Common Laws of England* in Hobbes, *Writings on Common Law and Hereditary Right* (Oxford: Clarendon Press, 2005, Alan Cromartie and Quentin Skinner, eds), 10. But this cannot affect the point that the task of interpreters of the law is to work out the content of the law which was made, not to impose their own views of what law should have been made.

95 *Leviathan*, 192.

permitting this state of affairs to persist. However, this marks no real practical disagreement with the common lawyers since they also think that the persistence of such precedent is conditional on the legislature not choosing to override the judgment. Nevertheless, Hobbes insisted that there can be no precedent when it comes to interpretation of 'immutable' laws – the laws of nature.[96] It is here that he offered Coke's dictum about the presumption of guilt as an example of why, with interpretation of the laws of nature, the judge's judgment has force only for the parties.

The implications of Hobbes's qualified hostility to precedent are immense. His theory of sovereignty is far from stripping judges of power. Rather, it proclaims that judges have the authority of their sovereign to interpret its laws in the light of the laws of nature even when the 'bare words of a written Law' appear to suggest that such an interpretation is not warranted.[97] This is as potent an authority as most lawyers in the common law tradition have ever claimed. That, more than any actual assertion of the authority of judges to void legislation, explains why the claim that judges must interpret all statute law in the light of some set of fundamental principles leads to the suspicion that the claim elevates those principles above sovereign authority. But the legality proviso does not establish a source of constraints on sovereignty which are independent of the sovereign, principles located in a morality external to law. Rather, it explains the way in which fundamental principles of legality are constitutive of sovereignty. Judges do not have this authority because of a doctrine of the separation of powers. Indeed, Hobbes regarded the idea that the sovereign power may be divided as one of the doctrines destructive of the state.[98] Rather, the authority is theirs because their judgments are an integral part of the exercise of sovereignty, as Hobbes indicated in his 'Introduction' to *Leviathan* when he said that the magistrates and other '*Officers* of Judicature and Execution' are the 'artificiall *Joynts*' of the artificial man who is the sovereign.[99]

Hobbes, however, took care to emphasize that while an 'incommodity' which arises when a written law seems inconsistent with a law of nature should set the judge on the path to find a reasonable interpretation of the law, nevertheless, 'no Incommodity can warrant a Sentence against the

[96] Ibid, 192.
[97] Ibid, 194.
[98] *Leviathan*, 225.
[99] Ibid, 9. His emphasis.

Law'.[100] I have already suggested that this qualification does not distinguish him from the common law tradition and at this point we can see that the real distinctions between Hobbes and the common lawyers are as follows.

First, Hobbes, unlike the common lawyers, explicitly advocated an institutional solution to problems which arise when judges cannot determine a reasonable interpretation for a statute. Judges, as we have seen him suggest, should suspend judgment until they have consulted the sovereign. Hobbes seemed to have in mind here a consultation of the sovereign in its adjudicative capacity. That is, the question to the sovereign is, 'Is a reasonable interpretation of the law possible, given that the "bare words of a Written Law" are so obviously inconsistent with a law of nature?' Such consultation presents the sovereign with an option. Either it can give a kind of advisory opinion as to an interpretation the judge could adopt or, because there is no way to avoid violating the law of nature while implementing the enacted law, it should initiate legislative reform.[101]

Second, Hobbes reached this position not by working up an account of judicial interpretation from the existing practices of a particular jurisdiction, as for example the common lawyers of his day did with the common law, and as Dworkin did centuries later. He did not, that is, offer a theory of law which grows out of a theory of interpretation. Rather, his account of the role of judicial interpretation is part of a more general inquiry into the modern legal state in which the sovereign is the one who rules by legal right.

2.2.4 *Liberty under a Regime of Public Laws*

As we have just seen, entailed in Hobbes's understanding of adjudication is that a subject is entitled to challenge an enacted law on the basis that its

[100] Ibid, 194. In addition, we can note that Coke's dictum from *Dr. Bonham's Case* was 'obiter', that is, delivered in a context where Coke ruled that the charter of the College of Physicians did not as a matter of statutory interpretation permit it to sanction Bonham – an unlicensed practitioner – in the ways that it had, and that more generally the college could not be a judge in its own cause. The authority to void statutes was not therefore in issue in the case.

[101] Hobbes did not indicate the institutional shape for these responses. Bentham, however, did put his mind to this kind of problem and advocated a parliamentary committee. See Gerald Postema, *Bentham and the Common Law Tradition* (Oxford: Clarendon Press, 1986), 434–9.

'literal' interpretation does not comply with natural law in the hope that a judge will find a way to interpret the law so that its meaning is more consistent with the laws of nature. The subject must take the judge's interpretation as definitive, though it has no force beyond the parties to the matter, as Hobbes seemed firmly opposed to any doctrine of precedent, at least in regard to the laws of nature.[102] But the point remains that the laws of nature, as interpreted by the judge, condition the content of the subject's legal obligations insofar as the text of the enacted law relevant to the matter permits and until such point as the sovereign overrules a subordinate judge. It is this process of interpretation which imparts a moral quality to the law, or, more accurately, makes the moral substance implicit in law explicit. For the deliberation involved is not about morality at large. It is about how best to understand the conditions of interaction which the sovereign has prescribed in its law in terms which live up to the assumption that judges must adopt: that all of the sovereign's law is intended to serve the interests of subjects viewed as equal before the law.

However, those interests are not confined to equality. They include liberty.[103] Hobbes began chapter 21 of *Leviathan*, 'Of the Liberty of Subjects', by saying that freedom is the 'absence of ... external Impediments of motion'. He went on to define a 'free man' as '*he, that in those things, which by his strength and wit he is able to do, is not hindered to doe what he has a will to*'.[104] It may seem from this chapter, and from elsewhere in *Leviathan*, that the point of entering the civil condition is to establish a sovereign who will enact laws which restrain the radical liberty of the state of nature so that individuals can interact on terms set by the sovereign, rather than by other individuals. Hence, the liberty an individual has in civil society is the liberty which one has through the 'silence' of the law 'to act according to his own discretion'.[105] This would amount to the same kind of liberty one had in the state of

102 *Leviathan*, 193–4.

103 My interpretation of Hobbes's views on liberty is much influenced by Oakeshott, especially his 'The Rule of Law'. See my 'Dreaming the Rule of Law'.

104 *Leviathan*, 146. His emphasis.

105 Ibid, 152. Hobbes continues: 'As for the other Lyberties, they depend on the Silence of the Law. In cases where the Soveraign has prescribed no rule, there the Subject hath the Liberty to do, or forbeare, according to his own discretion. And therefore such Liberty is in some places more, and in some lesse; and in some times more, in other times lesse, according as they that have the Soveraignty shall think most convenient.'

nature but now restricted by the law so that individuals can safely act on their desires within the restricted space.

This sketch is mistaken in one fundamental respect and also does not capture the full complexity of Hobbes's views on the liberty of the subject.[106] It is mistaken because it misconstrues the way in which civil laws bind. Hobbes called the civil law of the sovereign 'Artificiall Chains' which he said the subjects have themselves 'fastened at one end to the lips of the Man or Assembly to whom they have given the Soveraigne Power, and at the other end to their own Ears'. But, he added, the chains are in 'their own nature but weak', though they may 'be made to hold, by the danger, though not by the difficulty of breaking them'.[107]

Such chains are not, then, physical bonds of the sort which can literally restrict liberty. In addition, since fear is not an external impediment, fear of sanctions cannot, as in the command theory, be the basis of obligation to law. Rather, subjects recognize their duty to obey the law because they understand the normative basis of their prior obligation of obedience to the sovereign. As Hobbes said in *Behemoth*, 'the Power of the mighty has no foundation but in the opinion and the beleefe of the people'; further, 'if men know not their duty, what is there that can force them to obey the laws? An army you will say? But what shall force the army?'[108] However, it remains important that those who do not understand their obligation to the sovereign are motivated by fear of sanctions, so that those who do understand have the security permitting them to follow the law without making themselves prey to others.

The sketch also, as I said, does not capture the full complexity of Hobbes's views on the liberty of the subject because it conceives of the civil law as merely limiting the liberty individuals had in the state of nature. Hobbes's idea of being able to act at one's discretion does share something with the liberty one has in the state of nature, since it is the liberty to act on the basis of one's desires. But since laws cannot constrain

[106] This view also cannot properly account for what Hobbes calls the 'true Liberty of a Subject', ibid, 150. I discuss this kind of liberty in Section 2.4.

[107] Ibid, 147.

[108] Hobbes, *Behemoth*, 16, 58–9. See also *Leviathan*, 117: 'without the terrour of some Power' the Lawes of Nature ... of themselves ... are contrary to out Naturall Passions ... And covenants, without the Sword, are but Words, and of not strength to secure a man at all.' But such fear is still not the basis for obedience, as Hobbes clarified at 232, ibid, when he said that 'men cannot know the Right of any Law the Soveraign maketh' on the basis of the 'terrour of legall punishment'. Rather, they have to understand their 'natural obligation'.

in the physical way in which Hobbes conceived of external impediments to individual motion triggered by desire, civil liberty is constituted rather than constrained by law. Moreover, it is a liberty I have even when there are such external impediments. For even if I am physically obstructed from doing something I desire to do and which the law permits me through its silence to do, that obstruction does not take away the permission but merely prevents me from exercising it. I still have the liberty, even though I cannot execute my desire to use it. Civil liberty is the freedom of subjects to act on their own desires through subscribing to the conditions set out by the law.

Civil liberty thus has two aspects to it – the freedom to do as we desire and the conditions which make it possible for us to do as we desire. Hence, such liberty – freedom under an order of public laws – makes possible liberties which require legal constitution even if the substantive ends for which they are used is at the discretion of the subjects. It is, in my view, this kind of 'non-instrumental' law,[109] one which makes possible civil interaction between subjects, which Hobbes had in mind when he offered the following account of the function of law in civil society:

> For the use of Lawes, (which are but Rules Authorized) is not to bind the People from all Voluntary actions; but to direct and keep them in such a motion, as not to hurt themselves by their own impetuous desires, rashnesse, or indiscretion; as Hedges are set, not to stop Travellers, but to keep them in the way.[110]

Consider in this regard a law which seems a rather obvious example of a prohibition on action rather than a hedge-like direction, the law which proscribes murder. According to the hedge metaphor, such a law is better understood as setting out a condition for successful interaction with your fellows – refraining from acting murderously keeps people in the way, just as driving on the prescribed side of the road does. These kinds of constraints are thus better seen, as Michael Oakeshott described them, as the 'adverbial conditions' of successful interaction, and so as constitutive of civil liberty.[111]

If I am right that Hobbes saw law as constitutive of civil liberty in this way, it may appear difficult to make sense of his remarks to the effect that law is a restraint, notably, as he said in chapter 26 of *Leviathan*, a

[109] Oakeshott, 'The Rule of Law', 148.
[110] *Leviathan*, 239–40.
[111] Oakeshott, 'The Rule of Law', 148.

> Restraint . . . without the which there cannot possibly be any Peace. And Law was brought into the world for nothing else, but to limit the natural Liberty of particular men, in such manner, as they might not be hurt, but assist one another, and joyn together against a common Enemy.[112]

However, Hobbes also said in chapter 21 that it is absurd to clamour for liberty from the law if it is natural liberty at stake. His argument on this point was in part that to clamour for such liberty – for exemption from the law – is to demand a return to the anarchic state of nature in which 'all other men may be masters of their lives'.[113] It is this thought that lies behind the claim that if one lives under an order of public laws, whether made by an absolute monarch or democratic assembly, 'the Freedome is still the same',[114] by which I take Hobbes to have meant the quality, not the quantity of the freedom. His argument is not only about the precariousness of life in the state of nature – the 'dissolute condition of masterlesse men';[115] it is also about what we give up in not having a sovereign who rules us through public laws. That is, going beyond the security provided by the sword of the sovereign, we give up on the institution by law of civil liberty, which makes it possible for us to act on our desires and also to attach legal consequences to some of them in ways important to us as creatures who wish so to act.

For Hobbes, then, the point of individuals consenting to live under the authority of an all-powerful sovereign is to move from the natural condition in which the only freedom they can enjoy is a worthless pre-political freedom to the civil condition in which they enjoy civil liberty. That point requires not only that the sovereign has a monopoly on coercive power but also that when it exercises that power, it does so through law – by putting in place an order of public laws. With such an order in place, subjects will find that the law does more than leave to them a secure space in which to act on their desires – to exercise discretionary liberty. The law also constitutes the spaces of civil liberty, which are unavailable in the absence of law, and which are put at individuals' discretion, thus permitting peaceful interaction.

It follows that civil liberty does not consist in a freedom from external obstacles because the bonds of the law are not such obstacles.

[112] *Leviathan*, 185.
[113] Ibid, 147.
[114] Ibid, 149.
[115] Ibid, 128.

Rather, the bonds of the law create civil liberty; and as long the laws do that, they will create the same quality of liberty even though the space they make for the exercise of discretion by subjects will vary greatly across both time and place. Hobbes's concern was thus more the quality than the quantity of civil liberty. That a universal quality is secured, even though quantity will vary according to sovereign will, is important to understanding why for Hobbes sovereign rule is not arbitrary in the way contemporary 'republican' philosophers today allege,[116] even though their charge is accurate that he supposed that it is absurd to demand freedom from the law, whatever its political provenance, because freedom, considered qualitatively, is the same in any civil condition.[117]

2.2.5 Coercive Power versus Authority

In place at this point are the basic elements which made it plausible for Hobbes to claim that the law is a public conscience by which the legal subject has already undertaken to be guided. Legal subjects are to regard themselves as under an obligation of obedience to their sovereign so long as it provides them with a peaceful, stable order. But the order is not any old order. It is a legal order in which sovereign authority is legally constituted. Moreover, such an order does not have any old content since it serves the subject's interests in equality and liberty. Should subjects not be able to understand the law as serving these interests, they will have reason to regard themselves as not under an obligation of obedience to their sovereign.

Thus, for Hobbes the normal case of a legal order is one which serves such interests and his account of such order makes more plausible the claim that a sovereign is always de jure. That it is only the normal case suggests that there can be abnormal cases, legal orders in which the sovereign fails to serve the subjects' interests in equality and liberty.

[116] See, for example, Quentin Skinner, *Liberty before Liberalism* (Cambridge: Cambridge University Press, 1998), *Hobbes and Republican Liberty* (Cambridge: Cambridge University Press, 2008) and Philip Pettit, 'Liberty and Leviathan' (2005) 4 *Politics, Philosophy and Economics* 131.

[117] In Section 2.3, I deal with those places in Hobbes's work where he seems to give the sovereign a prerogative power to act without legal authorization or even against the law. For the case against my argument, see Thomas Poole, 'Hobbes on Law and Prerogative', in Dyzenhaus and Poole, eds, *Hobbes and the Law* 68.

This will happen when the sovereign either prospectively or retrospectively makes altogether explicit its intention not to provide equality- and liberty-serving protection to its subjects. As suggested at the end of Section 2.2.2, in doing so, the sovereign puts a strain on the subjects' understanding that they are getting the right kind of protection from the sovereign. And as suggested at the end of Section 2.2.1, this strain can manifest itself in two different ways: on the one hand, as a tension within legal order, so one which judges can help to moderate so long as the sovereign does not choose to overrule them; on the other hand, as a tension between governing by law and exercising superior coercive power outside of the law.

The first kind of tension does not pit legality against power since it points to a problem internal to legal government when the sovereign acts in a way which seems inconsistent with one of the laws of nature. It is not thus a tension between different arguments made by Hobbes. Rather, it is a tension illuminated by his argument about the legal constitution of sovereign authority. The other tension, in contrast, is a tension between that argument and the places in Hobbes's works where he asserted both the capacity of the sovereign to act in virtue of its greater power with no legal warrant for doing so and that subjects must acknowledge that they have authorized the sovereign so to act.

In Section 2.3, I work through three of Hobbes's own examples in order to further our understanding of these two tensions and thus of his political legal theory more generally. As we will see, the examples return us both to the themes of Chapter 1 which arise out of the puzzle of very unjust law and to the question which in the Introduction I claimed should be made central to philosophy of law, the legal subject's question 'But, how can that be law for me?'

2.3 Hobbes on Very Unjust Law

Even if one regards Hobbes as an uncompromising authoritarian because he held that there is no such thing as an unjust law, one must acknowledge his position that subjects are not obliged to obey certain commands to which they could not rationally have consented in their agreement to constitute the sovereign. His basic argument is that no individual can be taken to consent to an act which threatens the very survival which consenting to sovereign rule is meant to secure. Hobbes supposed that this argument entails that subjects are entitled to resist acts of punishment, and to disobey commands to kill or hurt themselves, or which put them in danger.[118] Moreover, he gave subjects a right to resist commands which bring dishonour on them;[119] and here the issue seems to be more the inhumanity of the command than its threat to the survival of the individual. In *Leviathan* he generalized the right of resistance to the extent that he was accused of creating a 'rebel's catechism'. He said that the subject may disobey the sovereign in any matter where 'the end for which the Soveraignty was ordained' is frustrated by the sovereign's commands; and that seems to make the subject's judgment the test of sovereign authority.[120]

The argument does lead to a problem in Hobbes's account of punishment. In chapter 28 of *Leviathan*, 'Of Punishments and Rewards', he distinguished between punishment and hostility. Punishment in Hobbes is an institution which respects the principle that there should no punishment for a crime which did not exist in the law at the time of the act – *nulla poena sine lege*. It also requires both a proper trial and attention by the judge to Law 7 of the laws of nature, which sets out a principle of proportionality when it comes to punishment.[121] Hostility, in contrast, is the visitation of force on an individual outside of this institution.[122] In the former case, the sovereign acts as sovereign, in the latter as a natural individual with superior power. So here we have a distinction between power, in the sense of superior coercive force, and authority.

But the distinction does not work cleanly when it comes to subjects who are properly, that is, legally, punished since they are entitled to regard the sovereign as not authorized to punish them. The sovereign's right to punish is, Hobbes said, derived from the individual's right of nature to do everything possible to preserve oneself and the subjects did not give the sovereign that right but only laid down their own right in order to strengthen the sovereign's. From the perspective of all the other subjects, the sovereign is authorized to act, but the relationship between the sovereign and the punished subject is a state-of-nature relationship.[123] This claim tells us that Hobbes found problematic the infliction of force on a subject even when such infliction is legally authorized.

[118] *Leviathan*, 98, 150–2.
[119] Ibid.
[120] Ibid, 151.
[121] Ibid, 106.
[122] Ibid, 214–15.
[123] Ibid.

He should therefore have been even more concerned about the use of force in the absence of such authorization.

On my interpretation of Hobbes, it is a necessary but not a sufficient condition for a state to exist that its coercive power be superior to that of any subject so that the sovereign can enforce its judgments. The condition does not suffice because superior force must also be legally authorized. Force exercised without such authorization takes place not in the civil condition but in the state of nature. Consequently, subjects should not acknowledge that they have authorized the sovereign so to act simply because the act is that of a much more powerful natural person or group of such persons.

With this in mind, we can return to the tension in Hobbes which arises because he asserted both the capacity of the sovereign to act in virtue of its power and that subjects must acknowledge that they have authorized the sovereign so to act. In my view, this tension is in large part the product of Hobbes's preference for locating the artificial person of the sovereign in one natural person, a monarch, on the basis that monarchical rule is likely to be more stable than other forms of rule, particularly democratic rule. This preference led Hobbes into confusions, best illustrated by his ill-advised reliance in chapter 21 of *Leviathan* on the biblical tale of David and Uriah, which provides the first example of what appears to be a sovereign command which both clearly violates the laws of nature, and is therefore unjust, and yet must be regarded by subjects, including the victim of the act, as just.[124]

2.3.1 Very Unjust Law, Example 1

Hobbes relied on the tale to make the point that the sovereign is accountable only to God for its infractions of the laws of nature, thus apparently defusing the strong and repeated claim that the sovereign, while not subject to civil law, is subject to natural law. Recall that David brings about the death of the innocent Uriah on the battlefield in order to conceal the fact that he has impregnated Uriah's wife, Bathsheba, while

124 Ibid, 148. Hobbes also appealed to the biblical story of Jeptha, whose vow to sacrifice 'whatever comes out of his door' if he should return victorious from battle leads to his sacrifice of his daughter. For an acute analysis of problems Locke encountered in relying on this story, and which are quite similar to those discussed in this chapter, see Andrew Rehfeld, 'Jeptha, the Hebrew Bible, and John Locke's "Second Treatise of Government"' (2008) 3 *Hebraic Political Studies* 60.

Uriah was away fighting in one of David's wars. David says to God, with Hobbes's approval, '*To thee only have I sinned.*'[125] So while Hobbes was clear that David violated the laws of nature, his point was that the subject is precluded from bringing the sovereign to account, that is, from punishing it, because whatever the sovereign does is authorized by the subject: 'Every Subject is Author of every act the Soveraign doth.'[126] Subjects cannot then claim that the sovereign has injured them or treated them unjustly. Hobbes drove home this point again in a later chapter, when he said that a breach by the sovereign of the law of nature, while a 'breach of trust', 'is not enough to authorize any subject, either to make warre upon, or so much as to accuse of Injustice, or any way to speak evill of their Soveraign'.[127]

However, the tale and the point Hobbes wished to take from it are difficult to square with his understanding of the artificial nature of the person of the sovereign in civil society. Properly understood, the tale contains a much more complex message about the inappropriateness, though not the unfeasibility, of locating sovereign authority in one natural individual, namely, in the person of a monarch.

There are two possible interpretations of how Hobbes understood this tale, both inconsistent with the account of political and legal order I have attributed to him. The first has it that David acts lawfully, which goes to show that an act which is unlawful in the eyes of God can at the same time be perfectly lawful as far as the subject is concerned. On this interpretation, in order for David to act justly from Uriah's perspective to bring about his death, he has to act lawfully since justice for Hobbes is a property of the sovereign's law. The second has it that David's demands of the other actors in the story were exercises of sheer power, not law, but still authorized by the other actors and thus not a fit subject for complaint. But Hobbes, despite what he himself said in chapter 21, should have rejected both interpretations for much the same set of reasons which come out of a closer examination of the actual story.

In the actual story, David brought about Uriah's death by secretly instructing Joab, his battlefield commander, to ensure that Uriah meets his death. One could say that his death was still lawfully brought about because Joab received the secret instruction in a letter carried by Uriah

125 *Leviathan*, 148. His emphasis. Hobbes added the 'only' to the standard translations, which are otherwise consistent with David having sinned also against Uriah.

126 Ibid.

127 Ibid, 172.

from David, which Joab knew to be an authentic communication from the sovereign, and so he was acting in terms of his lawful duty when he sent Uriah into battle. Moreover, there was a public communication to Uriah and his fellow warriors when Joab ordered them to go into a situation where they were doomed to die.

In giving this order, Joab in fact disobeyed David, who wanted Uriah and his fellow warriors to be put into danger and then the others to be withdrawn. Joab, however, was unwilling to single out Uriah in a way which would draw attention to the fact that Uriah was being sent to his death for a purpose which had nothing to do with the war. To avoid that result, he had to sacrifice not only Uriah but also other elite warriors. So his command was unlawful in that it went beyond his commission. That he did this to avoid making public the substantive illegality of David's command only increases the illegality because he sacrificed not just one but several warriors on the altar of David's lust. In addition, it is significant that Hobbes characterized the story as one about putting to death an innocent. He did not and could not say that it is about 'punishing' an innocent. Punishment for Hobbes is by definition an act which follows a proper finding of guilt for a crime set out in a public law before the act was done and which is both proportionate to the crime and directed at reform of the criminal and at the deterrence of others.

In this light, we can see that the secret order does not amount to a chain of artificial law which reaches from David's lips to Uriah's ears, such that Uriah can be said to have himself fastened it there. While there are two law-like elements in the series of events that lead to Uriah's death – the secret instruction and Joab's command – they do not add up to anything like a civil law, one which could guide him as a subject. Moreover, these elements could not be made into a chain, at least not one which had any authority over Uriah. Hobbes was adamant throughout *Leviathan* that a command to a subject requiring the subject to commit suicide is void from the outset. It is not, that is, like a general criminal law whose sanction one is entitled to resist once one has been convicted of the crime set out in the law. Such a law has authority over all subjects, except the subject who is due to be punished. In contrast, a command to kill oneself has no authority.

However, even if the story cannot be on Hobbes's own terms an exercise of power through law, one could still try to explain it as an exercise of sheer power which the subject must also take as by definition just, though this interpretation fails even more dismally than the first. If Uriah and the other actors would have to regard an exercise of non-legal power as by definition just, one would have to ask why David and others felt obliged to conceal David's deeds. The only answer is that Uriah would be as entitled to resist an extra-legal command to kill himself as he would a legal command and that the public spectacle created would undermine the normative basis of sovereignty. It would not be like a valid punishment inflicted under a properly imposed criminal law which the criminal is entitled to resist, an act which loses its authority only for the victim. Rather, the utterance is a failed attempt at issuing a valid order, an act which is ultra vires or outside the limits of sovereign authority.[128] Uriah is, on Hobbes's own terms, entitled to say to David that in issuing that order he has stepped out of his artificial role as sovereign and into a state-of-nature relationship of hostility with Uriah, in which, if David prevails, it will be by sheer power, not by right.

It is significant that the various attempts at concealment in the actual story do not work. Joab, perhaps even Uriah, and then the messenger who brings news to David of Uriah's death, know of David's sin. Indeed, the messenger does not obey Joab's instruction to convey the message of Uriah's death in a rather veiled fashion, since he rightly fears that he will incur David's wrath if he does not immediately highlight that David's aim was fulfilled, albeit not in the way David had ordered. So one has to add to an already complex story that the attempt by David to cover up his sin provokes two acts of disobedience on the part of those who are seeking to carry out their orders. Those acts signal the futility of the cover up, and knowledge of the sin soon infects David's household, leading to its destruction.

The actual story of David and Uriah is, then, one about the instability of monarchical power, just because sovereign authority is wielded by one natural individual, especially when added to the mix is the sense that the king rules in part by divine grace, in part by covenant, so that God plays an ambiguous role in the unfolding of the narrative. It is told in a context in which God is the guardian of the moral order and will see to it that order is restored by visiting David's sin on his household and, eventually, on David himself. This kind of pre-modern society is largely incommensurable with the one whose birth pangs Hobbes had witnessed in the civil war and whose elements he describes in *Leviathan* as the essential foundation of a building which an 'able Architect' would design, an architect with an eye on building something that is not 'crasie', doomed

[128] Ibid, 98.

to 'fall upon the heads of their posterity'.[129] One of the things which makes it incommensurable is that this society lacks both general laws and the institution of judicature, that is, of judges from whom the subject can ask for an answer to the question 'But, how can that be law for me?' It is a society which is at best 'primitive' in the sense used by Hart when he contrasted a 'developed legal society' with a 'primitive' one, in part because the latter lacks such institutions.[130] As I show in Section 2.3.2, things look very different when Hobbes dealt with examples of very unjust law in a modern legal state.

2.3.2 Very Unjust Law, Example 2

The second example of a very unjust law is the one from Coke which seems to require that the innocent man who fled trial be punished even though he had been declared innocent. Hobbes, we saw, used it to illustrate his argument against the common law tradition and its adherence to a doctrine of precedent.

Hobbes affirmed that it is against the law of nature 'To punish the Innocent; and Innocent is he that acquitteth himselfe Judicially, and is acknowledged for Innocent by the Judge.' He thus concluded that 'there is no place in the world, where … [Coke's dictum] can be an interpretation of a Law of Nature, or be made a Law by the Sentences of precedent Judges, that had done the same. For he that judged it first, judged unjustly; and no Injustice can be a pattern of Judgement to succeeding Judges.'[131] And just in case his reader had not appreciated the point, he repeated it in even stronger terms:

> If the Law ground upon his flight a Presumption of the fact, (which was Capitall,) the Sentence ought to have been Capitall: if the Presumption were not of the Fact, for what then ought he to lose his goods? This therefore is no Law of England; nor is the condemnation grounded upon a Presumption of Law, but upon the Presumption of the Judges. It is also against Law, to say that no Proofe shall be admitted against a Presumption of Law. For all Judges, Soveraign and subordinate, if they refuse to heare Proofe, refuse to do Justice: for though the Sentence be Just, yet the Judges that condemn without hearing the Proofes offered, are Unjust Judges, and their Presumption is but Prejudice; which no man ought to bring with him to the Seat of Justice, whatsoever precedent

[129] Ibid, 221.

[130] Hart, *The Concept of Law*, 91–9.

[131] *Leviathan*, 192.

> judgements, or examples he shall pretend to follow. There be other things of this nature, wherein mens Judgements have been perverted, by trusting to Precedents: but this is enough to shew, that though the Sentence of the Judge, be a Law to the party pleading, yet it is no Law to any Judge, that shall succeed him in that Office.[132]

The point so far is only about precedent and judge-made law. It is meant to support Hobbes's main argument against the common lawyers that a judicial interpretation of natural law binds only the parties before the judge and so has no force into the future. However, it is radical, as Hobbes clearly thought it applies to the sovereign in its judicial capacity as well as to subordinate judges. The question then arises as to what happens when the sovereign brings about the same result in its legislative capacity; and Hobbes contemplated such a law. He said that 'a written Law may forbid innocent men to fly, and they may be punished for flying: But that flying for feare of injury, should be taken for presumption of guilt, after a man is already absolved of the crime Judicially, is contrary to the nature of a Presumption, which hath no place after Judgement given'.[133]

This example is instructive as it shows that for Hobbes this law – one which makes it a crime to avoid one's trial by fleeing before the trial starts – is the only legitimate way the sovereign may regulate by law the actions of innocent people facing a criminal charge who may consider flight. That leaves Hobbes open to the challenge that legitimacy is one thing, legal validity another. For he did not in this discussion confront the example of a law which explicitly enacted the objectionable presumption; and we know from his treatment of the tale of David and Uriah, and from elsewhere in *Leviathan*, that he acknowledged that the sovereign can issue commands which violate the laws of nature.

Indeed, in one of these passages, Hobbes asserted that the sovereign's agents, which include subordinate judges, must implement such commands and that if they refuse they break Law 3 of the laws of nature, which forbids 'breach of covenant';[134] and which he said in chapter 15 is 'the Fountain and Originall of JUSTICE'.[135] So I turn, in Section 2.3.3, to my last example of a very unjust law in Hobbes, one in which he

[132] Ibid, 193.
[133] Ibid, 192–3.
[134] Ibid, 113.
[135] Ibid, 100.

confronted head-on the problems created by a law which explicitly implements the injustice.

2.3.3 *Very Unjust Law, Example 3*

This example illuminates the tension internal to legal government when the sovereign acts in a way which seems inconsistent with one of the laws of nature. It is of a son commanded to kill his father 'whether innocent or guilty and rightly condemned'.[136] Hobbes discussed it initially in *De Cive* (1642) and returned to it in *Behemoth or the Long Parliament* (1679), a reflection on the civil war some seventeen years after *Leviathan.*

In *De Cive*, Hobbes said that a son commanded to kill his father would not be obliged by the command 'since there are others who will do it if ordered to do so, and a son may prefer to die than to live in infamy and loathing'.[137] He then generalized the point by saying: 'There are many other cases in which commands are dishonourable for some people to carry out but not for the others; the former are right to refuse to do them but not the latter; and this will be without prejudice to the absolute right given to the ruler.'[138] One might well conclude that Hobbes was saying here that there is no way in which the sovereign's power is threatened by the son's right to refuse because someone else can easily be found to kill the father.[139] Thus Susanne Sreedhar, in a rare and illuminating analysis of this important piece of text, says that these are cases in which obedience cannot be 'systematically expected' because the 'threat of punishment is likely to be ineffective'; in addition, they are cases the 'sovereign can systematically permit'.[140] She plausibly supposes that the example shows that 'Hobbes's sovereign is absolute (and absolutely authorized) in that he can command with impunity . . . But unlike many absolutists Hobbes does not think that absolute sovereignty requires absolute obedience'.[141]

In order to solve the puzzle Hobbes created of the subject being entitled to consider himself not bound in this and other situations, Sreedhar relies on Raz's idea that an authoritative decision announces

136 Hobbes, *On the Citizen*, 83.
137 Ibid.
138 Ibid.
139 See Susanne Sreedhar, *Hobbes on Resistance: Defying the Leviathan* (Cambridge: Cambridge University Press, 2010), 125.
140 Ibid, 130.
141 Ibid, 129.

to its subjects an exclusionary reason, a reason which excludes reliance by subjects on the reasons which were in dispute before the authority decided. It thus excludes reliance on reasons within a certain scope.[142] Sreedhar argues that for Hobbes there is a determinate set of non-excludable reasons – reasons which preclude killing oneself, bringing dishonour on oneself, etc. Hobbes must concede that there is such a set because the premise of his whole argument for subjection to the sovereign is ensuring self-preservation. He could make that concession without undermining the argument because the concession does not threaten the absolute nature of sovereignty.[143]

Sreedhar's Razian solution does have a plausible basis in Hobbes's account in *De Cive*. But it does not work as well when Hobbes returned to this example in B*ehemoth*, a book in the form of a dialogue where B is the pupil and A his master, in which the sentence I relied on above is located:

> B: Must tyrants also be obeyed in everything actively? Or is there nothing wherein a lawful King's command may be disobeyed? What if he should command me with my own hands to execute my father, in case he should be condemned to die by the law?
>
> A: This is a case that need not be put. We have never read nor heard of any King so inhuman as to command it. If any did, we are to consider whether that command were one of his laws. *For by disobeying Kings, we mean the disobeying of his laws, those his laws that were made before they were applied to any particular person; for the King, though as a father of children, and a master of domestic servants command many things which bind those children and servants yet he commands the people in general never but by a precedent law, and as a politic, not a natural person.* And if such a command as you speak of were contrived into a general law (which never was, nor never will be), you were bound to obey it, unless you depart the kingdom after the publication of the law, and before the condemnation of your father.[144]

The passage is intriguing, first, because while A does not mention explicitly the distinction between a tyrant and a lawful king on which B relies in his question, neither does A explicitly reject it, whereas Hobbes in *Leviathan* and other earlier works was adamant that such a distinction

142 See especially, Joseph Raz, 'Authority, Law, and Morality', in Raz, *Ethics in the Public Domain: Essays in the Morality of Law and Politics* (Oxford: Oxford University Press, 1994) 194.

143 Sreedhar, *Hobbes on Resistance*, 108–22.

144 Hobbes, *Behemoth*, 51. My emphasis.

is both politically pernicious and conceptually confused.[145] It is intriguing, second, because A's remarks about why the case 'need not be put', especially when these are read in the light of the legal theory elaborated in *Leviathan*, reveal an account of law's authority which is very different from the positivistic account usually attributed to Hobbes. Third, notice that, in contrast to the description of the example in *De Cive*, here the father is not said to be either innocent of the crime or guilty. Rather, Hobbes focused on the case in which the father has been 'condemned . . . by the law'.

In this passage, Hobbes expressed doubt that any sovereign would enact the law proposed in B's question. This doubt is evidence of his optimism that sovereigns will not produce pathologies – situations which undermine legal subjects' basis for obedience or continuing consent to sovereign rule. Nevertheless, Hobbes deemed it important openly to confront an example of such a pathology. His first point is that we must be careful about what counts as a law. There is a difference between personal authority (the commands of a father to his children or to his servants) and political authority (the commands of the same individual who happens to be king when he wishes to fulfil his role as sovereign, as the artificial person with ultimate legal authority). In the latter case, his commands must be issued as laws, with the result that no command has any effect until it is in proper form.

Hobbes's second point is that proper form requires not only that the law precede any official act but also that it be couched in general terms, and only then applied to particular circumstances.[146] A law that commanded *me* to execute *my* father if he were found guilty of a particular offence would not count as a law. Hobbes did, however, suggest that the sovereign could 'contrive' to put such a command into general form. Such a law would have to set out a crime punishable by the death penalty

145 For discussion of Hobbes's changing views on this distinction, see Kinch Hoekstra, 'Tyrannus Rex vs. Leviathan' (2001) 82 *Pacific Philosophical Quarterly* 420.

146 Hobbes's commitment to the generality of law is not undermined by passages such as that in *Leviathan*, 183, where he gives his definition of civil law: 'In which definition, there is nothing that is not at first sight evident. For every man seeth, that some Lawes are addressed to all the Subjects in generall; some to particular Provinces; some to particular Vocations; and some to particular Men.' For every theory of the rule of law acknowledges the necessity of particular laws but requires that such laws be made only in terms of general laws. Consider, for example, Joseph Raz's third principle of the rule of law: '*The making of particular laws (particular legal orders) should be guided by open, stable, clear and general rules.*' Joseph Raz, 'The Rule of Law and Its Virtue', in Raz, *The Authority of Law* 210, at 215. His emphasis.

and stipulate that if the convicted criminal happened to have a son of a certain age in the country, the son must take on the office of executioner. This would be a cumbersome and curious law, cumbersome because of the conditional clauses piled on top of each other, curious because it would be a puzzle to subjects why the sovereign was going to such trouble to single out for special inhumane treatment criminals who happened to have sons. However, if the sovereign succeeded in enacting such a law I would be bound to obey, Hobbes said, unless I get out of the country before the condemnation of my father. So while it would be difficult to wrestle legal form into the right kind of shape to deliver a result which Hobbes clearly regarded as inhumane, he admitted that it could be done.

While Hobbes was bothered by the sheer inhumanity of the law, his analysis in *Behemoth* did not focus on that fact. Rather, his focus was on the legal complexities of the situation. This focus goes against the grain of the orthodox understanding of Hobbes as an early command theorist for whom law is a transmission mechanism for judgments made outside of the law by the sovereign to those subject to the sovereign's authority. On that understanding, law serves, as it does in Hartian legal theory, to transmit the factual content of the sovereign's judgments to his subjects. The idea of exclusionary reason, as well as the rest of the conceptual apparatus which goes with it, elaborates the claim that an authoritative decision's success in providing an exclusionary reason depends on it having a determinate content. 'Determinate' in this context means factually determinable, that is, determinable without having to rely on moral considerations and arguments.[147] A reason must have a factually determinable content for it to function as a content-independent reason. We saw in Section 2.1 that it is this claim which on Hart's account provides the essential continuity between early and contemporary legal positivism.[148]

But there is a gap between the claim that subjects must accept that they cannot challenge an authoritative decision by reopening the conflict of reasons which the decision is supposed to settle and the claim that the decision must have a factually determinable content in Raz's sense. This is the gap Hobbes exploited in his denial that an authoritative decision's success depends on its having such a content. The reasons for that denial explain why Hobbes thought it would be difficult for the sovereign to

[147] See Raz, 'Authority, Law, and Morality', 203.

[148] See my *Hard Cases in Wicked Legal Systems: Pathologies of Legality* (Oxford: Oxford University Press, 2010, 2nd ed.), chapters 8 and 9.

'contrive' to make the command discussed in *Behemoth* into law. His argument is that there are certain kinds of inhumanity which legal form resists, so that it is both difficult to make that kind of content legal and incumbent on legal officials to try to avoid ascribing that kind of content to the law. Indeed, the difficulty in part explains the possibility that the officials should be able to come up with a less problematic interpretation of the law.

Support for this argument can be found when the sovereign's command to the son to kill his father is set in the context of Hobbes's theory of legality – the theory about the commitments inherent in the idea that a king 'commands the people in general never but by a precedent law, and as a politic, not a natural person'. To take advantage of the time between publication of the law and the condemnation of my father, I would have to be pretty sure that he would be convicted despite the fact that he must first be tried and found guilty by a judge. For only after such a finding had been made could the judge issue the command that I execute my father. This factor complicates matters because, as we have seen, Hobbes has a rich understanding of the judicial role which combines with his account of the institution of punishment in this context in the following way.

The proposition that the son is under a legal duty to kill his father is true if and only if, prior to his father's deed, there existed the general law just sketched, and the father has been convicted in a full and fair trial. That entails that from law's own perspective the judge would have to take into account any argument which sought to show that a law of nature required him to interpret the law in a particular way, perhaps one which goes against what may have seemed at first the self-evident meaning of the law. For Hobbes's remark that judges insult the sovereign if they fail to interpret his law in light of the laws of nature requires that judges must take the meaning of any particular law to be the one which complies best with the laws of nature, even when another interpretation would seem the more obvious one outside of the interpretive context provided by natural law.

There are two laws of nature which should give the judge pause in interpreting the command literally. First, Hobbes elaborated Law 11, the law of equity, as forbidding '*Acception of Persons*'.[149] Law 11 thus seems to rule out the kinds of statutes which the common lawyers fitted into the

[149] *Leviathan*, 108. His emphasis.

category of Bills of Attainder, that is, laws which depart from generality in singling out particular individuals for penalties and punishments; and the law in the example singles out fathers and sons in a way which appears intended to expose both to grave dishonour, the son by being required to execute his father, his father by having to regard his son as if he were an enemy.

Second, Law 7 forbids the infliction of punishment 'with any other designe, than for correction of the offender, or direction of others'.[150] Hobbes must have supposed that the death penalty may be inflicted when this would help to direct others by deterring them from certain crimes, even though it cannot 'correct' the offender.[151] Thus, a judge could conclude that my knowledge that my own son will have to execute me should I be found guilty of committing a particular crime could be regarded as the basis of a plausible interpretation of this law of nature because the very inhumanity of the law might have a great deterrent effect.

But while judges may think they can make sense of their role in ordering that I execute my father, can they make sense of the claim that I am under a duty to do as commanded? Recall that in *De Cive*, Hobbes supposed there is no duty at all. In contrast, in the passage from *Behemoth* he said that I will be 'bound' unless I escape the country before my father's actual condemnation. Hobbes's vacillations create the kinds of puzzles which Sreedhar invokes the idea of exclusionary reason and a legal positivist account of authority to solve; for example, that I am entitled to resist the sovereign's punishments. I cannot consent not to resist because the punishment undermines the end of self-preservation for which I transferred to the sovereign my right to judge how best to preserve myself. In *Leviathan*, Hobbes called this the 'true Liberty' of the subject, and said that the words of the covenant giving the sovereign a complete authorization to govern cannot 'by themselves' bind a man 'either to kill himselfe, or any other man' or to 'execute any dangerous or dishonourable Office'.[152]

[150] Ibid, 106.

[151] Though Mario Cattaneo suggests that the logical conclusion of Hobbes's argument is that the death penalty should be outlawed because of its deep irrationality; 'Hobbes's Theory of Punishment', in KC Brown, ed., *Hobbes Studies* (Oxford: Basil Blackwell, 1965) 275.

[152] *Leviathan*, 151.

However, set in the context of Hobbes's discussion of the interaction of enacted and natural law in *Leviathan*, a different aspect of the command's problematic nature emerges. The command's inhumanity is legally problematic because it undermines the basis for law's claim to authority over me. This basis is not reducible, as is commonly supposed, to my interest in security – a trade of protection for obedience – though even on those terms one might argue that the law undermines security. For Hobbes is clear that a civil society is not merely one in which there is centralized power, as I explain in Section 2.4.

2.4 Towards a Political Legal Theory

In Hobbes's legal theory, what makes a society civil is in large part that power is exercised through law. We saw that he argued that to clamour for freedom from the law is absurd because that is to demand a return to the state of nature.[153] This argument is rightly taken to be an attempt to debunk the claim that people may legitimately rise up against their leaders in the name of liberty. But it is not only that. It is also an argument about the quality of civil liberty, a kind of liberty we can have only when a system of civil law is in place. Moreover, a system of civil law can be in place only if there is a legal order which makes it possible for laws to be enacted, interpreted, applied and enforced. Any such legal order will contain not only the enacted law, but also the fundamental principles of legality which make that order into a legal order, rather than an order of unmediated coercive power. If I am right that Hobbes was indeed committed to the legality proviso, two important conclusions follow.

First, the sovereign's subjection to the laws of nature is not only, as Hobbes sometimes said, a matter between the sovereign and God, with no effect on the relationship between the sovereign and its subjects.[154] The legality proviso tells us that it is not sufficient for an enacted law to be authoritative that it complies with the public criteria. The content of the enacted law must also be interpretable by judges in light of the laws of nature. These interpretations condition the content of the laws as the laws apply to particular subjects, and thus affect the relationship between

[153] Ibid, 147.
[154] For example, ibid, 148.

the subject and the sovereign on the basis of the laws of nature, the set of which Hobbes called 'the true and onely Morall Philosophy'.[155]

Thus, the sovereign as ultimate judge is constrained by the laws of nature, not because it owes duties to its subjects, and despite the fact that Hobbes rejected arguments for the separation of powers. Rather, the constraints come about because of the duty the judges owe to the sovereign to interpret enacted law in the light of their understanding of the laws of nature. Of course, the sovereign as first and ultimate judge can either preclude or override such interpretations. However, that does not make the constraints cease to be such; it simply makes them overridable by very explicit words.

The second important conclusion is that Hobbes is not a legal positivist at least in so far as he does not subscribe to the claim which creates the continuity between early and contemporary legal positivists – that the content of the law must be determinable by factual tests alone. At this point my argument has to contend with the point about the sovereign's ability to override subordinate judges. Those who hold the orthodox view of Hobbes emphasize that for him if a law makes sense, that is, it is intelligible and validly promulgated, that is enough. A lot turns, however, on whether my argument is contending with the strict positivist claim which is part and parcel of the orthodox interpretation of Hobbes or with a moderate position.[156]

On the strict position, an authoritative decision must have a factually determinable content, in which case the legality proviso plays no role at all in the interpretation of the law. This position has to ignore or explain away large parts of Hobbes's text. The moderate position, in contrast, takes these chunks of text into account but maintains that the legality proviso operates unless it comes into clear conflict with the determinate content of a law which is valid in terms of the validity proviso. At that point, the validity proviso trumps the legality proviso, so that, for example, if the sovereign commands that all mediators should be killed on sight, that command must be taken by subordinate judges as the correct interpretation of Law 15 of the laws of nature that all those who mediate peace should be granted safe passage.[157] Similarly, if the sovereign commands that judges should act partially, or against equity, or

[155] Ibid, 110.

[156] The strict position corresponds roughly to that of 'exclusive legal positivists' and the moderate position to that of 'inclusive legal positivists'. See Appendix I.

[157] *Leviathan*, 108–9.

should not take account of the evidence, they must treat the content of these commands as correct statements of the laws of nature. In addition, those subject to the laws interpreted in this manner must accept the laws as interpreted in accordance with right reason.

The moderate position thus leads to a rather odd conclusion. But there is something to it. The sovereign may explicitly override a law of nature. However, it is crucial to appreciate the legal complexity of the situation in which the sovereign effects such an override. Recall that there are two ways in which the sovereign can do this. It can do so retrospectively by overruling a decision of its subordinate judges, that is, in its judicial capacity, or it can do so prospectively through very explicit statutory text, that is, in its legislative capacity.

If we assume that the sovereign is a supreme legislature, and that it is operating in a context in which, as we take for granted in our day, there is a separation of powers between the legislature and the judiciary, this distinction may seem to make little difference. If the legislature chooses to overrule the apex court of the legal order, it will do so through a statute by making explicit in an amended statute what it could have done in the first place prospectively. However, even if the legal instrument is the same in this context, its function is different, a point which is important both as a matter of how to understand Hobbes's legal theory and of the relevance of that theory to contemporary debates.

While Hobbes was against a division of sovereign power – indeed, thought it in the nature of sovereign power that it cannot be divided – he clearly saw the need for a division of functions. As he put it in his discussion of interpretation, in claiming that the final arbiter of disputes over legal meaning is the supreme lawmaker: 'To [the legislator] . . . therefore there can not be any kind of knot in the Law, insoluble; either finding out the ends, to undoe it by; or else making what ends he will, (as *Alexander* did with his sword in the Gordian knot,) by the Legislative power; which no other interpreter can doe'.[158] Here Hobbes distinguished between two ways in which the legislator, who is also the final interpreter of the law, may deal with a seemingly insoluble problem of interpretation. The first finds a solution within the law which shows that the problem was not in fact insoluble – the knot is undone. The second does not so much find as impose a solution. It cuts through the knot. Only the first solution is properly interpretive of the law; and while both

[158] Ibid, 191. His emphasis.

solutions have authority because they emanate from the legislator, the authority they have is different: respectively, the authority to issue the definitive or final interpretation of the law and the authority to make new law.

We know from the variety of ways of constructing a legal order that it is perfectly possible to locate these two kinds of authority in institutions which are not only separate, but also in a constitutional scheme which secures the independence of each institution from the other. Indeed, in all well-functioning modern legal states there is in place some kind of more or less formal separation of powers between the legislative, the judicial and the executive branches of government. To the extent that there is no separation, or that the lines of separation are too blurred in practice, both lawyers and philosophers of law will think that the legal order is problematic.[159]

Hobbes's opposition to this kind of arrangement is clear. But it does create certain problems internal to his conception of legal order. The suggestion that the sovereign must always be able to overrule its subordinate judges in its judicial capacity is problematic because of the law of nature which precludes judges from being judge in their own cause.[160] In addition, in chapter 26 of *Leviathan*, Hobbes suggested that judges who find out that they have been witness to a fact on which an accused's innocence depends should ask the sovereign to appoint another judge.[161]

[159] Indeed, the fact that the international legal order does not instantiate such a separation, and may be not capable of ever doing so, means that its status as legal continues to be debated. Hobbes, in chapter 13 of *Leviathan*, 90, notoriously advised readers who might be sceptical that there could be such a thing as the state of nature because they live under the protection of a sovereign to look to the state of relationship between states, which he suggested presents an obvious example of a perpetual condition of potential war because there is no international sovereign. I deal with this issue in Chapter 4.

[160] Hobbes, *On the Citizen*, 52, and *Leviathan*, 109, Law 18. Johan Olsthoorn relies on *On the Citizen*, 85 where Hobbes suggests that if subjects bring suit against the sovereign, it is for the sovereign to choose – a matter of 'will' not law – whether to submit the dispute to legal settlement. Thus, Olsthoorn argues that 'individuals cannot invoke the principles of equity to seek redress'; 'Hobbes's Account of Distributive Justice as Equity' (2013) 21 *British Journal for the History of Philosophy* 13, at 31. Olsthoorn also suggests that the subjects do not sue *against* the sovereign because the sovereign is not party to the case. The sovereign can therefore adjudicate the case without violating natural law. But this claim is both at odds with what Hobbes explicitly said, as he had to, since in the nature of a legal action of this sort the sovereign or one of its delegates has to be named as the party. Of course, from the judge's perspective, all that matters is clarifying what the law requires, but that leaves in place the problem identified in the text.

[161] *Leviathan*, 194.

Finally, the sovereign could refrain from appealing against the judgment of its most senior subordinate judges, if the decision went against it. If it refrained, it would not be setting up this subordinate judge as a rival but simply affirming tacitly its own will, as interpreted by the subordinate judge. This may be considered preferable to the situation in which judges opt to be judges in their own cause, which Hobbes was clear is a decision to reinstate the state of nature of individual warring judgments.[162]

Thus, even if Hobbes insisted on no formal division of powers, he presupposed a division of functions because he understood that it is valuable from a normative point of view to keep functions conceptually distinct. Consider, for example, section 33 of the Canadian Charter of Rights and Freedoms, which gives Canadian legislatures the authority to override judicial interpretations of many of the rights entrenched in the charter, thus giving the legislatures the 'last word' (as long as the override is renewed every fifth year) in controversies about these rights. Several scholars have argued that section 33 instantiates a new model of constitutionalism which does not opt for either legislative or judicial supremacy.[163] But others have riposted that it does not, because the text of section 33 strongly suggests that an 'override' does not represent a final 'interpretation' of the charter (an undoing of the knot) but rather a brute legislative overriding of the court's last constitutional word (a cutting of the knot).

I do not think a lot turns on the claim about this being a new model, for reasons elaborated in Chapter 3. For the moment, I want only to highlight that it matters both politically and legally which function one thinks a Canadian legislature is exercising when it uses the override. If one thinks it is the legislative function, it matters politically because the legislature is signalling that it wishes to step outside of the usual constitutional limits of the legal order in a limited way; and the political costs to doing this are demonstrated by the fact that the override is hardly ever used. It also matters legally because the reason that the political cost is incurred is that the signal is that the supreme lawmaker is reneging on fundamental legal commitments. It is a signal to those subject to the sovereign's power that the legal order is in a partial state of transition to a different mode of government, one which makes its claim in the register of might not right. In contrast, if one thinks it is the judicial function, the

162 Ibid, 109.

163 Notably, Stephen Gardbaum, *The New Commonwealth Model of Constitutionalism* (Cambridge: Cambridge University Press, 2013).

sovereign's interpretation must be taken as representing the true content of the protected right, in which case there is no internal tension and it becomes difficult to distinguish might and right, unmediated coercive power from legal order.

Hobbes's institutional solution to the problem judges encounter when they cannot give a reasonable interpretation of one of the sovereign's laws sends the signal associated with the legislative function. The problem it occasions is generated internally in that it arises because the officials of the order assume that it is part of their role to ensure that the order lives up to its own most fundamental commitments. They do not so much attempt to confine their sovereign to such commitments as understand their role in the exercise of sovereignty as maintaining the principles which are constitutive of sovereign authority. Once the problem is understood as internally generated, it is incumbent on those with the power to do so to find an institutional solution to the problem. They must try to the extent possible to resolve the problem internally because it threatens not only the maintenance of the legal order in good shape but also the claim of those in power to be able to rule in the register of authority.

Recall that for Hobbes it is not order as such – the mere absence of conflict – which is in issue. Rather, it is the kind of order which makes possible a certain kind of interaction between subjects, one which puts in place a stable system of public laws under which individual subjects can live together as free and equal members of the jural community. This point establishes one end – the 'duty end' – of what we can think of as the interpretive spectrum. At this end, judges are under a duty to strike down a law, even though the law complies with the validity proviso, and even though they are not given any explicit authority by any other kind of enacted law to do so.

The other end – the 'aspiration end' – is established by Hobbes's claim in chapter 30 of *Leviathan* that the sovereign must make 'Good Lawes'. Hobbes did not mean by 'good' 'just' since his view was that all the sovereign's laws are by definition just. Rather, a good law is that which is '*Needfull*, for the *Good of the People*, and withall *Perspicuous*'.[164] Further, while one might think that the true end of a law is the benefit of the sovereign this is not the case, for 'the good of the Soveraign and People, cannot be separated'.[165] Finally, perspicuity consists not so much in the

164 *Leviathan*, 239. His emphasis.
165 Ibid, 240.

words of the law, but in a 'Declaration of the Causes, and Motives, for which it was made'.[166] It seems clear that for Hobbes law should have all of these features in order that it might be 'the publique Conscience, by which [the subject] ... hath already undertaken to be guided'.[167]

As one moves along the spectrum towards the aspiration end, matters become complex because when an enacted law is not clearly void but seems to undermine one or other law of nature, the judge is under a duty to try to find an interpretation of the statute which will make it less problematic from the perspective of legality. The duty end of the spectrum is where the lawmaker must conform in very particular ways with legality in order for its acts to be recognized as law. Correspondingly, when the lawmaker fails so to conform, judges must declare that the act fails to be law. As one moves away from this end, answers to the question of what legality requires will not be so clear; nevertheless, the judges remain under a duty. This is the duty to interpret the law to make it as consistent as possible with the aspirations of legality, thus ensuring that law lives up to its internal commitments to serving the equality and liberty of the subject.

It follows that any of the following examples would be legally speaking problematic from Hobbes's perspective on legality: a statute which flatly contradicted the content of one of the laws of nature; a statute which precluded judges from relying on a particular law of nature in interpreting the law; or, even more radically, a statute which prohibited judges from ever relying on the laws of nature. Judges are required in these cases to try to do what they can to preserve the interaction of the laws of nature with enacted law, even if Hobbes would not say that the judges are under a duty to declare the statute void. But he would say that each case requires some kind of institutional solution in order to maintain the legal order in good shape. That suffices to show that Hobbes has a rich and complex legal account of law's authority, one in which the complexities are generated from within. They are so generated because the principle of justification is always in play, a principle which requires judicial attention to the laws of nature as well as to enacted laws, and which thus requires judges to show that laws which meet the validity proviso also meet the legality proviso.

Put differently, the issue does not turn on whether judges have the authority to invalidate unconstitutional laws so that there is a mechanism

[166] Ibid.
[167] Ibid, 223.

internal to the legal order for resolving this kind of conflict. Rather, Hobbes helps us to understand that the kinds of conflicts resolved by this kind of judicial review will arise in any legal order because they are conflicts internal to the exercise of legal authority. Moreover, addressing such conflicts is part of the judicial role even when judges are confined to interpretation of the law and a legislative body has authority to override them by enacting an altogether explicit statute. The result will be that at times judges will find themselves on points of the spectrum towards the aspiration end and unable to decide a conflict between the two provisos in favour of the legality proviso.

The difference, therefore, between these two forms of judicial review in this context pertains only to whether there is a formal judicial remedy available in the limit case in which the validity proviso clashes with the legality proviso in such a way that the individual's interests in liberty and equality are threatened. Sreedhar's positivist argument is one way of responding to the limit case through a claim about non-excludable reasons, in essence inalienable rights against the sovereign.[168]

My account is different. The authority of the sovereign is not a matter of its being able to decide as it pleases with each individual subject unless the decision has a negative impact on the non-excludable reasons of that individual. Rather, the limit case reveals the fundamental norms of the jural community of which all legal subjects are members and which make it possible for the artificial person of the sovereign to have and to exercise authority, by which I mean de jure or legitimate authority.[169]

In the limit case, the subject is entitled to disobey because the sovereign has put into doubt the subject's membership of the community which is a precondition for the subject to recognize the sovereign as an authority. More accurately, such individuals no longer must regard themselves as subjects – as subject to an order of authority – since the issue seems like resistance to unmediated coercive power. In other words, while they might understand perfectly well that they are threatened with harm by the person or people who happen to have most of the power in the event of non-compliance with a directive, the directive is no longer

[168] See Yves Charles Zarka, 'The Political Subject', in Tom Sorell and Luc Foisneau, eds, *Leviathan after 350 Years* (Oxford: Clarendon Press, 2004) 167.

[169] See Stephen Darwall, *The Second-Person Standpoint: Morality, Respect, and Accountability* (Cambridge, MA: Harvard University Press, 2006), 12, note 25. While I cannot go into this issue here, Hobbes seems to me to supply the account of public political authority which Darwall needs in order to elaborate his second-personal account of moral authority.

intelligible to them as authoritative, as the command of one to whom they were formerly obliged.

As we have seen, not only is it the case that the laws of nature condition the content of the law but also they do so through their relationship to the reasons for obedience. The laws of nature are what they are because of the reasons underlying the creation of the sovereign–subject relationship. They have traction within civil society through the way in which they interact with enacted law, as it is applied by officials and interpreted by them and by judges, thus making the content of enacted law in part dependent on its compliance with the laws of nature. Before one gets to the limit case in Hobbes's civil society, officials and judges will have the opportunity to try to interpret the law in such a way as to make it conform to the moral commitments of the jural community, expressed in the laws of nature. Hence, because the laws of nature protect our interest in liberty and equality in a way which makes it rational for us in the first place to authorize the sovereign, the content of the enacted law will reflect those interests until the sovereign chooses explicitly to undermine those interests. At that point, this person ceases to act as sovereign, even if no judge has the legal resource to make a formal declaration to this effect.

Put differently, the content of the civil law must reflect subjects' interests in a way that is intelligible or 'perspicuous' to the legal subject. When intelligibility in this sense is not achievable, it will also be the case that the validity and the legality provisos are in conflict, which brings into question the most fundamental legal commitments of the well-functioning jural community which Hobbes calls a civil society. Hobbes's account of a civil society as one in which the legally constituted sovereign governs its subjects according to law thus goes a long way to showing how one might pass 'unwounded' between those 'who contend, on one side for too great Liberty, and on the other side for too much Authority'.[170]

This understanding of the constitution of sovereignty does imply limits of a kind. First, Hobbes insisted from the beginning of *Leviathan* that the individual human being as such is the subject of political order. In his view, there is only one pre-political right, the right which every individual has to self-preservation, including the right to judge for oneself how to exercise that right.[171] In the state of nature, it is a worse than

[170] *Leviathan*, 3.

[171] For example, ibid, 93–4, 151–2, 214.

useless right since its existence contributes to the precariousness of that state, so it is rational for individuals to authorize a sovereign to govern them. It is thus also rational for all subject to such government to understand that they should be taken to have consented so to be governed, to understand that they should adopt the stance of the Just Man. But it is rational only so long as the reciprocal relationship between protection and obedience is maintained in which protection is of the subject understood as a person who is free and equal before the law.

Hence, the pre-political right to preserve oneself survives into the civil condition as a political right, for Hobbes the right of rights, which is the right to demand a justification from public officials for any exercise of coercive power in terms of the reciprocal relationship between protection and obedience.[172] But it also survives as setting the limit of that political relationship by marking the point where justification runs out and political order turns into unmediated coercion, at which point the subject is no longer getting protection and is no longer bound to the sovereign.

Indeed, Hobbes's understanding of the institution of punishment no longer seems so peculiar when understood in this way, since we can see why he presented a double optic on the violence necessary to maintain order.[173] There is the private optic of the about-to-be-punished individual who is in a kind of mini-state of nature in relation to the officials. But there is also the public optic of fellow subjects for whom it is very important to observe that the individual got all of the protections afforded by the rule of law before being subject to coercion. It is crucial, in other words, for the spectacle of legality to be played out in the right way, not only for subjects directly impacted by the law, but for the general public who look on, so that the latter know that if they should have to confront the state, that confrontation will be mediated by legality.[174]

[172] Hobbes has immense difficulties with the idea of conscription for military service because of this idea. See, ibid, 151–2, immediately following the paragraph in which he sets out the rebel's catechism. In the very last chapter, 'A Review, and Conclusion', he resolves these difficulties by adding a new law of nature at 484, his emphasis: '*That every man is bound by Nature, as much as in him lieth, to protect in Warre, the Authority, by which he himself is protected in time of Peace.*' His emphasis.

[173] I owe these insights to the work of Alice Ristroph, for example, 'Criminal Law for Humans', in Dyzenhaus and Poole, *Hobbes and the Law* 97.

[174] On the importance of publicity in Hobbes, see Jeremy Waldron, 'Hobbes and the Principle of Publicity' (2001) 82 *Pacific Philosophical Quarterly* 447.

Hobbes's project was to construct a legal theory in service of a general political theory, one which explains the role of legal order in sustaining legitimate political authority, whatever the nature of the political regime – monarchy, democracy or aristocracy. In this respect, he is well described as a 'constitutional indifferentist',[175] since he is a political and legal philosopher who thinks that the choice for one kind of constitutional order over another is to be made on pragmatic grounds. The best example of Hobbes's indifferentism is that his argument for the superior nature of monarchy over democracy is not at the level of abstract political theory. Instead, he argued that in practice the former is more likely than the latter to conduce both to stability and the overall good of the people.[176] His argument against precedent should be understood in the same light. A legal order should not adopt such a doctrine as a matter of abstract political theory, for such a theory can tell one only that law must be interpretable in the light of the fundamental principles of legality. Rather, adoption should be on the basis of whether the doctrine promotes conformity to fundamental principles from the perspective of a 'very able Architect' who wishes above all to avoid designing 'a crasie building' that 'must assuredly fall upon the heads of . . . posterity'.[177]

Similarly, abstract political theory cannot decide between what kind of institution should confront the problems which arise when statute law is not interpretable in the right way. But there must be some such institution lest the legal order be incapable of vindicating its commitment to its principles, in which case it would cease to be a legal order and become some other mode of exercising power. Here there are various options.

First, there is Hobbes's own option which requires a judicial reference to the sovereign. Second, there is the common law tradition's option which gives judges an extensive interpretive authority, which Hobbes also adopted, save that he was clearly wary of the hint that the authority might extend to the voiding of flagrantly offensive laws. Indeed, it seems likely that he intended the first option as a way of avoiding placing judges in a situation of institutional face-off because the matter is channelled into the institutional structure of sovereignty.[178]

[175] Vinx, 'Constitutional Indifferentism and Republican Freedom'.

[176] *Leviathan*, 131–8.

[177] Ibid, 221.

[178] This double-barrelled institutional solution has an interesting contemporary analogue in the UK Human Rights Act (1998), which in section 3 requires that judges strain to interpret statutes to make them compatible with the human rights commitments of the statute, and in section 4 requires judges to make a declaration of incompatibility of the

A third option, which did not exist in Hobbes's time, and which it may seem he would have rejected outright, is the explicit grant of authority to judges to invalidate statutes on the basis of a bill of rights in an entrenched constitution. But even in this regard, his rejection might be best understood as nuanced. As we have seen, he explicitly stated that a formally valid sovereign act which undermines the essential rights of sovereignty would be void from the outset.[179] Moreover, constitutional mechanisms which require judges to consider that limits on rights can be justified by the government in a proportionality analysis or which allow legislative overrides of judicial declarations of unconstitutionality, or even mechanisms of constitutional amendment which do not make amendment politically impossible, can plausibly be understood as consistent with the interpretation of Hobbesian sovereignty presented here. Hobbes's sovereign is the legal sovereign.[180]

Hobbes can then be understood as the founder of the rule-of-law tradition in modern political and legal theory. But he is also one of the founders of the modern political discourse of constitutionalism about the reciprocal relationship between, on the one hand, the sovereign person of the state and the officials who implement and interpret the law and, on the other hand, the persons who are subject to the law. The sovereign as an artificial person speaks to the subjects through law, and legal language has its own grammar which requires that subjects be addressed in a way which respects them as responsible agents, each endowed with equal capacity to judge right and wrong. Hobbes's legal theory amounts to a superior articulation of, rather than an attempt to undermine, the idea that the rule of law is a moral good. Perhaps even more important is that the rule of law is a moral good because it is a political good, one which helps to make it possible for individuals to live together on stable and peaceful terms despite their very different views of the moral good for themselves.

Hobbes's theory is thus part of an even more general inquiry into the place of legal order in the construction of stable political order in a bid to answer what Bernard Williams called the 'Hobbesian question' of how to

statute with the human rights commitments, if they cannot find an interpretation under section 3. See Chapter 4.

179 *Leviathan*, 127.

180 Here it is worth considering the implications of Hobbes's idea of the 'sleeping sovereign', in *On the Citizen*, 98–100, an idea which inspired Richard Tuck, *The Sleeping Sovereign: The Invention of Modern Democracy* (Cambridge: Cambridge University Press, 2015).

secure 'order, protection, safety, trust, and the conditions of cooperation'.[181] This, Williams said, is the 'first' political question because 'solving it is the condition of solving, indeed posing, any others'.[182] As such, it is first and foremost a political theory of legal order. Perhaps more accurately, it is a theory of political order as legal order, since a political order is characterized by authority relationships in contrast with relationships of unmediated coercive power and mediation is achieved by law.

The point is not that a political order can do without coercive power, only that it wields such power in a way which makes plausible a claim that its officials have been authorized by subjects. Any exercise of coercive power by the state must therefore be recognizable as an authoritative act, which entails that it must meet the two provisos set out in Sections 2.2.1 and 2.2.2. That puts an onus of justification on officials which, if it cannot be discharged, raises the question whether the subject is without the reciprocal relationship of protection and obedience, which would imply that the relationship is not political but one of hostility or unmediated coercion between more and less powerful natural individuals. Hobbes's injunction to the subject is not 'Obey the law, whatever its content'. Rather, it is 'Obey the law because of the content it has', a content which can answer the question 'But, how can that be law for me?'

This account of the role of legal order in sustaining political order subtly changes the understanding of the relationship between sovereignty and fundamental legal principles. Often debate about this relationship seems structured by a binary option which I discuss at length in Chapter 3. Either the sovereign is subject to *legal* principles with judges as their guardian or the principles are *political* principles and the sovereign as the ultimate law maker is the sole judge of the content of the principles. Hobbes presented another option. Fundamental principles are the political principles intrinsic to the rule-of-law project and should not be seen primarily as limiting sovereign authority. Rather, the principles constitute sovereign authority. They are the right-giving principles of the legal state. As such, the subordinate officials of the state – those who work at levels below the level of supreme legislative power – must concretize the law or complete the exercise of sovereignty consistently

[181] Bernard Williams, 'Realism and Moralism in Political Theory', in Williams, *In the Beginning Was the Deed: Realism and Moralism in Political Argument* (Princeton: Princeton University Press, 2005, Geoffrey Hawthorn, ed.) 1.

[182] Ibid.

with those principles. Sovereignty, while often identified by Hobbes with the ultimate lawmaking power, is more complex than a one-off act because it involves a process of concretizing general laws until they can be applied to legal subjects consistently with the laws of nature.

Hobbes's legal theory shows, then, that any attempt to give an account of the authority of law must contain the three elements set out in the Introduction. First, it explains authority as compliance with fundamental principles of legality – the right-giving basis of the legal order. Second, it gives to judges and other officials a role in interpreting enacted law in the light of such principles. It thus offers a theory of the role of interpretation in maintaining legal order. Given the first and second elements, the principles make up a grammar of legality in that enacted laws which are not interpretable in the light of the principles have a dubious claim to authority. If enough dubious laws are enacted, the order begins to shift from one of legal right to one of unmediated coercive power. To be legal, to count as valid law, law must be interpretable in a way which respects these principles. Most concretely, that loss of authority will be manifested at the point at which a legal official is unable to answer the subject's question 'But, how can that be law for me?' Finally, Hobbes begins his analysis of the modern legal state by setting out a constitutionalist idea in the social contract. In Chapter 3, I turn to exploring how these elements of political legal theory can help us to understand and make progress in contemporary debates in philosophy of law.

3

The Constitution of Legal Authority / The Authority of Legal Constitutions

> This is more than Consent, or Concord; it is a reall Unitie of them all, in one and the same Person, made by Covenant of every man with every man, in such manner, as if every man should say to every man, *I Authorize and give up my Right of Governing my selfe, to this Man, or to this Assembly of men, on this condition, that thou give up thy Right to him, and Authorize all his Actions in like manner.* This done, the Multitude so united in one Person, is called a COMMON-WEALTH, in latine CIVITAS. This is the Generation of that great LEVIATHAN, or rather (to speake more reverently) of that *Mortall God*, to which wee owe under the *Immortall God*, our peace and defence.
>
> Thomas Hobbes[1]

The constitution of the state demarcates a jurisdiction, an area in which the law commands by right. This idea of constitution is immensely complex, first, because it is ambiguous between *constitution as act* and *constitution as achievement*. Constitution as act evokes the idea in the social contract tradition of the *Gesellschaftsvertrag* – the state is the product of an actual contract between free and equal individuals. Constitution as achievement evokes the idea in that same tradition that in every political order there is a *Herrschaftsvertrag* – an actual constitutional arrangement which sets out the relationship between ruler and ruled, whether in a written constitution, as in Germany, or an unwritten constitution, as in the UK. To use terms currently popular, the idea of constitution is ambiguous between the idea of constituent power, 'We, the people', and that of constituted powers, the artefact of 'We, the people'.

Second, as the epigraph from *Leviathan* tells us, the idea of constitution suggests not only that the achievement is greater than the sum of

[1] Thomas Hobbes, *Leviathan* (Cambridge: Cambridge University Press, 1996, Richard Tuck, ed.), 120. His emphasis.

its parts, but also that there is an almost magical transformation of these parts which takes place between act and achievement. Here Hobbes picks up on a thought, expressed in the first pages of *Leviathan*, that human individuals in making this 'Artificiall man' accomplish something we can take to 'resemble that *Fiat*, or the *Let us make man*, pronounced by God in the Creation'.[2] There is thus an element of artifice as well as of artefact in the creation of this artificial man, especially since Hobbes seems to imply by 'as if' that the contract is hypothetical. The individuals should conclude that they consented because, so long as they are rational, they would have consented.

Finally, the idea is complex because the act of constituting the internal space of the state necessarily affects the space outside of it. The outside is constituted in relation to the other constituted jurisdictions, just as that state's internal space is constituted in relation to them. The act of constitution is therefore Janus-faced. It looks both inwards and outwards.

In this chapter, I attend to just the first two complicating factors, the relationship between constitution as act and constitution as achievement within the modern legal state and the element of artifice. I thus leave to Chapter 4 the issue of the Janus-faced nature of the constitution, a division of labour which permits me to focus here on the issues of the constitution of authority and the authority of constitutions as if they arise only within one national legal order, and in Chapter 4 on the implications for the relationship between such an order and the other legal orders of the world.

Section 3.1 sets out Hart's and Kelsen's candidates for what I called in the Introduction a constitutionalist idea: the functional equivalents they propose to Hobbes's claim that a social contract explains the unity of legal order. As we know, Hart regarded the act of constituting legal authority as primarily a matter for legal officials, the group which must accept the authority of the legal order for it to be maintained. In addition, Hart claimed that official acceptance of the law does not require moral endorsement and that, he thought, supported his thesis that a legal order can be both authoritative and illegitimate. But I argue both that acceptance cannot be confined to officials and that authority cannot be disentangled from legitimacy. More precisely, legal authority is always de jure because of the role law plays in transforming might into right; and right is ultimately a matter of justification to legal subjects.

[2] Ibid, 9–10. His emphasis.

Section 3.2 turns to Kelsen to advance my argument, while Section 3.3 shows how it helps to reframe the debate in legal theory about the relationship between law and morality as one about the relationship between legal order and legitimacy. With that relationship established, I can turn in Sections 3.4–3.8 to an account of the authority of constitutions.[3]

3.1 On the Constitution of Authority

Hart's move away from the command theory of law was largely driven by his sense that law cannot be understood as a matter of coercion alone. It must be understood also and primarily as a matter of authority or legal right. In addition, as Hart explained in 1958, he rejected the command theory's claim that law is 'the creation of the legally untrammeled will of the sovereign who is by definition outside of the law'[4] because of what he took to be a fact about legal orders: 'nothing which legislators do makes law unless they comply with fundamental rules specifying the essential law-making procedures'. 'They lie', Hart said, 'at the root of a legal system' and he suggested that 'what was most missing in … [Bentham's and Austin's] scheme is an analysis of what it is for a social group and its officials to accept such rules.' He thus argued that his notion of accepted fundamental rules, 'not that of a command as Austin claimed, is the "key to the science of jurisprudence", or at least one of the keys'.[5]

In *The Concept of Law*, Hart began his parable of the emergence of legal order from a 'primitive' society by saying that it is 'of course possible to imagine a society without a legislature, courts, or officials of any kind'.[6] In such a society, the only rules are customary public norms which impose duties on its members.[7] Legal order emerges through the 'introduction … of rules enabling legislators to change and add to the

[3] Sections 3.1–3.3 are based on my 'The Janus-Faced Constitution', in Jacco Bomhoff, Dyzenhaus and Thomas Poole, eds, *The Double-Facing Constitution* (Cambridge: Cambridge University Press, 2020) 17. Sections 3.4–3.8 are based on my 'The Idea of a Constitution: A Plea for *Staatsrechtslehre*', in Dyzenhaus and Malcolm Thorburn, eds, *Philosophical Foundations of Constitutional Law* (Oxford: Oxford University Press, 2016) 9. I thank Oxford University Press for permission to reuse this material.

[4] HLA Hart, 'Positivism and the Separation of Law and Morals', in Hart, *Essays in Jurisprudence and Philosophy* (Oxford: Clarendon Press, 1983) 49, at 59.

[5] Ibid.

[6] HLA Hart, *The Concept of Law* (Oxford: Clarendon Press, 1994, 2nd ed.), 90.

[7] Ibid, 93.

rules of duty, and judges to determine when the rules of duty have been broken' – 'a step forward', Hart said, 'as important to society as the invention of the wheel'[8] because these rules solve problems in the public order of a primitive society: the 'uncertainty' about what social norms count as such rules; the 'static' nature of these rules since there is no clear way of changing them; and 'inefficiency' because of the lack of recognized means both of determining whether rules have been violated and of enforcing the rules.[9] The problems are solved by the introduction of 'secondary' rules: the problem of uncertainty by the 'rule of recognition' which specifies 'some feature or features possession of which by a suggested rule is taken as a conclusive indication that it is a rule of the group to be supported by the local pressure it exerts';[10] the static quality of primary rules by 'rules of change'; and the problem of inefficiency by 'rules of adjudication'.[11]

Now from the 1958 essay and also from Hart's description of the important step it may seem that among the three types of secondary rules the most fundamental are the rules of change. These rules show that even in a legal order in which the parliament is the supreme lawmaker, there are *legal* limits on what it may do, thus refuting the command theory's claim that the sovereign is legally unlimited. Hart was, however, a little ambivalent about the issue of limitation. It seemed to be the case both in his 1958 essay and in *The Concept of Law* that the rules of change do not so much *limit* what the legislature may do as *constitute* it as a body with power to do certain things, just as the rules of contract law do not so much limit what the contracting parties may do as make it possible for them 'to create structures of rights and duties for the conduct of life within the coercive framework of the law'.[12]

Moreover, in *The Concept of Law*, Hart clarified that of these secondary rules, it is the rule of recognition which is most fundamental since it specifies the lawmaking procedures. Its ultimate nature is indicated by the fact that its existence is not certified by any other rule. It exists as a matter of fact in the practice of the officials of the system and they apply it because they take the 'internal point of view' towards it. They accept

[8] Ibid, 41–2.
[9] Ibid, 92–3.
[10] Ibid, 94.
[11] Ibid, 95–7.
[12] Hart, 'Positivism and the Separation of Law and Morals', 60–1, and *The Concept of Law*, 27–8.

that it provides 'a public, common standard of correct judicial decision'.[13] According to Hart, his account enables philosophy of law for the first time properly to explain legal order in terms of a constitutive, authority-creating idea, something Bentham and Austin had failed to do because their theory reduced law to the commands backed by coercion of a legally unlimited sovereign. They thus did not so much replace the constitutionalist idea of the social contract with their own candidate as reject the thought that legal theory needs any such idea.

Austin, notably, argued that there is no such thing as constitutional law or international law.[14] What passes for these phenomena amounts, in his view, to rules of conventional morality, not legally binding rules. He substituted for the idea of social contract the fact of the 'habit of obedience' of the majority of those subject to the law. We identify the sovereign of a legal order by finding out who is habitually obeyed and does not obey any other person or body. All we need to know about why there is the habit is that there are sufficient sanctions attached to the sovereign's commands to motivate obedience. Hence, legal order can be fully explained as resting on coercion, in terms of might rather than right.

Hart's followers thus suppose his account of the rule of recognition to amount to a revolutionary moment in the history of legal theory which allows philosophy of law to discard much if not all of its prior theoretical attempts to articulate the 'key to legal science'.[15] However, on my argument to come, Hart's articulation of the rule of recognition does not amount to such a moment even within his own English tradition of legal positivism. Its novelty lies only in that the way in which he elaborated the rule reintroduced the constitutionalist idea to his own tradition. Moreover, that reintroduction requires much help from Kelsen's articulation of a similar idea almost half a century prior to Hart's initial forays into legal theory.

[13] Ibid, 116.

[14] John Austin, *Lectures on Jurisprudence or the Philosophy of Positive Law*, vol. 1 (London: John Murray, 1885, 5th ed.), 177, 204.

[15] For example, John Gardner, who succeeded Dworkin in the Chair of Jurisprudence in Oxford, reports that Hart was in a state of high excitement when he came up with this idea, fully justified, in Gardner's view, because '[n]othing in the way law has been theorized has been the same since. It is an authentic "Eureka!" moment in the history of ideas'; 'Why Law Might Emerge: Hart's Problematic Fable', in Luís Duarte D'Almeida, James Edwards and Andrea Dolcetti, eds, *Reading HLA Hart's The Concept of Law* (Oxford: Hart Publishing, 2013) 81, at 96.

Kelsen argued that at the base of every legal order is a *Grundnorm* – the basic norm – which must be hypothesized to make sense of the idea that there is a unified normative order. The *Grundnorm* tells the officials and subjects of the order that the constitutional norms of that order – from which all other norms derive their validity – must be obeyed.[16] Hart thus shared with Kelsen the claim that sovereignty – in the sense of the ultimate lawmaking power of a society – is a juridical idea, which must be explained as a matter of constituted authority, not in terms of an exercise of sheer or unmediated coercive power. They both attempted to explain how might is transformed into right through its mediation by law or, more precisely, by its exercise in the context of a legal order constituted by a candidate for the constitutionalist idea.

But Hart and his followers regard as redundant Kelsen's claim that the *Grundnorm* prescribes obedience to law. All one need observe (from the 'external point of view') is that there is as a matter of actual official practice a rule which stipulates criteria for the recognition of valid laws and that officials manifest their acceptance of this rule (from the 'internal point of view') by applying the criteria and criticizing those who do not. As Hart put the point:

> If a constitution specifying the various sources of law is a living reality in the sense that the courts and officials of the system actually identify the law in accordance with the criteria it provides, then the constitution is accepted and actually exists. It seems needless reduplication to suggest that there is a further rule to the effect that the constitution . . . is to be obeyed. This is particularly clear where, as in the United Kingdom, there is no written constitution: here there seems to be no place for the rule 'that the constitution is to be obeyed' in addition to the fact that certain criteria of validity (e.g. enactment by the Queen in Parliament) are to be used in identifying the law. This is the accepted rule and it is mystifying to speak of a rule that this rule be obeyed.[17]

Hart also rejected Kelsen's view that it is 'logically impossible to regard a particular rule of law as valid and at the same time to accept, as morally binding, a moral rule forbidding behaviour required by the legal rule'. He noted that 'no such consequences follow from the account of legal validity given in this book. One reason for using the expression "rule of

[16] Hans Kelsen, *Introduction to the Problems of Legal Theory* (Oxford: Clarendon Press, 1992, Bonnie Litschewski Paulson and Stanley L Paulson, trans.), 54–5.

[17] Hart, *The Concept of Law*, 293.

recognition" instead of a "*basic* norm" is to avoid any commitment to Kelsen's view of the conflict between law and morals.'[18]

In other words, Hart thought it an advantage of his approach that it permitted the preservation of what he regarded as a sound dualism or two-systems view about the legal and the moral domains, that is, his Separation Thesis.[19] Such dualism permits the good liberal citizen to decide whether to obey the law without being distracted by what Hart regarded as a natural law mindset which supposes that an unjust law is not law. That mindset, we have seen him suggest, issues in contrary stances: the anarchist stance that a law is invalid if unjust in the eyes of the beholder and the reactionary stance that if X is the law, it must also be just.[20] On this view, as I have pointed out, Kelsen might seem to fall into the trap of adopting the reactionary stance despite his positivist commitments.

Hart also thought that this dualism is sound for theoretical reasons. It permits one to appreciate that acceptance does not require moral endorsement. On the one hand, he was clear that legal authority is actively created:

> It is true ... that if a system of rules is to be imposed by force on any, there must be a sufficient number who accept it voluntarily. Without their voluntary co-operation, thus creating *authority*, the coercive power of law and government cannot be established.[21]

On the other hand, he emphasized that, once one understands that there is no necessary connection between the system of legal obligations and the system of moral obligations, one can also appreciate that the obligations of the legal system can be accepted on the basis of 'many different considerations':

> calculations of long term interest; disinterested interest in others; an unreflecting inherited or traditional attitude; or the mere wish to do as others do. There is no reason why those who accept the authority of the system should not examine their conscience and decide that, morally, they ought not to accept it, yet for a variety of reasons to continue to do so.[22]

[18] Ibid. His emphasis.
[19] Ibid, 293.
[20] Hart, 'Positivism and the Separation of Law and Morals', 53–4.
[21] Hart, *The Concept of Law*, 201. His emphasis.
[22] Ibid, 203.

This relationship of voluntary cooperation, he suggested, could be confined to legal officials, though he seemed unsure how to understand the situations in which this occurred, which he diagnosed variously as pathological, unhealthy and abnormal.[23]

On one account, obedience – the first condition for the existence of legal order – 'is the only one which private citizens *need* satisfy: they may obey each "for his part only" and from any motive whatever; though in a healthy society they will in fact often accept these rules as common standards of behaviour and acknowledge an obligation to obey them, or even trace this obligation to a more general obligation to respect the constitution'. In contrast, 'acceptance' or the 'second condition must also be satisfied by the officials of the system'. The officials 'must regard these as common standards of official behaviour and appraise critically their own and each other's deviations as lapses'.[24]

If, however, acceptance were confined to officials, this would present 'an extreme case', as we saw in Chapter 1: 'The society in which this was so might be deplorably sheeplike; the sheep might end in the slaughterhouse. But there is little reason for thinking that it could not exist or for denying it the title of a legal system.'[25] Here Hart's concern seemed to be with the displacement of acceptance from the primary rules of a primitive society to the secondary rules of a modern legal state and from individuals in general to possible confinement to officials. With such displacement a habit of obedience to primary rules whatever their content could arise. This habit amounts to a kind of acceptance though it is not the same as the active, critical acceptance which the official sector must display. It is the kind of passive stance of obeying rules whatever their content merely because they have been certified as valid, one which Hart decried throughout his work and which he argued legal positivism, correctly understood, could guard against.[26]

The situation seems to contrast with yet another where there is widespread disobedience, which Hart described as follows:

> The normal, unproblematic case where we can confidently say that a legal system exists, is just one where it is clear that the two sectors are congruent in their respective typical concerns with the law. Crudely put, the facts

[23] Ibid, 116–18.

[24] Ibid, 116–17. His emphasis.

[25] Ibid, 117.

[26] See Michael A Wilkinson, 'Is Law Morally Risky? Alienation, Acceptance and Hart's Concept of Law' (2010) 30 *Oxford Journal of Legal Studies* 441.

> are, that the rules recognized as valid at the official level, are obeyed. Sometimes, however, the official sector may be detached from the private sector, in the sense that there is no longer general obedience to the rules which are valid according to the criteria of validity in use in the courts. The variety of ways in which this may happen belongs to the pathology of legal systems; for they represent a breakdown in the *complex congruent practice* which is referred to when we make the external statement of fact that a legal system exists. There is here a partial failure of what is presupposed whenever, from within the particular system, we make internal statements of law.[27]

But notice that it does not seem likely that Hart would describe a stable slave-owning society in which enslaved persons were the majority of the population but kept in line by very efficient and cruel sanctions as healthy or normal, even if one were concerned only with the society's legal, not its moral, health. For enslaved persons cannot be said to 'acknowledge an obligation to obey' the rules of such a society 'or even trace this obligation to a more general obligation to respect the constitution'.[28] Missing in such a society is anything like Hart's idea of a 'complex congruent practice' which he took to be at the centre of a society which has made the step from a 'primitive' society into the world of the modern legal state. Hart, however, neither here nor elsewhere, elaborated his understanding of this phenomenon of, as he also put it, the 'complex, but normally concordant, practice of the courts, officials, and private persons in identifying the law by reference to certain criteria'.[29]

Hart thought he could avoid this issue because the 'existence' of the practice 'is a matter of fact'.[30] But, as we have seen, for legal positivists who wish to make sense of law as a matter of authority, reduction to facts which can be described in a prescriptively neutral way does not suffice. Indeed, both Hart and Raz were tempted in different ways to a kind of rapprochement with natural law just because it is difficult to explain law's authority without introducing some moral element.

Recall Raz's claim that Hart's ideas of acceptance and the internal point of view require the figure of 'the legal man', whom he claims to find in Kelsen, and who adopts 'the law as his personal morality, and as

27 Hart, *The Concept of Law*, 117–18. My emphasis.
28 Ibid, 116.
29 Ibid, 110.
30 Ibid.

exhausting all the norms he accepts as just'.[31] The legal man fits into Raz's general theory of legal authority in which to understand legal orders as authoritative involves understanding their claim to have legitimate authority, which requires the figure of the man who accepts the legitimacy of the legal order because he equates justice with the content the law happens to have. But, on Raz's view, one can presuppose this figure consistently with the claim that legal orders are rarely just, so that in general their claim to legitimate authority may fail.[32] He would, then, make no concession to the natural law claim that there is a necessary connection between law and morality.

Nevertheless, we saw that Hart worried that Raz's analysis of authoritative legal reasons threatened to undermine the Separation Thesis;[33] that is, he expressed a similar concern to the one we just saw him express about Kelsen's one-system or monist theory, and which he expressed rather vehemently in regard to Dworkin. In addition, Hart claimed that the analysis should be rejected because it is unrealistic for the reasons just set out. Judges need form no views about the moral merits of the law in accepting that they are under a standing duty to apply it, whatever the merits of its content; something he took Raz to recognize in the thought that the judges could be insincere in associating themselves with the legal man.

But Hart, as we also saw, recognized that his rejection of Raz's analysis left him unable to explain the force of authoritative legal reasons because it presupposed a non-cognitive account of legal reasons committed to the 'paradoxical', even confused, conclusion that 'judicial statements of a subject's legal duties need have nothing directly to do with the subject's reasons for action'.[34] Indeed, as I mentioned, in a philosophical obituary of Hart, Raz concluded that because Hart's rule of recognition is to be explained as a matter of the facts about its existence, including the fact that criticisms are made of those who deviate from its duties, he put

[31] Joseph Raz, 'Kelsen's Theory of the Basic Norm', in Raz, *The Authority of Law: Essays on Law and Morality* (Oxford: Clarendon Press, 1979) 122, at 142–3.

[32] Recall that in Chapter 1 I showed that Raz is rather ambiguous on this point in that he may think that in general legal orders lack authority, not only legitimate authority, in which case their claim to be legal would also be in doubt. See Joseph Raz, 'Authority, Law, and Morality', in Raz, *Ethics in the Public Domain: Essays in the Morality of Law and Politics* (Oxford: Oxford University Press, 1994) 194.

[33] HLA Hart, *Essays on Bentham: Jurisprudence and Political Theory* (Oxford: Clarendon Press, 1982), 153.

[34] Ibid.

forward a non-cognitivist 'sanction theory of rights and duties'.[35] In other words, Hart put forward a position of the sort he thought he had moved beyond in rejecting the command theory of law.

I pointed out that this is a big problem for Hart for reasons which go beyond a failure to break with the command theory of law. When Hart talked of 'official acceptance', he tended to think of the relationship as one between the officials, on the one hand, and the fundamental rules of the legal order, on the other. Acceptance refers to the voluntary cooperation of each official with every other which involves using the secondary rules to produce, determine the content of, apply and enforce the primary rules. But these officials do not have to have any regard for the individuals who are subject to their decisions. Once they have determined what the law is, they simply declare it, apply it or enforce it. However, if the figure of the legal subject is introduced, as Raz seemed to do with the legal man, the authority relationship becomes more complex because the officials must now have regard for the perspective of the person to whom the law is applied. On my argument so far, to take that perspective into account requires that officials can satisfactorily answer the legal subject's question 'But, how can that be law for me?' Raz finesses this possibility because his legal man accepts that whatever content is given to the answer to that question must be taken as just, which collapses justice into the content of positive law – precisely the reactionary view which is wrongly attributed to Hobbes.

Now while Hart rejected this rapprochement by Raz with natural law, we saw that he found another route to a rapprochement through his sketch of a minimum content of natural law which he thought leads to a qualification of the positivist claim that the law can have any content.[36] In addition, he gave an account of the 'judicial virtues' as 'impartiality and neutrality in surveying the alternatives; consideration for the interest of all who will be affected; and a concern to deploy some acceptable principle as a reasoned basis for decision'.[37]

In Chapter 1, I suggested that the combination of the claim about minimum content with the account of the role morality of judges is quite powerful. Judges are bound by their role to come up with an answer to

[35] Joseph Raz, 'HLA Hart (1907–1992)' (1993) 5 *Utilitas* 145, at 149. See further John Finnis, 'On the Incoherence of Legal Positivism' (2000) 75 *Notre Dame Law Review* 1597, at 1608–10.

[36] Hart, *The Concept of Law*, 199.

[37] Ibid, 205.

the legal subject's question which meets two criteria. First, they must demonstrate that their answer to legal subjects is respectful of the subjects' subjectivity – their ability to respond to reasons. Second, the answer must rest on a justice-like general principle supported by the legal materials relevant to the matter, a principle which shows that the legal subjects are such because they are within the class whose interests the law protects, even if the protection is rather minimal. In other words, Hart too felt at this moment compelled to bring the legal subject within the official gaze, which meant that the authority relationship could not be conceived as one only between officials and the secondary rules.

This is not only a rapprochement with natural law, but also with the kind of interpretive position in the natural law tradition which Dworkin was to set out. However, it does not come about through an argument which starts on Dworkin's preferred terrain of adjudication, in the thick of exploring rival accounts of how judges do and should decide hard cases. Rather, it starts on Hart's own terrain of an account of the authority of law. As I have argued, once one chooses to account for law in terms of the distinction between might and right and from the internal point of view, one inevitably approaches a position more accommodating of a natural law position on legal authority. Moreover, such a position recognizes that judges and other legal officials play an important role in mediating the legal relationship between lawmaker and legal subject, between ruler and ruled.

I now argue that it matters that this kind of natural law position is understood in political legal terms on the basis of an idea of legitimate legal authority which cannot be reduced to a moral position of the kind Hart seemed to have in mind when he articulated the Separation Thesis. Legitimacy, that is, does not amount to a coincidence between the content of the law and what the legal subject takes to be the standards of correct morality. Rather, it has to do with the actual acceptance by legal subjects of the de jure authority of a legal order in a way which constitutes that authority. One might say that there is more to the analogy we saw Hart draw between the rules of contract law and his secondary rules than he recognized, even a version of the social contract theory which we find in Hobbes and which Hart, following Bentham and Austin, rejected.

I show that it is important to hold on to Raz's insight as to how the perspective of the legal subject is implicated in the legal order's claim to legitimate authority, an authority with which judges must appear to associate themselves. But we need a more nuanced description of that perspective than that of the legal man who adopts 'the law as his personal morality, and as exhausting all the norms he accepts as just'. Here Kelsen indicated the way and revived for his century the figure we encountered in Chapter 2 of Hobbes's 'Just Man', whose will is 'framed' by the justice of the law.[38] The Just Man can get an answer to the question 'But, how can that be law for me?' because it is asked of officials mindful of their role to uphold the fundamental commitments of their legal order.[39]

3.2 The Legal Man versus the Just Man

When Kelsen in 1924 first set out his hierarchical theory of legal order, he explicitly recognized that his idea of the basic norm has a functional equivalence to the idea of the social contract in natural law theories:

> The concept of the basic norm of the constitution in the legal logical [*rechtlogischen*] sense corresponds to a certain degree with the concept so significant to natural law theory of the original contract or social contract that first and foremost constitutes the state. At bottom, we find the same theoretical need for a presupposition of unity on which the unity of the state order in the multiplicity of legal acts [*Rechtsakte*] of state could be grounded, and which could grasp actual power relationships as legal relationships [*Rechtsbeziehungen*], and which leads here necessarily to the basic norm as it does in natural law theory to the foundational contract.[40]

These lines contain three important insights. In reverse order: first, the task of philosophy of law is to grasp what otherwise might seem to be mere power relationships as legal relationships in the sense of legal right; second, such a grasp requires understanding the legal order as a unity, which in turn requires understanding the constitution in the sense of the basic norm which gives it unity; third, that task is roughly similar to the

[38] See Hobbes, *Leviathan*, 104.

[39] I am much influenced in this section by Lars Vinx's discussion of the figure he calls the 'law-abiding citizen' and of the need to recast the relationship as one between law and legitimacy rather than between law and a personal perspective on morality: Lars Vinx, *Hans Kelsen's Pure Theory of Law: Legality and Legitimacy* (Oxford: Oxford University Press, 2007), 76, 154–6, 209 and 41, note 50.

[40] Hans Kelsen, 'Die Lehre von den drei Gewalten oder Funktionen des Staates', in Hans Klecatsky, René Marcic and Herbert Schambeck, eds, *Die Wiener rechtstheoretische Schule: Hans Kelsen, Adolf Merkl, Alfred Verdross*, vol. 2 (Vienna: Europa Verlag, 1968) 1625, at 1652. (My translation.)

natural law project which seeks to give an account of the authority of the state in terms of a social contract between free and equal individuals.

The first, a mark of Kelsen's legal theory, is that law must be understood as a matter of authority, not sheer coercive power. Hence, philosophy of law must seek to explain how might is transformed into right through its mediation by law. The second is also a mark of his theory: an understanding of the authority of law presupposes the unity of the legal order and the idea of the fundamental norm which gives it this unity. Only the third insight surprises: Kelsen's acknowledgement that the first two bring his legal positivist theory of law close to natural law. Moreover, he went on to say that the idea of an original contract is more or less synonymous with 'the concept of a *foundational law* or of *fundamental law*, the so-called *lex fundamentalis*' which 'plays a most significant role in the theory of natural law' and which he said is given 'almost pure expression in the legal theoretical line of thought of the basic norm or the constitution in the legal logical sense'.[41] Kelsen was adamant, however, that there is no more than an affinity between the third insight and the others. He asserted that the idea of the social contract is a 'primitive' version of the hypothesis of the basic norm and should be in any case rejected because it requires supposing that there was an actual original act of consent on the part of those subject to the law, even if the political regime is autocratic.[42]

We will see, however, that if one accepts the first two insights, the rapprochement with natural law and the social contract idea in the third cannot so easily be rejected. One can, then, appreciate how legal positivist philosophies of law, including Hart's version, rest on a robust version of what I called in the Introduction a 'constitutionalist idea', the idea of an ongoing practice which constitutes legitimate authority of the sort early modern social theorists set out in versions of the social contract. At least, they so rest as soon as legal positivists embark on explaining law as a matter of authority. Such an explanation requires taking into account the internal point of view of those subject to law since a legal order is qualitatively different from the order of coercion which Hart called a 'gunman situation writ large'.[43] As a result, we can also recast the debate between legal positivists and natural lawyers about the nature of law and whether there is a necessary connection between law and morality as a

[41] Ibid, 1652–3.
[42] Ibid, 1652–4. (My translation.)
[43] Hart, 'Positivism and the Separation of Law and Morals', 59.

more productive debate about constitutionalism, about, that is, the implications of understanding legal order in terms of a constitutionalist idea.[44] And that recasting gives legal philosophy a new role in taking forward debates in constitutional theory.

I must acknowledge that my interpretation of Kelsen is unorthodox. For the most part he supplied the basis of what a leading Kelsen scholar calls a 'weak reading' of authority according to which, as in Hart, law's claim to authority seems mainly addressed to legal officials and not to legal subjects, since for Kelsen law's authority is a matter of giving the officials permission to apply sanctions to subjects when they fail to comply with the law.[45] Indeed, the element of sanctions in Kelsen's theory led Hart to charge him with adherence to a command theory of law which reduces law ultimately to coercion.[46] But, as we have seen, Hart also cannot escape the charge, this time put by Raz, that his own theory of authority is ultimately a sanction-based one because it relies on the informal sanction of criticism officials face when they deviate from the accepted practice of applying secondary rules, albeit not the sanctions which apply to subjects for non-compliance with primary rules.[47]

Raz's charge is reinforced when we recall that Hart said of the rules of change that they constitute the legislature as a body with the power to do certain things, just as the rules of contract law make it possible 'to create structures of rights and duties for the conduct of life within the *coercive* framework of the law'.[48] The problem is not only that Hart's account of the way in which the fact of official practice constitutes authority fails to escape his own charge of conceiving of law as the gunman situation writ large. In addition, the very thought that facts of social practice by themselves constitute authority attracted rather devastating criticism from Dworkin, who in an early analysis of Hart's idea of the rule of recognition showed that one cannot read duty off the fact of merely convergent behaviour.[49]

44 For a different but illuminating reading of Hart's book as an exercise in public law theory, see Peter Cane, 'Public Law in *The Concept of Law*' (2013) 33 *Oxford Journal of Legal Studies* 649.

45 For detailed discussion, see Stanley L Paulson, 'The Weak Reading of Authority in Hans Kelsen's Pure Theory of Law' (2000) 19 *Law and Philosophy* 131.

46 Hart, *The Concept of Law*, chapter 3, 'The Variety of Laws'.

47 Raz, 'HLA Hart (1907–1992)', 149.

48 Hart, *The Concept of Law*, 27–8. My emphasis.

49 Ronald Dworkin, 'Model of Rules II', in Dworkin, *Taking Rights Seriously* (London: Duckworth, 1981, 3rd impression) 46, at 49–50.

On one interpretation, this criticism of Hart's account of legal authority goes in the direction of asserting that law matters, perhaps even exists in the sense of providing authoritative legal reasons, when and only when it transmits moral reasons to us, as judged by moral theory. In short, we are back with the moral realist position I outlined at the end of Chapter 1 which says that there is no independent realm of legal duties, thus eliminating from our inquiry the thought that there is a distinctive domain of legal normativity.[50] If this suggestion were right, Austin would be correct to say that both international law and constitutional law were nothing more than morality, though he should have gone further and said that there is no more to law in general than what morality already requires.

So much seems also to be the upshot of Raz's critique of Hart, which resonated unusually with Dworkin's. In Raz's argument for bringing the legal man into legal positivism, he emphasized that part of the reason that Hart put himself in the predicament of not being able to explain the normative force of legal reasons is that, as Kelsen argued, 'judicial social practices do not confer binding force on the ultimate legal rules'.[51] Put differently, Hart's claim that it 'seems needless reduplication to suggest that there is a further rule to the effect that the constitution . . . is to be obeyed' is wrong. Even if it seems 'mystifying to speak of a rule that this rule be obeyed',[52] this is a mystery legal philosophy must attempt to solve if it is to hold on to the distinction between might and right, which Kelsen at least attempted to do.

This attempt requires the 'strong reading' of Kelsen's theory of authority in which the legal subject is front and centre in the authority relationship. Support for the strong reading is to be found in Kelsen's treatments of norm conflicts, and is given expression in the kinds of statements Raz adduces as evidence for his claim that the legal subject for Kelsen is the 'legal man'. For example, Kelsen argued that 'an individual who regards law as a system of valid norms has to disregard morals as such a

[50] Indeed, one of these legal theorists relies on this critique in asserting that Dworkin early on saw the light of a one-system theory which says that legal obligations are genuine obligations only when certified as such by independently correct morality, although in later work he went back to taking law too seriously: Scott Hershovitz, 'The End of Jurisprudence' (2015) 124 *Yale Law Journal* 1160, at 1196–7.

[51] Joseph Raz, 'The Purity of the Pure Theory', in Stanley L Paulson and Bonnie Litschewski Paulson, eds, *Normativity and Norms: Critical Perspectives on Kelsenian Themes* (Oxford: Oxford University Press, 2007) 237, at 252.

[52] Hart, *The Concept of Law*, 293.

system ... no viewpoint exists from which both morals and law may simultaneously be regarded as valid normative orders. No one can serve two masters.'[53]

I have already indicated that this argument troubled Hart, who criticized Kelsen in particular for his monistic view of the relationship between law and morality.[54] In response to the claim that it is not possible to serve two masters when it comes to law and morality,[55] Hart asserted that while this point addresses the situation of conflict in which individuals are subject to duties by two norms they accept as valid, it does not address the situation of individuals who wish to make a moral criticism of the law for, say, requiring military service, even though they themselves are not liable for such service.[56] He found 'alarming' that Kelsen's argument 'excludes the possibility of a moral criticism of law'.[57]

Hart's discussion omitted two significant details. First, Kelsen's claim about the law–morality relationship is invoked in support of his argument against dualism when it comes to the national law–international law relationship; second, he ended his discussion of the latter by saying that it 'is by juristic interpretation that the legal material is transformed into a legal system'.[58] I deal with the first in Chapter 4 and here explore the significance of Kelsen's emphasis on the role of juristic interpretation in making an order legal.

Like Hart, Kelsen did not offer a theory of adjudication since such a theory is, he thought, a political theory beyond the scope of legal science. He also emphasized that at each of the levels of legal activity below the level of legislation there is an irreducible moment of judicial or official creativity. But unlike Hart and his followers, Kelsen did not think that the moments of creativity fill in the gaps in the law which result when the positive law does not dictate an answer.[59] In this respect, Kelsen's legal theory is closer to Dworkin's than it is to the legal positivism of Hart and his followers as, on his view, a legal order provides seamlessly for an

53 Hans Kelsen, *Pure Theory of Law* (Cambridge, MA: Harvard University Press, 1945, Max Knight, trans.), 329.

54 HLA Hart, 'Kelsen Visited', in Hart, *Essays in Jurisprudence and Philosophy* 286, at 302–3.

55 Hart refers to Hans Kelsen, *General Theory of Law and State* (Cambridge, MA: Harvard University Press, 1945, Anders Wedberg, trans.), 373–5, 408–10.

56 Hart, 'Kelsen Visited', 302–3.

57 Ibid, 302.

58 Kelsen, *General Theory of Law and State*, 375. The discussion of national and international law is at 373.

59 Kelsen, *Pure Theory of Law*, 245–50.

authorized official to solve by a legal procedure any problem raised within the legal order.[60] Indeed, his legal theory goes further since it rejects Dworkin's distinction between legislation (the instrument of policy and the province of the legislature) and adjudication (the realm of principle and the province of the judiciary).[61] For Kelsen, the moment of creativity in legislation is much more heightened than in adjudication, but it is quantitatively rather than qualitatively different. Legislation is a legally authorized act which must respect the constitutional norms governing its production.[62]

In setting out this position, Kelsen was primarily concerned with explaining legal order from the internal point of view of one who accepts that the norms of that order are binding, not because of any threat of force but because they are part of an authoritative order. For if one adopts the internal point of view, one assumes that the answer to any legal question will be produced by legal procedures and will make sense of one's subjection to the substantive and formal norms of the legal order by displaying them as a unity. One assumes, in other words, that a principle of legality governs, and this assumption shows why Hart was wrong to claim that Kelsen's theory 'has a juristic Midas touch, which transmutes all questions about laws and their relationship into questions of the content of law or questions concerning what laws say; but the touch is perverse, for not all questions are of that kind'.[63] Rather, Kelsen was mostly concerned to answer questions about what makes an order legal: a polity governed in accordance with the rule of law in that law regulates its own production and all legal problems are solved in a dynamic law-governed process.

Moreover, Kelsen at times accepted, in line with his remarks about the basic norm and the social contract, that the assumption of the unity of legal order introduced a natural law element to his legal theory which

[60] For illuminating discussion of the similarities between Kelsen and Dworkin, see Tony Honoré, 'The Basic Norm of a Society', in Honoré, *Making Law Bind: Essays Legal and Philosophical* (Oxford: Clarendon Press, 2002) 89, at 106–14. Honoré argued that Kelsen's basic norm is best understood not as a norm ultimately about the constitution, but as a social norm of cooperation and as such should, where appropriate, influence judges in their decision of hard cases.

[61] Dworkin, 'The Model of Rules I', in Dworkin, *Taking Rights Seriously* 14.

[62] See Hans Kelsen, 'The Nature and Development of Constitutional Adjudication' (Lars Vinx, trans.), in Vinx, ed., *The Guardian of the Constitution: Hans Kelsen and Carl Schmitt on the Limits of Constitutional Law* (Cambridge: Cambridge University Press, 2015) 22, at 48–9.

[63] Hart, 'Kelsen Visited', 321.

transcended the limits of a 'strict positivism'.[64] He recognized that the same point had to apply to the assumption when made about the international legal order. 'In this sense', he said, 'there is absolutely no contradiction between natural law and positive law', although he also suggested that his theory's positivistic character was preserved because the content of the legal order would be filled by legislation. Hence, he thought his thesis that law can have any content could remain intact.[65] But that thesis must be qualified for reasons quite similar to the qualification we saw Hart inject into his own version of legal positivism in Chapter 1 when he found himself constrained to deny that law can have any old content.[66] Moreover, the affinity Kelsen perceived between the idea of a social contract and the basic norm goes deeper than he was willing to recognize, as he himself indicated when he said that the postulate of unity is not merely formal, since it is also a postulate of peace.[67]

Kelsen's argument for the postulate of peace is that every legal order must be effective to some degree before it can be said to be valid. If there were total compliance with its norms, it would be superfluous; too little compliance and it would not exist as a legal order. To be effective somewhere in between these two points, Kelsen asserted, it must represent a 'compromise' between 'conflicting interest groups in their struggle … to determine the content of the social order' and so it must be the case that none of these groups is 'wholly satisfied or dissatisfied'.[68] That is what makes a legal order an order of peace.[69]

Now on one view of such an order, peace is just the absence of conflict. On this view, and in line with the weak reading of authority, Kelsen's

[64] Hans Kelsen, 'Natural Law Doctrine and Legal Positivism', in Kelsen, *General Theory of Law and State*, 389, at 437. See Jochen von Bernstoff, *The Public International Law Theory of Hans Kelsen: Believing in Universal Law* (Cambridge: Cambridge University Press, 2010, Thomas Dunlap, trans.), 116 and Mathijs Notermans, 'Social Peace as *Conditio Tacita* for the Validity of the Positive Legal Order' (2015) 34 *Law and Philosophy* 201, at 213–14.

[65] Kelsen, *Das Problem der Souveränität und die Theorie des Völkerrechts: Beitrag zu Einer Reinen Rechtslehre* (Aalen: Scientia Verlag, 1981), 252. (My translation.)

[66] Hart, *The Concept of Law*, 199.

[67] For the most striking formulation see Hans Kelsen, *Law and Peace in International Relations: The Oliver Wendell Holmes Lectures, 1940–41* (Cambridge, MA: Harvard University Press, 1948), 1.

[68] Kelsen, 'Natural Law Doctrine and Legal Positivism', 438–9.

[69] See further Notermans, 'Social Peace as *Conditio Tacita* for the Validity of the Positive Legal Order', 213–14.

claim that a legal order is necessarily an order of peace could be said to be the result of the fact that an effective legal order is one in which the state's claim to a monopoly on coercion holds. But Kelsen had, like Hobbes, something else in mind in his reflection on a legal order as an order of peace, which has to do with the fact that the state's monopoly on coercion is necessary but not sufficient for an effective legal order to exist.[70] It is necessary because in every legal order there will be individuals who will conform to law only when they fear being sanctioned if they do not. But it is not sufficient. Long-term stability depends on most of those subject to the law being able to understand that monopoly as legitimate, which requires understanding their subjection as serving their interests, even when they disapprove of the content of some or many laws.

Put differently, the compromise between conflicting interest groups will not be achieved if the content of the law as determined by the relevant officials regularly relegates the individuals on the losing side of the conflict to second-class status. Such individuals will not be able to accept the compromise as a sufficient basis to make sense of their legal order as an order of legal right or authority, rather than one of unmediated coercive power. The kind of compromise which sustains a legal order is not a compromise on any terms whatsoever, one which permits the law to have any content. It is a compromise which maintains the individuals who are affected by the law in their status of equality before the law.[71]

[70] See Norberto Bobbio's insightful observations in Bobbio and Danilo Zolo, 'Hans Kelsen, the Theory of Law and the International Legal System: A Talk' (1998) 9 *European Journal of International Law* 355, at 358–9.

[71] Kelsen did say that '[o]nly one group may be interested in "peace," namely, the one whose interests are better preserved by this order than those of other groups. These other groups may also fail to violate the order. They may maintain the state of peace not because they consider it just, but because, in view of their own weakness, they must be satisfied with the minimum of protection which this order affords to their interests': 'Natural Law Doctrine and Legal Positivism', 441. But while his point is that one should not make too much of the fact that a legal order is an order of peace, if it is a *legal* order it will be maintained in part by the weaker group on the basis that it does protect their interests, albeit minimally. See further, Hans Kelsen, 'The Law as a Specific Technique', in Kelsen, *What Is Justice? Justice, Law and Politics in the Mirror of Science* (Berkeley: University of California Press, 1957) 231, at 238: 'The peace of the law is not a condition of absolute absence of force, a state of anarchy; it is a condition of a force monopoly of the community. . . . A community, in the long run, is possible only if each individual respects certain interests – life, health, freedom, and property of everyone else – that is to say, if each refrains from forcibly interfering in the sphere of interest of the other.' See also

As we have seen, Hart assumed that in a primitive society the internal point of view must be shared by the individuals of that society. They must accept the authority of the primary rules of their society. In contrast, once legal order with its secondary rules has emerged, only the officials need have that attitude of acceptance and the acceptance need not extend beyond the secondary rules. However, on my argument, the combination of Hart's minimum content of natural law with his account of the judicial virtues shows both that the acceptance of legal subjects is an essential component of legal order and that acceptance, whether of officials or of subjects, extends to the primary rules.

The very fact that law made at the higher levels of the legal hierarchy must be progressively concretized as it journeys down to the moment of actual application to a particular legal subject entails that officials must take the subject's perspective into account if they are to be faithful to their role. Moreover, in taking this perspective into account, acceptance is generated on condition that the officials observe their role morality in displaying the virtues on Hart's list: 'impartiality and neutrality in surveying the alternatives; consideration for the interest of all who will be affected; and a concern to deploy some acceptable principle as a reasoned basis for decision'.[72] Adapting Hart's formulation, one might say that the voluntary relationship constituting authority is not one which can be confined to the officials of the legal order since it requires the acceptance of the law by those to whom the law is applied – the legal subjects. Thus, among the essential building blocks of legal order is the perspective of the individual legal subject, one which Hart almost always portrayed as a perspective entirely external to law and deployed as a resource to criticize the settled content of the positive law.

When conceived as a perspective internal to law, it becomes explicit when the order of the modern legal state institutionalizes mechanisms of review of and appeal against the interpretations of the law adopted as the basis for official implementation of the law. But even in the absence of such mechanisms, officials must take into account this perspective because their own internal point of view is incomplete without it.

Notermans, 'Social Peace as *Conditio Tacita* for the Validity of the Positive Legal Order', 203, note 9: 'for Kelsen the peace of the law is not an "anarchical" order of absolute absence of force, nor a "utopian" state completely free from violence or conflict between individuals or groups; the legal order is rather a socially approved (be it "democratically" or "autocratically") state of compromise, in which the use of force is monopolized just to prevent, reduce and counteract individual violence and social conflict'.

[72] Hart, *The Concept of Law*, 205.

As Raz argues, officials cannot make the distinction between might and right without assuming that it holds for legal subjects. More precisely, their internal point of view is dependent on whether, in applying the law to legal subjects, they apply it by right *from the perspective of those subjects.*

Of course, if no mechanisms of review or appeal are available to subjects, there is no way within the legal order for testing the claim that the law is so applied, other than by observing that subjects have what Austin called the habit of obedience.[73] And just as the internal point of view is incomplete without the legal subject's perspective, so too the order of the modern legal state is incomplete without such mechanisms, as it is incomplete without mechanisms of enforcement for use against those who treat the legal order, not from the internal point of view but as a system of unmediated coercion – as a gunman situation writ large. It is incomplete in the first respect because it does not permit the vindication of the internal point of view. It is incomplete in the second respect because it fails to guarantee to those who take the internal point of view that their practice will not be undermined by those who regard the law as nothing more than commands backed by threats.

I want thus to suggest that the inclusion of this perspective in even its most austere form is the beginning of constitutionalism, of the discipline exerted by both formal and substantive legal principles on the exercise of state power. That inclusion is part of an attempt to understand legal order from the position of legal subjects who wish to make sense of the norms of their order as binding as well as valid, as norms they obey because they accept the norm's authority, not because they fear the sanctions following non-compliance. Their perspective is an essential component of what we saw Hart called the 'complex congruent practice' of acceptance constitutive of the authority of a legal order.

However, if the legal subject is the 'legal man' who adopts 'the law as his personal morality, and as exhausting all the norms he accepts as just', as Raz describes him, the introduction of this perspective into an account of legal order will seem to presuppose exactly Kelsen's monism about law and morality which Hart found so 'alarming', and which led him to express disquiet about the moral element in both Dworkin's and Raz's arguments.[74] But, on closer inspection, Raz's understanding of the legal

[73] See Austin, *Lectures on Jurisprudence*, vol. 1, Lecture VI. In general, Austin's analysis of this idea is far more sophisticated than Hart's cursory treatments of Austin's theory suggest.

[74] Hart, *Essays on Bentham*, 153–61.

man should not perhaps be so much a cause for alarm as for rejection of Raz's account of the legal subject.

As JW Harris pointed out, the analogy Raz draws between the legal man and the situation of a non-believer in a religion who adopts the point of view of a believer in order to explain the believer's religion to him is unconvincing. With the non-believer,

> there is a real point of view which he can adopt, whereas the 'legal man' does not exist. . . . [He] has, by assumption, no extra-legal moral system on which he bases the normativity of the law; for if he did there could be no guarantee that uniform moral force would be transmitted to every conceivable legal enactment. . . . So far as *substantive moral grounding* is concerned, the hypothetical 'legal man' stands in the air.[75]

Harris's analysis of what he calls Kelsen's 'pallid normativity' points us towards a more robust and helpful understanding of Kelsen's view of legal authority. Kelsen was, of course, fully aware that, as Hart put it in his criticism of Kelsen's rejection of dualism when it comes to the law–morality relationship: 'No human being is *just* a lawyer or *just* a moralist. Some at least think about both moral and legal norms and consider their meaning as norms and find that they conflict.'[76] Indeed, Kelsen could have retorted that this is not his but Hart's problem. Hart cannot explain why this individual should experience any normative conflict in the first place, given his general view that legal norms do not of themselves have any morally binding force.[77]

In contrast, the question for Kelsen is precisely how to make sense of legal order from the perspective of individuals faced with a conflict between their 'personal morality' – the moral norms they themselves hold dear – and the norms of their legal order, which they also accept as valid. Moreover, in the perspective of a legal theory which aims to

[75] James W Harris, 'Kelsen's Pallid Normativity' (1996) 9 *Ratio Juris* 94, at 112–13. My emphasis.

[76] Hart, 'Kelsen Visited', 306. His emphasis.

[77] As Lon Fuller pointed out many years before in a different context – his debate with Hart about the Grudge Informer Case: 'I hope I am not being unjust to Professor Hart when I say that I can find no way of describing the dilemma as he sees it but to use some such words as the following: On the one hand, we have an amoral datum called law, which has the peculiar quality of creating a moral duty to obey it. On the other hand, we have a moral duty to do what we think is right and decent. When we are confronted by a statute we believe to be thoroughly evil, we have to choose between those two duties'; Lon L Fuller, 'Positivism and Fidelity to Law: A Reply to Professor Hart' (1958) 71 *Harvard Law Review* 630, 656. See my Chapter 1 for extensive discussion of this issue.

understand law's authority, such individuals are the legal subject, and so do not stand on air, faced with a naked conflict between the norms of two valid orders. Rather, they are Hobbes's Just Men. They stand on the ground of someone already subject to the law – to the public order of law in which they happen to find themselves. They must then attempt to make sense of the presumption that they should subject themselves to the norms of that legal order, even when these conflict with their personal morality.

This is a kind of relativism.[78] Such legal subjects accept that the modern legal order is legitimate even when some or many of its norms do not correspond with their sense of justice, and so they should regard particular laws as binding on them, even when they do not endorse the content of the rules. They thus in a sense relativize their convictions in relation to both the convictions of their fellow subjects and the public judgments established as mandatory by the law. The idea here has something in common with Kelsen's claim that law can have any content as well as with Hart's account of the two features of the reasons law provides to its subjects – authoritative legal reasons.[79]

As we saw in Chapter 2, the first feature is that such reasons are 'peremptory' – a commander 'characteristically intends his hearer to take the commander's will instead of his own as a guide to action and so to take it in place of any deliberation or reasoning of his own'.[80] The second feature is that such reasons are 'content-independent' – they are 'intended to function as a reason independently of the nature or character of the actions to be done'.[81] The idea differs, however, from Hart's account in respect of a feature which for Hart, and Raz following him, is implicit in the second feature. They suppose that in order to function as a content-independent reason, the content of the law must be determinable as a matter of fact, that is, 'without using moral arguments'.[82] But as I argued in Chapter 2 on the basis of Hobbes's legal theory, for an authoritative legal reason to function as a content-independent reason its content must be both determinable and determined in such a way that

[78] See Joseph Raz, 'Legitimate Authority', in Raz, *The Authority of Law* 3, at 10–11, where, in order to reject the idea of 'relativized authority', he sketches a way of referring to 'what those people or societies accept or propose as legitimate authority without endorsing those views'.

[79] Hart, *Essays on Bentham*, 252–3.

[80] Ibid.

[81] Ibid, 254.

[82] Raz, 'Legal Positivism and the Sources of Law', in Raz, *The Authority of Law* 37, at 47–8.

legal subjects can make sense of their subjection to it, which requires that it is interpretable as consistent with fundamental principles of legality.[83]

The clue which provides the start to the solution to the puzzle of legal authority lies in Kelsen's political theory. Kelsen's first short but rich work on the nature of democracy reveals that the ground of the legal subject is very particular. It is the ground of individuals who, however sure they are of their moral convictions, know that in order to live on peaceful terms with others who are equally sure but of very different convictions, they must find with those others some common standards for public life despite their disagreements. That gives such individuals reason to accept that it is worth living under the political order of democracy in the knowledge that there is no guarantee that the content of individual enacted laws will correspond with their moral convictions.[84]

Kelsen argued further that a properly functioning democracy will govern in accordance with a 'principle of legality'. All political decisions backed by the state's monopoly on legitimate coercion will be put into legal form, and so will enter as legal norms into the structured hierarchy of the legal order.[85] As democratically produced norms, they carry with them whatever legitimacy accrues to norms merely because the majority has decided in their favour as a result of a political contest in which it prevailed over the opposition of what turned out to be the minority. Such legitimacy can be preserved only so long as the decision respects the conditions whereby the minority is itself preserved, so that not only is it capable of opposition in some future contest but also has the prospect of prevailing.[86]

Democratic or political legitimacy is not, however, the only legitimacy these norms have. They also accrue legal legitimacy, gained through the transformation of might into legal right which accompanies their conversion from political into legal norms. Successfully converted norms are norms capable of being concretized by legal officials in ways which display the norms' identity with the legal order understood as a

[83] Fuller pointed out against legal positivism that a 'statute [should be] ... seen, not as a message addressed into a void, but as a message whose meaning is dependent upon the interpretation its addressee, as a reasonable and sensible man, would put on it'; Lon L Fuller, 'The Justification of Legal Decisions' (1972) 7 *Archiv für Rechts- und Sozialphilosophie* (Beiheft Neue Folge) 77, at 78.

[84] Hans Kelsen, *The Essence and Value of Democracy* (Plymouth: Rowman and Littlefield, 2013, Nadia Urbinati and Carlo Invernizzi Accetti, eds, Brian Graf, trans.), 103–5.

[85] Ibid, chapter 7, 'Administration'.

[86] Ibid, 103.

meaningful whole. The basic norm must be presupposed in order to make sense of this idea.

This is not a mere logical requirement, necessary to make conceptual sense of the fact that there is a binding set of norms. It is also deeply pragmatic in nature. It is an achievement of constructive juristic activity which will depend on whether the content of particular norms can be interpreted so as to display this identity. It is best described as a regulative assumption – an assumption we need to make before we can make sense of our practice, but also one we must maintain by ensuring our practice conforms with it.

The more the legal order is not an order of peace in which subjects can recognize that the law protects their interests, the harder it will be to achieve this goal, and the more precarious the order will become. This factor sets both a sociological and a normative outer limit on legal order. The limit does not dictate what content the order should have. Rather, as we saw in Chapter 2 with Hobbes, it marks not very precisely a border crossed when a law or set of laws puts a class of legal subjects beyond the legal pale. The limit is thus more negative than positive in nature, suggesting what kinds of laws will subvert the basis of legal order. It is not, however, wholly negative because of the combination of two factors. The first factor is more formal, pertaining to the duties of officials in and the institutional make-up of any legal order, and the second more substantive, pertaining to the fund of values necessary for such an order to exist.

Officials who exhibit the kinds of virtues on Hart's list of judicial virtues, who adopt what Fuller called an 'ideal of fidelity to law',[87] have a duty to ensure that a law which might on a literal interpretation breach this limit is interpreted and applied in a way preserving to the greatest extent possible the subject status of those affected by the law. If officials are unable to come up with such an interpretation, the law will be suspect as law no matter how well it complies with the formal criteria of validity in that legal order. The limit does not dictate the institutional make-up of the legal order. But it does provide a kind of internal imperative to reform legal order in such a way as to make it better able to live up to the aspiration of legality; to deal, for example, with the category of laws which are legally suspect despite their apparent formal validity. Put differently, to the extent that a legal order lacks the institutions necessary

[87] Fuller, 'Positivism and Fidelity to Law'.

to implement, interpret and enforce the law, it will be defective legally speaking. From the perspective of legal subjects, there is a dynamic inherent to legal order which requires that they can both raise and get an adequate answer to questions of the form 'But, how can that be law for me?'

But just as there is an institutional transformation in the transition from what Hart called a primitive order to a complex legal order, so too there is a transformation in the internal point of view. Raz's description of the legal man applies only to the point of view of the individual of what they thought of as a 'primitive' society. As Hart and Kelsen both pointed out, in such an order the individual regards the public norms as directly binding in that there is a complete coincidence between the individual's sense of justice and these norms. More precisely, individuals have no sense of justice apart from the content of these public norms and so for them the issue of the legitimacy of the law does not arise. Indeed, for Hart it seems at times that there is no law present – only generally accepted public norms.[88]

The issue of the legitimacy of law can arise, therefore, only in a context in which at any time at least some individuals will find themselves subject to public mandatory norms the content of which they find unjust. Such subjection involves what Kelsen in his work on democracy called the 'torment of heteronomy':[89] the pain which accompanies conceiving of oneself as an autonomous individual who can and should decide for oneself how best morally speaking to live, but who accepts there is reason to abide by mandatory public norms one would not oneself choose if one had the power to do so and which may even strike one as unjust.

88 See, for example, Kelsen, 'Natural Law Doctrine and Legal Positivism', 422–3; Hart, *The Concept of Law*, 91–2. Note that Hart's and Kelsen's views about the transition from primitive to full-fledged legal orders are very different. Kelsen thought that primitive legal systems are systems and have basic norms, but lack centralized organs of application and enforcement. Hart seemed to argue that what is lacking in the regime composed exclusively of primary rules is not just his secondary rules but law itself; hence, it would be a misnomer to call someone a 'legal man' in a primitive order. Hart's view is forced on him because there cannot be legal duty in his theory in the absence of a rule of recognition, whereas for Kelsen the kind of institution Hart had in mind is important to help ensure that the basic norm will be vindicated, but not necessary for it. See my Chapter 4.

89 Kelsen, *The Essence and Value of Democracy*, 27, where the translator gives 'agony of heteronomy' as the translation. For a very careful account of how Kelsen's legal subject differs from Hart's and Raz's conception, see Vinx, *Hans Kelsen's Pure Theory of Law*, especially 47–77.

Democracy can alleviate the torment and help to explain why subjects should have this stance of acceptance because it preserves for them the equal chance of participating in making such norms. There is both a formal and a substantive aspect to such preservation. The formal aspect is that the political process is as open to their participation as it is to that of everyone else in the political community. The substantive aspect is that the maintenance of this openness recognizes their status as free and equal subjects.

But, as I have already indicated, that the norms decided on in the political process must enter into the legal order before they can be concretized, applied and enforced also plays an alleviatory role with equivalent formal and substantive aspects. Here the formal aspect pertains in part to the fact that an answer to the question 'But, how can that be law for me?' is one produced in accordance with legal procedures. It also pertains to both the formal and substantive criteria which must be met for a public policy to be converted into law.

The formal dimension is taken for granted by legal theorists, for example, the requirement that laws be general.[90] Substantively, the content of the norm must be interpretable as consistent with the content of other relevant substantive norms of the legal order. And since that content will be an order of peace – one reflective of a compromise of interests between the different social groups subject to law – if any particular norm is to support rather than undermine the postulate of unity, it must be interpretable as maintaining the individuals' subject status. Just as the democratic political order must maintain the political subject status of those who end up forming the opposition to a particular law, so the particular laws of a legal order must maintain the legal subject status of the individuals in the jural community.

The distinction between these two statuses should not be exaggerated. The legal subject status is not apolitical. The very conception of the individual as a legal subject is political in that it is formulated to explain why it might be rational for individuals to subject themselves to the public norms established in a legal order. As such, it is intrinsically connected to the status of the political subject of a democracy. This is the case even when one notes that some proponents of social contract

[90] These criteria get their most elaborate formulation in the work of Lon L Fuller, *The Morality of Law* (New Haven: Yale University Press, 1969, revised ed.), chapter 2. I discuss different conceptions of formalism in public law in 'Process and Substance as Aspects of the Public Law Form' (2015) 74 *Cambridge Law Journal* 284.

theory, prominently Hobbes, thought that democracy is only one of the forms of government capable of maintaining a stable political order. For while one can try to imagine an autocratic political order in which the leader governs in accordance with the rule of law, it is unclear why the leader would accept this kind of constraint, and even whether it is really accurate to call this political order autocratic.[91] Rulers' submission to this kind of constraint creates a tension within the autocratic system since they thereby accept that all their political judgments must be put into proper legal form and so be interpretable as answering the subject's question 'But, how can that be law for me?' They are no longer a tyrant or autocrat, a natural person with more power than anyone else who uses the form of law when and only when it is convenient to exercise political judgment that way. Rather, as we saw in Chapter 2, they are an artificial person, constituted by law, and relate to their subjects through law and so in a way which makes their judgments responsive to their subjects. One might say that constitutionalism is set in motion.

If the motion continues, the direction is democracy because of the combination of two ideas. The acceptance by legal subjects is constitutive of the authority of the legal order and the judgments made by public officials must seek to answer the subject's question 'But, how can that be law for me?' Any form of undemocratic political rule is in tension with this combination, which is why early modern writers, notably Hobbes, while concerned about the dangers they saw in democratic rule, could find only pragmatic arguments tied to their contexts to support the claim that political power is best concentrated in the hands of a monarch. The same reason explains why they at the same time insisted that the monarch enjoyed something like democratic legitimacy because he got his

[91] See John Finnis, *Natural Law and Natural Rights* (Oxford: Clarendon Press, 1980), 273: a 'tyranny devoted to pernicious ends has no self-sufficient *reason* to submit itself to the discipline of operating consistently through the demanding processes of the rule of law, granted that the rational point of such self-discipline is the very value of reciprocity, fairness, and respect for persons which the tyrant, *ex hypothesi*, holds in contempt'. His emphasis. As Finnis points out, Hans Kelsen claimed in his *Allgemeine Staatslehre* (Berlin: Springer, 1925), 335 that natural law was both 'naïve' and 'arrogant' in its denial of the fully legal character of despotism. Finnis also notes that this passage is omitted from the English translation. See Finnis, *Natural Law and Natural Rights*, 25, note 4. He does not mention that Kelsen, while he continued by saying that this can be the case 'even when legal subjects are fully enslaved, and have no subjective rights', also observed that this kind of situation is hard to find in actual legal orders. (Kelsen, *Allgemeine Staatslehre*, 335, my translation.) I explore this issue in Chapter 5.

authority from a social contract between the individuals who were transformed by it into subjects.[92]

But the other direction is always a practical possibility. Even when a democratic order is in place, there is no guarantee that the subject's legal status will be maintained. One way to try to secure such maintenance is to entrench a bill of rights – both political and individual – and give to a formally independent judiciary the authority to invalidate laws which violate the rights. In other words, one puts in place the kind of constitutional order which is nearly always presupposed in discussions of constitutionalism. Clearly, no guarantee comes with even this kind of constitutional dispensation.[93] Nor is it at all obvious that legal orders in which there is parliamentary supremacy do a worse constitutional job of maintaining these statuses. For this reason, legal theory can be agnostic on the question whether constitutional judicial review of the validity of statutes is necessary for maintaining the authority of legal order. But it is significant, as I discuss further in Section 3.5, that legal theorists generally agree about the following. In every national legal order, there should be a body of officials – a judiciary – independent of those who implement and enforce the law, who have the role of ensuring that the officials who implement and enforce the law act within the limits of the law. Moreover, such limits are understood as both formal and substantive.[94]

Such agreement strongly supports a claim that this kind of review authority is a necessary condition for the maintenance of legal authority within the modern legal state.[95] It is also usually taken as a necessary

[92] See Kinch Hoekstra, 'Early Modern Absolutism and Constitutionalism' (2013) 34 *Cardozo Law Review* 1079; Luc Foisneau, 'Sovereignty and Reason of State: Bodin, Botero, Richelieu and Hobbes', in Howell A Lloyd, ed., *The Reception of Bodin* (Leiden: Brill, 2013) 323; Daniel Lee, *Popular Sovereignty in Early Modern Constitutional Thought* (Oxford: Oxford University Press, 2016); Benjamin Straumann, *Crisis and Constitutionalism: Roman Political Thought from the Fall of the Republic to the Age of Revolution* (Oxford: Oxford University Press, 2016).

[93] See, notably, Wojciech Sadurski, *Poland's Constitutional Breakdown* (Oxford: Oxford University Press, 2019).

[94] Indeed, in Kelsen's view, the first step from a primitive order to a more complex, indeed properly functioning legal order, takes place with the establishment of courts, and so he emphasized the 'surprising fact that the centralization of the law-applying function – that is, the establishment of courts – precedes the centralization of the law-creating function – the establishment of legislative organs. Long before parliaments as legislative bodies came into existence, courts were established to apply the law to concrete cases'; Hans Kelsen, *Peace through Law* (Chapel Hill: University of California Press, 1944), 21.

[95] Hart's and Kelsen's disagreement, noted above, about whether a primitive order is a legal order will affect their views on whether this body is necessary for there to be legal order at

condition for the maintenance of the rule of law. For when a legal official makes a decision affecting the rights and interests of a subject, the subjects have no way of ensuring that the decision is according to law rather than personal whim unless they are able to get an answer from an official independent of the first to their question 'But, how can that be law for me?'

From a legal theory perspective, more important than the content of the actual debates about appropriate constitutional design is that the subject matter of these debates is about how to realize the project of constitutionalism set in motion by the very attempt to understand legal order as a matter of authority, which is to say from the point of view of the legal subject. As I have argued, this person is not Raz's airborne legal man. Rather, it is the legal subject – someone whose feet are planted firmly on the ground. I also suggested that this ground is very particular. One might say that it is political rather than moral ground so that the reasons that count in its space are more political than moral and that it is both sociological – based in acceptance in fact – and normative, a claim I elaborate in Section 3.3.

3.3 Acceptance, Legitimacy and the Social Contract

The claim that the ground is political more than moral so that the reasons which count in its space are more political than moral indicates an important but not hard and fast distinction. The Anglo-American debate in legal theory over the last fifty years or so has been shaped by a dualism about law and morality which assumes that the key issue for philosophy of law is whether a necessary connection can be demonstrated between the content of the positive law of any legal order and the personal morality of individuals. Left largely unaddressed within this debate are the questions 'Which individuals' personal morality is at stake?' and 'What amounts to such a morality?'

At times, legal positivists have supposed that the answers to such questions do not matter as the Separation Thesis holds for any set of values. But Hart usually assumed that the values are those of concerned liberal citizens, anxious to maintain a critical distance from the law so that they can bring to bear their moral judgment on the question of how

all. Hart's answer would be 'Yes' and Kelsen's 'No', which is why, as we will see in Chapter 4, Kelsen had no trouble accounting for public international law's status as law while Hart had considerable difficulty.

to react to the law, unclouded by natural law illusions of a necessary connection between law and morality.[96] Raz introduced a different dimension with his theory of authority, according to which a directive is authoritative only if it reflects the objective reasons which already apply to the subject. It can do so by solving coordination problems – which side of the road to drive on – or transmitting expert judgments, for example, environmental or public health regulations, or by reflecting the moral reasons already applicable to the subject which the authority figure is better at getting right than the subjects would be if left to their own devices. On this view, law is a transmission belt for objective reasons and its authority depends not on its being law but on (at least generally) transmitting right reason.

As we have seen, in Hart's legal theory, law has authority whether it is liberal in content or not, whereas for Raz the law merely claims authority, so that when it pronounces on moral matters it has authority only when its demands happen to coincide with the demands of liberal morality. Consequently, it is difficult to understand how Raz's position differs from the anarchist one which Hart saw as one of the two pitfalls inherent in natural law theories with their assertion of a necessary connection between law and morality.[97] Moreover, the non-cognitive alternative Hart offered, as we saw him acknowledge, is implausible since it makes the idea of right inherent in law's claim to authority vacuous. Since the individual should regard the law as creating obligations if and only if its content passes the test of moral evaluation, law as such does not give rise to obligations properly so-called. Much the same idea lies behind Raz's 'normal justification thesis' – that in moral matters a directive has authority when and only when it reflects the objective reasons already applicable to the subject of the directive.[98]

96 See Gerald J Postema, *Legal Philosophy in the Twentieth Century: The Common Law World* (Heidelberg: Springer Dordrecht, 2011), 339–40.

97 In retrospect, it is also difficult to understand why Raz thought he had managed to answer comprehensively the challenge posed by Robert Paul Wolff, *In Defense of Anarchism* (Berkeley: University of California Press, 1998). See, for example, Raz, 'Legitimate Authority', 11–10, 25–7. For it may turn out that Raz's cases of unproblematic legitimate authority, for example solving coordination problems and making judgments in certain complex technical areas, are not the issues which Wolff had in mind, and those cases where Raz thinks that there is unlikely to be legitimate authority – cases in which the state takes a stand on a moral issue, are precisely the ones which troubled Wolff.

98 Raz, 'Authority, Law, and Morality', 198.

Hart's and Raz's common theory of legal authority is, then, that it is de facto authority, based on the fact of official acceptance of a certain set of institutional arrangements for making, applying, interpreting and enforcing mandatory public norms. But, in line with the standard arguments that one cannot derive an 'ought' from an 'is', they conclude that law as such is not only morally but also 'normatively inert'.[99] Law becomes normatively active only when it has the content it should have according to liberal morality, in which case it is morality – not law – which is the activating agent. Both fear that if they were to concede any moral force to law as such, they would be forced to embrace the reactionary horn of the dilemma which Hart took to be the other pitfall of natural law theories. That fear then drives them in their different ways towards the anarchist position.[100]

Raz's position is more nuanced in that subjects who rightly accept law's authority do so not only because the law reflects reasons in any case applicable to them, but also because they know that those who make the law are generally better at making such judgments than they are themselves. The latter is the 'second-order' reason for not deciding for themselves on the content of certain 'first-order' reasons, those on which the law has pronounced.[101] The idea of a reason to submit oneself to reasons not of one's own determination brings Raz's subject of authority closer to Kelsen's legal subject.

But, on my argument in Section 3.2, Kelsen's legal subject contrasts with Raz's, because Kelsen has a political rather than moral conception of the legal subject. It includes subjects' personal morality, while explaining why they might find reason to subject themselves to laws which not only fail to reflect that morality but also should be rejected from the standpoint of liberal moral theory.[102] Subjects will have such reason when the constitutionally mandated, dynamic or constructive juristic activity which applies general norms to their concrete situation does so in a way which preserves their subject status.

[99] John Gardner's useful and telling phrase: Gardner, *Law as a Leap of Faith* (Oxford: Oxford University Press, 2012), 23.

[100] For a similar criticism, see Jacob Weinrib, *Dimensions of Dignity: The Theory and Practice of Modern Constitutional Law* (Cambridge: Cambridge University Press, 2016), 41–7. I differ from Weinrib in that, following Kelsen, I propose a political rather than a moral solution to the dilemma.

[101] See Joseph Raz, *Practical Reason and Norms* (Princeton: Princeton University Press, 1990), 39–40.

[102] See Chapter 6.

As we have seen, Hartian legal positivism consigns such activity to an extra-legal, political realm.[103] In so consigning it, this kind of legal positivism not only seems to evade the responsibility of offering a theory of the role of interpretation in constructing and maintaining legal order but also that of developing a theory of the role of constitutionalism in performing the same tasks. But, as I have tried to show, the evasion could not be total because Hart and his followers took it as incumbent on philosophy of law to offer an account of law's authority, one which does not reduce the explanation of law's bindingness to coercion. Hart's idea of the internal point of view and his short excursion into natural law in fact sow the seeds of constitutionalism and undermine the dualism of the Separation Thesis. If these seeds were permitted to sprout, Hartian legal positivism would have to move even further away from the command theory of law than Hart ever contemplated. However, I do not want to suggest that the terminus of the move would be either a full-blown liberal theory of how judges should decide 'hard cases' or the conventionalist or the fact-driven theory to which Dworkin claimed Hartian positivism is committed.[104] Indeed, the way in which Dworkin's challenge to Hartian legal positivism established the terrain for legal philosophical debate in English had unfortunate consequences for philosophy of law.

First, Kelsen, the most important figure in philosophy of law of the last century, was and remains largely marginalized. Second, the challenge led to a deadlock which, as I indicated in Chapter 1, some have tried to break by resurrecting versions of an Austinian, sanction-based theory of law.[105] But they do so at the cost that Hart had vividly pointed out in 1958: law is seen as the gunman situation writ large. Others have put forward a theory in which law matters only when, according to some full-blown independent moral theory, it makes a positive moral impact on its subjects.[106] Here the cost is that legal philosophy ceases to be interested in what is normatively distinctive about legal order.

My suggestion in this chapter is that a return to Kelsen could locate the debate on more productive terrain than that of theory of adjudication versus theory of law – the terrain of constitutionalism – and in this way

[103] Inclusive legal positivism sought to remedy this problem. See Appendix I.

[104] Ronald Dworkin, *Law's Empire* (London: Fontana, 1986).

[105] For example, Frederick Schauer, *The Force of Law* (Cambridge, MA: Harvard University Press, 2014).

[106] See Mark Greenberg, 'The Moral Impact Theory of Law' (2014) 123 *Yale Law Journal* 1289 and Hershovitz, 'The End of Jurisprudence'.

permit the arc of legality put in place by Hobbes to stretch to the twentieth and our century. On this terrain, one can properly address the topics of how law's de jure authority gets constituted by the acceptance in fact of those subject to it and how that acceptance in turn conditions the shape of the institutions of a legal order as well as the content of its laws. That acceptance does not quite amount to a social contract, in either the sense of the actual contract which Hume is generally thought to have successfully debunked, or a hypothetical social contract which is thought to have met the same fate as the actual one, this time under fire from Dworkin.[107] Rather, it partakes of elements of both the ideas of actual acceptance and the acceptance of the hypothetical reasonable person.[108]

The result is a kind of social contract, in the words of JW Gough in one of the best treatments of its history, an 'abbreviation for the idea that political obligation involves a relationship analogous to contract'.[109] Gough's monograph relied, as I have, on Ernest Barker's analysis of

[107] David Hume, 'Of the Original Contract', in Frederick Watkins, ed., *Hume: Theory of Politics* (Austin: University of Texas Press, 1953) 193; Ronald Dworkin, 'Justice and Rights', in Dworkin, *Taking Rights Seriously* 185.

[108] Hume's rejection of the social contract and consent theory is not as categorical as is often thought to be the case. See Peter Winch, 'Certainty and Authority', in A Phillips Griffiths, ed., *Wittgenstein: Centenary Essays* (Cambridge: Cambridge University Press, 1991) 223, at 227–8, commenting on Hume's case of a hereditary prince who returns after having been deposed by a usurper who remained unpopular and is greeted with enthusiasm by the people as their legitimate ruler. In this case, Hume says, 'they consent because they perceive him to be already by birth their lawful sovereign'. (See Hume, 'Of the Original Contract', 206.) Winch says (his emphasis):

> consent does indeed play a role in the relations between citizens and ruler in this case, but not the role described by social contract theorists. It is not the *source* of their sense of the ruler's legitimacy; rather, their recognition of his legitimacy is expressed in the role played by the thought of his birth in the way they consent to his rule, and the importance they attach to this is of course rooted in the hereditary institutions which belong to their form of political life. It goes without saying that this form of life involves certain ingrained habits of obedience towards people occupying certain positions within it.

On this interpretation of Hume, his views are not that different from the idea of 'attributed consent' developed by Kinch Hoekstra in a bid to understand the role of consent in Hobbes's theory of authority: 'The *de facto* Turn in Hobbes's Political Philosophy', in Tom Sorell and Luc Foisneau, eds, *Leviathan After 350 Years* (Oxford: Oxford University Press, 2004) 33, at 67–8.

[109] JW Gough, *The Social Contract: A Critical Study of Its Development* (Oxford: Clarendon Press, 1957, 2nd ed.), 248.

how the modern social contract tradition combined the ideas of the *Gesellschaftsvertrag* and the *Herrschaftsvertrag*.[110] Barker argued that the social contract tradition stood for two values: 'the value of Liberty, or the idea that will, not force, is the basis of government, and the value of Justice, or the idea that right not might, is the basis of all political society and of every system of political order'.[111] He acknowledged, however, that the state 'in general did not arise in a climate of contract' but 'was formed and developed by a variety of factors' including 'force'.[112]

This tells us that the social contract tradition does not aim to give us an account of the historical origins of the modern legal state. Rather, it seeks an explanation, which is at the same time a justification, of the state which in fact developed. As Barker put it:

> [I]f we look at the State in particular, as it exists in our own time and in the area of the Western world, we are equally bound to recognize that it lives and has its being in a climate of contract: mutual concession, mutual toleration, mutual discussion, and general give and take. The modern State of the Western world is a legal association. As such it depends upon, and is constituted by, a memorandum of association, or set of articles of association, or in other words 'a constitution', which states the contractual terms on which the association is made and under which it henceforth acts. The constitution of a State may thus be regarded as the contract on which its action, and the action of its members, in their capacity as members, is ultimately dependent; and from this point of view political obligation may be regarded as contractual obligation.[113]

On my argument in Chapter 2, this is precisely the account of the state which emerges from Hobbes's political legal theory. The political order of the modern legal state is distinctive because in it the monopoly of legitimate force the state enjoys is wielded through law with the result that might is converted into legal right. I have argued here that in combination the insights of Hart, Raz and Kelsen on how to understand the authority of that state from the internal point of view – from the

[110] Ibid, *passim*, and 250–4.

[111] Barker, 'The Theory of the Social Contract in Locke, Rousseau and Hume', 87.

[112] Hobbes, despite his central place in the social contract tradition, put this point even more forcefully in the last chapter of *Leviathan* when he said that the origins of most states lie in war, so that 'there is scarce a Common-wealth in the world, whose beginnings can in conscience be justified'; Hobbes, *Leviathan*, 486. See my Chapter 4.

[113] Ernest Barker, *Principles of Social and Political Theory* (Oxford: Oxford University Press, 1951), 190.

perspective of those involved in constituting such authority – show that we must include the perspective of legal subjects as well as that of the officials who apply the law to them.

That makes the contract between ruler and ruled a hybrid of actual and hypothetical acceptance. It partakes of actual acceptance in just the way that Austin's much maligned idea of a habit of obedience suggests, but understood in terms of the actual beliefs of those in the jural community about what it takes to vindicate claims of right, not fear of sanctions.[114] It partakes of the idea of the hypothetical reasonable person in that it postulates, or better bets, that the tacit habit of acceptance will become explicit if put to the test of scrutiny by the subject. This test is not altogether or even mostly hypothetical, however. It depends on the *fact* of widespread acceptance. The more legal subjects have institutional means of contesting mandatory or legal public norms whose content seems unreasonable *to them*, the less easy it will be to make the claim that acceptance is the product of coercion. As I suggested of Hobbes at the beginning of this chapter, individual consent is both hypothetical and actual, and the same is true of acceptance, manifested in a habit of obedience, which understood correctly may be taken to be collective consent.

In other words, consent is hypothetical because it is what we must hypothesize in order to make sense of the claim that legal authority is de jure. It is actual because, first, an order which rests on right rather than might will in fact be one in which most of those subject to law do accept the legitimacy of their order. But it is also actual because, second, acceptance is both produced and tested by the way in which the institutions of legal order are designed so as to be able to give an adequate answer to the subject's question 'But, how can that be law for me?' No 'ought' is derived from an 'is'. Rather, the order of the modern legal state is designed to elicit the consent of those subject to its law. The idea of a state machine designed to produce collective consent may of course seem rather ominous. But the consent here is that of individual legal subjects who will consent only when their state's laws make sense to them as serving their interest as equal before the law and the law can make such

114 On habit and legitimacy, see Cheryl Misak, 'A Pragmatist Account of Legitimacy and Authority', in David Rondel and Susan Dieleman, eds, *Pragmatism and Justice* (New York: Oxford University Press, 2017) 295.

sense because of its interpretability in light of the order's fundamental legal commitments.[115]

Philosophy of law does not, however, settle in the abstract the precise design of the institutions of legal order or the fine detail of constitutional order. For example, Barker noted after the passage in the long quotation earlier in this section that it is 'especially plain' that political obligation may be regarded as contractual obligation 'where there is a written constitution'. But, he added, 'it does not cease to be plain where the constitution is partly or even largely unwritten: there is, after all, no difference of kind between the "written" and the "unwritten" constitution'.[116] I have reconstructed the agenda of philosophy of law here in an attempt to show that, so long as it seeks to understand law as a matter of authority, particular positions do take stands on the terrain of constitutionalism. How they do so is complex, as these stands require an explanation of constitutional authority, the topic of the rest of this chapter.

3.4 The Constitution as Achievement

Philosophers of law and constitutional theorists generally agree that every national legal order has a constitution. However, it is notoriously difficult to answer the question of constitutionality: what all such legal orders share in having a constitution. The intuition here is that it is so fundamental that every national legal order must have one, whatever the content of its actual constitution – the rules one would collect in a textbook of the constitutional law of Canada, of Germany, and so on.

Of course, the rules of the actual constitution – the positive law of the constitution – will vary considerably as indeed the content of positive law more generally will vary from legal order to legal order. But just as philosophers of law think that the question 'What is law?' is worth trying to answer despite this variation, so it is worthwhile trying to answer the question of constitutionality. Moreover, my thesis in the rest of this chapter is that in answering the question of constitutionality we can get a better grip on an answer to the question about law.

Obvious candidates for what legal orders share in having a constitution are the constitutionalist ideas discussed so far: Hart's rule of recognition and Kelsen's basic norm. But the available literature does

[115] I elaborate the idea of the fund of values in Chapter 6.

[116] Barker, *Principles of Social and Political Theory*, 190–1.

not clarify how, if at all, such debates in philosophy of law relate to constitutional theory, in particular to the debate between 'political' and 'legal' constitutionalists, despite the fact that their debate is precisely about questions such as what the constitution is, what makes it authoritative and whether it is part of or beyond the law.

'Political constitutionalists' such as Richard Bellamy and Jeremy Waldron argue that the constitution is a set of democratic principles legitimating the legal order and they seem to suppose further that it is political rather than legal in that it lies beyond the legal order.[117] Conversely, 'legal constitutionalists' such as Trevor Allan and Ronald Dworkin argue that the constitution is legal, that is, within legal order, and contains substantive principles of political morality which make up its legitimating basis.[118]

Political constitutionalists focus on the issue of the legitimacy of judicial review of a particular sort, called either 'strong judicial review' or 'strong-form judicial review'. It occurs if judges are allocated the authority to overrule the legislature when they conclude that statutory provisions violate constitutionally protected rights. This allocation of authority to judges is illegitimate in the eyes of political constitutionalists since, in their view, in a well-functioning democracy, only our elected representatives in the legislature have the legitimacy and the competence to settle – to have 'the last word' about – deep societal disagreements about rights. But this is not a debate, as they see it, within philosophy of law as it takes place in prescriptive political theory, which allows them to criticize as illegitimate the 'is' of legal orders in which judges do in fact have the last word. Here they agree with Hart and his followers who suppose that there is no real joinder between the inquiry undertaken by philosophy of law, which is to work out the necessary and sufficient conditions for X to be law, and constitutional theory. Legal philosophical inquiry is, on their common view, descriptive and conceptual by contrast with the politically prescriptive inquiry of constitutional theory.

Allan and Dworkin, in contrast, do not see the debate as confined to a disagreement within constitutional theory since they also contest Hart's

[117] For example, Jeremy Waldron, 'The Core of the Case against Judicial Review' (2006) 115 *Yale Law Journal* 1346; Richard Bellamy, 'Political Constitutionalism and the Human Rights Act' (2011) 9 *International Journal of Constitutional Law* 86.

[118] TRS Allan, *The Sovereignty of Law: Freedom, Constitution and Common Law* (Oxford: Oxford University Press, 2013); Ronald Dworkin, *Freedom's Law: The Moral Reading of the American Constitution* (Cambridge, MA: Harvard University Press, 1996).

claim that at the base of a legal order one finds a rule of settled practice – the rule of recognition. Rather, there is a legal constitution containing substantive principles of political morality. It follows for them that the focus of political constitutionalists on strong judicial review is misplaced, since in every legal order judges have the duty to interpret the law in the light of substantive constitutional principles.

I agree with Allan and Dworkin and argue in what follows that there is already a joinder because Hartian legal positivists do have shared commitments with political constitutionalists. Most significantly, despite the fact that political constitutionalists think that the constitution lies beyond the legal order, both they and Hartian legal positivists are committed to an understanding of the constitution according to which the constitution is legal. In their shared view, a constitution should consist exclusively of legal and formal authorization rules – rules delegating authority to various institutional actors. That view depends on a more profound commitment which we have already encountered. It is to the idea that the legitimating source of the law of a legal order – what gives it de jure authority – lies beyond the order.

With these commitments in view, we can understand why Hartian legal positivists are political constitutionalists and political constitutionalists Hartian legal positivists. More accurately, they are the heirs and torchbearers of Bentham's and Austin's command theory of law.[119] However, as I argue, we encounter in regard to these issues the same kinds of ambivalence we encountered in Hart as he sought to understand law in the register of authority. These ambivalences allow us to see why otherwise arid-seeming questions in legal philosophy matter to fundamental questions about constitutionality, and why central questions of constitutional theory are important to a more general account of the authority of law. I also argue that once we see that every legal order has a legal constitution, it is difficult to confine an understanding of the constitution to formal authorization rules or to locate the source of legitimate authority outside of the legal order. For such rules imply substantive principles and the combination of the rules with substantive principles locates the source of legitimate legal authority within law.

However, my main object is to establish the kind of joinder in which this kind of argument can be properly contested. For with that joinder, we come to see much of philosophy of law as a kind of *Staatsrechtslehre*,

[119] Here I echo Raz, 'Authority, Law, and Morality', 194.

the theoretical tradition of public law in which Kelsen worked.[120] As I pointed out in the Introduction, the tradition approaches the question of constitutionality through a combination of philosophical and constitutional theory, since it is a question about the correct theory of public legal right, put differently, about the legitimacy of the modern legal state.

I start, in Section 3.5, with a sketch of three assumptions shared by philosophy of law and constitutional theory, as well as of some complications which attend them. Together the assumptions frame a space in which one can explore the joinder between philosophy of law and constitutional theory. My claim is not, however, that a legal order which failed to instantiate one or more of the assumptions would fail to be a legal order. After all, as we will see in Chapter 4, these assumptions can be made only about a national, not an international order. Nevertheless, in the case of national legal orders, it follows from these assumptions that the answer to the question of constitutionality is the one offered by the legal constitutionalists. The constitution is legal and contains both formal authorization rules and substantive principles of political morality which together help to make up the legitimating basis of legal order.

3.5 Three Assumptions and Some Complications

The first assumption is that all legal orders share something fundamental in having a constitution. It is easier to state what is not fundamental than what is. It is not whether the constitution is written or unwritten, or whether the legal order is federal or unitary, or whether it is presidential or parliamentary, and so on. Indeed, it should not matter to answering the question of constitutionality whether the legal order is a 'parliamentary legal order', one in which a supreme parliament may make or unmake any law it likes, or whether it is a 'bill-of-rights legal order' which has an entrenched bill of rights and authorizes judges to invalidate legislation which violates one of the rights. However, this last issue is a central topic in the debate in constitutional theory and I will suggest both

[120] 'Much of' because this kind of inquiry in philosophy of law does not seek to answer questions about the normative structure of particular fields of private law. It is inclined, however, to give public law priority over private law in understanding legal order, for reasons I sketch in 'Liberty and Legal Form', in Lisa Austin and Dennis Klimchuk, eds, *The Rule of Law and Private Law* (Oxford: Oxford University Press, 2014) 92. See further Appendix II.

here and in Chapters 4 and 5 that these two models of legal order frame implicitly debates in philosophy of law.

The second assumption is that the legal order of a modern legal state consists of the institutions associated with the doctrine of the separation of powers: there is a legislature, an executive and a judiciary, and there is some degree of separation between them. The legislature enacts statutes, the statutes delegate authority to the executive to implement the statutes and judges have the main role in interpreting the law, including the statutes delegating authority to the executive.

The third assumption falls out of the second. It is that in all national legal orders, judges have the authority to review state action even if their review authority is confined to what political constitutionalists consider to be a 'weak' form. Such review happens when judges do not question the validity of the statute which delegates authority to officials, but ask instead whether the officials in implementing the statute acted intra vires, within the limits of their authority. If the judges find that the officials acted outside such limits – ultra vires – they may declare the action invalid. I refer to this kind of authority as 'administrative law review' because, technically, it occurs within the field of administrative law – the body of law governing the activity of officials who administer the legal regimes created by statutes.[121]

We have already encountered one complication which gets in the way of answering the question of constitutionality: whether the constitution is in or outside the legal order. Another complication, as already indicated, is that there seem to be two rival versions of the basis of constitutionality, of its fundamentality. Is it a set of *formal authorization rules* authorizing legislators, judges and other legal officials to make, interpret and implement the law or is it a set of *substantive principles* materially limiting what officials, including legislators, are permitted to do, for example, by entrenching individual rights against the state, as in a bill-of-rights legal order?[122]

[121] I here ignore the fact that administrative law review has been expanded to include non-statutory bodies. Note that in a federal system, courts will usually have the task of policing the boundaries between the federal unit and the federated units. This kind of review also can be understood as formal review for *vires*, but like administrative law review, it is hard to keep substance out. Much of my analysis of the judicial role in administrative law review would thus apply to controversies about a federal division of powers.

[122] This idea of 'limit' is inaccurate in ways which I won't introduce into the text in order to avoid overcomplicating an already very complex set of issues. For example, a constitutional provision which says that legislation may not treat people unequally, but that affirmative action is not ruled out by this limit, does not limit the state but authorizes it

The answer 'both authorization rules and substantive principles' is vulnerable to the following challenge. In a parliamentary legal order, there are authorization rules: the formal and procedural rules of 'manner and form' the parliament must follow to make law. But there may seem to be no substantive principles, at least none which limits the parliament's authority to make a law with any content. So, the answer to the question of constitutionality might appear to be the one which Hart would offer: necessarily authorization rules and contingently, in addition, substantive principles. Hartian legal theory, that is, both rejects Austin's claim that a bill-of-rights constitution is not law properly so-called and purports to be agnostic on the question whether a legal order should have such a bill-of-rights constitution. However, Hartian legal theory is committed to the view that the legal order of a modern legal state will contain formal authorization rules in its 'secondary' rules.

This Hartian position will seem plausible if we contrast standard bill-of-rights legal orders and the UK order in which there is parliamentary supremacy and so, as the saying goes, the parliament may enact any law it pleases as long as it complies with the formalities, the rules of 'manner and form'. And if there are no substantive constraints on the legislature in a parliamentary legal order, legal positivism will seem to emerge victorious in its argument with thinkers in the natural law tradition who claim a necessary connection between law and morality.

Moreover, this victory may seem to establish the lack of a joinder between philosophy of law and constitutional theory mentioned in Section 3.4. Recall Austin's famous line: 'The existence of law is one thing; its merit or demerit another.' Austin followed that claim with, 'Whether it be or not is one enquiry; whether it be or not conformable to an assumed standard is a different enquiry.'[123] These two lines continue to shape Hartian legal positivism since the distinction between philosophy of law and constitutional theory tracks the distinction between the 'is' and the 'ought' of law, the distinction stated in Hart's Separation Thesis that there is no necessary connection between law and morality.

However, for reasons that will become clear in a moment, I refer to the distinction in the rest of this chapter as Hart referred to it in 1958 in his first major statement of legal positivism as the 'utilitarian distinction',[124]

to pursue an equality-seeking policy, and provisions which require the state to alleviate poverty, preserve the environment and so on, go even further than authorization.

123 Austin, *Lectures on Jurisprudence*, vol. 1, 233.

124 Hart, 'Positivism and the Separation of Law and Morals', *passim*.

thereby recognizing that Bentham and Austin, who had proposed it, were not only legal positivists but also founders of utilitarianism: a political philosophy about the common good which fundamentally shaped their view of the appropriate design of legal order. Notice that to make the distinction is not to declare the second kind of inquiry – whether the law is conformable to an assumed (moral or political) standard – to be less worth doing than the inquiry undertaken by philosophy of law. It is only to say that the second inquiry takes place within political theory, of which constitutional theory is a branch.

But at least three things should make us hesitate before we adopt the division of labour which Bentham, Austin and Hart recommended between legal and political theory. First, political constitutionalists usually adopt a positivistic understanding of law as determined as a matter of social fact, but do not espouse agnosticism about how legal orders should be designed or about how judges should interpret the law. Rather, they argue that it is illegitimate to give judges the last word on whether legislation conforms to rights because judges have no business second-guessing the outcomes of the legislators' deliberation on moral and political issues. For the same reason, they regard as highly suspect the legal constitutionalist suggestion that judges should interpret statutes in the light of their understanding of the substantive principles of their legal order. Rather, judges should adopt interpretive approaches to law which search for settled facts about legislative intent; and there are well-known examples of judges who profess allegiance to such approaches.

Second, and as Hart rather casually acknowledged in referring to the 'utilitarian distinction' between law and morality, Bentham and Austin deployed that distinction in the service of a conception of law which models legal order in such a way as to make law an effective instrument for the top-down transmission of the political judgments of utilitarian elites to legal subjects. Bentham, as we know, wished to avoid as much as possible giving judges the opportunity to impose their views on the content of legislation, whereas Austin differed mainly in that he worried that legislators are beholden to the uneducated public; so he thought it desirable to give a large role to the judicial elite.[125]

In other words, for Hart's positivist predecessors, while what the law is on any matter is a question of fact, and so not answerable to a moral or

[125] See, for example, Austin, *Lectures on Jurisprudence*, vol. 1, 65–6; and vol. 2, 348–55.

political standard, their conception of law and of legal order is so answerable. This is the standard set by utilitarianism requiring, as in political constitutionalism, that legal order be designed so as to ensure that political judgments made outside of law be transmitted by law in a way faithful to the content of the original judgment. Hence, questions about the content of the law must be resolvable to the extent possible without judges having to deliberate about the merits of that content. Judges should thus adopt interpretive methods which rely exclusively on facts about the law. In other words, like Hobbes's legal theory, Bentham's and Austin's legal theories are political legal theories in that both their understanding of law and their view of the proper design of legal order are shaped by the commitments of their political theory.

Third, as we have seen, Austin regarded constitutional law not as law properly so-called but as 'positive morality' – as a set of moral conventions standing outside of the legal order and which cannot affect the validity of law.[126] But that is because, with Bentham, Austin regarded as illegitimate judicial reliance on moral principles as criteria for the validity of statutes, though unlike Bentham he wanted to grant judges a large interstitial lawmaking role.[127]

Bentham and Austin are, then, the original political constitutionalists, at least in the English tradition of legal positivism. They differ from their descendants in Bellamy and Waldron only in that the descendants are not hostile to legally mandated rights commitments, so long as the legislature is recognized as the final interpreter of the rights. It might even be that if one sets contemporary Hartian legal philosophy in a tradition of positivist thinking about law which stretches from Bentham to Bellamy and Waldron, its mode of doing legal philosophy looks rather aberrant. For positivist legal philosophy before Hart and in the hands of contemporary political constitutionalists is a kind of *Staatsrechtslehre*, a theory about the legitimacy of the modern legal state.

Indeed, as we will see in Section 3.6, the rule of recognition might best be understood as an ambivalent placeholder for the normative commitments of this political constitutionalist tradition. If that is the case, as I suggested in Section 3.1, Hart did not so much discover a constitutionalist idea in sketching the rule of recognition as propose a new name for a phenomenon well known to his tradition. Moreover, as we saw in Chapter 2 with Coke, figures in the common law tradition have argued

[126] Ibid, vol. 1, 230.
[127] Ibid, vol. 2, 348–55.

for centuries that the authority of a supreme lawmaker in a parliamentary legal order is controlled by substantive principles which judges discern in interpreting the legal traditions of their political community. In their view, such principles are more fundamental in the constitution of legal order than authorization rules. This argument has been revived in our time in the work of Allan and Dworkin.

Notice that while we know that political constitutionalists think that it is a political mistake to establish a bill-of-rights legal order, it is not clear whether they think that, in such an order, the constitution is political or legal. Austin, as Hart noted, held the view that such a constitution is not law properly so-called whereas Bentham seemed to think it is law, but that it is a mistake to have one, as it authorizes judges to second-guess judgments made by utilitarian legislators.[128] As we will see in Section 3.6, the same kind of problem bedevils Hart's attempt to understand the fundamental or constitutional basis of legal order, that is, to answer the question of constitutionality. Moreover, as I also show, although there is some ambiguity in their position, both political constitutionalists and legal positivists seem committed to the claim that the legal constitution should ultimately be one which consists only of formal authorization rules. Put differently, it seems that both political constitutionalists and legal positivists must suppose that there are constitutional rules which determine what counts as valid legislation. Hence, the idea of a thin legal constitution is implicit in their position. The rule of recognition is an attempt to express a political commitment to confining the constitution to such rules in an apparently neutral fashion, an attempt which I argue fails.

3.6 Is the Rule of Recognition Mysterious?

Hart's idea of a rule of recognition may seem to enable legal positivism to account for the existence of both parliamentary and bill-of-rights legal orders in a way which was not open to Bentham and Austin, given their shared political opposition to such orders as well as Austin's legal theoretical opposition – his claim that even in a bill-of-rights legal order, the constitution amounts to no more than positive morality and that its sanctions are moral, not legal. The rule of recognition thus seems to supply to the question of constitutionality the answer that a constitution

[128] Hart, 'Positivism and the Separation of Law and Morals', 54–5.

contains necessarily authorization rules and contingently, in addition, substantive principles. The make-up of any actual constitution can, then, be a matter of description and legal positivism need take no stance on whether it is advisable to incorporate substantive principles into a constitution.

But the idea of a rule of recognition turns out to be just as mysterious as we saw Hart claimed is the case with Kelsen's basic norm. While Hart often spoke as if the rule of recognition of a legal order is its constitution, there are also indications in his work and in the work of his followers that the rule of recognition is more basic than the constitution. Consider, for example, the UK's parliamentary legal order, described as follows on the parliament's website:[129]

> Parliamentary sovereignty is a principle of the UK constitution. It makes Parliament the supreme legal authority in the UK, which can create or end any law. Generally, the courts cannot overrule its legislation and no Parliament can pass laws that future Parliaments cannot change. Parliamentary sovereignty is the most important part of the UK constitution.

On this description, the rules of change for statutes are the fundamental part of the UK constitution. As a result, in an inquiry into the validity of a statute, all that a court may have regard to is whether there has been compliance with those rules. But there must be something that makes it the case that judicial inquiries into validity are so confined. If it is the rule of recognition which makes it the case, are the rules of change really the ultimate rules of the constitution and does it follow that the rule of recognition lies beyond the constitution, outside of legal order?

Hart said that this kind of question 'extracts from some a cry of despair: how can we show that the fundamental provisions of a constitution which are surely law are really law?'[130] Others, he said, 'reply with the insistence that at the base of legal systems, there is something which is "not law", which is "pre-legal", "meta-legal" or is just "political fact"'. His solution is:

> The case for calling the rule of recognition 'law' is that the rule providing criteria for the identification of other rules of the system may well be thought a defining feature of legal system, and so itself worth calling 'law'; the case for calling it 'fact' is that to assert that such a rule exists is indeed

[129] Available at www.parliament.uk/about/how/sovereignty.
[130] Hart, *The Concept of Law*, 111.

> to make an external statement of an actual fact concerning the manner in which the rules of an 'efficacious' system are identified. Both these aspects claim attention but we cannot do justice to them both by choosing one of the labels 'law' or 'fact'. Instead, we need to remember that the ultimate rule of recognition may be regarded from two points of view: one is expressed in the external statement of fact that the rule exists in the actual practice of the system; the other is expressed in the internal statements of validity made by those who use it in identifying the law.[131]

On this account, there is no perspective-independent answer to the question whether the rule of recognition is law or fact. Rather, the answer depends on whether we take the external or the internal point of view. From the point of view of those outside of the legal system, all that is observed is convergent behaviour. From the internal point of view, the rule provides a reason for acting in a certain way.

Hart also acknowledged that the consensus on which the internal point of view seems to depend could break down because there could be disagreement about the 'ultimate criteria to be used in identifying a law'.[132] He went on to remark that when the courts have to settle such disagreements – 'previously unenvisaged questions concerning the most fundamental constitutional rules' – 'they *get* their authority to decide them accepted after the questions have arisen and the decision has been given. Here all that succeeds is success.'[133] This last claim is surely itself a cry of despair, as it pushes the answer to the question beyond the legal to the contingencies of politics. As Dworkin pointed out, it leaves Hart unable to explain even conventional morality. Hart's account of law cannot deal as a juridical matter with the fact that people both disagree about the scope of conventional rules and think that their disagreement is about what the rule requires, despite the fact that there is no consensus on this issue.[134]

Hart's successors do little to dispel the despair. John Gardner, for example, points out that Hart was uncertain whether to classify the rules of recognition as themselves legal. In Gardner's view, rules of recognition do not 'quite belong to' their legal systems. They 'lie beyond the constitution' since one needs rules of recognition in order to identify rules as constitutional rules. 'Even the constitution needs to be constituted

131 Ibid, 111–12.
132 Ibid, 122.
133 Ibid, 153. His emphasis. I examine this claim in Chapter 5.
134 Ronald Dworkin, 'Model of Rules II', 49–50.

somehow.' 'Is it constituted by law?' Kelsen, Gardner says, thought so, but then faced an infinite regress, which his fiction of the validity of basic norms as the first historical constitution was supposed to end. In contrast, Hart avoided this problem, Gardner claims, by presenting the ultimate rules of recognition as 'borderline legal rules'. They provide criteria, but 'by their nature' do not meet those criteria. They are, he says, to be found in the 'custom of law applying officials' but need not identify that custom as a source of law. 'In that sense they are above the law rather than part of it.' We can thus agree that there are 'ultimate rules of recognition that are, so to speak, above the constitution' and that 'there is no *law* that is above the constitution. Constitutional law is as high as the law goes.'[135]

Raz also becomes ambivalent on this issue. He rejects the thought that the constitution of a country is its rule of recognition because, while most constitutions can always be changed 'in accordance with procedures they themselves provide', the rule of recognition 'can change only as the practice that it is changes'. It 'cannot give way to statutory law'. It is unlike the rest of the law. 'It is the practice – that is, the fact – that the courts and other legal institutions recognize the validity, the legitimacy, of the law, and that they are willing to follow it and apply it to others.' 'It is the point . . . at which – metaphorically speaking – the law ends and morality begins.' 'If the rule of recognition exists . . . then the law exists. But only if . . . [the courts] are right in so conducting themselves is the law actually legitimate and binding, morally speaking.'[136]

Finally, Waldron argues that if we are looking for the ultimate rules of a legal order, rules of change are more worthy of our attention than the rule of recognition.[137] He suggests that the validity of a rule depends not on any rule of recognition, but on whether the rule was made in accordance with the rules of change. He also suggests that in a parliamentary legal order, the

135 Gardner, *Law as a Leap of Faith*, 107. His emphasis.

136 Joseph Raz, 'On the Authority and Interpretation of Constitutions: Some Preliminaries', in Larry Alexander, ed., *Constitutionalism: Philosophical Foundations* (New York: Cambridge University Press, 1998) 152, at 161.

137 Jeremy Waldron, 'Who Needs Rules of Recognition?', in Matthew Adler and Kenneth E Himma, eds, *The Rule of Recognition and the US Constitution* (New York: Oxford University Press, 2009) 327. Waldron might be thought to have an ambivalent relationship with the positivist tradition, but that thought depends, in my view, on supposing that the tradition starts with Hart. If the tradition is seen as including Bentham and Austin, and in line with my argument as a kind of *Staatsrechtslehre*, Waldron is more of a torchbearer of the tradition than most legal philosophers who work in broadly the positivist style of legal philosophy.

rule of recognition gets 'its distinctive content from the rule of change' which empowers the parliament to legislate, and that 'it is not clear ... that the rule of recognition actually does anything with that content that the rule of change has not already done'.[138] Further, contrary to the arguments made by most legal positivists, Waldron alleges that we do not need the rule of recognition to tell us that there is a duty to observe the rules of change, since the power that a rule of change confers on, say, the legislature to enact a statute implies that the duties of other actors in the system will be changed when the power is exercised. In Waldron's view, the claim that every legal order contains a rule of recognition might be driven by a perceived need for closure – that is, for a rule which would make it the case that a legal order produced a kind of certainty one might think desirable on normative or conceptual grounds. But there is, he says, 'some effrontery in the positivists' insistence that every legal system must contain a rule cast in terms that represent the positivists' own jurisprudential position!'[139]

Waldron could have called in aid Hart's own observation against Kelsen that in parliamentary legal orders we do not need to look beyond the constitution to find a rule that puts judges under a duty to apply the constitution: 'It seems a needless reduplication to suggest that there is a further rule to the effect that the constitution (or those "who laid it down") are to be obeyed.'[140] Gardner, however, thinks that the observation is mistaken in regard to written constitutions – constitutions which are 'laid down' – though it is true of unwritten constitutions. In the former case, there is no 'needless reduplication' but 'a separate rule of recognition without which there is no written constitution to contain those rules'.[141] In this view, the rule of recognition when there is a written constitution turns out to be nothing more than Kelsen's basic norm, as Gardner seems to acknowledge.[142] And Waldron himself reverts to Kelsen, though he suggests that we might try to understand the basic norm as a practice, that is, something more like Hart's claim about what we can observe from an external point of view. In line with his general argument, Waldron adds that the norm is better understood as a

138 Ibid, 342.

139 Ibid, 344.

140 Hart, *The Concept of Law*, 293.

141 Gardner, *Law as a Leap of Faith*, 109. See further Cane, 'Public Law in *The Concept of Law*', 669–73.

142 Gardner, *Law as a Leap of Faith*, 109.

dynamic process than a static recognition, since the basic norm empowers those who laid down the first constitution to make that change.[143]

One might well ask whether Waldron's remark about the effrontery of the positivist position does not come back to bite him, given his argument. Suppose that the fundamental or constitutional rules of a legal order are rules of change of the sort we associate with the rules of manner and form of the UK legislative process and that the main constitutional task of judges when confronted with a statute is to recognize it as valid if it complies with such rules of change. If the constitution contains only such rules of change, its content would be purely formal. It would contain only the rules strictly required to enable a supreme legislature to maintain its supremacy, which is exactly what political constitutionalists from Bentham to Bellamy and Waldron think appropriate.

Perhaps, then, the legal positivist answer to the question of constitutionality is that the constitution of every legal order is fundamentally its rules of change, that is, its formal authorization rules. Precisely this thought seemed to animate Austin's reflections on the US Constitution, the essence of which, he thought, lies in its amendment formula.[144] Austin held the view, which Gardner describes rather disparagingly, that in the USA 'the Presidency, Congress and the Supreme Court are ... mere administrative bodies regulated by a kind of jumped up administrative law'.[145]

That position is not, as political constitutionalists may allege, one which opposes legal constitutionalism. Rather, like Hart and his followers, political constitutionalists are 'political' only in that for political reasons they favour a particular kind of legal constitution, a formal one limited to rules of the manner and form sort which do not constrain the legislature's authority to effect any change by ordinary statute. In other words, they are formal legal constitutionalists for substantive reasons to do with this kind of constitutionalism's fit with the political theory of utilitarianism or with a theory of democratic legitimacy and competence requiring that the legislature have the last word when it comes to settling disagreements about rights.[146] Because this fit is with a source of

143 Waldron, 'The Core of the Case against Judicial Review', 346–8.

144 Austin, *Lectures on Jurisprudence*, vol. 1, 222.

145 Gardner, *Law as a Leap of Faith*, 115.

146 There are other theories of legitimacy which underpin this kind of constitutionalism, for example, the theory of constitutional monarchy.

legitimacy external to the legal order, they can understand all authority within the legal order as delegated authority, with 'the people' being the ultimate author.

Kelsen, moreover, did regard constitutional law as jumped-up administrative law.[147] In his view, the parliament in any legal order creates law at a very high level but still at a level below the constitution. So the parliament, just like an administrative body, exercises authority delegated by the level above. Indeed, Kelsen clearly distinguished between the basic norm, which is the '*constitution in the juridical-logical sense*' and 'the constitution of the positive law, adopted through the act of a legal body'.[148] He also – a theme of my Chapter 4 – argued that the state constitutional level is not ultimate since states have their authority delegated to them by public international law. Constitutional law is for him no more than the ultra vires principle of administrative law writ large: the principle that a body which wields delegated power may not go beyond the terms of its mandate.[149]

In this view, in every legal order there is not only a constitution but also a legal constitution, since every constitution will contain at least more or less complex rules of change. The choice as to the design of such rules is, Kelsen supposed, political.[150] The question of how political power should be distributed to bring into being the will of the community is a political not a legal theoretical question. But whatever the answer to that question, it will be expressed in the formal authorization rules of a legal constitution. When the actual legal constitution contains in addition what Kelsen calls 'material norms', for example a right to freedom of expression, and gives to judges the authority to determine whether such a norm has been violated by the legislature, the question of whether the norm has been violated is still formal rather than substantive or material. For in such an order, the answer to the question whether a statute is

[147] Kelsen, 'The Nature and Development of Constitutional Adjudication'.

[148] Hans Kelsen, 'The Concept of the Legal Order' (1982) 27 *American Journal of Jurisprudence* 64 (Stanley L Paulson, trans.), at 68. His emphasis.

[149] Note that Gardner himself struggles to escape this view in *Law as a Leap of Faith*, 109–16. In his view, bodies like legislatures and courts wield inherent not delegated power. In explaining why they have inherent power, he suggests that originally the power was delegated to them, but at a certain point they came to be viewed by relevant officials as wielding powers which are not revocable; from that point on, they have inherent power.

[150] See Kelsen's critique of Carl Schmitt: Hans Kelsen, 'Who Ought to Be the Guardian of the Constitution?' (Lars Vinx, trans.), in Vinx, ed., *The Guardian of the Constitution* 174.

unconstitutional depends ultimately on whether it was enacted in accordance with the amendment formula.[151] However, Kelsen warned sternly against the introduction of terms such as 'freedom' into the constitution unless these terms can be given a determinate content. If such terms are vague, a 'fullness of power' is conceded to judges which is 'altogether intolerable' as it involves a 'shift of power from parliament to an extra-parliamentary institution' and which might involve the judges becoming the 'exponent of political forces completely different from those that express themselves in parliament'.[152]

Notice that most features of this kind of position characterize Raz's account of the relation of the rule of recognition to the constitution. Recall that he says that most constitutions can be changed 'in accordance with procedures they themselves provide'; hence, the rule of recognition cannot be the constitution. Thus, he seems to envisage that the legal constitution is in most legal systems fundamentally a matter of formal rules of change. Why then is the rule of recognition necessary? Because, or so the answer seems to be, there must exist something that makes these rules authoritative for officials. But, as we have seen, it is not clear that the rule of recognition can do that job. For Raz, the source of official duty is morality, and so it is located beyond not only the legal order and its constitution but even beyond the rule of recognition. Indeed, on Raz's account of authority, actual legitimacy depends on whether the law is the effective instrument of moral judgments legal subjects should follow because this will serve their interests better than if they decided for themselves. Law lives up to its ideal as law when it conforms to fundamental formal norms which conduce to its service as an effective instrument of morality.[153] As a result, the constitution has the authority it claims only if its authors have done a better job of moral reasoning than its subjects would, if left to their own devices.

As we have seen, political constitutionalists also find a resting point for the source of legitimacy outside of law in the politics of sovereignty, though they insist that the sovereign is a supreme parliament.[154] But they

[151] Ibid, 187–8; and Kelsen, 'The Nature and Development of Constitutional Adjudication'.

[152] Ibid, 61–2. At this point, Kelsen may have begun to stray over the line demarcating a theory of law which gives an account of the role of adjudication within that theory and a theory of adjudication like Dworkin's.

[153] In my view, these two lines summarize the position that comes out of a combination of Raz, 'Authority, Law, and Morality' and his essays on authority in *The Authority of Law*.

[154] For further exploration, see David Dyzenhaus, 'Constitutionalism in an Old Key: Legality and Constituent Power' (2012) 1 *Global Constitutionalism* 229.

must manage the fact that the legislature is not a purely political construct – it is also a legally constituted institution. They do so, as we have seen, by claiming either that it is not legally constituted or that, if it is, it should not be subject to substantive constitutional limits, that is, through the claim that the legal constitution is or should be limited to a particular kind of formal authorization rule. Hence, they become ambivalent about the location of authority, whether it is located inside legal order in the formal rules of change of a particular kind of legal constitution, or located outside in what legitimates restricting the rules of change so as to ensure the supremacy of a democratically elected parliament.

Similarly, both Hart and Kelsen thought that behind the actual constitution is something more fundamental than positive law, something which gives rise to what Hart in a perhaps unguarded moment called 'legal legitimacy'.[155] It is what makes law into an authoritative order and not the gunman situation writ large. As they understand things, there must be a source of duty and that source cannot be the constitution, because there has to be something which validates that constitution. If there is no source of validation, we encounter the logical problem Hobbes set out of an infinite regress.

However, that problem arises only for those who make what I will call 'the assumption of linearity', after Mark Walters's perspicuous distinction between 'linear' and 'circular' theories of legal authority.[156] Linear theories assume 'that the authority of legal norms can be traced back along a line of increasingly higher norms until an originating source is located. Law from this perspective is held up by a string, and someone or something must hold the end of that string.'[157] Circular theories, in contrast, 'do not need to address the problem of infinite regress':

> Law from this perspective is embedded within a network of interlocking strands of normative value that bend back upon themselves never reaching an end. The relevant image on this account is not a string but a web of strings shaped into a globe or sphere.[158]

Political constitutionalists and legal positivist philosophers in Hart's tradition are, on this distinction, string theorists though both are

[155] See HLA Hart, 'Answers to Eight Questions', in Duarte D'Almeida, Edwards and Dolcetti, eds, *Reading HLA Hart's The Concept of Law* 279, at 298.

[156] Mark Walters, 'The Unwritten Constitution as a Legal Concept', in Dyzenhaus and Thorburn, eds, *Philosophical Foundations of Constitutional Law* 33, at 33–4.

[157] Ibid.

[158] Ibid.

ambivalent, albeit in different ways, when it comes to the question where the string ends, within or without the legal order. The best explanation for both the ambivalence and the difference is as follows. There is only one position in play. But it makes its argument within two registers, philosophy of law and political theory, and it is the movement between these registers which creates both ambiguity and mystery.

Legal positivism in its constitutional theory register is ambivalent about whether the constitution is political or legal, though it insists that the constitution ought to contain only formal authorization rules of the kind one finds in a parliamentary legal order. It also insists that legitimate authority resides outside of legal order, though when the constitution is limited to formal authorization rules it will be the case that the laws enacted by the (democratic) parliament are by definition legitimate.

In contrast, in its philosophy of law register, legal positivism holds that the constitution is legal, but is ambivalent about whether its authority is located in or outside of legal order. That ambivalence leads to another, about whether whatever gives the constitution authority (an ultimate rule or a basic norm) is itself in or outside the legal order. Moreover, in this register legal positivism still tends to cling to the claim that the constitution either should be or is in fact limited to formal authorization rules, though in its attempts to rise above the constitutional theory fray, it is usually compelled to concede that the constitution can contingently (though perhaps unwisely) contain substantive principles.

The way forward for legal positivism is to merge the two registers by arguing that the constitution is legal, that it should be confined to formal authorization rules of the kind one finds in a parliamentary legal order, and that once so confined, the law made by the parliament enjoys legitimate authority. 'The people' who delegate authority from the outside can then be identified with the democratically elected legislature, and de facto power becomes de jure authority. In other words, the way forward for legal positivism is to reconceive itself as a participant in the project of *Staatsrechtslehre*, as, that is, involved in the debate about the correct theory of public legal right.

But in Section 3.7, I show that legal positivism reconceived in this way encounters a different set of problems. Once the concession is made that the constitution is legal and that it is the locus of legitimate authority, it is difficult either to stick with a linear theory or to confine the constitution to formal authorization rules. In terms of Walters's distinction, the justification of authority becomes circular and answers the question of constitutionality with 'necessarily both authorization rules and substantive principles'. Moreover, with circularity the accusation of effrontery is stripped of its force. The values which legitimate legal order and which figure fundamentally in the theory of that order are to be found in a process of justification which circulates within the legal order.

3.7 Unity, Integrity and the Social Contract

Consider the claim that the constitution must be more than jumped-up administrative law. That claim is really a conclusion which depends on two premises: the major premise that the constitution can't be understood in terms of delegated power and the minor premise that there is no more to administrative law than delegated power. In Chapter 4, I argue that the first premise is wrong and here do the same for the second.

Administrative law is constitutional law writ small, for it is not just a matter of formal authorizations but, as I show here, also of values and principles governing administrative action.[159] As such, it shades into the kind of judicial review which political constitutionalists find objectionable. That's why, as I claimed earlier, it is significant that they and legal positivists are willing to assume that in any legal system with a rudimentary separation of powers, judges should have the authority to ensure that officials who wield delegated powers stay within their legislative mandate and that such authority is necessary if the rule of law is to be maintained.

My argument starts with what will seem to many legal positivists to be two parochial examples which cannot therefore form the basis for a claim which sounds in philosophy of law, for both are from one legal order, the UK. The first is the well-known dissent in the First World War by Lord Shaw in *R* v. *Halliday*, in which he reasoned that a blanket legislative authorization to the executive to make regulations to deal with a situation of wartime emergency should be read by judges to exclude the authority to make a regulation governing detention since there was no explicit authority to make such a regulation in the legislation.[160]

In Shaw's view, the Habeas Corpus Acts and other constitutional documents, for example, the Magna Carta, give expression to principles that are part of the constitution. They 'in one sense confer', he said, 'no rights upon the subject, but they provide whereby his fundamental rights shall be vindicated, his freedom from arrest except on justifiable legal process shall be secured, and arbitrary attack upon liberty and life shall

[159] See Dyzenhaus, 'Process and Substance as Aspects of the Public Law Form'.
[160] *R* v. *Halliday, ex p. Zadig* [1917] AC 260.

be promptly and effectually foiled by law'. He also said that if parliament had intended to make this colossal delegation of power it would have done so 'plainly and courageously and not under cover of words about regulations for safety and defence'. For judges to allow the right to be abridged is to 'revolutionize' the constitution, perhaps more accurately to undertake a counter-revolution. It amounts to what he called a 'constructive repeal of habeas corpus', a repeal by the executive which is then ratified by judges.[161]

Notice that in Kelsenian terms, this material or substantive norm is formally protected, because the legislature must be utterly explicit about its intentions to override that norm in any statute. Moreover, on some definitions of strong judicial review, Shaw would have exercised such review had he been able to persuade a majority of his fellow judges to join him. Waldron, for example, says such review exists not only when judges have the authority to decline to apply a statute, but also when they have the authority 'to modify the effect of a statute to make its application conform with individual rights (in ways that the statute does not itself envisage)'.[162] But that is precisely what judges do much of the time in administrative law, dramatically in the *Anisminic* case in which the Judicial Committee of the House of Lords found a path to sidestep a privative clause – a provision in a statute which precludes judicial review – but less dramatically in many decisions on the validity of administrative action.[163]

These are cases which political constitutionalists should not generally find problematic from the standpoint of democratic legitimacy because, in accepting the legitimacy of administrative law review, they accept the legitimacy of judges who choose not to read privative clauses literally. They accept, in other words, that executive officials are not permitted to be 'a law unto themselves' – to wield legally unconstrained power. As I have explained elsewhere, a general privative clause attempts to achieve this end by seeming to deny judges any review authority whatsoever, while a substantive privative clause seeks to preclude judges from reviewing executive action on particular grounds, for example, that the

161 Ibid, 293–4.

162 Waldron, 'The Core of the Case against Judicial Review', 1346.

163 *Anisminic Ltd.* v. *The Foreign Compensation Committee* [1969] 2 AC 147. See also *R (Privacy International)* v. *Investigatory Powers Tribunal* [2019] UKSC 22, in which the majority of the Supreme Court – the apex court which has replaced the Judicial Committee of the House of Lords – resisted the attempt, a reaction to *Anisminic*, to make a legislative intention to exclude judicial review even clearer.

official was biased, or failed to give a hearing to those affected by the decision.[164] I say 'should' because political constitutionalists may object that in these cases the judges are doing something other than applying the statutes as they were intended to be applied and that only if the judges were to stick to literal application would they be interpreting the statute faithfully.[165]

As I pointed out in Section 3.5, political constitutionalists may hold that judges should adopt interpretive approaches to law which search for facts about legislative intent. But that is to adopt a controversial stance about the correct interpretive theory which cannot appeal in any non-question begging way to facts, since what the relevant facts are is conditioned by fundamental, normative commitments; in their case, following Bentham, the thought that law's role is to transmit the factual content of legislative judgment to legal subjects. It is also, then, misleading to suppose, as political constitutionalists do, that the main issue is which institution gets the last word, so that the solution is to confine judges to administrative law or weak review. Whether the legal constitution consists of substantive principles as well as formal authorization rules does not depend on whether judges are recognized as having the authority to enforce the principles against the legislature.

Legal positivists in Hart's tradition are also misled by that false picture of the difference a bill-of-rights constitution makes to legal order. In contrast, Kelsen argued that if one accords to judges the authority to interpret statutes to guarantee the legality of executive action implementing those statutes, one should be likewise committed to according to judges the authority to interpret the norms of the constitution which govern the legality of statutes. To think that a statute is the guarantee of its own legality is, according to Kelsen, a kind of nonsense,[166] a point well illustrated by my second example – *Jackson* v. *Attorney General.*[167]

164 See my *The Constitution of Law: Legality in a Time of Emergency* (Cambridge: Cambridge University Press, 2006), 102–17. In the terms coined in Chapter 2 for analysing Hobbes's legal theory, the former preclude the operation of the validity proviso, while the latter fail to meet the legality proviso.

165 See Richard Ekins, commenting on *R (Privacy International)* v. *Investigatory Powers Tribunal*, 'Do Our Supreme Court Judges Have Too Much Power?', *The Spectator*, 14 May 2019, www.spectator.co.uk/article/do-our-supreme-court-judges-have-too-much-power-. See Appendix III.

166 Kelsen, 'The Nature and Development of Constitutional Adjudication', 22–7.

167 *Jackson* v. *Attorney General* [2005] UKHL 56.

That case was on the surface about formal rules of change. The judges had to decide whether the Hunting Act 2004, which criminalized certain kinds of hunting, was a lawful Act of Parliament. The House of Lords had refused to assent to the Act. Prior to the Parliament Act 1911, such a refusal was an effective veto, but the 1911 Act made it possible for the House of Commons to override the House of Lords after two years. The Parliament Act 1949 reduced the period to one year, but because the House of Lords opposed the 1949 Act, it had to be enacted in accordance with the requirements of the 1911 Act.

The appellants in *Jackson* argued that the 1911 Act could not lawfully be used to amend itself. The Act delegated authority to the House of Commons to override the House of Lords in certain circumstances which did not include changing the scope of those circumstances. As a result, the 1949 Act was not a validly enacted Act. It was ultra vires the authority of the House of Commons. Their argument thus depended on the claim that, because legislation made under the 1911 Act was a species of delegated legislation, its validity could be questioned in a way that the validity of primary legislation may not. This argument was designed to meet the counterclaim that when a statute is on its face valid, the courts may not, in testing its validity, look behind it at the process by which it was enacted.[168]

The government did not as a matter of fact make this counterclaim. Instead, it argued that so long as the House of Commons followed the procedure set out in the 1949 Act it could enact any statute whatsoever. Nevertheless, the judges did find it important to dismiss the counterclaim. Lord Bingham, for example, said that '[t]he appellants have raised a question of law which cannot, as such, be resolved by Parliament. But it would not be satisfactory, or consistent with the rule of law, if it could not be resolved at all. So it seems to me necessary that the courts should resolve it, and that to do so involves no breach of constitutional propriety.'[169]

[168] See, ibid, para. 7 (per Lord Bingham).

[169] Ibid, para. 27, and see para. 51 (per Lord Nicholls). For an argument that the judges had no jurisdiction, see Richard Ekins, 'Acts of Parliament and the Parliament Acts' (2007) 123 *Law Quarterly Review* 91. En route to this conclusion, Ekins asserts that the UK Parliament was 'not constituted by law and the way in which it may act is not prescribed by law', by which he means that its 'nature and action . . . is not stipulated by any set of rules': 101–2. This is question begging as he does not take into account the possibility that it is constitutional principle at stake. See Appendix III.

Moreover, the judges agreed that parliament as constituted under either of the Acts could not evade a prohibition in the 1911 Act against extending the life of parliament beyond five years. Lord Bingham and two others supposed that this was the only restriction on parliament's authority,[170] while four reserved judgment on this matter.[171] Lord Steyn and Lady Hale, in contrast, expressed their disquiet at the thought that the House of Commons, as long as it waited the requisite period, could do anything it liked, for example, enacting 'undemocratic and oppressive legislation', or abolishing the upper house or judicial review in cases where governmental action affects the rights of individuals.[172] As Allan has said, '[r]ather than treat these remarks as a threat to overthrow the established legal order, with which the courts have become disenchanted, we should interpret them – much more plausibly – as a reminder of qualifications already latent within the supremacy doctrine, awaiting elaboration if and when circumstances dictate'.[173]

In sum, *Jackson* shows that a statute can't guarantee its own legality. Judges cannot deal with claims of intra and ultra vires without relying, albeit often implicitly, on substantive constitutional principles. Thus, Kelsen's argument is right that the legal order of the modern legal state requires that judges should have the authority to interpret constitutional norms which govern the legality of statutes. But it cannot find a resting place in formal authorization rules, for it is only at the most superficial

[170] *Jackson*, para. 31 (per Lord Bingham), para. 61 (per Lord Nicholls), para. 127 (per Lord Hope). It is significant that Lord Hope invoked Hart's idea of the rule of recognition in support of the claim that the 'open texture of the foundations of our legal system ... defies precise analysis in strictly legal terms'. From that, he said, it followed that 'the rule of Parliamentary supremacy is ultimately based on political fact' (ibid, para. 120). But he also wanted to claim that there are limits on the 'power to legislate', limits which are a 'question of law for the courts, not for Parliament'. 'The rule of law enforced by the courts is the ultimate controlling factor on which our constitution is based' (ibid, para. 107). The tension between these two claims – that the constitutional limits are internal legal limits and that they are external political limits – became even more palpable when he asserted both in the same sentence: 'There is a strong case for saying that the rule of recognition, which gives way to what people are prepared to recognise as law, is itself worth calling "law" and for applying it accordingly' (ibid, para. 126).

[171] Ibid, para. 139 (per Lord Rodger), para. 141 (per Lord Walker), para. 178 (per Lord Carswell), para. 194 (per Lord Brown).

[172] Ibid, paras 100–2 (per Lord Steyn), para. 159 (per Lady Hale), though her remarks are inconsistent with the position she took at para. 158 and with her qualification in para. 159 that the 'constraints upon what Parliament can do are political ... rather than constitutional'.

[173] Allan, *The Sovereignty of Law*, 144.

level that we can regard disputes about formal rules of change as formal in nature. They are deeply substantive disputes about the nature of democracy and the role of law in it, even when judges do their best to treat the disputes as formal.[174]

When the substance rises to the surface, we find that there is no need for judges to reach outside of the law for constitutional authority. They do not engage in the kind of linear reasoning which requires an ultimate stopping point responsive to the problem of infinite regress. Rather, in relying on legal materials they engage in the kind of circular reasoning Walters describes because the authority must be sought within the legal order, which means that appeals must be made to the resources of normative value in the public record of that order. And it leads to seeing the authority of law as legitimate because in making the appeals and in organizing the resources into a sustained argument about what the requirements are of the actual constitution, one is necessarily involved in a process of justification. As Neil MacCormick put the point:

> Understanding a constitution is not understanding any single rule internal to it as fundamental; it is understanding how the rules interact and cross-refer, and how they make sense in the light of the principles of political association that they are properly understood to express. If there is a fundamental obligation here, it is an obligation toward the constitution as a whole. It is the obligation to respect a constitution's integrity as a constitution, an obligation that has significance both in moments of relative stasis and in more dynamic moments.[175]

This statement picks up on Dworkin's claim that the central value of legal order is 'integrity', a value requiring legal actors to find a way of interpreting the law so that it can be understood as the expression of a unified jural community.[176] The principles judges are required to invoke in public law to make sense of the law in this way are the constitutional, legitimating principles of the order.[177]

174 This is true also of the constitutional disputes in South Africa in the 1950s, to which Hart referred when dealing with the problem of disagreement about the 'ultimate criteria to be used in identifying a law' – see Hart, *The Concept of Law*, 122 and 153. On these disputes, see *Jackson*, para. 84 (per Lord Steyn). I discuss these disputes in Chapter 5.

175 Neil MacCormick, *Questioning Sovereignty: Law, State, and Nation in the European Commonwealth* (Oxford: Oxford University Press, 1999), 93.

176 Ronald Dworkin, *Law's Empire* (London: Fontana, 1986).

177 Dworkin at times rejected this interpretation of his position, but, as I argued in Chapter 1, it is the natural interpretation and I argue in Chapters 5 and 6 that it is one he had reason to maintain.

It is important to see that this idea is hardly new in philosophy of law. As we saw in Chapter 2, it goes back at least to Hobbes, who argued that sovereigns, however constituted, must speak with one voice as the representative of the people who are subject to their laws. In turn, subjects must understand themselves as owning their sovereign's laws as if they each had made the laws themselves, and for that reason the laws must be understandable as the product of a single person.[178] Put differently, the constitution of the people as a unity – as a unified political community – depends on the sovereign's laws being understood as the product of one person. Moreover, to understand the laws in that way is to understand them as legitimate.

We also saw in Chapter 2 that Hobbes was concerned with the problem of infinite regress, though he characterized the issue as a practical one of not subjecting the sovereign to the rule of any other sovereign.[179] There must be a stopping point within legal order for questions about what the law requires. Hobbes argued that, in the exit from the state of nature, sovereign authority comes about through the individuals agreeing to be bound by the one who will act in their name.[180] But it is important to recall that for him the one who acts is an artificial person, constituted by the agreement of individuals who, on entering that agreement, find themselves reconstituted from a state of individuals who make up a multitude into a unified people. The story of exit from the state of nature becomes a 'just so' one, though not in a pejorative sense. It is the story one is compelled to tell in order to make sense of the idea of the people who are at the same time the subjects of the law and its authors, and in which authority is to be understood reflexively, as determined within legal order in the circular fashion just described.[181] Put differently,

[178] Hobbes, *Leviathan*, 120.

[179] Ibid, 224.

[180] Ibid, Chapters 13–17.

[181] As Kelsen explained:

> At bottom, only a juristic fact is capable of circumscribing the unity of the People with some accuracy, namely: the unity of the state's legal order whose norms govern the behaviour of its subjects. A multiplicity of human actions is unified as the content of the norms making up the order. This unity, then, represents the 'People' as an element of a particular social order, the state. As such a unity, the 'People' is not, as is often naively imagined, a body or conglomeration as it were, of actual persons. Rather, it is merely a system of individual acts regulated by the state legal order.

Kelsen, *The Essence and Value of Democracy*, 36.

it is the kind of story one must tell if one makes the regulative assumption that legal authority is legally constituted.

Hobbes's thought here echoes faintly in Hart in that he insisted that there is only one rule of recognition, an insistence which is undermined only because he used the metaphor of a rule to capture what it is that gives unity to a legal order. For there is no one rule which can do that kind of work, as Dworkin argued in two of his earliest critiques of legal positivism,[182] and as is acknowledged by Hart's followers who try to save the idea by positing a multiplicity of rules.[183] It echoes more strongly in Kelsen in that the basic norm must be presupposed in order to make sense of the hypothesis of the unity of legal order and to explain why, from the perspective of the legal official and subject, the order must be understood as legitimate.[184] It echoes most strongly of all in Dworkin and Allan, perhaps too strongly in that they equate the constitution and its legitimacy with a set of substantive liberal principles.[185]

182 See Dworkin, 'The Model of Rules I' and 'The Model of Rules II'.

183 See Joseph Raz, *The Concept of a Legal System: An Introduction to the Theory of a Legal System* (Oxford: Clarendon Press, 1980, 2nd ed.), 197–200, who says at 200 that only some 'jurisprudential criterion', some 'general truth about law' can answer the question whether a law is a law of a system.

184 For insightful remarks along these lines, see Fuller, 'Positivism and Fidelity to Law', 638–43. By far the majority of Kelsen scholars would reject this interpretation; see, for example, the essays in Michel Troper, *Pour Une Théorie Juridique de L'État* (Paris: Presses Universitaires de France, 1994). But see Vinx, *Hans Kelsen's Pure Theory of Law*, in particular 157–63, where he seeks to make sense of Kelsen's rather bewildering set of definitions of 'constitution'.

185 And see MacCormick, *Questioning Sovereignty*, note 68, 93, where he follows the passage quoted above with:

> This, I think, shows that Kelsen was right in thinking that any fundamental norm underlying the whole of legal order has to be conceived as external to the constitution itself. The constitution is a totality of interrelated rules or norms that is historically given and yet dynamic in providing for the possibility of its own change by processes for which it itself makes provision. . . . [H]owever, there is no reason to follow Kelsen in treating this as a mere presupposition or transcendental hypothesis. Surely a working constitution requires this to be the kind of shared custom or convention held among those who treat the constitution as foundational of normative order. That is, then, a common social practice, and it is a practice that necessarily involves shared membership in what Dworkin calls a 'community of principle', not a mere chance overlap of practical attitudes among those who hold power . . . The idea of a *Grundnorm*, it is submitted, should be adapted to this sense.

It is unclear, however, how the basic norm can in this light be considered 'external'.

There are, of course, major differences between Kelsen and Hart, on the one hand, and Dworkin and Allan, on the other. Kelsen and Hart regarded judicial interpretation of the law as a kind of legislation, whereas Dworkin and Allan regard judges as under a duty to give the 'one right answer' which the best principled interpretation of the law can deliver.[186] But in retrospect debate about this issue may seem to have been rather a waste of energy.

The debate makes sense if one agrees with Bentham that judicial interpretation should be marginalized to the extent possible, for democratic utilitarianism holds that such interpretation is an arbitrary intervention in the lawmaking process. But from Austin on, legal positivists and political constitutionalists have conceded to judges a legitimate role in deciding cases when it is controversial what the law requires. As Hart's take on the judicial virtues shows, discretion seems to vanish from the positivist vocabulary when it comes to describing what judges do in such cases. Put differently, from the internal point of view of a legal official charged with interpreting the law, the answer to a question about what the law requires must be the judge's good faith and best shot at showing both that the legal order speaks with one voice on the question and that the answer is based on principles which justify it to those whom it affects.[187]

Examples such as *Halliday* and *Jackson* are thus parochial only in that they illustrate that the way in which judges in one jurisdiction dealt concretely with concrete legal questions can help to answer the more abstract question of constitutionality. In other words, that question will always be answered in the same way – by resort to both formal authorization rules and substantive principles – even though the content of the

[186] Dworkin, 'Hard Cases', in Dworkin, *Taking Rights Seriously* 81.

[187] Gardner claims that Dworkin's view is 'crazy' that the constitution's meaning never changes at the hands of judges, a claim so 'crazy', he says, that he is 'reluctant' to attribute it to Dworkin: Gardner, *Law as a Leap of Faith*, 38. However, far from being crazy, the claim is entailed when one adopts the internal point of view of a judge. Gardner also suggests, at 37, that Dworkin possibly never held the view, referring to Dworkin, *Justice in Robes* (Cambridge, MA: Belknap Press, 2006), 266; and that Dworkin seemed to have changed his mind when in Dworkin, *Law's Empire*, 255–63, he seemed to say that the 'right answer' is 'relativized to the convictions of each judge'. In *Justice in Robes*, however, at 266, note 3, Dworkin insisted that he did not change his mind about the thesis and he was clear in *Law's Empire* that his view was that the right answer thesis is consistent with recognizing both that the law changes over time at the hands of judges and that judicial convictions are an intrinsic element of working out the right answer.

actual answers must differ according to time and place.[188] In addition, one of the ways in which the examples are parochial is significant. They show that even in a parliamentary legal order there are, following Allan, constitutional and substantive 'qualifications already latent within the supremacy doctrine, awaiting elaboration if and when circumstances dictate'. That entails that while the content of the actual answers will vary greatly, there is a limit to that variation because the ultimate addressees of the circular process of justification are the legal subjects, who want to understand both why the legal order speaks with one voice on the question and why its answer is based on principles which justify it to them. As I have suggested, the juridical relationship between ruler and ruled which is thus established is also a political relationship, a governmental contract or *Herrschaftsvertrag*. Section 3.9 ends this chapter by setting out the implications of the political dimension of this relationship for our understanding of the authority of constitutions.

3.8 Constitutionalism and the Basic Legitimation Demand

Because the relationship is political as well as juridical, the answer to the question of constitutionality is part and parcel of satisfying what Bernard Williams called the 'Basic Legitimation Demand'.[189] This is the demand which every modern legal state must satisfy if it is to show that it wields authority, rather than sheer or unmediated coercive power, over those subject to its rule. To meet that demand, Williams said, the state 'has to be able to offer a justification of its power *to each subject*'.[190]

Constitutional law, on this view, is no more than jumped-up administrative law, so long as we understand that the implicit assumption behind this label is wrong.[191] The assumption is that there is a qualitative

188 In a bill-of-rights legal order when the issue is whether a statutory provision violates one of the protected rights, it might seem that only substantive principles are in play. But I think it is almost always the case that judges should consider that the legislature has issued a formal judgment on the matter, so in issue will be questions of deference and proportionality. In some jurisdictions, for example the USA, such 'formal' questions get submerged, just as in parliamentary legal orders issues of substantive principle often lurk below the surface of formalistic judgments.

189 Bernard Williams, 'Realism and Moralism in Political Theory', in Williams, *In the Beginning Was the Deed: Realism and Moralism in Political Argument* (Princeton: Princeton University Press, 2005, Geoffrey Hawthorn, ed.) 1.

190 Ibid, 5. His emphasis.

191 There is an intuitive difference between constitutional law and administrative law in that constitutional law largely concerns the conduct of the legislature while administrative

difference between administrative law and constitutional law because administrative law is a linear matter of delegated authority, whereas constitutional law is not. But this thought misperceives the quality of administrative law, as did the proponents of the 'ultra vires doctrine', who argued some years ago in the UK that the grounds of judicial review of administrative action must be sourced in a doctrine of actual legislative intent, that is, in judgments made outside of legal order the determinate content of which is then transmitted to subjects.

As the critics of the ultra vires doctrine showed, administrative law is best understood as a project in which judges and other legal officials seek to work out the constitutional principles which discipline the decisions taken by those who act on behalf of the state.[192] And as Kelsen argued, there is a quantitative, not a qualitative, difference between this kind of review and review of statutes for their constitutionality,[193] a powerful argument so long as one grasps the quality of administrative law review as constitutional review writ small. Indeed, with this qualification in place, and as I show in Chapter 4, one can go further with Kelsen and reject Gardner's assertion that '[c]onstitutional law is as high as the law goes' because public international law is higher still, and so is a necessary part of an account of the modern legal state's authority.[194]

On this view, every legal order must have a constitution because the constitution comes about through the complex interactions of institutions which have more or less differentiated roles to play in both producing and maintaining the order. That constitution must contain formal authorization rules delineating the roles. But it must also contain substantive principles of two sorts. First, the formal authorization rules are themselves justified by substantive principles which will come into view when an institution is challenged on the basis that it has not performed

law concerns the conduct of administrative officials charged with implementing the legislature's statutes. But the conduct of administrative officials is subject to constitutional norms which courts will enforce; and in jurisdictions like Canada where administrative tribunals are recognized to have a role in interpreting the constitution, the norms of the entrenched bill of rights become part of administrative law.

192 Many of the main interventions in this debate can be found in Christopher Forsyth, ed., *Judicial Review and the Constitution* (Oxford: Hart Publishing, 2000).

193 Kelsen, 'The Nature and Development of Constitutional Adjudication'.

194 Though the qualification requires that public international law be seen as circular and thus, as Evan Fox-Decent argues, as 'co-constituted by national and international law'; see Fox-Decent, 'Constitutional Legitimacy Unbound', in Dyzenhaus and Thorburn, eds, *Philosophical Foundations of Constitutional Law* 119, at 139. I elaborate a similar view in Chapter 4.

its role. Second, the norms of the public law of the order will require interpretation, that is, the norms explicitly articulated in different positive law materials and the norms of the unwritten constitution, both of which will overlap with the justificatory principles. When the institution or institutions charged with interpreting the law perform that role, the answer they give must present itself as the good faith and best shot answer described in Section 3.7.

Here too principles will come into view as a result of challenges to the way in which institutions are performing their roles. The point about challenge is important because a legal order orders relations both between the individuals subject to it and between those individuals and the state; and, as legal subjects, the individuals are entitled to get answers from the appropriate institution about the content of their legal rights and duties. The answers have to make the good faith attempt at making sense of the individuals' subjection to law – of the claim that order exists to make it possible for them to interact under conditions of stability and security.

This rather sparse Hobbesian constraint permits a wide variety of different institutional arrangements for determining the legal will of the political community and of different content for what I called in Section 3.4 the actual constitution. In a bill-of-rights legal order, the discussion of the content of the actual constitution will be framed but not determined by the abstract and general statements of the commitments in the bill. In a parliamentary legal order, the discussion will be framed but not determined by the public statements of rights commitments over time, including in a common law system by judicial pronouncements.

But in both cases, the content of the actual constitution is always a matter of both form and substance and, ultimately, a matter of argument and justification. In both cases, the legal constitutionalists recognize – as did Williams in his critique of utilitarianism – that value is partly constituted by our projects.[195] And when we regard ourselves as having united our wills with others to empower a sovereign, we find that we have done more than create a mechanism through which to exercise our unbounded will. We have created a collective self, defined (as human persons are) by commitments and projects which have normative force in our deliberations which are not reducible to 'what we have reason to do all things considered', whether this is established by utilitarian

[195] Bernard Williams, 'A Critique of Utilitarianism', in Williams and JJC Smart, *Utilitarianism: For and against* (Cambridge: Cambridge University Press, 1973) 76.

calculation or by one or other process of deliberation recommended by a moral realist position. Further, the deliberations confer authority on our collective decisions in a never-ending process of seeking to ensure the integrity of the public decisions to be found in our legal record. Coherence is a crucial aspect of 'integrity'. But another aspect which Williams highlighted is remaining true to one's long-held projects and substantive commitments.[196]

The issue of whether and how legality connects to certain constitutional substantive commitments is really part of a larger disagreement about the sources of public normativity. The legal positivist tradition, broadly understood, attempts to find the sources of law's authority outside of law and so wants to insist on a methodology for establishing binding public norms which makes it possible for law to transmit its results as a linear theory of legal authority prescribes. That builds into legal positivism a tendency to respond to the question of constitutionality with the answer 'formal authorization rules'. In contrast, the legal constitutionalists find the sources of law's authority within the law and so try to make sense of the fundamental, substantive, public commitments of their order in the way a circular theory of authority requires, and as is suggested by Williams's point about projects, commitments and integrity. In this light, the debate about the question of constitutionality can be reconceived as one to be approached within a *Staatsrechtslehre*, a combination of philosophical and constitutional theory, since it is a question about the correct theory of public legal right and the legitimacy of the modern legal state. In that same light, once legal positivism and political constitutionalism are merged, they can productively engage with the legal constitutionalism of Allan and Dworkin.[197]

One could explain Hart's lack of attention to these topics, as I do in Chapter 4, as due to the fact that he was writing in the context of a legal order in which the parliament is taken to be able to make any law it pleases, and so to his implicit assumption that he could base a general legal theory on a very partial account of his own legal order. For the moment, I want to note that there is in Hartian legal positivism not only the persistent theme that the content of the law is what is determinable as

[196] Ibid, 116–17.

[197] Jeffrey Goldworthy's work is a fine example of what I have in mind in this merger, though he may not see things quite this way. See, for example, Goldsworthy, *Parliamentary Sovereignty, Contemporary Debates* (Cambridge: Cambridge University Press, 2010).

a matter of fact, but also the legacy of Bentham's and Austin's distaste for entrenched bills of rights which limit the scope of legislation by giving authority to judges to determine the limits. Bentham provided a political argument based on the maximization of utility, while Austin suggested that such limits are conceptually unavailable since constitutional law is not law properly so-called, but merely positive or conventional morality. In addition, Bentham's efforts to find ways to diminish the opportunities for judges to impose their views on the content of legislation support the kind of theory of adjudication which requires that the content of the law be determinable by factual tests.[198]

Similarly, despite Hart's rejection of the command theory of law, the image of a supreme parliament which is legally constituted but may make any law that it pleases – a law with any content in positivist parlance – dominates his imagination not only in *The Concept of Law* but also in other writings. Like Bentham and Austin, he seems haunted by the potential in natural law theories to provide the resources for judges to impose substantive limits on the ability of such a body to make a law with any content. For example, he specifically warned against the temptation to 'exploit the moral implications latent in the vocabulary of the law and especially in words like *ius*, *recht*, *diritto*, *droit* which are laden with the theory of Natural Law', lest it lead to saying that 'enactments which enjoined or permitted iniquity should not be recognized as valid, or have the quality of law, even if the system in which they were enacted acknowledged no restriction upon the legislative competence of the legislature'.[199]

As a result, a major gap opened in Hart's thought as to why he ruled out the operation of constitutional principles if not found in a positive legal instrument. The gap can be plugged only by a version of what he took to be Kelsen's redundant idea of a basic constitutional norm, and which argues for the superiority of the kind of legal order in which

[198] They did disagree on some matters pertinent to my discussion. I have already mentioned that Austin did not share Bentham's faith in the wisdom of the judgments of 'the people', and so advocated a large role for judicial elites in legislating. In addition, Bentham not only coined the term 'international law', but wished to promote its development, while Austin denied that it was law properly so-called; like constitutional law, it is merely positive morality. See MW Janis, 'Bentham and the Fashioning of "International Law"' (1984) 78 *American Journal of International Law* 405.

[199] Hart, *The Concept of Law*, 208.

parliament is supreme.[200] If that gap is not plugged, Hart is left with an entirely static account of law of the sort Kelsen described when he argued that to adopt the static perspective as the sole perspective on law is the greatest flaw in what he called the 'analytical jurisprudence' of John Austin. Such a perspective 'regards law as a system of rules complete and ready for application, without regard to the process of their creation'. In contrast:

> The pure theory of law recognizes that a study of the statics of law must be supplemented by a study of its dynamics, the process of its creation. This necessity exists because the law, unlike any other system of norms, regulates its own creation. An analysis of positive law shows that the process by which a legal norm is created is regulated by another legal norm. Indeed, usually other norms determine not only the process of creation, but also, to a greater or lesser extent, the content of the norm to be created. Thus, a constitution both regulates the procedure by which statutes are created, and contains provisions, mostly negative, concerning their content.[201]

Now in his 1958 essay, Hart had on behalf of his positivist tradition emphatically rejected the view that it supports a theory of adjudication according to which 'the law was a closed logical system in which judges deduced their decisions from premises'. 'The root of this evil', Hart said, 'is preoccupation with the separation of powers and Blackstone's "childish fiction" (as Austin termed it) that judges only "find," never "make," law.'[202] For the same reason, Hart would have repudiated Kelsen's attribution of a static theory of law to his positivist tradition.

Recall, however, that the rule of recognition is supposed to be a cure for the 'uncertainty' of rules in a primitive society. Among the rules it identifies are the secondary rules of change and adjudication. Hart

200 See further Stephen Perry, 'Political Authority and Political Obligation', in Leslie Green and Brian Leiter, eds, *Oxford Studies in Philosophy of Law* (Oxford: Oxford University Press, 2013) 1. At 73, Perry cites Waldron, 'Who Needs Rules of Recognition?', and says that 'the priority Hart gives to the rule of recognition over power-conferring secondary rules seems to me to be clearly in tension with his fundamental insight that the "introduction into society of rules enabling legislators to change and add to the rules of duty, and judges to determine when the rules of duty have been broken, is a step forward as important to society as the invention of the wheel." In other words, at the foundational level of law, it is legislative and judicial powers . . . that are most important, not judicial duties.'

201 Hans Kelsen, 'The Pure Theory of Law and Analytical Jurisprudence' (1941) 55 *Harvard Law Review* 44, 49.

202 Hart, 'Positivism and the Separation of Law and Morals', 66.

claimed that the former cure the problem of the 'static' nature of the rules in a 'primitive' society, while the latter cure the problem of 'inefficiency'.[203] The former have to do with legislative change while the latter have to do with identifying adjudicative officials and prescribing the procedures they are to follow. It seems clear from Hart's brief account in chapter 5 of *The Concept of Law*, from his discussion of his core/penumbra model of adjudication in 'Positivism and the Separation of Law and Morals'[204] and from his sustained critique of Dworkin for offering a mere theory of adjudication,[205] that the rules of adjudication fall into two groups.

If judges decide that the rule in dispute has in fact a determinate content which answers the question posed by the dispute, they do no more than identify the law as it is in the core. In this way, they operationalize the rule of recognition. If, however, they find that there is no such determinate content, they are in the penumbra, and so they are operationalizing a rule of change in order to decide what the law ought to be by filling in a gap. In that case, they are not doing anything different from legislators.[206] Hence, the dynamic dimension of legal order, understood as legislative change, is not a topic for philosophy of law. It is relegated to other disciplines – a Dworkinian political theory of adjudication or social science. All that philosophy of law can say about the situation is that judges are exercising a discretion, as in the case of an actual legislature, though writ small in the case of judges. Of course, once the change has been made, assuming that the officials making it had the authority to do so, the rule of recognition will certify the new rule as valid.

It is this insistence on discretion which explains the fact that, as Waldron points out, at times Hart seems to suppose that the rules of change (not the rule of recognition) are the ultimate rules of legal order. In accordance with my argument in this chapter, it follows that Hart's rule of recognition is a needless reduplication of his rules of change. The ultimate norms of a legal order are, in Hart's theory, the rules which provide the criteria for making a valid change in the law.[207] Moreover, as

[203] Hart, *The Concept of Law*, 92–3.

[204] Hart, 'Positivism and the Separation of Law and Morals', 62ff.

[205] Hart, *The Concept of Law*, 239–44.

[206] It is also possible that there is a core or determinate answer, but the judges have the authority to depart from it.

[207] Norberto Bobbio, 'Pour un lexique de théorie générale du droit', in Bobbio, *Essais de Théorie du Droit* (Paris: Bruylant LGDJ, 1998, Michel Guéret, trans.) 55, at 59–61;

the brilliant Italian political and legal philosopher Norberto Bobbio pointed out, not only is it plausible that Hart's rules of change must in his scheme be ultimate but also there is something strange about calling them rules of *change*. On Bobbio's account, the novelty in Hart's theory of secondary rules is limited to the name he gave to a phenomenon long recognized by Kelsen-influenced European jurists under the title of 'juridical production'; that is, the 'norms by which the juridical order regulates the process of creation, of modification and of extinction of norms'.[208]

Bobbio argued that 'production' is more 'precise' than 'change' because it is capable of including a plurality of legal effects, for example the norms which govern contracts and the norms which govern the exercise of judicial power. He observed that Hart noted a 'kinship' between rules of change and the norms which govern 'the making of wills, contracts, transfers of property, and many other voluntarily created structures which typify life under law'.[209] But, said Bobbio, there is something more than a 'simple kinship'.[210] He argued further that a rule-of-recognition account of law is best suited to an order, if one has ever existed, of the kind Hart calls a 'primitive' society, in which 'the norm which has the function of permitting the identification of the norms of the system is confined to indicating a set of norms created once and for all, and which are, therefore, in the true sense of the word "recognized"'. But it is doubtful, Bobbio claimed, that that kind of society qualifies, on Hart's or any terms, as a legal society.[211]

Bobbio's analysis points in the following direction. There is one other kind of society, which, if it ever existed, would amount to a legal society, in which something like Hart's rule of recognition operated as he claimed it did for all legal societies. Imagine a legal society in which there is parliamentary supremacy and statutes are the only source of law. There the unwritten constitution would require that legal officials recognize as law only those artefacts which are produced in accordance with the criteria for recognizing a statute as valid. In addition, the rules of

Riccardo Guastini, 'The Basic Norm Revisited', in Luìs Duarte d'Almeida, John Gardner and Leslie Green, eds, *Kelsen Revisited: New Essays on the Pure Theory of Law* (Oxford: Hart Publishing, 2013) 63, at 72–4; Waldron, 'Who Needs Rules of Recognition?', 327.

208 Bobbio, 'Pour un lexique de théorie générale du droit', 60, quoting from a work by Tomaso Perassi. (My translation.)

209 Hart, *The Concept of Law*, 96.

210 Bobbio, 'Pour un lexique de théorie générale du droit', 60–1.

211 Ibid, 61.

adjudication would require judges to determine all cases in which the content of the law was disputed in accordance with factual tests as to legislative intention in order to avoid making their determinations a rival source of law, an objective supported by legislative efforts to draft clear and comprehensive codes of conduct and by stripping judgments of precedential force. In short, the society would approximate Bentham's vision of the ideal legal society in which law can serve as the instrument of unadulterated utilitarian judgments made by the legislature.[212]

In this society, the rules of adjudication serve the objective of preserving the content of legislative judgments, while the rule of recognition, which Bobbio suggested might be appropriate for a primitive society, differs only in that it is iterative. By 'iterative' I mean that each time the legislature effectuates a change in the law, an item in the collection of norms in the statically conceived legal system changes. It is a society which is legal in that there is only one mechanism – one mode of juridical production – recognized for bringing change in the law. The problem of the static nature of the rules is solved in a way which can be explained by a static model of law, since norm production happens in one way only and outside of its scope of inquiry. Hart, ironically, and as we saw in Section 3.1, thought that this kind of society provides the knockdown demonstration that Kelsen's basic norm is a 'needless reduplication' because it suggests there is 'a further rule to the effect that the constitution [is] to be obeyed'.[213]

Moreover, as Riccardo Guastini, relying on Bobbio, has pointed out, in the UK context such rules of change are 'but the *constitution itself*, which provides the criteria of validity of legislation and any further "lower" rules'.[214] There is, then, no further role for a rule of recognition, unless one thinks it important for philosophy of law to explain why those who accept the constitution as binding regard it as a legitimate authority over them, that is, as legitimated by something extra-legal, for example, a utilitarian theory of political morality, a thought Hart always vigorously resisted.

[212] See AWB Simpson, 'The Common Law and Legal Theory', in Simpson, ed., *Oxford Essays in Jurisprudence* (Oxford: Oxford University Press, 1973, 2nd series) 77 and Gerald Postema, *Bentham and the Common Law Tradition* (Oxford: Clarendon Press, 1986).

[213] Hart, *The Concept of Law*, 29.

[214] Guastini, 'The Basic Norm Revisited', 72–3, his emphasis. See also Gerald Postema, 'Law's System: The Necessity of System in Common Law' (2014) 69 *New Zealand Law Review* 69, at 85.

Notice also that the legal order here is a unified system of rules in only an external sense in that there is one ultimate or sovereign authority which is the source of all law, exactly the problem Raz diagnosed with Austin's command model of law.[215] Raz thus accepted Kelsen's argument that 'it is impossible to grasp the nature of law if we limit our attention to the single isolated rule', that is, the internal relationship between norms has to be explained.[216] But he rejected the dynamic theory Kelsen thought necessary if one wishes to understand the unity of legal order from the inside, from the internal point of view of the jurist or the judge.[217] That rejection is yet more evidence of the inability of the English tradition of legal positivism to move beyond Austin's command theory.

Kelsen, in contrast, did have a lot to say about the proper role of constitutional adjudication and the place and kind of constitutions in the construction of legal order. Again, context can be invoked as part of the explanation, since Kelsen was one of the designers of the Austrian Constitutional Court – the first of its kind – as well as a judge on its first bench.[218] But Kelsen argued that the commitment to legality inherent in the idea of the modern legal state is best fulfilled when there is an entrenched written constitution, with constitutional guarantees as narrowly framed as possible, and with an independent court which has full power to review both statutes and executive acts for their compliance with the constitution.[219] In addition, as we will see in Chapter 4, he argued for monism about public international law, for the position that the basic norm of the international legal order is also the basic norm of all national legal orders. He thus favoured the establishment of international courts which could decide conflicts between the norms of international law and those made by sovereign states.[220] He did, in short, provide a pretty full theory of constitutionalism, though in much of his work he portrayed the choice for a constitutional court as well as for monism of the sort he favoured as one for political, not legal theory.

[215] Joseph Raz, *The Concept of a Legal System: An Introduction to the Theory of a Legal System* (Oxford: Clarendon Press, 1980, 2nd ed.), 25–6.

[216] Ibid, 88, quoting Kelsen, *General Theory of Law and State*, 3.

[217] Ibid, 128ff.

[218] For Kelsen's own account of the court's work, see his 'Judicial Review of Legislation: A Comparative Study of the Austrian and the American Constitution' (1942) 2 *The Journal of Politics* 183.

[219] Kelsen, 'The Nature and Development of Constitutional Adjudication'.

[220] See for example, Kelsen, *Introduction to the Problems of Legal Theory*, 116–17.

It is highly plausible, then, to reconstruct Kelsen's thought so as not to understand him as a philosopher with two hats: a legal theory hat, on the one hand, and a constitutional-political hat, on the other. Rather, one should see his legal theory as not only a political legal theory but also as a theory of constitutionalism – as the quite seamless elaboration of his bid to understand the modern legal order in a 'pure' or non-ideological way.[221] It is an account of a peaceful and orderly testing ground for competing political ideologies, at least for those prepared to confine their contest to the terms adopted by one willing to take the perspective of the legal subject.

Given the current deadlock in philosophy of law, and the possibility of a productive exchange between legal philosophy, on the one hand, and theories of constitutionalism and political legitimacy, on the other, in which a range of common concerns are recognized, that suggestion has, in my view, much to recommend it. In Chapter 4, I follow through on the suggestion by elaborating the implications of philosophy of law reconceived as *Staatsrechtslehre* for an understanding of the relationship between national legal orders and 'law beyond the state'.

[221] See Vinx, *Hans Kelsen's Pure Theory of Law* and *The Guardian of the Constitution*, also Honoré, 'The Basic Norm of a Society' and Notermans, 'Social Peace as *Conditio Tacita* for the Validity of the Positive Legal Order'. See also Michael Stolleis, *A History of Public Law in Germany, 1914–1945* (Oxford: Oxford University Press, 2004), 155–6, on Kelsen and his school:

> These normativists set their sights on a legal order that was only normative and virtually purged of ancillary sciences and metaphysics, all in an effort to reach a level of scholarliness that was appropriate to the pure legal proposition ... This would make legal scholarship unassailable against objections derived from both the concrete reality of the multi-ethnic state, and from morality and natural law, which was in the purview of the Church. For a class of scholars in which many were of Jewish background, and thus usually opted for democracy, rights of freedom, emancipation, and social balance, 'scholarliness' was also the suitable platform to combat the anti-Semitism that had long since become virulent in Austria and the clericalism that to some extent went hand in hand with it. Consequently, the sharp separation of law from history, politics, and morality, and the corresponding insistence on 'purity', was also a political response – dressed in the garb of legal theory – to the crisis of the Hapsburg Empire that was affecting all spheres of society.

4

The Janus-Faced Constitution

In Chapter 3, I discussed the complicated relationship between constitution as act and constitution as achievement, as well as the idea that the constitution is greater than the sum of its parts. This chapter focuses on the remaining issue which complicates our understanding of constitutionality – its Janus-faced nature. The act of constitution, that is, looks both inwards and outwards.

Janus is usually thought of as the Roman god of doors and doors can be shut and barred against the outside. But he is also the god of door*ways*, thresholds, passages and transitions, which offers an alternative way of understanding the act of constitution as liminal rather than exclusionary, as establishing not so much a barrier as a threshold or point of transition. On this second understanding, the act of constitution not only affects the space outside of it. It is also affected by and affects the legal orders in that space, both with respect to the form in which it is constituted and in that the threshold marks a point which norms can and sometimes must cross to make their way from one space to another.

I want to use these images to explore three legal relationships in which the Janus-faced aspect of the constitution of the modern legal state seems central: first, the relationship between national law[1] and public international law; second, the relationship between states which gives rise to private international law, the field which concerns the application of the private law norms of one state to a dispute in another; finally, the reach of the public law norms of a national order beyond the territorial limits of the state in the field of 'foreign relations law', in which questions arise about whether public officials acting outside of a state's borders are governed by the public law of their country, for example, by the rights in a bill-of-rights constitution.

[1] I use 'national', 'municipal' and 'domestic' interchangeably, though with a preference for 'national', to describe the law and legal order of an individual modern legal state.

My argument requires a rather steep ascent to what James Crawford, an eminent public international lawyer, calls the 'glacial uplands of juristic abstraction',[2] the debate about international law between Hans Kelsen and HLA Hart. Kelsen devoted more attention to the theory and practice of international law than any other major twentieth-century legal theorist. However, a recent revival of interest in public international law among Anglo-American legal philosophers either ignores his contribution altogether or regards it largely through the lens of Hart's disparaging account in which, as I pointed out in the Introduction, he accused Kelsen of making 'perverse', 'confused', 'profoundly mistaken', 'highly idiosyncratic' and 'content-obsessed' arguments, and of putting forth a 'comic' theory based on a 'useless' central idea.[3] The revival also altogether ignores the division in international law between public and private international law; more accurately, it ignores the latter altogether, and so treats international law as if the issues it raises for philosophy of law were confined to its public dimension. It goes without saying that foreign relations law is also not generally part of the debate.

Hart's theory of law occupies centre stage in this resurgence and doctrinal public international lawyers usually adopt his theoretical vocabulary, in particular his account of the rule of recognition, when they feel the need for some theoretical tools. This is a puzzle because Hart saw philosophy of public international law as peripheral to the main task of jurisprudence – to analyse the 'distinctive structure of a municipal

[2] James Crawford, *Brownlie's Principles of Public International Law* (Oxford: Oxford University Press, 2012, 8th ed.), 50.

[3] HLA Hart, *The Concept of Law* (Oxford: Clarendon Press, 1994, 2nd ed.), 236, and HLA Hart, 'Kelsen Visited' and 'Kelsen's Doctrine of the Unity of Law', in Hart, *Essays in Jurisprudence* (Oxford: Clarendon Press, 1983) 286 and 309, at 302, 313, 321. And I pointed out in the Introduction that, in an interview in 1988, Hart said that Kelsen's 'central error was his … "content-obsession"; this led him to attempt to determine the question whether laws belong to the same or different systems solely by an examination of their content'. Hart, 'Answers to Eight Questions', in Luís Duarte D'Almeida, James Edwards and Andrea Dolcetti, eds, *Reading HLA Hart's The Concept of Law* (Oxford: Hart Publishing, 2013) 279, at 290. Things are very different in work by European scholars. See, notably: Jochen von Bernstoff, *The Public International Law Theory of Hans Kelsen: Believing in International Law* (Cambridge: Cambridge University Press, 2010, Thomas Dunlap, trans.); Lars Vinx, *Hans Kelsen's Pure Theory of Law: Legality and Legitimacy* (Oxford: Oxford University Press, 2007); Alexander Somek, 'Kelsen Lives' (2007) 17 *European Journal of International Law* 4; Alexander Somek, 'Monism: A Tale of the Undead', in Matej Avbelj and Jan Komárek, eds, *Constitutional Pluralism in the European Union and beyond* (Oxford: Hart Publishing, 2012) 343; and Paul Gragl, *Legal Monism: Law, Philosophy, and Politics* (Oxford: Oxford University Press, 2018).

legal system'[4] – and deemed its study 'only a relatively small and unimportant part of the most famous and controversial theories of law'.[5] In addition, his own analysis of public international law is widely considered problematic.[6] But while Hart is thought not to have been quite on his game when it came to public international law, it may seem that his is the only game in town when it comes to the place of such law in a general theory of law.[7]

I argue here that Hart not only disparaged Kelsen, but also distorted his key ideas because of his own parochial understanding of legal order. With these distortions corrected, we can see that it is high time for philosophy of law to return to Kelsen if it is to make progress, not least because Kelsenian legal theory shows us the benefits of reversing the order of argument about public international law. Instead of, first, constructing a theory of the law of a national legal order – the internal law of the modern legal state – and, second, asking whether public international law is law in its light, we should see that understanding the legality of international law – both public and private – illuminates how philosophy of law might productively address some of its central problems.

[4] Hart, *The Concept of Law*, 17.

[5] Ibid, 4.

[6] See Jeremy Waldron, 'International Law: "A Relatively Small and Unimportant Part of Jurisprudence"', in D'Almeida, Edwards and Dolcetti, eds, *Reading HLA Hart's The Concept of Law* 209.

[7] Liam Murphy notes the same phenomenon, including Kelsen's prominence, but takes Hart as his foil in 'Law beyond the State: Some Philosophical Questions' (2017) 28 *European Journal of International Law* 203. Even Ronald Dworkin's posthumously published 'A New Philosophy for International Law' (2013) 41 *Philosophy and Public Affairs* 1, which seeks to show that his interpretive theory provides an answer to the question of public international law's legal status, takes place on Hart's terrain. To apply his approach to international law, Dworkin had to imagine that the international legal order has gone a long way to establishing the institutions we associate with the separation of powers in a domestic legal order, that is, that the General Assembly of the UN takes a legislative role and there is an international court which plays an integral part in advising the General Assembly on the legality of its proposed legislation. Since his proposal gives the court a compulsory jurisdiction in some legal disputes – all those in which the General Assembly is exercising its legislative jurisdiction – his thought experiment puts in place the institutions which would allow not only Hart's rule of recognition, but also Hart's other two secondary rules to operate – the 'rules of change' or of law-making and the 'rules of adjudication' which pertain to the role of those who interpret, apply and enforce the law. Dworkin's foray into international law thus invites a reprise of the deadlocked Hart–Dworkin debate about the adjudication of 'hard cases' in domestic law in which he sought to replace a rule of recognition, validity-based account of the law with his interpretive model.

I examine these issues through the lens of the debate about whether the relationship between public international law and national law should be understood as 'monists' or as 'dualists' urge. According to the former, 'national and international law form one single legal order, or at least a number of the interlocking orders which should be presumed to be coherent and consistent'.[8] In contrast, the latter emphasizes 'the distinct and independent character of the international and national legal systems'.[9] As Crawford explains, on this view, '[n]either legal order has the power to create or alter rules of the other. When international law applies in whole or in part within any national legal system, this is because of a rule of that system giving effect to national law.'[10] He further observes that in cases of conflict between public international law and national law, 'the dualist would assume that a national court would apply national law, or at least that it is for the national system to decide which rule is to prevail'.[11]

In this debate, Kelsen defended monism while Hart adopted, albeit mostly implicitly, dualism. I show that once Kelsen's position is freed from Hart's distortions there is a surprising twist to this debate. It turns out, as Kelsen always argued, that dualism does not exist as a theory of the relationship between national law and public international law. Rather, it is a dualistic practical set of arrangements a national legal order may adopt for structuring its monistically conceived relationship with public international law.

Moreover, monism here is the position I call 'international law monism' which, following Kelsen, holds that the basic norm of public international law grounds the validity of all national legal orders. In contrast, Hart's rule of recognition account of national legal order, while officially endorsing dualism, in fact presupposes the position I call 'national law monism'. According to that position, it is the rule of recognition of Hart's own legal order which grounds the validity of public international law. Hart's legal theory proves not only parochial because it is a theory of what I called in Chapter 3 a 'parliamentary legal order'; it is also unable to escape the clutches of Austin's command theory of law and his denial that public international law is law properly so-called.

[8] Crawford, *Brownlie's Principles of Public International Law*, 48.
[9] Ibid.
[10] Ibid.
[11] Ibid.

Section 4.1 situates Kelsen's basic norm and Hart's rule of recognition in the debate between monism and dualism in order to begin my argument that the basic norm does better in philosophy of law's attempt to account for the legality of public international law. I continue in this vein in Section 4.2, a discussion of the conflicts between legal norms in both private and public international law which may seem at first sight to provide evidence for dualism, but which in fact tells in favour of Kelsenian international law monism. Section 4.3 elaborates the juristic method I take to underpin Kelsen's approach and about which Hart was profoundly ambivalent. Section 4.4 indicates the promise of this method for an understanding of the reach of the public law norms of a national order outside its borders. Section 4.5 completes the arc of legality by taking the discussion back to Hobbes in order to introduce the topic of Section 4.6, the 'politics of recognition' inherent in a Kelsenian understanding of international law.

4.1 Monism versus Dualism in Hart and Kelsen

We saw in Chapter 3 that Kelsen, with Hart following him, sought to restore a constitutionalist idea to a central place in legal theory as an integral part of their attempt to explain law as a matter of authority. As a result, they both rejected Austin's denial that public international law is law properly so-called. Once sovereignty in the sense of ultimate law-making power was seen as not necessarily legally unlimited but rather always juridically constructed or legally constituted, both constitutional law and public international law are no longer ruled out as conceptually possible.[12] I suggested that the idea can be restored only if the authority of the constitution of a legal order is located within that order and the justification of that authority becomes circular rather than linear. Here I extend this argument to the modern legal state's relationship with law 'beyond the state'.

In the history of legal theory, both monism and dualism responded to the Austinian position that law beyond the state, in particular public

[12] The issue is not only conceptual. The claim that sovereignty is legally unlimited may be political as well as conceptual because the conceptual exclusion is done for political reasons, as I have suggested from Chapter 1 on. The idea that to be subject to law is to be subject to the sanctions of some institution is primarily motivated by political reasons not to have ultimate law-making power legally unconstrained and it works by appealing to the fact that such power is not subject to sanctions.

international law, is not law properly so-called because there is no world sovereign, in the sense of an ultimate lawmaking power not subject to anyone else's command but to which every national state is subject, and which can enforce international legal norms by threatening sanctions for non-compliance and effectively visiting them on delinquent states. The first attempt to move away from this position was made at the end of the nineteenth century when legal theorists sought to understand law both as a matter of authority and as the product of a legally unconstrained sovereign will. For them, there was the inward-looking face of sovereignty (the law of the sovereign which governs relationships between it and its subjects as well as between its subjects) and there was the outward-looking face (the law which governs its relationships with other sovereigns). With both national and public international law, the law binding the sovereign comes about because the sovereign chooses to be bound. Public international law is, on this view, interstate law – the product of combined sovereign wills – which becomes part of a national legal order only when the sovereign of that order chooses to make it so.

These theorists thus adopted dualism, a position which attempts to avoid denying that public international law is law. Instead, it asserts that the international and national legal orders are distinct in that public international law norms enter national space only when expressly incorporated by positive law. Their attempt failed as a matter of theory as it amounted to an uneasy compromise between the conceptual claim that the sovereign is a legally unlimited entity and their recognition that, as a matter of fact, sovereigns are legally bound by public law, whether national or international.

Because Kelsen and Hart opposed this unlimited conception of sovereignty, they did not foreclose the conceptual space for public international law (or for that matter national constitutional law) to be genuine law. It could even be said that they argued that legal theory should rid itself to the extent possible of the concept of sovereignty because in political and legal thought it is so bound up with the idea of a legally unlimited political entity. As Kelsen said at the end of his 1920 book on public international law, the 'concept of sovereignty should be radically supressed'.[13] The question for both was whether the space

[13] Hans Kelsen, *Das Problem der Souveränität und die Theorie des Völkerrechts: Beitrag zu Einer Reinen Rechtslehre* (Aalen: Scientia Verlag, 1981), 320. (My translation.) See Hart, *The Concept of Law*, 221 for similar doubts. As Hermann Heller argued in 1927, this is a flawed view of the history of political thought as early modern writers like Bodin and

opened by constructing sovereignty as a juridical concept permits a positive answer to the question whether public international law is law. Both answered 'Yes' to the question, though they also both found public international law problematic because it is 'primitive'.[14]

In one respect, their reason for using this label was similar. Although primitive societies lack legislatures and centralized law-enforcement agencies, the main mark of primitiveness is the lack of a judiciary – officials who can make authoritative determinations of the law.[15] But they differed radically in that Hart supposed that this institutional lack shows that there is no rule of recognition, which entailed for him that there is no legal order: 'there is no basic rule providing general criteria of validity for the rules of international law, and . . . the rules which are in fact operative constitute not a system but a set of rules, among which are the rules providing for the binding force of treaties'.[16] Hence, the analogy with the primitive society, though Hart asserted that the analogy goes only so far: 'In form, international law resembles such a regime of primary rules, even though the content of its often elaborate rules are very unlike those of a primitive society, and many of its concepts, methods and techniques are the same as those of modern municipal law.'[17]

Hart's analysis of public international law was largely driven by the Separation Thesis, by his determination to forestall any thought that the 'formal differences between international and municipal law can best be

Hobbes did not think of the sovereign as acting outside the scope of law. Moreover, attempts to radically suppress sovereignty must backfire, leaving the sovereign to reappear in Schmittean form. See my 'Introduction: The Politics of Sovereignty' to Herman Heller, *Sovereignty: A Contribution to the Theory of Public and International Law* (Oxford: Oxford University Press, 2019; David Dyzenhaus, ed., Belinda Cooper, trans.).

[14] Kelsen was unabashed about the use of 'primitive' to describe the international legal order, while Hart was a little more wary in *The Concept of Law*, 227. See Terry Nardin, *Law, Morality, and the Relations of States* (Princeton: Princeton University Press, 1983), 150–8. Hart's reliance on the idea of a primitive society is an example of the way in which his legal philosophy was parochial in that it was tied to time and place. He relied, that is, on the social evolutionary theory of British anthropologists at the time he wrote. See Coel Kirkby, 'Law Evolves: The Uses of Primitive Law in Anglo-American Concepts of Modern Law, 1861–1961' (2018) 58 *American Journal of Legal History* 535.

[15] For Hart, see *The Concept of Law*, 93–4. For Kelsen, see, for example, Hans Kelsen, *General Theory of Law and State* (Cambridge, MA: Harvard University Press, 1945, Anders Wedberg, trans.), 327.

[16] Hart, *The Concept of Law*, 236.

[17] Ibid, 227.

described by classifying the former as "morality"'.[18] Public international law is law and not morality, first, because when states reproach each other for lapses from it they do not resort to the moral language of 'conscience' but to 'technical' arguments based on relevant legal materials.[19] Second, in public international law, as in national law, there are many rules of the sort 'drive on the left' or 'a valid will requires two witnesses' which are morally neutral but important in order to ensure predictability and certainty.[20] Third, Hart repeated one of his main objections based on the Separation Thesis to any analogy between national law and morality: 'the very idea of change by human legislative *fiat* is repugnant to the idea of morality ... because we conceive of morality as the ultimate standard by which human actions (legislative or otherwise) are evaluated'. But, despite the fact that there is no legislature for public international law, he said there is 'nothing similarly inconsistent with the idea that the rules might be subject to legislative change'.[21] Fourth, while it is often said that the system as a whole must rest on 'a generally diffused conviction that there is a moral obligation to obey its rules', Hart thought that one can dismiss this claim for the same reason that he had dismissed it in the national context. While some states may indeed morally endorse public international law, there is a wide range of other reasons for endorsement: 'calculation of long-term interest, or ... the wish to continue a tradition or ... disinterested concern for others'.[22]

This argument is rather strange.[23] Its direction suggests that public international law is law and not morality both because its subjects accept it as mandatory and engage in law-like arguments about its requirements. However, Hart had earlier in *The Concept of Law* denied that there is law properly so-called in the primitive societies from which national legal orders emerge, despite the fact that such societies have customary public rules which express their most important values, rules maintained by criticism of lapses as well as by sanctions, albeit meted out inefficiently by self-help or collective group action. Moreover, Hart did not contemplate

18 Ibid.

19 Ibid, 228.

20 Ibid, 228–30.

21 Ibid, 230. For the earlier discussion, see, ibid, 177.

22 Ibid, 230–2.

23 A rather mild judgment, compared to Waldron's claim that it 'presents a frustrating combination of insight and obtuseness' in 'International Law: "A Relatively Small and Unimportant Part of Jurisprudence"', 209.

the possibility that where such customary norms exist in primitive societies, the group and individuals will deploy the kinds of legalistic techniques to determine their obligations which he finds in the international domain.[24] Finally, his third reason – the lack of a legislature – should speak on his understanding of morality to an analogy, not a disanalogy, between the rules of public international law and those of morality; and it is unclear why within his fourth reason, 'disinterested concern for others', is not a moral motive, while 'long-term interest' is surely a candidate for one.

Legal theorists sympathetic to Hart's general position but critical of his rather nonchalant treatment of public international law have sought to show that, contrary to his claim, public international law has much more developed secondary rules than he had detected.[25] The path not taken is Kelsen's, perhaps because it is thought that Hart had successfully shown why Kelsen's must fail.[26]

Unlike Hart's, Kelsen's path is via his constitutionalist idea, the basic norm. Kelsen did not think that a society in which there are only customary norms lacks a legal order. It has one, so long as the members of that society both accept the norms as binding and seek to understand each norm as part of a meaningful unity. The members will presuppose the basic norm and there is in place a legal order, albeit a primitive one. Similarly, so long as one can hypothesize a basic norm for the norms of

[24] See the perfunctory references to anthropological literature in Hart, *The Concept of Law*, 291–2. See also A Campbell, 'International Law and Primitive Law' (1988) 8 *Oxford Journal of Legal Studies* 169.

[25] This is Waldron's strategy, 'International Law: "A Relatively Small and Unimportant Part of Jurisprudence"'. For a more elaborate argument along these lines, see Mehrdad Payandeh, 'The Concept of International Law in the Jurisprudence of HLA Hart' (2010) 21 *European Journal of International Law* 967. As Payendeh points out, there is much better evidence for public international law's institutional maturity some fifty years after Hart published *The Concept of Law*. See also Murphy, 'Law beyond the State: Some Philosophical Questions'.

[26] In 'What Makes a Social Order Primitive? In Defense of Hart's Take on International Law' (2017) 23 *Legal Theory* 258, 262, David Lefkowitz argues that Hart's understanding of a primitive order depends not on a 'functional distinction' which turns on the absence of secondary rules, but on a 'specialization distinction' which turns on whether there is a division of labour in identifying, altering, applying and enforcing law. I agree with Lefkowitz that a focus on a division of labour can be helpful, as I argue in Section 4.5; and his discussion of the ambiguities in Hart's account of public international law is valuable. But, in my view, the way to disambiguate is to move Hart's theory in the direction of a Kelsenian de jure account of authority, something which Lefkowitz almost acknowledges, especially when he talks about 'de facto legitimacy'. See 279, note 80.

public international law, there is in place a legal order, one demanding obedience from all those subject to it. In the international legal order, as in a primitive society, the subjects – respectively, states and individual human beings – are at the same time the officials, responsible as they are for interpreting as well as enforcing the public norms of their order.

This difference in turn affects Hart's and Kelsen's answer to the question whether there is public international law. Hart's answer is 'Yes, there is public international law in the sense of discrete binding rules, but no international legal order', while for Kelsen there is public international law because there is international legal order. It is precisely this conception of legal order which led to Kelsen's opposition to dualism about the relationship between the international order, on the one hand, and national orders, on the other. He distinguished between what I call 'national law monism' and 'international law monism'. The former insists that only one national legal order exists so that valid legal norms are only those norms which can trace their validity to its own basic norm. The latter states that there are many valid national legal orders but they are all part of the international legal order and so trace the ultimate validity of their norms back to its basic norm.

Kelsen argued for international law monism, qualified by the suggestion in much of his work that his preference for this kind of monism is a political one for cosmopolitanism over nationalism and imperialism, and so not dictated by legal theory.[27] But in his 1920 book on public international law, he indicated that only international law monism provides a coherent account of the juridical relationship between public international law and national law and argued as follows:

> There is a generally accepted understanding of the nature and concept of international law that it constitutes a community of states with equal rights. The proposition of the coexistence of a multiplicity of communities, which despite their actual differences in size, population, and effective means of exercising power are from the perspective of legality [*rechtlich*] of equal value and, when it comes to their mutually delimited spheres of power, bound in a higher community is an eminently ethical idea and one of the few really valuable and uncontested components of contemporary cultural consciousness. But this proposition is only possible

[27] See for example, Hans Kelsen, *Introduction to the Problems of Legal Theory* (Oxford: Clarendon Press, 1992, Bonnie Litschewski Paulson and Stanley L Paulson, trans.), 116–17. This is the translation of Kelsen, *Reine Rechtslehre: Einleitung in der rechtswissenschaftliche Problematik* (1934).

> with the help of a juristic hypothesis: that above the communities understood as states stands a legal order [*Rechtsordnung*] which mutually delimits the spheres of validity of the individual states in that it hinders incursions by one into the sphere of the others, or at least subjects them all to equal conditions for such incursions.[28]

He concluded this set of thoughts by saying that 'when the primacy of international law fulfils this function, the concept of law [*Rechtsbegriff*] is simultaneously perfected in a formal and substantive sense. The law [*Recht*] attains the organization of humanity and thereby a unity with the highest ethical idea.'[29]

In the Concept of Law, Hart did not discuss this argument, perhaps because he thought he had already shown that the basic norm is a redundant idea. He confined himself to the dismissive observation that one can do without the 'obstinate search for unity', once one sees that public international law consists of discrete rules that states accept as binding.[30] But in two later essays, he attempted to refute Kelsen's international law monism, as well as Kelsen's general opposition to dualism of any kind.

On Hart's understanding, Kelsen's 'central argument' for international law monism is the principle of effectiveness in public international law – the principle that so long as a state has an effective legal order, it will be recognized as a valid or legitimate order by public international law. Hart called this relationship 'the relationship of validating purport': for example, a statute of the UK legal order purports to validate the norms of the Soviet order.[31] He thought that this argument can be quite easily shown to be wrong. While this statute would validate Soviet law for UK courts, it would not validate Soviet law. Kelsen thus confused, Hart claimed, questions about the content of the law, with questions about the identity of legal systems, which turn not on the content of the law but on their 'mode of recognition'.[32] He concluded, as we saw in Chapter 3, that Kelsen's theory 'has a juristic Midas touch, which transmutes all

[28] Kelsen, *Das Problem der Souveränität*, 204. (My translation.)

[29] Ibid, 205. (My translation.) See Gragl, *Legal Monism* for an argument that Kelsen was committed to international law monism, though one put on an epistemological, positivistic basis different from the political one I advance here.

[30] Hart, *The Concept of Law*, 235.

[31] Hart, 'Kelsen's Doctrine of the Unity of Law', 317–21.

[32] Ibid, 319–21.

questions about laws and their relationship into questions of the content of law or questions concerning what laws say; but the touch is perverse, for not all questions are of that kind'.[33] But, as we also saw, this criticism misses entirely the dynamic dimension of Kelsen's theory – that Kelsen's theory is about juridical production. Hart, that is, because of the static nature of his theory, failed to see that the issue is about the dynamic production of content and hence about the relationship between legal form, process and content.[34]

For Kelsen, the principle of effectiveness is the principle of public international law which validates national legal orders, that is, all those orders which qualify as legal because they meet, among other criteria, a criterion of efficacy. Hart's supposed counterexample is not a norm of public international law but a positive law enacted in one of the plurality of national legal orders which purports to validate the law of another. It resembles more a choice-of-law rule in private international law than it does a norm of public international law. It looks, that is, like the rule of a jurisdiction which picks out the substantive private law norm which should decide an issue when a norm of its private law conflicts with a private law norm of another jurisdiction and both private law norms are relevant to the issue.

Moreover, the principle of effectiveness is not the basis of Kelsen's argument for monism. Its function in Kelsen's argument is as a recognized norm of public international law which can't be explained as a matter of state consent since it explains why there is in the first place a state which can bind itself by consent. Its validity has therefore to be based on something other than a state-made law. The best explanation is that it is valid because it is part of the unified whole made up of the norms of public international law plus the norms of the different national orders. To conceive of those norms as a unified order, one must presuppose the basic norm of public international law. Kelsen's position is thus that for there to be a plurality of valid national legal orders, there must be in place an overarching legal order. In this regard, there is only one candidate – the international legal order.

[33] Ibid, 321.

[34] For a robust Kelsenian response to Hart, to which I am much indebted, see Lars Vinx, 'The Kelsen–Hart Debate: Hart's Critique of Kelsen's Legal Monism Reconsidered', in Jeremy Telman, ed., *Hans Kelsen in America: Selective Affinities and the Mysteries of Academic Influence* (Switzerland: Springer, 2016) 59. My own response differs in that it drives to the surface Hart's national law monism.

For Hart, it transpires, the issue is whether a national legal order, because it is subject only to law certified by its rule of recognition, is thereby sealed off from other national orders as well as from the list of public international law norms. His example of laws of validating purport plays no role in Kelsen's theory of public international law and is the product of Hart's own mindset – one which claims that public international law applies in whole or in part within any national legal system only when there is a rule of that system giving effect to the former. As a result, he could only imagine the entry of a norm from one legal space into another by dint of a national law of validating purport.[35] He thus embraced the dualism of the late nineteenth- and early twenty-century positivistic theories, despite his rejection of their conception of public international law as will-based interstate law, and despite his attempt to show against Austin that the positivist tradition is not committed to the denial of the legal status of public international law.

One does not have to read between the lines to discern Hart's dualism, for he had this to say in one of his endnotes:

> Kelsen's account (op. cit, pp. 373–83) of the possible relationships between municipal law and international law ('primacy of national law or primacy of international law') assumes that the statement that a legal system exists *must* be a statement of law, made from the point of view of one legal system about another, accepting the other system as 'valid' and as forming a single system with itself. The common-sense view that municipal law and international law constitute separate legal systems, involves treating the statement that a legal system (national or international) exists, as a statement of fact. This for Kelsen is unacceptable 'pluralism'.[36]

This endnote is to chapter 6 of *The Concept of Law*, 'The Foundations of a Legal System', in which Hart discussed the problem of how to explain the transition of a colony from a subordinate part of the legal system to independent statehood; that is, from a condition in which the UK rule of recognition is the ultimate rule to one where one can say that the entity no longer owes its 'contemporary legal status' to the UK statute which first established the colony. Hart's answer was that while the basic 'constitutional structure' of the entity remains the same, its enactments

[35] See Somek, 'Kelsen Lives', 426–7.
[36] Ibid, 296–7, note to 121.

are now valid because 'under the rule of recognition locally accepted, enactment by the local legislature is an ultimate criterion of validity'.[37]

Hart's reference in the note is to Kelsen's *General Theory of Law and State*, to the section with the title, 'The Unity of National and International Law as a Postulate of Legal Theory', which is also Hart's main source for his critique of Kelsen's philosophy of public international law and of his account of norm conflict. In placing this note as a comment on his chapter 6, Hart took a problem Kelsen saw as about the relationship of national and public international law and recharacterized it as one exclusively to do with national law, thus asserting the pluralism which Kelsen rejected, one which sees national legal orders as spaces sealed until a political decision is taken to permit or require entry by a norm from outside.[38] Hart's working assumption was therefore that the problems of philosophy of law, including the legal status of public international law, are to be addressed from the perspective of the internal point of view of a jurist who takes the rule of recognition of his national legal system to have primacy.

Hart did not suppose that this assumption ruled out the possibility of monistic national law systems, where it might make sense to say that 'international law and the law of that state form parts of a single system of law'. But that, he said, will depend 'on the manner in which and extent to which a given state recognizes international law'.[39] It will ultimately depend, that is, on the contingent content of the rule of recognition. He did not, however, say 'on *whether* a given state recognizes international law' since he assumed that the claim that public international law is law entails that states will differ only as to *how* they recognize it. If they are monistic in practice, the norms of public international law will be directly binding within the states; if they are dualistic in practice, the norms of public international law will bind the states only in the international domain unless they choose to incorporate a norm by statute.

In putting forward this view, Hart appeared oblivious to the argument of Hersch Lauterpacht, the most eminent public international lawyer of

[37] Ibid, 120–1. Hart's discussion in these pages laid the basis for his later critique of Kelsen's philosophy of public international law and his example of a law which 'purports' to confer validity.

[38] That this was a recharacterization not only went unnoticed, but also had far-reaching consequences for philosophy of law and more generally legal scholarship, which I sketch in Chapter 5.

[39] Hart, 'Kelsen's Doctrine of the Unity of Law', 321.

the time, that public international law is 'part of the law of England' as evidenced by the 'doctrine of adoption'.[40] According to this doctrine, public international law norms are automatically adopted by the UK legal order, which gives rise to a rule of construction such that judges consider themselves under a duty to interpret national law in light of those norms, unless in issue is a UK statute the content of which can only be understood as overriding a particular norm.[41] It is only treaties which after ratification must be incorporated by statute before judges will deem them to have direct domestic application.

The 'common-sense view that municipal law and public international law constitute separate legal systems' is thus wrong. The 'fact' of the matter is that any particular national legal order in the plurality of states in the international order accepts the international order as 'valid' and as forming a single system with itself. It will differ from other national orders only in that, as we just saw Hart say, the way in which that relationship with international law is regulated will 'depend on the manner in which and extent to which ... [the] state recognizes [public] international law'. In other words, states have different ways of managing their relationship with public international law. But, given that they recognize its legality, they must manage their internal affairs so as to give effect to the assumption that the international legal order 'forms a single system' with the national order.

It follows that Hart, far from refuting Kelsen's monism, affirmed it in one variant: national law monism.[42] There are binding norms of customary international law because the rule of recognition of one's state will deem the recognized norms of international law to be legally binding. All the norms of public international law can then be accounted for. The rule of recognition will include criteria for validating the norms of customary international law including the *pacta sunt servanda* maxim that

[40] Hersch Lauterpacht, 'Is International Law a Part of the Law of England?', in Lauterpacht, *International Law: Collected Papers: The Law of Peace*, vol. 2 (Cambridge: Cambridge University Press, 2009, E Lauterpacht, ed.) 537, first published in (1939) 25 *Transactions of the Grotius Society* 51. Hart was well aware of Lauterpacht's work, as the references in *The Concept of Law* at 305–6 show. But he appears not to have taken the time to get to grips with Lauterpacht's theoretically sophisticated, though practice-based, arguments.

[41] Hart was surely aware of this feature of judicial practice, though he does not mention it. I explore the likely reason for this omission later in this chapter.

[42] See Somek, 'Kelsen Lives' and 'Monism: A Tale of the Undead'.

agreements between states must be maintained and the peremptory norms of *jus cogens*.[43]

This position is in itself problematic for two distinct reasons. First, Hart no less than Kelsen should have regarded national law monism as flawed because it is committed conceptually to the proposition that there can only be one valid legal order – one's own national legal order – on whose basic norm or rule of recognition the validity of all other legal orders depends. Second, if one's national law monism is, as in Hart's legal theory, based on the rule of recognition, public international law norms are recognized as law because one's rule of recognition says so. They will bind states at least externally, and as well internally, depending on whether such norms have been explicitly incorporated, either wholesale (by the constitution, that is, the system is monistic) or retail (by a particular statute, that is, the system is dualistic). However, as with Hart's account of the role of customary law in a national legal system, while he thought it an advantage of the rule of recognition that it can account for such law whereas a command theory of law cannot, his own theory has great difficulty in so accounting, as does the English tradition of legal positivism in general for the legal status of common law.[44] The difficulty arises because at most Hart's legal positivism can say of customary law that it is accepted because it is accepted, which makes the rule of recognition account of customary law as redundant as Hart claimed of the basic norm. Indeed, the difficulty goes deeper than Hart's account of customary law, or of public international law, or of the common law, since at bottom the rule of recognition is *itself* a customary rule: 'officials

[43] Defined by Article 53 of the Vienna Convention on the Law of Treaties as 'a norm accepted and recognized by the international community of States as a whole from which no derogation is permitted and which can only be modified by a subsequent norm of general international law having the same character'; for example, prohibitions on slavery, genocide and torture. In addition, there are obligations *erga omnes* which are owed to the international community of states as a whole, and are more a matter of state responsibility for violations of the obligations than is the case with *jus cogens* obligations. See, for example, Stefan Kadelbach, '*Jus Cogens*, Obligations *Erga Omnes* and other Rules: The Identification of Fundamental Norms', in Christian Tomuschat and Jean-Marc Thouvenin, eds, *The Fundamental Rules of the International Legal Order: Jus Cogens and Obligations Erga Omnes* (Leiden: Martinus Nijhoff Publishers, 2005) 21. There is some overlap between the last two categories.

[44] For the classic demonstration, see AWB Simpson, 'The Common Law and Legal Theory', in Simpson, ed., *Oxford Essays in Jurisprudence* (Oxford: Oxford University Press, 1973, 2nd series) 77. In *Reflections on 'The Concept of Law'* (Oxford: Oxford University Press, 2011), Simpson points out, at 165–8, that Hart not only failed in *The Concept of Law* to discuss the common law, but did not even mention it.

must apply as valid the norms of their own customary behavior (and not, for example, norms of other people's customary behaviour, or moral norms, etc.)'.[45]

These problems are internal to Hart's attempt to explain public international law as a matter for the rule of recognition of the national legal order. There is, in addition, a tension between that attempt and his claim that in fact 'municipal law and international law constitute separate legal systems'. This claim goes much further than asserting a fact since it turns the way in which Hart's own legal system interacts with public international law into a theoretical claim. It is here that we begin to see most clearly Hart's parochialism.

For Hart, the normal case of legal order was his own parliamentary legal order. He inflated its practical, dualistic arrangements for interacting with some of the norms of public international law into dualism as a theoretical position, albeit one designed to explain what he took to be the fact of the matter – that legal systems exist as separate valid orders. That position is in tension with recognizing public international law's legality, whether from the perspective of national law or international law monism.

It is of course possible that neither the basic norm nor the rule of recognition helps to explain the legality of public international law. But for the moment I wish only to register the point that if one wants, as Hart despite his ambivalences did, to account for both the fact that public international law is law properly so-called and the fact of pluralism – of the existence of multiple national legal orders – Kelsen's argument is compelling that one should move up the legal hierarchy and opt for international law monism. Alternatively, one can subtract either factor and make do with just one. If one subtracts authority, there is no problem coping with the fact of pluralism, but one gives up on the task of

[45] Here I adopt the formulation of this point (emphasis removed) in Michael Giudice, 'Hart and Kelsen on International Law', in Leslie Green and Brian Leiter, eds, *Oxford Studies in Philosophy of Law* (Oxford: Oxford University Press, 2013) 148, at 159–60. Once one sees this, it becomes in fact very difficult to distinguish Hart's legal theory from Austin's. As Austin would have said of the rule of recognition, it is a rule of positive morality which states that the criteria for the validity of law in the national legal system must be observed if parliament is to make law. Austin's claim that it is a mistake to think of such a rule as constitutional law properly so-called echoes in Hart's own hesitations about the legal status of the rule of recognition discussed in my Chapter 3. See Hart, *The Concept of Law*, 111–12.

explaining public international law as a matter of authority. If one subtracts the fact of pluralism, one can be a national law monist.

This does not yet show that Kelsen's argument succeeds. It still needs to respond both to the fact that legal orders exist which are officially dualistic and that evidence for dualism goes beyond any official stance because of the fact of norm conflicts between legal orders, whether between the private law norms of two national legal orders, or between the international legal order and a national legal order. It also needs to deal with Kelsen's insistence after 1920 that legal philosophical considerations cannot decide between international law and national law monism. But for the moment we can recognize that Kelsen, unlike Hart, tried to follow through on the project of restoring a constitutionalist idea to legal theory without giving up on that idea when it comes to public international law.

4.2 Norm Conflict in Private and Public International Law

In Hart's view, the fact of norm conflict between different legal orders, as well as between law and morality, is highly significant in showing that Kelsen's monism is mistaken.[46] In addition, we saw in Chapter 3 that he was concerned that monism excluded the possibility of a moral criticism of a valid law, that is, that it undermined the Separation Thesis.[47]

However, Hart adduced conflicts between the private law norms of two orders as a problem for his own, not Kelsen's legal theory. In Section 4.2.1, I show that his account of private international law, in contrast with his view of public international law, presupposes Kelsen's international law monism, so that the question becomes whether the latter kind of monism can respond to norm conflicts between a national order and the international order. I argue in Section 4.2.2 that it can.

4.2.1 Norm Conflict in Private International Law

Once Hart had 'refuted' Kelsen through the example of a law of validating purport, he turned to various problems he thought attended his own

46 Hart, 'Kelsen Visited', 302.

47 Ibid, 302–3. As I pointed out in Chapter 3, Hart signalled this concern in *The Concept of Law*, at 293 (his emphasis): 'One reason for using the expression "rule of recognition" instead of a "*basic* norm" is to avoid any commitment to Kelsen's view of the conflict between law and morals.'

account of the rule of recognition as candidate for the constitutionalist idea. One such problem arises out of the existence of private international law. As Hart described this field:

> All civilized systems contain special rules for dealing with cases containing a foreign element . . . These special rules determine both when courts have jurisdiction to try cases with such foreign elements and which legal systems should guide the courts in the exercise of their jurisdiction.[48]

The problem private international law poses for the rule of recognition is that it indicates that the rule of recognition of one state validates within a certain scope rules from another. Hart's view thus subordinates the rule of recognition of one state to that of another. As Hart put it, private international law suggests that 'the laws of one country that are recognized and applied by the courts of another country belong to the legal system of the latter country as well as of the former'.[49] His response to this problem was that when UK courts apply the private law of another legal order they do not really '*apply*' the foreign law 'but . . . a law of their own with a similar content to that of the foreign law that they recognize'.[50] According to Hart, this suggestion avoids the conclusion, destructive of the idea of the rule of recognition, that 'laws of one country that are recognized and applied by the courts of another belong to the legal system of the latter country as well as of the former'.[51]

Here is an example of what Hart appeared to have in mind. Suppose that a couple gets married in state A where the only marital property regime is community of property and divorced in state B where the only regime is separation of property. The wife argues to the divorce court in B that the law of A should apply, while the husband argues that the law of B should. The court finds that the private international law rule of B is that on divorce the law of the state where the couple were married governs the division of property. Hart's suggestion seems to be that B's court, in applying the legal principles of community of property of A, is applying B's law of separation of property, despite the fact that B's own substantive law on this matter requires a different property regime.[52]

48 Hart, 'Kelsen's Doctrine of the Unity of Law', 340–1.

49 Ibid.

50 Ibid. His emphasis.

51 Ibid.

52 One way of avoiding this strangeness is adopted by Joseph Raz. Raz denies that the norms of another state become part of the law of the state in which they are applied even though the courts are under a legal duty so to apply them. And he uses this claim to buttress his

This is not an immediately intuitive conclusion and Hart supplied no argument to explain it. All he offered was a hesitant suggestion, clearly prompted by the concern that the court is subordinating the operation of its rule of recognition to A's, so that within a limited scope B's rule is no longer ultimate.

Recall that Hart did not say in his treatment of public international law that 'all civilized systems contain special rules for responding to the obligations imposed by public international law'.[53] If he had, he would have committed his legal theory to the proposition that there is an international legal order, anchored by his constitutionalist idea. On his account of that idea, the anchor would have to be understood as lodged in each existing national legal order, with the implication that those who take the internal point of view to their own rule of rule of recognition must deny the existence of the similar anchor in every other national legal order. In other words, he would have committed his legal theory to the juridically strange and politically unattractive view of the world entailed in national law monism.

I argued in Section 4.1 that Hart is in fact committed to that view. Here I start by pointing out that Kelsen's account of private international law is similar to Hart's, though Hart does not refer to it, which is odd given that it appeared in a book which is one of his main sources in his two essays critical of Kelsen. Kelsen, in contrast, supplied an argument for the account. It shows that the kind of solution to which Hart was drawn for norm conflicts in private international law supports international law monism, which puts Hart's accounts of the legality of private international law and public international law into tension with each other. As a result, the question becomes whether Kelsen's international law monism can deal with norm conflicts between public international law and national law. If it can, to put things crudely, Kelsen won the debate.

In terms of my example, one can understand Kelsen's argument as follows. The courts of B are obliged to apply the law of A in a private dispute when and only when there is a rule validated by the constitution of B requiring them so to act. It follows that the 'reason of validity' of the

general argument that moral values do not become incorporated into law simply because judges have a duty to give effect to them. See Joseph Raz, 'Incorporation by Law' (2004) 10 *Legal Theory* 1, at 10–11. For earlier references, see in Raz, *The Authority of Law: Essays on Law and Morality* (Oxford: Clarendon Press, 1983) 'The Institutional Nature of Law' 103, at 119–20, 'Legal Validity' 146, at 149, and Raz, *Practical Reason and Norms* (Princeton: Princeton University Press, 1990), 152–4. See my Appendix I.

[53] Hart, 'Kelsen's Doctrine of the Unity of Law', 340.

law from A is that it is a 'norm of the legal system of that State', that is, of B.[54] There is no difference between this situation and that obtaining when a revolutionary constitution stipulates that some of the statutes of the old regime 'should continue to be in force under the new constitution'. Likewise, 'the norms of so-called private international law prescribing the application of norms of a foreign law to certain cases "refer" to norms of another legal system instead of reproducing the contents of these norms'.[55]

The claim that private international law is 'so-called' is there solely to alert us to Kelsen's argument that there is no issue of public international law at stake here, only a matter of what B's law requires. He also objected to the alternative label for the field of 'conflict of laws' because there is no conflict.

> [T]he foreign law does not claim to be applied by the organs of the State whose private international law is in question; and the latter does not refuse the application. On the contrary. . . . [T]he law of one state prescribes the application of the law of another State; and the latter does not object or demand it. It has no right to do so since it is not really its own law which is applied by the other State. The latter applies norms of its own law. The fact that these norms have the same contents as corresponding norms of another State does not concern the latter.[56]

Finally, Kelsen objected to the term 'choice of law' because there is no choice when a rule of one state requires its courts to refer to the law of another in resolving a dispute. Hence, he preferred 'reference rules' or 'incorporation rules'.[57] Such a reference rule is distinguished from the 'norm to be applied' but, 'from a functional point of view, the one is essentially connected with the other. Only if they are taken together do they form a complete rule of law.'[58]

Notice that the reference rule, which need not be a statute, is not a rule of validating purport. It is not a rule which purports to confer validity, but a rule which does confer validity. It can be understood as such because B's reference rule validates another rule of B's private law, albeit one with a content similar to a private law norm of A, for B's jurisdiction only. As a result, a kind of legal pluralism is introduced to the legal order

[54] Kelsen, *General Theory of Law and State*, 244.
[55] Ibid.
[56] Ibid, 246–7.
[57] Ibid, 247.
[58] Ibid.

of B. Within B community of property governs the couple married in A, while separation of property governs couples married in B. That pluralism is made possible by the constitution of B, itself validated by the basic norm of the international legal order.

Things are quite different with public international law, because there we move up a level. Indeed, on a Kelsenian conception of legal order, one needs to move up to that level to understand why it might be the case that, if there are two national legal orders, one would expect to find that in both there are norms validated by their constitutions requiring their courts to apply norms with the same content as the private law norms of the other jurisdiction. It follows that the norms of private international law are not norms of public international law. But, as Hart acknowledged, in all mature legal orders we find rules about how to deal with a dispute when an individual seems to be subject to the conflicting private law norms of two jurisdictions. This tells us that while regimes of private international law will have different contents, that there is such a regime is required if a national legal order is to take its place in the overarching international order of legality.[59]

Just as international law monism explains how we can understand the distribution of public law authority between states such that they are authorized to make law for those subject to their jurisdictions, so it explains why public international law authorizes states to make private international law rules for the adjudication of conflicts between the private law norms of one jurisdiction with another.[60] If we are to make sense of the passage of private law norms from one national order to another which create such conflicts, we can do so only if we do not assume the truth of national law monism, which from B's perspective would require the denial of the existence of A as a separate order.

Nor can it happen, at least it could not happen as a matter of legal requirement, if the two orders were, as dualism requires, seen as solitudes sealed off one from the other until an authority in one breaks – a political act – the seal. If that were the case, some non-juridical explanation of why the sovereign permits entry would have to be supplied, which may

[59] In Section 4.5 I respond to Kelsen's claim that a legal order can do without private international law altogether. See Hans Kelsen, 'Le Renvoi' (1957) *Annuaire of the Institute of International Law* 115.

[60] See Michael S Green, 'Legal Monism: An American History', in Christopher Bezemek, Michael Potacs and Alexander Somek, eds, *Legal Positivism, Institutionalism and Globalisation* (Oxford: Hart Publishing, 2018) 23.

account for the popularity of comity-based explanations these days, that is, explanations based on an idea of mutual respect or reciprocity between states. But such explanations are no more than relics of Austinian positivism about public international law.[61]

Moreover, dualism cannot be a coherent theory of how the private law of two national legal orders relate *legally* to each other. Rather, as a theory, it is a compromise forged by a national law monism which cannot ignore the fact of the existence of other legal orders and so reaches for a non-juridical explanation of why there might be norm travel between them. Nor, as already suggested, can dualism be a coherent theory of how the law of any national legal order relates *legally* to the public international law order.

In sum, if we find that legal orders relate to each not as sealed solitudes but as juridically connected in ways which permit or require the passage of norms from one to another, Hart's rule of recognition is of no help. I have diagnosed as the reason that it is an account of legal order suited to a national law monism which must resort to highly implausible explanations in a bid to account for the binding quality of norms from other

[61] See, for example, Timothy Endicott, 'Comity among Authorities' (2015) 68 *Current Legal Problems* 1, for a dualist approach to authority in general. See also Hersch Lauterpacht, 'Diplomatic Protection and Criminal Jurisdiction over Aliens' (1947) 9 *Cambridge Law Journal* 330, at 331:

> This is not the proper occasion for enquiring in detail into the reasons of the fascination which the term 'comity of nations' has exercised over judges and practising lawyers. It is possible that the lingering influence of Austinian positivism which rejects the claim of the law of nations to be law 'properly so-called' may have given added attraction to a vague, non-committal and somewhat pretentious form of words which is on occasions strangely out of keeping with the reality of international relations. However that may be, it is suggested that the term 'comity of nations' is misleading and that there is no such antiquity about it as to make its abandonment impracticable.

Alex Mills traces the emergence of the comity concept, and the broader idea that private international law is exclusively domestic law, to 'the positivist theoretical emphasis on sovereignty' in the development of thinking about private international law; Mills, *The Confluence of Public and Private International Law: Justice, Pluralism and Subsidiarity in the International Constitutional Ordering of Private Law* (Cambridge: Cambridge University Press, 2009), 71. The ambiguous nature of comity as neither law nor policy, but a 'bridging' mechanism between the two, is also discussed in Joel R Paul, 'Comity in International Law' (1991) 32 *Harvard International Law Journal* 1, at 44–55. In my view, 'comity' as a bridging concept often plays a highly ambiguous role, much like Hart's rule of recognition. It signals a jurist's unresolved dilemma when it comes to the choice between national and international law monism.

legal orders. It can resort, for example, to the non-juridical idea of comity or to Hart's own attempt to understand public international law in a way weakly analogous to the mandatory norms of a primitive society. But that these explanations are implausible does not yet show that Kelsen's argument for a legal relationship succeeds. Even if I am right that Kelsen can explain why conflicts between the private law of national legal orders are only apparent, nothing yet follows for conflicts between the legal norms of a national order and the norms of public international law.

4.2.2 *Norm Conflict in Public International Law*

Since Kelsen's argument about private international law relies on what he thought of as the 'reference rules' validated by the national constitution, which is in turn validated by public international law, his position may seem vulnerable to exactly the criticism Hart levelled against him.[62] In a parliamentary legal order, the constitution permits parliament to enact a law with a content which contradicts the content of a norm of international law, and the UK courts will regard themselves under a duty to uphold that law. For example, one identifies a valid norm of the international legal order which has content X (protect minorities) and a valid statutory norm of the national legal order with content −X (oppress this minority) and a court within the national order is under a duty to uphold the latter norm. Do we have here an example of norm conflict, created by a norm validated by the constitution, which testifies to the falsity of international law monism and hence to the superiority of Hart's constitutionalist idea?

Hart did notice that Kelsen recognized that in practice conflicts arise. As in the example just offered, state A and state B enter into a treaty which provides equal protection for the rights of a minority in B after which B enacts a statute depriving the minority of all political rights. Kelsen suggested that one has to understand the situation as 'exactly analogous' to that which obtains in a national system in which there is a written constitution which safeguards rights by stipulating that the officials responsible for enacting a statute which violates one of the rights will be punished by an institution in the legal order other than the judiciary. In this case, the 'so called unconstitutional statute … is and

[62] Hart, 'Kelsen's Doctrine of the Unity of Law', 333–4.

remains a valid law, without the constitution having to be suspended or changed because of it' and there is, Kelsen argued, no conflict between a 'norm of a lower level and a norm of a higher level'. Rather, the correct understanding is 'that the validity of the lower norm may be abolished or the responsible organ punished'. The lower norm is a 'delict', but not a negation of the higher norm. It is only a condition to which 'the law attaches certain consequences'. Similarly, in the public international law example, the enactment of the discriminatory law 'is the condition to which international law attaches its sanctions: reprisals or war'. However, the norm of the national order remains valid 'even from the point of view of international law, because international law provides no procedure in which the norm can be abolished'.[63]

Hart's view of this argument was that, while 'ingenious', it 'merely locates the conflict at a different point' – 'between rules prohibiting and *permitting* the same action, i.e. the enactment of the statute'.[64] But this response misses altogether that Kelsen's account of norm conflicts presupposes a dynamic model of legal order, while Hart's criticism of Kelsen is based on a static model which regards a legal order as if a snapshot could be taken of all its positive law at a particular moment in time. Hart's mistake is of the order which he and his successors accused Dworkin of making, of seeking to contest the positivist theory of law on the basis of a theory of adjudication about how judges should decide hard cases. Indeed, as indicated in Chapter 3, once Hart's mistake comes into view, one can see not only why the positivist accusation against Dworkin fails because Dworkin, like Kelsen, argued for a dynamic model of law. One can also see that the fundamental divide in philosophy of law is neither between legal positivism and natural law theory, nor between theories of law and theories of adjudication. Rather, the divide is between dynamic models which include the process of juridical production within the scope of legal theory, and static models which consign dynamic production to some extra-legal space on which philosophy of law must remain silent.

When Kelsen presented his example of a valid but unconstitutional national law, he assumed that for the judiciary to have no authority to invalidate an unconstitutional law within the national legal order, it must be the case that the constitution explicitly stipulates that judges do not

[63] Hans Kelsen, *Pure Theory of Law* (Cambridge, MA: Harvard University Press, 1945, Max Knight, trans.), 331.

[64] Hart, 'Kelsen's Doctrine of the Unity of Law', 333–4. His emphasis.

have this authority and that some other institution is given authority, not to invalidate the statute, but to inflict a sanction on those who brought about the delict. If there is no such provision, he claimed, judges will have the authority to invalidate the statute even if the constitution explicitly does not give it to them. The reason is that if judges 'are authorized to apply the statutes, they have to determine whether something whose subjective meaning is to be a statute has objectively this subjective meaning; and it does have the objective meaning only if it conforms to the constitution'.[65]

In making this assumption, Kelsen also assumed that the normal case in a national legal order is that judges will have jurisdiction in disputes about what the law requires. Hence, if there is a constitution which protects the rights of minorities, and it has the force of law, hence, is not purely cosmetic, it will fall to judges to decide whether a statute which affects the rights of a minority violates the constitution. However, it is possible for the constitution to stipulate an exception to this normal case by not only excluding judicial review of statutes but also by providing a remedy other than invalidation to another institution within the legal order. Here as elsewhere this additional assumption evokes Kelsen's 'ideal of "due process" of law'.[66] From the perspective of legality there should be an institutional mechanism which ensures that all unconstitutional and illegal acts are invalidated. By turning what should be a 'voidable' legal act into a delict – a legal wrong subject to sanction but not voidable – the national legal order creates a defect in legality.

The situation in public international law is not 'exactly analogous', then, to national law's normal case. Rather, it is analogous to the abnormal case because in public international law there is no court with compulsory jurisdiction over the application of the law. Instead, public international law delegates to states the task of both interpreting and enforcing it, with enforcement effected not by invalidation but by sanctions. That states have this double role is problematic. Not only is enforcement in the international domain inefficient and fraught. It is also the case, to adapt Kelsen above, that the question 'whether something whose subjective meaning is to be a public international law norm has objectively this subjective meaning' is left to the judgment of states, including that of the allegedly delinquent state.

65 Kelsen, *Pure Theory of Law*, 272.

66 Kelsen, *General Theory of Law and State*, 278.

Now that the analogy is to the abnormal case in a national legal system, and that Kelsen, like Hart, deemed the international system to be 'primitive', may seem to indicate that when all is said and done for both him and Hart public international law is similarly flawed. So much is true in that they shared the view that the principal institutional defect is the absence of a court with compulsory jurisdiction over disputes about what the law requires.[67] But it makes a big difference that Hart's theory of law disqualified public international law as a legal order because of this institutional lack, while Kelsen saw it as a defect in the legality of public international law, though one which does not go to its status as such.

There are two things to note about this kind of defect. First, Kelsen's example of no norm conflict in a national legal system to which he thought the public international law–national law relationship is analogous is not as contrived as it might appear. Consider that he used the term 'the ideal' of due process in his detailed discussion of the place of administrative law in legal order in his *General Theory of Law and the State*. A theme of that discussion is how legality can be preserved in the administrative state despite the fact that the legal order might find it convenient to delegate functions ordinarily associated with the judiciary to organs within the administrative state and may choose mechanisms of enforcement different from the mechanism of invalidation.[68]

Nor is this kind of example confined to administrative law. Consider that the UK Human Rights Act (1998) does not authorize judges to invalidate statutes which offend the rights it protects. Rather, in section 3 it requires judges to try to interpret the statutes so as to remove the offence or, if this is not possible, in terms of section 4, to declare the statute incompatible with the Act, which puts the ball in parliament's and the government's court. If action is not forthcoming from those institutions, the matter ends up in the European Court of Human Rights. If that court rules against the UK, and the UK government still refuses to take action, the matter becomes one for the state parties to the European Convention on Human Rights.[69]

[67] Hart, *The Concept of Law*, 232–3. And, for example, Kelsen, *General Theory of Law and State*, 338–9.

[68] Kelsen's inclusion within the scope of philosophy of law of administrative law, as well as the law of federalism and the law of entrenched bills of rights, also marks an important difference between his theory and Hart's which speaks to Hart's parochialism.

[69] Similarly, section 33 of the Charter of Rights and Freedoms of the Canadian Constitution permits a legislature to maintain as valid a law which violates some of the rights it protects 'notwithstanding' that judges have declared the law invalid. See Chapter 2.

The second and more important thing to note, which this last example indicates, is the dynamic dimension of the problem. The incompatibility of the offending statute with fundamental legal commitments of the order is a standing *legal* rebuke to the organ which has brought it about. The offending state should legally speaking cure the problem by bringing its internal law into compliance with public international law, just as the legislature should amend or annul the unconstitutional statute to come into compliance with the constitution. On a dynamic understanding of law, while the remedy of sanctions is far from ideal in international affairs, it is still the case that the point of the remedy is the same as having an institution with the authority to invalidate. Until the incompatibility is cured, the organ capable of curing it is in continuing dereliction of duty at the level at which the incompatibility manifests.[70]

Hence for Kelsen the conflict arises only if one adopts the static perspective on law, and he could explain the nuances of this legally problematic situation because he offered a dynamic perspective. The fact that a UK court has to uphold the statute which requires at this point in time −X is not determinative of the claim that there is a conflict in the legal order which includes at the international level a norm prescribing X. The reason is that the legal process has not yet come to an end. As Kelsen said of such conflicts at the end of his discussion of international law monism: 'The specific function of juristic interpretation is to eliminate these contradictions by showing that they are merely sham contradictions. It is by juristic interpretation that the legal material is transformed into a legal system.'[71]

With this dynamic view of the function of juristic interpretation, we can understand how public international law may both prescribe X and allow organs within a national order to prescribe −X. For it remains the case that while at the national level −X will prevail for the time being, at the international level the state is bound to bring its national law into line with public international law. There may be no independent body which can pronounce definitively on this issue, nor a body other than another state which is entitled to force compliance. But that would show only that the international legal order is defective from the internal perspective of legality because it failed to provide the institutional resources which help

[70] There is a difference, then, between the delicts of individuals who break the law of their national states and the delict of an organ of state, which is that the former do not amount to this kind of standing rebuke.

[71] Kelsen, *General Theory of Law and State*, 375.

to ensure that states fulfil their obligations. Indeed, the dynamic process unleashed by the presupposition of the basic norm brings such institutional problems to the surface. Further, it is only when the problems are on the surface that those who are committed to the constitutionalist project of subjecting all state action to the rule of law can and should address them by considering what reforms would ensure that legal obligations are vindicated.

Notice that, as was the case with private international law, in order even to conceive of this kind of conflict, one has to abandon national law monism. Far from denying the possibility of a conflict arising between norms from different legal orders, international law monism makes it possible to understand how there *could* be such a conflict in the first place by postulating an intrinsic connection between the orders because they are both *legal* orders.[72] This is not to say that states cannot be more or less dualistic in practice, if all that is meant by this label is that states will have different ways of giving shape to their relationship with the order of public international law. From a theoretical perspective which seeks to understand law's normativity, however, this is not really dualism because international law monism is the theory which explains why states are under a prior obligation to give shape to that relationship. States can do a better or worse job of this, just as they can do a better or worse job of arranging their national constitutional order, or their rules of private international law under that order.

We must therefore be careful to distinguish between dualism as a description of dualistic actual state practice and dualism as a theory of public international law. The former is an account of how various states in fact order their relationship with public international law, given an international monist view of the obligation so to do. The latter, as in Hart, conflates that account with a theory of public international law in a way which perpetuates the problems of the command theory of law. As a result, and despite Kelsen's frequent suggestions to the contrary, the choice for national law monism is not suspect on grounds of political morality alone. It is also suspect because legal orders are only dualistic in practice and then only to some extent. Dualism as a theoretical position is an attempt to abandon national law monism without embracing

[72] See, for example, the contrasting positions set out in Avbelj and Komárek, eds, *Constitutional Pluralism in the European Union and beyond* by Mattias Kumm, 'Rethinking Constitutional Authority: On the Structure and Limits of Constitutional Pluralism' 39, and by Alexander Somek, 'Monism: A Tale of the Undead'.

international law monism. That leaves it uneasily perched between a conception of sovereignty as pre-political and legally unlimited, as in Austin's command theory of law, and a conception in which sovereignty is understood as legally constituted.[73]

In sum, Hart's difficulties with accounting for public international law are symptomatic of a more general problem with his constitutionalist idea. The rule of recognition cannot perform the task he set for it of moving legal theory from Austin's reductive account of law as a matter of command and coercion to an account of legally constituted authority. As I now show, this problem persists into Hart's criticism of Kelsen when it came to the latter's opposition about dualism on another relationship, this time the relationship between law and morality. From Kelsen's position on this issue, I can draw some tentative conclusions about the legal relationship not yet addressed: the reach of the public law norms of one national order into the jurisdictions of other states in the field of foreign relations law.

4.3 Content, Concepts, Methods and Techniques

Recall that Hart said of public international law that '[i]n form, it resembles ... a regime of primary rules, even though the content of its often elaborate rules are very unlike those of a primitive society, and many of its concepts, methods and techniques are the same as those of modern municipal law'.[74] By 'form' Hart had in mind that there is no rule of recognition for public international law. It followed that the test whether a particular norm is law turns on whether it happens to be one on a list of discrete norms which happen to be accepted by states. In that respect, the rules of public international law are like the primary rules of a primitive society.

As Hart stated, he did not wish to push the analogy too far for two reasons. First, the content of the rules of public international law is much more elaborate than that of the norms of a primitive society, more akin to the legal rules of a national legal order. Second, the practice of determining the content of these rules looks very much like that of national legal orders because sophisticated legal techniques are required, wielded (he seemed to assume) by bodies of professional lawyers, including the

[73] Hart, 'Positivism and the Separation of Law and Morals', 58–62.

[74] Hart, *The Concept of Law*, 227.

lawyers who staff the various international administrative bodies, judicial bodies and arbitration courts, when these exist.

We also know that Kelsen did not suppose that there is a difference in form. His formal requirement is not that there exists a judicial institution which can pronounce finally on whether a rule is a rule of public international law. Rather, it is that those who wish to work out their legal obligations must presuppose that the norms which give rise to these obligations are part of a unified meaningful whole, which in turn requires presupposing the basic norm. Legal order exists when juristic interpretation of this sort can occur.

His position and Hart's are similar in that they both see as a necessary but not sufficient condition for the existence of legal order that there are norms which are effective in that those subject to them comply with them most of the time. But they differ when it comes to the other necessary condition for there to be legal order. For Hart, it is acceptance by officials of a rule of recognition, while for Kelsen it is the ability to presuppose a basic norm. As I have suggested, this makes Hart's position incoherent. On the one hand, he asserted that there is no law properly so-called in primitive societies – only a 'primitive or rudimentary form of law' – because there is no rule of recognition.[75] On the other hand, he asserted that there is public international law despite the fact that there is no rule of recognition. That left him unable to explain how states are under a legal obligation to obey public international law since for him legal obligation presupposes the existence of a rule of recognition. In contrast, Kelsen was not troubled by any incoherence. For him, there must be legal order before there can be law and the ability to presuppose the basic norm in attempting juristic interpretation, not any institutional fact, is all that is needed besides the sheer existence of effective norms.

Put in this way, Kelsen's emphasis on the dynamic nature of legal order, the importance of juristic interpretation in creating that order understood as a meaningful whole and the role of unity in the process of interpretation, makes his legal theory start to look, as I observed in Chapter 3, quite similar to Dworkin's interpretivism.[76] Indeed, Dworkin, early in his career, noted an affinity between his theory and

[75] Ibid, 86.

[76] For a rare discussion of the similarities between Kelsen and Dworkin, see Tony Honoré, 'The Basic Norm of a Society', in Honoré, *Making Law Bind: Essays Legal and Philosophical* (Oxford: Clarendon Press, 2002) 89.

Kelsen's in a little-known response to Hart's critique of Kelsen's monism on the basis of conflicts between norms.[77]

Dworkin argued that Hart had failed to recognize two different senses of validity at play in Kelsen's work. First, there is the sense which attaches to the statement that a norm is valid because it is created in accordance with the basic norm of a legal order. It responds to the kind of problem which the rule of recognition seems designed to solve. The second sense, Dworkin said, has to do with the '*dynamics* of legal reasoning, and in particular with the structure of an argument that ends in the decision that some man or some official ought to do something, meaning not that he has good reasons for doing it, but that it is, on balance, what he must do'. Here validity attaches to a 'conclusory statement' which presupposes the validity of one basic norm, that is, one norm which '"is binding" on the particular official and persons concerned'.[78]

Dworkin then offered his own analysis of a passage in Kelsen to which Hart objected for the reason we have encountered, namely, that Hart thought that Kelsen's monism required that there could be no moral criticism of valid law, thus undermining the Separation Thesis. As we saw in Chapter 3, Kelsen, addressing possible conflicts between law and morals, said that 'an individual who regards law as a system of valid norms has to disregard morals as such a system . . . [since] no viewpoint exists from which both morals and law may simultaneously be regarded as valid normative orders. No one can serve two masters.'[79]

According to Dworkin, the 'key words here are "viewpoint" and "simultaneously"; Kelsen's position is that one person cannot regard both norms as valid in the sense of deciding the issue of what he ought to do on some occasion'. Hence, '[w]hen Kelsen says that if international law and municipal law conflicted, we could not speak of them both as valid at the same time, he means that someone who had to decide what he ought to do – a judge for instance – could not treat them both as valid in the

[77] HLA Hart, 'Kelsen's Doctrine of the Unity of Law', in Howard E Kiefer and Milton K Munitz, eds, *Ethics and Social Justice* (Albany: State University of New York Press, 1968) 171; Ronald Dworkin, 'Comments on the Unity of Law Doctrine (a Response)', in ibid, 200. As before, I refer to Hart's essay as reprinted in Hart, *Essays in Jurisprudence and Philosophy* 309. Dworkin illustrated his argument by relying on examples drawn from private international law, which he was teaching at that time in the Yale Law School.

[78] Dworkin, 'Comments on the Unity of Law Doctrine', 200. My emphasis.

[79] Kelsen, *Pure Theory of Law*, 329.

conclusory sense, could not, in Kelsen's phrase, serve two masters'.[80] Hart thus confused two different contexts: the context in which clearly consistent statements are made, like 'according to international law one must not wage war' and 'according to American law one must wage war', and the context in which statements are made like 'because international law so provides, you are forbidden to fight and 'because American law so provides, you are required to fight' and in which the statements are inconsistent.[81]

Dworkin's point was that the issue here is not for deontic logic – the logic of normative argument – in the abstract. Rather, it is about what kind of deontic logic illuminates legal reasoning, given that in the case of a conflict between two valid rules, a court may not keep silent but 'must subordinate one rule, or fashion a new one'. It follows, Dworkin suggested, that Kelsen's view 'seems better to record our practices of adjudication than does a deontic logic that would permit' the existence of such a conflict.[82]

[80] Dworkin, 'Comments on the Unity of Law Doctrine (a Response)', 201. His point shows, in my view, why Alexander Somek's illuminating work on these issues goes wrong in one respect. Somek says that legal positivists such as Hart fail to see that the relevant question for Kelsenian monism is always 'What can happen next?' See Somek, 'Monism: A Tale of the Undead', 354–5. But Kelsen's question is not about prediction. It is: 'What *should* happen next?'

[81] Ibid.

[82] Dworkin, 'Comments on the Unity of Law Doctrine (a Response)', 201–2. Dworkin added that he was speaking, with Kelsen and Hart, 'of legal rules, not legal principles and policies, which follow a rather different logic'. This addition indicates that Dworkin thought that his response on Kelsen's behalf to Hart could be pushed in the direction of the theory of adjudication he had begun developing in the paper, first published as 'The Model of Rules' (1967) 35 *University of Chicago Law Review* 14, in which he first put forward the claim that judges must decide hard cases on the basis of their best understanding of the principles that underpin and justify the positive law relevant to answering the legal question. Their answers must, as he was to put things later, satisfy both a dimension of 'fit' with relevant positive law and a dimension of 'soundness' or 'justification'; Ronald Dworkin, *Law's Empire* (London: Fontana, 1986). His response to Hart does not require by itself that one go in that direction since it has to do with something much more basic, with 'the dynamics of legal reasoning'. However, his idea of fit does have something in common with the role that a static model of law plays in Kelsen's legal theory, as does the idea of justification with the dynamic model. In addition, the role of unity in Kelsen has more in common with Dworkin's idea of integrity than it does with Hart's rule of recognition. See my Chapter 3 and Honoré, 'The Basic Norm of a Society'. For discussion of Kelsen's theory of interpretation, see Jochen von Bernstoff, 'Specialized Courts and Tribunals as the Guardians of International Law? The Nature and Function of Judicial Interpretation in Kelsen and Schmitt', in Andreas Føllesdal and Geir Ulfstein, eds, *The Judicialization of International Law: A Mixed Blessing?* (Oxford: Oxford

In making this point, Dworkin signalled his commitment to the dynamic model of law he later developed in his interpretive theory. However, as I noted in Chapter 3, there are subtle differences between Dworkinian interpretivism and a Kelsenian account of adjudication since Kelsen rejected a distinction between legislation (the instrument of policy and the province of the legislature) and adjudication (the realm of principle and the province of the judiciary).[83] For Kelsen, the moment of creativity in legislation is much more heightened than in adjudication, but it is quantitatively rather than qualitatively different. Legislation is a legally authorized act which must respect the constitutional norms governing its production. Similarly, the executive implementation of legislation requires official creativity, though a quantitatively smaller amount than legislation since it must respect both constitutional norms and whatever legislated norms officials are charged with concretizing.[84]

These differences permitted Kelsen to navigate between two extremes. On the one hand, in Hart's legal theory the arbitrary individual at the apex of the political order – the legally unlimited sovereign of the command theory of law – is repressed in his elaboration of a complex legal society only to pop up whenever an official has to make a decision.[85] Law's control seems to evaporate at the moment of interpretation or application of law. On the other hand, Dworkin's theory is often accused of falling prey to the opposite problem. Law's control becomes total but in an implausible way as he equates law with the rule of liberal principles, as interpreted by judges. As a result, it is in his theory that Kelsen's ambition of the radical suppression of sovereignty is achieved, though at the cost of equating law's control with control by a substantive position in liberal theory.

I sketched above Dworkin's criticism of Hart for having confused Kelsen's two distinct conceptions of validity: the conception which attends to certification of a norm as a valid member of a legal order

University Press, 2018) 9. And for discussion relevant to this issue see the exchange between him and Liam Murphy: von Bernstoff, 'Law beyond the State: A Reply to Liam Murphy' and Murphy, 'Law beyond the State: A Rejoinder' (2017) 28 *European Journal of International Law* 257 and 265.

83 Ronald Dworkin, *Taking Rights Seriously* (London: Duckworth, 1981, 3rd impression).

84 See Vinx, *Hans Kelsen's Pure Theory of Law*, 48–9.

85 See my 'Positivism and the Pesky Sovereign' (2011) 22 *European Journal of International Law* 363. I point out there that Hersch Lauterpacht accused Kelsen of a similar consignment and I agreed. I indicate in Section 4.5 why this accusation is inaccurate.

and validity in the 'conclusory' sense pertaining to what an individual, apparently subject to the conflicting norms of two different normative orders, must do. Dworkin's criticism of Hart is correct. But he failed to see that these two dimensions imply a third, one which not only bridges the two identified but also serves to bring his position and Kelsen's even closer to each other.

First, and corresponding to validity as certification, there is the dimension of vertical validity, which can be understood as a ladder of formal authorization stretching from the lowest rung at which legal norms are concretized to the highest rung at which the most constitutional authorizing norms reside. The second dimension of validity – the one missing from Dworkin's account at this point in his work – derives from the idea of the unity of the legal system, which tells us that an act must be more than formally authorized. Its content must be one which can cohere with the content of other relevant legal norms – substantive norms as well as formal authorizing norms – within a unified field of legal meaning. This second dimension of validity thus accrues to a norm through being part of a unified field of meaning.

The third dimension of validity corresponds to the conclusory conception and it arises out of the way in which the other two dimensions work in combination. When a legal official is deciding on what someone must legally speaking do, the official's duty is to justify the directive issued, backed as it is by the state's coercive power, as being in accordance with the law. It is a necessary condition of such justification that the official in fact is legally authorized to issue that directive. But this formal condition – the ultra vires condition specified by UK administrative law – does not suffice. The content of the norm must also be justifiable as a norm which fits within the unified field of legal meaning made up of substantive as well as formal norms.

In other words, besides the ladder of formal authorization there is what we can think of as the ladder of material concretization. When legal officials exercise their formal interpretive authority, they are also giving further content to the norm or norms they are interpreting, which requires an act of creative judgment. But, while creative, the judgment is constrained by the requirement that its content is understandable as a norm within a unified field of legal meaning.

Kelsen usually portrayed this requirement as epistemological, driven by the scientific need to demonstrate that the norms of the order cohere. But that suggestion raises the question of the audience for the demonstration. The first possible candidate is the officials themselves, which we should recall is the audience Hart identified when it comes to the rule of recognition. It appears also to be the audience for Kelsen if one accepts the 'weak reading' of his theory of authority according to which law's claim to authority is mainly addressed to legal officials and not legal subjects. This kind of authority is a matter of giving the officials permission to apply sanctions to subjects when they fail to comply with the law.

I argued in Chapter 3 for the 'strong reading' of Kelsen's theory of authority in which the legal subject is front and centre in the authority relationship. In the perspective of a legal theory which understands law as a matter of authority, this individual is the legal subject, and so is not faced in situations of norm conflict with an abstract conflict between the norms of two valid orders. Rather, legal subjects stand on the very particular ground of someone who needs to find out what their obligations are, given that they are already subject to the rule of law – to the public order of law in which they happen to find themselves. They must be able to find an answer to their question 'But, how can that be law for me?' which also makes sense of the presumption that they should subject themselves to the norms of that legal order even when the norms conflict with their personal moralities.

As I pointed out, this is a kind of relativism. Legal subjects accept that the modern legal order is legitimate when some or even many of its norms do not correspond with their sense of right and wrong, and so they should regard particular laws as binding whatever their content. They in a sense relativize their convictions in regard to both the convictions of their fellow subjects and the public judgments established as mandatory by the law. But, as I argued, for an authoritative legal reason to function as a content-independent reason its content must be both determinable and determined in such a way that legal subjects can make sense of their subjection to it.[86]

This figure has much in common with the person Karen Knop has argued is at the heart of private international law. Standardly, private international law is taken to be a matter of working out conflicts between the private law norms from different systems. Knop suggests that this view has to be refined. In her view, private international law is about a private side of citizenship captured in the figure of the 'legal citizen' – the

[86] See Lon L Fuller, 'The Justification of Legal Decisions' (1972) 7 *Archiv für Rechts- und Sozialphilosophie* (Beiheft Neue Folge) 77, at 78.

person who is entitled to sue and be sued in certain courts.[87] She shows how what she calls private international law's 'cosmopolitan form' – its 'techniques' for dealing with the applicability of foreign law – allows it to bring a very concrete focus to contentious moral questions about 'inclusion and exclusion'.[88] More recently, in a discussion of the application of public international law norms by domestic courts, Knop, Ralf Michaels and Annelise Riles have argued that such techniques offer an alternative to the binary options that courts must always apply such norms or not apply them unless required by national law to do so.[89] They call this alternative 'theory through technique':

> We do not resolve the question of whether international law applies in all circumstances, or even whether this international law applies in all circumstances. We seek to answer only the question of whether this international law applies to these litigants with respect to these specific legal rights and this particular dispute. For example, whereas countless scholars ask whether international law is democratically legitimate, we ask whether its application in the particular context is justified. This does not make the question small; it makes it concrete.[90]

In their view, this approach requires what they call a 'submission' to 'the constraint of legal form', though they add that their invocation of formalism should be understood in the spirit of Fuller and his argument that legal fictions are devices we adopt not because we think them to reflect reality but rather because we need them in our attempt to make sense of reality.[91] In Section 4.4, I elaborate the idea of form at stake.

[87] Karen Knop, 'Citizenship, Public and Private' (2008) 71 *Law and Contemporary Problems* 309. She relies on JGA Pocock, 'The Ideal of Citizenship since Classical Times' (1992) 99 *Queen's Quarterly* 33.

[88] Knop, 'Citizenship, Public and Private', 313.

[89] Karen Knop, Ralf Michaels and Annelise Riles 'International Law in Domestic Courts: A Conflict of Laws Approach' (2010) 103 *American Society of International Law Proceedings* 269, at 273, responding in part to Mattias Kumm, 'The Legitimacy of International Law: A Constitutionalist Framework of Analysis' (2004) 15 *European Journal of International Law* 907.

[90] Knop, Michaels and Riles 'International Law in Domestic Courts: A Conflict of Laws Approach', 273.

[91] Ibid. See Lon L Fuller, *Legal Fictions* (Stanford: Stanford University Press, 1967) and his reliance on Hans Vaihinger's 'as if' philosophy.

4.4 Against Geographical Legality

The lines just quoted from Knop, Michaels and Riles respond to an actual example of norm conflict which is a twist on Kelsen's example of a public international law norm which requires −X (the morally admirable norm of non-discrimination) when a national law norm requires X (the morally repugnant norm of discrimination). In this actual example, −X, a resolution of the Security Council, requires that individuals who are considered by a special committee of the council to be connected to terrorist networks should be subject to criminal-like sanctions which affect important rights and interests without being offered any opportunity to contest or even to know the case against them. In contrast, X is the constitutional norm of the national order, generally agreed to be a universal norm of legality, which requires that no one should be subject to sanctions which affect important rights and interests unless one first had an appropriate opportunity to contest the case against one before an impartial tribunal. A challenge is raised by an individual in a court of state A to a regulation enacted in that jurisdiction which implements the international law norm by subjecting him to the sanctions.[92]

This example might seem to pose a particular problem for international law monism, if the position requires that public international law norms always trump national law norms in cases of conflict. In that case, the court in A would have to apply the constitutionally repugnant norm in deciding a case within its national jurisdiction. But the example

[92] Such was the effect of a resolution of the Sanctions Committee of the United Nations Security Council which required states to freeze the assets of individuals placed on a list of those suspected of having links to Al Qaeda and the Taliban. If states were to comply with the obligation imposed on them by the public international law norm imposed by the Security Council, they would have to override national constitutional norms of fairness or due process. See *Kadi* – Case C-402/05 P and C-415/05, *P. Kadi and Al Barakaat International Foundation* v. *Council and Commission* [2008] ECR I-6351, as discussed by Gráinne de Burca, 'The European Court of Justice and the International Legal Order after *Kadi*' (2010) 51 *Harvard International Law Journal* 1. See in particular 23–4, 29–30, for her analysis of the problematically dualist approach of the European Court of Justice and 41–9 for a sketch of how a 'soft constitutionalist' approach would have served the court better in getting to its conclusion that the public international norm should not be implemented. On my argument here, such an approach presupposes international law monism. For an exploration of a similar approach, one which seeks to provide a middle ground between a national constitutionalism akin to national law monism and a full-blown international constitutionalism akin to international law monism, see Kumm, 'The Legitimacy of International Law: A Constitutionalist Framework of Analysis'. In my view, and following Somek, 'Monism: A Tale of the Undead', Kumm's approach requires a kind of monism, the kind which makes legal pluralism thinkable as legal.

poses such a problem only if one visualizes the union of the international legal order and national legal orders as existing on a plane levelled out by public international law because its norms cause to be ejected from the plane any national law norm the content of which contradicts a public international law norm. In this vision, the duty of a domestic court or any other law-applying and -interpreting institution is to decide in favour of public international law whenever such a conflict arises, and whatever the content of the norm.

This way of understanding the problem is not the product of the kind of international law monism developed here. Rather, it is the product of an international law monism which is the mirror image of a national law monism which seeks to come to terms with the fact of existence of public international law, but whose static conception of law results in theoretical dualism and its dogma of incorporation. In both, all that matters is whether the content of a norm of the order to which it gives priority appears to contradict the content of a norm from another order which has a claim to be applicable in the matter. In that case, the norm from the privileged order must always and automatically win.

By contrast, an international law monism which adopts a dynamic conception of the law will not readily assume that either the norm of public international law (which seems to require −X) or the national law norm (which seems to require *X*) have a content which makes it impossible to produce a conclusory norm. Rather, the issue will be what content should be imputed to the conclusory norm which the court in A should issue, so that the norm can display its identity with all other relevant legal norms. My emphasis on the dynamic aspect of this kind of international law monism is of course meant to alert us to the possibility that a court might find an interpretive way out of the problem. In the oft-cited words of a common law judge in a case in 1863, where the legislation under review did not provide for a hearing prior to the state's demolition of property: 'although there are no positive words in a statute requiring that the party shall be heard yet the justice of the common law will supply the omission of the legislature'.[93] A judge may, that is, try to find a way to interpret the national constitutional norm so as to make it consistent with the public international law norm with the result that no sanctions could be imposed without the person being given an opportunity to contest the case.

[93] Byles J in *Cooper* v. *Wandsworth Board of Works* (1863) 14 CB (NS) 180, at 194.

My emphasis also alerts us to more than the interpretive option, as it is not the only one available, nor even – depending on the circumstances – the best one. The judge may find that the problem is not resolvable by interpretation at the national level, so has to be moved to the international level. That can be done by making the equivalent of a declaration of incompatibility under the Human Rights Act. The judge can recognize the formal validity of the regulation while pointing out very explicitly its constitutional flaw, which is not a flaw merely because of a contingent feature of A's constitution, but also a flaw from what we might think of as the very commitment to constitutionalism.

Now there are differences, notably, there is by assumption no national political body which can respond legislatively, nor any court at the international level which has the authority to provide an interpretive solution. There is, however, the Security Council, the international body which issued the resolution, and which is capable of reforming the institutional set up for listing individuals in ways which conform to norms of fairness or due process. That body is under no legal obligation to respond in the sense that there is no other body which can order it to do so. But it is important to recall that we need not be confined in our understanding of fidelity to law by the theoretical blinkers of the command theory of law. As those who could make these reforms look down the ladders of formal authorization and material concretization, they will have to contemplate that national courts and other bodies are having constitutional and legal difficulty concretizing the positive norm they have created. The criticism these difficulties elicit, as well as the occasional decision in which national or other courts find an interpretive solution precluding application of the norm, provide significant incentives for those who could make the reforms, *if* they wish to be seen as ruling by law and not by means of unmediated coercive power.[94]

Three features of dynamic international law monism fall out of this example. First, whichever solution seems appropriate – interpretive, institutional or some combination – its motivation is the regard which must be displayed for the legal subjects whose interests are affected by an official decision and wish to make sense of their subjection to law as a matter of authority or legal right rather than unmediated coercive power. Second, institutions located at the lower levels of the ladder of formal

[94] For an account and astute analysis of the actual story, see Devika Hovell, *The Power of Process: The Value of Due Process in Security Council Sanctions Decision-Making* (Oxford: Oxford University Press, 2016).

authorization are under a duty to apply and interpret the law as if those with authority to enact legislative or quasi-legislative norms intended those norms to be interpreted as part of a unified field of meaning which includes constitutional norms of legality. Third, as this interpretive presumption suggests, the task of upholding the rule of law is not one which is exclusively the preserve of the judiciary, since it is as much the task of executive and legislative institutions. That judges are either not authorized to deal with a certain kind of dispute, nor should be authorized, in no way entails that the dispute is one to be settled politically, where 'political' settlement is equated with extra-legal action.

As Campbell McLachlan has pointed out in his pioneering work on the rule of law in foreign relations law, the fact that the judiciary might be excluded from a certain area of law may mean only that the law has allocated guardianship of rule of law in that area to some other institution, not that the institution has been permitted to enter some extra-legal space.[95] In addition, as I have suggested here, that the judiciary might be excluded from providing interpretive solutions for certain kinds of problems does not mean that judges are excluded from enjoining in their judgments other institutions to perform their role of providing such solutions.

The term 'enjoinment', trading as it does on both 'urging' and 'compelling', is meant to capture something that 'comity' reaches for but stops short of – the legal obligation which exists albeit no institution exists that can force another to act. Those who claim to rule by law rather than by some other means can be held to the commitments implicit in that claim even if they cannot be forced to do so.[96] The idea that a nation's conduct

[95] See Campbell McLachlan, *Foreign Relations Law* (Cambridge: Cambridge University Press, 2014), 5, quoting Lauterpacht as follows:

> [E]very international dispute is of a political character, if by that is meant that it is of importance to the State in question. Thus viewed, the proposition that some legal questions are political is an understatement of what is believed to be the true position. The State is a political institution, and all questions which affect it as a whole, in particular in its relations with other States, are therefore political . . . [but] . . . it is equally easy to show that all international disputes are, irrespective of their gravity, disputes of a legal character in the sense that, so long as the rule of law is recognized, they are capable of an answer by an application of legal rules.

[96] We can note here that Fuller rejected the idea of a social contract for explaining the commitment by the lawgiver 'implicit in the concept of law' and suggested in its place the 'old fashioned legal term' 'intendment' – that is, that 'our institutions and our formalized

of its foreign affairs is law-governed and that one source of the legal norms which govern it is the nation's own public law or constitutional norms is anathema only to those who adopt national law monism. For them, the public law of a modern legal state stops at its territorial borders unless a political decision is made to extend its reach. But if one adopts the Kelsenian juridical conception, that 'geographical' understanding of the reach of public law norms must be rejected.[97]

With that rejection, we can begin the task of working up a legal theory which has at its centre legal subjects whose mark is that they are entitled to ask of a legal official 'But, how can that be law for me?' and to get an answer which fully displays its legal basis, which may be in national law or public international law, or both. As Knop's invocation of the 'legal citizen' suggests, such figures are not the citizens of the political community of a nation state, nor the subjects of democratic political theory. Rather, they are members of a jural community – the community of legal subjects bound together by *Recht*.

The constitution of such a community will include the legal norms which are considered part of its national constitution, whether written or unwritten or both. But there are also the compulsory norms of public international law (*jus cogens* and obligations *erga omnes*), customary international norms and treaty-based norms. At the same time, the public law norms of the national legal order will presumptively apply to any challenge raised by someone who is directly subject to an act of state power, whether or not that individual is within the borders of the nation state. They must so apply if the state is to claim that it acts by authority rather than by unmediated coercive power, since to act with authority is to claim authorization on the part of those subject to one's

interactions with one another are accompanied by certain interlocking expectations that may be called intendments'; Lon L Fuller, *The Morality of Law* (New Haven: Yale University Press, 1969, revised ed.), 33. See my Chapter 6.

97 In the course of his speeches in the cause of the impeachment of Warren Hastings, governor-general of Bengal from 1773 to 1785, Edmund Burke protested against the view that morality is 'geographical' – the view that one set of public standards governed the way British public officials should act in Britain and another less exacting or hardly exacting at all governed their actions when abroad. On that view, Hastings should not be tried and convicted for his abuses of authority while in office because he was entitled to act in ways which would be regarded as violations of fundamental standards of law and morality at home. See Jennifer Pitts, *A Turn to Empire: The Rise of Imperial Liberalism in Britain and France* (Princeton: Princeton University Press, 2005), 78–85, and Thomas Poole, *Reason of State: Law, Prerogative and Empire* (Cambridge: Cambridge University Press, 2015), 151–64.

power, even if the authorizing subject is, at least in part, constituted through the process of challenge.

Just as the legal subject is in a process of at least partial reconstruction, so is the constitution itself both act and achievement. As achievement, it provides the framework within which discussion begins about what is legally required. As act, the conclusion as to the content of that norm may require adopting an innovative understanding of that framework. While this requires immense complexity, it is hardly more than the complexity already in place in any actual private international law matter, when – as we saw Kelsen suggest – a norm from one order refers to a norm of another order in a bid to form a 'complete rule of law'; and, as Knop, Michaels and Riles suggest, this does not make the problems of constitutionalism explored here small; rather it makes them concrete.

But while the problems become concrete, and in this way resolvable, their solution does require presupposing something a good deal more robust than an austerely formal basic norm. Indeed, from the discussion thus far we can glean that the basic norm transforms power into legal right in such a way that legal subjects are in some sense citizens, in both the private and public aspects, and that as such they are, as we saw Kelsen put it, bound together 'in a higher community'.[98]

Kelsen was, recall, speaking about states in the international legal order, not individuals in a national order. But his observations apply with equal force to the subjects of a national order, so that we can substitute 'individual' for 'state' and 'national' for 'international', with other changes made to follow suit, to get the following:

> There is a generally accepted understanding of the nature and concept of national law that it constitutes a community of individuals with equal rights. The proposition of the coexistence of a multiplicity of individuals, which despite their actual differences in strength and resources are from the perspective of legality [*rechtlich*] of equal value and, when it comes to their mutually delimited spheres of power, bound in a higher community is an eminently ethical idea and one of the few really valuable and uncontested components of contemporary cultural consciousness. But this proposition is only possible with the help of a juristic hypothesis: that above the individuals understood as legal subjects stands a legal order [*Rechtsordnung*] which mutually delimits the spheres of lawful action of

[98] Kelsen, *Das Problem der Souveränität*, 204.

> the individuals in that it hinders incursions by one into the sphere of the others, or at least subjects them all to equal conditions for such incursions.[99]

Recall also that Kelsen concluded this set of thoughts by saying that 'when the primacy of international law fulfils this function, the concept of law [*Rechtsbegriff*] is simultaneously perfected in a formal and substantive sense. The law [*Recht*] attains the organization of humanity and thereby a unity with the highest ethical idea.'[100] This may seem to make Kelsen both a not so closeted liberal and, which may seem more of a surprise, an anti-positivist. We might then choose to regard his statement as well as the other points in his work where he admitted an affinity between his position and natural law as aberrations, rather than clues, in the same way as we might regard Hart's apparent concessions to natural law. In addition, at least in the abstract, this statement of the jural community of the modern legal state may seem to presuppose a conception of community as composed of liberal citizens. Transposed back to the international level, the presupposition would be of a community of liberal states, that is, exactly the discourse of civilization which seems so problematic when one appreciates its role in the construction of empire and colonialism.

In Section 4.5, I take the arc of legality back to Hobbes in order to introduce the topic of Section 4.6 – the 'politics of recognition' inherent in the Kelsenian understanding of international law. That section in turn provides a bridge to Chapters 5 and 6, which explore more generally the political contours of legal theory in a way which shows that these passages in Kelsen and Hart are not aberrations. Rather, they are evidence of the natural law features of any legal theory which embarks on explaining law in the register of authority.

4.5 Hobbes on the International Rule of Law

Hobbes is often credited with putting in place the original conception of the constitution as a sealed space. In chapter 13 of *Leviathan* he described the miserable condition of mankind in the state of nature and remarked to readers who might be sceptical that such a state ever existed that they need only look to international relations to observe one:

[99] Adapted from the passage, ibid, as translated in the text to note 28.
[100] Ibid, 205.

> But though there had never been any time, wherein particular men were in a condition of warre one against another; yet in all times, Kings, and Persons of Soveraigne authority, because of their Independency, are in continuall jealousies, and in the state and posture of Gladiators; having their weapons pointing, and their eyes fixed on one another; that is, their Forts, Garrisons, and Guns upon the Frontiers of their Kingdomes; and continuall Spyes upon their neighbours; which is a posture of War.[101]

The passage is influential because international relations 'realists' take Hobbes not only to be describing international relations as they are but also as they must be – an arena where individual states relentlessly pursue goals which they take to serve their particular interests. Public international law must be that way because the conditions which make the rule of law possible within a state – namely, an absolute sovereign with a monopoly on the power to make, enforce and interpret the law – are so conspicuously lacking in the international arena. Yet public international law exists, and critics of such realism can point not only to general compliance with it but also to examples of compliance which seems plausibly to be against state interest. Hence, these critics argue, since public international law constrains the power of sovereign states, there is an international rule of law, even though the international legal order lacks the institutional framework we consider essential for the rule of law within states.

This argument from actual examples is problematic because the practice of state compliance with public international law is not that easily demonstrated to be the product of legal constraint. Indeed, the problem goes beyond public international law since the practice whereby a state generally complies with its own public law is hardly different in this respect. But, as I now argue, this phenomenon does not so much demonstrate the truth of realism as that the ultimate questions in debates between these realists and their critics are normative questions about how best to construct practice, and not merely debates about how best to describe it. To think that Hobbes, to take just one prominent example, was providing a simple description of state practice in the quotation above is to misunderstand what question he was asking when he inquired into whether the rule of law is possible, in national affairs or at the international level.

[101] Thomas Hobbes, *Leviathan* (Cambridge: Cambridge University Press, 1996, Richard Tuck, ed.), 90.

It mattered a great deal to Hobbes that the rule of law could be realized in practice. As he said, *Leviathan* was written in large part as a book of instruction so that people with the help of a 'very able Architect' (the sovereign) can avoid constructing a 'crasie building ... such as hardly lasting out of their own time, must assuredly fall upon the heads of their posterity'.[102] So part of Hobbes's inquiry into the rule of law has to do with how it can help to sustain the edifice of civil society over time. But his main question is how it is possible that those subject to the de facto power of a sovereign could consider its enacted law as obligatory, as having de jure or legitimate authority over them. In short, the question is mainly a normative one: why should the law be considered a source of obligations in the first place?

Hobbes, we saw, gave the following clear answer to this question. If one is living under the protection of a de facto sovereign, one can be presumed to have consented to recognize its law as authoritative over oneself because it is rational to prefer the protection of any sovereign to the chaos of the state of nature.[103] On the standard view, Hobbes reconfigured the venerable contrast between the rule of law and the arbitrary rule of men into a contrast between being subject to the arbitrary rule of one person or group of persons – the sovereign – and being subject to the arbitrary will of all other individuals in the state of nature. The former is rationally preferable to the latter because, as the product of just one person or group with a monopoly on coercion, it can provide legal subjects with the order which makes secure and peaceful interaction between them possible.

It is easy to see how such realism might be thought to be consistent with this normative position. Since there is no international sovereign, all we have in international relations is the jostling for power of individual states, each seeking to impose its will on the others. To the extent that there is public international law, it constrains states only insofar as they find it in their interest to abide by its rules, which means that the most powerful states in the international order are more or less unconstrained. On this view, public international law is no more than the instrument of legally unconstrained (though perhaps politically constrained) state power, an instrument which sovereigns use to promote their interests. Because the law is no more than an instrument, sovereigns may act

102 Ibid, 221.

103 Ibid, 128–9.

outside public international law or even against it if they deem it useful and have the political power to do so.

But if realism is right about public international law, the rule of law is no more possible within states than it is in the international order. Realism of this sort if true is true all the way down. That conclusion of course supports rather than refutes realism. But my broader point is that this kind of realism, whether about the national or the international order, is ultimately not a descriptive account of practice but a normative theory. Practice can be made to correspond to it but that is a matter of normative choice. It is possible to construct a political world, whether national or international, along realist lines. But it is also possible to construct it along rule-of-law lines. Since we live in a world which is an admixture of realist and legalist elements, there is a normative choice to be made about whether to make our world more or less subject to the rule of law.

I argued in Chapters 2 and 3 that there is much more to the content of the choice for the rule of law and to Hobbes's answer to the normative question about law's authority than is commonly supposed. Submission to a sovereign is not submission to the arbitrary rule of one person. It is submission to the rule of one artificial person whose identity is legally constituted, and who not only rules through law but also in accordance with the rule of law.[104] Submission to sovereignty is ultimately submission to the rule of law. That explains both why law can be treated domestically as a source of obligations and why international relations are governable by the rule of law.

Recall from Chapter 2 that Hobbes, while he thought it in the nature of sovereign power that it cannot be divided, clearly saw the need for a division of functions. As Hobbes put it in his discussion of interpretation in claiming that the final arbiter of disputes over legal meaning is the supreme lawmaker: 'To [the legislator] . . . therefore there can not be any kind of knot in the Law, insoluble; either finding out the ends, to undoe it by; or else making what ends he will, (as *Alexander* did with his sword in the Gordian knot,) by the Legislative power; which no other interpreter can doe.'[105]

As I pointed out, Hobbes was here distinguishing between two ways in which the legislator, who is also the final interpreter of the law, may deal

[104] See my 'Hobbes on the Authority of Law', in Dyzenhaus and Thomas Poole, eds, *Hobbes and the Law* (Cambridge: Cambridge University Press, 2012) 186.

[105] Hobbes, *Leviathan*, 191. His emphasis.

with a seemingly insoluble problem of interpretation. The first finds a solution within the law which shows that the problem was not in fact insoluble – the knot is undone. The second does not so much find as impose a solution – it cuts through the knot. Only the first solution is properly interpretive of the law and while both solutions have authority because they emanate from the sovereign, the authority they have is different. The first is the authority to issue the definitive or final interpretation of the law, the second the authority to make new law. This distinction by itself puts in place all we need to understand why public international law may be regarded as an obligation-creating legal order. For what it does is to establish what Georges Scelle, an eminent international lawyer, called 'the juridical phenomenon of the role splitting function'.[106]

Consider, for example, a group of five children playing a winner-takes-all, war-like game with several general but complex rules which raise difficult issues of interpretation in particular situations.[107] At a certain point in the game, one of the children, Luke, whose turn it is, offers a sophisticated argument about why one of the rules should be interpreted

[106] Georges Scelle, 'Le phénomène juridique du dédoublement fonctionnel', in Walter Schätzel and Hans-Jürgen Schlochauer, eds, *Rechstfragen der Internationalen Organisation: Festschrift für Hans Wehberg zu Seinem 70 Geburstag* (Frankfurt am Main: Vittorio Klostermann, 1956) 342. I adopt this translation from Antonio Cassese, 'Remarks on Scelle's Theory of "Role Splitting"' (dédoublement fonctionnel) in International Law' (1990) 1 *European Journal of International Law* 210. For an overview of Scelle, see Hubert Thierry, 'The European Tradition in International Law' (1990) 1 *European Journal of International Law* 193. For contemporary application, see Evan J Criddle and Evan Fox-Decent, *Fiduciaries of Humanity: How International Law Constitutes Authority* (Oxford: Oxford University Press, 2016), 321–2. Jeremy Waldron argues for something like this view in 'Are Sovereigns Entitled to the Benefit of the International Rule of Law?' (2011) 22 *European Journal of International Law* 315. For my critique, see 'Positivism and the Pesky Sovereign'. Waldron, responding to the critique, rejects among my claims the suggestion that his legal theory, in which there is the tight relation between the rule of law and the concept of law often rejected by Hartian positivists, must accept a more natural law account of immanent principles of legality. See Waldron, 'Response: The Perils of Exaggeration' (2011) 22 *European Journal of International Law* 389, at 395. As he points out, he has argued elsewhere that such a tight relation 'is compatible with the separation of the validity conditions of law from the bottom-line moral evaluation of a given edict'; ibid, referring to his 'The Concept and the Rule of Law' (2008) 43 *Georgia Law Review* 1. The general argument of that paper is hugely influential, including on my own work, even though I contest his compatibility claim.

[107] I set out 'Luke's game', and much of the argument of this section, in 'Hobbes on the International Rule of Law' (2014) 28 *Ethics and International Affairs* 53.

in a way significantly advantageous to him. The argument relies on the text and an interpretation of the same rule in a somewhat analogous situation in a previous iteration of the game where the group had all agreed on how to proceed. The others, who stand to lose if Luke is right, offer an equally sophisticated argument in response. The debate rages over several minutes until Luke agrees that the majority interpretation is correct and the game proceeds with Luke correspondingly disadvantaged.

One way of understanding this example is in purely realist terms. The majority simply outvoted Luke because it happened to be in their interest to do so at that particular point in time, a crucial juncture in the game of a sort which often attracts such interpretive disputes. Further, Luke fell in with their decision because he had to if he were to continue in that game and if he wanted to be trusted to be a participant in future games. The only norm which could be extracted from the example would be that in cases of controversy the actor with the most power could, because of that position, legislate a self-interested answer. In the context of this game, that actor turns out to be the majority of the group.

The distinction between interpretation and legislation is necessary if we are to respond to the fact that Luke and the other children in the game regard themselves as not only players bent on winning but also as judges – interpreters of the rules legislated by a supreme legislator, the maker of the game. When they occupy the judicial role, they accept certain commitments: to be bound by the text of the rules; to offer reasonable interpretations of what a rule requires in cases where it is controversial; to take into account for the sake of fairness the way in which the rule has been previously interpreted in analogous situations; to treat each participant as an equal when it comes to interpretation. In other words, they accept they must act in accordance with what we saw Hart called the 'judicial virtues'.[108] The difference is that the players do not regard these so much as the marks of being a good judge but of being a judge at all.

Such commitments make it possible for the players to adopt as a regulative assumption of the game that its rules make up a unified system which contains an answer to all possible questions which might arise about the application of the rules. Because there is only one level of judges – there is no court of appeal – such commitments have to be taken all the more seriously in order to maintain trust, in particular the requirement to offer only reasonable interpretations of the rule. Those

[108] Hart, *The Concept of Law*, 204–5.

locked in dispute with each other are judges in their own cause, with the result that there is much more pressure on them to achieve agreement on the most reasonable interpretation of the rules than in a legal order with a separation of powers and a hierarchically organized judiciary.

While one can explain, then, why the majority *qua* judges offered interpretation X while Luke *qua* judge offered Y in terms of the fact that X advances the majority's interests and Y Luke's, neither X nor Y is reducible to those interests. Indeed, during the course of the interpretive dispute, the players *qua* judges accepted the onus of showing precisely why the different interpretations were not reducible to any given player's interests. Put differently, the interests provide *motives* for preferring one interpretation to another, but they do not qualify as *reasons* which justify either interpretation. If Luke insisted on an unreasonable interpretation, that interpretation would be reducible to interest – more accurately, it would not even count as an interpretation – and he would be taken by the others as unfit to be trusted to play the game. If Luke, that is, were playing the 'primitive society' game of self-help, he would have shown that he cannot be 'received into any Society', as Hobbes said of the 'Foole', who says there is no such thing as justice, and so considers himself entitled to ignore the law when he thinks it expedient.[109]

Notice that in the game all the participants have equal freedom to decide what is in their best interests as well as equal authority as interpreters of the rules. We could say that they are sovereign in these respects and that the fact that they regard themselves as obligated by rules not of their making does not detract from their sovereign status. Were it not for these rules – the rules constitutive of the game – they would have no such status. But it is important to see that when they play the game, they do more than subscribe to a set of authoritative rules. They also subscribe to the principles of interpretation which permit them to consider themselves as free and equal participants, even when they submit to an interpretation with which they disagree. These principles are not themselves an explicit part of the rules of the game. Rather, they discipline the content of the rules through the interpretive process. As such, they make up what we can think of as the natural law of the game and while the game lasts, the players are a self-constituting jural community in which each is at times a free and equal subject, at other times a public official.

[109] Hobbes, *Leviathan*, 102–3.

Kelsen shared much the same view. In *Peace through Law*, a work published during the height of the Second World War, he said that 'it is the essential characteristic of the law as a coercive order to establish a community monopoly of force'.[110] He added that even in a 'primitive legal community' there is such a monopoly. While the principle of 'self-help' prevails in that it is up to individuals in the community rather than institutions to interpret and enforce the law, the individuals still think of themselves as interpreting and enforcing the law of the community, which means that what they do is 'the exercise of the community monopoly of force'.[111]

Kelsen's main argument was that the international order needed to develop a system of compulsory adjudication if it were to escape from a state equivalent to a 'primitive' legal community. Similarly, Hersch Lauterpacht, Kelsen's most eminent student as well as the leading international lawyer of his time, argued in *The Development of International Law by the International Court*[112] that submission to compulsory jurisdiction goes a long way to solving the problem of international law's 'immaturity'.[113] But Lauterpacht, like Kelsen, thought that the order of public international law has no less a claim to be a legal order than does national law, even if it is in an immature state. This idea depends on a claim both shared that there is a distinction between legislation and adjudication, even in what we saw Hart thought of as a pre-legal or 'primitive' order.

Indeed, Kelsen made almost exactly this point, though without using the language of natural law, in his argument in *Peace through Law* that sovereignty is fully compatible with submission to the jurisdiction of an international tribunal. Judicial decisions, he said, are 'objective and impartial', 'not political decrees issued according to the principle, which is a negation of law, that might goes before right'.[114] He continued:

> Even if the decision of an international tribunal does not constitute the strict application of a pre-existing legal rule, it is supposed to be founded on at least the idea of law – that is, on a rule which although not yet positive law, ought, according to the conviction of independent judges, to

[110] Kelsen, *Peace through Law*, 3–4.
[111] Ibid.
[112] Hersch Lauterpacht, *The Development of International Law by the International Court* (London: Stevens and Sons, 1958).
[113] Ibid, 158.
[114] Kelsen, *Peace through Law*, 48.

> become law and which really becomes positive law for the case settled by the particular judicial decision. It is the submission to the law, to the law not as a system of unchangeable values, but as a body of slowly and steadily changing norms, which is not incompatible with the principle of sovereign equality since it is only this law that guarantees the co-existence of the States as sovereign and equal communities.[115]

I want thus to suggest that the position of states in the international order is much like the position of the players in this game. The point is deeper than that the sovereign states of the international order find themselves always entangled in public international law as they consider how best to advance their interests. It is that they are themselves creatures of public international law. To maintain their status as sovereign states, they must treat as binding the law which constitutes the jural community of which they are a part. Hence, when one state raises a question about the legality of another's action or proposed action, that state must accept the onus of justifying its action as having a warrant in a reasonable interpretation of the law.

The major difference between the children's game and the relationship between states is that while the goal of the game (as with many such games) is to be the only player left standing, the goal of any legal order, no matter how primitive, is to secure, as in Kelsen's title, peace through law. When interpretive disputes break out in a legal order, the participants are under an obligation *qua* judges to show that their understanding of the rules advances the goal of securing peace.[116] That goal also provides the impetus for developing the institutions which make legal orders, including the international order, more mature. To the extent that the international legal order has developed such institutions, it is less fragile than the order of the game. But one must take into account that, as Hobbes pointed out, even in a national legal order one can make the claim that the laws are no more than 'cobwebs' because 'potent men' have got away with breaking them, leaving only the 'weaker sort' to be caught.[117] According to Hobbes, those who make this claim reason as follows: '*Justice is but a vain word: That whatsoever a man can get by his own Industry, and Hazard, is his own: That the Practice of all Nations*

[115] Ibid.

[116] For a treatment of public international law which elaborates this kind of theme, see Jutta Brunnée and Stephen J Toope, *Legitimacy and Legality in International Law: An Interactional Account* (Cambridge: Cambridge University Press, 2010).

[117] Hobbes, *Leviathan*, 204. His emphasis.

cannot be unjust: That Examples of former times are good Arguments of doing the like again.'[118]

In this passage, Hobbes not only rejected the main premise of international relations realism, which he regarded as the position adopted by the 'Foole' who thinks that his perception of self-interest is the measure of appropriate action, but also made it clear that this premise does not necessarily hold in international relations. The direct implication is both that the practice of any nation can be judged according to standards of justice and that, as there are the Just Men we encountered in Chapter 2 whose will is framed by justice in the civil condition, so, in 'the practice of all nations', there are just states. Since for Hobbes justice is a property of law, the practice of nations can be law-governed and in *Leviathan* he said that sovereigns are governed by the same law that governs men who have 'no Civil Government', namely, by 'the law of Nations', the 'same thing' as natural law. Both sovereigns and such men are thus subject to the laws of nature, but subject in the sense that they are bound 'in the Conscience onely', there 'being no Court of Naturall Justice'.[119]

This sense of being bound is elaborated in a passage in one of the two chapters in which Hobbes set out his extensive account of the laws of nature, where he distinguished between being bound only by one's conscience, *in foro interno*, and being bound to act by some public constraint, *in foro externo*.[120] It may seem, as we saw in Chapter 2, that the former sense of obligation is empty since Hobbes emphasized that in civil society the sovereign's interpretation of what the laws of nature require is definitive, as is the individual's interpretation in the state of nature. However, as Noel Malcolm has argued, Hobbes is not a realist in that he thought that no moral rights and duties exist in international relations, but only in that he did not think that international relations could ever achieve the presumed 'harmony' of civil society.[121]

Malcolm points out that Hobbes did not confine the situation where the laws of nature bind *in foro externo* to that of civil society, that is, to the situation of the modern legal state. One is bound *in foro externo* as long as one has assurance of performance from the other party to a contract, which means that if the other party performs its part of the

[118] Ibid. His emphasis.
[119] Ibid, 244.
[120] Ibid, 110.
[121] Noel Malcolm, 'Hobbes's Theory of International Relations', in Malcolm, *Aspects of Hobbes* (Oxford: Clarendon Press, 2004) 431, at 455–6.

contract in the state of nature, one is bound to reciprocate.[122] In other words, *in foro externo* obligation is not confined to the situation in which state coercion will follow failure to perform. It also arises where failure to perform is immoral because one is under an obligation to respond to another's performance.

Malcolm shows that there are important lessons to be learned from Hobbes's theory of international relations. Moral laws do exist both in the state of nature and in international society. But, generally, one will have the right to act in ways which violate those laws unless there are special circumstances, notably when one has entered into an agreement with another and the other has performed its part of the agreement.[123] In addition, Malcolm shows that Hobbes not only saw how treaties and agreements could stabilize international relations but also how a common culture of shared values could provide a basis for stability. In this second respect, Malcolm observes that when it came to culture, Hobbes thought it just as important that the sovereign make political education part of the internal project of achieving stability within the state.[124]

Hobbes then was no more a realist about public international law than he was about domestic law. His position has much in common with Kelsen and Lauterpacht, both of whom regarded public international law as the law which governs all those states which have made a normative commitment to being part of a jural community. Such commitment requires that the states understand that they bear the onus of justifying their actions on the basis of reasonable interpretations of existing law. The only serious difference between Kelsen and Lauterpacht was that Kelsen officially rejected natural law. But, as Lauterpacht argued, it is difficult to make sense of Kelsen's legal theory without the idea of principles of natural law which stem from the project of achieving peace through law between free and equal individuals, whether natural individuals or states. In addition, he argued that Kelsen's preference for international law monism was the 'back door' by which the 'ghost of natural law' had 'crept into the cast-iron logic of . . . [Kelsen's] system'.[125]

[122] *Leviathan*, 102. Malcolm, 'Hobbes's Theory of International Relations', 438.
[123] Ibid, 445–6.
[124] Ibid, 449–55.
[125] Hersch Lauterpacht, 'Kelsen's Pure Science of Law', in Lauterpacht, *International Law: Collected Papers – The Law of Peace*, vol. 2 (Cambridge: Cambridge University Press, 2009, E Lauterpacht, ed.) 404, at 423.

Lauterpacht pointed out that Kelsen's qualification that it is juridically permissible to choose between the hypothesis that the basic norm of a national legal order is the basic norm of public international law and its converse is odd, given that the former is incompatible with the ultimate unity of legal knowledge. For it follows from national law monism that each national state has to be conceived as ultimately sovereign over and at the same time subordinate to every other. It is also incompatible with the idea of public international law as regulating the relations of coordinated and equal states, which presupposes the existence of a higher authority, as well as with accepted rules of public international law, for example, the rule of the continuity of the state. On this view, the affirmation of the primacy of state law is an affirmation of mere force.[126]

Hence, Lauterpacht suggested that Kelsen's preference for international law monism is evidence of his attraction to natural law. It is difficult, he observed, otherwise to comprehend Kelsen's 'proud insistence' that the initial juridical hypothesis transforms power into right. But for its peace-creating effectiveness, the achievement would be of doubtful value. Nevertheless, Kelsen in his later work asserted that the primacy of public international law is merely a matter of choice in order to maintain his distance from natural law. He wished to maintain that distance because he thought that the attraction to natural law is of a piece with the attraction to an ideal which transcends human experience, and so to something inconsistent with the dignity and autonomy of the individual. But, said Lauterpacht, while we may 'have abandoned the theory that statutes repugnant to natural justice are void, . . . that does not mean that we have ceased to shape positive law and to interpret it, sometimes out of recognition, by ideas for which the term natural law is an elastic and convenient expression'.[127] To the extent that positivism disregards this phenomenon, namely, the phenomenon of dynamic juridical production, it

> becomes a dogma divorced from the general trend of legal thinking. The manner in which judges have recourse to the 'law above the law' or the 'law behind the law' in order to obliterate the gap between law and justice has been for a long time the persistent and central theme of legal philosophy . . . This is the problem of reconciling the antinomy of rule

[126] Ibid, 422.
[127] Ibid, 425–6.

> and discretion, of security and justice, of stability and change. But it is a problem which is outside the range of Kelsen's writing.[128]

We can see, however, that Lauterpacht's claim here, while broadly true of Hart and his successors, does not attend to the way in which Kelsen's Pure Theory includes the dynamic dimension of juridical production within its scope. Kelsen, on my reconstruction of his theory, would have agreed with Lauterpacht's positive answer to the question he posed in an address to the Grotius Society – 'Is International Law a Part of the Law of England?' There Lauterpacht took as his epigraph the following lines from Blackstone's *Commentaries*:

> [T]he law of nations (whenever any question arises which is properly the object of it's jurisdiction) is here adopted in it's full extent by the common law, and is held to be a part of the law of the land. And those acts of parliament, which have from time to time been made to enforce this universal law, or to facilitate the execution of it's decisions, are not to be considered as introductive of any new rule, but merely declaratory of the old fundamental constitutions of the kingdom; without which it must cease to be a part of the civilized world.[129]

Lauterpacht was not fazed by the doctrine of parliamentary supremacy in giving a positive answer to the question in his title. As we saw earlier in Section 4.1, he pointed out that there is a commonly accepted rule of statutory construction that statutes are to be interpreted 'so as not to be in conflict with international law'.[130] Any affirmation of the absolute supremacy of parliament is, given this rule of construction, a 'theoretical affirmation', one which has 'the probably not unintended effect of stressing the duty of judges to do their utmost to interpret statutes so as not to impute to the Legislature the intention of disregarding international law'.[131] He argued that the insistence in the UK parliamentary legal order on an incorporating statute was not a reaction to a common law claim that public international law is part of national law. Rather, it was a reaction to the uncertainty of public international law in particular areas. That is, where the requirements of public international law are uncertain, and given that public international law is part of the law of the land, the

[128] Ibid, 426.

[129] Sir William Blackstone, *Commentaries on the Laws of England*, fifth chapter of the Fourth Book, quoted in Lauterpacht, 'Is International Law a Part of the Law of England?', 537.

[130] Ibid, 542.

[131] Ibid, 543.

way to resolve uncertainty is for parliament to clear up the uncertainty.[132]

Lauterpacht still stressed that the will of individual states mattered when it came to the binding quality of public international law. But such an act of will, he argued, is a general submission to public international law – a voluntary act of submission which as long as it lasts 'has the effect of elevating to the authority of a legal rule the unity of international and municipal law'.[133] From the 'point of view of municipal law' that submission may, Lauterpacht said, be 'validly refused or withdrawn, but the sanction of such action must be, in Blackstone's words, that the State would "cease to be part of the civilized world"'.[134]

Such voluntary submission is needed to maintain what Lauterpacht called 'a fundamental jurisprudential identity' between national law and public international law even in officially dualist legal orders.[135] That identity is manifested in various ways, including the recognition of the importance of public international law in the interpretation of statutes, of the force of customary international law in the absence of an explicit statutory override, and of the category of *jus cogens* and other mandatory norms. It is also manifested in the fact that, as we saw Hart say of private international law, '[a]ll civilized systems contain special rules for dealing with cases containing a foreign element'.[136]

Helpful here is the argument of Martin Wolff, an eminent private international lawyer, that while private international law is not itself public international law, the 'lawgiver' must bear in mind the community, 'neither the community of his own nationals nor that of the various states or nations, but the community of all individuals, of mankind, the *société international des individus*'.[137] He continued: 'The aim of the lawgiver must be to establish *such rules as he can reasonably wish to see introduced by the legislators or courts of other countries.* Private International Law is not itself international, but it should certainly be drawn up in an international frame of mind.'[138]

Kelsen was badly placed to deny this, despite his claim in an essay of 1957 that a legal order need make no provision for private

[132] Ibid, 546.
[133] Ibid, 549.
[134] Ibid.
[135] Ibid.
[136] Hart, 'Kelsen's Doctrine of the Unity of Law', 340–1.
[137] Martin Wolff, *Private International Law* (Oxford: Clarendon Press, 1962, 2nd ed.), 16.
[138] Ibid. His emphasis.

international law.[139] The international frame of mind is entailed in international law monism and is central to his legal theory. He did not suppose that the legal philosopher should first construct a theory and only then ask whether by its criteria either public or private international law are law. Rather, given the existence of both, one should understand how these fields inform legal theory, which requires seeing the centrality of public international law to legal order and thus the necessity of international law monism. A state may decide to do without private international law and may also enact statutes which explicitly exclude unwritten or written constitutional norms, or public international law norms, or judicial and other review of the implementation of the law, and so on. But with each such decision, the order's claim to be a legal order is put under stress at the same time as its officials become less able to give adequate answers to the legal subject's question 'But, how can that be law for me?'

So much is required as soon as one begins to move beyond the image of sovereignty as the absolute unlimited authority of an 'uncommanded commander'.[140] As Lauterpacht argued, the root of dualism is to be found in the rise of positivistic doctrines of absolute state sovereignty.[141] Just as it is not asserted that the common law fails to be part of the law of the land because statutes may override the common law, so one should reject the claim that public international law is not part of the law of the land because statutes may override it. But, he claimed, with each such overriding, the 'fundamental jurisprudential identity' of law with its aspirations is in peril.[142] In short, the problem of the identity of public international law and domestic law is no different from the problem of the identity or unity of statute and common law, unless one adopts what Lauterpacht described as a 'barren type of legal positivism'.[143]

As I have indicated here and argued in Chapter 3, on the strong reading of Kelsen's theory of authority the problem is not outside Kelsen's range. The strong reading is required by the hypothesis of the basic norm which makes the hypothesis itself not arbitrary. Rather, as I elaborate in Chapter 6, it is a 'regulative assumption', a 'claim about inquiry and what those engaged in inquiry must assume'.[144]

139 Kelsen, 'Le Renvoi'.
140 Hart, 'Positivism and the Separation of Law and Morals', 59.
141 Lauterpacht, 'Is International Law a Part of the Law of England?', 555.
142 Ibid, 558–9.
143 Ibid, 568.
144 See Cheryl Misak, *The American Pragmatists* (Oxford: Oxford University Press, 2013), 50–5, at 51.

In philosophy of law the fundamental choice is whether to inquire into law as primarily a normative practice or as a practice of coercion. Once the choice is made for the former, for understanding law as a matter of authority, one cannot stop short of the strong reading.

We have seen that Kelsen did at times and Hart at nearly all times stop at an understanding of the authority relationship as one between officials who do not have to have regard for the legal subject. It is this resting place which leaves Hart's theory stuck between an account of law as authoritative and one of law as the gunman situation writ large and which creates the ambivalences in both his and Kelsen's constitutional theories explored in Chapter 3. But once we accept, for Kelsenian reasons, that the authority relationship includes the perspective of legal subjects, reasons which we saw Raz argued had to apply to Hart's legal theory, there is no longer a choice available within a juridical account of the authority of law between the hypotheses of international law and national law monism.

International law monism prevails because only that hypothesis renders intelligible the place of the legal subject, whether an individual person subject to the rule of a state or a state subject to international law, in the constitution of legal authority. Moreover, as Kelsen clearly saw – the point which Lauterpacht drives home – the choice for national law monism is a political one for what Hart called the 'uncommanded commander',[145] the figure in the command theory of law who is both at the apex of the legal hierarchy and not within the purview of its law. As such it is a political choice against the rule of law and the idea of a jural community.

Kelsen did qualify his thought that there is a natural law foundation to international law by saying that it must be understood as 'confined' to the role of the basic norm in juridical production, the way in which the juristic hypothesis makes possible a legal order 'between coordinated subjects', with its content developed by positive legal acts.[146] Implicit in this statement is Kelsen's oft-repeated slogan that the positive law can have any content, his equivalent of Hart's Separation Thesis that there is no necessary connection between law and morality. In other words, there is no concession to natural law because public international law, just like national law, can be given any content.

[145] Hart, 'Positivism and the Separation of Law and Morals', 59.

[146] Kelsen, *Das Problem der Souveränität*, 252–3.

However, because Kelsen conceived public international law as a legal order, we can see more clearly in international relations than in the case of a national legal order why law cannot be given any content. To conceive the order of public international law as a legal order, one must hypothesize the basic norm, which is a postulate of peace in that it organizes public international law so as to enable the interaction of states understood as legally speaking equal. It is hardly, then, a coincidence that the material or substantive norms of international law, whether developed by custom or through consent, are norms which sustain – or at least are not in conflict with – the postulate of peace between equals.

States are given the task of concretizing those norms, whether to govern their own interaction in the international domain, or to govern the interaction of subjects within the space of a national legal order. That concretization process happens through 'will' more than 'intellect', in the sense that the process of concretizing the norms involves creative judgment, but one that is law-governed both in that it is formally authorized and must take into account relevant material norms. It follows that the content of positive legal norms which undermine equality-preserving peace are legally (as well as morally) suspect, and give rise to problems which will be channelled through legal institutions.[147] The unity afforded by the basic norm is therefore both an assumption of Kelsenian legal theory and an achievement. It is a regulative assumption which we make about our practice in order to give it the point we take it to have.

I discussed in Chapter 3 the analogy Kelsen saw between the basic norm in his theory and the social contract in natural law theory. As he said, it serves the 'same theoretical need for a presupposition of unity on which the unity of the state order in the multiplicity of legal acts of state could be grounded, and which could grasp actual power relationships as

[147] Exactly this point was elaborated in different ways by two of Kelsen's students who became leading international lawyers, Alfred Verdross and Lauterpacht. Verdross pushed Kelsen's theory of international law in a natural law direction via a more deductive kind of reasoning from its premise in the basic norm, and is widely credited with getting accepted in the twentieth century the idea that there is within public international law a core of mandatory fundamental norms – *jus cogens* – whose binding force is not owed to either treaties or custom, but to their fundamentality in the international legal order. See my 'A Monistic Approach to the Internationalization of Constitutional Law', in Julia Motoc, Paulo Pinto de Albuquerque and Krzysztof Wojtyczek, eds, *New Developments in Constitutional Law: Essays in Honour of Andras Sajo* (The Hague: Eleven International Publishing, 2018) 97 and Alfred Verdross, 'Forbidden Treaties in International Law: Comments on Professor Garner's Report on the "The Law of Treaties"' (1937) 31 *American Journal of Intentional Law* 571.

legal relationships'.[148] On my argument, Kelsen's point is that when political judgments are put into legal form, they accrue legal legitimacy, gained through the transformation of might into legal right. Successfully transformed norms are norms capable of being concretized by legal officials in ways which display the norms' identity with the legal order understood as a meaningful whole, which requires presupposition of the basic norm.

This requirement is deeply pragmatic, an achievement of constructive juristic activity which depends on whether the material content of particular norms can be interpreted so as to display this identity. The basic norm thus substitutes for the social contract of early modern legal theory by making unity an achievement enabled by the requirement that politics, whether international or domestic, be conducted by legal means. On this account, national law monism is just the displacement from the individual onto the state of the anarchic stance that one should obey the law only when one's perception of self-interest counsels one so to do.[149]

Kelsen's argument that pluralism, whether within the state or between states, is made possible by monism is thus based at bottom on a political commitment which requires a rejection not only of dualism but also of national law monism. As he recognized, international law monism requires in addition a rejection of all dualisms, including that between law and morality. While his conception of the legal subject may well strike many as so thin as not to be able to do the work of achieving the 'organization of humanity and thereby a unity with the highest ethical idea', it is of the individual who accepts the authority of law because only under legal order is it possible to ensure the peaceful interaction of a plurality of formally equal legal subjects. As such, it helps to explain the authority of public international law, national public law and the private law of particular national orders. It also helps to explain the reach of national public law norms beyond the borders of the nation state in the field of foreign relations law.

It does so on condition that one rejects dualist theories of law because they reduce to a kind of monism which amounts to a politically

[148] Kelsen, 'Die Lehre von den drei Gewalten oder Funktionen des Staates', 1652.

[149] In our time, it is the kind of libertarianism that finds congenial the slogan 'America First'. For a chilling history of this slogan, see Sarah Churchwell, *Behold America: The Entangled History of 'America First' and 'The American Dream'* (New York: Basic Books, 2018).

dangerous denial of the authority of law. Far from excluding (as Hart thought) the moral criticism of law, it explains how within legal order conflicts between norms are resolved either by interpretation or by channelling the conflict to different levels within the legal hierarchy so that conflicts at a particular level are eliminated. That, Kelsen emphasized, is a dynamic process which requires an understanding of the unity to which legal order aspires as an ethical achievement of continual human effort.[150] Theories of adjudication such as Dworkin's are not, then, discontinuous with general theories of law, as Hartian legal positivists claim. Rather, they are local accounts of how law is optimally concretized, of how the law should be applied by officials to legal subjects.[151]

Kelsenian theory does not attempt to fill out the details of such a theory. But because it requires that the dynamic process of concretization be performed in a way which respects legality's aspiration to unity, it also requires that officials develop such a theory, one which seeks to maintain peaceful interaction between legally speaking equal subjects. Such theories are part of 'the law of the land' and they seek to achieve the unity of legal order, understood in terms of the postulate of equality-preserving peace. That legal order is premised on this postulate is, of course, in some deep sense contingent, for example, on the parties to the Treaties of the Westphalia having decided on such terms at those moments. In that sense Kelsen's legal theory is just as parochial as Hart's, since he thought it incumbent on philosophy of law to understand the international legal order of the Westphalian state system.[152] That committed his legal theory to a particular politics of recognition – the topic of Section 4.6.

150 One can't therefore have a legal positivist account of public international law based on normative values without a theory of interpretation which seeks to vindicate those values, which may show that such an account cannot be strictly positivist. This would, I think, be Kelsen's criticism of the account in Benedict Kingsbury, 'Legal Positivism as Normative Politics: International Society, Balance of Power and Lassa Oppenheim's Positive International Law' (2002) 13 *European Journal of International Law* 401.

151 Lauterpacht, in my view, erred much as Dworkin was to do later, in seeking to build his general theory of international law from a theory of adjudication as practiced in common law jurisdictions. See my 'A Monistic Approach to the Internationalization of Constitutional Law'.

152 See Benjamin Straumann, 'The Peace of Westphalia as a Secular Constitution' (2008) 15 *Constellations* 173.

4.6 The Politics of Recognition

In Section 4.5, I observed that Kelsen's conception of the legal subject may well strike many as so thin as not to be able to do the work of achieving the 'organization of humanity and thereby a unity with the highest ethical idea'. Here I highlight the opposite claim: the conception can't do that work because it is so thick. Perhaps more accurately, its thinness is deceptive since it conceals the normative commitments of Western individualism and its conception of the modern legal state. This is a claim I must accept.

My argument throughout has been that such a state has legitimate authority because its legal order makes it possible for its officials to answer the legal subject's question 'But, how can that be law for me?' The answer is adequate only when it preserves the subject's place as a free and equal member of the jural community, a topic elaborated in Chapter 6. In this chapter, I have extended that argument to include law beyond the state and tried to show how my Kelsenian conception of international legal order makes it possible for modern legal states – the subjects of public international law – to interact with each other on peaceful, stable and equal terms, thus enabling the states to create similar conditions for the individuals subject to them.

On this view, not only the law within the state but also the law without exists for the benefit of the individuals within. Public international law delegates to states the authority to make law for the legal subjects within the states. The authority thus delegated is very wide. But it is not a blank cheque. It is underwritten by the social contract which exists in each state which means that the state and the whole apparatus of public international and national law exists for the sake of the individuals within the states.

I am thus vulnerable to the charge that my theoretical commitments shape the contours of the space for legal argument in ways which rig things in favour of the West, the family of self-styled 'civilized nations', as illustrated by the role of such arguments in imperialism, colonialism and neocolonialism. Luke's game sketched in Section 4.5 would, on this critique, be just one example of the way we educate our children in the political culture of the West; and the international order would look more like a winner-takes-all game than like the maintenance of an order of peace between legally speaking equal sovereign states. The West, that is, always wins the game and will continue to do so until the states born in the postcolonial era find a way of reshaping that order, perhaps under the leadership of a new global power.

In international law theory, this critique comes out of the work of Critical Theorists, Feminist Theories of public international law and perhaps most prominently of TWAIL scholars, that is, Third World Approaches to International Law, who can point to the glaring fact that in the nineteenth century a standard of 'civilization' was used as the bar to entry into the 'family' of states, with the states which considered themselves civilized determining who got admitted.[153] As a matter of doctrine, it plays out in the persistent debate in public international law about how a state-like entity acquires international legal personality. In its pure form, the 'declaratory theory' argues that whether or not an entity is a state is a matter of fact which, once established, requires recognition by existing states of its legal status, while the 'constitutive theory' in its pure form argues that the entity's legal status is conferred on it by the political acts of recognition of existing states.[154]

In all the other debates we have covered so far – very unjust law, constitutionality and law beyond the state – a persistent theme has been the relationship between politics and law and a persistent question whether the role of facts in establishing law has the result that politics drives law – that political might drives legal right. At times, as for example when Kelsen claimed that political preference determines the contest between national and international law monism, it will seem that the fundamental issues in philosophy of law are in some important sense relative to subjective political judgment.

This problem of relativity of judgment looms largest of all in the debate between the declaratory and the constitutive theory. Indeed, in this case the political element may seem so large that it overwhelms the legal. This may seem inevitable. As Kelsen said of his Pure Theory, 'the problem of the origin of the law – the law in general or a particular legal order – meaning the causes of the coming into existence of the law in general or a particular legal order with its specific content, are beyond the

153 For an excellent sketch of these positions, see Rose Parfitt, 'Theorizing Recognition and International Personality', in Anne Orford and Florian Hoffmann, eds, *The Oxford Handbook of the Theory of International Law* (Oxford: Oxford University Press, 2016) 583. See also in the same volume, Florian Hoffmann, 'International Legalism and International Politics' 954.

154 James Crawford, *The Creation of States in International Law* (Oxford: Clarendon Press, 2006).

scope of this theory'.[155] Moreover, the classics of political theory also tend to treat it as beyond their scope. For example, Hobbes argued that we should not in general inquire into the origins of a political and legal order because 'there is scarce a Common-wealth in the world, whose beginnings can in conscience be justified',[156] a thought Kant echoed in asserting that '[a] people should not *inquire* with any practical aim into the origin of the supreme authority to which it is subject'.[157]

But if one is going to have a legal theory of the relations between states, the question of origins cannot be altogether avoided, as illustrated by Kelsen himself. He is reputed to have moved from advocacy of the declaratory theory to adoption of the constitutive position. But rather, as with the national and international law monism issue, he was for most of his career mainly concerned to find a position consistent with the primacy of public international law. If public international law is to be considered as law, as authoritative over states, the question whether a new entity is going to be considered a state is a legal question no different in nature from any question of law. As Kelsen put it in an essay on this topic: 'It is a fundamental, though often overlooked, principle of jurisprudence that in the province of law there are no absolute, directly evident facts, facts "in themselves", but only facts established by the competent authority in a procedure prescribed by the legal order.'[158] He thus argued that

> [i]nternational law has to determine its subjects just as national law has to determine who are the subjects of the rights and obligations laid down by it; e.g., only human beings, not animals, or, only free men, not slaves.

[155] Hans Kelsen, 'Law, State, and Justice in the Pure Theory of Law', in Kelsen, *What Is Justice? Justice, Law and Politics in the Mirror of Science* (Berkeley: University of California Press, 1957) 288, at 294. He went on, ibid, to emphasize that this exclusion did not mean that the problem was unsusceptible to scientific inquiry since it could be studied historically or sociologically.

[156] Hobbes, *Leviathan*, 486.

[157] Immanuel Kant, *The Metaphysics of Morals*, in Kant, *Practical Philosophy* (Cambridge: Cambridge University Press, 1996, Mary J Gregor, ed. and trans.) 353, at 461. His emphasis.

[158] Hans Kelsen, 'Recognition in International Law: Theoretical Observations' (1941) 35 *American Journal of International Law* 605, at 606. Kelsen is supposed to have espoused the declaratory theory in earlier work, notably in *Das Problem der Souveränität*, 224–41. See, for example, Joseph L Kunz, 'Critical Comments on Lauterpacht's Recognition in International Law' (1950) *American Journal of International Law* 713, at 714.

> If international law did not determine what a state is, then its norms, which obligate and empower the states, would not be applicable.[159]

We saw in Section 4.5 that it is at precisely this point that we encounter the problem elaborated through Luke's game: states are judges in their own cause because there is no independent international tribunal with compulsory jurisdiction over disputes around statehood. Indeed, the constitutive theory was associated in the nineteenth century with the kind of positivist legal theory which understands sovereignty as legally unlimited, denies therefore that public international law is law properly so-called and concludes that recognition by one state of another is constitutive in the sense that it is a purely political act.[160]

But as Kelsen explained, the statement 'A has committed a theft' is a mere 'subjective opinion of an individual' unless there exists a legally 'decisive' and 'authentic' opinion, namely, that of the 'authority instituted by the legal order to establish the fact'.[161] On this analogy, the existing states are authorized by public international law to determine that an entity is a state in terms of that same body of law, just as judges in a national legal order are authorized by their state's law to determine that an act is a theft in terms of that same body of law. There must exist facts like that person A has an object which B once had or that there is a defined territory over which one entity exercises effective control. These brute facts – observable facts about the world – are, however, not legal facts until they have been characterized as such by a competent authority. Kelsen's allegiance to the constitutive theory thus requires explaining why the constitutive act is both legal and a matter of duty on the recognizing state. The constitutive theory can achieve this goal only if there are in most cases a stable set of facts about statehood which require recognition.

For this reason, as Kelsen acknowledged even in his early work on this topic, any theory is going to give a role to facts, law and politics; the theory, that is, will contain elements of both the declaratory and constitutive positions. Similarly, Lauterpacht took the constitutive side because he wished to emphasize that recognition is a juridical matter, not something that can be simply read off a set of facts. But he also acknowledged that 'while recognition is constitutive in one sphere, it is declaratory in

159 Kelsen, 'Recognition in International Law', 606.

160 Hersch Lauterpacht, *Recognition in International Law* (Cambridge: Cambridge University Press, 1947), 61–3.

161 Hans Kelsen, 'Recognition in International Law', 606.

the other. It is declaratory in the meaning that its object is to ascertain the existence of the requirements of statehood and the consequent right of the new State to be treated henceforth as a normal subject of international law.'[162]

That those who start off on one side of this debate seem to end up with a theory which imports the other side is often thought to lead to the conclusion that we should eschew theory and embrace a kind of pragmatism which regards practice as the only site where this issue can be resolved.[163] For it remains the case that whether or not an entity can exercise its statehood depends on its recognition by other states, and that it remains open to each state to decide whether or not to treat an entity as a state in their relations with it. Furthermore, recognition patterns are treated as playing an evidentiary role, which introduces an element of circularity. As a result, there are many examples of inconsistent practice which illustrate (1) the political dimensions of recognition both when states for political reasons decide to withhold recognition of entities which meet the criteria (e.g. Taiwan) or to recognize entities that do *not* meet the criteria (e.g. Kosovo), and (2) the frequently invoked rationale for the declaratory theory, namely, that recognition is a political decision for each state to make, and that the declaratory theory allows for that by liberating the existence of the entity in question from the recognition by others.[164]

Moreover, while Lauterpacht regarded as a 'grotesque spectacle' the prospect of a 'community being a State in relation to some but not to other States' and said this prospect was a 'grave reflection upon international law', he also fully conceded that this problem resulted from the lack of 'political integration of international society'.[165] Because he knew that precisely this lack made impracticable an international tribunal with

[162] Lauterpacht, *Recognition in International Law*, 75.

[163] Crawford, *The Creation of States in International Law*, 19–28.

[164] For discussion, see Campbell McLachlan, *Foreign Relations Law*, 401–2. Note that it is possible for there to be territorially bound spaces which are fully law governed but which do not amount to a modern legal state. In fact, without the existence of such spaces prior to the formation of the modern legal state after the Treaties of Westphalia, there would not have been the raw material out of which the modern state system could be built. Once in place, that system – the beginning of the international legal order – transformed the spaces into states, much as I have argued from Chapter 2 on individuals in a hypothetical state of nature are transformed when they become legal subjects, constituted as such by the public order of law of their state.

[165] Lauterpacht, *Recognition in International Law*, 78.

compulsory jurisdiction, he resorted to the rather vague idea that the constitutive theory was tempered by a duty on all states owed to the international community at large to grant recognition.[166] His suggestion, that is, was that the acts of recognition are not merely political but also legal.

For this he came under fire from Josef Kunz, like Lauterpacht one of Kelsen's students. Kunz, who had established himself as a distinguished public international lawyer in the USA, observed that Kelsen's reasons for preferring the constitutive theory were logical whereas as Lauterpacht's were ethical, and he accused Lauterpacht of wishful thinking in his claim to have found a basis for the theory in doctrine.[167] Lauterpacht, he said, had forgotten that 'the science of international law cannot by its fiat correct the structural defects of the primitive international legal order',[168] and he thought that both practice and doctrine support the declaratory theory, a position also advanced by James Crawford in the leading recent treatment.

Crawford, after setting out the flaws in both theories, especially when stated in their pure forms, says that one might conclude that in practice the differences between the theories do not amount to much. But this conclusion 'assumes that there exist in international law and practice workable criteria for statehood. If there are no such criteria, or if they are so imprecise as to be practically useless, then the constitutive theory will have returned, as it were, by the back door.'[169]

The major attempt to establish such criteria was in 1933 in the Montevideo Convention on the Rights and Duties of States which set out four in its Article 1: 'a permanent population'; 'a defined territory'; 'government'; and 'capacity to enter into relations with other states'. As Arnulf Becker Lorca explains, this initiative was led by Latin American states in a bid to substitute objective criteria for the exclusionary standard of 'civilization' which had prevailed up until that point. He regards their success as evidence of the ability of states hitherto regarded as 'peripheral' to make their presence felt in international law, thus paving the way for other peripherals – namely, the states which emerged in the post-

[166] Ibid, 74–5.
[167] Kunz, 'Critical Comments on Lauterpacht's Recognition in International Law', 715–16.
[168] Ibid, 716.
[169] Crawford, *The Creation of States in International Law*, 27.

colonial era after the Second World War – to succeed partially in securing 'formal autonomy and equality'.[170]

The convention is taken by many as a sign of the victory of the declaratory theory. In contrast, critical theorists suppose that public international law is doomed to swing between the declaratory theory and the constitutive one as lawyers craft their arguments to suit one or other political objective.[171] This critical stance is hardly different from the more cynical versions of international relations realism except that its practitioners often hanker after something very different.[172] For example, Martti Koskenniemi, one of the leading practitioners of critical theory, observes that '[u]njust entities have been regarded as states, and since the Peace of Westphalia, that they have been so regarded has been a cornerstone of the international system'.[173] If, he continues, they were not recognized as states, the result would be that the international system 'had become based on principles of justice'.[174] Since he regards principles of justice as highly contested, we need '[d]ecision processes . . . through which they can be translated into social action', 'processes which are prior to the principles and delimit how they can be applied'. He thus relies on Kelsen for a distinction 'between an ethical and a juridical conception of the state – the state as the realization of Utopia, and the state as the form in which different Utopias clash today – in order to mold the social reality in which we live'.[175] For Kelsen, he continues, 'it is the very formality, or artificiality, of states that provides their best *raison d'être*. As pure form – legal system – the state provides that position of retreat in which we can reflect upon our sociological and ethical

[170] Arnulf Becker Lorca, *Mestizo International Law: A Global Intellectual History, 1842–1933* (Cambridge: Cambridge University Press, 2014), 355.

[171] See, notably, Martti Koskenniemi, *From Apology to Utopia: The Structure of International Legal Argument* (Cambridge: Cambridge University Press, 2005, reissue with new epilogue), 272–82. For criticism of this mode of argument, see my 'Formalism, Realism, and the Politics of Indeterminacy', in Wouter Werner, Marieke De Hoon, and Alexis Galàn, eds, *The Law of International Lawyers: Reading Martti Koskenniemi* (Cambridge: Cambridge University Press, 2017) 39.

[172] As in the work of a pioneer of TWAIL, Antony Anghie, *Imperialism, Sovereignty and the Making of International Law* (Cambridge: Cambridge University Press, 2012).

[173] Martti Koskenniemi, 'The Wonderful Artificiality of States' (1994) 88 *Proceedings of the Annual Meeting (American Society of International Law)* 22, at 28.

[174] Ibid.

[175] Ibid.

conceptions and their relations to the truth or acceptability of our preferred ways of life'.[176]

Koskenniemi here fully embraces a Kelsenian conception of legality. And I have argued, contra Kunz, both that Kelsen adopted that conception for ethical as well as logical reasons and that such a conception cannot be merely formal; it must include principles of *Recht* – the fundamental principles of legality. Recall Lauterpacht's remark that Kelsen's preference for international law monism was the 'back door' by which the 'ghost of natural law' had 'crept into the cast-iron logic of . . . [Kelsen's] system'.[177] There is, I suggest, more than an echo of the remark in Crawford's worry that the criteria for statehood may be 'too imprecise as to be practically useless', in which case 'the constitutive theory will have returned, as it were, by the back door'. But the theory has to make an entrance. Only the constitutive theory is capable of preserving the idea that recognition as a state is of what I have called a modern *legal* state – a state with a well-functioning legal order which enables the officials who act in its name to answer adequately the legal subject who asks 'But, how can that be law for me?'

In doing that, the constitutive theory preserves the normative dimension of the civilizational standard in that it invites states to take stands on recognition premised on the fact that an entity's claim to be recognized as a state is undermined because it is undemocratic, or systematically oppresses part of its population, or does not abide by the rule of law. None of these standards is among the Montevideo criteria though the rule of law is perhaps the best candidate as it is plausibly implied in 'government'. In this regard, Crawford observes that '[n]o doubt "legal order" is an important element of government, hence an indication of statehood. But its status as a distinct criterion is open to doubt.'[178] He also says, in regard to the requirement that there must be a government in general control of its territory, that public international law 'lays down no specific requirements as to the nature and extent of this control, except that it include some degree of maintenance of law and order and the establishment of basic institutions'.[179]

Recall Lauterpacht's claim that there is an element of voluntary submission in a state's subjection to public international law. He could not

[176] Ibid, 29.
[177] Lauterpacht, 'Kelsen's Pure Science of Law', 423.
[178] Crawford, *The Creation of States in International Law*, 93.
[179] Ibid, 59.

have meant by this claim to deny the authority of public international law. Indeed, the whole point of the constitutive theory in his or Kelsen's hands is not that the existing states constitute the new state through their political acts of recognition. Rather, it is public international *law* which does the constitutive work. For the work to be done, the agency of states is required. But within a national legal order so does the authoritative characterization of an act as a theft require agency, the agency of a judge as the competent authority.

We meet again here the problem sketched in Section 4.5 in Luke's game of 'the juridical phenomenon of the role splitting function'. When it comes to public international law, states both make and interpret the law which binds them and, moreover, constitutes them as international legal persons. For Kelsenian legal theory this problem points, as I observed in Chapter 3 and will come back to in Chapter 6, to a quantitative not a qualitative distinction. The political element in legal judgment becomes larger as one moves up the hierarchy of norms. It is no surprise that when one moves from the space of national legal order to the space of international legal order the political element gets bigger, especially when one notices that there is one qualitative difference between the situation where an act is determined to be a theft and an entity is determined to be a state.

Both determinations are, to adopt Robert Cover's useful term, 'jurisgenerative' in that they create legal meaning.[180] However, while the determination that B stole something from A tells us that someone who is assumed to be a person in the eyes of the law has done something to which certain consequences are attached, the question whether B is such a person is different. It is a question about whether there exists an actor capable of producing or incurring legal consequences and the generation of a legal person is a qualitatively different act from the determination that a person committed theft.[181]

180 Robert Cover, 'Nomos and Narrative', in Martha Minow, Michael Ryan and Austin Sarat, eds, *Narrative, Violence, and the Law: The Essays of Robert Cover* (Ann Arbor: Michigan University Press, 1995) 95, at 103.

181 Indeed, the idea of jurisgeneration is not only a central theme of Hobbes's *Leviathan*, but he also named it as such, when, as we saw in the epigraph to my Chapter 3, he talked of 'the Generation of that great LEVIATHAN'. Hobbes, *Leviathan*, 120. He picked up here on his claim in his Introduction that the creation by natural individuals of the artificial person of the state resembles 'that *Fiat*, or the *Let us make man*, pronounced by God in the Creation'; ibid, 9–10. His emphasis.

This is still not a qualitative difference between the international legal order and national legal orders, since in the latter a crucial question is which natural individuals will be recognized as full legal subjects. As we just saw Kelsen say, 'international law has to determine its subjects just as national law has to determine who are the subjects of the rights and obligations laid down by it; e.g., only human beings, not animals, or, only free men, not slaves'. However, on my argument, the thought that it is legally permissible for a modern legal state to institute slavery is hardly unproblematic, and the same is true of the use of law as an instrument of oppression beyond the state. Indeed, Lauterpacht pointed out that to compare the problem of the recognition of states to the ability of national law to create slavery is to rely on a 'questionable' analogy to private law. While he did not thereby deny the existence of slavery as an institution of positive private law, he also remarked that '[a]part from slavery, private law knows of no cases in which persons, physical or juridical, possess legal personality in relation to some members of the community but not to others'.[182]

A final qualitative difference is that the thief does not want to be so characterized whereas an entity seeks recognition as a state and within states those in conditions of second-class citizenship or worse are at some point likely to engage in struggle to achieve first-class status. In this light, Lauterpacht's emphasis on voluntary submission tells us that when an entity chooses to attempt to enter as a state into the space of the international legal order, it accepts that part of the cost of the ticket of entry is its acceptance of the authority of public international law. The same is true of an oppressed class of individuals within a modern legal state who choose to conduct their struggle within its legal space, that is, they reject armed and extra-legal struggle.

When in issue is entry of an entity as a state into international space, the ticket cannot be made too expensive, as was the case with the monopolistic practice of the 'civilized' states of the nineteenth century; and the achievement of the Montevideo Convention was to lower the cost in such a way as to permit a much greater pluralism, one which would be threatened if too much normativity were built in.[183] But there has to be some normativity. The criteria are never, as it were, brute facts. Rather, they are legally established facts which requires at least, to borrow

[182] Lauterpacht, *Recognition in International Law*, 78.

[183] As is the case in John Rawls, *The Law of Peoples* (Cambridge, MA: Harvard University Press, 2002).

from Hart, a 'minimum content' of *Recht*. And with entry comes exposure to more substantive principles which is why individual states may make the political decision not to recognize a new candidate. As Crawford observes, beyond criteria which express the principle of effectiveness, there will always be criteria which 'either supplement or in certain cases contradict this principle on grounds of legitimacy'.[184] Of course, such political decisions may be and are sometimes made on purely expedient grounds. States can be the equivalent of Fooles as well as of Just Men. But that only tells us that the order of the modern legal state is not a necessary way of organizing our common life.

That the space within the modern legal state and the space in which such states interact are shaped by the conception of the legal subject advanced by my argument tells us that there is a politics to legal space. Most human individuals do not have any choice about whether to live subject to some state, and state-like entities may have very little choice when it comes to the decision to aspire to the status which will make them subjects of public international law. The association of the politics of legal space with oppression within the state and subjugation of others beyond the state is not only undeniable; it also needs continual reminders, and legal theorists should follow Hart's lead and make it their task to issue such reminders. However, while it is the case that entry to legal space is always fraught with risk, it is also full of opportunity; hence, the topic of Chapter 5 – an inquiry into the politics of legal space.

[184] Crawford, *The Creation of States in International Law*, 46.

5

The Politics of Legal Space

Central to philosophy of law, I have argued, is the legal subject's question 'But, how can that be law for me?' Chapter 4 explored that argument in an investigation of the interaction between the space of the modern legal state and law 'beyond the state'. Here I investigate the difference made to the answer to the question when it is given in two different contexts: first, a context in which a legal space – one both constructed by law and ruled by law – interacts with another legal space; and, second, in a context in which a legal space interacts with a space of no-law. As we will see, the definition of a legal space as both constructed by law and ruled by law is important because law can be used to construct a space of no-law, a legal void or 'black hole', as Lord Steyn described the situation of detainees at the US base of Guantanamo.[1] In such a space, prerogative or legally unmediated power rules.

I pointed out in Chapter 4 that Hart, in the course of his critique of Kelsen's monistic account of the relationship of national and public international law, recharacterized the issue of the continuity of legal order as one exclusively to do with national law. In issue was the transition of a colony from a subordinate part of the legal system in which the UK rule of recognition was the ultimate rule to independent statehood with the result that the entity no longer owed its 'contemporary legal status' to the UK statute which established the colony. Hart suggested that, while the fundamental rules of the entity remain the same, its enactments were valid after the transition because 'under the rule of recognition locally accepted, enactment by the local legislature is an ultimate criterion of validity'.[2]

[1] Johan Steyn, 'Guantanamo Bay: The Legal Black Hole' (2004) 53 *International and Comparative Law Quarterly* 1.

[2] HLA Hart, *The Concept of Law* (Oxford: Clarendon Press, 1994, 2nd ed.), 121, and see the note to this page at 296–7.

The title of the chapter is 'The Foundations of a Legal System' and the section in which this discussion takes place is titled 'The Pathology of a Legal System'. In it, Hart was rather ambiguous about whether the discussion is from the 'external point of view', that is, from the point of view of a social scientist or historian surveying events across time, or from the 'internal point of view' of a jurist or judge trying to work out what the law required at a particular point.[3] But the argument seems to be about the inevitable movement from the internal to the external – from the inside of law to the outside of politics – when there is uncertainty in the rule of recognition, a topic to which Hart returned in the next chapter, 'Formalism and Rule-Scepticism'.

Hart's recharacterization goes unnoticed in philosophy of law with only vague allusions to the fact that *The Concept of Law* was written during the era of decolonization and the end of empire, and so also during the backlash against these 'winds of change' in the aggressive assertion of white supremacy in southern Africa. The sense that such issues can remain largely at the subtextual level, and that philosophy of law can address its topics from the perspective of national law without being troubled by them, profoundly shaped one of the most interesting debates in legal theory in the second half of the twentieth century – how to understand the status of the Rhodesian legal order after Ian Smith's white minority government issued its Unilateral Declaration of Independence (UDI) from the British state in 1965.

Kelsen's legal theory was much discussed in that debate, in large part because in 1968 the Rhodesian High Court in *Madzimbamuto* v. *Lardner-Burke* relied on a passage from Kelsen's work to justify its conclusion that the order in which it operated was a valid legal order despite the rupture UDI had effected.[4] But in these discussions, public international law was treated as irrelevant, despite its importance to Kelsen and indeed to the judges in *Madzimbamuto*.[5]

For example, Peter Oliver's fine study of the problems sparked by Hart's chapter on these issues does not consider the role of public

[3] Ibid, 117.

[4] *Madzimbamuto* v. *Lardner-Burke* (1968) 2 SA 284 (RAD). I discuss this case in Appendix III.

[5] For example, John Finnis, 'Revolutions and Continuity of Law', reprinted in Finnis, *Philosophy of Law: Collected Essays*, vol. 4 (Oxford: Oxford University Press, 2011) 407. See Appendix III.

international law.[6] His neglect follows in the footsteps of Geoffrey Marshall's magisterial work on the Commonwealth constitutional theory of the mid-twentieth century.[7] Marshall, in turn, was influenced by RTE Latham's 1937 pioneering essay on the constitutional law of the Commonwealth, in which he denied that public international law had any relevance to constitutionalism within the state despite his own heavy reliance on Kelsen.[8] Marshall and Latham then influenced Hart's development of the idea of the rule of recognition.[9]

The point here is not that if the matter is characterized with Kelsen as about the relationship between public international law and national law from the internal point of view that the problems Hart addressed are solved. In fact, they become more complex. For example, one has to take account of the persistent debate I discussed in Chapter 4 between the 'declaratory theory', which argues that recognition of an entity as a state merely confirms its legal status, and the 'constitutive theory', which argues that an entity which aspires to legal statehood requires the recognition of other states. That debate has implications for the question of the interaction between private and public international law in this situation. Should a court in state B enforce rights acquired in state A which would be enforced but for the fact that B does not recognize A?[10] More broadly, it implicates the issue of legal theory, empire and decolonization.[11]

Most important of all for my argument is the implication of that debate for the link between legality and the recognition of the individual

[6] Peter Oliver, *The Constitution of Independence: The Development of Constitutional Theory in Australia, Canada, and New Zealand* (Oxford: Oxford University Press, 2005).

[7] Geoffrey Marshall, *Parliamentary Sovereignty and the Commonwealth* (Oxford: Clarendon Press, 1957).

[8] RTE Latham, *The Law and the Commonwealth* (London: Oxford University Press, 1949). Latham was intrigued briefly, at 609–10, by the question of the relationship of what he called 'imperial fundamental law' (576ff.) to public international law. But he seems to have understood the Commonwealth as a distinct international legal order, premised on a national law monism in which the basic norm was the supremacy of the imperial parliament.

[9] Marshall's *Parliamentary Sovereignty and the Commonwealth* had a prominent role in Hart's endnotes to chapter 6 of *The Concept of Law* and Hart also at 296 acknowledged Latham's account in *The Law and the Commonwealth* of the constitution of the Commonwealth countries in terms of a basic norm.

[10] See Campbell McLachlan, *Foreign Relations Law* (Cambridge: Cambridge University Press, 2014), chapter 10.

[11] See, for example, Dylan Lino, 'Albert Venn Dicey and the Constitutional Theory of Empire' (2016) 36 *Oxford Journal of Legal Studies* 751 and 'The Rule of Law and the Rule of Empire: AV Dicey in Imperial Context' (2018) 81 *Modern Law Review* 739.

human being as a full legal subject, or first-class citizen. As we have seen from Chapter 2 on, the legal subject is as much an artificial person as the modern legal state. Both are legally constructed and so can be deconstructed. On my argument thus far, construction happens in a process of juridical production subject to the discipline of legal norms which condition the content of the law. The production of the legal person of the human individual is, like that of the person of the state, a highly political process, which means that it has the inherent potential to be abused when human individuals are constructed as less than full subjects, even as non-persons, that is, consigned to slavery. But since it is also a legal process, abuse leads to tensions internal to the legal order in which it happens, in the case of second-class citizens because they have one foot in the first-class space, the other in the space constructed by the discriminatory law.

There is thus a politics to legal space which makes the use of law to undermine the status before the law of human individuals an abuse – which is problematic from the perspective of legality. It also makes problematic the abuse of law to render human individuals into the condition of non-personhood or slavery, even though that kind of law might appear to eliminate the legal tensions occasioned by second-class citizenship. For unlike the tension which comes from the interaction of two legal spaces which produces second-class citizenship, slavery is produced by an interaction between a legal space and a legally created space of no-law. Nevertheless, as we will see, legal tensions do arise.

I return to these issues in Sections 5.3 and 5.4. Section 5.1 begins by setting out the issues which directly haunted these pages of *The Concept of Law*: the 'Voters Rights Cases' decided by South Africa's apex court of the time, the Appellate Division. These cases starkly raise the problem of the politics of legal space which is the focus of this chapter and in which I sketch several ideal types of the modern legal state, with the Voters Rights Cases offering the 'Apartheid State'. Section 5.2 indicates why consideration of this ideal type matters for philosophy of law and in particular for the debates between Hart, Fuller and Dworkin about the Separation Thesis. I show that the Apartheid State may provide the basis for a better Dworkinian response to Hart than Dworkin himself managed, one which relies, as Dworkin was loath to do, on Fuller. Section 5.3 elaborates that basis through a consideration of three other ideal types: the 'Dual State', the 'Rule-of-Law State' and the 'Parallel State'. I also discuss there the possibility that in fact most, perhaps all, states turn out to be a mixture of these types, a 'Hybrid State'. Section 5.4 returns to the topic of the politics of recognition, this time focused on the human individual rather than the state, which prepares the way for the discussion of political legal theory in Chapter 6.

5.1 We, the People?

In 1948 the National Party became the majority party in South Africa and formed the government which set about turning the system of white supremacy there into the version it named 'apartheid'. A priority was to remove those 'Coloureds' – mixed-race South Africans – who still had the vote from the common electoral roll. In 1909 the UK parliament had enacted the South Africa Act which put in place the Constitution of the Union of South Africa. Section 152 of the Act required that certain of its provisions could be changed only by a two-thirds vote of both houses of the South African parliament – the House of Assembly and the Senate – sitting together. One such provision was Section 35, which protected the right to vote of all those entitled to vote under 'laws existing in the Colony of the Cape of Good Hope at the establishment of the Union' and precluded their disqualification from being registered as voters 'by reason of ... race or colour only' unless the special procedure was followed. The provision was designed to protect the male Coloured and African voters of the Cape Province and was anathema to any government intent on ensuring a more complete white domination.[12] The provisions of the Act had been negotiated at a National Convention by thirty white delegates of the four South African colonies, who decided to maintain in the Constitution the franchise rules of each colony, which ranged from not permitting any non-white participation in the franchise to permitting a limited participation.[13]

Only Coloured voters were in issue after 1948 because in 1937 the parliament, using the special unicameral procedure, enacted the Representation of Natives Act to remove protected black voters from the common roll and give them separate representation.[14] In 1951, the

[12] At that time, the franchise was limited to men.

[13] See Ian Loveland, *By Due Process of Law: Racial Discrimination and the Right to Vote in South Africa, 1855–1960* (Oxford: Hart Publishing, 1999).

[14] A challenge to this statute was dismissed by the Appellate Division on the basis that the parliament had become the supreme and sovereign law-making body as a result of the Statute of Westminster, and so the court had no power to pronounce on the validity of a duly promulgated statute: *Ndlawana* v. *Hofmeyr, N.O.*, 1937 AD 229. The Statute of Westminster was a 1931 Act of the UK Parliament which removed the power of the

National Party government brought about the enactment of the Separate Representation of Voters Act providing that Coloured voters who were on the common roll be represented separately from whites. The government could not muster the two-thirds majority of both houses of parliament required by the South Africa Act to effect this change, so the parliament passed the statute using the bicameral procedure for ordinary legislation, a simple majority in separate sittings of the two houses.

In *Harris* v. *Minister of the Interior*,[15] the Appellate Division declared the statute invalid. Chief Justice Centlivres, giving the unanimous judgment of the court, held that, while it was correct to assert that the parliament was a supreme and sovereign lawmaking body, the fact that it could validly enact certain laws only when sitting unicamerally did not affect its sovereign status. This, he claimed, was a result reached in a completely ordinary process of statutory interpretation:

> The Court in declaring that such a Statute is invalid is exercising a duty which it owes to persons whose rights are entrenched by Statute. Its duty is simply to declare and apply the law and it would be inaccurate to say that the Court in discharging that duty is controlling the Legislature. It is hardly necessary to add that Courts of law are not concerned with the question whether an Act of Parliament is reasonable or unreasonable, politic or impolitic.[16]

The parliament responded by enacting, again by the bicameral ordinary procedure, the High Court of Parliament Act of 1952. It provided that when the Appellate Division declared a statute invalid, its decision would be subject to review by the 'High Court of Parliament' on the application of a member of the cabinet. Every member of the two houses would be a member of this 'court'; one would be appointed as president by the governor-general (the head of state); the president would select a ten member 'judicial committee' from the members of parliament to make a

parliament to enact laws for the Dominions such as Australia, Canada, the Union of South Africa and New Zealand. In particular, section 2(2) provided that no law made by one of their parliaments 'shall be void or inoperative on the ground that it is repugnant to the law of England, or to the provisions of any existing or future Act of Parliament'. Ndlawana's lawyers used an ingenious argument based on the claim that the Statute of Westminster removed the constitutional protections in the South African Constitution because a statute enacted after 1931 bicamerally was merely repugnant to a British statute. Hence, the Representation of Natives Act was invalid because *not* enacted at separate sittings.

15 *Harris* v. *Minister of the Interior* 1952 (2) SA 428 (A).

16 Ibid, 456.

recommendation to the full body; the full body would then decide the matter by majority vote and that decision would be taken as final and binding, to be executed as if it were a decision of a division of the Supreme Court.[17]

The High Court of Parliament Act was challenged in *Minister of the Interior* v. *Harris*.[18] In the main judgment, Centlivres held that the Constitution envisaged that the rights protected by section 152 would be enforceable by the sanction of invalidity exercised by a 'Court of Law', and that while the parliament had the power to enact laws that established courts, the bodies had to be courts in substance not just in form. Since in substance the High Court of Parliament was no different from a select committee of parliamentarians, it was not a 'Court of Law'. Rather, it was a court only in name, which stripped the constitutional protections of any force. Hence, the statute was invalid.

It is important to note that the term 'Court of Law' was not used in the Constitution. But Centlivres pointed out that section 152 entrenched a right and provided the sanction of invalidity for a statute which infringed the right unless it were enacted in proper form. Since it is judges who in the course of deciding disputes determine whether an enactment is invalid, the issue in such cases must be decided by a 'Court of Law'.[19] He thus rejected the government's 'startling proposition' that the High Court Act affected only unentrenched 'procedural law', and not the entrenched 'substantive right'.[20]

I want to emphasize just one passage from Justice Schreiner's concurring judgment because it both prepared the way for his dissent in the next case and proved a shrewd anticipation of what was on the cards. He stated that he did not wish to proceed on the lines that the High Court of Parliament was not a 'Court of Law' because that would permit an Act passed bicamerally to nominate, for example, a magistrate's court as the final court in constitutional cases. That would be a 'Court of Law' but nevertheless 'a radical departure from the judicial hierarchy set up in the Constitution and a grave impairment of the protective system implicit in sec. 152'.[21] In his view, an 'entirely sufficient and convincing reason … for holding that the High Court of Parliament Act is invalid' was that

[17] Ibid, 496.
[18] *Minister of the Interior* v. *Harris* 1952 (4) SA 769 (A).
[19] Ibid, 780.
[20] Ibid, 780–1.
[21] Ibid, 788.

'implicit' in the Constitution was 'a protective judicial system . . . with the Appellate Division set up at the apex'.[22]

The government responded by getting the parliament to enact the Senate Act of 1955, which provided for the reconstitution of the Senate in such a way that the government secured the two-thirds majority it needed in a unicameral session. The South Africa Act Amendment Act of 1956 was then passed. It disenfranchised the Coloureds and 'compensated' them with a separate roll which elected four members to the House of Assembly and one to the Senate.[23] In addition, the Appellate Division Quorum Act of 1955 enlarged the Appellate Division from six to eleven judges and provided that all eleven had to sit in cases to determine the validity of a statute. In defending the Senate Act in parliament, the minister of justice said that by it the government intended to 'reinstate the sovereignty of Parliament'.[24]

The Senate Act was challenged in *Collins* v. *Minister of the Interior*.[25] Centlivres held that although the purpose of the Senate Act was plain, it was irrelevant as the parliament sitting bicamerally had 'plenary power to reconstitute the Senate'.[26] He recognized that the Act rendered the rights protected by the Constitution 'nugatory' in the same way as had the High Court of Parliament Act. But he reasoned that the Senate Act did not affect protected rights since a further legislative step was required and the reconstituted Senate was a 'senate', while the High Court of Parliament was not a 'Court of Law'.[27] Eight of the judges concurred with this result, including all of the judges from the old bench, save for Schreiner.

In his dissent, Schreiner focused on what he called the 'proviso' to section 152 of the Constitution: that a statute amending the section has to be 'passed by a two thirds of the total number of members of both Houses . . . at [a] joint sitting'. For the purposes of the proviso, he reasoned, the Senate was the body as contemplated by the Constitution, even if the parliament could for other purposes constitute the Senate in any way it liked. The parliament could no more use the two-step process than it could if, acting bicamerally, it first set out an education requirement for the franchise, and, second prohibited persons of a particular

[22] Ibid, 788–9.

[23] In 1968 this representation was abolished by the Separate Representation of Voters Amendment Act of 1968.

[24] 1955 House of Assembly Debates, columns 4425–7.

[25] *Collins* v. *Minister of the Interior* (1957) (1) A 552 (A).

[26] Ibid, 565.

[27] Ibid, 568–9.

race from attaining that qualification. There are, he said, 'only two separate fields if they are really kept separate, not if they are only separate as a matter of form. Once legislation in the one field is used as a stage preparatory to legislation in the other, there ceases to be real separation and in substance they become one field'.[28] In response to the argument that purpose was irrelevant, he reasoned that if in issue is a 'legislative plan to do indirectly what the Legislature has no power to do directly . . . the purpose may be crucial to validity'.[29]

At the end of Hart's chapter 'The Foundations of a Legal System', he discussed the first two cases and said:

> Had this process not been stopped (because the Government found it unwise to pursue this means of getting its way), we should have had an endless oscillation between two views of the competence of the legislature and so of the criteria of valid law. The normal conditions of official, and especially of judicial, harmony, under which alone it is possible to identify the system's rule of recognition, would have been suspended. . . . All we could do would be to describe the situation as we have done and note it as a substandard, abnormal case containing within it the threat that the legal system will dissolve.[30]

In sum, uncertainty in the rule of recognition threatens the dissolution of the legal order which is why Hart's next chapter has the title 'Formalism and Rule-Scepticism'. In it, he sought to allay the concern that the fact there will be such abnormal cases affects the viability of legal order. He relied on much the same argument we encountered in Chapter 1 from his 1958 article, which distinguished between the 'core' of settled law and the 'penumbra' of unsettled law. His suggestion was that because the core is much bigger than the penumbra, the existence of

[28] Ibid, 575.

[29] Justice Steyn, one of the newly appointed judges, delivered a separate judgment in which he claimed that the rationale of the High Court decision turned on there being a necessary inference from the sanction of invalidity in the proviso that a Court of Law had to decide the issue of invalidity. He then reasoned that no such inference could be drawn from the use of the words 'Houses of Parliament'; ibid, 586–7. When Centlivres retired, Steyn was appointed to his position, leapfrogging over the more senior judges including Schreiner, the most senior. He presided over a court bent on providing juridical support for the legislative entrenchment of apartheid. See Edwin Cameron, 'Legal Chauvinism, Executive-Mindedness and Justice: LC Steyn's Impact on South African Law' (1982) 99 *South African Law Journal* 38.

[30] Hart, *The Concept of Law*, 122–3. Other than an allusion to the Grudge Informer Case – see my Chapters 1 and 6 – I believe this may be the only occasion when an actual case figures in Hart's argument in the text of *The Concept of Law*.

uncertainty in the penumbra not only fails to undermine the stability afforded by the core but also can be beneficial as it permits judges to adapt the law to changing economic and social circumstances.[31] Still, he recognized that uncertainty in the most fundamental rule when 'vital social issues' are at stake raises a much more dramatic problem for the legal order. Returning to the Voters Rights Cases, he observed that when courts decide 'previously unenvisaged questions concerning the most fundamental constitutional rules, they *get* their authority to decide them accepted after the questions have arisen and the decision has been given. Here all that succeeds is success.'[32] In contrast, with 'less vital social issues', it could happen that

> a very surprising piece of judicial law-making concerning the very sources of law may be calmly 'swallowed'. Where this is so, it will often in *retrospect* be said... that there always was an 'inherent' power in the courts to do what they have done. Yet this may be a pious fiction, if the only evidence for it is the success of what has been done.[33]

It is somewhat strange that Hart, writing some years after the third case was decided, seemed aware only of the first two decisions.[34] But it may be that the only difference the third case would have made is to his sense of how the political battle had been won. More important is that, as I already suggested, a trawl through the text and his long endnotes reveals how deeply his book is marked by the death throes of empire including the white supremacist backlash in southern Africa.

The most agonized, passionate and, in my view, best passages in Hart's otherwise austere work in philosophy of law are prompted by the 'pathologies' which arise when law is used as the instrument of oppression to the extent that either the consensus about constitutional fundamentals needed to sustain legal order breaks down or, which may be worse, the oppressed become sheeplike and are passively led to the 'slaughter-house'.[35] However, as I have observed before, because these issues are consigned by Hart's static model of law to the penumbra, and so deemed

[31] HLA Hart, 'Positivism and the Separation of Law and Morals', in Hart, *Essays in Jurisprudence and Philosophy* (Oxford: Clarendon Press, 1983) 49, at 62–72.

[32] Hart, *The Concept of Law*, 153. His emphasis.

[33] Ibid. His emphasis.

[34] Indeed, even this is unclear. Hart cites directly only one of the cases and gives a different date in the text – 1954 – for a case cited as decided in 1952. Ibid, 122.

[35] Ibid, 117.

outside the scope of philosophy of law, he could not explain what is juridically interesting about them.

A South African lawyer of the time did better. DV Cowen, a law professor at the University of Cape Town, had in a short monograph published in 1951 set out the basis for the Appellate Division's reasoning in the first two cases.[36] He relied, he claimed, on 'accepted statutory canons of interpretation' of the South Africa Act considered as 'being no more than an Act of the United Kingdom Parliament'. He also thought that 'the same conclusion could be reached on the basis that the South Africa Act is a fundamental declaration of the will of the South African people. That Act was forged after much travail at a National Convention. At the request of the four self-governing colonies, it embodied the essential terms of a contract entered into between them to unite for the purposes of government. Accordingly, it would not be a contention without force that the South Africa Act is a British Act in form only, but in substance a constitution created by the will of the South African people.'[37] He added that such 'a contention would . . . raise difficult legal problems. Jurisprudentially, the ultimate nature of what Kelsen would call the *grundnorm* of the South African legal system is involved.'[38]

Cowen was quite right that such a contention raises very complex theoretical questions, for example, the question of what exactly was the will of the South African people in 1909, indeed, of who *were* the South

[36] DV Cowen, *Parliamentary Sovereignty and the Entrenched Provisions of the South Africa Act* (Cape Town: Juta and Co., 1951). Hart did not refer to this short monograph. But he did refer to two papers by Cowen in the long endnote at 299 of *The Concept of Law*; a note to his discussion in the text at 150 of 'Formalism and Rule Scepticism'. Both papers, the first dealing with the first decision, and the second with the implications of the first and second decisions for our understanding of parliamentary sovereignty, made a juridical Kelsenian argument from the internal point of view of a South African jurist, though one informed by a deep sense of constitutional history, legal theory and comparative law. (Cowen had the Chair in Comparative Law at the University of Cape Town at that time.) Hart made no mention of the fact that Cowen's argument and its basis in a constitutionalist idea indebted to Kelsen were in serious tension with his own arguments in the text. See DV Cowen, 'Legislature and Judiciary – Reflections on the Constitutional Issues in South Africa: Part I' (1952) 15 *Modern Law Review* 282 and 'Legislature and Judiciary – Reflections on the Constitutional Issues in South Africa: Part II' (1953) 16 *Modern Law Review* 273, especially 294.

[37] Cowen, *Parliamentary Sovereignty*, 49.

[38] Ibid, note 125. Cowen's Kelsenian thought is clearly inspired by Latham; see 6, referring to the Kelsenian conception of sovereignty set out in Latham, *The Law and the Commonwealth*, 522–5.

African 'people'. In a penetrating analysis of these cases, the Canadian constitutional scholar Edward McWhinney pointed out that in 1953 the National Party had been re-elected with a greatly increased majority, albeit one not large enough to exploit the unicameral procedure. He suggested that in 'none of the crisis situations in the great English-speaking countries where courts have been involved in power conflicts with executive or legislative authority, have the courts for any considerable length of time withstood a co-ordinate authority that has a substantiality of public opinion behind it'.[39] Despite this counsel of doom, McWhinney did not endorse the court's reasoning, nor deem it a 'pious fiction' designed to cover up an inevitable piece of judicial legislation. Rather, he found that Centlivres and most of the judges resorted to a positivistic mode of reasoning in the vain hope that it would help them to avoid a confrontation with the government. As he pointed out, that mode in the end made it impossible for them to find legal resources to continue their resistance. In relying on what Centlivres in a 1955 lecture called a 'strict and complete legalism'[40] – very formal modes of reasoning which left the substantive issues of principle buried below the surface – the judges put themselves in a position which the government could exploit by manipulating form.

In this light, one can appreciate the significance of Schreiner's disagreement with Centlivres in the second case. His rationale in 'the judicial hierarchy set up in the Constitution', which he took to be implicit in a rights-protecting section, gave him the resources he needed for his dissent in the third. He connected form to substance in a way which permitted him to keep substance in place as the basis for repudiating future manipulations of form. Lorraine Weinrib, also a Canadian

[39] Edward McWhinney, *Judicial Review in the English-Speaking World* (Toronto: University of Toronto Press, 1960, 2nd ed.), 195–6.

[40] In September 1955, Centlivres attended a conference at Harvard Law School on 'Government under Law'. In his paper, he kept carefully away from direct comment on the Voters Rights Cases, though he did set out the constitutional protection in section 152. He adopted from a speech of Sir Owen Dixon, the Chief Justice of Australia, who also attended the conference, the idea that there is no 'other safe guide to judicial decisions in great conflicts than a strict and complete legalism'. In a system with an omnipotent parliament, he asserted, the sole question for the courts is whether 'an enactment is *intra* or *ultra vires* the Constitution', a question which has nothing to do 'with the merits or demerits of legislation'. See Albert van de Sandt Centlivres, 'The Constitution of the Union of South Africa and the Rule of Law', in Arthur E Sutherland, ed., *Government under Law* (Cambridge, MA: Harvard University Press, 1956) 423, at 427.

constitutional scholar, in the course of a Schreiner Memorial Lecture, aptly commented that 'Schreiner's remarkable vision was to see in the South Africa Act the components of a modern constitutional instrument protecting fundamental rights and freedoms, as higher law, against encroachment by the ordinary political process'. She continued:

> in exercising the role of guardian of these entrenched rights . . . , Schreiner invoked the deepest values of modern constitutional ordering. He recognized the interests at stake as subjective legal entitlements, protected by courts as impartial adjudicators of disputes between the rightholders and the state. He rejected arguments that rendered these claims as fragile, formal interests. He evaluated the legitimacy of state power by the purposes and effects of its exercise. He persevered in his role as guardian of the freedom and equality of all members of the political community, especially the weakest members. He constrained the temporarily elected government to the higher law strictures of the South Africa Act, understood, to the extent possible, as the framework of a polity of free and equal citizens.[41]

Weinrib's qualification 'to the extent possible' is important. As McWhinney had pointed out, an 'activist' judicial approach maintained beyond the first two cases would eventually have had to consider 'principles of political representation going beyond the 50,000 "coloured" voters affected by the Separate Representation of Voters Act of 1951, and in this regard both major contending European factions (English and Afrikaner) seemed to be agreed on fundamentals', which he summed up as 'the general principle of political *non*-representation of the non-European majorities in the Union of South Africa'.[42]

In sum, it may seem that at best the judges could have done more to keep alive the glimmer of an idea of the unity of the people not based on racial grounds. But they were incapable of challenging the basic fact of apartheid and the system of racial segregation which preceded it, both designed to maintain white supremacy in the political domain in order to ensure continued dominance in the economic and social domains. In addition, it may seem to follow that these decisions teach us about the futility of relying on constitutional protections and adjudication to resist a determined and powerful elite, even when (like the National Party) the

[41] Lorraine E Weinrib, 'Constitutionalism in the Age of Rights: A Prolegomenon' (2004) 121 *South African Law Journal* 278, at 283.

[42] McWhinney, *Judicial Review in the English-Speaking World*, 197. My emphasis.

elite at least wishes to pay lip service to respecting the rule of law.[43] As long as the elite is willing to make its actual intentions ever more public and articulate in the law, the form of law can be used to implement any content.

I have tried to resist that argument throughout this book at the abstract level of legal theory. There is also the actual South African experience. Apartheid South Africa was a deeply divided society in which the Constitution both recognized the division and sought to preserve by entrenchment some idea, however fragmentary, of the unity of the people in which all adult legal subjects were subject to the same general law. The dominant white minority was determined to move to the Westminster model of parliamentary supremacy in order to preserve the division on its own supremacist terms. They wished, that is, to move decisions about constitutional fundamentals from the space formally delimited by higher law constitution-making to the space of ordinary parliamentary politics in order to maintain and even strengthen the division.[44] And that was because they assumed that in a parliamentary legal order the parliament may make a law with any content.

However, it was not the case in South Africa that without the formal constitutional protections of Coloured voters, there was nothing substantive left. What Schreiner called the 'protective judicial system . . . with the Appellate Division set up at the apex' remained intact. There remained in place in apartheid South Africa an unwritten constitution which gave to judges the resource to interpret statutes in such a way as to preserve, as we saw Weinrib put it, 'to the extent possible . . . the framework of a polity of free and equal citizens'.[45] The content of the constitution was no

[43] See the excerpts from the parliamentary debates quoted by Marshall in his chapter on South Africa in *Parliamentary Sovereignty and the Commonwealth*, 182–248.

[44] See Hanna Lerner, *Making Constitutions in Deeply Divided Societies* (Cambridge: Cambridge University Press, 2011). I explore this theme in 'Exemplary But Not Canonical: The South African Voters Rights Cases', in Sujit Choudhry, Michaela Hailbronner and Mattias Kumm, eds, *Global Canons in an Age of Uncertainty: Debating Foundational Texts of Constitutional Democracy and Human Rights* (Oxford: Oxford University Press, forthcoming).

[45] See John Dugard, *Human Rights and the South African Legal Order* (Princeton: Princeton University Press, 1978); Anthony S Mathews, *Freedom, State Security and the Rule of Law: Dilemmas of the Apartheid Society* (Cape Town: Juta, 1986); Richard Abel, *Politics by Other Means: Law in the Struggle against Apartheid* (New York: Routledge, 1995); Jens Meirhenrich, *The Legacies of Law: Long-Run Consequences of Legal Development in South Africa, 1652–2000* (New York: Cambridge University Press, 2008); David Dyzenhaus, *Hard Cases in Wicked Legal Systems: Pathologies of Legality* (Oxford: Oxford University Press, 2010, 2nd ed.).

more (but also no less) than the resources of a legal tradition which had inherited from both English common law and Roman Dutch law presumptions of the liberty and equality of the individual legal subject which were supposed to inform judicial interpretation of statutes.

It should be noted that only a minority of the judges were determined to deploy these presumptions and these judges were generally in the lower courts so were often overruled on appeal. In addition, the parliament was astute to react by closing what the government saw as a gap in the legislation and by ensuring that new legislation did not provide similar opportunities. To achieve that end, the parliament had to be either explicit in its legislation that certain groups of people were not to be treated as free and equal or to prohibit in very explicit statutory provisions judicial review of the implementation of those decisions. These strategies, often combined, had the effect of putting those affected beyond the reach of the rule of law. They were governed not by law but by the diktat of the officials who staffed the particular legal regimes, which threatened to turn the order from a legal one into something else. But to the extent this was not done, apartheid South Africa continued to be a modern legal state, though of a particular kind – the Apartheid State.

All inhabitants of apartheid South Africa were subject to the same general law. The racial laws of apartheid carved out vast exceptions to the rule of general law by creating the legal regimes which dominated the lives of the majority population of black South Africans, subjecting them to severe discrimination. These regimes were for the most part run by specialized agencies and officials and they relegated black South Africans to an inferior status in almost all aspects of life. Nevertheless, the ideal that all South Africans were equal before the law – the specifically legal ideal of human dignity – was maintained as an abstract ideal of the legal order throughout the apartheid era even as particular apartheid laws made it ever clearer that the animating political ideology of the ruling party was one of white supremacy. Black South Africans were as a result second-class citizens.

I suggested in Chapter 1 that if one is legally recognized as having status as a legal subject for some purposes but not for others, the parts of the law which seem to relegate one to inferior status are put into question by those parts which do not when a legal challenge is mounted to the subject's inferior status. Here I explore the way in which a legal order can go in very different directions, depending on the answers given by its officials. On the one hand, the answers may enhance the subjects' status, in which case the order becomes more rule-of-law like. On the other, the answers may diminish status to the point where the inferior status of the group is so entrenched that individuals in it are no longer second-class citizens because they are governed by an entirely different regime of law, or even by an order quite different from legal order. I start by relocating my discussion so far in the more general themes of my book to prepare the way for an exploration of the ideal types of state which help to guide this exploration.

5.2 Dworkin Revisited

Recall from Chapter 1 that Dworkin expressed some doubt that the situation of a judge starkly faced with a clearly unjust law would easily arise. In a long footnote to that claim, Dworkin said that he needed to distinguish more sharply than he had in his earlier work between 'explanation' and 'justification'.[46] In his view, an explanation does not 'provide a justification of a series of political decisions if it presents, as justificatory principles, propositions that offend our ideas of what even a bad moral principle must be like'.[47] He also said that he had more confidence than he had suggested in earlier work in what he called the 'screening power of the concept of a moral principle'. He claimed that the requirement his theory imposes on judges – that they provide an argument which shows the legal record in its best moral light – will tend to screen out or exclude morally unacceptable principles.[48]

Dworkin did not pursue this line of inquiry, other than by offering hypotheticals in an illegitimate system like the Nazi one in which he argued that a judge could and should resist reasoning by analogy from an explicitly unjust law. For example, in a private law dispute, an 'Aryan' German claims that in tort law Jews are subject to strict liability while Aryans are not, because in contract law a statute stipulates that only Aryan Germans have remedies available to them in disputes with Jews. In such examples, it seems clear that the case is hard because a discriminatory ideology evidently explains or fits one area of private law, and perhaps much of the law of the order. But in the area in which the

[46] Ronald Dworkin, 'A Reply by Ronald Dworkin', in Marshall Cohen, ed., *Ronald Dworkin and Contemporary Jurisprudence* (London: Duckworth, 1984) 257, at 299, note 4.

[47] Ibid.

[48] Ibid.

dispute occurs, it is still possible to claim that individuals are entitled to equal concern and respect.[49]

However, the resource of a screening principle in tort law may seem removable by the stroke of a legal pen, whether by a discriminatory statute or by a 'Dworkinian' judgment which finds that Aryan ideology overwhelmingly explains the bulk of Nazi private law, not to mention public law, and hence requires that in a hard case a judge should extend that ideology. At that point, as we saw, Dworkin advised that in a legal order which is arguably wholly illegitimate, the judge should decide that the law-like artefacts of the political system supply no moral reasons and are therefore not law. We are thus returned to the positivist claim that the existence of moral resources in the law which make genuine justification possible is contingent. In addition, the idea that moral principles will screen out repugnant principles brings Dworkin's position uncomfortably close to Hart's understanding of natural law positions as what I called positivism with a minus sign: the law of any legal order is its positive law with extremely unjust laws subtracted. Still, as I argue here, there is something to the screening idea as long as it is not understood as a kind of contingently 'inbuilt moral filter',[50] but rather, as suggested in Chapters 3 and 4, as what happens in a dynamic process of juridical production.

I describe that process more fully in Chapter 6. Here I prepare for that discussion by explaining why the existence of legal order makes the production process possible, an explanation not available to Hartian positivists or Dworkin, because neither inquired into what happens to *legal order* when particular laws are used to consign a whole group to second-class status. Their neglect in this regard was driven by their assumption that the dispute between them is, as Dworkin liked to say, about law in the 'doctrinal' sense: what makes claims true or false about the law of a particular place.[51]

It is the combination of the assumption that the debate is entirely doctrinal with the assumption that philosophy of law must explain law's authoritative nature which leads to the puzzle of very unjust law. The first

[49] Ibid. Compare Ronald Dworkin, *Law's Empire* (London: Fontana, 1986), 105–8.

[50] See Martin Stone, 'Legal Positivism as an Idea about Morality' (2011) 61 *University of Toronto Law Journal* 313, at 323, for discussion of the idea that law has 'a kind of in-built moral filter, such that injustice of certain kinds or degrees renders a rule incapable of being a true proposition of law of a given time and place'.

[51] Ronald Dworkin, *Justice in Robes* (Harvard: Belknap Press, 2006), 2.

assumption has the same kind of consigning effect as Hart's static conception of the law of a legal order, as we can see when we note that Dworkin identified a second, 'sociological' concept, which he took to be Lon Fuller's. Such a concept, Dworkin said, seeks to set out precisely 'what kind of social structure counts as a legal system'. But he asserted that 'we would think it silly to argue about whether . . . [an alien group on a distant planet] *really* had a legal system when we discovered that they had no enforcement institutions, or that *ex post facto* legislation was the norm there rather than the rare exception, or that their officials never claimed morally legitimate authority'.[52]

Dworkin also identified a third 'taxonomic' concept, which asks questions such as whether moral principles can count as principles of law, which he attributed to Joseph Raz and rejected as a 'scholastic fiction'.[53] Finally, he identified an 'aspirational' conception, 'which we often refer to as the ideal of legality or the rule of law', and which he endorsed. This, he said, is a politically contested concept, with the lines of contest drawn between more substantive rights-based conceptions and more 'formal conceptions'.[54]

Dworkin's dismissal of Fuller's legal theory as 'silly' betrayed, as we have seen is the case with Hart is his dismissive moments, his own sense of vulnerability when it came to Fuller's attempt to explain law in terms of a self-styled 'aspirational' theory of the morality inherent in legality.[55] Moreover, as we saw in Chapter 1, Dworkin himself seemed to accept a 'sociological' concept in his attempts to explain how very unjust law might give rise to moral reasons of some kind in the context of the antebellum USA when the issue arose as to whether a judge should send an enslaved person who had escaped to the North back to slavery in the South.

First, Dworkin argued that if an unjust legal system is a source of moral reasons for judges to apply its laws that arises from the fact that there is a 'general political situation' such that 'the central power of the community has been administered through an articulate constitutional structure the citizens have been encouraged to obey and treat as a source

[52] Ibid, 3. His emphasis.
[53] Ibid, 4.
[54] Ibid, 5.
[55] See Lon L Fuller, *The Morality of Law* (New Haven: Yale University Press, 1969, revised ed.), 41.

of rights and duties, and that the citizens have in fact done so'.[56] As I pointed out, that makes the fact of acceptance – we might even say an Austinian 'habit of obedience' – part of the explanation of why the artefacts produced by the system amount to obligation-creating laws.

Second, Dworkin said that the distinction between the political rights people think they have whatever the law contains and their legal rights – the rights they 'are entitled to enforce on demand, without further legislative intervention, in adjudicative institutions that direct the executive power of sheriff or police'[57] – can only be made 'in a community that has developed some version of what Hart called secondary rules: rules establishing legislative, executive, and adjudicative authority and jurisdiction'.[58] That seems to make the existence of legal rights dependent on the existence of the institutions of the modern legal state.

In addition, the question whether moral principles can count as principles of law is not a 'scholastic fiction', as Dworkin well knew, when it is asked as a political question. As we saw in Chapters 1 and 3, it becomes aspirational when asked in the utilitarian command theorists' advocacy for a kind of formalistic legal order because such an order would best suit the top-down transmission of judgments of overall utility made outside of law. It is at that level of abstraction that joinder is achieved between more substantive rights-based conceptions and such very thin conceptions of legality. We have also seen that Dworkin's theory of law falters precisely when he tries to build it out of an account of adjudication which presupposes that within the positive law of any legal order are the interpretive resources of late twentieth-century liberalism.[59]

To move forward, we should return to a modified version of one of the alternatives for a judge faced with an unjust law which in Chapter 1 we saw Dworkin discarded under fire from Hart: the judge who stays in office and applies the law under explicit protest, hoping, 'against odds, that his appeal based on moral grounds will have the same practical effect as a lie would'.[60] But we must substitute 'legal grounds' for 'moral grounds' and to do this we need to see that there were more differences

56 Dworkin, 'A Reply by Ronald Dworkin', 258.

57 Ronald Dworkin, *Justice for Hedgehogs* (Cambridge, MA: Belknap Press, 2011), 405.

58 Ibid.

59 See my 'The Rule of Law as the Rule of Liberal Principle', in Arthur Ripstein, ed., *Ronald Dworkin* (Cambridge: Cambridge University Press, 2007) 56.

60 Ronald Dworkin, 'Appendix: A Response to Critics', in Dworkin, *Taking Rights Seriously* (London: Duckworth, 1981, 3rd impression) 291, at 326–7.

between Nazi law and, say, American law than that the Nazis used their laws to achieve ends odious to an American.

This last sentence adapts Fuller's acute charge against Hart in their exchange in 1958 that Hart in his analysis of Nazi law focused exclusively on the immorality of the ends of which particular laws were made the instrument and thus neglected the damage done to legality and legal order.[61] As we know from Chapter 1, Fuller subsequently identified eight 'desiderata' or principles of legality: generality, promulgation, non-retroactivity, clarity, non-contradiction, possibility of compliance, constancy through time and – the one which he took to be the most complex – 'congruence' between official action and declared rule.[62] A system which fails completely to meet one of these principles, or fails substantially to meet several, would not, in his view, be a legal system. It would not qualify as government under law – as government subject to the rule of law.

Fuller's claim was that compliance with the principles imbues law with an 'inner' or 'internal' morality which makes a positive moral difference to all legal systems. Even a tyrant who wanted to govern through the medium of law would have to comply and this would preclude rule by arbitrary decree and secret terror, which, Fuller said, is the most effective medium for tyranny.[63] However, Dworkin, in tandem with legal positivists, argued in response both that only prudential reasons prevent tyrants from making their unjust aims altogether explicit in the law at their command and that compliance serves only to make those commands more effective. In short, they argued that the principles could not exert a moral discipline on law which provides a legal obstacle to such aims.[64]

Notice, however, that Fuller's legal theory presents a kind of one-system picture since the morality in question is internal, already immanent in the law. In addition, Fuller's morality is not at the level of positive law but at the level of principles of legality, though his claim is that the compliance with these principles will condition the content of positive

[61] Lon L Fuller, 'Positivism and Fidelity to Law: A Reply to Professor Hart' (1958) 71 *Harvard Law Review* 630, at 650.

[62] These are set out in detail in Fuller, *The Morality of Law*, chapter 2.

[63] Ibid, 157–9.

[64] Ronald Dworkin, 'Philosophy, Morality, and Law: Observations Prompted by Professor Fuller's Novel Claim' (1965) 113 *University of Pennsylvania Law Review* 672; Hart, *Concept of Law*, 206–7. See further, Joseph Raz, 'The Rule of Law and Its Virtue', in Raz, *The Authority of Law: Essays on Law and Morality* (Oxford: Clarendon Press, 1983) 210, at 223–6.

law. Indeed, Fuller could be taken to agree with Hart against Dworkin that philosophy of law must start by addressing this level.[65] There are, in Hart's words, 'minimum conditions necessary and sufficient for the existence of a legal system',[66] which may be why he at times seemed to agree that the principles were among such conditions, though then hastened to add that they exert no discipline on the content of the law.[67]

In making this kind of response, Dworkin and Hartian positivists overlooked the possibility that if law must comply with such principles to a significant degree, it will in fact be the case that an interpretive model of the kind Dworkin advocated gains significant traction in the positive law of any particular legal order. If that were the case, the model would not produce the perverse results Hart thought undermined Dworkin's position, because, as Dworkin himself suggested, one should have more confidence in the 'screening power' of principles, though conceived in Kelsenian terms as a dynamic process of juridical production. The basis for that confidence is that the principles are not merely moral but also legal: they are the principles of legality with which positive law must comply to count as law. Hence, if legislators follow the ethos of law-making set out by the principles, the law they make will be interpretable by judges in a way which treats the individual subject to the law as someone with, in Fuller's words, 'dignity as a responsible agent'.[68]

These are theoretical claims, but I have elsewhere marshalled considerable evidence in favour of them: studies of the apartheid legal order,[69] of

65 See Hart's remark in *The Concept of Law*, vii, that the book is an exercise in 'descriptive sociology'.

66 Ibid, 116–17.

67 See Jeremy Waldron, 'Positivism and Legality: Hart's Equivocal Response to Fuller' (2008) 83 *New York University Law Review* 1135.

68 Fuller, *The Morality of Law*, 162. See Kristen Rundle, 'Form and Agency in Raz's Legal Positivism' (2013) 32 *Law and Philosophy* 767, especially at 771, where Rundle sets out two dimensions of Fuller's argument, the 'distinctive ethos of legislation' which requires law to take a particular form and the way in which that form 'presupposes the legal subject's status as a responsible agent'. My argument adds a third dimension, implicit in the combination of the first two, that the law must be interpretable in a way which vindicates that presupposition. (Rundle also provides an illuminating analysis of a tension between Raz's account of authority, which has the rational agent at its heart, and his account of the rule of law which argues that the rule of law serves only to make law into a more effective instrument of policy, including policies which deny agency, for example, by enslaving people.)

69 See my *Hard Cases in Wicked Legal Systems*.

the legal order of Weimar[70] and of legal responses to the threat of terrorism in the post 9/11 era.[71] As I have already suggested, such studies of legal experience show that legislators who wish to address the individuals subject to their power as lacking 'dignity as a responsible agent' must adopt either one or both of two strategies. Either they can explicitly state that aim, or they can delegate power to officials permitting the officials to achieve the same end, not because this end is explicitly stated in the empowering statute, but because official implementation of the statute is explicitly stated to be unreviewable by judges.

Both strategies use law to place individuals or groups of individuals beyond the reach of the law. But they do so in a way which does not comply with law's form, in the first case by negating generality and its implicit commitment to formal equality before the law, in the second case by ensuring that there is no law with which official action must be congruent. If the legislators adopt one or both the strategies in a not altogether explicit fashion, judges are under a duty to treat the law the legislators made as if it were intended to comply with their legislative ethos, just as we saw in Chapter 2 Hobbes advised. As a result, if the form of law is to some extent respected, to that extent it will be interpretable in a way which respects the dignity as a responsible agent of those subject to the law. It will meet, that is, Hobbes's legality proviso.

This conclusion shows why the principle of publicity exercises a moral discipline on the content of the law, and thus, as Fuller argued, why tyrants who wish to govern through law will find themselves both legally and morally constrained. In addition, it helps to show why it is not merely a contingent fact that where law is present, so is this discipline. I also show in these studies that even in a legal order where there is no entrenched bill of rights, such defects in form can provide the legal basis for a judicial conclusion that the law is void[72] or support treating an explicit provision in a statute as a legal nullity.[73]

Finally, the studies show that even when it is not the case that a judge has the legal resources available to declare invalid a statute that offends principles of legality, or to interpret the statute in such a way that the

[70] See my *Legality and Legitimacy: Carl Schmitt, Hans Kelsen and Hermann Heller in Weimar* (Oxford: Clarendon Press, 1997).

[71] See my *The Constitution of Law: Legality in a Time of Emergency* (Cambridge: Cambridge University Press, 2006).

[72] Consider the common law view that a bill of attainder is void.

[73] Consider how judges in the common law world have sidestepped or read down privative clauses which strip them of review power of official action.

offence is either mitigated or removed, this does not mean that the statute is legally speaking unproblematic. Such a statute might be formally speaking valid in that it complies with rule-of-recognition-type tests. It meets, that is, Hobbes's validity proviso. But it will offend against legal form in another sense of the principles of legality inherent in his legality proviso, observance of which gives law a particular form. If judges find that they must uphold this statute, they can stay in office and take up Dworkin's third option from his initial response to the challenge of a judge faced with applying an unjust law. They can make an explicit protest but not only on moral grounds, since it is on grounds which are at the same time legal.

Such a protest is quite powerful. Recall from Chapter 4 that an analogue of it is effective under the UK Human Rights Act (1998), which in section 3 requires that judges strain to interpret statutes to make them compatible with the human rights commitments of the statute, and in section 4 requires judges to make a declaration of incompatibility of the statute with the human rights commitments, if they cannot find an interpretation under section 3. If a section 4 declaration is made, a minister of the Crown may in terms of section 10 of the Act amend the statute. The legislature may of course amend it, or do nothing, though doing nothing puts the state in violation of its international legal commitment to the European Convention on Human Rights, a matter on which the European Court of Human Rights will eventually pronounce. But while it is significant that in one jurisdiction such declarations have generally received positive responses from the legislature, more significant is why there have been such responses.

Even in a legal order which lacks these formal remedies, judges have the interpretive option open until the point that the legislature rules it out. At that point, they have the option of an informal declaration of incompatibility, a claim in the judgment that what the legislature has done is offensive to legality and the rule of law. It is worth noting that such informal declarations are often to be found in dissenting opinions which live on in legal memory just because they capture legality's rebuke to a legislature which has sought to undermine the conditions necessary for successful government according to law.

Moreover, as I argued in Chapter 4, it is important to take into account the relationship between national law and public international law. If the issue is decided within the modern legal state in a way which conflicts with public international law, there is still a question about how that issue will be resolved in the international legal order, or, as in the case of the

Human Rights Act, within the legal order which binds together a particular community of states. A legal positivist retort would be that any overlap in content between the norms of a national legal order and those of a supra-national order is purely contingent, just as the overlap between positive law and morality is contingent. But as we have seen, both Hart and Kelsen find it difficult to stick to this position, and this book as a whole seeks to set out the argument for non-contingency.

For the moment, I want to note than when a legislature responds positively to such declarations, whether formal or informal, the responses have much to do with the message otherwise sent to those affected by the offending statute that they are not fully within the jural community constituted by the legal commitments of the political and legal order to which they are subject. Of course, as I have acknowledged again in this chapter, the powers that be may choose to reinforce the exclusionary message. If they do not, that leaves intact a resource for lawyers who wish to contest the exclusion legally, and it was on precisely this basis that human rights lawyers during the apartheid era put their challenges to the laws of apartheid. It is worth remarking that such lawyers claimed Dworkin's theory as a source of inspiration for their work in the standard example of the legal order which was often claimed by legal positivists to refute Dworkinian interpretivism.[74] My suggestion in this section has been that we need Fuller to understand how Dworkin's theory could so serve.

That this conclusion is supported by a mix of appeals to practical experience and theoretical arguments will render it unphilosophical according to many philosophers of law today who, to adapt Hersch Lauterpacht's point in Chapter 4, till the 'barren' fields of conceptual analysis.[75] But, as we have seen here, the vision of law implicit in the long arc of legality goes back at least to Hobbes, and the ways in which Hart and Kelsen were drawn to it as they joined in the quest to understand law

[74] See François du Bois, 'Preface', in du Bois, ed., *The Practice of Integrity: Reflections on Ronald Dworkin and South African Law* (Cape Town: Juta, 2004) xi. This collection contains the proceedings of a conference held in Cape Town to honour Dworkin's outsize influence on the practice of human rights lawyering during the apartheid era.

[75] Hersch Lauterpacht, 'Is International Law a Part of the Law of England?', in Lauterpacht, *International Law: Collected Papers – The Law of Peace*, vol. 2 (Cambridge: Cambridge University Press, 2009, E Lauterpacht, ed.) 537, at 568. John Gardner accused those like Ronald Dworkin and Gerald Postema who think important this kind of attention to legal experience of creating a 'fundamentally anti-philosophical climate'; Gardner, *Law as a Leap of Faith* (Oxford: Oxford University Press, 2012), 24.

in the register of authority are evidence of its power. It speaks to the virtues of 'integrative jurisprudence' – a method of doing legal philosophy which combines inquiry into politics, morality and history.[76] As I understand it, this method takes seriously the pragmatist claim that all inquiry must be answerable to experience. Philosophy of law's answerability requires a mix of painstaking attention to actual legal experience, as well as painstaking attention to the minutiae of debates within legal philosophical positions which attend to the relevant aspects of the experience. I have acknowledged that such attention will also reveal that experience can go in the exclusionary direction. But then we need Fuller too, in order to understand that an illegitimate legal system is a 'botched legal order',[77] indeed, on the path to becoming something other than legal order, an experience of illegality or even of unmediated coercion, as I explain in Section 5.3.

5.3 Legal Geography

In Chapter 4 I mentioned my opposition to 'geographical legality', the idea that the public law of a modern legal state stops at its borders. That was in the context of a more general discussion of the juridical relationship between public international and national law and between the private law norms of one state and another. Here I explore that opposition further through introducing the ideal types of the modern legal state which help to illuminate the issues raised by the Apartheid State. Since these are ideal types, my account is not meant to reflect all the complexity of the states which are their exemplars. Still, just as it is important for my argument that the Apartheid State is rooted in the actual experience of the apartheid legal order, so is it important that the other types discussed in this section are rooted in such experience, for the type abstracts from and simplifies experience only in order to illuminate it.[78] The inspiration

[76] See Harold J Berman, 'Towards an Integrative Jurisprudence: Politics, Morality, History' (1988) 76 *California Law Review* 779.

[77] Scott Shapiro, *Legality* (Cambridge, MA: Belknap Press, 2011), 391.

[78] See Max Weber, *Economy and Society* (Cambridge, MA: Harvard University Press, 2019, Keith Tribe, ed. and trans.), 85. Interestingly, Weber adapted this idea from one of the classic texts on the juridical nature of the modern legal state, Georg Jellinek, *Allgemeine Staatslehre* (Berlin: Verlag O Häring, 1905, 2nd ed.). See Tribe at 473 of Weber, *Economy and Society*, and Jellinek, *Allgemeine Staatslehre*, 32–40. My usage here is perhaps closer to Jellinek, as he viewed the ideal type of the state as one which lives up to its ideal, whereas Weber was concerned, as Tribe puts it at 473, to find a 'heuristic device': a

for this part of my argument is the classic analysis of the Nazi state in Ernst Fraenkel's *The Dual State*.[79]

5.3.1 *The Dual State and the Rule-of-Law State*

That Fraenkel's work, first published in English in the USA in 1941, informed neither the exchange between Hart and Fuller in the 1958 *Harvard Law Review* nor subsequent debate in philosophy of law is, in my view, one of the great missed opportunities in philosophy of law. The work is, moreover, based on a particularly rich experience: Fraenkel's legal practice in Berlin from 1933 to 1938, which he was permitted to do despite being Jewish because of his front-line service in the First World War.[80]

According to Fraenkel, the Nazi state was a 'Dual State' in that it consisted of two states which existed side by side. On the one side was the 'normative state', which contained whatever remained of the law and institutions of the Weimar legal order together with the statutory regimes enacted after 1933 and implemented through those institutions. On the other side was the 'prerogative state', which consisted of the apparatus of the Nazi Party wherein the leader's will (his actual will or his will as interpreted by subordinate officials) was the ultimate source of authority.[81] Fraenkel observed that the law of the normative state governed relationships between individuals and between individuals and state institutions only so long as officials in the prerogative state did not find such government inconvenient. Put positively, an official could override the law or the institutions of the normative state whenever this was thought to be in the interests of the Nazi Party.

Fraenkel contrasted the Dual State with what I will refer to as the 'Rule-of-Law State', which, following the foremost English public lawyer

'thought image of the leading characteristics associated with a form or institution employed in ordering historical reality'. For discussion of Weber's reliance on Jellinek, see Andreas Anter, *Max Weber's Theory of the Modern State: Origins, Structure, Significance* (Basingstoke: Palgrave, 2014), 13–14.

[79] Ernst Fraenkel, *The Dual State: A Contribution to the Theory of Dictatorship* (Oxford: Oxford University Press, 2017).

[80] See Douglas G Morris, *Legal Sabotage: Ernst Fraenkel in Hitler's Germany* (Cambridge: Cambridge University Press, 2020).

[81] I reserve capitalization in the text for the ideal types of state, and so will have 'normative state' and 'prerogative state' since these are not, on my account, ideal types of states, but the way Fraenkel described the spaces within the Dual State.

Albert Venn Dicey, he took to be a state in which all official action is subject to law, the officials are answerable for their actions before the ordinary courts, and the law to which officials are answerable includes both the positive law which authorizes their actions and legal principles embedded in the law protective of individual rights.[82] Fraenkel concluded that the rule of law did not obtain in Nazi Germany because the protections of the normative state were subject to the discretion of officials in the prerogative state.[83]

The Rule-of-Law State is, on my argument here, at one end of a continuum of legality. So long as a state is on that continuum, those who are subject to its law will be part of a jural community – the community of subjects bound together by law. These bonds are in the first place constituted by the enacted or positive law made by the state. However, they are also constituted by the fundamental legal principles which are to be found in any state on the continuum. To the extent that these bonds are lacking in a state, the closer it will move to the other end of the continuum, until the point where it falls right off, as Fraenkel argued the Dual State did.

The example of the Dual State shows why the kind of realism about public international law discussed in Chapter 4 cannot be refuted by pointing out that states comply with public international law most of the time. For if the more powerful states comply with the law only when they find it convenient, even if they happen to do so most of the time, the international legal order is the equivalent of the legal order of the normative state and the more powerful states are best understood as competing prerogative states. Even if one can plausibly claim that in particular cases a state seemed to forego some advantage by complying with law, it is all too easy to explain such cases as procuring another advantage, for example, through a state encouraging other states to enter into trade relationships with it which are beneficial in the long term.

It is important to see that this version of a realist argument goes much further than seeking to debunk the claim that international relations are governed by the rule of law, since it also seeks to debunk the claim that domestic relations are governable by the rule of law. It takes Fraenkel's description of the Dual State to apply to all states, so that the Nazi state differed from liberal democratic states only in that the prerogative state

[82] Ibid, 156. See Albert Venn Dicey, *The Law of the Constitution* (Oxford: Oxford University Press, 2013, John Allison, ed.), 119.

[83] Fraenkel, *The Dual State*, 70–1.

was completely visible in it, whereas in liberal democracies it recedes into the background, concealed by what realism supposes is a thin veneer of business-as-usual legality. That the rule of law is no more than this veneer is 'proved' by the fact that when business can no longer be conducted as usual because a situation arises which existing law does not regulate, an official will have to make a legally unconstrained decision about how to respond to that situation. According to this argument, while such situations pervade all legal orders, the veneer of legality can be maintained because these situations do not generally pose a dramatic challenge to the sense that business is as usual. When dramatic emergency situations do arise, in the form of existential challenges to the order, law recedes and the prerogative state comes to the fore.

Fraenkel was not only fully aware of this argument but also confronted it directly in his book in his discussions of the fascist legal theory of Carl Schmitt.[84] In order to appreciate why he thought it could and should be rejected, one must take into account the difference made by the fact that the interaction between the normative state and the prerogative state was one between a legal space and a space of no-law. On Fraenkel's account, the lawlessness of the prerogative state was complemented by the lawfulness of the normative state. As he put the point,

> The Normative State . . . is by no means identical with a state in which the 'Rule of Law' prevails, i.e., with the *Rechtsstaat* of the liberal period. The Normative State is a necessary complement to the Prerogative State and can be understood only in that light. Since the Prerogative and Normative States constitute an interdependent whole, consideration of the Normative State alone is not permissible.[85]

This analysis is more nuanced than, but still fully compatible with, a claim about Nazi 'lawlessness' which Fuller, following Radbruch, made.[86] For neither Fuller nor Radbruch claimed that such lawlessness amounted to a total legal void, only that there were pockets of lawlessness; and Fuller thought it was not shocking to suppose that at a certain point the pockets could swallow the whole. These insights are important if we wish

[84] See the many references to Schmitt, ibid, but especially the discussion at 60–4. See also Carl Schmitt, *Political Theology: Four Chapters on the Concept of Sovereignty* (Cambridge, MA: MIT Press, 1988, George Schwab, trans.).

[85] Fraenkel, *The Dual State*, 71.

[86] Lon L Fuller, 'Positivism and Fidelity to Law', 660. Gustav Radbruch, 'Statutory Lawlessness and Supra-Statutory Law' (2006) 26 *Oxford Journal of Legal Studies* 1 (Bonnie Litschewski Paulson and Stanley L Paulson, trans.).

to understand how the Rule-of-Law State can be hollowed out from within.

Consider that in his Preface to the 1974 German edition of *The Dual State*, Fraenkel said that in the final phase of his legal practice in Berlin he frequently described his work to friends as that of a 'switchman':

> That is, I regarded it an essential part of my efforts to ensure that a given case was dealt with under the auspices of the 'normative state', and not end up in the 'prerogative state'. Colleagues with whom I was on friendly terms confirmed that they, too, had repeatedly worked towards making sure that their clients were punished in a court of law.[87]

It was, in other words, still possible to enforce the law and the rule of law in Nazi Germany in the late 1930s, though that enforcement was a precarious business because it was contingent on decisions in the prerogative state.

Moreover, from what is known about the detail of Fraenkel's legal victories, Douglas Morris has suggested that they did not depend on the residual legal rights available within the normative state. Rather, they depended entirely on the effective use of legal procedures to Fraenkel's clients' advantage in cases in which judges were not subject to direct pressure from officials in the prerogative state or were prepared to try to resist such pressure and do their jobs.[88] This was all that was possible because the 'always cramped space' of the normative state contracted as the Nazi grip on power increased until the point when 'the normative state meant not the rule of law but the technical administration of the law'.[89]

Indeed, Fraenkel pointed out that the existence of the prerogative state did more than make the protections afforded by the normative state precarious. It also made the protections less robust. The 'mere existence of arbitrariness, as embodied in the [p]rerogative [s]tate', he remarked, 'has dulled the sense of justice to such a degree that the existence of an agency with limited jurisdiction is considered as a legal institution even though the government exercises enormous discretionary power'.[90] In a footnote to this claim, he quoted Dicey to this effect: 'the predominance of regular law, as opposed to the influence of arbitrary power, excludes

[87] Fraenkel, *The Dual State*, xix.

[88] Douglas G Morris, 'The Dual State Reframed: Ernst Fraenkel's Political Clients and His Theory of the Nazi Legal System' (2013) 58 *Leo Baeck Institute Year Book* 5.

[89] Ibid, 5 and 19.

[90] Fraenkel, *The Dual State*, 70.

the existence of arbitrariness, of prerogative, or even wide discretionary authority';[91] and he complained that this idea 'was never accepted in Germany'.[92]

Now Dicey equated the administrative state, as he observed it in France, with the absence of the rule of law because that state is composed of agencies and officials to whom the legislature has delegated discretion, not only as to how to implement the programme of the statute but also often to decide on the content of the programme by making rules to concretize an abstractly stated legislative mandate. Because this activity was supervised by specialized administrative tribunals, not the ordinary courts exercising the controls of ordinary law, Dicey claimed that '[a]-mong modern Englishmen the political doctrines which have in France created the system of *droit administratif* are all but unknown'.[93]

The idea of unknowability echoes in another of Dicey's claims – that martial law 'in the proper sense of that term, in which it means the suspension of ordinary law and the temporary government of a country or parts of it by military tribunals, is unknown to the law of England'.[94] One interpretation of these claims is that Dicey naïvely believed that there were in fact no administrative law regimes in England in existence in the late nineteenth century and that officials had never established regimes of martial law – regimes of legally unlimited military force within an area on the basis that an official response to civil unrest would be inadequate if it were confined to action in terms of the ordinary law as policed by the ordinary courts.

But this interpretation cannot be correct, since Dicey's legal practice was in administrative law,[95] and since he dealt at some length in a note to the sixth edition of *The Law of the Constitution* with the historical record of martial law.[96] In the latter, his concern was to show that the claim about the necessity of martial law, in effect a claim to the necessity of manifestations of the prerogative state in times of stress, is false because

91 Dicey, *The Law of the Constitution*, 119. I have corrected small errors in Fraenkel's quotation in *The Dual State*, 223, note 218.

92 Dicey, *The Law of the Constitution*, 119.

93 Ibid, 111.

94 Ibid, 161.

95 See Mark Walters, *AV Dicey and the Common Law Constitutional Tradition: 'A Legal Turn of Mind'* (Cambridge: Cambridge University Press, 2020), chapter 11, 'Dicey's Administrative Law Blindspot'.

96 Dicey, *The Law of the Constitution*, 352–66. See Walters, *AV Dicey and the Common Law Constitutional Tradition*, 277–85.

legality not only should but also can govern official action in times of stress, even though this might require more reliance on the legislature than on courts and perhaps, in addition, some institutional innovation.[97] He had thus to be committed to the same conclusion about administrative law regimes; and his view of administrative law regimes in England and of the French system of *droit administratif* moderated along the same lines.[98]

Fraenkel had a similar view of, on the one hand, both martial law and its equivalent in the emergency powers provision of the Weimar Constitution – Article 48 – and, on the other, of administrative law. In regard to the former, he traced the origins of the prerogative state in Nazi Germany to the abuse of Article 48 by the conservative politicians who governed Germany in the early 1930s as well as to the Weimar judges who had not accepted what he took to be a principle of English law that martial law is unconstitutional.[99] In regard to the latter, he observed that 'a clear distinction exists between administrative agencies and the organs of the Prerogative State': '[h]owever extensive the discretion of an administrative agency . . . its discretion can be exercised only within the limits of its clearly defined jurisdiction'.[100]

As I understand Dicey's and Fraenkel's view, martial law and unconstrained administrative discretion are constitutionally unknowable, but that does not amount to a denial of the existence of actual examples of the use of law to create spaces of legally unlimited power. Take the principle that no one should be a judge in their own cause. It has no application in the prerogative state as well as no application in an administrative state if there is no independent review of whether officials have transgressed the limits on their authority. As Fuller argued, if such a principle is generally unobserved, we should not think only that our legal order has changed in some important way but also that we are on the path to no longer living in a legal order.[101] We need, however, to see that such a conclusion applies only if an order is journeying to the extreme end of the continuum of legality. In between that end and the rule-of-law

[97] For an extended analysis, see my 'The Puzzle of Martial Law' (2009) 59 *University of Toronto Law Journal* 1.

[98] See Walters, *AV Dicey and the Common Law Constitutional Tradition*, 275–98 and chapter 11; Dicey, *The Law of the Constitution*, appendix II, 'The Development of Administrative Law in England'.

[99] Fraenkel, *The Dual State*, 3–6.

[100] Ibid, 70.

[101] Fuller, 'Positivism and Fidelity to Law', 660.

end, the relationship between the spaces of legality and the spaces of illegality is complex.

Fraenkel's legal practice was precarious because of the place of the Dual State off the legality continuum. He could not count on his client's case being dealt with by a judge who operated in the normative state. Further, if Morris is right, even within that space a lawyer could count only on properly applied legal procedures, not residual legal rights, because the relationship between the prerogative state and the normative state negatively affected the space of legality within the normative state. Finally, one has to take into account that even those procedures could turn out sometimes to be an utter sham, in which case there was a pocket of lawlessness within the normative state.[102]

Still, had the legal procedures been properly applied, victories would have been possible. This marks the difference between the normative state and the prerogative state. The latter was not bounded by even thin legality, unless one were to count Hitler's Enabling Act of 1933 – the statute which made his will into the fundamental 'legal' norm – as prospectively validating anything done within the prerogative state, which would be to evacuate the idea of legality of all content. Fraenkel said of the Act that 'it would be futile to deny the significance of this legislation in the transformation of the German legal order'.[103] His argument about that significance was twofold.

First, the Act was in itself lawless – the product of an 'illegal *coup d'état*'.[104] Now illegality can be the foundation of legality. But Fraenkel was clear that this was not the case in Nazi Germany. Rather, the second point, the Act brought about the 'abolition of the rule of law'.[105] Relying on Charles McIlwain's work on medieval and early modern conceptions of absolutism, Fraenkel emphasized the distinction between the arbitrary power of a dictator who makes law in 'accordance with his will' and the absolute sovereign whose will is valid only if 'expressed in a way prescribed by law and tradition' and 'restricted to certain purposes'. Here he found telling the 'formula: "The king is bound by the Law of God and the Law of Nature"'.[106] As he explained, the distinction was between the

[102] See HO Pappe, 'On the Validity of Judicial Decisions in the Nazi Era' (1960) 23 *Modern Law Review* 260, a rather devastating critique of Hart's treatment of the Grudge Informer Case.

[103] Fraenkel, *The Dual State*, 4.

[104] Ibid.

[105] Ibid, 8–9.

[106] Ibid, 113.

conception of antiquity that law is a 'matter of politics' and the modern conception which 'attaches politics to law'.[107]

That the prerogative state was not so bound meant that what held the two states together was not legality but something else, some complex mix of prudential factors which made it expedient for the Nazis to maintain the normative state: for example, the importance of a somewhat stable life for 'Aryan', heterosexual, not mentally disabled Germans who had not been involved in anti-Nazi political activities; perhaps some sense that the existence of the normative state could be the basis for legitimacy claims both within and without Germany; and the fact that some of the Nazi goals were better achieved using properly applied law as their instrument rather than arbitrary official action. Because the two states were held together by prudential factors and not by law, the jural community within the normative state was entirely precarious. One could be moved across the boundary between the two spaces at the will of a Nazi official. Moreover, once moved across that boundary, one was no longer a legal subject. Rather, one was an object of discretion, to be used as some official thought fit, which in the case of millions in Germany and in Germany's Occupied Territories meant fit for extermination.

The significance of the construction of the legal space by prudential considerations rather than by law can be appreciated by contrasting the Dual State with two other kinds of state. First, there is the Apartheid State, a perverse variant of a Rule-of-Law State. As I already pointed out, the ideal that all South Africans were equal before the law was maintained as an abstract ideal of the legal order throughout the apartheid era, even as particular apartheid laws made it ever clearer that the animating political ideology of the ruling party was one of white supremacy. I also observed that the parts of the law which seemed to relegate second-class citizens to inferior status could be used to throw into doubt those parts that did not, to the point where inferior status for a group was so entrenched that individuals in the group were no longer second-class citizens because they were governed by an entirely different regime of law. In that case, the order would change into one in which there are two separate spaces of legality though held together by law. It would become what I call a 'Parallel State', the topic of Section 5.3.2.

[107] Ibid, 114. I come back to this distinction in Chapter 6.

5.3.2 *The Parallel State*

A prominent example of a Parallel State is the one which governs both Palestinians in the Occupied Territories and the inhabitants of Israel.[108] Before I begin my analysis of this kind of state, two clarifications are in order.

First, while I claim that it is a distinct ideal type of state, and thus deny that it is an Apartheid State, my denial does not pertain to the issue whether the actual Israeli state is guilty of the crime of apartheid, as that crime is stated in public international law.[109] On my argument the fact that a state has committed the crime of apartheid does not suffice to make it an Apartheid State because such a state is characterized by the fact that all legal subjects are regarded as equal before the law even though its statutory regimes go a long way to undermine the equality of the oppressed parts of the population.[110] In other words, a state which commits the crime of apartheid but does not regard its oppressed subjects as formally equal before the law is not, in my terms, an Apartheid State.[111]

Second, there is the issue of occupation. Palestine is officially supposed one day to become a fully independent state. But de facto it is subject to Israeli control and de jure it is (with the possible exception of Gaza)

[108] For relevant use of this term, see Mark LeVine and Mathias Mossberg, eds, *One Land, Two States: Israel and Palestine as Parallel States* (Berkeley: University of California Press, 2014). I assume in this section that the regime of law in one state within a Parallel State is inferior to the regime in the other. One can conceive of a Parallel State in which the regime in both is different but equally benign. But this kind of Parallel State would be juridically uninteresting.

[109] The *International Convention on the Suppression and Punishment of the Crime of Apartheid* declares apartheid to be a crime against humanity (Article I) and defines it as 'inhumane acts committed for the purpose of establishing and maintaining domination by one racial group of persons over any other racial group of persons and systematically oppressing them', with relevant acts listed (Article II). For arguments to the effect that the Israeli state is guilty of this crime, see Michael Sfard, 'The Occupation of the West Bank and the Crime of Apartheid: Legal Opinion', June 2020, https://s3-eu-west-1.amazonaws.com/files.yesh-din.org/Apartheid+2020/Apartheid+ENG.pdf and B'Tselem, 'A Regime of Jewish supremacy from the Jordan River to the Mediterranean Sea: This Is Apartheid', www.btselem.org/sites/default/files/publications/202101_this_is_apartheid_eng.pdf.

[110] If my argument is correct, the situation in Israel/Palestine is in one respect worse than that in apartheid-era South Africa. The legal resources available to lawyers to contest the legality of the officials who implement the occupation do not include the fundamental norms of the Israeli legal order.

[111] It is, however, the case that any Apartheid State will be guilty of the crime of apartheid as it by definition uses law to maintain a system of racial or ethnic supremacy.

subject to the public international law of belligerent occupation, notably to Article 43 of the Hague Regulations: 'The authority of the legitimate power having in fact passed into the hands of the occupant, the latter shall take all the measures in his power to restore, and ensure, as far as possible, public order and safety, while respecting, unless absolutely prevented, the laws in force in the country.' Such occupation is supposed to be subject to three principles: the inalienability of sovereignty vested in the occupied territory (that is, no legal taking of land by conquest); management of the occupation as a form of trust; and, implicit in the first two, the temporary nature of the occupation.

Now that occupation has lasted for over fifty years and politically speaking there is no end to it in sight. Moreover, the 'facts on the ground' established by Israeli settlers within the Occupied Territories, the infrastructure of roads and security put in place by Israel to secure these settlements including the wall or 'Separation Barrier', as well as the extension of the protection of Israeli law to these settlements and the enactment of statutes to facilitate further settlement activity, indicate an ongoing de facto annexation which the current government seems to regard as the prelude to a formal act of annexation, an act of conquest illegal under public international law. I do not deal with this issue except to note that, were there to be such an act of formal annexation, one would still not have in place an Apartheid State unless the government were, first, to establish equality before the law for all subjects and, second, to enact statutes which in significant respects made Palestinian subjects into second-class citizens.

The fiat which brought the Palestinian and Israeli orders together, thus creating the Parallel State, was effected by Meir Shamgar, who had held the office of attorney general during the initial period of occupation and had in that role designed the system of military law which governed the occupation.[112] It unified the two legal orders by making the Israeli Supreme Court the apex court for both legal orders. But within this unified legal order a fairly clear distinction is maintained between the

[112] In an early legal analysis (1990), Eyal Benvenisti suggested this was a Dual State – Benvenisti, *Legal Dualism: The Absorption of the Occupied Territories into Israel* (New York: Routledge, 2018). This label was not, however, based on Fraenkel, but on a paper by Shamgar. Ibid, unnumbered Preface. For a different view, though one based on considerable lapse of time, see Aeyal Gross, *The Writing on the Wall: Rethinking the International Law of Occupation* (Cambridge: Cambridge University Press, 2017). Gross argues that the Supreme Court navigates the parts of public international law most suitable for shoring up the legality of the occupation while avoiding those which do not.

two suborders, except in so far as the court applies principles of Israeli administrative law in light of its perception of appropriate application in the context of military occupation, which is in line with Shamgar's official reason for this fiat – that it was important that there was some form of external control over the military so as to prevent arbitrariness and maintain the rule of law.[113]

On the one hand, within the Israeli legal order (ILO), the supreme legislative authority is the parliament, the Knesset, which legislates subject to the regime of constitutional law developed out of Israel's Basic Laws by the court under the leadership of powerful chief justices. On the other hand, within the legal order of the Occupied Territories (OTLO), the supreme lawmaker is the military which legislates subject to the regime of law developed by the same court, though the court, while curbing some kinds of arbitrariness, in general defers to the military's say-so in security matters when it came to the facts and to the controls which are considered appropriate to apply. Hence, in this Parallel State, the law which governs the lives of Palestinians in the OTLO is not an exception to the general law of the ILO but the system of law developed by the military under the supervision of the Supreme Court.[114]

This Parallel State is thus unlike the Apartheid State because it is not held together by fundamental legal principles. But within it, the OTLO is not a prerogative state in which individuals are subject to the totally arbitrary will of those with power over them. The officials of the system may not disobey the standing commands or orders of the military authorities. Further, there is even less arbitrariness because of the Israeli Supreme Court's jurisdiction. More procedural protections have been put in place than the military authorities thought appropriate. Occasionally, the court finds that public international law is relevant to its deliberations. Further, there have been some decisions, especially

[113] I say fairly clear because it appears that recently the Supreme Court has started to rely more on constitutional law than on public international law in its rulings on Palestinians in the OTLO. See Tamar Hostovsky Brandes, 'The Diminishing Status of International Law in the Decisions of the Israeli Supreme Court concerning the Occupied Territories' (2020) 18 *International Journal of Constitutional Law* 767. She argues that this shift is consistent with a deliberate eradication of the distinction between Israel and the Occupied Territories by the parliament and the government.

[114] The military is of course also subject to parliamentary legislation which in some cases orders the military commander to legislate in particular ways. Note that appeals can be made from the OTLO to the Israeli administrative courts.

those brokered between lawyers in the shadow of the court, which have made a substantive difference.[115]

The tensions in issue here arise because that court presides at the same time over the Israeli state, a Rule-of-Law State, which it has had a prominent role in designing. Within the OTLO, Palestinians are neither quite second- nor quite first-class citizens. To be a second-class citizen, there has to be a group of first-class citizens in whose status the second-class citizens to some extent partake and the inhabitants of the OTLO are not subject to the fundamental principles which lie at the basis of the ILO. They are also not quite first-class citizens within the OTLO because while all the subjects of the OTLO are equally subject to the law, the law they are subject to is the commands of those who occupy their land by force, who in that respect are more like the uncommanded commander of Austin's theory of law than like a legislature which legislates by enacting the general laws which together could be said to make up a public order of law. To be a first-class citizen is to be treated with dignity as a responsible agent and within the OTLO that ideal is reduced to what Joseph Raz describes as the 'guidance function' of law – the law just tells people what they must do. This is not nothing. To the extent that the law is not arbitrarily enforced, Palestinians can plan their lives, which, as Raz concedes, does provide for some measure of freedom and dignity, and indeed without which there can be neither freedom nor dignity.[116]

That there is some measure of freedom and dignity is, of course, important. It shows that even as law oppresses, it has to enable something of moral worth. This point applies also to the pockets of inequality established by apartheid law and it is worth noting that two of the major victories won by human rights lawyers against the actual South African Apartheid State arose out of exercises in statutory interpretation which stabilized apartheid law so that those subject to it could know with some certainty what their rights were under that law.

In *Komani NO* v. *Bantu Affairs Administration Board, Peninsula Area*,[117] the Appellate Division held that a black man qualified to live in an urban area was entitled to have his wife live with him, while in

[115] David Kretzmer, *The Occupation of Justice: The Supreme Court of Israel and the Occupied Territories* (Albany: State University of New York Press, 2002), 187–98.

[116] Joseph Raz, 'The Rule of Law and Its Virtue', in Raz, *The Authority of Law* 210, at 213–14, 219–23.

[117] 1980 (4) SA 448 (A).

Oos-Randse Administrasieraad v. *Rikhoto*,[118] the same court held that workers who were sent back annually from the cities to the rural areas and then had to enter into a fresh contract with their employers were, nevertheless, continuously employed and thus had a right to live in the urban area in which they worked.

In both cases, the urban areas were the townships, ghettoes for black South Africans established on the outskirts of cities set aside for whites so that the whites, who lived in vastly superior areas, would have the benefit of cheap labour. Still, the difference these decisions made in the lives of those black South Africans they affected was immense and served to undermine the myth of apartheid – the ideology of 'apartness' in which black South Africans in white urban areas were sojourners, 'guest workers' who came alone from their own states (the infamous Bantustans or 'homelands') on temporary contracts to work in officially 'white' South Africa.

As I indicated, these decisions were presented by the Appellate Division as standard exercises in statutory interpretation. That is, no fundamental principles of law were explicitly invoked. Nevertheless, the fact that South Africa remained an Apartheid State made it possible for the court to conceptualize black South Africans as full legal rights holders, albeit under a regime of substantively discriminatory law. In other words, their first-class status in some respects affected positively the legal space in which their inferior status was entrenched, unlike in the Dual State, in which the space of the prerogative state negatively affected the space of the normative state, and unlike in the Parallel State, in which the legal orders are joined together in a way which seeks to ensure that the fundamental principles of the ILO do not underpin the legal bond between them.

That second-class citizenship is constructed both by the enacted law which creates the status and by the fundamental legal principles which undermine it is instructive, as we can see by returning to the example of slavery. As I pointed out in the Introduction, second-class status is much more *legally* problematic than the status of slavery, so long as the enslaved persons are relentlessly consigned to the status of objects or things. Slavery is of course morally a very problematic status. But the proviso is important because it is very difficult to create the status of utter slavery by law.

[118] 1983 (3) SA 595 (A).

The development of the Roman law of slavery is an example here, as when enslaved persons assumed tasks on behalf of their masters, for example, entering into contracts, it became difficult to maintain them in the class of things without any subjective rights. In addition, the possibility of manumission – the emergence of an enslaved person by dint of an act of the owner from no-status to full status – made it more difficult to hold intact the category of no-status.[119] A slave-owning society is like a Dual State in that enslaved persons live in a space where prerogative rules, but private individuals wield the prerogative, not state officials. Moreover, it is a prerogative granted by law and so subject to legal regulation or abolition. The relationship between the space of legality and the space of private prerogative is thus bounded by law in a way which over time may constrict the prerogative space, the opposite of what we find in the Dual State, and more akin to the situation just described of the Apartheid State.

An example much closer in time illustrates this point vividly, though, as I show, in it the distinctions between my ideal types of state blur to the point where we have in place not only a 'Hybrid State' but also the suggestion that all modern legal states are hybrids. Nevertheless, the ideal types remain helpful for understanding where a state should be placed on the continuum of legality.

5.3.3 *The Hybrid State?*

In the antebellum USA, 'Fugitive Slaves' fled from slavery in southern states to what they hoped would be freedom in northern states. But they were required to be returned to their owners by the constitutional compact which established Union through a set of compromises which permitted and secured slavery. The requirement was given concrete expression in a succession of federal Fugitive Slave Acts, designed in part to overcome the resistance by abolitionists in northern states to the return of fugitives, a resistance often fought out by legal means in the courts.[120]

[119] See Alan Watson, *Roman Slave Law* (Baltimore: Johns Hopkins University Press, 1987).

[120] Article 4, section 2 provided that 'No Person held to Service or Labour in one State, under the Laws thereof, escaping into another, shall, in Consequence of any Law or Regulation therein, be discharged from such Service or Labour, but shall be delivered up on Claim of the Party to whom such Service or Labour may be due.' It did not expressly permit the enactment of the federal legislation, but did provide a basis for it.

The abolitionists and those judges who listened sympathetically to their arguments were often inspired by the ruling of the Court of King's Bench in the 1772 case of *Somerset* v. *Stewart* which held that an enslaved person brought to England could not be compelled to leave and was entitled to a writ of habeas corpus. Lord Mansfield stated in his judgment a wide-reaching jurisprudential basis for his decision: 'The state of slavery is of such a nature that it is incapable of being introduced on any reasons, moral or political, but only positive law . . . It's so odious, that nothing can be suffered to support it, but positive law.'[121]

The politics of legal space in the USA during this period were immensely complex as can be shown, even if one simplifies things greatly, by imagining the Union as divided into just two blocks, the North in which slavery was abolished, and the South in which slavery was an institution. One can try to conceive of the antebellum USA, that is, as a kind of Parallel State. This Parallel State would differ from a Dual State in that the North was on the rule-of-law end of the legality continuum and the same was true of the South, as long as one was not an enslaved person. Within the South, enslaved persons did not live in law-created spaces in which they had an inferior status which made them second-class citizens, with one foot in the first-class space, the other in the inferior space. Rather, they were in a law-created space of no-status. Moreover, if they exited from that space, whether by emancipation, or by order of law, or by successful escape, they emerged in both the South and the North into inferior status, a kind of Apartheid State, unlike in Rome where slavery was not race-based.[122]

[121] I rely here on the report of the judgment in (1772) Lofft 1, 98 ER 499, as reproduced in Andrew Lyall, *Granville Sharp's Cases on Slavery* (Oxford: Hart Publishing, 2017) 232, at 233. For extensive discussion of the influence of Mansfield's dictum, see James Oakes, *Freedom National: The Destruction of Slavery in the United States, 1861–1865* (New York: WW Norton and Company, 2014).

[122] On the contrast between Roman and American slavery, see A Leon Higginbotham, 'Foreword', in Watson, *Roman Slave Law*, ix. That free blacks lived in an Apartheid State was confirmed by the Supreme Court in 1859 in *Dred Scott* v. *Sandford* 60 US 393, a decision which in 1986 it failed to overturn in *Plessy* v. *Ferguson* 163 US 53. The court finally dealt with the issue in 1954, at least at the level of formal constitutional interpretation, in *Brown* v. *Board of Education* 347 US 487. On *Dred Scott*, see Paul Finkelman, *Supreme Injustice: Slavery in the Nation's Highest Court* (Cambridge, MA: Harvard University Press, 2018) and on the journey from slavery through *Dred Scott* to *Plessy*, Steve Luxenberg, *Separate: The Story of Plessy* v. *Ferguson and America's Journey from Slavery to Segregation* (New York: WW Norton and Company, 2019).

This Parallel State also differs from the one which unites the ILO and the OTLO. Enslaved persons could cross legally from the South to the North if they travelled with their owners, in the same way that the owners' baggage could. But once in the North questions arose, testable in court, whether, as in *Somerset's Case*, the enslaved person became free under local law. The issues here, again as in *Somerset's Case*, arose in private international law where, as we saw in Chapter 4, the legal question is whether a court in jurisdiction B should recognize jurisdiction A's private law rules respecting ownership of property when a legal subject of A is involved in litigation in B concerning a situation created under A's law.[123]

In the USA the problem was that the Constitution, although it infamously dared not call the institution of slavery by its name, made a compromise with the institution through articles about the protection of property which both permitted slavery in the South as well as the forcible rendition of enslaved persons back to their owners if either they had escaped to the North, or been taken by their owners to the North and tried to seek their freedom with the help of abolitionists and the courts. The ability to litigate on the basis of Lord Mansfield's dictum operated in the shadow cast by the constitutional compromise which permitted the odious institution. At the same time, it operated in the light cast by the Preamble of the Constitution: 'We the People of the United States, in Order to form a more perfect Union, establish Justice, insure domestic Tranquility, provide for the common defense, promote the general Welfare, and secure the Blessings of Liberty to ourselves and our Posterity, do ordain and establish this Constitution for the United States of America'. In addition, the situation of enslaved persons brought into the North was susceptible to being regulated by local statute, for example a statute which required that if owners stayed for longer than a prescribed period of time in the North enslaved persons in their possession would become free by force of law.

[123] See Paul Finkelman, *An Imperfect Union: Slavery, Federalism, and Comity* (Chapel Hill: University of North Carolina Press, 1981). The leading legal theoretical treatment remains Robert M Cover, *Justice Accused: Antislavery and the Judicial Process* (New Haven: Yale University Press, 1975). And see Ronald Dworkin's perceptive review of Cover's book, 'The Law of the Slave-Catchers', *Times Literary Supplement*, 5 December 1975, 1437. For an analysis of how private international law matters play out in the Parallel State which binds the ILO and the OTLO, see Michael Karayanni, *Conflicts in Conflict: A Conflict of Laws Case Study on Israel and the Palestinian Territories* (Oxford: Oxford University Press, 2014).

Perhaps, then, the North and the South made up not so much a Parallel State as a Hybrid State, one held uneasily together by fundamental legal principles as well as by positive law, including the positive law of the Constitution, in ways which made the space of no-status sanctioned by the Constitution and established by enacted law highly problematic, as it did the law-created spaces of inferiority in which free blacks lived. Indeed, it may be the case that all states on the continuum of legality turn out to be hybrid in that they are at least to some extent Rule-of-Law States, otherwise they would have no place on the continuum of legality. But to some extent some subjects will be second-class citizens and to that extent the state will be an Apartheid State. In addition, it is likely that to some extent a state will try to prevent general principles reaching from one legal space to another; hence, it will be to that extent a Parallel State; or will, whether deliberately or unwittingly, attempt to create spaces in which prerogative rules and to that extent be a Dual State.

If this conclusion is warranted it indicates not the defects but the advantages of my ideal types. Modern legal states may, that is, differ more in the extent to which they contain elements of the ideal types than in conforming altogether to one or other. However, the types are, in my view, most helpful in that they point to the problems of legality which arise in particular states and which will indicate both their place on the continuum of legality and the kind of jural community they create.

Consider, for example, the problems attending the capture of Fugitive Slaves in the North who contested their rendition in court. When lawyers sought their release through applications for habeas corpus or other legal devices, were the Fugitive Slaves litigating as free legal subjects in a space in which slavery had been abolished, or were they pieces of property which, once certified as such, required despatch back to the South? This tension could be viewed as one between, on the one hand, the norms of the Constitution other than the slavery-permitting Articles which transcended the enacted law of both the North and the South and, on the other, private international law with the South claiming that its property law regime should govern. But the legal situation was made even more complex by other considerations.

First, public international law was itself in play. The anti-slavery principle in *Somerset's Case* was seen by abolitionists and argued in court by their lawyers to be one common to both natural law and public international law. Second, the Constitution was argued to include such principles despite the tension within it created by the combination of the slavery-permitting property articles with the promise of freedom. Third, there was no strict division at that time between these branches of law and private international law, so that, as in *Somerset's Case*, the anti-slavery principle resisted the reach of the odious rules of the South's enacted law into the space of the North.[124] Finally, within the North 'personal liberty' laws were enacted which sought to ensure that Fugitive Slaves were given all the procedural rights of a free person when they litigated, which significantly improved their chances of a favourable verdict.

It was precisely to address these tensions that the South caused to be enacted a new federal Fugitive Slave Law in 1850 which, as Andrew Delbanco says, 'denied the most basic right enshrined in the Anglo-American tradition: habeas corpus – the right to challenge, in open court, the legality of their detention'.[125] Delbanco describes it as an 'act without mercy'. It forbade defendants to testify in their own defence, ruled out trial by jury and disallowed all forms of exonerating evidence including rape, beatings and other kinds of abuse, put the power of extradition in the hand of federal officers, criminalized the act of sheltering a fugitive and required local authorities to assist the claimant in recovering his property. Once ownership was proved according to the property laws of the South, the person was rendered back to captivity, which is why only proof of freedom that the person was not owned in the eyes of that law, for example, emancipation papers signed by the owner, could save the enslaved persons from this fate.[126]

The 1850 law had, in light of the analysis so far, two important and interrelated dimensions. First, it sought to turn public law cases about liberty into pure private international law matters with a foreordained result. Second, it sought to ensure that result by reducing the public law dimension of the litigation by stripping litigants' procedural rights to the bone. Recall here from Chapter 4 Karen Knop's suggestion that private international law is about a private side of citizenship captured in the figure of the 'legal citizen' – the person who is entitled to sue and be sued

124 In private international law these days, such principles tend to be cabined off into a 'public policy exception'. For my argument against this practice, see my 'Not an Isolated, Exceptional, and Indeed Contradictory Branch of Jurisprudence', in Roxana Banu, Michael Green and Ralf Michaels, eds, *Philosophical Foundations of Private International Law* (Oxford: Oxford University Press, forthcoming).

125 Andrew Delbanco, *The War before the War: Fugitive Slaves and the Struggle for America's Soul from the Revolution to the Civil War* (New York: Penguin Press, 2018), 5.

126 I follow Delbanco, ibid, 5, closely here save for my emphasis on the dimension of private international law.

in certain courts.[127] Knop shows how what she calls private international law's 'cosmopolitan form' – its 'techniques' for dealing with the applicability of foreign law – allows it to bring a very concrete focus to contentious moral questions about 'inclusion and exclusion'.[128]

The 1850 law sought, that is, to deal with the problem of public citizenship which the Constitution fudged in its 'property' provisions by diminishing private citizenship through stripping litigants of the procedural rights that make it possible to present their case. It thus sought to deal with the internal legal tensions of the US constitutional order by making it almost impossible to raise these in a judicial forum. But that attempt served only to intensify political tensions in the North, often leading to violent resistance to the enforcement of the law, given that the legal avenues of resistance had been so narrowed.[129] In addition, new liberty laws were enacted in the North which sought to ensure jury trials for Fugitive Slaves in the face of the 1850 law, which as one southern senator complained, amounted to a 'practical denial of the whole right of the slaveholder over his slave, if he gets beyond the Jurisdiction of his own State'.[130]

It was thus of immense political significance that Abraham Lincoln made part of his campaign for the presidency the problem which would attend a free black who would be deprived of the opportunity of proving his status. In his inaugural address, Lincoln claimed that anyone who had sworn an oath to uphold the Constitution was committed to upholding the Fugitive Slave clause which had been taken to permit the enactment of the rendition legislation. But he objected to the 1850 law in these terms:

> In any law upon the subject ought not all the safeguards of liberty known in civilized and humane jurisprudence be introduced, so that a free man be not, in any case, be surrendered as a slave? And might it not be well, at the same time, to provide by law for the enforcement of that clause of the

[127] Karen Knop, 'Citizenship, Public and Private' (2008) 71 *Law and Contemporary Problems* 309, at 310.

[128] Ibid, 313.

[129] RJM Blackett, *The Captive's Quest for Freedom: Fugitive Slaves, the 1850 Fugitive Slave Law, and the Politics of Slavery* (New York: Cambridge University Press, 2018). See also James Oakes's very perceptive review, 'The Power of Running Away' (2018) *New York Review of Books*, 6 December issue. My account in the following two paragraphs follows Oakes.

[130] Ibid.

> Constitution which guarantees that 'the citizens of each State shall be entitled to all the privileges and immunities of the citizens of the several states?'[131]

As James Oakes has commented, '[d]ue process was widely regarded as one of the "privileges and immunities" of citizenship, so the demand that accused fugitives be guaranteed a jury trial was an implicit recognition of black citizenship'.[132] Moreover, in a trial with a jury of northerners opposed to slavery, it was not only the case that free blacks would be better guarded against rendition under a false claim that they were owned but also possible that individuals would be freed despite the fact that they were owned under the property rules of the South.

These legal issues brought the Union to the brink of the war which began the same year in which Lincoln delivered his address. That local enactments like personal liberty laws and litigation could have these results had of course everything to do with the fact that the legal issues implicated the existential moral problem of the Union – the tension between its constitutional commitments to 'blessings of liberty' and to the idea that there could be property in man. But that the moral issues were implicated as *legal* issues was politically significant, as can be illustrated by recalling Dworkin's distinction between 'legislative rights' which are 'rights that the community's lawmaking powers be exercised in a certain way' and 'legal rights' which are 'political rights, but a special branch because they are properly enforceable on demand through adjudicative and coercive institutions without need for further legislation or lawmaking activity'.[133]

The idea of enforceability 'on demand' is important because it specifies what is distinctive about the politics of legal space. Within that space, as long as legal officials exhibit what Fuller called an attitude of 'fidelity to law', those subject to law are entitled to be shown a legal warrant for the interpretation of the law on which an official acted.[134] The subject can ask the question 'But, how can that be law for me?' and is entitled to get an answer from an official independent from the one who acted.

The analysis above shows that the range of possible answers is restricted by the construction of the particular legal space in which the question is asked. In a state on the rule-of-law end of the legality continuum, the subjects can in principle get an answer which, while it

131 Ibid.
132 Ibid.
133 Dworkin, *Justice for Hedgehogs*, 407.
134 Lon L Fuller, 'Positivism and Fidelity to Law'.

may not always be what they want, and may even be one of which they morally disapprove, does not undermine their status as first-class citizens in the jural community. Such a state exists when its enacted law which draws distinctions between groups of peoples does so in ways which can be justified to individuals in those groups on the basis of the fundamental legal principles of the order.

In a Parallel State such as the combination of Israel with the Occupied Territories, because it is bound together by a *fiat* and not by fundamental principles, subjects in the OTLO are denied access to the fundamental legal principles in the ILO and so are governed by a system of enacted law enforced in accordance with principles of administrative law, though adapted to the context of military rule so as to make its subjects' interests subordinate to the military's sense of the demands of security. The jural community in this context is one which, as Hobbes said in *Leviathan*, preserves a 'bare Preservation' but not all the 'other Contentments of life' which, he argued, the 'safety of the people' required if they were to trade their obedience for their sovereign's protection.[135] Its members know that they do not own, to continue with Hobbes, the acts of their sovereign as if these were their acts. They have not fastened the artificial chains of the law from the sovereign's lips to their ears.[136] Those chains are imposed on them by a regime which looks increasingly like military conquest rather than temporary legal occupation, a phenomenon which the actions of the Supreme Court serve both to obscure and legitimize. Moreover, the spectre of the prerogative state hovers over the community since in almost any case in which the state invokes security considerations, the Supreme Court will defer. If, as Carl Schmitt said, 'The sovereign is he who decides on the exception',[137] this practice of the court maintains in an uneasy alliance a legal idea of sovereignty under the rule of law and a Schmittean idea of legally unlimited sovereignty, with the court providing a veneer of legality over the latter since it will decide when to defer to the military, even if its test is that it will usually defer whenever the military claims this is necessary.[138]

[135] Thomas Hobbes, *Leviathan* (Cambridge: Cambridge University Press, 1996, Richard Tuck, ed.), 231.

[136] Ibid, 147.

[137] Schmitt, *Political Theology*, 5.

[138] See Hassan Jabareen, 'Can the Court Normalize the Exception in Non-emergency Cases? Palestinian Cases before the Israeli Supreme Court' (2020) 18 *International Journal of Constitutional Law* 788. For examination of the problem of exception in the occupation, see Orna Ben-Naftali, Michael Sfard and Hedi Viterbo, *The ABC of the OPT: A Legal*

Finally, there is a way in which Palestinian subjects in this Parallel State are virtual second-class citizens in the legal sense sketched above, and which complicates my argument. The Israeli Supreme Court presides over a state – the ILO – in which there are first-class citizens, although the Palestinian citizens of Israel are in significant respects second-class citizens.[139] Within the Occupied Territories, while Palestinians are all subject to the same law, it is also the case that they live side by side with the Israeli settlers in the fortified enclaves which are illegal extensions of the Israeli state and subject to the protection of that state. Dramatic examples here are the separate systems of roads established by the Israeli Defence Forces for settlers and Palestinians, and the wall built to cut Palestinians off from contact with Israel and settler enclaves, as well in many cases from their means of livelihood.[140] Palestinians in the Occupied Territories are, that is, virtual second-class citizens because they live under an occupation which provides full status for settlers and an inferior status for them while the Supreme Court's jurisdiction over them gives them a toehold if not a foothold in the first-class space. But even that toehold is at best precarious since the court both offers and withdraws the protections of legality. It gives them procedural rights to contest official action, but at the same time narrows dramatically the substantive resources available for that contest. Indeed, it narrows them so dramatically that, as indicated, I would resist the argument that there now exists an Apartheid State since there is hardly even lip service to the ideal that all subjects are equal before the law.

This is in a way the converse of the situation under the Fugitive Slave Law of 1850 in which procedural rights were drastically reduced in order to block access to the substantive legal resources, albeit that these were deeply compromised. During the apartheid era, both strategies were used in particular laws – a reduction in procedural rights or a narrowing of substantive legal resources, or a combination of both. With the last, the situation of legal subjects became perilously close to pockets of

Lexicon of the Israeli Control over the Occupied Palestinian Territory (Cambridge: Cambridge University Press, 2018).

139 See Hassan Jabareen, 'Hobbesian Citizenship: How the Palestinians Became a Minority in Israel', in Will Kymlicka and Eva Pföstl, eds, *Multiculturalism and Minority Rights in the Arab World* (Oxford: Oxford University Press, 2014) 189.

140 See John Dugard and John Reynolds, 'Apartheid, International Law, and the Occupied Palestinian Territory' (2013) 24 *European Journal of International Law* 867; Hassan Jabareen, 'How the Law of Return Creates One Legal Order in Palestine' (2020) 21 *Theoretical Inquiries in Law* 459.

lawlessness within that example of a perverse Rule-of-Law State, perhaps akin to the situation of those individuals in whose matters Fraenkel achieved his victories between 1933 and 1938.

But still there was a difference in that the normative state in which Fraenkel's victories were won was contiguous with the prerogative state which was not an exception to the order of the normative state in the sense that apartheid laws created exceptions – often vast – to the fundamental legal principles of the Rule-of-Law State. Rather, as Fraenkel pointed out, the prerogative state was exceptional in that it was Schmitt's 'state of exception' writ large, a space unbounded by law in which those who wielded power were like the bounty hunters and federal commissioners who in the antebellum USA rendered people into a space of lawlessness, though the space was unlike the prerogative space of slavery in that it had no legal boundaries.[141]

In sum, legal contiguity matters to those who wish to use resources within the law to challenge particular laws or the actions of officials implementing those laws, and they find themselves at points on the continuum of legality between the rule-of-law and the extreme ends. That they can make the challenge as of right – on demand – depends not only on the resources of principle available within their own space but also on the contiguity of the law-created space within which they find themselves and which creates the problematic status they wish to contest with another law-created space which makes the first space legally as well as morally problematic.

Of course, physical contiguity also matters. Suppose that in the antebellum USA the North and the South fractured into independent states, which was in fact the threat the Union faced on the brink of the war as individual southern states either threatened secession or seceded. There would be extreme moral and political tensions about slavery which would arise from the fact that the North and the South shared a physical border, in just the way that such tensions were most intense between the actual

[141] The space of the Nazi prerogative state may have been legally more complex than is assumed in the text. See Herlinde Pauer-Studer and J David Velleman, *Konrad Morgen: The Conscience of a Nazi Judge* (London: Palgrave MacMillan, 2015), which describes the career of a legal official in the SS who, on discovering the existence of the extermination camps, began prosecuting with some success the officials who staffed the camps when they committed infractions of the SS military code. Morgen's view was that the mass killing was itself lawful, since it was being carried out by secret order of Hitler and the Enabling Act made lawful such an order, but the order did not affect 'ordinary' crimes committed by the SS in the camps.

northern and southern states that bordered each other in the antebellum period.[142]

The difference between this situation and that in the Union of both states is that in the latter the moral and political tensions manifest themselves legally in that judges have to answer conflicting claims of legal right which arise from within the domestic law of their own legal order, while in the former the tensions would arise from sheer physical contiguity. Moreover, in the former situation it matters more that the two states are firmly on the continuum of legality than that they share a physical border. For if they are both firmly on the continuum, as we can see from *Somerset's Case*, the moral tensions can become legal if an enslaved person either escapes to or is brought to a state which does not permit slavery. In such a case, as long as one adopts Mansfield's premise in his dictum in *Somerset's Case*, the application of the property rule of the slave-owning state is defeated by the legal norm of the other state which does not allow the law of slavery to reach into its space.

The more abstract point at stake here is that these two states, because they are *legal* states, are legally contiguous, whether or not they are physically contiguous, because of the international dimension of private international law. The difference physical contiguity makes is only that it is more likely that these moral problems will arise as legal problems. Similarly, the norms of public international law apply to states because that body of law binds them together as states subject to the same rule of law without regard to their physical location.

Both public and private international law thus make vivid for all legal states a phenomenon which was perhaps uniquely vivid in the antebellum USA. Dworkin's distinction between legal and legislative rights is of the utmost importance because it focuses attention on the way in which legal rights exist as a matter of demand within the institutional structure within which they are asserted. In contrast, legislative rights are rights which get contested in the domain of debate over what legislation ought to be enacted in order to make a society better off. They only become legal rights once the legislature has enacted them into its positive law. But if legislative rights in state A are legal rights in state B, and A and B are legally contiguous, the ties of legality between A and B – what unites them as *legal* states – will raise the question whether the legal rights of A must be interpreted in light of the relevant legal rights of B. Similarly,

142 For discussion of the particular tensions which arose in states on the borders between the North and the South, see Oakes, *Freedom National.*

in the international legal order certain norms, while not of the status of *jus cogens*, are nevertheless considered *erga omnes* – obligations owed to all – and thus hierarchically superior to customary international law.[143] While the status of such norms is controversial, their existence along with *jus cogens* norms as well as the norms of customary international law raise legal questions about what rights obtain in any national order, whether or not that state is in practice monistic or has explicitly assented to or incorporated the obligation.

5.4 The Politics of Recognition Again

In *The Occupation of Justice*, a pioneering study of the legal regime created by Israel's occupation, David Kretzmer comments that it is 'fair to assume . . . that a further reason [for creating the Parallel State] could well have been that petitions to the Supreme Court of Israel by residents of the Occupied Territories would imply the recognition of Israel by the petitioners, as well as political legitimization of Israeli rule over the Territories'.[144] Whether or not this reason motivated Shamgar, the implication is built into the structure of the Parallel State and its instantiation in this context. But it is also built into the structure of the modern legal state, if, as I just suggested, all such states are hybrid.

Recall from Section 4.6 the debate in public international law between the 'declaratory theory', which argues that recognition of an entity as a state merely confirms its legal status, and the 'constitutive theory', which argues that an entity which aspires to legal statehood requires the recognition of other states. The 'politics of recognition' is inherent in the legal constitution of space and a decision to enter that space entails subjecting oneself to the authority of its legal norms and thus to accepting their legitimacy.

The Palestinian inhabitants of the Occupied Territories did not make such a decision. It was foisted on them by the Israeli state. But to the extent that they choose the path of legal resistance to the occupation, they opt for the politics of legal struggle, not armed illegal struggle, and that

[143] See Stefan Kadelbach, '*Jus Cogens*, Obligations *Erga Omnes* and Other Rules: The Identification of Fundamental Norms', in Christian Tomuschat and Jean-Marc Thouvenin, eds, *The Fundamental Rules of the International Legal Order: Jus Cogens and Obligations Erga Omnes* (Leiden: Martinus Nijhoff Publishers, 2005) 21.

[144] See Kretzmer, *The Occupation of Justice*, 19–20. On the practice of human rights lawyering within the OTLO, see Michael Sfard, *The Wall and the Gate: Israel, Palestine, and the Legal Battle for Human Rights* (New York: Metropolitan Books, 2018).

choice is, on my argument, one which implies acceptance of legitimacy. For an individual to resile from the order of modern legal state is to take up, as Hobbes tells us, a relationship of hostility with the state, just as for a state to resile from the international legal order is to forego juridical relationships with all other states, which need not henceforth treat it as a legally speaking equal member of their jural community. In both cases, the individual or the state resile at the same time from the laws of nature of which Hobbes said are the 'true and onely Moral Philosophy. For Moral Philosophy is nothing else but the Science of what is *Good*, and *Evill*, in the conversation, and Society of man-kind.'[145]

This idea of a conversation about good and evil within a community will seem of course ominous, as I acknowledged in Chapter 4. The discourse between 'civilized' members of the jural community of modern legal states became a justificatory basis for imperialism and colonialism. If Hobbes's laws of nature, or the idea of fundamental principles of legality, are no more than the principles which justified the power grab by Western nation states, the legacy of which still bedevils our world today, then the rule of law is no more than a veneer over naked power. The same problem occurs with the space or spaces of the modern legal state. To accept to play by the politics of legal space within the modern legal state is to subject oneself to the political power of its elites.

But, as I have argued throughout, the acceptance is not of unmediated power. It is acceptance of power mediated by law where law means both enacted or positive law and fundamental principles of legality. Moreover, there is the legal subject and the question 'But, how can that be law for me?' That issue reaches a heightened political intensity when at stake is whether there is an entity which meets the criteria for full membership of a jural community, whether the jural community of states or the jural community of subjects within a state.

In the discussion of this issue as it pertains to states in Chapter 4, we saw that the political stakes were lowered somewhat by the move away from the Western 'civilizational' standard to the more factual criteria set out in the Montevideo Convention. But as we also saw, there can be no solution by brute facts as in the Convention's Article 1: 'a permanent population'; 'a defined territory'; 'government'; and 'capacity to enter into relations with other states'. Such facts don't become relevant as legal facts until they have been characterized as such by an authoritative institution,

[145] Hobbes, *Leviathan*, 110.

which makes the characterization of entities as states or human individuals political as well as legal. Nevertheless, the facts do make for a stabilizing element. There is, as the great German jurist Georg Jellinek put it, a 'normative force to the factual'.[146]

I want to suggest that when it comes to the recognition of human individuals as full legal persons or first-class citizens there is an analogue, indeed an easier one than in the case of the factual elements of statehood. It is, simply put, looking like a human: *Ecce Homo* or 'Behold the Man', the title of the painting on my cover. I rely here on the philosopher Avishai Margalit who argues that '[m]oral honour has only one dimension – horizontal. It is respect accorded to all humans, even to the obnoxious cruel criminals, or to the miserably retarded' and that the 'trait in which humans deserve moral respect is their being human, nothing more and nothing less'.[147] Respect is due, in his terms, because we humans are 'icons' of each other: 'The human trait that provides justification for according respect to each and every human being is that each and every human being is capable of standing in an iconic relation to all humans.'[148] Further, 'it is our human body that makes us capable of standing in iconic relations to other humans. The iconic relation is a mixture of natural history and normative exercise, but whatever it is, it makes morality go round.'[149]

In the context of my argument, the last sentence should be adapted to 'the iconic relation is a mixture of natural history and normative exercise, but whatever it is, it makes legality go round', so that in law, as in morality, 'the idea of horizontal respect is that each human being, no matter of what shape or colour or age, can stand in an iconic relation to the rest of humanity'.[150] When a political elite deploys positive law to disturb that relationship, it will find that its exercise of power is mediated by law, both positive law and fundamental principles of legality, and also by the requirement that legal officials be able to answer the legal subject's question 'But, how can that be law for me?' For the relationship is no more, but also no less, than the one in which first-class citizens stand to each other. With that disturbance, the subject has standing to require a

146 Jellinek, *Allgemeine Staatslehre*, 330.

147 Avishai Margalit, 'Human Dignity between Kitsch and Deification', in Christopher Cordner, ed., *Philosophy, Ethics and a Common Humanity: Essays in Honour of Raimond Gaita* (Abingdon: Routledge, 2011) 106, at 108, 118.

148 Ibid.

149 Ibid, 119.

150 Ibid.

justification.[151] And here we can note that Hermann Heller, one of the leading public lawyers and legal theorists of Weimar, argued that Jellinek's insight into the normative force of the factual must be matched with another, that there is a factual force to the normative – the 'power formative character of law'.[152]

But even if my argument is correct that such legal mediation makes a moral difference, it is still a difference within the confines of the law. As Michael Sfard argues in his book on practising human rights law in the Occupied Territories, regime change cannot be an aim of human rights lawyers because they accept the limits the law imposes on their practice.[153] Not only do their losses in court help to shore up the legitimacy of the regime but also their occasional victories, because the latter support the authorities' claim to be ruling in accordance with the rule of law. That fact has made Sfard and others wonder whether they should discontinue their practice because overall the calculus is that they do more harm than good. But they find themselves unable to give up because the victims of the oppressive regime turn to them for help.

There is another reason for continuing. The experience of human rights lawyers in apartheid South Africa looms large in Sfard's

[151] In his main essay on the rule of law, Raz argues that FA Hayek's claims on behalf of the principle of generality lead to an 'absurdity' which Hayek tried to modify by suggesting that while distinctions will be made by law between groups, these distinctions will not be arbitrary if justified. See Joseph Raz, 'The Rule of Law and Its Virtue', 226–7, criticizing Hayek, *The Constitution of Liberty* (Chicago: University of Chicago Press, 1960), 153–4. Raz suggests ('The Rule of Law and Its Virtue', 227) that Hayek here transforms the rule of law 'to encompass a form of government by consent and it is this which is alleged to guarantee freedom. This is the slippery slope leading to the identification of the rule of law with the rule of good law.' Raz is correct in that all of this is entailed by Hayek's theory of the rule of law with its emphasis on the importance of generality. What Raz fails to see is that precisely all of this is part and parcel of a theory of law as a matter of authority, and his failure is entirely due to the fact his 'exclusive legal positivism' reinstates Austin's model of law, a point I will elaborate in Appendix I. Once we see this, we can also understand why Raz's attempt to strip Fuller's principles of legality of their moral quality fails. For an excellent treatment of the tensions internal to Raz's argument against Fuller, see Rundle, 'Form and Agency in Raz's Legal Positivism'.

[152] Hermann Heller, *Staatslehre*, in Heller, *Gesammelte Schriften*, vol. 3 (Tübingen: JCB Mohr, 1992, Christoph Müller, ed.) 92, at 393–5. For my translation of part of this posthumously published and unfinished project, see Hermann Heller, 'The Nature and Structure of the State' (1996) 18 *Cardozo Law Review* 1139, at 1214–16. Heller, who died in 1933 aged forty-two, is hardly known outside of Germany. I return to his legal theory at the end of Chapter 6.

[153] Sfard, *The Wall and the Gate*, especially the concluding chapter, 'Sand on the Slope'.

understanding.[154] On the last page of his book, he asserts that 'one day the occupation will end, like apartheid in South Africa' and when it does 'we'll find that we are not entirely bereft of a culture of good government, that we do have moral foundations to draw on'. That provides the reason why 'human rights lawyers must hold their heads high and know that they have a role in the appearance of cracks in the occupation'.[155]

Sfard does not note that just such a culture of good government was the basis for constitutionalism in post-apartheid South Africa and has proved of the utmost importance at a time when trust in government is low, because of widespread corruption and incompetence which has infected all levels during a decade of 'state capture'. The human rights lawyers of the apartheid era maintained the idea that the law embodied an ideal of the unity of the people which transcended the political divisions of the day, and which was worth struggling for against the odds. It is significant that the roots of such struggle go back to the turn of the last century, to the commitment to an ideal of constitutionalism which profoundly informed the practice of the founders of South Africa's main liberation movement, the African National Congress.[156]

Without the example of a few cases in which the judges upheld fundamental principles of legality, there would have been no basis for these lawyers' practice. The ideal for which they strove required them to adopt the regulative assumption in the ideal just sketched. Such an assumption does not aim to reflect all the brute facts about the world. It seeks instead to shape the world by engaging in a practice that builds on some elements in it in order to make the world live up to the ideal which informs the assumption. I argued in Chapter 3 that it is this kind of idea which Kelsen was after when he asserted that jurists must hypothesize a basic norm if they are to make sense of legal order as a unified order of norms.

There is an element of choice in the 'if', as there is in the decision to be a human rights lawyer in an unjust regime, or for a political entity to struggle on substantively unequal terms to join the system of modern legal states. Similarly, for some political entities, for example Indigenous

[154] Ibid, 443–4 and 447–8.

[155] Ibid, 455.

[156] See my 'The African National Congress and the Birth of Constitutionalism' (2020) 18 *International Journal of Constitutional Law* 284, reviewing Tembeka Ngcukaitobi, *The Land Is Ours: South Africa's First Black Lawyers and the Birth of Constitutionalism* (Cape Town: Penguin, 2018) and Bongani Ngqulunga, *The Man Who Founded the ANC: A Biography of Pixley ka Isaka Seme* (Cape Town: Penguin, 2017).

nations which cannot aspire to be modern legal states and may have good reason in any case not to entertain such an aspiration, there are difficult choices to be made about how and to what extent to participate in the legal spaces of the state in which they find themselves or in the space of the international legal order.

Here we should recall that in the early 1960s the leaders of the African National Congress, most notably Nelson Mandela, turned to armed struggle because the legal space for oppositional politics had been severely constricted by the apartheid regime, a turn which reflected similar decisions made by other political leaders in the course of the struggle for self-determination in the postwar period. However, at least in the case of the African National Congress, the ideal of constitutionalism and the rule of law continued to animate their activity, as it did the activity of those who chose to continue the struggle within the space afforded by the fact that South Africa remained for the most part an Apartheid State. In Chapter 6, I turn to set out a complete sketch of the political legal theory which can explain why the legal order of the modern legal state holds out an indelible and substantive promise to its subjects at the same time, as Hart reminds us, that the 'centrally organized power' it gathers 'may well be used for the oppression of numbers with whose support it can dispense'.[157]

[157] Hart, *The Concept of Law*, 202.

6

Legality's Promise

In this chapter, I bring together the themes explored in the preceding chapters. In particular, I elaborate the main implication of Dworkin's remark in the manuscript version of *Justice for Hedgehogs* that it would be counterintuitive to think that 'most of the subjects of most of the political communities over history had no moral duty to obey the laws of their community'.[1] As I suggested at the end of Chapter 1, the implication is that the moral record of the law of a society, the fund of values in fact established over time, amounts to what Hobbes told us is 'the publique Conscience, by which . . . [the subject] hath already undertaken to be guided'.[2]

'Moral' in this formulation is, however, subject to at least three interpretations. First, it could mean the values which a particular society happens to take as moral in that they were considered important enough to be legislated or otherwise made into law. That interpretation is consistent with HLA Hart's insistence that 'the idea of a moral legislature with competence to make and change morals, as legal enactments make and change law, is repugnant to the whole notion of morality'.[3] It is consistent, that is, with the thought that what Hart called 'critical

[1] Quoted in Susanne Sreedhar and Candace Delmas, 'State Legitimacy and Political Obligation in *Justice for Hedgehogs*: The Radical Potential of Dworkinian Dignity' (2010) 90 *Boston University Law Review* 737, at 746. In his initial response to this paper, given at the symposium on the manuscript of *Justice for Hedgehogs*, Dworkin said that the legitimacy of a legal order is 'a matter of degree' and that while it is possible to say in the abstract what a perfectly legitimate government would be, one that treats all citizens in accordance with the best moral conception of equal concern and respect, it is 'harder to state a floor beneath which any purported government is wholly illegitimate'. See www.bu.edu/law/journals-archive/bulr/documents/dworkin_r.pdf. Unfortunately, this more nuanced view did not make it into the published versions of either his response or the book.

[2] Thomas Hobbes, *Leviathan* (Cambridge: Cambridge University Press, 1996, Richard Tuck, ed.), 223.

[3] HLA Hart, *The Concept of Law* (Oxford: Clarendon Press, 1994, 2nd ed.) 175, 177.

morality' – 'the general moral principles used in the criticism of actual social institutions including positive morality'[4] – might condemn the values in the public record, but still one should suppose that there is a duty to obey the law. For example, one could make the exclusively prudential argument mistakenly attributed to Hobbes that any order is better than disorder.

Hart's insistence is, however, inconsistent with a second interpretation of 'moral' – with the apparently relativistic thought that there is no more to morality than the values in the contingently established legal record of a society. On this view, legal subjects should obey the law not for content-independent reasons – reasons apart from the content of the law – but because of the moral content the law contingently has. Surely, any liberal position must join Hart in finding this view repugnant?

Dworkin was a staunch defender and leading articulator of liberal ideals. However, he seemed to adopt this second interpretation when, as we saw in Chapter 1, he declared it a mistake for legal theory, one he himself had made, to engage in an exercise of bridge-building between 'two different intellectual domains' or 'systems': (1) law, which 'belongs to a particular community'; and (2) morality, which does not, because 'it consists of a set of standards that have imperative force for everyone'. Law, on this mistaken view, is 'made by human beings' and it is a contingent fact what its content is, whereas morality is 'not made by anyone . . . and it is not contingent on any human decision or practice'.[5] Hence, he suggested that we should replace the 'two-systems' picture of legal theory with a 'one-system picture'.[6] 'Legal rights are political rights, but a special branch because they are properly enforceable on demand through adjudicative and coercive institutions without need for further legislation or lawmaking activity'.[7] His rejection of a dualistic account of the relationship between law and morality seems, that is, to imply that morality is made by human beings in the same way as they make law. Did he as a result also accept that the content of morality is, like that of law, contingent, and that the idea of a moral legislature with competence to

4 HLA Hart, *Law, Liberty and Morality* (Oxford: Oxford University Press, 1981) 20. These terms were deployed in Hart's debate with Lord Devlin about the legal enforcement of morals, but he relied on the same ideas in his legal theory.

5 Ronald Dworkin, *Justice for Hedgehogs* (Cambridge, MA: Belknap Press, 2011), 412.

6 Ibid, 402.

7 Ibid, 407.

make and change morals is not repugnant to the whole notion of morality?

In this chapter, I defend this implication of a one-system legal theory, though my defence seeks to allay the liberal concern about dangerous moral relativism by setting out a third interpretation of 'moral', one I argue Hart went a long way to endorsing. My response to the liberal concern continues the argument of the book as a whole that one goes wrong in assuming that the issue at stake can be reduced to one about the content of positive law. The reduction leaves out that there is more to law than positive law, in Latin *lex* and in German *Gesetz*; namely, it leaves out *jus* or *Recht* as these other languages describe fundamental principles of legality. Positive law can only be made in a legal order and in such an order the discipline of such principles conditions its content.

Put differently, the concern, at least in Hart's hands, stems from legal positivism's exclusive focus on positive law, which does not, it turns out, even account for the role of such law in legal order. For the content of the positive law of a legal order is answerable to the experience of the subjects who live under its rule. It is this answerability which makes the conception of morality presupposed by a theory of law's authority defensible and it is best articulated by the philosophical tradition of pragmatism. I will not, however, offer anything like a full defence of the pragmatist account of morality, only that it is the conception of morality one should adopt if one wishes to explain law in the register of authority.

In this way, I can follow through on my support for the 'strong reading' of Hans Kelsen's theory of legal authority – one which makes the legal subject a participant in the constitution of authority. We have seen that Kelsen's constitutionalist idea in the basic norm is far from being, as Hart claimed, redundant to the explanation of the authority of law. Rather, it is a regulative assumption, a claim about inquiry and what those engaged in inquiry must assume, if their inquiry is into the authority of law.[8] As such, the idea has both theoretical and practical dimensions.

As a matter of theory, it requires an elaboration of authority as legitimate or de jure authority and attention to the way in which the relationship between those who wield authority and those subject to it can be said to be one of right rather than might. As a matter of practice, it requires attention to the way in which, in the light of legal subjects'

[8] See Cheryl Misak, *The American Pragmatists* (Oxford: Oxford University Press, 2013), 50–2, at 51, discussing the idea, central to CS Peirce's pragmatism, of 'abductive inference'.

experience of law, legal order is and should be designed with a view to vindicating its intrinsic commitment to the rule of law and its concomitant commitment to constitutionalism.

But why must both these requirements be in place? The answer is in Hart's assertion in 1958 that '[l]aw surely is not the gunman situation writ large'[9] and in his analysis in *The Concept of Law* of the authority elements of legal order which support the claim that a philosophical inquiry into law is primarily an inquiry into the authority of law. A strike against the idea of law as a matter of coercion is that one's legal theory would have to reduce the authority elements to others, as in the command theory of law, which, as Hart argued, makes the theory implausible at least because judges and other legal officials must operate in the register of authority.

The coercive elements of legal order are no less real and irreducible. Hence, a theory of law which acknowledges their place without attempting to reduce them away is a better theory than one which negates them. However, theories of law as a matter of authority need not reduce the coercive elements of law to anything else. Rather, they relegate the coercive elements to a secondary position. Law's primary mode is to address legal subjects in the register of authority, and coercion is necessary only to provide the addressees with the assurance that they will not fall prey to those who reject the claim of right. Put differently, coercion is there to ensure that potential non-compliers will be brought into line by threat of sanctions. Hence, if law seems irreducibly composed of both authority and coercion elements, a theory which can account for both in a non-reductive way is superior to one which cannot.

The issue here is not only what we can think of as descriptive superiority – the ability to explain more of the elements of the object of the inquiry than rival theories. There are also normative issues at stake. Recall that Hart claimed that the positivist 'wider' concept of law is superior to a natural law 'narrow' conception because it permits the study of the complex moral issues raised by iniquitous laws in a way the latter cannot; for example, the question of obedience to immoral law or the question faced by the postwar German courts who had to decide whether to punish the Grudge Informers when doing so would require violating the principle against retroactive punishment: 'A concept of law

9 HLA Hart, 'Positivism and the Separation of Law and Morals', in Hart, *Essays in Jurisprudence and Philosophy* (Oxford: Clarendon Press, 1983) 49, at 59.

which allows the invalidity of law to be distinguished from its immorality, enables us to see the complexity and variety of these separate issues; whereas a narrow concept of law which denies validity to iniquitous rules may blind us to them.'[10]

A concept of law which can respond to moral complexity is of course better than one that cannot. But I have argued from Chapter 1 that Hart's positivism does not do so well on this dimension precisely because of the way in which his static theory narrows the inquiry. He treated most of his examples of complexity as if the problem were created by a law with a determinate unjust content which a subject must consider obeying or a judge applying. He thus excluded from the scope of legal philosophical inquiry the question of how judges and other officials should interpret a law when faced with a situation in which it seems to require a very unjust result. This exclusion is in tension with Hart's own emphasis on judges as officials who regard the law as working in the register of authority, as well as with his claim that they should display the virtues he sketched.

I argue here that the 'complex congruent practice'[11] constitutive of the authority of the modern legal state requires that the legal order be seen as affording a 'laboratory' for working out the content of the morality of the society ruled by its law. That morality is the fund of the society's values which have been transformed in the process of juridical production into law. Acceptance, by both officials and legal subjects, is of the transformation process as appropriate for establishing a public record of the values – the public conscience of the law. The process is, as I indicated in Chapter 3, the equivalent of an actual social contract. But it is a constantly renewed contract because the legal order is dynamic not static and provides to its subjects the opportunity to ask 'But, how can that be law for me?' This is a question invited by the institutional structure of legal order. Attempts to answer it may require new interpretations of the law, changes to positive law and even reforms to the transformation process if no satisfactory answer to the question can be determined.

In Section 6.1, I revisit Radbruch to show that Hart did not so much reject Radbruchian natural law theory as reinvent it in a way he thought could preserve the Separation Thesis. Since that move made his position contradictory, the question arises why the Separation Thesis has such an

[10] Hart, *The Concept of Law*, 210–11, at 211.
[11] Ibid, 118.

influence on philosophy of law, despite the denials of Hart's followers that they or Hart himself ever propounded it. The explanation offered by my account so far is twofold.

First, there is the fact that Dworkin's main response to the problem of very unjust law failed. Second, any rejection of the Separation Thesis seems to require accepting Hobbes's claim that the law is a public conscience so that legal subjects should obey the law because of the content it contingently has. I suggest that only a pragmatic account of morality can justify Hobbes's claim and allow legal theory to shed the blinkers imposed by the Separation Thesis, which it must do if the deadlock between legal positivism and natural law is to be broken; and Section 6.2 sketches such account based mainly on chapter 8 of *The Concept of Law*.

Section 6.3 sets out the place of the account in the political legal theory which explains the legitimate authority of the modern legal state in terms of the 'Basic Legitimation Demand' we saw articulated by Bernard Williams in my Chapter 3: the demand which every legitimate state must satisfy if it is to show that it wields authority rather than sheer coercive power over those subject to its rule.[12] I argue that law's authority is always only provisional, at most a punctuation point in a process of juridical production in an autonomous legal sphere.[13]

I conclude with a sketch of how the book as a whole explains legality's promise by focusing in Section 6.4 on the idea mentioned in the Introduction of the 'individual legal conscience'. I focus, that is, on the appropriate stance of one subject to the law of a modern legal state. The state must do more than recognize the subject as a person to be addressed with 'dignity as a responsible agent'.[14] It must also accept that such address requires recognizing the priority of the individual legal conscience; and that returns me to the issues discussed at the end of Chapters 4 and 5 – the politics of recognition of states in the international legal order and of legal subjects within national orders.

12 Bernard Williams, 'Realism and Moralism in Political Theory', in Williams, *In the Beginning Was the Deed: Realism and Moralism in Political Argument* (Princeton: Princeton University Press, 2005, Geoffrey Hawthorn, ed.) 1, at 15. His emphasis.

13 For this way of formulating the point, see Cheryl Misak, 'A Pragmatist Account of Legitimacy and Authority', in David Rondel and Susan Dieleman, eds, *Pragmatism and Justice* (Oxford: Oxford University Press, 2017) 295, at 306.

14 Lon L Fuller, *The Morality of Law* (New Haven: Yale University Press, 1969, revised ed.), 162.

6.1 Radbruch Revisited

We saw in Chapter 1 that Hart thought that Radbruch, because of his experience of Nazism, had recanted his prewar commitment to legal positivism and embraced a natural law position. In 'Positivism and the Separation of Law and Morals', Hart described this position as follows:

> [Radbruch's] ... considered reflections led him to the doctrine that the fundamental principles of humanitarian morality were part of the very concept of *Recht* or Legality and that no positive enactment or statute, however clearly it was expressed and however clearly it conformed with the formal criteria of validity of a given legal system, could be valid if it contravened basic principles of morality.[15]

Hart added that this 'doctrine can be appreciated fully only if the nuances imported by the German word *Recht* are grasped'.[16] He had in mind the distinction English elides between enacted law or *Gesetz* and *Recht* with its connotation of legal right. But, as I noted, he did not think it worthwhile to explore the nuances in this part of his essay because of the 'stark nonsense' and 'extraordinary naïvety' demonstrated by such natural law positions.[17]

While Radbruch was the direct target of Hart's harsh criticism in this part of the essay, Fuller was at least collateral damage. Fuller was Hart's main interlocutor during his visit in 1957 to Harvard which prompted their exchange in the *Harvard Law Review*, and the whole of Hart's 1958 essay appears carefully structured to nip in the bud the jurisprudential position Fuller was developing, though Hart mentioned Fuller in the text only at the very end. It is Fuller's account of adjudication which Hart saw in part III of the essay as providing the challenge to the Separation Thesis, because Fuller adopted the premise that such adjudication is based on values, while denying that the action takes place in what Hart termed a 'penumbra' of discretion.[18] In addition, it was Fuller's early hints that there is an internal morality to law with which law must comply which preoccupied Hart in part V on the legality of legal order.[19]

15 Hart, 'Positivism and the Separation of Law and Morals', 74.

16 Ibid.

17 Ibid, 75, 74.

18 Ibid, 68–71.

19 See Fuller's first discussion of 'The Problem of the Inconsiderate Sovereign', in Lon L Fuller, *The Law in Quest of Itself* (Boston: Beacon Press, 1940), 34–41. Hart, 'Positivism and the Separation of Law and Morals', 50, note 3.

Finally, it was Fuller's early critique of legal positivism which disturbed Hart. When Hart began his defence of the Separation Thesis by portraying legal positivism as under attack for its tendencies to blind 'men to the true nature of law and its roots in social life', to be 'corrupting in practice', 'as its worst apt to weaken resistance to state tyranny or absolutism', 'at its best apt to bring law into disrepute',[20] he could cite as evidence for this proposition only two postwar essays by Radbruch[21] and a work on legal theory by Wolfgang Friedmann.[22] When it came to positions which generally contest the Separation Thesis, Hart could find only three:[23] Fuller's book *The Law in Quest of Itself* and a short essay by him,[24] AP d'Entrèves's classic *Natural Law*[25] and a short philosophical essay by Arnold Brecht in the 1942 *Harvard Law Review*.[26]

However, Brecht's essay barely mentioned legal positivism, as it is a critique of the distinction between 'is' and 'ought' in general philosophy. And while Fuller and d'Entrèves did discuss legal positivism, they were

[20] Ibid, 50–1.

[21] Hart refers, ibid, 50, note 5, to Gustav Radbruch, 'Die Erneuerung des Rechts', 1947, and 'Gesetzliches Unrecht und Übergesetzliches Recht', 1946. The latter is translated as 'Statutory Lawlessness and Supra-Statutory Law' (2006) 26 *Oxford Journal of Legal Studies* 1 (Bonnie Litschewski Paulson and Stanley L Paulson, trans.).

[22] Hart, 'Positivism and the Separation of Law and Morals', 50, note 4, cited Wolfgang Friedmann, *Legal Theory* (London: Stevens and Sons, 1953, 3rd ed.), 154, 294–5. But 154 was a criticism of Austin's distinction between law as it is and law as it ought to be when it amounts to the 'denial that legal ideals were of any concern to the lawyer', while 294–5 made basically the same point. Hart's footnote goes on to pour scorn on Friedmann for asserting, at 416 and 163, that Austin's legal positivism was both cause and product of the rise of a national state able to 'assert its authority undisturbed by juristic doubts'. But there is no contradiction in a claim that an ideology could not have been born but for certain political conditions which the ideology then helped to take hold and become stronger. For an excellent account of Friedmann, with the bonus of an account of Radbruch, see John Bell, 'Wolfgang Friedmann (1907–1972), with an Excursus on Gustav Radbruch (1878–1949)', in Jack Beatson and Reinhardt Zimmermann, eds, *Jurists Uprooted: German-Speaking Émigré Lawyers in Twentieth-Century Britain* (New York: Oxford University Press, 2004) 517.

[23] Hart, 'Positivism and the Separation of Law and Morals', 49–50.

[24] Lon L Fuller, 'Human Purpose and Natural Law', cited by Hart as (1956) 53 *Journal of Philosophy* 697, but referred to here in its reprint in (1958) 3 *Natural Law Forum* 68. Hart, 'Positivism and the Separation of Law and Morals', 49, note 2.

[25] AP d'Entrèves, *Natural Law: An Introduction to Legal Philosophy* (London: Hutchinson's University Library, 1951). In 'Positivism and the Separation of Law and Morals', 49, note 2, Hart refers to the second edition of 1952, 116.

[26] Arnold Brecht, 'The Myth of Is and Ought' (1941) 54 *Harvard Law Review* 811. See Hart, 'Positivism and the Separation of Law and Morals', 50, note 3, where Brecht is referred to as 'Brech'.

not in the business of, as Hart alleged, using 'legal positivism' as 'terms are as missiles in intellectual battles', and thus 'to stand for a baffling multitude of different sins'.[27] Rather, their books contain measured discussions of figures they took to be important to the positivist tradition – Hobbes, Bentham and Austin – and principally of the figure who was at that point the leading philosophical exponent of legal positivism in the twentieth century: Hans Kelsen.

When it came to Kelsen, these authors made the following point, one I have elaborated in the preceding pages. Kelsen was drawn to finding a basis for law's authority in a norm which transcends positive law and which brings his position closer to a natural law one. But he then shied away from developing this basis, which left him with the claims that there is no more to law than positive law and that positive law in and of itself has authority over those subject to it. It is precisely the conjunction of these two claims which d'Entrèves thought landed legal positivism with the unwelcome conclusion that might makes right,[28] that is, with the position Hart diagnosed as one of the traps into which natural law positions fall.[29]

It is also worth noting that, other than Fuller, all these scholars were like Ernst Fraenkel in that they had had direct experience of totalitarianism. D'Entrèves fought as a partisan in his native Italy during the Second World War.[30] Friedmann practised as a private lawyer in Germany, then as a labour court judge, until forced as a Jew to leave his post in 1934. Radbruch had been minister of justice in the Social Democratic government in the early years of the Weimar Republic and was forced into retirement from his academic position in 1933. Brecht held various senior positions in the German civil service from 1910 to 1927, and appeared for Prussia in the landmark case in 1932 when the right-wing federal government mounted a coup against the Socialist-dominated, Prussian government, thus preparing the way for the Nazi seizure of

[27] Ibid, 50–1.

[28] Fuller, *The Law in Quest of Itself*, 66–77; d'Entrèves, *Natural Law*, 110–11.

[29] Hart, 'Positivism and the Separation of Law and Morals', 53–4.

[30] He claimed in a letter to Fuller in the wake of the debate in the *Harvard Law Review* that while positivism had prevailed in Italy it would be 'absurd to make it responsible for Fascism', while in Germany lawyers did tend to take the slogan 'law is law' 'as an adequate, a sufficient, and indeed a metaphysical ground of obligation itself'. Quoted in Nicola Lacey, 'Out of the Witches' Cauldron: Reinterpreting the Context and Reassessing the Significance of the Hart–Fuller Debate', in Peter Cane, ed., *The Hart–Fuller Debate in the Twenty-First Century* (Oxford: Hart Publishing, 2010) 1, at 39.

power.[31] These were not men likely to be guilty of the 'extraordinary naïvety' of which Hart accused the natural law tradition.[32]

Moreover, not only did Hart set up something of a straw man in order to make his argument. He also structured the argument in such way as to divide his natural law foils into compartments in which he could more easily dismiss the components of their positions.[33] We saw in my Chapter 1 that Hart sought to drive a final nail home in the coffin of Radbruch's position through showing the bad consequences of the adoption of the Radbruch Formula in the Grudge Informer Case. But only in the next part – part V – did Hart proceed to discuss the nuances of legality, which he treated as if it were a distinct topic.

This was a consequential deferral. As I have pointed out, Hart's argument depends on robbing Radbruch's position of its nuances by conceiving it as positivism with a minus sign: the law of a legal order is its statically conceived positive law, as certified by the criteria of legal validity in its most fundamental rules, minus those positive laws which we judge to be extremely unjust by the standards of a moral position external to the law. If this were correct, Radbruch would differ from Hart only in that Hart says that citizens should disobey extremely unjust laws, while for Radbruch there is no issue of disobedience to law since there is no law to be disobeyed. Radbruch's position would in fact lead to the dire confusions which Hart diagnosed and which can be avoided only if we 'speak plainly' and say 'that laws may be law but too evil to be obeyed'.[34]

But Hart was not responding to Radbruch's actual position, as one can tell from the translation of the key passage in which Radbruch is taken to state the formula and in which I have inserted the variations on *Recht* where the reader might otherwise infer that 'law' is being used in the sense of *Gesetz*:

[31] Hart, 'Positivism and the Separation of Law and Morals', 74. For discussion of the case and its significance, see my 'Legal Theory in the Collapse of Weimar: Contemporary Lessons?' (1997) 91 *American Political Science Review* 121.

[32] Hart, 'Positivism and the Separation of Law and Morals', 74. D'Entréves wrote to Fuller that he shared his 'feelings about Hart's "strokes of the oar." I confess that in both hearing and reading his strictures on Radbruch [. . .] I could not help feeling sorry for the incurable smugness of our English friends".' Lacey, 'Out of the Witches' Cauldron', 22.

[33] For discussion of this strategy in Hart's responses to Fuller's more developed position, see Jeremy Waldron, 'Positivism and Legality: Hart's Equivocal Response to Fuller' (2008) 83 *New York University Law Review* 1135.

[34] Hart, 'Positivism and the Separation of Law and Morals', 77.

> The conflict between justice [*Gerechtigkeit*] and legal certainty [*Rechtssicherheit*] may well be resolved in this way: The positive law [*Recht*], secured by statutory enactment and power, takes precedence even when its content is unjust [*ungerecht*] and fails to benefit the people, unless the conflict between statute and justice [*Gerechtigkeit*] reaches such an intolerable degree that the statute, as 'flawed law' [*unrichtiges Recht*], must yield to justice. It is impossible to draw a sharper line between cases of statutory lawlessness [*Unrechts*] and statutes which are valid despite their unjust content [*trotz unrichtigen Inhalts*]. One line of distinction, however, can be drawn with utmost clarity: Where there is not even an attempt at justice [*Gerechtigkeit*], where equality, the core of justice [*Gerechtigkeit*], is deliberately betrayed in the enactment of positive law [*Rechts*], then the statute is not merely 'flawed law', [*unrichtiges Recht*] it lacks completely the very nature of law [*Rechtsnatur*]. For law, including positive law [*positives Recht*], cannot be otherwise defined than as a system and an institution whose very meaning is to serve justice [*Gerechtigkeit*].[35]

Discussion of this passage is often preoccupied with the question whether it contains two distinct formulas, the first having to do with the tricky issue of whether enacted law has a content so extremely unjust that it cannot be considered law, the second with enacted law which explicitly states its commitment to injustice of a kind which clearly betrays law's 'core' mission of protecting equality, in which the law clearly fails to be law. But attention to Radbruch's use of *Recht*, set in the context of his discussion which immediately precedes it, provides a sound basis for supposing both that there are not two parts and that he did not intend his position to be formulaic.

When Radbruch complained that positivistic legal thinking had dominated lawyers in Nazi Germany, he had in mind a position we can term 'ideological positivism',[36] the view that 'A law is a law' (*Gesetz ist Gesetz*)

[35] Radbruch, 'Statutory Lawlessness and Supra-Statutory Law', 7. For the German original see Radbruch, 'Gesetzliches Unrecht und Übergesetzliches Recht', in Radbruch, *Rechtsphilosophie* (Stuttgart: KF Koehler Publishing, 1973, Erik Wolf and Hans-Peter Schneider, eds) 339, at 345–6. In writing 'Positivism and the Separation of Law and Morals', Hart used a good translation of this essay from the materials for Fuller's Jurisprudence course at Harvard during the year Hart was a visitor to the Harvard Law School. See Hart, 'Positivism and the Separation of Law and Morals', 74, note 42. I thank Kenneth Winston for supplying me with a photocopy of the translation both Hart and Fuller relied on in their debate.

[36] For this term, see Norberto Bobbio, 'Sur le Positivisme Juridique', in Bobbio, *Essais de théorie du droit* (Bruylant: Paris, 1998, Michel Guéret, trans.) 23, at 27–8. I discuss this term in 'Positivism and Totalitarianism', in Torben Spaak and Patricia Mindus, eds, *The*

and thus that anything which has the form of law ought to be enforced. This view, he said, excluded the ideas of 'statutory lawlessness' (*Gesetzliches Unrecht*) and 'supra-statutory law' (*übergesetzliches Recht*). But, he pointed out, obligation and validity cannot be based simply on power and compulsion. They must be based 'on a value inherent in the statute'.[37]

This, Radbruch argued, is the value of justice, itself the reason we value the certainty which statutes afford us. Even the fact that we value the certainty only enacted law can achieve must be understood as a requirement of justice, as serving the public good of legal subjects, because without the certainty brought by enacted law, subjects could not have that service. He named this good 'purposiveness' and emphasized that 'what benefits the people is, in the long run, only that which law is, namely, that which creates legal certainty and strives towards justice [*Recht*]'.[38] As the passage just quoted makes clear, part of law's striving for justice is that 'equality' – the 'very core of justice' – is respected.

Hence, Radbruch found three values inherent in law – certainty, purposiveness and justice – with certainty occupying a 'curious middle place' since it is there in order to facilitate both purposiveness and justice.[39] The two parts of the passage do not, then, set out two formulas. Rather, they presuppose an interpretive spectrum akin to the one I sketched in Chapter 2 in Hobbes. In Radbruch, the spectrum ranges from minor to major value conflicts and it is only in the exceptional case of blatant extreme injustice that a judge should make justice the test for the validity of law. What gives the exceptional case its character is that the law is not interpretable in a way which can avoid finding that its purpose is to be an instrument of extreme injustice.[40] Until that point, the judge should attempt to find an interpretation reconciling the certainty which positive law brings with the demands of justice, in the sense we must recall of *Recht*, the justice inherent in legality.[41]

Cambridge Companion to Legal Positivism (Cambridge: Cambridge University Press, 2021) 764.

37 Radbruch, 'Statutory Lawlessness and Supra-Statutory Law', 6.

38 Ibid.

39 Ibid.

40 In the terms elaborated in my account of Hobbes's legal theory, such a law, while satisfying the validity proviso, fails to satisfy the legality proviso.

41 Here it is important to clear up a possible misconception: that when Radbruch speaks of the 'service' and 'certainty' which positive law brings he was articulating an early version of Raz's theory of legal authority in which law has authority when it serves to transmit

Moreover, as Radbruch knew, the legal arguments in cases which confronted the Nazi past sought for the most part to find within German law the interpretive resources necessary to get to the conclusion which served justice without resorting to invalidating Nazi statutes. Thus, Radbruch did not set out his position to provide a 'Formula' for later deployment by judges. Rather, he wished to understand from a juridical point of view the legal arguments German lawyers and judges were already engaged in making.[42]

These arguments were set out in a long extract Radbruch quoted from the legal opinion of a prosecutor in a Grudge Informer Case and which formed part of the materials Hart read in preparing his essay.[43] There is an interesting question, then, about why Hart distorted not only Radbruch's position by ridding it of its nuances but also the situation which faced German lawyers and judges in postwar Germany. In addition, had Hart consulted Radbruch's *Philosophy of Law* of 1930, available in a Harvard University Press translation of 1950, he would have found that Radbruch, far from recanting his prewar positivism, did little more than bring out an implication of his prewar position. For Radbruch had already stated there that 'even the validity of positive law that is unjust and wrong cannot be maintained unqualifiedly; hence the question of validity may be considered nor only from the standpoint of legal certainty but also that of justice and . . . [purposiveness]'.[44]

reasons to legal subjects which reflect the reasons which already apply to them and which the legislator is better at determining than the subjects. The better understanding is that Radbruch was setting out a complete theory of legal authority, one which accounts for the dynamic process of norm production in which judges have a role and which should not be consigned to extra-legal space, outside of the scope of legal theory. Raz's theory of authority can in this light be seen to continue the command theory of law's exclusive focus on positive law, statically conceived, and thus to present only a very partial account of law's authority.

42 For discussion of the actual cases, see my 'The Case of the Grudge Informer Revisited' (2008) 83 *New York University Law Review* 1000 and HO Pappe 'On the Validity of Judicial Decisions in the Nazi Era' (1960) 23 *Modern Law Review* 260.

43 Radbruch, 'Statutory Lawlessness and Supra-Statutory Law', 2–4.

44 Gustav Radbruch, *Legal Philosophy*, in *The Legal Philosophies of Lask, Radbruch, and Dabin* (Cambridge, MA: Harvard University Press, 1950, 20th Century Legal Philosophy Series, vol. 4, Kurt Wilk, trans.) 47, at 111. The translator has 'expediency' for Radbruch's 'Zweckmässigkeit' and, following the Paulsons' translation of 'Statutory Lawlessness and Supra-Statutory Law', I prefer 'purposiveness'; Radbruch, *Rechtsphilosophie*, 168–9. Hart referred to this work in the German 4th edition of 1950 in 'Positivism and the Separation of Law and Morals', 50, note 8, but (as far as I can tell) only to provide a source for the translation in Fuller's materials which he discussed in part IV.

In that work, Radbruch put forward an explicitly Hobbesian argument that in the circumstances of deep disagreement about the good in a modern legal state enacted law provides subjects with public standards which permit them to interact with each other on stable and peaceful terms.[45] Enacted law can do that job only if the individuals subject to the law are prepared to treat it as binding on them. For this reason, it is the 'professional duty of the judge to validate the law's claim to validity, to sacrifice his own sense of the right to the authoritative command of the law, to ask only what is legal and not if it is also just'.[46]

Now this argument might seem to make Radbruch's prewar position a version of the orthodox interpretation of Hobbes's legal theory, that is, a version of ideological positivism. But, as in my account of Hobbes in Chapter 2, Radbruch wanted us to be alert to the distinction between legal right and statute and so to be careful not to equate the idea of justice according to law with plain facts about the content of the value judgments which those with the power to do so think they have legislated. Rather, legal justice or justice according to law, much like Hobbes's laws of nature and Fuller's idea of an 'internal morality' of law, has to do with the internal value structure of a legal order when law is understood as a matter of authority.

Radbruch argued that law can be authoritative only if it serves the values of justice and purposiveness, as well as the value of certainty, with the last a value only because of its service to justice. Moreover, these values are in the structure of legal order because of the peculiar quality of legal justice, at the core of which is equality. It is peculiar because what equality requires must be determined extra-legally, as it is a highly contested political value. But once the value judgment has been made and law enacted, the law must be applied in a way which respects the relational demands of equality before the law.

> For while justice directs us to treat equals equally, unequals unequally, it does not answer the question of the viewpoint from which they are deemed equal or unequal in the first place; moreover, it determines solely the relation, and not the kind, of the treatment. Both questions may be answered only by referring to the purpose of the law.[47]

45 Radbruch, *Legal Philosophy*, 116–17. For the view that Radbruch did change his stance significantly, see Stanley L Paulson, 'On the Background and Significance of Gustav Radbruch's Post-war Papers' (2006) 26 *Oxford Journal of Legal Studies* 17.

46 Radbruch, *Legal Philosophy*, 119.

47 Ibid, 108.

It is for this reason that purposiveness becomes part of the structure of legality. The content of purposiveness must be settled for law to do its job of providing a supra-individual order. Hence, legal certainty enters the value structure, which Radbruch observed has the result 'most oddly' that 'the positivity of the law itself becomes a prerequisite of its rightness; to be positive is to be implicit in the concept of right law just as much as rightness of content is a task of positive law'.[48] Of the three values, Radbruch said that only purposiveness is 'relativistic' while '[j]ustice and legal certainty are above the conflicts between views of law and the state, above the struggles of the parties'.[49]

Hart's distortion of Radbruch is remarkable. Even more remarkable is that, as we saw in Chapter 2, Hart in effect reinvented Radbruch in the next part of 'Positivism and the Separation of Law and Morals', and went on to offer an even more elaborate account of the natural law elements to which any positivist theory of law must attend in his argument about the 'minimum content' of natural law in chapter 9 of *The Concept of Law*, 'Laws and Morals'. His deferral of discussion of natural law in *The Concept of Law* to his penultimate chapter mirrors the similar deferral in 'Positivism and the Separation of Law and Morals' to the penultimate part of the essay, and it has the same effect, as we can see in light of my argument so far. It permitted Hart to set out a static theory of law with legal order's dynamic elements noted but their operation consigned to extra-legal space.

Hart achieved this aim largely through the implicit assumption, a relic of the utilitarian command theory of law, that legislation is the product of a supreme legislature which is legally unlimited in the sense of not subject to substantive constraints. That in turn provided the model for understanding judicial interpretation as a quasi-legislative, gap-filling exercise in a penumbra. But it is also achieved through the attempted subordination of all rules, including the secondary rules of change and adjudication, to the 'ultimate' rule of recognition, which Hart attempted to strip of the mysteries of Kelsen's basic norm, only to introduce mysteries of his own, as we saw in Chapter 3.

Had Hart placed his part V discussion of legality at the beginning of 'Law and the Separation of Law and Morals', or his chapter 9 discussion of natural law at the beginning of *The Concept of Law*, he would have been able to present a different and much more convincing account of

[48] Ibid.
[49] Ibid.

law's authority. That he did not had everything to do with the Separation Thesis: namely, with his conviction that the claim that law has no necessary moral quality is both obvious because of the existence of unjust laws and morally important because it facilitates a candid response to the complex moral situation raised by such laws.

I claimed in the Introduction that the Separation Thesis has misdirected philosophy of law from 1958 to this day, despite the fact that Hart's successors assert not only that there are all sorts of necessary connections between law and morality but also that Hart himself never subscribed to the Separation Thesis.[50] In light of my argument, we can see that Hart's claims which are in tension with the Separation Thesis show only that he put forward a contradictory position by combining two components in his legal theory. First, there is Hart's claim that law must be understood as a matter of authority. Second, there is his claim that the Separation Thesis tells the good liberal citizen that law is no more than positive law and that, therefore, *qua* law it has no authority.

That legal philosophy has been able for sixty years to live with this contradiction has much to do with the fact that Dworkin's interpretivism has been taken to be the main challenge to the Separation Thesis. As my Chapter 1 demonstrated, Dworkin's main response to the existence of unjust laws and very unjust legal systems remained vulnerable to the point Hart made in 1958 that the moral resources on which interpretivism relies are contingent on the history of particular legal orders. In Section 6.2, I explain how that vulnerability can be cured by attending to the way in which an appropriate Dworkinian response relies on a pragmatist conception of morality, one which Hart himself came close to elaborating.

6.2 Law's Laboratory

I argued in Chapter 1 that the puzzle of unjust law complicates the division in legal theory between natural law and legal positivism. The central figure here is the judge because of the obligation of judges to apply law based on facts which are contingent and may not be morally good. How can we square what seems like a standing judicial obligation to apply the law with the idea that that law has no guarantee to be something which ought to be applied? Hart, as we saw, tried to deal with

[50] See, for example, John Gardner, *Law as a Leap of Faith* (Oxford: Oxford University Press, 2012), 48–51.

this problem by minimizing the account of law's authority so that there is no moral requirement to apply it. In contrast, Dworkin subordinated the factual dimension of law to its moral dimension and argued that the criteria in the moral dimension determine the law. But the difficulties each encountered had the result that both were tempted to wander over to the other side of the divide between legal positivism and natural law.

In Chapter 5, I suggested that the solution to the puzzle can rely on the way in which principles of legality condition the content of law. For the discipline of legality makes more plausible Dworkin's claim that an answer to a question of law which shows the legal record in its best moral light will not include morally unacceptable principles. This suggestion entails that what remains after the conditioning or transformation process is done is moral, the idea which Hart said is repugnant to the whole notion of morality because it implies that there is such a thing as a moral legislature. However, a particular version of this idea is not at all repugnant, so long as we are prepared to adopt a pragmatist account of moral inquiry.

It is noteworthy in this regard that in *Justice for Hedgehogs*, Dworkin endorsed the pragmatist view of inquiry as aimed at getting right answers, a position which was put forward by the founder of pragmatism, CS Peirce.[51] It holds that true or rational beliefs in any field of inquiry are those which survive the tribunal of experience and argument, against the background of our current beliefs and principles. The settled beliefs arising from this process of inquiry are always provisional since they must be left vulnerable to revision in light of further experience. It follows that much of our compulsory public morality – the morality we feel is settled and important enough that it was made into law – is no more than the judgments which have survived the tribunal of experience and inquiry.[52] As I put things at the beginning of this chapter, positive

[51] In *Justice for Hedgehogs*, Dworkin describes his account of truth as 'pragmatist' since he argues, following Peirce, that 'truth is the intrinsic goal of inquiry': 177. And in his work on moral inquiry, he seems to argue, with pragmatists, that the test for the objectivity of our judgments is that they are the best we can achieve for the time being in light of our experience, at the same time as we insist that inquiry be kept open in case we should revise those judgments. Fuller preferred to think of himself as a pragmatist rather than a natural lawyer, as I point out in Section 6.3. See Kenneth I Winston, 'Is/Ought Redux: The Pragmatist Context of Lon Fuller's Conception of Law' (1988) 8 *Oxford Journal of Legal Studies* 329. But there is no need to accept this dichotomy. See Philip Selznick, 'Sociology and Natural Law' (1961) 6 *Natural Law Forum* 84.

[52] See Dworkin's response to Lord Devlin's conservative argument that a political community is entitled to use the criminal law to enforce its moral views: Dworkin, 'Liberty and

law makes law answerable to the experience of the subjects who live under law's rule. It is this answerability which makes the conception of morality presupposed by a theory of law's authority defensible.

We will see later in this section that this kind of pragmatism is hardly new to legal theory, since Oliver Wendell Holmes was a prominent figure in pragmatism's founding, both as a general philosophical doctrine and as highly conducive to understanding the relationship between law and morality. For the moment, I want to sketch how the best account of this pragmatist idea at work in the law is to be found in *The Concept of Law* in the very section in which Hart asserted that the idea of a moral legislature is repugnant to the whole notion of morality.

In chapter 8 of *The Concept of Law*, 'Justice and Morality', Hart set out the four 'formal' features of what he called 'social morality'. The assertion forms part of the discussion of the second feature, '*Immunity from deliberate change*'.[53] The first is '*Importance*' – that the standards are maintained despite the fact they restrict 'the drive of strong passions . . . at the cost of sacrificing considerable person interest'; are enforced by

Moralism', in Ronald Dworkin, *Taking Rights Seriously* (London: Duckworth, 1981, 3rd impression) 240. Dworkin suggested that Hart's earlier response in *Law, Liberty, and Morality* to Devlin neglected the insight worth taking seriously in Devlin's position – that a 'community must take the moral responsibility' to protect what it considers to be its core values and 'must therefore act on its own lights – that is, on the moral faith of its members'; ibid, 247. Dworkin thus argued that the problem in Devlin was his conception of morality, not the claim about legal enforcement: 'What is shocking and wrong is not . . . [Devlin's] idea that the community's morality counts, but his idea of what counts as the community's morality'. Ibid, 255. Dworkin went on to describe a process of community argument which 'sifts' positions for 'prejudices and rationalizations'; ibid. He did not in this essay address the role of law in this process. My argument in this book is that legal order plays precisely this role, though one better described as conversion or transformation in a process of juridical production than as 'sifting' or 'screening'. Note that some saw Dworkin's argument as a bad compromise with conservatism – see Joel Feinberg, *Harmless Wrongdoing: The Moral Limits of the Criminal Law* (Oxford: Oxford University Press, 1990), 47–8. In my view, an even more charitable (and I think more accurate) reading of Devlin's conservatism shows that his position was that the common law method provides the kind of testing ground for moral experience which a pragmatic conception of morality advocates. See his discussion of the 'elastic principles' which should govern moral inquiry in Patrick Devlin, *The Enforcement of Morals* (Oxford: Oxford University Press, 1965), which starts at 16 with the statement: 'I do not think that one can talk sensibly of public and private morality any more than one can of a public and private highway. Morality is a sphere in which there is a public interest and a private interest, often in conflict, and the problem is to reconcile the two.'

53 Hart, *The Concept of Law*, 175. His emphasis. For rare and illuminating discussion of Hart's views about morality, see Peter Cane, 'Morality, Law and Conflicting Reasons for Action' (2012) 71 *Cambridge Law Journal* 59.

'social pressure' and it is recognized that a change in the standards would bring about 'far-reaching and distasteful changes in the lives of individuals'.[54] The third is the '*Voluntary character of moral offences*' – that moral blame is excluded when the action was unintentional and not negligent.[55] Finally, there is '*The form of moral pressure*', as the typical form of pressure is 'appeals to the respect for the rules, as things important in themselves, which is presumed to be shared by those addressed'.[56]

In setting out these features, Hart wanted to 'evade . . . [the] philosophical difficulties' which surround the decision whether morality 'amounts to immutable principles which constitute part of the fabric of the Universe, not made by man, but awaiting discovery by the human intellect' or whether it amounts to 'expressions of changing human attitudes, choices, demands, or feelings'.[57] In other words, he wished to avoid the kind of problem sketched at the end of my Chapter 1 whereby philosophers of law must decide on the correct legal theory on meta-ethical grounds, and so must choose between moral realism – the theory that moral judgments reflect certain objective facts in the world – and some version of emotivism. As I pointed out there, either choice is reductive in a way which distorts our experience.

For moral realists, when it comes to law, all that is important to study is its moral impact, with the result that law is lost to legal inquiry. For legal positivism in its command theory version, a bare emotivist account of morality suffices. Since law's task is to transmit correct judgments of utility to legal subjects, the role of morality in legal theory amounts to nothing more than the calculus of pain over pleasure in order to calibrate the sanctions attached to non-compliance. Hence, morality is lost to legal inquiry. With both moral realism and the command theory, whether the law of any state is in fact legitimate depends on an external fact. It depends on either getting moral theory right or on moral arithmetic, a calculus of emotional responses.[58]

54 Hart, *The Concept of Law*, 174. His emphasis.
55 Ibid, 178. His emphasis.
56 Ibid, 180. His emphasis.
57 Ibid, 168.
58 In this light, we can see the deep tension in Raz's legal theory. On the one hand, it seems a marriage of the command theory with moral realism: law's claim to legitimate authority is vindicated only when it transmits the reasons, an external fact certified by correct moral theory, which already apply to subjects. But on the other hand, it is a Kelsenian account of the legal reasons which officials must offer to the legal subject in order to answer the question 'But, how can that be law for me?'

Hart, we know, was clear-eyed about the problem for philosophy of law when law's authority is located outside legal order. On the one hand, sanction-based accounts of law will not do since legal theory must attend to the way in which law provides reasons of a special kind to subjects – authoritative legal reasons. On the other hand, if authoritative legal reasons were always moral reasons of some kind, their force would be more easily explained. But since Hart was not willing to countenance that such reasons always have a moral quality to them, he admitted that he was in a difficult position, in effect a two-systems or dualist view that there are 'two independent "worlds" or sets of objective reasons, one legal and the other moral'. He thus conceded that his 'non-cognitive' account seems committed to the 'paradoxical' and even confused conclusion that 'judicial statements of a subject's legal duties need have nothing directly to do with the subject's reasons for action'.[59]

Hart's position can be rescued from these problems. The solution is to liberate him from both non-cognitivism and the Separation Thesis through understanding how his attempt to avoid both moral realism and emotivism leads to a pragmatic account of morality.[60] The account

[59] HLA Hart, *Essays on Bentham: Jurisprudence and Political Theory* (Oxford: Clarendon Press, 1982), 266–7.

[60] A different attempt finds in Hart's legal theory the more sophisticated version of emotivism developed by philosophers under the label 'expressivism': see, for example, Kevin Toh, 'Hart's Expressivism and His Benthamite Project' (2005) 11 *Legal Theory* 75 and Matthew X Etchemendy, 'New Directions in Legal Expressivism' (2016) 22 *Legal Theory* 1. But expressivism is a theory of moral statements which depends on exactly the kinds of meta-ethical commitments which Hart thought raised the 'philosophical difficulties' legal theory should try to avoid. The issue is not merely that one should avoid such difficulties if possible. Rather, many of the pieces of evidence from Hart's own work which Toh adduces in favour of his claim for Hart's expressivism fit just as well with a claim that Hart was a pragmatist. Most important, though, is that a pragmatic account of the conception of morality appropriate to a theory of legal authority both does not rest on anything 'meta', that is, anything which transcends human experience, and makes sense of morality as an appropriate object of 'cognition', when cognition is understood as inquiry into moral experience. Note that Kelsen at times adopted an explicitly emotivist view. See, for example, Hans Kelsen, 'Law, State, and Justice in the Pure Theory of Law', in Kelsen, *What Is Justice? Justice, Law and Politics in the Mirror of Science* (Berkeley: University of California Press, 1957) 288, at 295:

> There is not, and cannot be, an objective criterion of justice because the statement: something is just or unjust, is a judgment of value referring to an ultimate end, and these value judgments are by their very nature subjective in character, because based on emotional elements of our minds, on our feelings and wishes. They cannot be verified by facts, as can statements about reality.

emerges from his attempt in *The Concept of Law* to identify what is distinctive about morality when we refer to '"*the* morality" of a given society or the "accepted" or "conventional" morality of an actual social group'.[61]

Hart's aim here, in line with his commitment to the Separation Thesis, was to distinguish social morality from the value content of the positive law of *any* legal order. In a 'primitive' society, that is, there is no more to compulsory social rules than the content of social morality. Only in a developed legal society is it possible to distinguish the rules of social morality from the values embedded in legal rules because the primary legal rules are determined by reference to the secondary rules of recognition, change and adjudication. As a result, the primary rules are subject to change, their content can be morally unimportant by the standards of social morality, offences can be legislated so that there is involuntary culpability and there need be no presumption that pressure to conform appeals to the respect for the rules.[62]

This distinction was important to Hart for two reasons. First, the Separation Thesis is not confined to a claim about the relationship between law and immutable morality. Rather, it is the thesis that there is no necessary connection between law and any set of values which a society has ever endorsed or could ever endorse. It follows that, if the standards of immutable morality could be identified, there would be no necessary connection between those standards and law. The second reason is exactly the same as that advanced by Hart for adopting the positivist conception of law. It widens the scope of inquiry by not requiring us to adopt a conception of immutable morality, one which utterly transcends social mores, thus excluding social moralities which exhibit these formal features, but which would be condemned by the immutable standards.[63]

Still Hart, as we have seen, thought that there is a distinction between critical and positive morality, with the former containing the standards a society adopts in order to evaluate the duties 'recognized in the actual practice of social groups'.[64] This is a distinction between the duties and

[61] Hart, *The Concept of Law*, 169. His emphasis.
[62] Ibid, 173–80.
[63] Ibid, 181.
[64] Ibid, 182.

obligations a group in fact recognizes and the standards by which these are evaluated by the same group. According to Hart, critical morality has its own 'formal conditions, one of rationality and the other of generality'. Implied in criticism in these terms is 'first that social arrangements should not rest on beliefs which can be shown to be mistaken, and secondly that the protections from harm, which morality characteristically affords through the actions and forbearances it demands, should be extended at least to all men who are able and willing themselves to observe such restrictions'.[65]

In calling these conditions 'formal', Hart indicated, as does the context in which he introduced them, that rationality and generality are part of social morality, though they belong to its critical department. The social morality Hart described is not, then, the compulsory values of a 'primitive' society in which there is no distinction between social and legal mores. Rather, it is the social morality which exists apart from the content of the law in a modern legal state. Put differently, it is the kind of social morality one finds in a jural community, as the third of his formal features – the voluntary character of moral offences – makes plain. For the idea that one is not responsible for events over which one has no control is not a feature of all or perhaps even many premodern belief systems. It may even be the case that the idea owes its prominent place in modern social moralities in large part to the influence of ideas of responsibility first concretely articulated in criminal or civil trials. Indeed, as Tony Honoré pointed out, our moral terms such as 'right', 'duty' and 'obligation' are 'derived from Roman law (*ius*, *debitum*, *obligatio*), the system that first conceived law as a balance of rights and obligations subsisting between individuals and between them and the state'.[66] Similarly, the idea that the social mores of a society can and should change must become more acceptable when a society moves from one in which there is only customary law, that is, generally accepted mandatory social norms, to one in which legislation is viewed as a legitimate means of producing new compulsory norms.[67]

65 Ibid, 183.

66 Tony Honoré, 'The Necessary Connection between Law and Morality' (2002) 22 *Oxford Journal of Legal Studies* 489, at 491.

67 See Peter Cane, *Responsibility in Law and Morality* (Oxford: Hart Publishing, 2002), especially 12–15, and Honoré, 'The Dependence of Morality on Law'. It is consistent with the claim in the text that, once the norm of responsibility developed in the law has influenced social morality, legislation may subsequently properly oust the norm in certain areas of the law, for example, by criminalizing driving when drunk.

In addition, Hart noted a causal role for law in changing morality in the very section in which he argued against this proposition. He acknowledged there that the fact that 'morals and traditions cannot be directly changed, as laws may be, by legislative enactment must not be mistaken for immunity from other forms of change'. For example, 'legal enactments may set standards of honesty and humanity, which ultimately alter and raise the current morality; conversely, legal repression of practices thought morally obligatory may, in the end, cause the sense of their importance and so their status as morality to be lost'.[68] But this effect, he emphasized, is contingent. While change in the law is direct, 'ingrained morality' may survive the change and 'continue in full vigour side by side with laws which forbid what it enjoins'.[69]

Hart regarded the claim about contingency as self-evident and did not therefore notice that much of what he said in chapter 8 shows that it is not entirely so. First, while he pointed out distinctions between the content of the positive law and of the social morality of a particular modern society, he also emphasized the significant overlap which will necessarily exist between the two in any such society. Social morality 'always includes certain obligations and duties, requiring the sacrifice of private inclination and interest which is essential to the survival of any society, so long as men and the world they live in retain some of their most familiar and obvious characteristics'.[70] These will include rules restricting violence, protecting property and 'requiring honesty and truthfulness in dealings with others'; hence, social morality will have the same kind of content which we saw Hart set out when in chapter 9, 'Laws and Morals', he made a similar Hobbesian argument about the 'minimum' natural law content of any legal order.[71] Indeed, it is in chapter 8 that he made the Hobbesian remark I quoted in my Chapter 1, which set the stage for his chapter 9 discussion:

> It seems clear that the sacrifice of personal interest which such rules *demand* is the price that must be paid in a world such as ours for living with others, and the protection they *afford* is the minimum which, for beings such as ourselves, makes living with others worth while. These simple facts constitute . . . a core of indisputable truth in the doctrines of Natural Law.[72]

[68] Hart, *The Concept of Law*, 177.
[69] Ibid, 177.
[70] Ibid, 172.
[71] Ibid.
[72] Ibid, 181. His emphasis.

Second, the fact of overlap plus distinction puts in place a symbiotic relationship between law and social morality of which Hart was aware but could not take fully on board because of the static model of law he generally adopted. Recall from my Chapter 1 that in 'Positivism and the Separation of Law and Morals' Hart, in responding to Fuller's early work on principles of legality, said that 'justice in the administration of the law' is 'not justice of the law'.[73] He made this distinction in order not only to preserve but even to strengthen the Separation Thesis. If the content of the law is unjust by some external moral standard, the 'just' administration of the law by law's own internal standard of 'treat like cases alike' can make things morally worse. Laws 'that are hideously oppressive' can be applied with the 'most pedantic impartiality'.[74] Recall also that he later accused Dworkin of making a 'last-ditch' and 'hopeless' defence on the basis that individuals in a wicked legal system have a moral right that judges treat like cases alike.[75]

In chapter 8 of *The Concept of Law*, Hart explored further what he called 'the specific idea of justice and the special features which account for its peculiarly intimate connection with law' and devoted most of his discussion to 'treat like cases alike'.[76] His treatment started from the same position he articulated in 1958. He claimed that

> the resemblances and differences between human beings which are relevant for the criticism of legal arrangements as just or unjust are quite obvious. This is pre-eminently the case when we are concerned not with the justice or injustice of the *law* but of its *application* in particular cases. For here the relevant resemblances and differences between individuals, to which the person who administers the law must attend, are determined by the law itself.[77]

From this, and in line with the claim about pedantic impartiality, he asserted that 'there is no absurdity in conceding that an unjust law forbidding the access of coloured persons to the parks has been justly administered, in that only persons genuinely guilty of breaking the law were punished under it and then only after a fair trial'.[78]

[73] Hart, 'Positivism and the Separation of Law and Morals', 81.
[74] Ibid.
[75] Hart, *Essays on Bentham*, 152–3.
[76] Hart, *The Concept of Law*, 157.
[77] Ibid, 160. His emphasis.
[78] Ibid, 161.

But this assertion fails to take into account precisely the kind of Radbruchian analysis sketched in Section 6.1, according to which 'the law' includes principles of *Recht* which condition the content of the law. Impartial judges, mindful of what Hart called the judicial virtues,[79] will not when faced with a precedent which seems to require an unjust result be 'most pedantic' and simply reproduce the result of the earlier decision. Rather they will understand impartiality as requiring them to try to find an interpretation of the law which both exhibits their fidelity to law and gives a satisfactory answer to 'But, how can that be law for me?'

In this regard, Hart exhibited the very ambiguity he relied upon when it came to the question of the role of legality in legal order. As I indicated in Chapter 1, this ambiguity permitted him at times to acknowledge that Fullerian principles of legality are moral while denying that law must by and large comply with them, while at other times he acknowledged that law must by and large comply with the principles but denied that compliance imparts any moral quality to law. Thus, in *The Concept of Law* he began his discussion of the connection between the specific idea of justice and the principle of like treatment by saying that it 'lies in the fact that outside the law there is a moral conviction that those with whom the law is concerned have a right to mutual forbearance from certain kinds of harmful conduct'.[80] This was for Hart an indelible feature of social morality in the modern legal state, as he acknowledged by immediately saying that 'a structure of reciprocal rights and obligations proscribing at least the grosser sorts of harm, constitutes the basis, though not the whole, of the morality of every social group. Its effect is to create among individuals a moral, and, in a sense, an artificial equality to offset the inequalities of nature'.[81] The norm of equality is thus a human artefact, developed to regulate interaction between individuals in a civil society. Moreover, the principle that 'prima facie human beings are entitled to be treated alike' is 'so deeply embedded in modern man' that 'almost universally where the laws do discriminate by reference to such matters as colour and race at least lip service is still widely paid to this principle'.[82]

Now Hart noted that it is possible for a social morality to openly disavow equality, as in the ideology of a slave-owning society.[83] But he

[79] Ibid, 204–5.
[80] Ibid, 164–5.
[81] Ibid.
[82] Ibid, 162.
[83] Ibid.

did not note that if there is reason to suppose, as he himself did, that the principle of equality is an indelible principle of legality as well as of social morality, it will be the case that any positive law discriminations on the basis of colour or race are subject to legal challenge. As I showed in Chapter 5, in an Apartheid State the formal commitment to the equality of all legal subjects before the law makes it possible for the discriminated-against second-class citizens to challenge their status. A judge who hears such a challenge, and who wishes to maintain fidelity to law, should not treat the formal commitment to the principle as mere lip service, but must try to determine the content of the law so as to make it answer the question 'But, how can that be law for me?'

For example, in the actual apartheid legal order, the Group Areas Act 1950 gave to officials the authority to set aside an area of South Africa for residence by one racial group and made it a criminal offence for members of other groups to reside there. Since there was no entrenched bill of rights, the statute could not be challenged on the basis that it was invalid because of its violation of the right of all South Africans to equal treatment. However, when officials designated the biggest and best areas for white South Africans, their decisions could be and were challenged on the basis that the statute did not give officials the authority to act unreasonably by creating a situation of gross inequality for racial groups. In other words, unless the statute explicitly told officials that they did not have to respect the right of individuals to equal treatment in the way in which the law was administered, they were under a legal duty to respect that right.[84]

I have described elsewhere how this kind of challenge generally failed. On the few occasions when lower courts upheld the challenges, a higher court would overrule them. Moreover, a government which enjoyed the support of the great majority of its all-white electorate could be counted on to use its grip on the legislature to ensure that the statute in question was amended to preclude further challenges, and that new statutes were drafted in ways which pre-empted similar challenges.[85] But such failure does not show, as Hart seemed to think, that 'all that succeeds is success' in political contests about legality in which the determinate content of a rule does not settle the answer.[86] Rather, as we saw in Chapter 5, the

[84] See my *Hard Cases in Wicked Legal Systems: Pathologies of Legality* (Oxford: Oxford University Press, 2010, 2nd ed.), chapter 2.
[85] Ibid.
[86] Hart, *The Concept of Law*, 153.

failure shows that if politics of a certain sort is to run roughshod over the rule of law, legislators must adopt either one or both of two strategies. Either they can explicitly state their aim of rendering a whole group of subjects to second-class status, or they can delegate power to officials permitting the officials to achieve the same end, not because this end is explicitly stated in the empowering statute, but because official implementation of the statute is explicitly stated to be unreviewable by judges. Both strategies use law to place individuals or groups of individuals beyond the reach of the law. But they do so in a way which does not comply with law's form, in the first case by negating generality and its implicit commitment to equality before the law, in the second case by ensuring that there is no law with which official action must be congruent.

In order to appreciate this insight, one has to drop an allegiance to both the Separation Thesis and to a static model of law. Put positively, one must accept that principles of legality or *Recht* are intrinsic to legal order, that they are moral as well legal and that for legal order to be maintained in good shape, officials must manifest their fidelity to law by interpreting the positive law in light of such principles. Justice in the administration of the law requires officials to reject 'pedantic impartiality' because judges mindful of what Hart called the judicial virtues, a role morality which includes impartiality, will attend to the way in which principles of legality condition the content of the law.

Hart almost got to this conclusion at several points, each of which is an attempt to grapple with the legacy of legal oppression – with the pasts of colonialism and Nazism, or the present at the time of writing of apartheid South Africa and the Jim Crow laws of the USA. For example, in chapter 8 of *The Concept of Law* he considered how the principle 'treat like cases alike' applies in regard to laws which provide for the compensation by one person of another for civil injuries. Such laws, he said, might be considered unjust for two different reasons. 'They might, on the one hand, establish unfair privileges or immunities', for example, 'if no white person were liable to a coloured person for trespass or assault'.[87] On the other hand, the law might provide no remedy for certain types of injury inflicted, 'even though morally compensation would be thought due. In this matter the law might be unjust while treating all alike.'[88]

[87] Ibid, 164.
[88] Ibid.

But in the first case, Hart missed that there would be a problem internal to legality which is at or close to the point at which Radbruch stated that because 'there is not even an attempt at justice . . . the statute is not merely "flawed law", [*unrichtiges Recht*] it lacks completely the very nature of law [*Rechtsnatur*]'.[89] In other words, at this point the judge must consider either invalidating the law or informing the legislature and other branches of government, by whatever means (including an informal declaration of incompatibility), of the problem. The problem is one from the perspective of legality with the substantive content of the law. It arises because a positive law makes plain that a class of persons is not to be rendered merely into just second-class status but also into a category in which they lose their very status as persons.[90]

In the second case, there is also a failure internal to legality. But here it is of the legal order failing to do its job of providing for peaceful and stable interaction between all individuals.

Hence, it differs from the first case in which one group gets that kind of protection but not another in a way which gives the first the power to dominate the other. For it makes all subject to the arbitrary power of each, in effect producing within civil society a partial Hobbesian state of nature. In both cases, tensions will arise. In the first, it is because an attempt to prescribe by law a discriminatory practice endorsed by some powerful social group collides directly with the legal principle. In the second, it arises because a prerogative space exists within the law which is inconsistent both with critical morality and with the way in which law, positive law as well as legal principles, governs other areas of social interaction. The impetus for reform in each case has to do with the symbiotic relationship between social morality and the values in the

[89] Radbruch, 'Statutory Lawlessness and Supra-Statutory Law', 7.

[90] As Julius Ebbinghaus put the point in his illuminating reflection on the Nazi era, speaking of the example of a group of individuals deprived of the right to own property:

> [T]hey have lost, in this respect, their condition as human beings, and have been reduced to the status of mere objects. In respect of the use of things they have become mere objects of the arbitrary power of men, because they have lost by law all capacity to restrict this power in favour of their own freedom of action. Can anyone fail to recognise that to be deprived of this is a violation quite different in kind from any mere act of injustice? The law informs them, so to speak, that having no rights, they cannot even be treated unjustly; and this is precisely what the state power can never say to any of its subjects.

Ebbinghaus, 'The Law of Humanity and the Limits of State Power' (1953) 10 *The Philosophical Quarterly* 14, at 21.

public legal record, a relationship which stems from the fact that the principle of equality specific to *Recht* or legal right is entrenched in each. A change in social morality which, in Hart's words, would 'openly reject the principle that prima facie human beings were to be treated alike' could not without severe tension coexist with the legal order of a modern legal state. As Hart said of social morality, '[i]f conformity with these most elementary rules were not thought a matter of course among any group of individuals, living in close proximity to each other, we should be doubtful of the description of the group as a society, and certain it could not endure for long'.[91]

Another place where Hart almost reached the conclusion that justice in the administration of the law conditions the content of the law was in 'Scandinavian Realism', his 1959 review article of Alf Ross, *On Law and Justice*.[92] Ross's 'realism', as sketched by Hart, involves too relentless a reduction of law to facts and to predictions about how such facts cause legal subjects to behave. He shared, though, Hart's view that moral values are not 'part of the fabric of the universe waiting our discovery by rational methods' and thus the non-cognitivism which Hart thought followed from that view, that is, that moral values 'cannot be proved or disproved by rational argument'.[93] But Hart also suggested, using one of his favourite pejoratives, that Ross's reductionism led him to 'absurdities', notably the claim that the words '"just" and "unjust" applied to a legal rule as distinct from a particular decision are "devoid of meaning"'.[94]

91 Hart, *The Concept of Law*, 172.

92 HLA Hart, 'Scandinavian Realism', in Hart, *Essays in Jurisprudence and Philosophy* 161.

93 Ibid, 163.

94 Ibid. As is the case when Hart resorted to claims like 'absurdity', he was more than likely attacking a bit of a straw man. For an argument to this effect in respect of Ross, see Jakob v H Holtermann, 'Introduction' to his edition of the new translation, by Uta Bindreiter, of Ross, *On Law and Justice* (Oxford: Oxford University Press, 2019), at xxviii–ix, and xxxvi–vii. Ross came up with the most striking dismissal of natural law I have seen, which Hart quoted without comment at 163 of 'Scandinavian Realism': 'Like a harlot, natural law is at the disposal of everyone. There is no ideology that cannot be defended by an appeal to the law of nature'. Kelsen's formulation is, however, a close contender: 'The question on which natural law focuses is the eternal question of what stands behind the positive law. And whoever seeks the answer will find, I fear, neither an absolute metaphysical truth nor the absolute justice of natural law. Who lifts the veil and does not shut his eyes will find staring at him the Gorgon head of power.' Hans Kelsen, 'Comment', in *Veröffentlichungen der Vereinigung der Deutschen Staatsrechtslehrer*, vol. 3 (Berlin: Walter de Gruyter and Co., 1927) 54, at 55. (My translation.)

Hart criticized Ross as follows:

> When we assert that a rule forbidding black men to sit in the public park is unjust we no doubt use, as our criterion of just treatment, the unstated principle that, in the distribution of rights and privileges among men, differences in colour should be neglected. In any full defence of this assertion the implicit criterion would have to be made explicit. But the dependence of concepts like justice on implicit, varying and challengeable criteria does not render them meaningless when applied to law.[95]

He continued that when legal actors make such claims about the application of rules,

> they are internal statements in the sense that they manifest acceptance of the standards and use and appeal to them in various ways. But the internal character of these statements is not a mere matter of the speaker having certain 'feelings of compulsion'; for though these may indeed often accompany the making of such statements they are neither necessary nor sufficient conditions of their normative use in criticizing conduct, making claims and justifying hostile reactions by reference to the accepted standard.[96]

In these quotations, Hart set out the logic which informs the legal inquiry into the content of law which an official working in an order of authority must undertake. For he suggested against Ross that the application of legal rules to particular cases requires attention to justice in determining the content of the relevant rules, a suggestion which gathered strength when Hart claimed that the 'dimensions of legal language are far richer than [Ross] ... allows' and that this claim is true even in the 'penumbra' of unsettled meaning.[97] This logic is peculiar to the necessary relationship between law and social morality where the latter is taken to include, as did Hart, the department of critical morality. As Honoré asked, 'What is the content of critical morality in this context?'[98] Dworkin's interpretive theory, he said, can't supply the answer because there may be 'no moral justification for some or many' of the rules and decisions of the system. Nor can it refer to any particular candidate for correct moral theory because any contender is going to be controversial. Still, in Honoré's view, there is a 'rational answer in the context in which ... [the question] arises':

95 Hart, 'Scandinavian Realism', 163.
96 Ibid, 167.
97 Ibid, 168–9.
98 Honoré, 'The Dependence of Morality on Law', 492.

> Law seeks to supplant unregulated violence, both within societies and between them, by fostering the values of co-operation and peaceful coexistence . . . The critical morality to which the law-maker implicitly appeals relates to these values, and to any more specific values consistent with them that the society in question may embrace. That the society embraces them does not make the appeal to them a social fact about that society. They are relevant to legal argument not because the society embraces them, or some of them (it may reject others) but because they tend to promote co-operation and peaceful co-existence.[99]

My argument in this section, and in this book as whole, supports Honoré's answer. It shows that the richness of legal language to which Hart alluded resides, on his own arguments, in law's normativity – the moral resources legal order affords just in being a legal order and which together make the law into a public conscience. But I have also shown that these critical resources of legal language go well beyond the legal order of any state. For there is a symbiotic relationship between the inside and the outside of the law of a modern legal state, one which is juridically required by Kelsenian international law monism when it comes to public and private international law, and which is not merely formal since social morality and law have the same minimum content.

The resources include:

1. The substantive rules within a modern legal state which make possible peaceful and stable interaction between legal subjects, namely, Hart's 'minimum content of natural law'.
2. The substantive principles which undergird these rules, that is, the idea that such interaction is between free and equal subjects, an idea which finds its formal expression in the requirements that law be general, that like cases should be treated alike so that differences in treatment must be justified and that the law should be impartially and fairly administered. In other words, there is a necessary connection between substantive content and many of Hobbes's laws of nature, which are, as Michael Oakeshott observed, 'no more than an analytic break-down of the intrinsic character of law, . . . the *jus* inherent in genuine law',[100] a connection which Fuller revived for philosophy of law in his principles of legality.

[99] Ibid.

[100] Michael Oakeshott, 'The Rule of Law', in Oakeshott, *On History and Other Essays* (Indianapolis: Liberty Fund, 1999) 129, at 173.

3. The equivalent of Hart's secondary rules which make possible authoritative juridical production, as well as law-governed coercion in the event of non-compliance with norms.
4. The constitutionalist idea, better expressed by a Kelsenian basic norm than a Hartian rule of recognition, since the former captures both the dynamic dimension of the production of legal norms and the official attitude of fidelity to law which requires that officials answer the legal subject's question 'But, how can that be law for me?' Such a norm is the functional equivalent of the Hobbesian social contract, and is to be found in Fuller and Dworkin in their arguments that legal order must aspire to 'integrity'. But it is also to be found in Austin's 'habit of obedience' and Hart's practice of official 'acceptance', though distorted by the static model of law they adopt.

In addition, there are:

5. The norms of public international law.
6. The private law norms of other national orders made relevant by a legal order's own private international law rules.

Finally, there are:

7. The principles in the critical department of the social morality of any modern legal state.

It is this complex of factors which makes plausible the thought that the law is a public conscience, a thought which echoes closer to our own time in Oliver Wendell Holmes's claim in 'The Path of the Law' that '[t]he law is the witness and external deposit of our moral life'.[101] Holmes added that the 'practice of it . . . tends to make good citizens and good men' and that he emphasized 'the difference between law and morals' only in order to facilitate 'learning and understanding the law'.[102]

Holmes is, of course, better known in philosophy of law for his claim that we should understand law from the point of view of the 'bad man', the figure who is concerned with the law only in so far as 'disagreeable consequences' might follow from his actions and thus that the law is no more than the 'prophecies of what the courts will do in fact, and nothing

[101] Oliver Wendell Holmes, 'The Path of the Law' (1897) 10 *Harvard Law Review* 457, at 459.

[102] Ibid, 549.

more pretentious'.[103] It is statements such as these which made Holmes one of Hart's foils both in 'Positivism and the Separation of Law and Morals' and *The Concept of Law*, and more generally led to Holmes's perceived role in American legal thought as the main founder of American Legal Realism. While no one could deny Holmes's place in this 'realist' pantheon, he also played an important role in the founding of pragmatism and it is the pragmatic dimension of his argument about the relationship between law and morality which I emphasize here.[104]

Both Hart and Kelsen criticized Holmes for his reductionism, for reducing, as had the command theorists, authority to the prediction that sanctions will be visited on those who fail to obey the sovereign's commands. They argued that we cannot understand statements of legal duty as simple predictions of what courts will do because a successful prediction will take a stand on how the court will get to its conclusion in reasoning about what the law requires, a stand, that is, on how the judge ought legally speaking to decide the matter.[105] Holmes, however, could not have agreed more and he is better understood as a pragmatist than as the kind of realist who reduced law to predictable facts.[106]

When Holmes said in lecture I of 'The Common Law' that '[t]he life of the law has not been logic: it has been experience',[107] the sentences preceding the remark made clear his view that logic is still one of the tools we need to make sense of law; and, in 'The Path of the Law', he stated that his opposition to the view that law is a matter of logic was reserved for the position that logic is the 'only force at work in the development of the law'.[108] Far from advancing a reductionist view, Holmes was explaining why it is plausible to regard the law as 'the

[103] Ibid, 461.

[104] See Misak, *The American Pragmatists*, and Frederic R Kellogg, *Oliver Wendell Holmes, Jr. and Legal Logic* (Chicago: University of Chicago Press, 2018).

[105] Hart, *The Concept of Law*, 38–42 and Hans Kelsen, *General Theory of Law and State* (Cambridge, MA: Harvard University Press, 1945, Anders Wedberg, trans.), 166–8.

[106] See Misak, 'A Pragmatist Account of Legitimacy and Authority' and *The American Pragmatists*, 77–81. Hart was generally more generous to Holmes than he was to Kelsen, Dworkin, Radbruch and Fuller, perhaps because he felt more affinity with Holmes's legal theory. He also saw that Holmes was far from dismissing the role of logic in legal argument. See HLA Hart, 'American Jurisprudence through English Eyes: The Nightmare and the Noble Dream', in Hart, *Essays in Jurisprudence and Philosophy* 123, at 128–31.

[107] Oliver Wendell Holmes, 'The Common Law', in Richard A Posner, ed., *The Essential Holmes* (Chicago: University of Chicago Press, 1992) 229, at 237.

[108] Holmes, 'The Path of the Law', 465.

witness and external deposit of our moral life' because of the kind of experience the legal experience is. As he said of theories like the command theory of law,

> [e]ven if every decision required the sanction of an emperor with despotic power and a whimsical turn of mind, we should be interested none the less, still with a view to prediction, in discovering some order, some rational explanation, and some principle of growth for the rules which he laid down. In every system there are such explanations and principles to be found.[109]

In this light, even the bad man who wishes to know what the courts will legally speaking do in order to avoid unpleasant consequences is counting on the judges' fidelity to law. Recall from my Chapter 1 that Hart offered an example of an immoral though legal norm, one which he thought could have informed the interpretation of the Nazi judges who convicted and sentenced to death the husband of the Grudge Informer: 'What sentence would both terrorize the public at large and keep the friends and family of the prisoner in suspense so that both hope and fear would cooperate as factors making for subservience?'[110] Hart noted that the 'prisoner of such a system would be regarded simply as an object to be used in pursuit of these aims'. But, he said, this would 'still be an intelligent and purposive' decision and 'from one point of view the decision would be as it ought to be'.[111]

In light of my account of the Dual State in Chapter 5, a lawyer who advised the husband that this was his fate would be advising that he would be condemned to death by an official in the prerogative not the normative state, and that the official did not care about either the law or the facts, only about the efficient operation of a regime of terror. The rule of such officials does not produce an experience of legality but of prerogative rule, something which Hart had trouble grasping because of his commitments both to the Separation Thesis and to a static model of law.

Holmes, by contrast, would have had no such trouble because his conception of morality was pretty much the one articulated in this section and his model of law was dynamic. As he put it:

> The language of judicial decision is mainly the language of logic. And the logical method and form flatter that longing for certainty and for repose which is in every human mind. But certainty generally is illusion, and

109 Ibid.

110 Hart, 'Positivism and the Separation of Law and Morals', 70.

111 Ibid.

> repose is not the destiny of man. Behind the logical form lies a judgment as to the relative worth and importance of competing legislative grounds, often an inarticulate and unconscious judgment, it is true, and yet the very root and nerve of the whole proceeding. You can give any conclusion a logical form. You always can imply a condition in a contract. But why do you imply it? It is because of some belief as to the practice of the community or of a class, or because of some opinion as to policy, or, in short, because of some attitude of yours upon a matter not capable of exact quantitative measurement, and therefore not capable of founding exact logical conclusions. Such matters really are battle grounds where the means do not exist for the determinations that shall be good for all time, and where the decision can do no more than embody the preference of a given body in a given time and place. We do not realize how large a part of our law is open to reconsideration upon a slight change in the habit of the public mind.[112]

Fuller is helpful in this regard. In *The Law in Quest of Itself*, the book which is Hart's main though implicit foil in 1958, he declared 'false'

> the common picture according to which there exists outside the law, and wholly independent of it, a body of moral precepts which exerts a kind of one-way gravitational pull on the law, against which the law opposes a constant inertia, so that it lags always behind morality and only meets those minimum ethical demands which relate to the most pressing social needs. ... Actually, if we look to those rules of morality which have enough teeth in them to act as a serious deterrent to men's pursuit of their selfish interests, we will find that far from being 'extra-legal', they are intimately and organically connected with the functionings of the legal order.[113]

Fuller proceeded to set out a nuanced relationship between law, morals and coercion. He was not, he said, claiming that 'men are, in the ordinary affairs of life, consciously deterred by legal penalties' as his view 'concedes that the effective deterrents which shape the average man's conduct derive from morality, from a sense of right and wrong'. Instead, what his view 'asserts is that these conceptions of right and wrong are themselves significantly shaped by the daily functionings of the legal order, and that they would be profoundly altered if this legal order were to disappear'.[114] The role of the judge in all of this is 'not merely laying down a system of

[112] Holmes, 'The Path of the Law', 466. On the dynamic dimension of Holmes's legal theory in contrast to static kinds of legal positivism, see Kellogg, *Oliver Wendell Holmes, Jr. and Legal Logic*, chapter 8, 'Positivism'.

[113] Fuller, *The Law in Quest of Itself*, 135–6.

[114] Ibid, 137.

minimum restraints designed to keep the bad man in check, but . . . in fact helping to create a body of common morality which will help define the good man'.[115]

Fuller himself noted that the idea of inquiry here is basically pragmatic,[116] and his idea of the usefulness of fictions is very like the pragmatist claim that we need to make regulative assumptions in order to engage in inquiry of any kind. In this light, the technical or, if you like, formal tools law provides in any field have been constructed to further inquiry about right answers to questions posed in that field.

Consider in this light the role of law in nineteenth-century Britain in consigning women to second-class status. In order to have second-class status, recall, one has to have one foot in the first-class space, the other in the discriminatory space. Thus, those bits of the law which recognized women's formal equality made problematic the bits which did not. Just this kind of issue led to debate and legislation in Britain about whether 'he' in statutory language was gender neutral, an issue which resurfaced in Canada and in the Privy Council in the *Persons Case*, about whether women counted as 'persons' appointable to the Senate.[117] The same kind of story can and has been told of the struggle for gay rights, notably, the right to same-sex marriage, in many liberal democratic states.[118]

Moreover, in mandating legal reforms which address such problems law provides a kind of laboratory for the testing of moral ideas. The kinds of social prejudices which help to maintain a group in second-class status might wither in the face of the experience made available when the law helps to begin to bring that group into a condition of equality. Such change comes about because the positive law of any legal order is always saturated with the morality of the society in which the order is located. In one sense, the moral content of the law will amount to positive morality, what some number of individuals in the society happen to think should be made into legal public morality and have the power to get incorporated into positive law, enforced by sanctions. But in order for such a legal norm to be made, it has to enter into the process of dynamic juridical production, and as Hart himself told us, that permits a negative response

115 Ibid.

116 See, ibid, 96, where Fuller likens the 'as if' method to the pragmatist approach to inquiry.

117 *Edwards* v. *Canada (Attorney General)* [1930] AC 124.

118 See, for example, David Boies and Theodore B Olson, *Redeeming the Dream: The Case for Marriage Equality* (New York: Viking, 2014) and Walter Frank, *Law and the Gay Rights Story: The Long Search for Equal Justice in a Divided Democracy* (New Brunswick: Rutgers University Press, 2014).

to the 'positivist thesis that "law may have any content"'.[119] Hart was therefore wrong to suppose that 'immunity from deliberate change' is a formal feature of social morality. The 'complex congruent practice'[120] of acceptance which is constitutive of the authority of the modern legal state requires that the legal order be seen as a laboratory for working out the content of the morality of the society ruled by its law. That morality is the fund of the society's values which have been transformed into law.

I have suggested here that only a pragmatic idiom is capable of accurately describing the way in which law understood as a dynamic process of juridical production shapes our inquiry about what moral judgments we should as legal subjects make. As Cheryl Misak puts it in her account of Holmes's pragmatism:

> It explains the idea of authority – of when it is legitimate, and then, *why* it is legitimate. It tells us that there is a fund of inherited social value that is unavoidable, and is itself the product of experience. But what the values are, how they should evolve, or be revised or replaced, and even how to understand them, is open to experience. Hence, authoritative pronouncements are provisional punctuation points in a process of inquiry.[121]

In Section 6.3, I bring together the main themes of this book in an exploration of how juridical production in an autonomous legal sphere can help to explain how the law can be authoritative, but only as marking 'provisional punctuation points in a process of inquiry'.

6.3 The Autonomy of the Legal

In introducing his discussion of 'Justice and Morality' in *The Concept of Law*, Hart said of natural law positions which contest his Separation Thesis that, while they might concede that his rule-of-recognition analysis of legal order is a 'starting point for the understanding of law', they would claim that it is not enough.

> Far more questionable from this point of view is the title to be treated as law of those municipal legal systems which exhibit the full complement of *juge, gendarme et legislateur* but fail to conform to certain fundamental requirements of justice or morality. In the words of St. Augustine 'What are states without justice but robber-bands enlarged?'[122]

[119] Hart, *The Concept of Law*, 199.
[120] Ibid, 118.
[121] Misak, 'A Pragmatist Account of Legitimacy and Authority', 306. Her emphasis.
[122] Hart, *The Concept of Law*, 156.

In alluding to Montesquieu's veneration for the separation of powers between the judiciary, the executive and the legislature in the same breath as he quoted Augustine's influential dictum, Hart signalled his aim of using Augustine to debunk Montesquieu's claim that the law of the modern legal state will have a moral quality to it just because of the separation of powers. His suggestion was that natural lawyers acknowledge that for the law of that state to have this kind of quality, it must conform to something more fundamental, either justice or morality. But with that acknowledgement, they also concede, he thought, that justice of the sort they have in mind is a standard external to legal order, not a condition an order has to meet to count as legal.[123]

The problems Hart's legal theory encountered in resisting the claim that the law of the modern legal state will have a moral quality to it arise because he and his successors accepted Augustine's distinction between de facto authority and de jure authority. For Augustine followed his question 'What are states without justice?' with another: 'What are bands of robbers themselves but little kingdoms?'[124] The second question arises because a band, like a kingdom, 'is governed by the authority of a ruler; it is bound by a pact of association; and the loot is divided according to an agreed law'. Augustine then reported the 'pertinent and true answer' given by a pirate seized by Alexander the Great when asked what the pirate intended by 'infesting the sea': 'The same as you do when you infest the whole world; but because I do it with a little ship I am called a robber, and because you do it with a great fleet, you are an emperor.' The difference between the robber band and the kingdom is, Augustine concluded, quantitative not qualitative: 'If, by the constant addition of desperate men, this scourge grows to such a size that it acquires territory, establishes a seat of government, occupies cities and subjugates peoples, it assumes the name of kingdom more openly. For this name is now manifestly conferred upon it not by the removal of greed, but by the addition of impunity.'[125] Since, that is, both a robber band and a kingdom wield the same kind of authority, a kingdom is merely a robber band – Hart's 'gunman' – writ large. We need, on this account, to distinguish between the kind of de facto authority robbers and kings

[123] We saw in Chapter 1 that Dworkin at one point made exactly this concession in response to positivist criticism.

[124] Augustine, *The City of God against the Pagans* (Cambridge: Cambridge University Press, 1998, RW Dyson, ed. and trans.), 147–8.

[125] Ibid.

wield – a mode of exercising power built on a pact and regulated by laws obeyed because of the penalties for disobedience – and legitimate authority, which is authority wielded justly; and justice in Augustine's view is unattainable by an earthly power.

As we have seen, Hart and his successors also suppose that it follows from the distinction between de facto and de jure authority that the content of the positive law of a legal order is simply the content which those with power to make law have injected into the law. The main difference between them and Augustine is that they, as by and large secular thinkers, think that the unattainability of de jure authority results from the fact that it is highly unlikely that the content of the positive law of any actual legal order will coincide fully or even mostly with the demands of humanly but correctly determined moral principles. As a result, their legal theory cannot distinguish between law and the gunman situation writ large. To the extent that the commands of the sovereign and its officials are considered authoritative, the commands are, to use the wonderfully evocative description of one of Hart's successors, 'normatively inert'.[126]

While my book is structured by the way in which Hart bequeathed this problem to philosophy of law, we have also seen its roots in Hobbes, and I have pointed out here that it goes back even further, to Augustine, more than a thousand years before Hobbes wrote *Leviathan*. In fact, it goes even further back because Augustine's telling of the tale of Alexander and the pirate was his response to Cicero's argument in *On the Commonwealth* that there is a kind of justice intrinsic to the legal order of a state, itself a response to the cynic philosopher Carneadas and his notorious duo of speeches in Rome in which he first proved the existence of justice and then disproved it.[127]

Benjamin Straumann has recently argued that Augustine failed to appreciate that the Ciceronian response to Carneadas does not rely on the idea that there are immutable principles of justice with which the law of the state must accord if it is to be legitimate. Rather, it offers a constitutionalist idea of a normative hierarchy at the top of which are the higher-order norms which together with 'statutory law (*lex*)' make up a '*jus publicum*', a public order of legal right.[128] Straumann adds that

[126] John Gardner, *Law as a Leap of Faith*, 23.

[127] Cicero, *Cicero on the Commonwealth and on the Laws* (Cambridge: Cambridge University Press, 2017, 2nd ed., James EG Zetzel, ed. and trans.).

[128] Benjamin Straumann, *Crisis and Constitutionalism: Roman Political Thought from the Fall of the Republic to the Age of Revolution* (Oxford: Oxford University Press, 2016), 147.

Cicero's constitutionalist idea is driven by a concern 'with norms that could be justified *outside* the framework of any given polity – in a pre-political state of nature'.[129]

That the norms must be justified 'outside' would to Hart only serve to confirm his view that his main natural law foils amount to positivism with a minus sign – that a legal order consists of its positive law with laws unjust by an external standard subtracted. But I have also shown that Hart's own position is closer to one which says that these higher-order norms are both inside and outside legal order, as we have seen from his two-step argument in chapters 8 and 9 of *The Concept of Law*.

In chapter 8, 'Justice and Morals', Hart argued that there is an ideal of justice intrinsic to both legal order and an order of social morality. But the former, he suggested, not only is consistent with great iniquity, but it can also serve to make more efficient the infliction of iniquity on those subject to law. Then, in chapter 9, 'Laws and Morals', while he conceded that there is minimum natural law content to the law of any legal order, he insisted that because this content need not be extended to all legal subjects, for example a class of enslaved persons, its existence is consistent with the Separation Thesis.

I argued in Section 6.2 that when one drops Hart's commitment to a static model of law, the Separation Thesis is no longer tenable, as he came close to recognizing. If juridical norm production, including the element of official interpretation, is a complex and dynamic mix of attention to enacted law, minimum natural law content and intrinsic principles of legality, there is a necessary connection between law and morality. The conception of morality here is that proposed by pragmatists and it is the conception we need to make sense of law's claim to authority, which can't be anything but a claim to legitimate authority.

This idea of authority is true to Hart's own philosophical instincts. The claim about necessity is not about 'immutable principles', nor about how we are always progressing to some inevitable ideal state, nor about correspondence with a natural order of things. Rather, as Hart put the point in chapter 8 of *The Concept of Law*, it is about 'a truth of some importance that for the adequate description not only of law but of many other social institutions, a place must be reserved, besides definitions and ordinary statement of facts, for a third category of statements: those the

129 Ibid. His emphasis.

truth of which is contingent on human beings and the world they live in retaining the salient characteristics they have'.[130]

In addition, in both chapters 8 and 9 of *The Concept of Law*, Hart argued, as we have seen, that a wider conception of social morality and of legal order is preferable to a narrower conception on two grounds. First, it is a mistake from the perspective of theoretical understanding to exclude orders which function in accordance with their formal features merely on the ground that their norms have a morally suspect content. Second, from the perspective of morality, a wider conception will respond better to conflicts between the norms of the orders and other external norms, for example the norms of liberal morality, because it does not wish away the conflict but approaches it with candour. Indeed, the grounds combine very effectively when one notes that most legal orders have had at times deeply illiberal content, as do many today in an increasingly illiberal world, and so it would be decidedly odd if philosophy of law were devoted exclusively to the study of liberal legal orders. And we know that Hart and his followers accused Dworkin of putting forward not a theory of law but a mere theory of adjudication appropriate only for contingently liberal legal orders.

I have indicated my view that Hart's argument for a wider conception is sound at an abstract level but goes awry in its details. His static model of law prevented him from addressing the moral complexity occasioned by such conflicts as he consigned them to other disciplines, while his adherence to the Separation Thesis left him unable to articulate how a

[130] Hart, *The Concept of Law*, 199–200. In 'Positivism and the Separation of Law and Morals', Hart reached for the same point, but both did not make it as perspicuously and relied on it in his main response to Fuller in the manner which helped to create the problems which have since deadlocked legal theory. At 80, he suggested that we could conceive of a world in which we are like giant armoured crabs, so that we would not have the vulnerabilities of us soft-skinned human beings that lead us to make rules prohibiting violence, and so on. This thought experiment helped, he thought, to show that on the 'contingent fact' of the makeup of human beings as we are 'rest huge structures of our thought and principles of action and social life'. He seemed to suggest that this fact also helped to demonstrate the Separation Thesis – no *necessary* connection – since in the world of crab law those structures would be very different. In one sense he was right. The connection between law and morality for which this book argues is based on this contingent fact since the question for philosophy of law is: what is law in our world as we find it, populated by beings like us with the vulnerabilities we happen to have? But we simply don't care about crab-law. Nor did Hart most of the time, since he was deeply concerned with analysing both the benefits and the dangers for individuals who find themselves in fact subject not only to the sheer centralized power of the modern legal state, but also to its claim to rule as a matter of right.

normatively inert legal norm could ever come into a conflict with a norm from outside the order of the modern legal state. The abstract argument is sound, that is, only once rid of the features which impede it, as we can see by elaborating it in light of insights from Bernard Williams's essay 'Realism and Moralism in Political Theory', an account of the problems encountered by liberal theories of legitimate political authority.[131]

In Williams's view, legitimacy is a matter of the actual acceptance of a political order's authority by those subject to it. He thus opposed liberal political theories which make morality prior to politics, either by adopting an 'enactment model', which 'surveys society to see how it may be made better' (e.g. the utilitarian command theorists and Raz's theory of political and legal authority), or in the form of the 'structural model' (e.g. Dworkin's rights-based theory). The latter set 'conditions in which power can be justly exercised'. In contrast to these versions of 'political moralism', Williams advocated 'political realism' which he thought gives a 'greater autonomy to distinctively political thought'[132] and thus does not suppose that legitimacy reduces to one or other version of liberal moral theory, which would have the result that very few political societies which have ever existed were legitimate.[133] In other words, he argued for the 'autonomy of the political' – a deliberate and provocative echo of Carl Schmitt's fascistic legal and political theory.[134] Realism counsels, in Williams's view, that what counts as legitimate in a particular political order is relative to what is accepted as a matter of fact in that order, not what some theory has determined as the moral standards which any order has to meet to count as legitimate; for example, and as many liberals would argue, that its laws respect some predetermined list of individual rights.

Hart's objection to what we can think of as liberal legal theories such as Dworkin's can be put in very similar terms. His analysis of law as an order of authority and his explanation of authority in terms of actual acceptance clearly resonate with Williams's analysis of the legitimacy of political order. He also shared with Williams the sense that something goes wrong both theoretically and morally speaking when one's study of order is restricted to orders which one happens morally to

131 Williams, 'Realism and Moralism in Political Theory', 1.
132 Ibid, 3.
133 Structural models belong to the family of Kantian political theory. See Appendix II.
134 See also his remarks in 'From Freedom to Liberty: The Construction of a Political Value', in Williams, *In the Beginning Was the Deed* 75, 77–8.

endorse.[135] And while, as we saw in the Introduction Raz describe Hart's contribution, his legal theory was 'realist and unromantic in outlook',[136] it was not realist in the way in which the command theory of law reduced law to facts about coercion, nor in the way in which certain versions of Legal Realism reduced (or are taken to reduce) law to facts to do with the prediction of official behaviour.

But we know that Hart feared that talk of legitimacy imports a moral component to the analysis of legal order which one should avoid if one is to preserve the wide scope of one's inquiry. For him, there was a clear distinction between the authority a legal order has as a matter of fact and legitimate authority, whereas Williams supposed that acceptance is constitutive of legitimacy. Williams was willing to make that supposition because, as we saw in Chapter 2, he took as the main mark of 'the political' that a society had found an answer to the 'first political question' – the Hobbesian question of how to secure 'order, protection, safety, trust, and the conditions of cooperation'.[137] It is the 'first' political question because 'solving it is the condition of solving, indeed posing, any others'.[138] A society which has solved the problem of order etc. is by that token legitimate. Williams's account of acceptance is, however, nuanced, as it requires actual acceptance but under the right conditions. It requires one to navigate between the Scylla and Charybdis of social contract theory; between, that is, actual and hypothetical consent, a dilemma which in legal theory manifests itself in the question whether the higher-order 'legal' norms are inside or outside legal order.

I already noted in Chapter 3 that Williams argued that a political order differs from a mere or 'unmediated' coercive order in that it seeks to satisfy the 'Basic Legitimation Demand' (BLD) which every legitimate state must satisfy if it is to show that it wields authority rather than sheer coercive power over those subject to its rule. To meet that demand the state 'has to be able to offer a justification of its power *to each subject*', which means to every individual in its power, 'whom by its own lights it can rightfully coerce under its laws and institutions'.[139] For this reason,

[135] Hart, *The Concept of Law*, 209–12. For a more detailed exploration of the similarities between Williams and Hart, see my 'The Inevitable Social Contract' (2021) 27*Res Publica* 187.

[136] Joseph Raz, 'Authority, Law, and Morality', in Raz, *Ethics in the Public Domain: Essays in the Morality of Law and Politics* (Oxford: Oxford University Press, 1994) 194.

[137] 'Williams, 'Realism and Moralism in Political Theory', 3.

[138] Ibid.

[139] Ibid, 4. His emphasis.

Williams said that 'first' should not be understood as implying that the first question 'once solved ... never has to be solved again'. 'Because a solution to the first political question is *required all the time*, the character of the solution is affected by historical circumstances: it is not a matter of arriving at a solution to the first question at the level of state-of-nature theory and then going on to the rest of the agenda.'[140]

In addition, Williams thought that if the solution were to avoid reintroducing the problem it was meant to address, for example, by provoking danger and distrust thus undermining cooperation, one needed in addition to the BLD 'the critical theory principle': 'the acceptance of justification does not count if the acceptance is produced by the coercive power which is supposedly being justified'.[141] That principle reinforced the tension in his position between the 'acceptability' of reasons, that is, reasons that in principle should be accepted but may not be, and reasons that are as a matter of fact accepted, even though they should not. Finally, he conceded a little enigmatically that the BLD may be a 'moral principle', at least in that 'it is inherent in there being first a political question'.[142]

On my argument, positivistic legal theory helps to show that the critical theory principle can be given an institutional expression which both explains the role of moral principle in a political realism and why the line between acceptable and in-fact-accepted reasons should be blurred. For positivism teaches us, against its intentions, that once one embarks on the path of explaining the authority of a de facto legal order – a legal order which exists as a matter of fact – the distinction between legitimate or de jure authority and de facto authority is difficult to sustain. Morality comes into the picture, 'inherent', as Williams just said, in 'there being first a political question'. The point is not only one of similarity in what might be thought of as any attempt to explain the logic of political and legal authority. In addition, my reconstruction of legal theory displays the resources of legal order without which Williams's challenge to liberalism will seem either a reduction of legitimacy to what people happen to believe, however the belief is produced, or no challenge

140 The quote is from 'Human Rights and Relativism', in Williams, *In the Beginning Was the Deed* 62, at 62. His emphasis. But the same thought is to be found in 'Realism and Moralism in Political Theory', 3.

141 Ibid, 6.

142 Ibid.

at all because what matters is the legitimacy of the political order onto which the beliefs latch and not the beliefs themselves.

Chapter 2 took the first step in this reconstruction, which does not seek to resolve the tension in the abstract, but only to show how the institutional structure of the modern legal state provides a space in which it can be productively addressed. Williams adopted the orthodox interpretation of Hobbes, in his terms, asserting that Hobbes thought that it was a sufficient condition for an order to be legitimate that it had successfully answered 'once and for all' the first political question.[143] But, as we saw, the contracting individuals in the state of nature, through forming themselves into the unity of the state and at the same time subjecting themselves to sovereign rule, transform themselves from natural individuals into legal subjects. With that transformation, they establish a relationship of reciprocity between subject and sovereign: the 'mutuall Relation between Protection and Obedience', as Hobbes put it in the last paragraph of *Leviathan*.[144]

That relationship is not between the natural individuals who hold sovereign office and the natural individuals who are party to the covenant. It is between two kinds of artificial person – the person of the sovereign and the persons who are legal subjects – and in it is the essence of the political, of the fact that a political order has been established in which rule is by right and the natural realm of rule by might has been left behind. Put differently, a political order is characterized by authority relationships by contrast with unmediated coercive power. It is not that a political order can do without coercive power, only that when it wields such power it does so on the basis of authority in a way which provides a foundation for the claim by legal officials to have been authorized by those subject to that power. Any exercise of coercive power by the state must therefore be recognizable as an authoritative act, which entails that it must, according to Hobbes's legal theory, meet two conditions of legality. The first condition is formal, as I termed it, the 'validity proviso' that any exercise of power must show a legal warrant in a law made in accordance with the formal public criteria for recognizing a law as such in the legal order. The second condition is substantive: any exercise of power must meet the 'legality proviso': the laws the sovereign makes have

143 Ibid, 3.

144 Hobbes, *Leviathan*, 491. For a full Hobbesian response to Williams, see my 'Emergencies and Human Rights: A Hobbesian Analysis', in Bardo Fassbender and Knut Traisbach, eds, *The Limits of Human Rights* (Oxford: Oxford University Press, 2019) 89.

to be interpreted, and so must be interpretable, in light of Hobbes's extensive list of the laws of nature. And both provisos will receive institutional expression.

As Straumann's study of Roman constitutionalism shows, central to the Roman juridical mode of responding to crises was the preservation of, first, the institution of *provocatio* – the citizens' right of appeal against decisions which affected them negatively by those who held high office – and, second, of the principal legislative institutions of the state and their modes of lawmaking. Such preservation was seen as a matter of the higher order of natural law which expressed the normative core of the republican idea of 'the people' of a political and legal order.[145]

In his analysis of these institutions, Straumann brings to the surface the Roman idea of political community as a jural community. As he explains, the jural conception of politics emerged against a backdrop of the decay of Roman political institutions which made vivid the possibility of the disintegration of society into the anarchy of a state of nature and so raised as urgent questions the location of sovereignty in – as well as the fundamental commitments of – the political order. Simply put, the question was raised of the nature of the Roman political order. The Roman answer, as formulated principally by Cicero, rejected Greek theories which asserted a continuity between ethics and politics such that there is some highest ethical good at which politics aims and in which, as Charles McIlwain put it, 'the law in a state [is thought of] only as one part or rather as one aspect of the polity itself, never as something outside or apart from the state to which that polity must conform, nor even any special provision within the state to which other laws are subordinate'.[146] Instead, it was based on the argument that the political order is constituted by 'law-like constitutional principles' so that the highest officers of state are in charge of 'the people' only because it is the case that these principles are in charge of the officers.[147]

That the Roman legal order already has this conception is significant. As Straumann shows, the jural conception was first conceived by the Romans; and no one would accuse the Romans of liberalism. As a result, the jural conception of politics is not liberal, except in the following

145 Straumann, *Crisis and Constitutionalism*, 129–39.

146 Charles Howard McIlwain, *Constitutionalism: Ancient and Modern* (Ithaca, NY: Cornell University Press, 1961, revised ed.) 37, quoted in Straumann, *Crisis and Constitutionalism*, 191.

147 Ibid, 25.

sense. The very idea that individuals do not have to consider themselves as striving to achieve some highest ethical good, but simply as members of a community in which coercive state action must be justified as being in accordance with law, may in our era favour liberal ideologies over others. Indeed, the claim that authority is a matter of reasoned justification is strongly associated with both liberalism and the constitutionalist tradition, as Williams in fact acknowledged.[148]

Notice that this claim opens up the prospect of a realm of politics which is independent of any conception of the highest ethical good for individuals and that the alternatives in the 'reason-of-state' tradition to which Schmitt belonged are all about closing down political conflict by a legally unconstrained decision.[149] One can consequently argue that if Schmitt was right that political theory needs a conception of the autonomy of the political,[150] it is to be found in the constitutionalist vision first articulated by Roman political theorists and jurists. Even more important is that the constitutionalist tradition established both the right to reasoned justification as the mark of the political relationship and that a juridical institutional structure be put in place which seeks to ensure that such justification is available. As Straumann shows, in the hands of Bodin and Hobbes the ruling out of a constitutional right of resistance is matched by the installation within the political order of the legal institutions of a well-ordered society, one which militates against a sovereign's need to resort to the secret policies and acts of illegal violence that form part of the *arcana* or 'dark matter'[151] which is the stuff of Schmitt's reason-of-state tradition.[152]

The constitutionalist tradition cannot of course claim to have eliminated such dark matter from any particular legal order. Rather, its ambition is to strive for its elimination through a continual process of experimentation in light of experience. It is thus deeply hopeful as well as pragmatic in spirit and, in the latter half of the twentieth century, has

148 Williams, 'Realism and Moralism', 9–11.

149 See my *Legality and Legitimacy: Carl Schmitt, Hans Kelsen and Hermann Heller in Weimar* (Oxford: Clarendon Press, 1997).

150 Carl Schmitt, *The Concept of the Political* (Chicago: University of Chicago Press, 1996, George Schwab, trans.).

151 See Thomas Poole, *Reason of State: Law, Prerogative and Empire* (Cambridge: Cambridge University Press, 2015), 56 and 'The Law of Emergency and Reason of State', in Evan Criddle, ed., *Human Rights in Emergencies* (New York: Cambridge University Press, 2016) 148.

152 See Straumann, *Crisis and Constitutionalism*, 306–7.

developed an apparatus both internationally and domestically around human rights regimes which is immensely complex in comparison to the constitutional instruments which typified the period before the Second World War, let alone those of the Roman Republic. It includes distinctions between derogable and non-derogable rights, different kinds of supervisory bodies at the international and national levels, doctrines of deference, proportionality, reasonableness and margin of appreciation.

This apparatus is a thick and complex institutional expression of the critical theory principle through legal mechanisms which require public reasons for decisions and independent checks on both the accuracy and cogency of the reasons. But all this complexity can be distilled down to the constitutional fundamentals of the Roman political and legal order: the subject's right of appeal to a body independent of the official who wields coercive power and the claim that the law – both enacted law and constitutional principle – is in charge of the officials, no matter how elevated their office. These two fundamentals make up the necessary institutional basis of what we can think of as the legal subject's political right of rights, the right in virtue of being subject to state coercive power to have justified any exercise of such power.

The constitutionalist idea advanced in my Chapter 3 thus has its origins in the break Roman lawyers effected with the Greek equation of the constitution with the whole political framework of a community. The constitution becomes the idea of *jus publicum*, a public law which includes fundamental principles of legality which link the autonomous space of politics with the autonomous space of law. But the autonomy of the former requires the autonomy of the latter. Legal order is the principal means of mediating might so that it is transformed into right. To be autonomous, a political order must therefore respect the autonomy of legal order. In so doing, it puts in place the core of constitutionalism – the political project of ensuring that the government of a polity is accountable to its subjects in terms of a scheme of constitutional principle. On this argument, one should, as we saw Hobbes advise at the end of Chapter 4, refrain from seeking to say how a modern legal state could ever acquire the right to rule. Rather, given that such states will claim that right, one should inquire into how the legal mediation of states' coercive power, tested by actual acceptance, is necessary to vindicate their claim.

As we have seen, on Hart's view, legal order cannot be understood other than in terms of law's authority – its special normativity – which he acknowledged involved the distinctive kinds of arguments which lawyers will make in seeking an answer based on the public record of law in a particular jural community.[153] My claim in this chapter is that philosophy of law can help to show why that idea is plausible, as it shows us how fundamental principles of legality shape our inquiry. For our confidence in these compulsory moral judgments is in part built upon the principles contained in the institutional make-up of law, in the vision of constitutionalism first formulated by the Romans.

First, there is the institutional expression of the principle which requires that legal subjects have the right to ask an independent official for reasons why the law applies to them in a way which addresses them as persons with dignity as responsible agents. Second, there is the institutional expression of the principles which underpin legal mechanisms for changing law in a way which makes the judgments embedded in the law revisable in light of further experience. These kinds of principle make it both possible for those who find themselves relegated by the law to second-class status to ask a judge 'But, how can that be law for me?' and, if no adequate answer can be provided, for an internal legal imperative to kick in which requires reform.[154] The commitment to legality entailed in the construction of the modern legal state requires a 'progressive realization of constitutionalism' in a bid to keep the solution legal order offers from reintroducing the problem of disorder it is designed to solve.[155]

The foremost contemporary articulation of this idea remains, as I have indicated in several places, Fuller's exposition of the principles of legality in *The Morality of Law*.[156] Fuller said his principle of congruence – that the 'actual administration' of rules must be 'congruent' with the 'rules as announced' – was the 'most complex' of the eight principles. For it 'may

[153] Even in public international law, as we saw in Chapter 4, despite the fact that Hart denied that it was law properly so-called.

[154] For an exploration of similar ideas, with reliance on Fuller, see Jeremy Waldron, 'How Law Protects Dignity' (2012) 71 *Cambridge Law Journal* 200.

[155] CJ Friedrich, *Constitutional Reason of State* (Providence: Brown University Press, 1957), 90. Friedrich, who had observed the travails of the Weimar Republic as a student in Germany before he embarked on a career which made him one of the USA's most influential political scientists, wrote that while the Kantian solution of a world state was unattainable, there was nevertheless something to be learned from it. It had 'the advantage of providing a developmental model and a pragmatic, if not a practical projection into the future, by which concrete political action programs may be inspired and policy shaped'; ibid, 89. For an exploration of similar ideas in the international domain, see Evan Criddle and Evan Fox-Decent, *Fiduciaries of Humanity: How International Law Constitutes Authority* (Oxford: Oxford University Press, 2016).

[156] Fuller, *The Morality of Law*, chapter 2.

be destroyed or impaired in a great variety of ways: mistaken interpretation, inaccessibility of the law, lack of insight into what is required to maintain the integrity of a legal system, bribery, prejudice, indifference, stupidity, and the drive toward personal power'.[157] In addition, he said that 'procedural devices designed to maintain it take, of necessity, a variety of forms'.[158]

Fuller's discussion of these forms connects his argument to his essay on 'The Forms and Limits of Adjudication' in which he emphasized the importance of impartial adjudicators in a rule-of-law order, in which the issues submitted to the adjudicators '[tend] to be *converted* into a claim of right or an accusation of guilt. This conversion is effected by the institutional framework within which both the litigant and the adjudicator function'.[159] This process of presenting 'proofs and reasoned arguments' requires, as we saw in Chapter 4 in 'Luke's game', the person making the arguments to present them as more than a 'naked demand'. They must be presented as a 'claim of right', that is, as 'supported by a principle'. As a result, 'issues tried before an adjudicator tend to become claims of rights or accusations of fault'.[160] The 'object of the rule of law is to substitute for violence peaceful ways of settling disputes. Obviously peace cannot be assured simply by treaties, agreements, and legislative enactment. There must be some agency capable of determining the rights of the parties in concrete situations of controversy.'[161]

I have shown that for this adjudicative conversion process to take place the law must be convertible, and that requires a prior conversion process. Legislation requires the reduction of a political programme to the explicit terms of a statute and thus a conversion of policy into legal public standards, which produces a kind of legal surplus value. By this I mean that the legitimacy of official action in compliance with the statute is not simply compliance with a political policy which the powers that be have

157 Ibid, 39, 81.

158 Ibid, 81.

159 Lon L Fuller, 'The Forms and Limits of Adjudication', in Kenneth I Winston, ed., *The Principles of Social Order: Selected Essays of Lon L Fuller* (Oxford: Hart Publishing, 2001) 101, at 111. My emphasis.

160 Ibid, 111.

161 Ibid, 114. Fuller also claimed, ibid, that courts and other adjudicative institutions are 'essential to the rule of law' and such a claim casts doubt on the legal status of public international law. But, as I argued in Chapter 4 via the story of Luke's game, one does not need the institutional division of labour to find adjudication in the international order.

determined appropriate. It is also the case that this conversion process *adds* value because it brings into being a particular type of *public* standard, one permitting the operation of the principles identified by Fuller as the desiderata of the inner morality of law, and which enables claims of right based on legal principle to be adjudicated. As I argued from Chapter 2 on, if the law is not convertible in this way, a problem is raised internal to legal order which requires those charged with maintaining the integrity of legal order to consider reform.

In addition, for legislators to attempt to effect moral change through law requires submission to the discipline of legality at several points. First, their policy must be made into a legal policy, which requires its conversion into standards which are general, etc. Second, there is the point of application. Third, there is the point when an individual asks a judge for an interpretation of the law which justifies its application in a way which answers the question 'But, how can that be law for me?' It is this discipline which, as Hart recognized, permits the response to the 'positivist thesis that "law may have any content"'.[162] Looking back at the history of the legal subordination of women or any other group can thus make us more aware of the possibility of injustice in our present situation which we find difficult to see. Here legality can be useful against law, as it were. We might be able to detect moral problems which we should address because of inconsistencies and tensions in our *legal* treatment of groups.

In this section I adapted the Marxist term of surplus value to describe this process and, to take another expression from the Marxist lexicon, we can say that quantity turns into quality. Recall from Chapter 4 my description of the two Kelsenian ladders: the ladder of formal authorization stretching from the lowest rung, at which legal norms are concretized, to the highest rung at which the most constitutional authorizing norms reside, and the ladder of material concretization. When legal officials exercise their formal interpretive authority, they are also giving further content to the norm or norms they are interpreting, which requires an act of creative judgment. But, while creative, the judgment is constrained by the requirement that its content is understandable as a norm within a unified field of legal meaning.

This substantive condition might not at first seem to amount to much, given Kelsen's admonition that the law can have any content. But that is

[162] Hart, *The Concept of Law*, 199.

in a way part of the substantive point. The formality of the procedures permits public policy appropriately determined outside the law to be enacted into law. Further, in understanding how public policy makes its way into law, one must avoid the positivistic mistake, highlighted by dynamic models of legal order, in supposing that law is merely a means for transmitting political/policy judgments from top to bottom, though no one should deny that law plays this important role. The point is rather to see that law does more than merely transmit public policy. It also converts it into legal form.

Put differently, the suggestion is that the ladder of formal authorization and the ladder of material concretization should be seen as one. This is not to say that the action on each rung of the ladder is the same and there are political choices to be made about how to structure the action on each rung. Rather, the crucial political choice is whether to have the ladder at all. For in putting the ladder in place, one makes the decision to have what, on the eve of South Africa's transition from apartheid to constitutional democracy, Etienne Mureinik, the country's leading public lawyer at that time, described as a 'culture of justification'. This is a culture in which 'every exercise of power is expected to be justified; in which leadership given by government rests on the cogency of the case offered in defence of its decisions, not the fear inspired by the force at its command'.[163]

The ladder constitutes such a choice because on it reasons travel in both directions, from top to bottom and from bottom to top. This may conjure up the image of a two-way conveyor belt, which in line with points made earlier in this section captures an important part of what is going on, though only a part. It captures only a part because from the top-to-bottom perspective of a legislator, judge or public official looking down the ladder at the legal subject, to get on to any of the rungs requires conversion, as I have already sketched. But it is important to know that conversion is required from the bottom-to-top perspective, that is, it is required of the legal subject who, looking up the ladder, wishes to bring a legal challenge.

As Lars Vinx has explained, Kelsen's category of 'voidable legal norms' – laws which are valid until declared invalid by an official with authority so to declare – has important implications for both the legal subject and for the design of legal order. So long as the legal order

[163] Etienne Mureinik, 'A Bridge to Where? Introducing the Interim Bill of Rights' (1994) 10 *South African Journal on Human Rights* 32.

introduces mechanisms of internal review sufficient to provide to legal subjects the opportunity to get an authoritative determination of the legality of a decision affecting their rights and interests, subjects should provisionally give up their right to judge whether the norm is binding. That there are officials with such authority who are independent of the officials who have issued the contested norm, and that the former will inquire into the norm's material as well as its formal validity, argues even more strongly in favour of the claim that legal subjects should adopt the stance that the laws of their legal order are binding on them. Since in every legal order the state will claim that its laws are so binding, the issue becomes whether the legal order through which the state speaks is designed so that those subject to it can make sense of that claim.[164]

Vinx also argues that it is the case for Kelsen both that the full legitimacy of the legal order can be achieved only in a democracy and that a democratic political order can vindicate its claim on the obedience of its subjects only if it puts in place a legal order designed in the way just described.[165] I indicated in Chapter 3 that explicit in Kelsen's political theory is the conception of the legal subject as the autonomous citizen. Such citizens suffer from the 'torment of heteronomy' in surrendering their judgment to the will of the majority and thus should have justified to them why the institutional structure of democracy alleviates that torment. That tension is alleviated in the political realm by putting in place a system of representative government which preserves through the competition of political parties the principle of opposition, thus ensuring that legislation is the product of appropriate compromise.[166]

Kelsen did not make that same conception explicit in his legal theory. But I also suggested in Chapter 3 that it is difficult to understand his account of legal order in its absence. Since in all legal orders, however designed, the state will claim that the design in fact in place suffices to provide an appropriate justification to each subject who brings a legal challenge, it is that conception of the subject which affords the lens for understanding legal order as such and for evaluating individual legal orders. In other words, and as I have argued, what Hart called the 'internal point of view' of the participants in legal order cannot be

164 Lars Vinx, *Hans Kelsen's Pure Theory of Law: Legality and Legitimacy* (Oxford: Oxford University Press, 2007), 89–94.

165 Ibid, chapter 4.

166 See Hans Kelsen, *The Essence and Value of Democracy* (Lanham: Rowman and Littlefield, 2013, Nadia Urbinati and Carlo Invernizzi Accetti, eds, Brian Graf, trans.).

confined, as Hart thought it could be, to the officials of the legal order. The official point of view is intrinsically linked to the point of view of the legal subjects because the officials bear the onus of justification when subjects ask an official 'But, how can that be law for me?' To accept that onus is to accept that the law brought to bear must be understandable as treating the legal subject as someone with dignity as a responsible agent.

There are some important implications to this merger of Kelsen and Fuller. First, however legal order is designed, the view down from the top of the ladder is committed to the claim that the conversion of public policy into law can be justified in a way that answers a subject's challenge. Put differently, citizens (or at least their legislative representative at the top of the ladder), in taking on the role of a free and equal maker of law, must consider themselves in another role, that of the legal subjects, who think of their subjection as one to an order of laws which can be justified to them conceived as agents who enjoy freedom and equality before the law. Second, as Kelsen tells us, legal order and its different regimes of law, both public and private, can be designed in more or less autocratic ways, that is, more or less democratically.[167] To the extent that design is democratic, subjects become ever more active participants in determining the content of the law, albeit that they have to accept that they have provisionally given up their right to judge whether the norm as authoritatively determined is binding.

Third, from the top-to-bottom perspective of the legislator, the norm issued is in the nature of what Hobbes called a command – a reason to be obeyed merely because someone in authority has said it. But we know from Chapter 2 that he emphasized not only that all laws require interpretation but also that a condition of their authority as law is that they are interpretable in accordance with the laws of nature. The content of the command will get progressively filled as one goes down the ladder, with its content not determined until the law has been applied. In this understanding, the sovereign's act of making a law is only completed when the provisional resting point has been reached at which the norm has been applied and is, at least for the moment, unchallenged.

In this light, and as I argued in Chapter 3, one can see that the category of legal subject is not politically neutral.[168] The legal subject is a political

[167] See Appendix II for my discussion of the kind of Kantian legal theory based on an a priori distinction between private law and public law in which the former is asserted to be normatively superior and of which Kelsen was deeply suspicious.

[168] For further discussion, see Appendix III.

construction whose personality informs the whole design of legal order. Legal subjects are the individuals in the jural community whom particular laws must address by offering reasons for action which make sense to them as free and equal before the law. The process of converting public policy to legal form has the political point of making it possible for the justification of that policy to be undertaken in just this fashion.

The conveyor belt on the way down the ladder of formal authorization is constructed to facilitate such justification. To the extent that such justification is difficult or not possible, it is the task of those charged with interpreting the law to alert those higher up the ladder of formal authorization. In this way, the lived experience of subjects under the regime of laws is placed on the conveyor belt on the way up the ladder of formal authorization, which puts those with legislative authority under an onus to consider legal reform because enacted law has been claimed to be incapable of being justified in the requisite fashion. To be a subject of legal order is thus to be endowed with some aspects of citizenship because one is entitled to the kind of justification to which legal order in its nature is committed. And, as Kelsen pointed out, the ladder can be designed in ways which increase the burden of justification on the state, which would endow the legal subject with ever greater aspects of citizenship.[169]

If only the ladder of formal authorization were in place, one would have what we saw in Chapter 3 Mark Walters describe as a 'linear theory' of legal authority.[170] Recall that such theories assume 'that the authority of legal norms can be traced back along a line of increasingly higher norms until an originating source is located. Law from this perspective is held up by a string, and someone or something must hold the end of that string.'[171] But both because the ladder of formal authorization and the ladder of material concretization are as one, and because the traffic on that ladder is always two way, a linear theory will not do. Instead, we need what Walters calls a 'circular theory', which sees law as 'embedded within a network of interlocking strands of normative value that bend back upon themselves never reaching an end. The relevant image on this

[169] Kelsen, *Introduction to the Problems of Legal Theory*, 92–6.

[170] See Mark Walters, 'The Unwritten Constitution as a Legal Concept', in David Dyzenhaus and Malcolm Thorburn, eds, *Philosophical Foundations of Constitutional Law* (Oxford: Oxford University Press) 33, 33–4.

[171] Ibid.

account is not a string but a web of strings shaped into a globe or sphere.'[172]

Walters perceptively shows that Kelsen's attempt to develop a theory of constitutionalism was at odds with the linear dispositions of legal positivism with its insistence on the idea that law can have any content. The theory of constitutionalism put Kelsen onto the path of developing a circular theory, while his legal positivism held him back.[173] I have argued here that Kelsen goes much further along that path than Walters supposes.[174] Kelsen constructed a multi-level monistic theory of legal order, one which both includes public international law and requires that the norms of the legal order be reconstructed by officials as the norms of a unified field of legal meaning which can justify official claims to legal subjects about what the subjects ought to do. All one need add to this picture is the observation that the legal subject is to be conceived in this process as free and equal before the law. The subject is, that is, the same person who is at the centre of Kelsen's theory of democracy and who was first conceived by Hobbes as the 'Just Man', the subject whose will is 'framed' by the justice of the law.[175]

In Chapter 3 we saw that Kelsen understood that this reconstructive effort is the functional equivalent of the social contract in natural law theory; and I have argued that a theory of law's authority cannot do without such an idea, the constitutionalist idea as I have termed it. Fuller's legal theory is no exception in this regard, despite a disclaimer to the contrary.[176] He prefaced the chapter in which he introduced his principles of legality with the following quotation from John Lilburne, the Leveller and parliamentary rights activist, from his 1645 pamphlet 'England's Birth-Right Justified': 'It is desired that our learned lawyers would answer these ensuing queries . . . whether ever the Commonwealth, when they chose the Parliament, gave them a lawless unlimited power, and at their pleasure to walk contrary to their own laws and ordinances before they have repealed them?'[177]

Fuller came back to this quotation at the end of the book at the point where he claimed that Hart had in *The Concept of Law* (in a passage

[172] Ibid.
[173] Ibid, 42–6.
[174] Or, indeed, as I supposed in *Legality and Legitimacy*.
[175] See Hobbes, *Leviathan*, 104.
[176] Fuller, *The Morality of Law*, 217.
[177] Ibid, 33.

pivotal to my argument in Chapter 3) recognized that there had to be some voluntary cooperation on the part of citizens in creating the authority of law.[178] '[I]f a system of rules is to be imposed by force on any, there must be a sufficient number who accept it voluntarily. Without their voluntary co-operation, thus creating *authority*, the coercive power of law and government cannot be established.'[179]

Fuller could also have adduced in evidence that in 1958 Hart said that one reason that law cannot be understood in terms of commands backed by threats is that many of the rules of private law are 'presented to society in quite different ways and have quite different functions. They provide facilities more or less elaborate for individuals to create structures of rights and duties for the conduct of life within the coercive framework of the law.'[180] Subsequently, in *The Concept of Law*, Hart applied this insight to public law since if officials are to legislate, adjudicate and administer, they must abide by such 'power conferring rules', just as a private individual has to act in accordance with the law of contracts to succeed in contracting. It follows, so Hart argued, that even the highest legislative authority has to be understood as legally constituted. He did note some differences. The rules governing legislation are, he said,

> very much more complex and the bilateral character of a promise is not present. Moreover, there is no person in the special position of the promisee *to whom* the promise is made and who has a special, if not the only claim, to its performance. In these respects, certain other forms of self-imposition known to English law, such as that whereby a person declares himself trustee of property for other persons, offer a closer analogy to the self-binding aspect of legislation. Yet, in general, making of law by enactment is something we shall understand best by considering such private ways of creating particular legal obligations.[181]

Thus, Hart wished to analogize public to private law, minus the element of reciprocity or bilateralism one finds in private law, which led Fuller to point out that Hart failed to acknowledge 'a corresponding cooperative effort on the part of government', that is, that 'maintaining a legal system in existence depends upon the discharge of interlocking responsibilities – of government toward the citizen and of the citizen toward

[178] Ibid, 216.
[179] Hart, *The Concept of Law*, 201. His emphasis.
[180] Hart, 'Positivism and the Separation of Law and Morals', 60–1.
[181] Hart, *The Concept of Law*, 43–4. His emphasis.

government'.[182] In line with Fuller, I have argued that Hart could not explain law's authority without dropping his claim that this cooperative relationship constituting authority could be confined to the officials of the system. Further, once legal subjects are understood as essential to the relationship of 'voluntary co-operation . . . creating authority', we can see that the social contract idea, or at least the *Herrschaftsvertrag* or governmental contract component of it, enters into any explanation of law's authority.

Now, as suggested in this section, Fuller rejected the idea of a social contract for explaining the commitment by the lawgiver 'implicit in the concept of law'. He advocated in its place the 'old fashioned legal term' 'intendment' – that is, that 'our institutions and our formalized interactions with one another are accompanied by certain interlocking expectations that may be called intendments'.[183] He took Lilburne to be suggesting 'that underlying the institution of parliamentary government there is an intendment – that is, a generally shared tacit expectation – that parliament will act towards the citizen in accordance with its own laws so long as those laws remain unrepealed'.[184]

By intendment, Fuller had in mind that the law must be interpreted in light of these expectations, in particular the expectation that the law when so interpreted will manifest a relationship of reciprocity between ruler and ruled or individual and individual. Such a relationship is exactly equivalent to Hobbes's sketch of the protection–obedience nexus which amounts to a governmental contract. With that in place, the other component of social contract theory, the *Gesellschaftsvertrag*, is implied, namely, the idea that the state is the product of an actual contract between free and equal individuals. It is implied because the acceptance by legal subjects is not only constitutive of legitimate legal authority but also ongoing. Acceptance is not a one-off act because, as Williams emphasized, 'a solution to the first political question is *required all the time*'.[185]

My claim here is reinforced by Fuller's argument that the government is the 'guardian of the integrity' of a system in which law provides citizens 'with a sound and stable framework for their interactions with one

[182] Ibid, 216.
[183] Fuller, *The Morality of Law*, 217.
[184] Ibid, 218, and see my 'Liberty and Legal Form', in Lisa M Austin and Dennis Klimchuk, eds, *Private Law and the Rule of Law* (Oxford: Oxford University Press, 2014) 92.
[185] Williams, 'Human Rights and Relativism', 62. His emphasis.

another'.[186] Moreover, Lilburne, like Fuller, thought that the judiciary and other adjudicative institutions had an essential role to play through interpretation of statutes in bringing the immanent morality of the legislative office – analogized to private law doctrines such as trusteeship or guardianship – to the surface.[187] In this regard, they both looked to Coke's invocation of the common law as a repository for interpreting statutes in such a way as to ensure that this immanent morality was realized. Finally, both thought that the civil condition which government under the rule of law brings about is one characterized by a particular kind of liberty, civil liberty or liberty under an order of *jus publicum*.

On the argument of this section, then, Augustine was both right and wrong. He was right to suppose that there is no qualitative distinction between a robber band and a small kingdom *if* the robber band indeed 'is governed by the authority of a ruler; it is bound by a pact of association; and the loot is divided according to an agreed law'. He was wrong in that he failed to see that a robber band which has made a pact to set up a system of legal authority which will govern their interactions both with their ruler and with each other into the future is not merely a differently organized robber band. In taking these steps, the band has begun to transform itself from an order of unmediated coercion into an order of legal right.[188]

6.4 The Individual Legal Conscience

Over the course of this book, we have encountered several figures designed to capture the stance, even the predicament, of someone subject to the law of the modern legal state whose officials claim legitimate authority to tell that person what to do. There is Hart's 'anarchist' who refuses to recognize the validity of any law which is wrong by his moral standards and the reactionary who thinks the law is moral just because it is valid.[189] Hart, we know, rejected both of these figures, as he did Holmes's 'bad man' who wants to know what the law requires, only so

[186] Fuller, *The Morality of Law*, 210.

[187] See Diane Parkin-Speer, 'John Lilburne: A Revolutionary Interprets Statutes and Common Law Due Process' (1983) 1 *Law and History* Review 276 and Monicka Patterson-Tutschka, 'Leveller John Lilburne and the Liberal-Republican Tradition' (2014) 43 *Perspectives on Political Science* 213.

[188] As Cicero pointed out in *On Duties* (Ithaca, NY: Cornell University Press, 2016, Benjamin Patrick Newton, trans.), 101–2.

[189] Hart, 'Positivism and the Separation of Law and Morals', 53.

that he can know what he can get away with. Hart also rejected the figure Raz claimed to be essential to an understanding of law's authority, and whom Raz suggested could be found in Kelsen – the 'legal man' who adopts 'the law as his personal morality, and as exhausting all the norms he accepts as just'.[190] The legal man, on Hart's analysis, is no different from the reactionary.

Hart's preferred figure thus seemed to be the 'puzzled man', who is 'willing to do what the law requires if only he can be told what it is'.[191] This figure is not, Hart thought, to be equated with the legal man. He may happen to approve of the law's content, but we need not assume moral endorsement because the obligations of the legal realm can be accepted on the basis of 'many different considerations':

> calculations of long term interest; disinterested interest in others; an unreflecting inherited or traditional attitude; or the mere wish to do as others do. There is no reason why those who accept the authority of the system should not examine their conscience and decide that, morally, they ought not to accept it, yet for a variety of reasons to continue to do so.[192]

This claim, Hart suggested, applied with as much force to the question of why states accept the authority of international law. There he listed 'calculation of long-term interest, or ... the wish to continue a tradition or ... disinterested concern for others' and said there 'seems no good reason for identifying any of these as a necessary condition of the existence of law either among individuals or states'.[193]

Driving Hart's selection of the figure of the puzzled man, or when it comes to public international law what we can think of as the 'puzzled state', is not only what he took to be a self-evident fact but also a moral consideration. We saw that when he rejected Kelsen's argument that the norms of two valid orders – including the moral and a legal order – cannot conflict, one reason was that there are as a matter of fact such conflicts. But Hart also found 'alarming' that Kelsen's argument 'excludes the possibility of a moral criticism of law', that is, if one recognized the validity of a legal norm, one must deny the possibility of criticism in terms of a norm of a valid moral order.[194] In other words, Hart was

[190] Raz, 'Kelsen's Theory of the Basic Norm', in Raz, *The Authority of Law: Essays on Law and* Morality (Oxford: Clarendon Press, 1983) 122, at 142–3.

[191] Hart, *The Concept of Law*, 40.

[192] Ibid, 203.

[193] Ibid, 230–2.

[194] Ibid, 302.

anxious that a theory of legal order from the internal point of view not rule out in any way the need for candid moral criticism of law by legal subjects. And in 1958 he offered as a way of understanding the 'specific character of the authority of a legal order' Bentham's 'simple' 'recipe' for 'life under a government of laws': '"*to obey punctually; to censure freely*"'.[195]

As I pointed out in the Introduction, Bentham himself called the recipe the 'motto of a good citizen',[196] and it is hardly, despite Hart's claim, 'simple'. The motto requires that legal subjects obey the law while maintaining their freedom to criticize it, which assumes that the law of a modern legal state has an authority to which the good citizen must accord weight. In Bentham, the assumption depends on a fact external to legal order – whether it is a legal order whose laws serve the interests of subjects determined in accordance with the axiom of utility, just as Raz later offered a conception of authority in which the external fact is a correct moral judgment. For Hart, in contrast, the problem is how to understand law's authority as generated by something internal to legal order. In this he joined Hobbes, Kelsen, Radbruch, Fuller and Dworkin, though he was hampered in the quest to set out a theory of authoritative legal reasons by his career-long allegiance to the Separation Thesis.

Hobbes, we saw, described the project of *Leviathan* as providing a theory of the modern legal state which steers between the dangers of according the state too much and too little authority, exactly as Hart in 1958 wanted a theory of law which avoids the stances of both the anarchist and the reactionary.[197] They differed in that Hart thought that these stances inhere in natural law positions because they suppose that law necessarily has a moral quality to it, whereas Hobbes argued that they can be avoided once one sets out the way in which the institutional order of the modern legal state permits the interaction of enacted law and the laws of nature: 'The Law of Nature, and the Civill Law, contain each other, and are of equall extent.'[198]

Hobbes called the figure who accords the state too little authority the 'Foole', who asserts that even in an established civil society he is entitled to disobey the law when he calculates that disobedience will better serve

[195] Hart, 'Positivism and the Separation of Law and Morals', 53. Bentham's emphasis.

[196] Jeremy Bentham, *A Fragment on Government* (Cambridge: Cambridge University Press, 1988), 10.

[197] Hobbes, *Leviathan*, 3; Hart, 'Positivism and the Separation of Law and Morals', 53–4.

[198] Hobbes, *Leviathan*, 185.

his interests, and opposed to him the 'Just Man' whose will is 'framed' by the justice of the law,[199] and I have argued that this figure captures better the nuances of Kelsen's legal subject who, contrary to Raz, does not regard 'the law as his personal morality, and as exhausting all the norms he accepts as just'. Rather, the Just Man has a conception of the justice of the law which permits him to criticize it from the internal point of view, from the perspective of the law's own standards. It is only when law by and large meets those standards that the Just Man will think that he should obey the law despite the fact that he disagrees with its moral content. He will think that he should obey the law because he can get satisfactory answers to the question 'But, how can that be law for me?' Thus, as I argued in Chapter 2, the Just Man, unlike the Foole, accepts that the law is a public conscience.

The Just Man is the key to Hobbes's response to the Carneadean problem, and in Chapter 4 we saw that Hobbes thought this response appropriate even in international relations.[200] The Foole, that is, denies that there can be justice both within and without a modern legal state and Hobbes, in rejecting the first denial commits himself, as he recognized, to rejecting the second. In the context of my Kelsenian argument that a theory of legal order must be a monistic theory of the relationship between public international and domestic law, the second denial is significant.

Hobbes, despite his claim early in *Leviathan* that international relations are doomed to being the war of one against all of the state of nature, saw that an affirmation of justice within the modern legal state requires the same when it comes to relations between states. Moreover, the debate between Cicero and Carneadas was not only about justice within the state but also and (perhaps even primarily) about whether there could be justice in the Roman imperial project.[201] The debate was, that is, about

199 Ibid, 104.

200 Ibid, 204. There is some controversy about whether the Just Man is a direct response to Carneadas. What matters more is that Hobbes's response is to the Carneadean problem represented by the Foole.

201 James EG Zetzel, 'Natural Law and Poetic Justice: A Carneadean Debate in Cicero and Vergil' (1996) 91 *Classical Philology* 297. See further Benedict Kingsbury and Benjamin Straumann, 'State of Nature versus Commercial Sociability as the Basis of International Law: Reflections on the Roman Foundations and Current Interpretations of the International Political and Legal Thought of Grotius, Hobbes, and Pufendorf', in Samantha Besson and John Tasioulas, eds, *The Philosophy of International Law* (Oxford: Oxford University Press, 2012) 33, at 36–40.

whether justice in the sense of *Recht* or legality is 'geographical' or can and must extend beyond the state's borders.

That same debate provides the context for Augustine's tale of Alexander the Great and the pirate. It surfaced again in 1625 in Grotius, in his attempt to provide a Ciceronean and thus juridical justification for Dutch imperialism in the first part of the seventeenth century.[202] And in the nineteenth century, the issue of geographical legality gripped England when John Stuart Mill and others sought to prosecute the governor of colonial Jamaica for his brutal suppression of a rebellion in the colony. Mill's 'Jamaica Committee' clearly saw that if their state permitted the operation of a prerogative state in a region under its control abroad, it might not be long before it was found convenient to resort to prerogative rule at home.[203] Put in terms of Ernst Fraenkel's analysis of the Dual State which animated Chapter 5, permitting such operation abroad would make the state at home into something more like a normative state in which the rule of law operates at the whim of officials in the prerogative state with the result that there is no rule of law.

The stance of the legal subject, conceived as Hobbes's Just Man, cannot therefore be one with respect only to the legality of the home state. We encountered in Chapter 4 Martin Wolff's observation that while private international law is not itself public international law, the 'lawgiver' must bear in mind the community, 'neither the community of his own nationals nor that of the various states or nations, but the community of all individuals, of mankind, the *société international des individus*'.[204] He continued: 'The aim of the lawgiver must be to establish *such rules as he can reasonably wish to see introduced by the legislators or courts of other countries.* Private International Law is not itself international, but it should certainly be drawn up in an international frame of mind.'[205]

My claim here is that both legal subjects and legal officials must share that frame of mind. In Chapter 2, I pointed to the apparent strangeness of Hobbes's theory of punishment, since the individual subject to

[202] See Hugo Grotius, *On the Law of War and Peace* (Cambridge: Cambridge University Press, 2012, Stephen C Neff, ed.), 2, 5, 6 and Benjamin Straumann, *Roman Law in the State of Nature: The Classical Foundations of Hugo Grotius's Natural Law* (Cambridge: Cambridge University Press, 2015).

[203] See RW Kostal, *A Jurisprudence of Power: Victorian Empire and the Rule of Law* (Oxford: Oxford University Press, 2005) and my extended response, 'The Puzzle of Martial Law' (2009) 59 *University of Toronto Law Journal* 1.

[204] Martin Wolff, *Private International Law* (Oxford: Clarendon Press, 1962, 2nd ed.), 16.

[205] Ibid. His emphasis.

punishment is entitled to resist its infliction even though every safeguard of legality has been observed. I argued that this account of the institution of punishment no longer seems so peculiar when we understand that Hobbes presented a double optic on the violence necessary to maintain order. There is the private optic of the about-to-be-punished individual who is in a kind of mini-state of nature in regard to the officials. But there is also the public optic of fellow subjects for whom it is very important to observe that the individual got all of the protections afforded by the rule of law before being subject to coercion. It is crucial, in other words, for the spectacle of legality to be played out in the right way, not only for subjects directly affected by the law but also for the general public who look on, so that the latter know that if they should have to confront the state, that confrontation will be mediated by legality.

Following Chapters 4 and 5, we can appreciate how the public optic needs to be enlarged to include individuals beyond the subjects' own state who are affected by their state; for example, the brutal and illegal suppression by British officials of the Jamaica Uprising, or, during the Iraq war, the Iraqi citizens who were treated by UK armed forces in ways which would be deemed abuses of legal commitments to human rights at home. Indeed, my argument in Chapter 4 against the idea that legality can be geographical – that its reach can be confined within the borders of the state – drew on Edmund Burke's polemic against the idea of 'geographical morality' in the impeachment trial of Warren Hastings, the former governor of Bengal, for the criminal practices of his colonial rule.[206]

Even this enlarged internal point of view must, however, retain the idea so central to Hart's whole project that final judgment when it comes to legal subjects' obedience to law must be reserved to the subject. Unlike Raz's legal man, the Just Man does not think that all there is to justice is the content of positive law. We learned from Chapter 2 that he is entitled to bring a challenge to the law on the basis of his judgment as to its iniquity – a judgment framed by his understanding of fundamental principles of legality – and to judge when the law has lost authority over him because the law renders him into a state-of-nature condition in which he is no longer properly protected.

In the twentieth century, this stance was, in my view, most eloquently described by Hermann Heller, the Weimar-era legal theorist I introduced

[206] See Jennifer Pitts, *Boundaries of the International: Law and Empire* (Cambridge, MA: Harvard University Press, 2018), chapter 4, 'Critical Legal Universalism in the Eighteenth Century'.

in Chapter 5, at the end of a 1927 book on sovereignty in public and international law.[207] His book responded to the so-called paradox of sovereignty, the question which preoccupied public lawyers of the time: if the sovereign is the highest authority, and hence not answerable to any other authority, how can the sovereign be subject to law, whether the public law the sovereign state itself makes, or public international law?

As Heller observed, that very question faces individuals who regard themselves as sovereign, as an autonomous lawgiver, but then wish to understand how that autonomy is compatible with treating the law of their state as authoritative. And as I remarked in the Introduction, some philosophers argue that autonomy is incompatible with political authority. Notably, in *In Defense of Anarchism*,[208] Robert Paul Wolff argued that if one follows Kant in supposing that the 'autonomous man' is one who 'gives laws to himself, or who is self-legislating', it seems to follow that a 'morally legitimate state is a logical impossibility'.[209]

I drew there a distinction between the puzzle of legal authority – how to explain the authority law has just in being law – and the puzzle of moral authority as Wolff depicts it. The latter is of wider scope because Wolff denies not only that law has any intrinsic authority but also that it cannot be endowed with authority by some external source, for example, a Hobbesian (though not Hobbes's) argument that order is better than disorder, or a utilitarian argument about maximizing happiness, or a Razian argument about law which transmits moral reasons better to legal subjects than if they were to rely on their own judgment.[210]

I undertook to try to show that solving the puzzle of legal authority can help in responding to, though not resolving, the puzzle of moral authority. Indeed, the solution to the puzzle of law's authority indicates why the puzzle of moral authority should be left unresolved because there is a moral worth to supposing, as Hart urged, that 'however great the aura of majesty or authority the official system may have, its demands must in

[207] Hermann Heller, *Sovereignty: A Contribution to the Theory of Public and International Law* (Oxford: Oxford University Press, 2019, David Dyzenhaus, ed., Belinda Cooper, trans.), 182–5, and see my 'Introduction: The Politics of Sovereignty' 1, at 54–7.

[208] Robert Paul Wolff, *In Defense of Anarchism* (Berkeley: University of California Press, 1998).

[209] Ibid, 14, vii.

[210] Raz, 'Legitimate Authority', in Raz, *The Authority of Law*, 3, at 25–7. As I noted in the Introduction, Raz's theory of legal authority was developed initially as an attempt to respond to Wolff.

the end be submitted to a moral scrutiny'.[211] In this regard, Heller, who was much influenced by Hobbes, emphasized that the modern condition is one in which we must make decisions in a deeply uncertain secularized world, one in which ethical certainty exists only in highly personal spheres. The only other source of certainty is that which law offers through providing a regular, predictable framework for common life. To have that certainty, we must subject ourselves to the state, to the sovereign organization which is both constituted by law and which makes law in this condition possible, because it is law which makes a common life possible. In subjecting ourselves, we should keep in mind that all the organization does is positivize ethical prescriptions. It cannot pronounce on them finally, for it is not the ultimate ethical authority, and might even act in such a way that it violates the very ethical presuppositions of its own existence. But such a violation would also amount to a violation of legality, since among these ethical presuppositions are also fundamental principles of legality.[212]

It is significant in this regard that Heller called this stance the 'individual legal conscience' – '*das individuelle Rechtsgewissen*' – a theme he elaborated in his last major work.[213] The individual legal conscience includes not only the prescription that in the last resort individuals must decide for themselves whether to obey the law but also the weight that individuals must accord to law in making that decision because of the element of *Recht* inherent in a government under law. Such a conscience includes, that is, a sense of the authority law has in virtue of the way in which it sustains the kind of political community I term a jural community – one where subjects are able to get adequate answers to the question 'But, how can that be law for me?' because the answers do not undermine their status as equal before the law.

Heller thus differed from Kelsen in his time, and from Hart thirty years later, because on his view there is more to a legal order than its positive law and its criteria for certifying valid law in that any legal order is also made up of fundamental principles of legality. But Heller shared with these positivist thinkers the rejection of the assumption behind the

[211] Hart, *The Concept of Law*, 210.

[212] Ibid, 201–2.

[213] See Hermann Heller, *Staatslehre*, in Heller, *Gesammelte Schriften*, vol. 3 (Tübingen: JCB Mohr, 1992, Christoph Müller, ed.) 92, 335–6. For my translation of part of this posthumously published and unfinished project, see Hermann Heller, 'The Nature and Structure of the State' (1996) 18 *Cardozo Law Review* 1139, at 1160–1.

question just posed about sovereignty: the assumption that the sovereign – the ultimate legal authority – is not and cannot be subject to any legal limit since it is a political entity which stands outside of legal order.

Chapter 4 set out how both Kelsen and Hart, in reintroducing a constitutionalist idea to legal theory, showed that the modern legal state is legally constituted with the result that the state is itself subject to law – a *legal* state. In this way, they opened up the conceptual space for legal theory to recognize both constitutional law and public international law as law properly so-called: law which binds the state in its interactions with individual subjects and with other states. But, as Heller argued against Kelsen, such an idea could not do the task set for it unless it both introduced fundamental legal principles into the picture and recognized that the task was political as well as legal.[214] It is a task in what I have called 'political legal theory'.

Heller thus foreshadowed Fuller's and Dworkin's criticisms of Hartian positivism for neglecting the role of principles in legal order and for supposing that philosophy of law is somehow apolitical. But, as I suggested in the Introduction, and have argued throughout this book, only Kelsen's legal theory is capacious enough to accommodate and make work together the following pivotal ideas of philosophy of law of the last sixty years or so: Hobbes's idea that the law is a public conscience; Hart's idea of the authority law has in terms of practice-based acceptance and his concern about preserving the space for moral criticism; Kelsen's idea of legal order as a hierarchy of norms unified by the basic norm; Radbruch's claim that extreme injustice is no law; Fuller's idea that any legal order will to some large extent comply with formal principles of legality which condition the content of law; and Dworkin's elaboration of the role of substantive moral principles implicit within the positive law in judicial interpretation.

In order to make these ideas work together, Kelsen's theory cannot remain 'pure', or at least not pure in the way he understood this attribute, that is, as apolitical. It must be adapted along the lines suggested by Heller to become a political legal theory. This theory does not depict law

[214] For an exploration of the project of situating the central questions of legal theory within a political theory along lines suggested by Heller, see Martin Loughlin, 'In Defence of *Staatslehre*' (2009) 48 *Der Staat* 1. Loughlin, however, offers an account of Heller's theory which reduces law to politics and Heller's juridical theory to Carl Schmitt's political theory. See my 'The End of the Road to Serfdom?' (2013) 63 *University of Toronto Law Journal* 310, a review of Martin Loughlin, *Foundations of Public Law* (Oxford: Oxford University Press, 2010).

as standing above politics. Rather, legal order is a way of constructing political order in a bid to answer the 'first political question', in Williams's description, the Hobbesian question of how to secure 'order, protection, safety, trust, and the conditions of cooperation'.[215] As he said, it is 'first' because 'solving it is the condition of solving, indeed posing, any others'.[216]

I hope to have shown here that the legal order of the modern legal state is more than a large part of the solution to the Hobbesian problem. Its legality prompts and often requires that questions about the law's treatment of those subject to the state's power be asked and answered, with the answers based on legal reasons which make sense to subjects of their subjection. In so doing, the legal order preserves peaceful interaction between legal subjects on terms of equality before the law. The Kelsenian legal theory I have elaborated thus perfects the long arc of legality which starts in Hobbes's argument that it is a social contract which underpins the authority of law under conditions of modernity. Only that kind of constitutionalist idea can explain the official duty to interpret enacted law in the light of fundamental principles of legal order which makes it possible for officials to answer the subject's question and provides the basis of the corresponding duty of the subjects to obey the law.

It is also the idea which ultimately underpins the authority of public international law. But it does not reduce such authority to the fundamental norm of one national legal order in the manner of the position I called national law monism, according to which a norm from outside the order lacks authority until a rule of recognition requires its incorporation. Rather, it adopts the position I called international law monism which holds that the basic norm of the international legal order grounds the validity of the legal orders of the plurality of the states, the subjects of the international jural community. Those legal orders in turn make possible the peaceful interaction of a plurality of legal subjects within the state.

I have thus suggested that international law monism enables an explanation of how three claims which may appear both internally inconsistent as well as inconsistent with each other in fact make a coherent whole: (1) how states are both constituted by public international law and constitute the international legal order; (2) how legal subjects are both constituted by the public law of their state and

[215] 'Williams, 'Realism and Moralism in Political Theory', 3.
[216] Ibid.

constitute its legal order; and (3), why (1) and (2) together show that the individual legal subject is ultimately the figure constitutive of the international legal order. As Hobbes said in *De Cive*, 'a commonwealth is formed not for its own sake but for the sake of the citizens'.[217]

This explanation requires a return to the discussion of the difficulties which attend the issue of the recognition of states in the international legal order and of the legal subject within a national order. As I acknowledged, the political element looms large in such decisions. Because they determine whether an entity is a full legal person, and thus a member of the jural community, they are existential decisions, made at the very limit of the juridical. But I have also suggested that three features of the decisions make the politics of such decisions amenable to legality.

First, in the international legal order, most cases will fall into the category of Hart's 'core' of 'settled law' on his distinction between 'core' and 'penumbra', or into the category of 'easy cases' on Dworkin's distinction between 'hard' and 'easy cases'. Second, argument about penumbral or hard cases is constrained by the duty on the competent legal authorities to accept that they are acting in the judicial capacity and must give reasons responsive to the kinds of legal considerations which figure in the core or easy cases. Third, this is not the only constraint since the judgment must be oriented by the basic norm to making sense of the relevant legal norms – both formal and material – as a unified whole. Finally, the basic norm is to be understood in this context, as Kelsen suggested, as a postulate of peace, moreover, as the postulate of an order in which the legal personalities are able to interact as free and equal subjects before the law, before *jus publicum*. Even in the limit case, then, the decision is a legal one, at least if, as Heller made clear in his own discussion of this problem, it is a decision for legality, not against it.[218]

I also argued in Chapter 5 that much the same analysis applies to the individual as the legal subject within a national legal order. A state's decision regarding which human individuals to include in the jural community of full or first-class legal subjects is both political and a limit case. In one way, it is even more intensely political than the equivalent

217 Thomas Hobbes, *On the Citizen* (Cambridge: Cambridge University Press, 1998, Richard Tuck and Michael Silverstone, eds), 143. Hobbes went on to emphasize, ibid, his emphasis, that the sovereign provides by 'universal laws' for the citizen, that is, the laws do not take notice of '*this or that individual* citizen'. But that emphasis is both required by the rule of law and consistent with the requirement that applications of such laws be justified in particular cases.

218 Heller, *Sovereignty*, 163–7 and my 'Introduction: The Politics of Sovereignty', 44–7.

decisions in the international realm because such distinctions will in the modern legal state generally be made legislatively, that is, not by states acting in their judicial capacity. But that does not make the distinctions political in what we can think of as the Schmittean sense of a quintessentially political distinction which demarcates 'friends' from 'enemies'.[219]

All of the following decisions about legal status are highly political, but they have nothing to do with demarcating friend from enemy: decisions about the ages at which children become full legal subjects for different purposes; decisions about how to respond to adult legal subjects whose capacity to act rationally is diminished; decisions about how to respond to refugees and how to regulate immigration; decisions about the rights of incarcerated subjects. Of course, politicians can choose to portray immigrants, refugees, criminals and even the rationally incapacitated as enemies of the people, to be rooted out of the body politic.[220] But to make that choice is to move towards the politics of a prerogative state, as will be revealed when judges and other officials begin to find it not only hard but even impossible to answer the question 'But, how can that be law for me?'

I have thus argued in this book that the law of a modern legal state does amount to a public conscience, for it contains the fund of the society's values which have been transformed into law. On this view, the law is a part of our moral fabric. It may require revision, even overthrow, as experience dictates. But this does not distinguish it from other beliefs and theories interwoven into that moral fabric. It is only within an idiom which takes this interweaving into account that we can describe perspicuously what otherwise seem to be two intuitions which conflict in situations of legalized injustice – that law is both a matter of fact and of authority.

We can now see that Dworkin should have retained in the final version of *Justice for Hedgehogs* the thought from the manuscript version that it is counterintuitive to suppose that 'most of the subjects of most of the political communities over history had no moral duty to obey the laws of

219 Schmitt, *The Concept of the Political*, 26–7.

220 Heller poured scorn on Schmitt's claim because under scrutiny it turns out to be an attempt to get rid of politics within the state. See Hermann Heller, 'Political Democracy and Social Homogeneity' (David Dyzenhaus, trans.), in Arthur J Jacobson and Bernard Schlink, eds, *Weimar: A Jurisprudence of Crisis* (Berkeley: University of California Press, 2000) 256, at 258. He pointed out there that the distinction 'indicates nothing essentially political', but rather allows for constructing the unity of the people on an 'altogether unpolitical' basis. In addition, its unity is static whereas political unity is 'something that daily has to be formed anew'.

their community'.[221] The pulling apart of moral duty from legal duty is only apt when massive revision or revolution is being undertaken. In the absence of the need for such revolution, our moral and legal lives are completely and utterly intertwined. It is in that intertwinement that legality's promise resides. For when the long arc of legality from Hobbes through Kelsen to Hart is fully in view, we can see that it does bend towards justice – the justice of *jus* or *Recht*.

[221] Quoted in Sreedhar and Delmas, 'State Legitimacy and Political Obligation in *Justice for Hedgehogs*', 746.

Appendix I

Exclusive and Inclusive Legal Positivism

One of the major debates in philosophy of law in the last twenty or so years of the twentieth century occurred when Hartian legal positivism broke into two camps. On the one hand, 'inclusive legal positivists' argue that if the rule of recognition of a legal order contingently includes moral criteria for the identification of law, and if in any hard case on the application of the criteria there is one answer to the legal question posed in the case, that answer should be deemed fully determined by law. On the other hand, 'exclusive legal positivists' resolutely hold on to the Separation Thesis, not only in HLA Hart's version that there is no necessary connection between law and morality but also in a version advanced by Bentham's and Austin's command theory – that law properly so-called is law determined by facts. If moral considerations are involved, judges by definition have discretion and their decisions are not determined by law. This is so even if it is the case both that the constitution obliges judges to take the considerations into account and there is an obvious 'right answer'.

Recall that legal positivists standardly claim that Ronald Dworkin's interpretive theory of law should be dismissed because he was offering a theory of adjudication not a theory of law, and, moreover, a theory of adjudication tied to legal orders which happen to be legitimate by liberal standards. However, as one can see from the structure of this internal debate, it is born out of the need for Hartian legal positivists, despite their claims to the contrary, to find an answer to Dworkin's powerful critique of their position. Indeed, Dworkin complained that inclusive positivists had 'wholly decamped from the philosophical heritage … [they] wished to defend'.[1] In his view, the success of his challenge to Hartian positivism was proved by the combination of, first, the fact that the exclusive camp's insistence that judges exercise a quasi-legislative discretion in hard cases is at odds with the legal practice of judges, and second, the inclusive camp's concession that in practice (at least in the jurisdictions familiar to them) more or less his interpretive theory of law is correct.

[1] Ronald Dworkin, *Justice in Robes* (Cambridge, MA: Belknap Press, 2006), 198.

However, both camps could point out that the positivist position did not rest on purely conceptual grounds. Even if inclusive positivism decamped, it was only from that part of the heritage which insisted that moral grounds are never law properly so-called, and hence, that when judges rely on them, their decisions are within the penumbra. More important, even if Dworkin won the battle in the jurisdictions with which he and Hartian positivists were most familiar, the USA and the UK, it might seem that he had lost the war when one looked at very unjust legal systems in which the content of the law is hostage to the undoubted fact of the immoral policies of the legislators. The preceding chapters contain my answer to the challenge put on the basis of very unjust law. Here I consider the way in which this internal debate further illuminates issues discussed there, particularly in Chapter 4.

The two camps differ for the most part about what to make of moral norms once they have gained entry to a legal order. For inclusive positivists, the norms figure among the grounds of law. They are, as it were, citizens. For exclusive legal positivists, in contrast, the norms are at best permanent residents, incapable of achieving full status, and Joseph Raz, the main proponent of exclusive positivism, supports this claim by an analogy with his understanding of private international law. According to Raz, the private law norms of one legal order do not achieve the status of law when they are applied by the courts of another, any more than do 'legally binding contracts, which are also binding according to law and change people's rights and duties without themselves being part of the law of the land'.[2] He thus suggests that the same point applies to moral standards in general as well as to moral standards in entrenched bills of rights and the rights protected by the UK Human Rights Act (1998).[3]

Raz's view of private international law is mistaken, and as we know from Chapter 4 both Hart and Kelsen would have agreed. Indeed, his claim was rejected in a debate about private international law in the nineteenth century, when WG Hammond[4] responded to an earlier case note by Albert Venn Dicey, the jurist who some years later published the first English treatment of private international law, now in its 15th edition.[5] Dicey had argued that 'the general principle of at least half the rules' of private international law is

[2] Most recently, Joseph Raz, 'Incorporation by Law' (2004) 10 *Legal Theory* 1, 10.

[3] Ibid, 10–12.

[4] William Gardner Hammond was an American law professor, educated in Germany, who became a 'key figure in the historical school of jurisprudence that dominated American legal thought in the nineteenth century'; see David M Rabban, 'Hammond's Blackstone and the Historical School of American Jurisprudence', in Anthony Page and William Pest, eds, *Blackstone and His Critics* (Oxford: Hart Publishing, 2018) 173, at 175.

[5] Albert Venn Dicey, *A Digest of the Law of England with Reference to the Conflict of Laws* (London: Stevens and Son, 1896).

that 'a right duly acquired under the law of another country must be enforced in other countries in accordance with that law'.[6] Hammond liked the idea of 'general principle', as it was 'a great improvement over the old fiction of foreign laws enforced when they are not laws by a supposed comity of nations'.[7] But he objected to the idea that only 'half' the rules could be so explained. He offered the example of a testator who, instead of stipulating in his will that his money should be divided in accordance with the law of France, stipulates the 'rules of Plato's "Republic" or of Cicero's "De legibus" or for that matter of Sir Thomas More's "Utopia"'.[8] Dicey's limit, he worried, would have the result that the law of France might in the other 'half' have the same status as such rules, that is, no legal status. This, he said, was a conclusion which Austin but not Dicey should reach.

Dicey's response shows not only that Hammond was right but also that Raz's exclusive legal positivism leads to the same conclusion.[9] And that suggests that Raz, even more than Hart, has trouble escaping the grip of the command theory of law. Dicey agreed that in Hammond's example judges apply French law as a matter of duty and that 'a fiction of supposed "comity" leads to mere confusion'.[10] In his textbook, he was even more vehement in his rejection of comity, saying that the disputes it provokes are 'little better than idle logomachy' and that anyone who supposed that when English judges apply French law they do so out of 'courtesy' would afford 'a singular specimen of confusion of thought produced by laxity of language'.[11] He continued:

> The application of foreign law is not a matter of caprice or option; it does not arise from the desire of the sovereign of England, or of any other sovereign, to show courtesy to other states. It flows from the impossibility of otherwise determining whole classes of cases without gross inconvenience and injustice to litigants, whether natives or foreigners.[12]

Dicey thus rejected Raz's gloss a century later on private international law by affirming the intertwined ideas that a jurist must reject non-juridical accounts of legal obligation and that the application of foreign private law is a matter of judicial duty not discretion. Moreover, he said of the public policy exception – that in common law jurisdictions, judges may refuse to apply an otherwise binding foreign norm because of its extreme injustice – that, while

[6] Quoted in WG Hammond, 'Note' (1887) 3 *Law Quarterly Review* 101.
[7] Ibid.
[8] Ibid, 101.
[9] Ibid, 102.
[10] AV Dicey, 'Note' (1887) 3 *Law Quarterly Review* 102.
[11] Dicey, *A Digest of the Law of England*, 10.
[12] Ibid, 10–11.

the 'expression "policy of English law" is very vague', its basis was not morality at large but 'fundamental ideas on which English law is grounded'.[13] Thus, under the heading 'Status', he said that 'English Courts do not recognise in England any penal (or privative) status arising under a foreign law, as, for example, the status of civil death, or the civil disabilities or incapacities which may be imposed on priests, nuns, Jews, Protestants, slaves, or others, by the law of the country to which they may belong'.[14]

The logic of Dicey's argument is juridical in that it is based wholly on legal reasons. As a result, it is also profoundly anti-positivist. This last claim will strike many private international law scholars as wrong. Dicey's private international law theory is regarded as the pinnacle of English legal positivism in the field and of the view that its rules are national, not international in character.[15]

Indeed, in his preface to *The Law of Domicile as a Branch of the Law of England: Stated in the Form of Rules*, Dicey said the title 'private international law' is an 'unfortunate misnomer' so that he would consider its rules 'solely as part of the laws of England'; further, that while the rules are 'in strictness "laws"', they are not 'international', and so should not be confused with the 'principles of international law properly so-called, which are "international" since they regulate the conduct of nations towards each other, but are not in the strict sense of the term "laws"'.[16] In addition, in his *A Digest of the Law of England*, Dicey stated his preference for what he called the 'positive method' over the 'theoretical method'. The former is inductive, worked up from the positive law of a particular state, whereas the latter is deductive, an attempt to distil general principles common to the private international law systems of all 'civilised' nations, epitomized in Savigny's claim that private international law is an 'international common law of nations having intercourse with each other'.[17]

[13] Ibid, 35.

[14] Ibid, 36. For an analysis of the public policy exception, see my 'Not an Isolated, Exceptional, and Indeed Contradictory Branch of Jurisprudence', in Roxana Banu, Michael Green and Ralf Michaels, eds, *Philosophical Foundations of Private International Law* (Oxford: Oxford University Press, forthcoming).

[15] For example, Alex Mills, 'The Private History of International Law' (2006) 55 *International and Comparative Law Quarterly* 1, 30–1. Mills points out at 23–4 and 44–50 that there is a connection between positivism about public international law and the classification of private international law as 'national law'. I agree. But, as I argued in Chapter 4, Kelsenian positivism shows why the classification is correct.

[16] Albert Venn Dicey, *The Law of Domicile as a Branch of the Law of England: Stated in the Form of Rules* (London: Stevens and Sons, 1879), iv–v.

[17] Dicey, *A Digest of the Law of England*, 16–23.

It may seem from these observations that Dicey opposed Savigny's 'internationalist' view of private international law with a 'nationalist' one.[18] It may then also seem that Judith Shklar's charge that Dicey's account of the rule of law in his lectures on constitutional law amounted to 'an unfortunate outburst of Anglo-Saxon parochialism' applies with equal force to his view of private international law.[19] In addition, in these lectures, Dicey said that a 'modern judge would never listen to a barrister who argued that an Act of Parliament was invalid because it was immoral' or that it violated the principles of international law because he, following Austin, regarded public international law as no more than 'international morality'.[20] Finally, he may also seem to be an inclusive legal positivist since in his *Digest* he affirmed, consistently with his view about 'fundamental ideas on which English law is grounded', that the 'law of every country . . . consists of all the principles, rules, or maxims enforced by the Courts of that country under the authority of the state', and emphasized that '[i]t makes no difference whether these principles be written or unwritten'.[21]

But Dicey's discussion of method is more complex than the secondary literature suggests. While he preferred the positive method, he highlighted the 'danger' that English lawyers, because of their allegiance to that method, would ignore 'two great merits' of the deductive approach: first, the actual 'agreement between the different countries of Europe as to the principles to be adopted for the choice of law'; second, that the 'choice of one system rather than another for the decision of a particular case is dictated by reasons of logic, of convenience, or of justice, and is not in any matter in any way of mere fancy or precedent'. His preference for the positive method was based only on what he took to be the theoretical method's tendency to presuppose 'certain self-evident principles of right whence can be deduced a system of rules, the rightness of which will necessarily approve itself to all judges'. The danger was that jurists would treat as law what they think ought to be law, a problem mitigated by his positive method since it starts from the assumption that the rules of private international law are to be worked up by scholars from the actual rules in their country 'with regard to a special topic, namely, the extra-territorial recognition of rights'.[22] He remained concerned, however, that the

[18] FA Mann, 'International Delinquencies before Municipal Courts' (1954) 70 *Law Quarterly Review* 181.

[19] Judith N Shklar, 'Political Theory and the Rule of Law', in Shklar, *Political Thought and Political Thinkers* (Chicago: University of Chicago Press, 1998, Stanley Hoffmann, ed.) 21, at 26.

[20] Albert Venn Dicey, *The Law of the Constitution* (Oxford: Oxford University Press, 2013, John Allison, ed.), 38–9.

[21] Dicey, *A Digest of the Law of England*, 3.

[22] Ibid, 18–21.

positive method did not take into account 'the extent to which civilised nations do in reality recognise certain common principles' and that, because there are only a small number of rules of private international law, when no rule is to be found in statute or precedent, 'judges must legislate, and do in fact legislate, with an eye to the principles which, being adopted in other countries, may, by an allowable fiction, be styled the common law of Europe'.[23] Finally, Dicey noted that Savigny and the other main exponents of the theoretical method were not that methodologically distinct from the 'positive' English jurist. Not only did they look to actual laws and allow that the 'actual practice of the Courts tests the correctness of theoretical speculation'. They also relied primarily on the law of their own jurisdiction or of very similar jurisdictions, for example, those influenced by Roman Law.[24]

Dicey's true view was, then, that it makes little difference whether one works up inductively from the law of one's own jurisdiction or down deductively from a set of rationally justified principles. There are risks inherent in each: with the former, parochial neglect of the common experience of other municipal systems which, if taken into account, would permit one to extrapolate general principles of private international law; with the latter, distortion of one's own law in assuming it simply reflects such principles. Moreover, in avoiding the first risk, one can see that merely because the private international law rules of one's own system do not supply an answer, it fails to follow that the law supplies no answer. Just as the law of England includes the fundamental principles of the common law of the land, so it includes the fundamental private international law principles of the 'common law of Europe'.

One must also be careful not to read Dicey's use of 'legislation' to describe what judges do in such cases as endorsing Hart's more extravagant claims that judicial interpretation is legally unlimited discretion. Rather, as Dicey recognized, and as Dworkin was to argue, if judges are to avoid deciding on the basis 'of caprice or option', they must discharge a duty fully to justify their decisions by recourse to the stock of available legal reasons, no matter how creative they have to be in that exercise. In addition, it is important not to elide Dicey's preference for a method focused on decided cases with Austin's claim that the 'existence of law is one thing; its merit or demerit another'. As we have seen, Hart made this claim central to his tradition, though he expressed it rather differently in his Separation Thesis that there is no necessary connection between law and morality.[25] Inclusive legal positivists then reformulated the

[23] Ibid.
[24] Ibid.
[25] HLA Hart, 'Positivism and the Separation of Law and Morals', in Hart, *Essays in Jurisprudence and Philosophy* (Oxford: Clarendon Press, 1983) 49, at 51, 54–5.

thesis as a 'Separability Thesis': 'Positivism is true ... just in case we can imagine a legal system in which being a principle of morality is not a condition of legality for any norm.'[26] That is, even if in every existent legal system law and morality are connected, one can imagine a legal system in which only facts count among the grounds of law.

Dicey's description of the positive method is at odds with both Austin's claim and Hart's Separation Thesis together with its reformulation. While he accepted that law as it is bounds the juristic inquiry in private international law, he emphasized that within that inquiry there can be no hard and fast distinction between the 'is' and the 'ought' of law because of the presence of fundamental moral ideas within the law which should inform the jurist's perception of what law is. He also, as we saw, claimed that, in the private international law context, fundamental ideas are to be found beyond the state's borders in 'the common law of Europe'. Since such ideas count as law in his taxonomy, there is some tension here with his denial in his work on constitutional law of the legal status of public international law norms, which parrots Austin's claim that public international law is not law because a norm is legal only if it is the product of sovereign will. Moreover, as we have seen, Austin extended his conclusion about public international law norms – that they are no more than norms of 'positive morality' – to constitutional law.[27]

Austin was thus the true founder of exclusive legal positivism, with Raz his main heir.[28]

[26] Jules Coleman, 'Negative and Positive Positivism', in Marshall Cohen, ed., *Ronald Dworkin and Contemporary Jurisprudence* (London: Duckworth, 1984) 28, at 31.

[27] John Austin, *Lectures on Jurisprudence or the Philosophy of Positive Law*, vol. 1 (London: John Murray, 1861, 5th ed.), 177, 204.

[28] In the posthumously published Postscript to *The Concept of Law* (Oxford: Clarendon Press, 1994, 2nd ed.), 251–4, Hart declared himself an inclusive positivist: he was influenced here by the major statement of this position in Wil Waluchow, *Inclusive Legal Positivism* (Oxford: Clarendon Press, 1994), a work which he had supervised as a DPhil thesis. His willingness to join the inclusive camp was based, in my view, on the commitment I have explored in preceding chapters to explaining law as a matter of the authority law has, in contrast to Raz's argument that law merely claims authority.

Appendix II

Kantian Private Law Theory

One of the most significant advances in philosophy of law in the late twentieth century is the account of the normativity of private law developed by my colleague Ernest Weinrib, in which he argues that attention to the formal features of a private law regime will bring to light the moral structure intrinsic to it.[1] More recently, this kind of account has been firmly nested by another colleague, Arthur Ripstein, in an exposition of Kant's political and legal philosophy, in which purposive agents whose freedom to enact their own purposes is made consistent with the same freedom of all other agents.[2] Only such consistency, he argues, can achieve the ideal of non-domination – that individuals are to be their own master, not subject to the will of any other; and legal institutions have to be in place for the ideal to be realized. Their theory thus presents a powerful 'one-system' account of the relationship between law and morality, one in which, as we have seen Ronald Dworkin argued, the connection between law and morality is not well represented by a dualistic picture of two separate systems because the morality in question is intrinsic to legal order.[3]

My account of law in the preceding chapters has therefore much in common with theirs, since I also argue that legal order puts in place a civil condition in which its subjects can interact with each other peacefully and on terms of equality which promote liberty. My account differs though in two respects.

First, the choice for Hobbes over Kant as my main philosophical guide is one for a thinker who found it important to locate argument ultimately in experience of the empirical world, not the world of conceptual argument, and that has an impact on many details of the two accounts. The more important difference, though, is the second. Ripstein and Weinrib suggest that the same Kantian ideal of non-domination can underpin public law, but that it and

[1] Ernest J Weinrib, *The Idea of Private Law* (Cambridge, MA: Harvard University Press, 1995).

[2] Arthur Ripstein, *Force and Freedom: Kant's Legal and Political Philosophy* (Cambridge, MA: Harvard University Press, 2009).

[3] Ronald Dworkin, *Justice for Hedgehogs* (Cambridge, MA: Belknap Press, 2011), 402.

private law have their own immanent moralities or normative structures, respectively, public right or distributive justice, and private right or corrective justice.[4] Moreover, in their scheme, private right has priority since public right comes into being primarily in order to make it possible for individuals to interact rightfully within the normative space established by private law. Legal order properly so-called is, on this view, an order in which horizontal relationships between individuals are governed by corrective justice, as guaranteed by the state. That makes it difficult for Weinrib and Ripstein to offer any account of a legitimate role for the state in redistributing resources in ways which may disturb the kind of order which would obtain were the state to confine itself to doing what is strictly necessary to maintain private order. The state, that is, seems limited by the priority of private right to ensuring the conditions under which the immanent morality of private law can thrive, and public law exists as an uneasy adjunct to private law order, both its guarantor and a constant threat.[5]

For this kind of reason, Kelsen was deeply suspicious of any legal theory based on an *a priori* distinction between private law and public law in which the former is asserted to be normatively superior. He saw its flaw as akin to the Schmittean claim that the state is a pre-political subject which can use the law as an instrument to advance its own interests, in that it conceives of the individual as a pre-political bearer of rights which the state's laws must respect. That distinction, Kelsen said, 'tends to take on the import of an opposition between law and power … the opposition, especially, between law and state'.[6]

I think it significant in this regard that Ripstein has suggested that a Kantian account of authority is consistent with Joseph Raz's analysis of political and legal authority which, as we have seen, argues that an authority is legitimate if the reasons which law transmits to legal subjects are reasons which already apply to them and which they do better following than if they relied on their own judgment.[7] It is consistent, Ripstein suggests, 'so long as "reason applying" is understood in the right way':

[4] See Ernest J Weinrib, *Corrective Justice* (Oxford: Oxford University Press, 2012), chapter 8, 'Poverty and Property in Kant's System of Rights' and Ripstein, *Force and Freedom*, chapter 9, 'Public Right III: Redistribution and Equality of Opportunity'.

[5] See my 'Liberty and Legal Form', in Lisa M Austin and Dennis Klimchuk, eds, *Private Law and the Rule of Law* (Oxford: Oxford University Press, 2014) 92.

[6] Hans Kelsen, *Introduction to the Problems of Legal Theory* (Oxford: Clarendon Press, 1992, Bonnie Litschewski Paulson and Stanley L Paulson, trans.), 92–3.

[7] Joseph Raz, 'Authority, Law, and Morality', in Raz, *Ethics in the Public Domain: Essays in the Morality of Law and Politics* (Oxford: Oxford University Press, 1994) 194.

> For Kant, the only relevant reasons are duties of right, and the state's authority extends only to those duties ... which cannot be coherently followed except in a rightful condition. All of the acts of a rightful condition, including the state's entitlement to decide how to achieve various public purposes, can be described as enabling people to 'do better' at conforming to their duties of right.[8]

On Ripstein's view, the differences between Raz and Kant are mainly that for Raz 'rights are based on interests that can be specified non-relationally, and that law is a tool for achieving purposes that can be fully specified without reference to law'.[9] Kant, then, is taken to argue that law is a tool for specifying rights conceived not as interests but as relational and legal. Since such rights can be articulated in a Kantian state of nature, though neither guaranteed nor fully specified there, the work that law does is to provide both the guarantee and the necessary specificity. One might say that the difference between Kant and Raz is that for Kant the moral order the law puts in place makes it possible for people to do their thing, whereas for Raz the law tells people what things to do.

As I pointed out in preceding chapters and in Appendix I, Raz's theory of authority does not depart significantly from Austin's command theory of law. Law will have the authority it claims not because of anything internal to legal order but only if its content is correct by some set of standards external to legal order. In this light, the question raised by Ripstein's concession to Raz's theory is whether his Kantian account of legitimacy turns out to have the same problem. I think it does.

Recall from Chapter 6 Bernard Williams's criticism of liberal political theories which make morality prior to politics. On his account, they either adopt an 'enactment model', which 'surveys society to see how it may be made better', or a 'structural model', which sets 'conditions in which power can be justly exercised'.[10] On this distinction, Raz and the command theorists adopt an enactment model while Kantians adopt the structural model. The models work in different ways. The enactment model transmits content which directly governs interaction, while the structural model stipulates conditions for interaction. But the latter, no less than the former, draws its standards for legitimate authority from outside of legal order.

The difficulty Kantian legal theory encounters in its prioritization of private right is reflected in a distinction in the architecture it proposes for legal order.

8 Ripstein, *Force and Freedom*, 197, note 24.

9 Ibid.

10 Bernard Williams, 'Realism and Moralism in Political Theory', in Williams, *In the Beginning was the Deed: Realism and Moralism in Political Argument* (Princeton: Princeton University Press, 2005, Geoffrey Hawthorn, ed.) 1, at 1–3.

This is between a constitutive principle of authority, which accords de jure or legitimate authority to the law enacted in an established legal order, and a regulative principle of justice, which imposes a duty on the state to regulate the private realm in accordance with corrective justice and the public realm in accordance with distributive justice. On this distinction, the work that 'relational' and 'legal' in Ripstein's formulation above do is to postulate a limit on political and legal authority, which becomes a legal limit only when a society puts in place what I called in Chapter 3 'a bill-of-rights constitution'. But then the limit is, as legal positivists argue, a moral limit, which may contingently be made a legal limit by positive constitutional law in order to secure the place of judges as the guardians of the order of private right.[11]

[11] For a defence of these two principles, as well as an argument that a legal order is defective if it is not a bill-of-rights legal order, see Jacob Weinrib, *Dimensions of Dignity: The Theory and Practice of Modern Constitutional Law* (Cambridge: Cambridge University Press, 2016).

Appendix III

John Finnis and 'Schmittean Logic'

In the preceding chapters, I dealt quite extensively with three twentieth-century natural law theories – those of Gustav Radbruch, Lon Fuller and Ronald Dworkin. Conspicuously absent is what may well be supposed to be the leading natural law position articulated in the last fifty years, the position set out by John Finnis in *Natural Law and Natural Rights*.[1] I have omitted Finnis from my account of legality's long arc despite the fact that I find many of his insights profound, especially his Fuller-influenced discussion of the rule of law in chapter X of *Natural Law and Natural Rights* – 'Law' – and despite the fact that, at times, his argument seems to come very close to mine.[2]

The reason for Finnis's absence is that, as I explain here, his theory is not a theory of legality. Rather, it is a political theory in which law's role is confined to transmitting a moral good determined outside of legal order. In this, it resembles the utilitarian command theories of law, as well as the Kantian legal theory discussed in Appendix II. But it differs substantively from both Bentham's utilitarian command theory and Kantian liberalism in that its vision of the moral good is troubling because it is profoundly reactionary.

[1] John Finnis, *Natural Law and Natural Rights* (Oxford: Clarendon Press, 1980).

[2] Consider, for example, that Finnis argues that 'no fact or set of facts, however complex, can by itself provide a *reason for* acting, let alone an "ought" of the kind that could speak with authority against an individual's self-interest'; John Finnis, 'On the Incoherence of Legal Positivism' (2000) 75 *Notre Dame Law Review* 1597, at 1608. His emphasis. He then asks, 1609, his emphasis, how any 'fact of convergent official behaviour [could] ... make the law not merely *accepted as* legally authoritative but actually *authoritative as law* for ... [an official] or anyone else who recognizes its injustice'. It follows, in his view, that '[j]udges appointed to office under a written constitution, which provides certain fundamental laws and restricts the manner in which those laws can be altered, must not allow rights under that constitution to be violated'. And he suggests, ibid, his emphasis, that

> In jurisprudence, there is a name for a theory of law that undertakes to identify and debate, openly and critically, the moral principles and requirements which respond to *deliberating persons'* requests to be shown why a legal rule, validly enacted, is binding and authoritative *for them*, precisely as law: That name (for good and ill) is 'natural law theory'.

In fact, as I suggest, it is so reactionary that it is plausible to view it as not only anti-liberal but also as anti-legal, in much the same way that Carl Schmitt's theory is both those things. If my suggestion is right, Finnis's theory is, unlike the command and Kantian theories, not even a candidate for what I have called 'political legal theory'.

HLA Hart pointed out long ago that Finnis's legal theory is bifurcated between a positivistic inquiry into law as it is and a naturalist identification of law as it ought to be.[3] Moreover, Finnis, unlike Hart, or at least unlike Hart's official position, appears to suggest that the judges must follow a positivistic method of determining the law on any matter, which relegates the naturalist perspective to the role of external critic of the law. I say 'appears' because it very difficult to pin down Finnis's exact position on this issue if one takes into account only his work in the more abstract reaches of philosophy of law, as he becomes vague at the crucial points.[4]

This bifurcation can, in my view, be explained and the difficulty resolved in the following way. On the one hand, Finnis's theory is positivistic in the sense that law is conceived for the most part as an instrument of the moral good conceived outside of the law. On the other hand, it is naturalist only in that his conservative vision of the good is somehow supposed to be mirrored in both a weak version of Fullerian legality and a British colonial-era view of the virtues of the common law in upholding the status quo.

The latter view comes across strongly in some of Finnis's early work in the context explored in Section 5.1. Recall that after Ian Smith's white minority government in Rhodesia issued its Unilateral Declaration of Independence (UDI) from the British state in 1965, the Rhodesian High Court decided in *Madzimbamuto* v. *Lardner-Burke* that the order in which it operated was a valid legal order despite the rupture UDI had effected.[5] In 'Revolutions and Continuity of Law' (1971), an influential treatment of issues raised in this and other decisions of that era, Finnis came to the following conclusion about *Madzimbamuto*:

> As soon as the Rhodesian judges had decided that Rhodesia was, as a matter of 'fact', a distinct society with its own accepted power structure and intelligible commonweal, not merely a fragment of imperial power and commonweal, their decision (if not their reasoning) became almost inevitable. The reason for this inevitability was expressed, as we saw, by lawyers of Edward IV: 'it is necessary that the realm should have a king

[3] HLA Hart, 'Introduction', in Hart, *Essays in Jurisprudence and Philosophy* (Oxford: Clarendon Press, 1983) 1, at 10–12.

[4] For an illuminating treatment of this difficulty, see Hillary Nye, 'Finnis's Divided View of Law: Problems for Adjudicative Theory' (2020) 11 *Jurisprudence* 503.

[5] *Madzimbamuto* v. *Lardner-Burke* (1968) 2 SA 284 (RAD).

> under whose authority laws should be held and upheld'. It is indeed possible to speak of a legal system growing, flourishing, and withering away – but only if one considers it as something importantly more than a set of rules, however profoundly analysed.[6]

In my view, once unpacked, this conclusion both contains Finnis's legal theory in a nutshell and explains the trajectory of his thought from the 1960s to the present. Some context, omitted in Finnis's essay, is required for this exercise.

With the proclamation of the UDI, Smith's government purported to create a new Constitution for the country to replace the 1961 Constitution, which had been made under the Southern Rhodesia (Constitution) Act 1961 of the British Parliament. The latter was the result of a complex negotiation between the minority white government of Rhodesia, African nationalists and Britain. The Rhodesian government wanted to have the British parliament's power to disallow Rhodesian legislation abolished, the British government wished to disengage from Rhodesia at the same time as ensuring that black Rhodesian advancement though constitutional means was secured, while African nationalists wanted to secure the best possible deal for black Rhodesians. In the end, Britain gave up its power of disallowance and the nationalists were allocated fifteen of the sixty-five seats in the parliament and a complex system of franchise was established which would delay majority rule, perhaps indefinitely.[7] The 1961 Constitution was repudiated by the African nationalists once they realized its implications and a period of political unrest began which led to the UDI, a declaration to prepare the way for ensuring white supremacy in perpetuity.[8]

The 1965 Constitution purported to constitute the sitting Rhodesian High Court, a creature of the 1961 Constitution, as the High Court of Rhodesia, and provided that judges who refused to accept the 1965 Constitution would automatically lose their office. But other than asserting Rhodesia's independence, it reproduced in large part the 1961 Constitution, though it did introduce new methods of constitutional amendment which, together with its abolition of the right to appeal to the Judicial Committee of the Privy Council in

[6] John Finnis, 'Revolutions and Continuity of Law', reprinted in Finnis, *Philosophy of Law: Collected Essays*, vol. 4 (Oxford: Oxford University Press, 2011) 407, at 429. Footnote and paragraph break omitted.

[7] The UDI was modelled after the US Declaration of Independence except that it did not assert that 'all men are created equal' nor did it claim that governmental power was derived 'from the consent of the governed'; Claire Palley, *The Constitutional History and Law of Southern Rhodesia, 1888–1965* (Oxford: Clarendon Press, 1966), 750, note 4. See 416–32 for a detailed account.

[8] See Martin Meredith, *The Past is Another Country: Rhodesia UDI to Zimbabwe* (London: Pan Books, 1980), 31–42.

London, had the effect of 'rendering the safeguards in the "Constitution" nugatory'.[9]

In *Madzimbamuto*, the Rhodesian High Court was faced with a challenge to Daniel Madzimbamuto's detention under emergency power regulations. Although he had been initially detained before 1965, his continued detention was under emergency regulations issued under the 1965 Constitution. Madzimbamuto's wife claimed that the declaration of the state of emergency and the detention order were invalid because the government was illegal.

Madzimbamuto's lawyer contended that the court had to decide between accepting the 1961 Constitution or the 1965 one, with the latter choice entailing that the judges had 'joined the revolution'. But two of the judges in the majority, including Chief Justice Beadle in the main judgment, relied on Kelsen's legal theory because they thought that his claim that at the basis of legal order is a basic norm showed that they did not face this dilemma.[10] They took his argument to be that a successful legal revolution takes place when the usurping government is effective. At that point, the basic norm which authorizes the constitution is simply presupposed.

Beadle suggested that this Kelsenian reasoning made possible a 'positivist' and politically neutral approach – one which looked to the way law is rather than how it ought to be. The approach did not in this case lead to the conclusion that the revolution had been successful. However, it was successful enough for him to consider the government to have de facto if not de jure authority.[11] The issue, he claimed, was not whether the change had come about by illegal revolution but only the efficacy of the new government.[12]

In his lone dissent, Justice Fieldsend staked out a clearly contrary position, based on his view that the 1961 Constitution 'was not only granted by the Sovereign on the authority of the British Parliament, but accepted by the electorate of this country acting on behalf of the country as a whole'.[13] The Constitution, he reasoned, 'assured' 'both the country's connection with the United Kingdom, and the protection of the various races that make up the population against their being overreached by any one racial group, whether it be a majority in the country, or whether it has a majority in the Legislative Assembly'.[14] He also pointed out that

[9] Palley, *The Constitutional History and Law of Southern Rhodesia*, 5, 751; though as she points out at 628 the protection of rights and liberties under the 1961 Constitution was precarious at best.

[10] For example, *Madzimbamuto*, 315–17.

[11] Ibid, 322–6.

[12] Ibid, 328.

[13] Ibid, 422.

[14] Ibid, 423.

> [i]n order that a *de facto* government be set up it is necessary that all the powers of sovereignty or government should be actually exercised by the body purporting to be a *de facto* government ... The usurper of a government constituted under a written Constitution must take the responsibility of replacing the legitimate court and its judges – yet a further illegal act – before he can be said to have usurped all the powers of sovereignty. To hold otherwise is merely to assert that the repository of one part of the sovereign power must acquiesce in the illegal assumption of power by the repository of another part.[15]

Moreover, relying on the first two Voters Rights Cases in South Africa, discussed in Chapter 5, in particular on Schreiner's judgment in the second, he reasoned that the courts are the 'guardians of the constitution' but also derive their authority from the 'legal supremacy' of the constitution. 'The natural corollary of this', he said, 'is that the Court cannot sit to determine whether the constitution under which it was created has disappeared. Nor can it continue to exist to enforce some other constitution.'[16]

> This is a lasting duty for so long as they hold office, whether the violation be by peaceful or revolutionary means. If, as in South Africa, the Courts were obliged to stand resolutely in the way of what might be termed a legitimate attempt to override the constitution, *a fortiori* must a court stand in the way of a blatantly illegal attempt to tear up a constitution. If to do this is to be characterised as counterrevolutionary, surely an acquiescence in illegality must equally be revolutionary. Nothing can encourage instability more than for any revolutionary movement to know that, if it succeeds in snatching power, it will be entitled *ipso facto* to the complete support of the preexisting judiciary in their judicial capacity. It may be a vain hope that the judgment of a court will deter a usurper, or have the effect of restoring legality, but for a court to be deterred by fear of failure is merely to acquiesce in illegality. It may be that the court's mere presence exercises some check on a usurper who prefers to avoid a confrontation with it.[17]

In his essay, Finnis made no mention of Fieldsend's dissent, and, while he clearly indicated that he did not endorse the majority's reasoning, he fully endorsed their conclusion. Recall that he endorsed it because it upheld a vision of a 'distinct society with its own accepted power structure and intelligible commonweal'. This claim in context is far more radical than anything to be found in the majority judgments. The 'distinct society' was that of the white minority who 'accepted' the oppressive 'power structure' because it was

[15] Ibid, 427–8.
[16] Ibid, 429.
[17] Ibid, 430.

'intelligible' to them as serving their economic and caste interests. The 'king' whose 'authority' was 'necessary' in order that 'laws should be held and upheld' was the executive headed by Smith which had ruptured the old legal order because it restrained their supremacist view of the order of things, much as we saw in Chapter 5 the first apartheid governments were determined to free themselves of the constitutional protection of the Coloureds' voting rights afforded by the 1909 South African Constitution.

Fast forward to the present and we can find that the same constellation of views underpins the arguments made during Brexit by Finnis and his followers for the constitutional legitimacy of an executive which acts free of legal and democratic constraints when fundamental constitutional questions must be resolved.[18] The main vehicle for these arguments is the website of the 'Judicial Power Project', which was originally set up to oppose judicial review on the human rights basis required by the UK's ratification of the European Convention on Human Rights and the subsequent incorporation of the rights through the Human Rights Act (1998).[19] When the political turmoil around Brexit started to raise issues of high constitutional law, it became the vehicle for the 'Leave' views of Finnis and his main protegé Richard Ekins, also an Oxford law professor.

Their main claim is that judicial review undermines parliamentary sovereignty, a claim which became especially strained when they argued that parliamentary sovereignty was undermined when the parliament sought to

[18] If one wants to proceed more slowly, a good guide is Richard Ekins, 'Constitutional Principle in the Laws of the Commonwealth', in John Keown and Robert George, eds, *Reason, Morality, and Law: The Philosophy of John Finnis* (Oxford: Oxford University Press, 2013) 396. Ekins details several of Finnis's interventions over the years in a bid to persuade courts to uphold the executive's place as the guardian of a constitutional order based on his conception of a 'distinct society'.

[19] For example, John Finnis, 'Judicial Power: Past, Present and Future', 2018, https://judicialpowerproject.org.uk/john-finnis-judicial-power-past-present-and-future/. Finnis has in the past argued for what he euphemistically calls a 'reversal of the inflow' of 'immigrant, non-citizen Muslims'. See John Finnis, 'Endorsing Discrimination between Faiths: A Case of Extreme Speech', in Ivan Hare and James Weinstein, eds, *Extreme Speech and Democracy* (Oxford: Oxford University Press, 2009) 430, at 440. He has also opposed the right to same sex marriage on the basis that 'homosexual conduct' is immoral – 'Law, Morality, and "Sexual Orientation"', in John Corvino, ed., *Same Sex: Debating the Ethics, Science, and Culture of Homosexuality* (Lanham, New York and London: Rowman and Littlefield, 1997) 31. Ekins has objected to the protection of the rights of those affected by the actions of the UK's armed forces: Richard Ekins, Patrick Hennessey and Julie Martineau, 'Protecting Those Who Serve', 28 June 2019, https://judicialpowerproject.org.uk/protecting-those-who-serve-richard-ekins-patrick-hennessey-and-julie-marionneau/.

control Theresa May's and Boris Johnson's attempts to exit the European Union without parliamentary sanction.[20] On both occasions, the UK Supreme Court found against the government.

The constitutional issue in these cases was complicated because the government was acting under prerogative not statutory powers, powers inherited from a time when the monarch was the political sovereign. *Miller 1* asked whether the government could notify the European Union of the UK's intention to withdraw via the foreign relations prerogative. 'No', answered the majority of the court, because on the agreed facts the withdrawal would definitely change domestic law, and rights and duties under that law, and prerogative doesn't allow you to do that, at least since 1688.[21] *Miller 2* asked whether Johnson's exercise of the prerogative to shut down Parliament during Brexit negotiations could be reviewed and, if it could, whether it was lawful. 'Yes' it could review, said a unanimous court, and this exercise was unlawful because it had 'the effect of frustrating or preventing, without reasonable justification, the ability of parliament to carry out its constitutional functions as a legislature and as the body responsible for the supervision of the executive'.[22] While the issues were novel in both cases, the principles were not. The lawyers for Gina Miller, who brought both cases, were able to build their reasoning on a firm and centuries-old foundation of fundamental legal principles.

My claim here is not that the cases were easy – that lawyers could not reasonably disagree about the correct answer. Rather, it is that the legal arguments Finnis, Ekins and those allied with them made were faux legal arguments in that they were designed to undermine legality in order to preserve a certain view of British society as the kind of 'distinct society' which Finnis had found preserved by the majority in *Madzimbamuto*.

Consider that in the aftermath of the *Miller* decisions, Finnis and his followers have argued that it is consistent with the rule of law for the UK parliament to break the rule of law, so leaving the executive free of the obligations the same government had negotiated in an international treaty.[23] This 'risible' argument, as one eminent UK constitutional lawyer called it,[24] is

[20] For example, Richard Ekins, 'Brexit and Judicial Power', 21 July 2016, http://judicialpowerproject.org.uk/wp-content/uploads/2016/07/R-Ekins-Brexit-and-judicial-power-21-July-2016.pdf.

[21] [2017] UKSC 5 www.supremecourt.uk/cases/uksc-2016–0196.html.

[22] [2019] UKSC 41 www.supremecourt.uk/cases/uksc-2019–0192.html, para. 50.

[23] For an early version, see Richard Ekins and Guglielmo Verdirame, 'The Ministerial Code and the Rule of Law', 6 November 2015, https://ukconstitutionallaw.org/2015/11/06/richard-ekins-and-guglielmo-verdirame-the-ministerial-code-and-the-rule-of-law/.

[24] https://twitter.com/profmarkelliott/status/1304076133827309569.

premised on the view that international law is not really law, it is 'defective' as Finnis has proclaimed.[25] It is risible because no jurist should take seriously the claim that government ministers and the parliament are legally authorized to violate the rule of law simply because they have the power to do so.[26]

Indeed, on this particular issue, the arguments are motivated by the national law monist position I discussed in Chapter 4; and, as we saw there, Kelsen regarded it as the position with an elective affinity to nationalistic political views. The affinity, that is, is to the views which oppose, in Finnis's words, a 'discourse in law schools and courts' which 'increasingly locates its participants in a universe of standards of correct thought and decision, and of the incorrect and unacceptable, which are generated and shared among persons who speak as if they were nowhere in particular'.[27]

The arguments of these lawyers in what Thomas Poole has aptly dubbed the 'Executive Power Project'[28] seem designed to set the UK on a path which leads to the undermining of both the rule of law and democracy. We can note here Ekins's astonishing claim that the judges of the UK Supreme Court who used reasoning long familiar to common lawyers to read a privative clause as not ousting all judicial review should be removed from office, a step which he asserted would not compromise judicial independence. In making this argument, he advocated the kind of tactic so successfully deployed in Orbán's Hungary and in Poland over the last few years of using mechanisms of judicial discipline to ensure a compliant judiciary at the same time as maintaining a façade of the rule of law.[29]

Elsewhere I have pointed out that the arguments deploy a 'Schmittean logic'.[30] This is not a logic which requires one to have read Carl Schmitt and his polemics during the last years of the Weimar Republic in his debate with

[25] John Finnis, 'Ministers, International Law, and the Rule of Law', 2 November 2015, https://judicialpowerproject.org.uk/ministers-international-law-and-the-rule-of-law/.

[26] See Dapo Akande and Eirik Bjorge, 'The United Kingdom Ministerial Code and International Law: A Response to Richard Ekins and Guglielmo Verdirame', 11 December 2015, www.ejiltalk.org/the-united-kingdom-ministerial-code-and-international-law-a-response-to-richard-ekins-and-guglielmo-verdirame/.

[27] John Finnis, 'Judicial Power: Past, Present and Future', 59.

[28] Thomas Poole, 'The Executive Power Project', 2 April 2019, www.lrb.co.uk/blog/2019/april/the-executive-power-project.

[29] Richard Ekins, 'Do Our Supreme Court Judges Have Too Much Power?', *The Spectator*, 14 May 2019, www.spectator.co.uk/article/do-our-supreme-court-judges-have-too-much-power-.

[30] David Dyzenhaus, 'Lawyer for the Strongman', 12 June 2020, https://aeon.co/essays/carl-schmitts-legal-theory-legitimises-the-rule-of-the-strongman.

Kelsen about who was the 'guardian' of the Weimar Constitution.[31] Rather it is the logic of the kind of 'legal' argument which is deployed when jurists want to reach the conclusion that the executive is the 'guardian of the constitution' in matters in which existential questions about the identity of the political community arise as legal questions.

In Chapters 5 and 6, I introduced Hermann Heller, one of the leading public law and legal theorists of Weimar-era Germany. In his 1927 book on sovereignty in public and international law, Heller pointed out that Schmittean logic is born of a wish to replace legal theory with a 'political theology' in which the executive is endowed with magical powers.[32] It results in a theory which he called 'organ sovereignty', according to which the will of the executive is made the source of law on the most important constitutional issues.[33] We find this theory in the USA today in the talk of the 'unitary executive'.[34] It also animates, in my view, Finnis's natural law theory; hence, his absence from the preceding chapters.

[31] See Lars Vinx, *The Guardian of the Constitution: Hans Kelsen and Carl Schmitt on the Limits of Constitutional Law* (Cambridge: Cambridge University Press, 2015). There is, however, a link through the German political theorist Eric Voegelin, whose thought is one of the major sources for Finnis and his followers. (See, for example, the many references to Voegelin in *Natural Law and Natural Rights* and in 'Revolutions and Continuity of Law', including the substantial quotation at 431.) Voegelin did his doctorate under Kelsen's supervision but, under the influence of Schmitt and other thinkers of the German and Austrian right, became a prominent figure in 'Austrofacism'. (See Janek Wasserman, *Black Vienna: The Radical Right in the Red City, 1918–1938* (New York: Cornell University Press, 2014), 209–12.) Those who take him seriously recognize Schmitt's influence on his thought. But they seek to distinguish between the two by emphasizing Voegelin's more mystical openness to transcendence, whatever that may mean, in contrast to Schmitt's worship of the sovereign decision which puts a stop to the uncertainties of the secular, disenchanted world. (For a recent example, see Thierry Gontier, 'From "Political Theology" to "Political Religion": Eric Voegelin and Carl Schmitt' (2013) 75 *Review of Politics* 25.) Kelsen thought this was a distinction without a difference and pointed out the totalitarian implications of Voegelin's political theory in 'Foundations of Democracy' (1955) 66 *Ethics* 1, at 6–14.

[32] Hermann Heller, *Sovereignty: A Contribution to the Theory of Public and International Law* (Oxford: Oxford University Press, 2019, David Dyzenhaus, ed., Belinda Cooper, trans.), 101–4.

[33] Ibid, 103–4.

[34] For my critique of the similar phenomenon in the USA, exemplified in explicit fealty to Schmitt in the work of the Harvard law professor Adrian Vermeule, see my 'Schmitten in the USA', 4 April 2020, https://verfassungsblog.de/schmitten-in-the-usa/.

BIBLIOGRAPHY

In the footnotes, I refer when appropriate to the title of the original essay in a collection instead of to the title of the collection. Here I list the titles of such essays in order of appearance immediately after the title of the collection.

Abel, Richard, *Politics by Other Means: Law in the Struggle against Apartheid* (New York: Routledge, 1995).

Akande, Dapo and Bjorge, Eirik, 'The United Kingdom Ministerial Code and International Law: A Response to Richard Ekins and Guglielmo Verdirame', 11 December 2015, www.ejiltalk.org/the-united-kingdom-ministerial-code-and-international-law-a-response-to-richard-ekins-and-guglielmo-verdirame/.

Alexy, Robert, 'On Necessary Relations between Law and Morality' (1989) 2 *Ratio Juris* 167.

Allan, TRS, 'Law, Justice and Integrity: The Paradox of Wicked Laws' (2009) 29 *Oxford Journal of Legal Studies* 705.

The Sovereignty of Law: Freedom, Constitution and Common Law (Oxford: Oxford University Press, 2013).

Anghie, Antony, *Imperialism, Sovereignty and the Making of International Law* (Cambridge: Cambridge University Press, 2012).

Anter, Andreas, *Max Weber's Theory of the Modern State: Origins, Structure, Significance* (Basingstoke: Palgrave, 2014).

Augustine, *The City of God against the Pagans* (Cambridge: Cambridge University Press, 1998, RW Dyson, ed. and trans.).

Austin, John, *Lectures on Jurisprudence or the Philosophy of Positive Law* (London: John Murray, 1885, 5th ed.).

Barker, Ernest, *Principles of Social and Political Theory* (Oxford: Oxford University Press, 1951).

'The Theory of the Social Contract in Locke, Rousseau and Hume', in Barker, *Essays on Government* (Oxford: Clarendon Press, 1960, 2nd ed.) 86.

Becker Lorca, Arnulf, *Mestizo International Law: A Global Intellectual History, 1842–1933* (Cambridge: Cambridge University Press, 2014).

Bell, John, 'Wolfgang Friedmann (1907–1972), with an Excursus on Gustav Radbruch (1878–1949)', in Jack Beatson and Reinhardt Zimmermann, eds,

Jurists Uprooted: German-Speaking Émigré Lawyers in Twentieth-Century Britain (New York: Oxford University Press, 2004) 517.

Bellamy, Richard, 'Political Constitutionalism and the Human Rights Act' (2011) 9 *International Journal of Constitutional Law* 86.

Ben-Naftali, Orna, *Sfard, Michael and Viterbo, Hedi, the ABC of the OPT: A Legal Lexicon of the Israeli Control over the Occupied Palestinian Territory* (Cambridge: Cambridge University Press, 2018).

Bentham, Jeremy, *A Fragment on Government* (Cambridge: Cambridge University Press, 1988).

Benvenisti, Eyal, *Legal Dualism: The Absorption of the Occupied Territories into Israel [1990]* (New York: Routledge, 2018).

Berlin, Isaiah, 'Two Concepts of Liberty', in Berlin, *Four Essays on Liberty* (Oxford: Oxford University Press, 1969) 118.

'The Hedgehog and the Fox', in Berlin, *Russian Thinkers* (London: The Hogarth Press, 1978) 22.

Berman, Harold J, 'Towards an Integrative Jurisprudence: Politics, Morality, History' (1988) 76 *California Law Review* 779.

Blackett, RJM, *The Captive's Quest for Freedom: Fugitive Slaves, the 1850 Fugitive Slave Law, and the Politics of Slavery* (New York: Cambridge University Press, 2018).

Bobbio, Norberto, *Thomas Hobbes and the Natural Law Tradition* (Chicago: Chicago University Press, 1993, Daniela Gobetti, trans.).

'Pour un lexique de théorie générale du droit', in Bobbio, *Essais de Théorie du Droit* (Paris: Bruylant LGDJ, 1998, Michel Guéret, trans.) 55.

Bobbio, Norberto, and Zolo, Danilo, 'Hans Kelsen, the Theory of Law and the International Legal System: A Talk' (1998) 9 *European Journal of International Law* 355.

Boies, David and Olson, Theodore B, *Redeeming the Dream: The Case for Marriage Equality* (New York: Viking, 2014).

Brecht, Arnold, 'The Myth of Is and Ought' (1941) 54 *Harvard Law Review* 811.

Brunnée, Jutta and Toope, Stephen J, *Legitimacy and Legality in International Law: An Interactional Account* (Cambridge: Cambridge University Press, 2010).

B'Tselem, 'A Regime of Jewish supremacy from the Jordan River to the Mediterranean Sea: This Is Apartheid', www.btselem.org/sites/default/files/publications/202101_this_is_apartheid_eng.pdf.

Cameron, Edwin, 'Legal Chauvinism, Executive-Mindedness and Justice: LC Steyn's Impact on South African Law' (1982) 99 *South African Law Journal* 38.

Campbell, A, 'International Law and Primitive Law' (1988) 8 *Oxford Journal of Legal Studies* 169.

Cane, Peter, *Responsibility in Law and Morality* (Oxford: Hart Publishing, 2002).

'Morality, Law and Conflicting Reasons for Action' (2012) 71 *Cambridge Law Journal* 59.

'Public Law in *The Concept of Law*' (2013) 33 *Oxford Journal of Legal Studies* 649.

Cassese, Antonio, 'Remarks on Scelle's Theory of "Role Splitting"' (dédoublement fonctionnel) in International Law' (1990) 1 *European Journal of International Law* 210.

Cattaneo, Mario, 'Hobbes's Theory of Punishment', in KC Brown, ed., *Hobbes Studies* (Oxford: Basil Blackwell, 1965) 275.

Centlivres, Albert van de Sandt, 'The Constitution of the Union of South Africa and the Rule of Law', in Arthur E Sutherland, ed., *Government under Law* (Cambridge, MA: Harvard University Press, 1956) 423.

Churchwell, Sarah, *Behold America: The Entangled History of 'America First' and 'The American Dream'* (New York: Basic Books, 2018).

Cicero, *On Duties* (Ithaca, NY: Cornell University Press, 2016, Benjamin Patrick Newton, trans.).

Cicero on the Commonwealth and on the Laws (Cambridge: Cambridge University Press, 2017, 2nd ed., James EG Zetzel, ed. and trans.).

Coke, Edward, *The Selected Writings and Speeches of Sir Edward Coke* (Liberty Fund: Indianapolis, 2003, Steve Sheppard, ed.).

Coleman, Jules, 'Negative and Positive Positivism', in Marshall Cohen, ed., *Ronald Dworkin and Contemporary Jurisprudence* (London: Duckworth, 1984) 28.

Cover, Robert M, *Justice Accused: Antislavery and the Judicial Process* (New Haven: Yale University Press, 1975).

'Nomos and Narrative', in Martha Minow, Michael Ryan and Austin Sarat, eds, *Narrative, Violence, and the Law: The Essays of Robert Cover* (Ann Arbor: Michigan University Press, 1995) 95.

Cowen, DV, *Parliamentary Sovereignty and the Entrenched Provisions of the South Africa Act* (Cape Town: Juta and Co., 1951).

'Legislature and Judiciary – Reflections on the Constitutional Issues in South Africa: Part I' (1952) 15 *Modern Law Review* 282.

'Legislature and Judiciary – Reflections on the Constitutional Issues in South Africa: Part II' (1953) 16 *Modern Law Review* 273.

Crawford, James, *The Creation of States in International Law* (Oxford: Clarendon Press, 2006).

Brownlie's Principles of Public International Law (Oxford: Oxford University Press, 2012, 8th ed.).

Criddle, Evan J and Fox-Decent, Evan, *Fiduciaries of Humanity: How International Law Constitutes Authority* (Oxford: Oxford University Press, 2016).

Darwall, Stephen, *The Second-Person Standpoint: Morality, Respect, and Accountability* (Cambridge, MA: Harvard University Press, 2006).

Daston, Lorraine, *Against Nature* (Cambridge, MA: MIT Press, 2019).

D'Entrèves, AP, *Natural Law: An Introduction to Legal Philosophy* (London: Hutchinson's University Library, 1951).

De Burca, Gráinne, 'The European Court of Justice and the International Legal Order after *Kadi*' (2010) 51 *Harvard International Law Journal* 1.

Delbanco, Andrew, *The War before the War: Fugitive Slaves and the Struggle for America's Soul from the Revolution to the Civil War* (New York: Penguin Press, 2018).

Dicey, Albert Venn, *The Law of Domicile as a Branch of the Law of England: Stated in the Form of Rules* (London: Stevens and Sons, 1879).

'Note' (1887) 3 *Law Quarterly Review* 102.

A Digest of the Law of England with Reference to the Conflict of Laws (London: Stevens and Sons, 1896).

The Law of the Constitution (Oxford: Oxford University Press, 2013, John Allison, ed.).

Devlin, Patrick, *The Enforcement of Morals* (Oxford: Oxford University Press, 1965).

Dindjer, Hasan, 'The New Legal Anti-Positivism' (2020) 26 *Legal Theory* 18.

Dugard, John, *Human Rights and the South African Legal Order* (Princeton: Princeton University Press, 1978).

Dugard, John, and Reynolds, John, 'Apartheid, International Law, and the Occupied Palestinian Territory' (2013) 24 *European Journal of International Law* 867.

Du Bois, François, 'Preface', in du Bois, ed., *The Practice of Integrity: Reflections on Ronald Dworkin and South African Law* (Cape Town: Juta, 2004) xi.

Dworkin, Ronald, 'Philosophy, Morality, and Law: Observations Prompted by Professor Fuller's Novel Claim' (1965) 113 *University of Pennsylvania Law Review* 672.

'Comments on the Unity of Law Doctrine (a Response)', in Howard E Kiefer and Milton K Munitz, eds, *Ethics and Social Justice* (Albany: State University of New York Press, 1968) 200.

'The Law of the Slave-Catchers', *Times Literary Supplement*, 5 December 1975, 1437.

Taking Rights Seriously (London: Duckworth, 1981, 3rd impression).

'Introduction' vii.

'Model of Rules I' 14.

'Model of Rules II' 46.

'Hard Cases' 81.

'Justice and Rights' 185.

'Liberty and Moralism' 240.

'Appendix: A Reply to Critics' 291.

'A Reply by Ronald Dworkin', in Marshall Cohen, ed., *Ronald Dworkin and Contemporary Jurisprudence* (London: Duckworth, 1984) 247.

Law's Empire (London: Fontana, 1986).

Freedom's Law: The Moral Reading of the American Constitution (Cambridge, MA: Harvard University Press, 1996).

'Keynote Address', in François du Bois, ed., *The Practice of Integrity: Reflections on Ronald Dworkin and South African Law* (Cape Town: Juta, 2004) 1.

Justice in Robes (Cambridge, MA: Belknap Press, 2006).

'Response' (2010) 90 *Boston University Law Review* 1059. Draft version at www.bu.edu/law/journals-archive/bulr/documents/dworkin_r.pdf.

Justice for Hedgehogs (Cambridge, MA: Belknap Press, 2011).

'A New Philosophy for International Law' (2013) 41 *Philosophy and Public Affairs* 1.

Dyzenhaus, David, *Hard Cases in Wicked Legal Systems: South African Law in the Perspective of Legal Philosophy* (Oxford: Clarendon Press, 1991).

'Legal Theory in the Collapse of Weimar: Contemporary Lessons?' (1997) 91 *American Political Science Review* 121.

Legality and Legitimacy: Carl Schmitt, Hans Kelsen and Hermann Heller in Weimar (Oxford: Clarendon Press, 1997).

The Constitution of Law: Legality in a Time of Emergency (Cambridge: Cambridge University Press, 2006).

'The Rule of Law as the Rule of Liberal Principle', in Arthur Ripstein, ed., *Ronald Dworkin* (Cambridge: Cambridge University Press, 2007) 56.

'The Grudge Informer Case Revisited' (2008) 23 *New York University Law Review* 1000.

'How Hobbes met the "Hobbes Challenge"' (2009) 72 *Modern Law Review* 488.

'*The Puzzle of Martial Law*' (2009) 59 *University of Toronto Law Journal* 1.

Hard Cases in Wicked Legal Systems: Pathologies of Legality (Oxford: Oxford University Press, 2010, 2nd ed.).

'Austin, Hobbes, and Dicey' (2011) 26 *Canadian Journal of Law and Jurisprudence* 411.

'Positivism and the Pesky Sovereign' (2011) 22 *European Journal of International Law* 363.

'Constitutionalism in an Old Key: Legality and Constituent Power' (2012) 1 *Global Constitutionalism* 229.

'Hobbes on the Authority of Law', in Dyzenhaus and Thomas Poole, eds, *Hobbes and the Law* (Cambridge: Cambridge University Press, 2012) 186.

'Legality without the Rule of Law? Scott Shapiro on Wicked Legal Systems' (2012) 25 *Canadian Journal of Law and Jurisprudence* 183.

'*The End of the Road to Serfdom?*' (2013) 63 *University of Toronto Law Journal* 310.

'Hobbes on the International Rule of Law' (2014) 28 *Ethics and International Affairs* 53.

'Liberty and Legal Form', in Lisa Austin and Dennis Klimchuk, eds, *The Rule of Law and Private Law* (Oxford: Oxford University Press, 2014) 92.

'The Public Conscience of the Law' (2014) 43 *Netherlands Journal of Legal Philosophy* 115.

'Dreaming the Rule of Law', in Dyzenhaus and Thomas Poole, eds, *Law, Liberty and State: Oakeshott, Hayek and Schmitt on the Rule of Law* (Cambridge: Cambridge University Press, 2015) 234.

'Process and Substance as Aspects of the Public Law Form' (2015) 74 *Cambridge Law Journal* 284.

'The Public Conscience of the Law: From Hobbes to Hart' (2015) 45 *Ragion Pratica* 565.

'Dworkin and Unjust Law', in Wil Waluchow and Stefan Sciaraffa, eds, *The Legacy of Ronald Dworkin* (Oxford: Oxford University Press, 2016) 131.

'The Idea of a Constitution: A Plea for *Staatsrechtslehre*', in Dyzenhaus and Malcolm Thorburn, eds, *Philosophical Foundations of Constitutional Law* (Oxford: Oxford University Press, 2016) 9.

'Formalism, Realism, and the Politics of Indeterminacy', in Wouter Werner, Marieke De Hoon and Alexis Galàn, eds, *The Law of International Lawyers: Reading Martti Koskenniemi* (Cambridge: Cambridge University Press, 2017) 39.

'A Monistic Approach to the Internationalization of Constitutional Law', in Julia Motoc, Paulo Pinto de Albuquerque and Krzysztof Wojtyczek, eds, *New Developments in Constitutional Law: Essays in Honour of Andras Sajo* (The Hague: Eleven International Publishing, 2018) 97.

'Emergencies and Human Rights: A Hobbesian Analysis', in Bardo Fassbender and Knut Traisbach, eds, *The Limits of Human Rights* (Oxford: Oxford University Press, 2019) 89.

'Introduction: The Politics of Sovereignty', in Hermann Heller, *Sovereignty: A Contribution to the Theory of Public and International Law* (Oxford: Oxford University Press, 2019, Dyzenhaus, ed.) 1.

'The African National Congress and the Birth of Constitutionalism' (2020) 18 *International Journal of Constitutional Law* 284.

'The Inevitable Social Contract' (2021) 27 *Res Publica* 187.

'The Janus-Faced Constitution', in Jacco Bomhoff, Dyzenhaus and Thomas Poole, eds, *The Double-Facing Constitution* (Cambridge: Cambridge University Press, 2020) 17.

'Lawyer for the Strongman', 12 June 2020, https://aeon.co/essays/carl-schmitts-legal-theory-legitimises-the-rule-of-the-strongman.

'Schmitten in the USA', 4 April 2020, https://verfassungsblog.de/schmitten-in-the-usa/.

'Exemplary But Not Canonical: The South African Voters Rights Cases', in Sujit Choudhry, Michaela Hailbronner and Mattias Kumm, eds, *Global Canons in an Age of Uncertainty: Debating Foundational Texts of Constitutional*

Democracy and Human Rights (Oxford: Oxford University Press, forthcoming).

'Positivism and Totalitarianism', in Torben Spaak and Patricia Mindus, eds, *The Cambridge Companion to Legal Positivism* (Cambridge: Cambridge University Press, 2021) 764.

'Thomas Hobbes and the Rule by Law Tradition', in Martin Loughlin and Jens Meirhenrich, eds, *The Cambridge Companion to the Rule of Law* (Cambridge: Cambridge University Press, 2021) 261.

Ebbinghaus, Julius, 'The Law of Humanity and the Limits of State Power' (1953) 10 *The Philosophical Quarterly* 14.

Ekins, Richard, 'Acts of Parliament and the Parliament Acts' (2007) 123 *Law Quarterly Review* 91.

'Constitutional Principle in the Laws of the Commonwealth', in John Keown and Robert George, eds, *Reason, Morality, and Law: The Philosophy of John Finnis* (Oxford: Oxford University Press, 2013) 396.

'Brexit and Judicial Power', 21 July 2016, http://judicialpowerproject.org.uk/wp-content/uploads/2016/07/R-Ekins-Brexit-and-judicial-power-21-July-2016.pdf.

'Do Our Supreme Court Judges Have Too Much Power?', *The Spectator*, 14 May 2019, www.spectator.co.uk/article/do-our-supreme-court-judges-have-too-much-power-.

Ekins, Richard, and Hennessey, Patrick, and Martineau, Julie, 'Protecting Those Who Serve', 28 June 2019, https://judicialpowerproject.org.uk/protecting-those-who-serve-richard-ekins-patrick-hennessey-and-julie-marionneau/.

Ekins, Richard, and Verdirame, Guglielmo, 'The Ministerial Code and the Rule of Law', 6 November 2015, https://ukconstitutionallaw.org/2015/11/06/richard-ekins-and-guglielmo-verdirame-the-ministerial-code-and-the-rule-of-law/.

Endicott, Timothy, 'Comity among Authorities' (2015) 68 *Current Legal Problems* 1.

Etchemendy, Matthew X, 'New Directions in Legal Expressivism' (2016) 22 *Legal Theory* 1.

Feinberg, Joel, *Harmless Wrongdoing: The Moral Limits of the Criminal Law* (Oxford: Oxford University Press, 1990).

Finkelman, Paul, *An Imperfect Union: Slavery, Federalism, and Comity* (Chapel Hill: University of North Carolina Press, 1981).

Finnis, John, *Natural Law and Natural Rights* (Oxford: Clarendon Press, 1980).

'Law, Morality, and "Sexual Orientation"', in John Corvino, ed., *Same Sex: Debating the Ethics, Science, and Culture of Homosexuality* (Lanham, New York and London: Rowman and Littlefield, 1997) 31.

'On the Incoherence of Legal Positivism' (2000) 75 *Notre Dame Law Review* 1597.

'Endorsing Discrimination between Faiths: A Case of Extreme Speech', in Ivan Hare and James Weinstein, eds, *Extreme Speech and Democracy* (Oxford: Oxford University Press, 2009) 430.

'Revolutions and Continuity of Law', in Finnis, *Philosophy of Law: Collected Essays*, vol. 4 (Oxford: Oxford University Press, 2011) 407.

'Ministers, International Law, and the Rule of Law', 2 November 2015, https://judicialpowerproject.org.uk/ministers-international-law-and-the-rule-of-law/.

'Judicial Power: Past, Present and Future', 2018, http://judicialpowerproject.org.uk/wp-content/uploads/2018/01/Judicial-Power-and-the-Balance-of-Our-Constitution.pdf.

Foisneau, Luc, 'Sovereignty and Reason of State: Bodin, Botero, Richelieu and Hobbes', in Howell A Lloyd, ed., *The Reception of Bodin* (Leiden: Brill, 2013) 323.

Forsyth, Christopher, ed., *Judicial Review and the Constitution* (Oxford: Hart Publishing, 2000).

Fox-Decent, Evan, 'Constitutional Legitimacy Unbound', in David Dyzenhaus and Malcolm Thorburn, eds, *Philosophical Foundations of Constitutional Law* (Oxford: Oxford University Press, 2016) 119.

Fraenkel, Ernst, *The Dual State: A Contribution to the Theory of Dictatorship* (Oxford: Oxford University Press, 2017).

Frank, Walter, *Law and the Gay Rights Story: The Long Search for Equal Justice in a Divided Democracy* (New Brunswick: Rutgers University Press, 2014).

Friedrich, CJ, *Constitutional Reason of State* (Providence: Brown University Press, 1957).

Fuller, Lon L, *The Law in Quest of Itself* (Boston: Beacon Press, 1940).

'Human Purpose and Natural Law' (1958) 3 *Natural Law Forum* 68.

'Positivism and Fidelity to Law: A Reply to Professor Hart' (1958) 71 *Harvard Law Review* 630.

Legal Fictions (Stanford: Stanford University Press, 1967).

The Morality of Law (New Haven: Yale University Press, 1969, revised ed.).

'The Justification of Legal Decisions' (1972) 7 *Archiv für Rechts- und Sozialphilosophie* (Beiheft Neue Folge) 77.

'The Forms and Limits of Adjudication', in Kenneth I Winston, ed., *The Principles of Social Order: Selected Essays of Lon L Fuller* (Oxford: Hart Publishing, 2001) 101.

Gardbaum, Stephen, *The New Commonwealth Model of Constitutionalism* (Cambridge: Cambridge University Press, 2013).

Gardner, John, *Law as a Leap of Faith* (Oxford: Oxford University Press, 2012).

'Why Law Might Emerge: Hart's Problematic Fable', in Luís Duarte D'Almeida, James Edwards and Andrea Dolcetti, eds, *Reading HLA Hart's The Concept of Law* (Oxford: Hart Publishing, 2013) 81.

Gaus, Gerald, 'Hobbes's Challenge to Public Reason Liberalism: Public Reason and Religious Convictions in Leviathan' (2010), in SA Lloyd ed., *Hobbes Today: Insights for the 21st Century* (Cambridge: Cambridge University Press, 2012) 155.

Giudice, Michael, 'Hart and Kelsen on International Law', in Leslie Green and Brian Leiter, eds, *Oxford Studies in Philosophy of Law* (Oxford: Oxford University Press, 2013) 148.

Goldsworthy, Jeffrey, *Parliamentary Sovereignty, Contemporary Debates* (Cambridge: Cambridge University Press, 2010).

Gontier, Thierry, 'From "Political Theology" to "Political Religion": Eric Voegelin and Carl Schmitt' (2013) 75 *Review of Politics* 25.

Gough, JW, *The Social Contract: A Critical Study of Its Development* (Oxford: Clarendon Press, 1957, 2nd ed.).

Gragl, Paul, *Legal Monism: Law, Philosophy, and Politics* (Oxford: Oxford University Press, 2018).

Green, Leslie, 'Positivism and the Inseparability of Law and Morals' (2008) 23 *New York University Law Review* 1035.

'The Morality in Law', in Luís Duarte D'Almeida, James Edwards and Andrea Dolcetti, eds, *Reading HLA Hart's The Concept of Law* (Oxford: Hart Publishing, 2013) 177.

Green, Michael S, 'Legal Monism: An American History', in Christopher Bezemek, Michael Potacs and Alexander Somek, eds, *Legal Positivism, Institutionalism and Globalisation* (Oxford: Hart Publishing, 2018) 23.

Greenawalt, Kent, 'Policy, Rights and Judicial Decisions' (1977) 11 *Georgia Law Review* 991.

Greenberg, Mark, 'The Moral Impact Theory of Law' (2014) 123 *Yale Law Journal* 1289.

Gross, Aeyal, *The Writing on the Wall: Rethinking the International Law of Occupation* (Cambridge: Cambridge University Press, 2017).

Grotius, Hugo, *On the Law of War and Peace* (Cambridge: Cambridge University Press, 2012, Stephen C Neff, ed.).

Guastini, Ricardo, 'The Basic Norm Revisited', in Luís Duarte d'Almeida, John Gardner and Leslie Green, eds, *Kelsen Revisited: New Essays on the Pure Theory of Law* (Oxford: Hart Publishing, 2013) 65.

Hammond, WG, 'Note' (1887) 3 *Law Quarterly Review* 101.

Harris, JW, 'Kelsen's Pallid Normativity' (1996) 9 *Ratio Juris* 94.

Harrison, Ross, *Bentham* (London: Routledge and Kegan Paul, 1983).

Hart, HLA, *Law, Liberty, and Morality* (Oxford: Oxford University Press, 1962).

Essays on Bentham: Jurisprudence and Political Theory (Oxford: Clarendon Press, 1982).

Essays in Jurisprudence and Philosophy (Oxford: Clarendon Press, 1983).

'Introduction' 1.

'Positivism and the Separation of Law and Morals' 49.

'American Jurisprudence through English Eyes: The Nightmare and the Noble Dream' 123.

'Scandinavian Realism' 161.

'Kelsen Visited' 286.

'Kelsen's Doctrine of the Unity of Law' 309.

The Concept of Law (Oxford: Clarendon Press, 1994, 2nd ed.).

'Answers to Eight Questions', in Luís Duarte D'Almeida, James Edwards and Andrea Dolcetti, eds, *Reading HLA Hart's The Concept of Law* (Oxford: Hart Publishing, 2013) 279.

Hayek, FA, *The Constitution of Liberty* (Chicago: University of Chicago Press, 1960).

Heller, Hermann, *Staatslehre*, in Heller, *Gesammelte Schriften*, vol. 3 (Tübingen: JCB Mohr, 1992, Christoph Müller ed.) 92.

'The Nature and Structure of the State' (1996) 18 *Cardozo Law Review* 1139 (David Dyzenhaus, trans.).

'Political Democracy and Social Homogeneity' (David Dyzenhaus, trans.), in Arthur J Jacobson and Bernard Schlink, eds, *Weimar: A Jurisprudence of Crisis* (Berkeley: University of California Press, 2000) 256.

Sovereignty: A Contribution to the Theory of Public and International Law (Oxford: Oxford University Press, 2019, David Dyzenhaus, ed.).

Hershovitz, Scott, 'The End of Jurisprudence' (2015) 124 *Yale Law Journal* 1160.

Higginbotham, A Leon, 'Foreword', in Alan Watson, *Roman Slave Law* (Baltimore: Johns Hopkins University Press, 1987) ix.

Hobbes, Thomas, *Behemoth or the Long Parliament* (London: Frank Cass, 1969, Ferdinand Tönnies, ed.).

On the Citizen (Cambridge: Cambridge University Press, 1998, Richard Tuck and Michael Silverthorne, eds).

A Dialogue between a Philosopher and a Student, of the Common Laws of England, in Thomas Hobbes, Writings on Common Law and Hereditary Right (Oxford: Clarendon Press, 2005, Alan Cromartie and Quentin Skinner, eds).

Leviathan (Cambridge: Cambridge University Press, 1996, Richard Tuck, ed.).

Hoekstra, Kinch, 'Tyrannus Rex vs. Leviathan' (2001) 82 *Pacific Philosophical Quarterly* 420.

'The *de facto* Turn in Hobbes's Political Philosophy', in Tom Sorell and Luc Foisneau, eds, *Leviathan After 350 Years* (Oxford: Oxford University Press, 2004) 33.

'Early Modern Absolutism and Constitutionalism' (2013) 34 *Cardozo Law Review* 1079.

Hoffmann, Florian, 'International Legalism and International Politics', in Anne Orford and Hoffmann, eds, *The Oxford Handbook of the Theory of International Law* (Oxford: Oxford University Press, 2016) 954.

Holmes, Oliver Wendell, 'The Path of the Law' (1897) 10 *Harvard Law Review* 457.

'The Common Law', in Richard A Posner, ed., *The Essential Holmes* (Chicago: University of Chicago Press, 1992) 229.

Holtermann, Jakob v H, 'Introduction', in Alf Ross, *On Law and Justice* (Oxford: Oxford University Press, 2019, v H Holtermann, ed., Uta Bindreiter, trans.).

Honoré, Tony, 'The Basic Norm of a Society', in Honoré, *Making Law Bind: Essays Legal and Philosophical* (Oxford: Clarendon Press, 2002) 89.

'The Necessary Connection between Law and Morality' (2002) 22 *Oxford Journal of Legal Studies* 489.

Hostovsky Brandes, Tamar, 'The Diminishing Status of International Law in the Decisions of the Israeli Supreme Court concerning the Occupied Territories' (2020) 18 *International Journal of Constitutional Law* 767.

Hovell, Devika, *The Power of Process: The Value of Due Process in Security Council Sanctions Decision-Making* (Oxford: Oxford University Press, 2016).

Hume, David, 'Of the Original Contract', in Frederick Watkins, ed., *Hume: Theory of Politics* (Austin: University of Texas Press, 1953) 193.

Jabareen, Hassan, 'Hobbesian Citizenship: How the Palestinians Became a Minority in Israel', in Will Kymlicka and Eva Pföstl, eds, *Multiculturalism and Minority Rights in the Arab World* (Oxford: Oxford University Press, 2014) 189.

'Can the Court Normalize the Exception in Non-emergency Cases? Palestinian Cases before the Israeli Supreme Court' (2020) 18 *International Journal of Constitutional Law* 788.

'How the Law of Return Creates One Legal Order in Palestine' (2020) 21 *Theoretical Inquiries in Law* 459.

Janis, MW, 'Bentham and the Fashioning of "International Law"' (1984) 78 *American Journal of International Law* 405.

Jellinek, Georg, *Allgemeine Staatslehre* (Berlin: Verlag O Häring, 1905, 2nd ed.).

Kadelbach, Stefan, '*Jus Cogens*, Obligations *Erga Omnes* and Other Rules: The Identification of Fundamental Norms', in Christian Tomuschat and Jean-Marc Thouvenin, eds, *The Fundamental Rules of the International Legal Order: Jus Cogens and Obligations Erga Omnes* (Leiden: Martinus Nijhoff Publishers, 2005) 21.

Kant, Immanuel, *The Metaphysics of Morals*, in Kant, *Practical Philosophy* (Cambridge: Cambridge University Press, 1996, Mary J Gregor, ed. and trans.) 353.

Karayanni, Michael, *Conflicts in Conflict: A Conflict of Laws Case Study on Israel and the Palestinian Territories* (Oxford: Oxford University Press, 2014).

Kellogg, Frederic R, *Oliver Wendell Holmes, Jr. and Legal Logic* (Chicago: University of Chicago Press, 2018).

Kelsen, Hans, 'Comment', in Veröffentlichungen der Vereinigung der Deutschen Staatsrechtslehrer, vol. 3 (Berlin: Walter de Gruyter and Co., 1927) 54.

'The Pure Theory of Law and Analytical Jurisprudence' (1941) 55 *Harvard Law Review* 44.

'Recognition in International Law: Theoretical Observations' (1941) 35 *American Journal of International Law* 605.

'Judicial Review of Legislation: A Comparative Study of the Austrian and the American Constitution' (1942) 2 *The Journal of Politics* 183.

Peace through Law (Chapel Hill: The University of California Press, 1944).

General Theory of Law and State (Cambridge, MA: Harvard University Press, 1945, Anders Wedberg, trans.).

'Natural Law Doctrine and Legal Positivism' 389 (Wolfgang Herbert Kraus, trans.).

Pure Theory of Law (Cambridge, MA: Harvard University Press, 1945, Max Knight, trans.).

Law and Peace in International Relations: The Oliver Wendell Holmes Lectures, 1940–41 (Cambridge, MA: Harvard University Press, 1948).

'Foundations of Democracy' (1955) 66 *Ethics* 1.

'Le Renvoi' (1957) *Annuaire of the Institute of International Law* 115.

What Is Justice? Justice, Law and Politics in the Mirror of Science (Berkeley: University of California Press, 1957).

'The Law as a Specific Technique' 231.

'Law, State, and Justice in the Pure Theory of Law' 288.

'Die Lehre von den drei Gewalten oder Funktionen des Staates', in Hans Klecatsky, René Marcic and Herbert Schambeck, eds, Die Wiener rechtstheoretische Schule: Hans Kelsen, Adolf Merkl, Alfred Verdross, vol. 2 (Vienna: Europa Verlag, 1968) 1625.

Die philosophischen Grundlagen der Naturrechtlehre und des Rechtspositivismus, in Hans Klecatsky, René Marcic and Herbert Schambeck, eds, Die Wiener rechtstheoretische Schule: Hans Kelsen, Adolf Merkl, Alfred Verdross, vol. 1 (Vienna: Europa Verlag, 1968) 281.

Das Problem der Souveränität und die Theorie des Völkerrechts: Beitrag zu Einer Reinen Rechtslehre (Aalen: Scientia Verlag, 1981).

'The Concept of the Legal Order' (1982) 27 *American Journal of Jurisprudence* 64 (Stanley L Paulson, trans.).

Introduction to the Problems of Legal Theory (Oxford: Clarendon Press, 1992, Bonnie Litschewski Paulson and Stanley L Paulson, trans.).

The Essence and Value of Democracy (Lanham: Rowman and Littlefield, 2013, Nadia Urbinati and Carlo Invernizzi Accetti eds, Brian Graf, trans.).

'The Nature and Development of Constitutional Adjudication', in Lars Vinx, ed., *The Guardian of the Constitution: Hans Kelsen and Carl Schmitt on the Limits of Constitutional Law* (Cambridge: Cambridge University Press, 2015, Vinx, trans.) 22.

'Who Ought to Be the Guardian of the Constitution?', in Lars Vinx, ed., *The Guardian of the Constitution: Hans Kelsen and Carl Schmitt on the Limits of Constitutional Law* (Cambridge: Cambridge University Press, 2015, Vinx, trans.) 174.

Kingsbury, Benedict, 'Legal Positivism as Normative Politics: International Society, Balance of Power and Lassa Oppenheim's Positive International Law' (2002) 13 *European Journal of International Law* 401.

Kingsbury, Benedict, and Straumann, Benjamin, 'State of Nature versus Commercial Sociability as the Basis of International Law: Reflections on the Roman Foundations and Current Interpretations of the International Political and Legal Thought of Grotius, Hobbes, and Pufendorf', in Samantha Besson and John Tasioulas, eds, *The Philosophy of International Law* (Oxford: Oxford University Press, 2012) 33.

Kirkby, Coel, 'Law Evolves: The Uses of Primitive Law in Anglo-American Concepts of Modern Law, 1861–1961' (2018) 58 *American Journal of Legal History* 535.

Knop, Karen, 'Citizenship, Public and Private' (2008) 71 *Law and Contemporary Problems* 309.

Knop, Karen, and Michaels, Ralf, and Riles, Annelise, 'International Law in Domestic Courts: A Conflict of Laws Approach' (2010) 103 *American Society of International Law Proceedings* 269.

Koskeniemmi, Martti, 'The Wonderful Artificiality of States' (1994) 88 *Proceedings of the Annual Meeting (American Society of International Law)* 22.

From Apology to Utopia: The Structure of International Legal Argument (Cambridge: Cambridge University Press, 2005, reissue with new epilogue).

Kostal, RW, *A Jurisprudence of Power: Victorian Empire and the Rule of Law* (Oxford: Oxford University Press, 2005).

Kretzmer, David, *The Occupation of Justice: The Supreme Court of Israel and the Occupied Territories* (Albany: State University of New York Press, 2002).

Kumm, Mattias, 'The Legitimacy of International Law: A Constitutionalist Framework of Analysis' (2004) 15 *European Journal of International Law* 907.

'Rethinking Constitutional Authority: On the Structure and Limits of Constitutional Pluralism', in Matej Avbelj and Jan Komárek, eds, *Constitutional Pluralism in the European Union and beyond* (Oxford: Hart Publishing, 2012) 39.

Kunz, Joseph L, 'Critical Comments on Lauterpacht's Recognition in International Law' (1950) *American Journal of International Law* 713.

Lacey, Nicola, *A Life of HLA Hart: The Nightmare and the Noble Dream* (Oxford: Oxford University Press, 2004).

'Out of the Witches' Cauldron: Reinterpreting the Context and Reassessing the Significance of the Hart–Fuller Debate', in Peter Cane, ed., *The Hart–Fuller Debate in the Twenty-First Century* (Oxford: Hart Publishing, 2010) 1.

Latham, RTE, *The Law and the Commonwealth* (London: Oxford University Press, 1949).

Lauterpacht, Hersch, 'Diplomatic Protection and Criminal Jurisdiction over Aliens' (1947) 9 *Cambridge Law Journal* 330.

Recognition in International Law (Cambridge: Cambridge University Press, 1947).

The Development of International Law by the International Court (London: Stevens and Sons, 1958).

International Law: Collected Papers – The Law of Peace, vol. 2 (Cambridge: Cambridge University Press, 2009, E Lauterpacht, ed.).

'Kelsen's Pure Science of Law' 404.

'Is International Law a Part of the Law of England?' 537.

Lee, Daniel, *Popular Sovereignty in Early Modern Constitutional Thought* (Oxford: Oxford University Press, 2016).

Lefkowitz, David, 'What Makes a Social Order Primitive? In Defense of Hart's Take on International Law' (2017) 23 *Legal Theory* 258.

Lerner, Hanna, *Making Constitutions in Deeply Divided Societies* (Cambridge: Cambridge University Press, 2011).

LeVine, Mark and Mossberg, Mathias, eds, *One Land, Two States: Israel and Palestine as Parallel States* (Berkeley: University of California Press, 2014).

Lino, Dylan, 'Albert Venn Dicey and the Constitutional Theory of Empire' (2016) 36 *Oxford Journal of Legal Studies* 751.

'The Rule of Law and the Rule of Empire: AV Dicey in Imperial Context' (2018) 81 *Modern Law Review* 739.

Lloyd, SA, 'Hobbes's Self-effacing Natural Law Theory' (2001) 82 *Pacific Philosophical Quarterly* 187.

Morality in the Philosophy of Thomas Hobbes: Cases in the Laws of Nature (Cambridge: Cambridge University Press, 2009).

Loughlin, Martin, 'In Defence of *Staatslehre*' (2009) 48 *Der Staat* 1.

Foundations of Public Law (Oxford: Oxford University Press, 2010).

Loveland, Ian, *By Due Process of Law: Racial Discrimination and the Right to Vote in South Africa, 1855–1960* (Oxford: Hart Publishing, 1999).

Luxenberg, Steve, *Separate: The Story of Plessy v. Ferguson and America's Journey from Slavery to Segregation* (New York: WW Norton and Company, 2019).

Lyall, Andrew, *Granville Sharp's Cases on Slavery* (Oxford: Hart Publishing, 2017).

MacCormick, Neil, *Questioning Sovereignty: Law, State, and Nation in the European Commonwealth* (Oxford: Oxford University Press, 1999).

Malcolm, Noel, 'Hobbes's Theory of International Relations', in Malcolm, *Aspects of Hobbes* (Oxford: Clarendon Press, 2004) 431.

Mann, FA, 'International Delinquencies before Municipal Courts' (1954) 70 *Law Quarterly Review* 181.

Margalit, Avishai, 'Human Dignity between Kitsch and Deification', in Christopher Cordner, ed., *Philosophy, Ethics and a Common Humanity: Essays in Honour of Raimond Gaita* (Abingdon: Routledge, 2011) 106.

Marshall, Geoffrey, *Parliamentary Sovereignty and the Commonwealth* (Oxford: Clarendon Press, 1957).

Mathews, Anthony S, *Freedom, State Security and the Rule of Law: Dilemmas of the Apartheid Society* (Cape Town: Juta, 1986).

McIlwain, Charles Howard, *Constitutionalism: Ancient and Modern* (Ithaca, NY: Cornell University Press, 1961, revised ed.).

McLachlan, Campbell, *Foreign Relations Law* (Cambridge: Cambridge University Press, 2014).

McLean, Janet, *Searching for the State in British Legal Thought: Competing Conceptions of the Public Sphere* (Cambridge: Cambridge University Press, 2012).

McWhinney, Edward, *Judicial Review in the English-Speaking World* (Toronto: University of Toronto Press, 1960, 2nd ed.).

Meirhenrich, Jens, *The Legacies of Law: Long-Run Consequences of Legal Development in South Africa, 1652–2000* (New York: Cambridge University Press, 2008).

Mertens, Thomas, 'Radbruch and Hart on the Grudge Informer: A Reconsideration' (2002) 15 *Ratio Juris* 186.

Mill, John Stuart, *On Liberty*, in *John Stuart Mill, Three Essays: On Liberty, Representative Government, The Subjection of Women* (Oxford: Oxford University Press, 1984, Richard Wollheim, ed.) 5.

Mills, Alex, 'The Private History of International Law' (2006) 55 *International and Comparative Law Quarterly* 1.

The Confluence of Public and Private International Law: Justice, Pluralism and Subsidiarity in the International Constitutional Ordering of Private Law (Cambridge: Cambridge University Press, 2009).

Misak, Cheryl, *The American Pragmatists* (Oxford: Oxford University Press, 2013).

'A Pragmatist Account of Legitimacy and Authority', in David Rondel and Susan Dieleman, eds, *Pragmatism and Justice* (New York: Oxford University Press, 2017) 295.

Morris, Douglas G, 'The Dual State Reframed: Ernst Fraenkel's Political Clients and His Theory of the Nazi Legal System' (2013) 58 *Leo Baeck Institute Year Book* 5.

Legal Sabotage: Ernst Fraenkel in Hitler's Germany (Cambridge: Cambridge University Press, 2020).

Mureinik, Etienne, 'A Bridge to Where? Introducing the Interim Bill of Rights' (1994) 10 *South African Journal on Human Rights* 32.

Murphy, Liam, 'Better to See Law This Way' (2008) 23 *New York University Law Review* 1088.

What Makes Law: An Introduction to Philosophy of Law (Cambridge: Cambridge University Press, 2014).

'Law beyond the State: A Rejoinder' (2017) 28 *European Journal of International Law* 265.

'Law beyond the State: Some Philosophical Questions' (2017) 28 *European Journal of International Law* 203.

Murphy, Mark C, 'Was Hobbes a Legal Positivist?' (1995) 105 *Ethics* 846.

Nardin, Terry, *Law, Morality, and the Relations of States* (Princeton: Princeton University Press, 1983).

Neiman, Susan, *Evil in Modern Thought: An Alternative History of Philosophy* (Princeton: Princeton University Press, 2002).

Ngcukaitobi, Tembeka, *The Land Is Ours: South Africa's First Black Lawyers and the Birth of Constitutionalism* (Cape Town: Penguin, 2018).

Ngqulunga, Bongani, *The Man Who Founded the ANC: A Biography of Pixley ka Isaka Seme* (Cape Town: Penguin, 2017).

Notermans, Mathijs, 'Social Peace as Conditio Tacita for the Validity of the Positive Legal Order' (2015) 34 *Law and Philosophy* 201.

Nye, Hillary, 'Finnis's Divided View of Law: Problems for Adjudicative Theory' (2020) 11 *Jurisprudence* 503.

Oakes, James, *Freedom National: The Destruction of Slavery in the United States, 1861–1865* (New York: WW Norton and Company, 2014).

'The Power of Running Away' (2018) *New York Review of Books*, 6 December issue.

Oakeshott, Michael, 'The Rule of Law', in Oakeshott, *On History and Other Essays* (Indianapolis: Liberty Fund, 1999) 129.

Oliver, Peter, *The Constitution of Independence: The Development of Constitutional Theory in Australia, Canada, and New Zealand* (Oxford: Oxford University Press, 2005).

Olsthoorn, Johan, 'Hobbes's Account of Distributive Justice as Equity' (2013) 21 *British Journal for the History of Philosophy* 13.

Palley, Claire, *The Constitutional History and Law of Southern Rhodesia, 1888–1965* (Oxford: Clarendon Press, 1966).

Pappe, HO, 'On the Validity of Judicial Decisions in the Nazi Era' (1960) 23 *Modern Law Review* 260.

Parfitt, Rose, 'Theorizing Recognition and International Personality', in Anne Orford and Florian Hoffmann, eds, *The Oxford Handbook of the Theory of International Law* (Oxford: Oxford University Press, 2016) 583.

Parkin-Speer, Diane, 'John Lilburne: A Revolutionary Interprets Statutes and Common Law Due Process' (1983) 1 *Law and History Review* 276.

Patterson-Tutschka, Monicka, 'Leveller John Lilburne and the Liberal-Republican Tradition' (2014) 43 *Perspectives on Political Science* 213.

Pauer-Studer, Herlinde and Velleman, J David, *Konrad Morgen: The Conscience of a Nazi Judge* (London: Palgrave Macmillan, 2015).

Paul, Joel R, 'Comity in International Law' (1991) 32 *Harvard International Law Journal* 1.

Paulson, Stanley L, 'The Weak Reading of Authority in Hans Kelsen's Pure Theory of Law' (2000) 19 *Law and Philosophy* 131.

'On the Background and Significance of Gustav Radbruch's Post-war Papers' (2006) 26 *Oxford Journal of Legal Studies* 17.

Payandeh, Mehrdad, 'The Concept of International Law in the Jurisprudence of HLA Hart' (2010) 21 *European Journal of International Law* 967.

Perry, Stephen, 'Political Authority and Political Obligation', in Leslie Green and Brian Leiter, eds, *Oxford Studies in Philosophy of Law* (Oxford: Oxford University Press, 2013) 1.

Pettit, Philip, 'Liberty and Leviathan' (2005) 4 *Politics, Philosophy and Economics* 131.

Pitts, Jennifer, *A Turn to Empire: The Rise of Imperial Liberalism in Britain and France* (Princeton: Princeton University Press, 2005).

Boundaries of the International: Law and Empire (Cambridge, MA: Harvard University Press, 2018).

Pocock, JGA, 'The Ideal of Citizenship since Classical Times' (1992) 99 *Queen's Quarterly* 33.

Poole, Thomas, '*Hobbes on Law and Prerogative*', in David Dyzenhaus and Poole, eds, *Hobbes and the Law* (Cambridge: Cambridge University Press, 2012) 68.

Reason of State: Law, Prerogative and Empire (Cambridge: Cambridge University Press, 2015).

'The Law of Emergency and Reason of State', in Evan Criddle, ed., *Human Rights in Emergencies* (New York: Cambridge University Press, 2016) 148.

'The Executive Power Project', 2 April 2019, www.lrb.co.uk/blog/2019/april/the-executive-power-project.

Postema, Gerald, *Bentham and the Common Law Tradition* (Oxford: Clarendon Press, 1986).

Legal Philosophy in the Twentieth Century: The Common Law World (Heidelberg: Springer Dordrecht, 2011).

'Law's System: The Necessity of System in Common Law' (2014) 69 *New Zealand Law Review* 69.

Rabban, David M, 'Hammond's Blackstone and the Historical School of American Jurisprudence', in Anthony Page and William Pest, eds, *Blackstone and His Critics* (Oxford: Hart Publishing, 2018) 173.

Radbruch, Gustav, *Legal Philosophy*, in *The Legal Philosophies of Lask, Radbruch, and Dabin* (Cambridge, MA: Harvard University Press, 1950, 20th Century Legal Philosophy Series, vol. 4, Kurt Wilk, trans.) 47.

'Gesetzliches Unrecht und Übergesetzliches Recht', in Radbruch, *Rechtsphilosophie* (Stuttgart: KF Koehler Publishing, 1973, Erik Wolf and Hans-Peter Schneider, eds) 339.

'Statutory Lawlessness and Supra-Statutory Law' (2006) 26 *Oxford Journal of Legal Studies* 1 (Bonnie Litschewski Paulson and Stanley L Paulson, trans.).

Rawls, John, *The Law of Peoples* (Cambridge, MA: Harvard University Press, 2002).

Raz, Joseph, *The Concept of a Legal System: An Introduction to the Theory of a Legal System* (Oxford: Clarendon Press, 1980, 2nd ed.).

The Authority of Law: Essays on Law and Morality (Oxford: Clarendon Press, 1983).

'Legitimate Authority' 3.

'Legal Positivism and the Sources of Law' 37.

'The Identity of Legal Systems' 78.

'The Institutional Nature of Law' 103.

'Kelsen's Theory of the Basic Norm' 122.

'Legal Validity' 146.

'The Rule of Law and Its Virtue' 201.

Practical Reason and Norms (Princeton: Princeton University Press, 1990).

'HLA Hart (1907–1992)' (1993) 5 *Utilitas* 145.

'Authority, Law, and Morality', in Raz, *Ethics in the Public Domain: Essays in the Morality of Law and Politics* (Oxford: Oxford University Press, 1994) 194.

'On the Authority and Interpretation of Constitutions: Some Preliminaries', in Larry Alexander, ed., *Constitutionalism: Philosophical Foundations* (Cambridge: Cambridge University Press, 1998) 152.

'Incorporation by Law' (2004) 10 *Legal Theory* 1.

'The Purity of the Pure Theory', in Stanley L Paulson and Bonnie Litschewski Paulson, eds, *Normativity and Norms: Critical Perspectives on Kelsenian Themes* (Oxford: Oxford University Press, 2007).

Between Authority and Interpretation (Oxford: Oxford University Press, 2009).

Rehfeld, Andrew, 'Jeptha, the Hebrew Bible, and John Locke's "Second Treatise of Government"' (2008) 3 *Hebraic Political Studies* 60.

Ripstein, Arthur, *Force and Freedom: Kant's Legal and Political Philosophy* (Cambridge, MA: Harvard University Press, 2009).

Rundle, Kristen, 'Form and Agency in Raz's Legal Positivism' (2013) 32 *Law and Philosophy* 767.

Sadurski, Wojciech, *Poland's Constitutional Breakdown* (Oxford: Oxford University Press, 2019).

Scelle, Georges, 'Le phénomène juridique du dédoublement fonctionnel', in Walter Schätzel and Hans-Jürgen Schlochauer, eds, *Rechstfragen der Internationalen Organisation: Festschrift für Hans Wehberg zu Seinem 70 Geburstag* (Frankfurt am Main: Vittorio Klostermann, 1956) 342.

Schauer, Frederick, *The Force of Law* (Cambridge, MA: Harvard University Press, 2014).

Schmitt, Carl, *The Concept of the Political* (New Jersey: Rutgers University Press, 1976, George Schwab, trans.).

Political Theology: Four Chapters on the Concept of Sovereignty (Cambridge, MA: MIT Press, 1988, George Schwab, trans.).

Selznick, Philip, 'Sociology and Natural Law' (1961) 6 *Natural Law Forum* 84.

Sfard, Michael, *The Wall and the Gate: Israel, Palestine, and the Legal Battle for Human Rights* (New York: Metropolitan Books, 2018).

'The Occupation of the West Bank and the Crime of Apartheid: Legal Opinion', June 2020, https://s3-eu-west-1.amazonaws.com/files.yesh-din.org/Apartheid+2020/Apartheid+ENG.pdf.

Shapiro, Scott, *Legality* (Cambridge, MA: Belknap Press, 2011).

Shklar, Judith N, 'Political Theory and the Rule of Law', in Shklar, *Political Thought and Political Thinkers* (Chicago: University of Chicago Press, 1998, Stanley Hoffmann, ed.) 21.

Simpson, AWB, 'The Common Law and Legal Theory', in Simpson, ed., *Oxford Essays in Jurisprudence* (Oxford: Oxford University Press, 1973, 2nd series).

Reflections on 'The Concept of Law' (Oxford: Oxford University Press, 2011).

Skinner, Quentin, *Liberty before Liberalism* (Cambridge: Cambridge University Press, 1998).

Hobbes and Republican Liberty (Cambridge: Cambridge University Press, 2008).

Somek, Alexander, 'Kelsen Lives' (2007) 17 *European Journal of International Law* 4.

'Monism: A Tale of the Undead', in Matej Avbelj and Jan Komárek, eds, *Constitutional Pluralism in the European Union and beyond* (Oxford: Hart Publishing, 2012) 343.

Sreedhar, Susanne, *Hobbes on Resistance: Defying the Leviathan* (Cambridge: Cambridge University Press, 2010).

Sreedhar, Susanne, and Delmas, Candace, 'State Legitimacy and Political Obligation in *Justice for Hedgehogs*: The Radical Potential of Dworkinian Dignity' (2010) 90 *Boston University Law Review* 737.

Stavropolous, Nicos, 'Legal Interpretivism', in *Stanford Encyclopedia of Philosophy*, http://plato.stanford.edu/entries/law-interpretivist/, first published 14 October 2003; substantive revision 8 February 2021.

Steyn, Johan, 'Guantanamo Bay: The Legal Black Hole' (2004) 53 *International and Comparative Law Quarterly* 1.

Stolleis, Michael, *A History of Public Law in Germany, 1914–1945* (Oxford: Oxford University Press, 2004).

Stone, Martin, 'Legal Positivism as an Idea about Morality' (2011) 61 *University of Toronto Law Journal* 313.

Straumann, Benjamin, 'The Peace of Westphalia as a Secular Constitution' (2008) 15 *Constellations* 173.

Roman Law in the State of Nature: The Classical Foundations of Hugo Grotius's Natural Law (Cambridge: Cambridge University Press, 2015).

Crisis and Constitutionalism: Roman Political Thought from the Fall of the Republic to the Age of Revolution (Oxford: Oxford University Press, 2016).

Thierry, Hubert, 'The European Tradition in International Law' (1990) 1 *European Journal of International Law* 193.

Toh, Kevin, 'Hart's Expressivism and His Benthamite Project' (2005) 11 *Legal Theory* 75.

Troper, Michel, *Pour Une Théorie Juridique de L'État* (Paris: Presses Universitaires de France, 1994).

Tuck, Richard, *The Sleeping Sovereign: The Invention of Modern Democracy* (Cambridge: Cambridge University Press, 2015).

Verdross, Alfred, 'Forbidden Treaties in International Law: Comments on Professor Garner's Report on the "The Law of Treaties"' (1937) 31 *American Journal of Intentional Law* 571.

Vinx, Lars, *Hans Kelsen's Pure Theory of Law: Legality and Legitimacy* (Oxford: Oxford University Press, 2007).

'Constitutional Indifferentism and Republican Freedom' (2010) 38 *Political Theory* 809.

The Guardian of the Constitution: Hans Kelsen and Carl Schmitt on the Limits of Constitutional Law (Cambridge: Cambridge University Press, 2015).

'The Kelsen–Hart Debate: Hart's Critique of Kelsen's Legal Monism Reconsidered', in Jeremy Telman, ed., *Hans Kelsen in America: Selective Affinities and the Mysteries of Academic Influence* (Switzerland: Springer, 2016) 59.

Von Bernstoff, Jochen, *The Public International Law Theory of Hans Kelsen: Believing in Universal Law* (Cambridge: Cambridge University Press, 2010, Thomas Dunlap, trans.).

'Law beyond the State: A Reply to Liam Murphy" (2017) 28 *European Journal of International Law* 257.

'Specialized Courts and Tribunals as the Guardians of International Law? The Nature and Function of Judicial Interpretation in Kelsen and Schmitt', in Andreas Føllesdal and Geir Ulfstein, eds, *The Judicialization of International Law: A Mixed Blessing?* (Oxford: Oxford University Press, 2018) 9.

Wacks, Raymond, 'Judges and Injustice' (1984) 101 *South African Law Journal* 266.

Waldron, Jeremy, 'Hobbes and the Principle of Publicity' (2001) 82 *Pacific Philosophical Quarterly* 447.

'The Core of the Case against Judicial Review' (2006) 115 *Yale Law Journal* 1346.

'The Concept and the Rule of Law' (2008) 43 *Georgia Law Review* 1.

'Positivism and Legality: Hart's Equivocal Response to Fuller' (2008) 83 *New York University Law Review* 1135.

'Can There Be a Democratic Jurisprudence?' (2009) 58 *Emory Law Journal* 675.

'Who Needs Rules of Recognition?', in Matthew Adler and Kenneth E Himma, eds, *The Rule of Recognition and the US Constitution* (New York: Oxford University Press, 2009) 327.

'Are Sovereigns Entitled to the Benefit of the International Rule of Law?' (2011) 22 *European Journal of International Law* 315.

'Response: The Perils of Exaggeration' (2011) 22 *European Journal of International Law* 389.

'How Law Protects Dignity' (2012) 71 *Cambridge Law Journal* 20.

'International Law: "A Relatively Small and Unimportant Part of Jurisprudence"', in Luís Duarte D'Almeida, James Edwards and Andrea Dolcetti, eds, *Reading HLA Hart's The Concept of Law* (Oxford: Hart Publishing, 2013) 209.

Walters, Mark, 'The Unwritten Constitution as a Legal Concept', in David Dyzenhaus and Malcolm Thorburn, eds, *Philosophical Foundations of Constitutional Law* (Oxford: Oxford University Press, 2016) 33.

AV Dicey and the Common Law Constitutional Tradition: 'A Legal Turn of Mind' (Cambridge: Cambridge University Press, 2020).

Waluchow, Wil, *Inclusive Legal Positivism* (Oxford: Clarendon Press, 1994).

Wasserman, Janek, *Black Vienna: The Radical Right in the Red City, 1918–1938* (New York: Cornell University Press, 2014).

Watson, Alan, *Roman Slave Law* (Baltimore: Johns Hopkins University Press, 1987).

Weber, Max, *Economy and Society* (Cambridge, MA: Harvard University Press, 2019, Keith Tribe, ed. and trans.).

Weinrib, Ernest J, *The Idea of Private Law* (Cambridge, MA: Harvard University Press, 1995).

Corrective Justice (Oxford: Oxford University Press, 2012).

Weinrib, Jacob, *Dimensions of Dignity: The Theory and Practice of Modern Constitutional Law* (Cambridge: Cambridge University Press, 2016).

Weinrib, Lorraine E, 'Constitutionalism in the Age of Rights: A Prolegomenon' (2004) 121 *South African Law Journal* 278.

Wilkinson, Michael A, 'Is Law Morally Risky? Alienation, Acceptance and Hart's Concept of Law' (2010) 30 *Oxford Journal of Legal Studies* 441.

Williams, Bernard, 'A Critique of Utilitarianism', in Williams and JJC Smart, *Utilitarianism: For and against* (Cambridge: Cambridge University Press, 1973) 76.

In the Beginning Was the Deed: Realism and Moralism in Political Argument (Princeton: Princeton University Press, 2005, Geoffrey Hawthorn, ed.).

'Realism and Moralism in Political Theory' 1.

'Human Rights and Relativism' 62.

'From Freedom to Liberty: The Construction of a Political Value' 75.

Winch, Peter, 'Certainty and Authority', in A Phillips Griffiths, ed., *Wittgenstein: Centenary Essays* (Cambridge: Cambridge University Press, 1991) 223.

Winston, Kenneth I, 'Introduction', in Winston, ed., *The Principles of Social Order: Selected Essays of Lon L. Fuller* (Oxford: Hart Publishing, 2001) 11.

'Is/Ought Redux: The Pragmatist Context of Lon Fuller's Conception of Law' (1988) 8 *Oxford Journal of Legal Studies* 329.

Wolff, Martin, *Private International Law* (Oxford: Clarendon Press, 1962, 2nd ed.).

Wolff, Robert Paul, *In Defense of Anarchism* (Berkeley: University of California Press, 1998).

Zarka, Yves Charles, 'The Political Subject', in Tom Sorell and Luc Foisneau, eds, *Leviathan after 350 Years* (Oxford: Clarendon Press, 2004) 167.

Zetzel, James EG, 'Natural Law and Poetic Justice: A Carneadean Debate in Cicero and Vergil' (1996) 91 *Classical Philology* 297.

INDEX

To fit with the argument of the book, the index is constructed mainly under the names of the principal figures considered. Where a name figures in the text in relation to just one topic, the topic is indicated in brackets.

For EU product safety concerns, contact us at Calle de José Abascal, 56–1°,
28003 Madrid, Spain or eugpsr@cambridge.org.

www.ingramcontent.com/pod-product-compliance
Lightning Source LLC
LaVergne TN
LVHW052019200926
848481LV00005B/1528
* 9 7 8 1 0 0 9 0 4 8 8 6 6 *